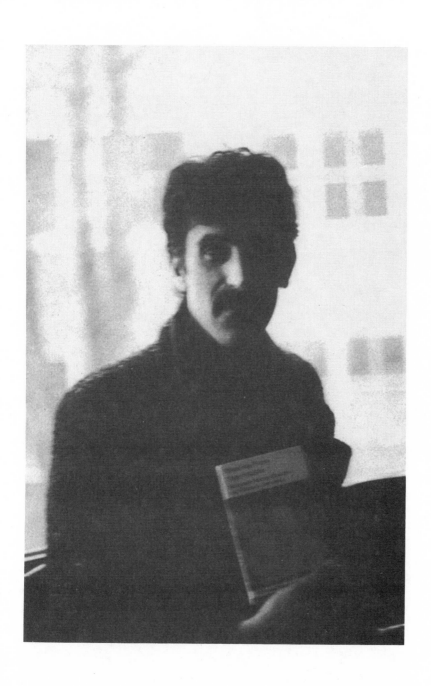

FRANK ZAPPA: THE NEGATIVE DIALECTICS OF POODLE PLAY

For Jeremy Prynne and Danny Houston,
the true gurus on this one

FRANK ZAPPA: THE NEGATIVE DIALECTICS OF POODLE PLAY

BEN WATSON

St. Martin's Press
New York

Frontispiece: Frank Zappa holding *Breeding From Your Poodle*, the book by Margaret Rothery Sheldon and Barbara Lockwood, Oslo, 13th January 1980. Photograph taken by Mårten Sund. See 'Shut Up 'N Play Yer Guitar' in Chapter Nine: More Guitars.

FRANK ZAPPA: THE NEGATIVE DIALECTICS OF POODLE PLAY.
Copyright © 1993 by Ben Watson.
'Oh No' © 1970 Frank Zappa Music
'Your Mouth' © 1972 Munchkin Music
'Stink-Foot' © 1974 Munchkin Music
'Debra Kadabra' © 1975 Munchkin Music

Library of Congress Cataloging-in-Publication Data

Watson, Ben
    Frank Zappa : the negative dialectics of poodle play / Ben Watson.
        p.   cm.
    ISBN 0-312-11918-6
    1. Zappa, Frank—Criticism and interpretation.   2. Music and society.
I. Title.
ML410.Z285W38   1995
782.42166'092—dc20   94-36294
                                                                  CIP
                                                                  MN

First published in Great Britain by Quartet Books Ltd.

First U.S. Edition: January 1995
10 9 8 7 6 5 4 3 2 1

LIST OF CONTENTS

ACKNOWLEDGEMENTS

I should like to thank the editors who have nurtured the writings of Out to Lunch: Ian Patterson, Ken Edwards, Paul Brown, Mårten Sund, John Wilkinson, Rod Mengham, Steven Holt, Harry Gilonis, Fred Tomsett; Caroline Arscott for discovering *Weasels Ripped My Flesh* and helping me formulate the mix of Marxism and punk that underlies this work; the rock musicians who have discussed Zappa with me: Tim Beckham of A. C. Temple, Andy Gill of the Gang of Four, Michael Rooney of the Primevals; the composers Martin Archer, Richard Barrett and Simon Fell; Leeds SWP members Martin Bennell, Matthew Caygill, Steve Edwards, Dave Ferris and Steve Skinner for the continuing art-political debate; Zappa fans Pancho Rodriguez Baez (get in touch, man!), Jorge Carretto, Simon Cliff, Chris Dean, Mike Laurence, Liz Leney, Frank Mabbitt and Gas Price for thought-provoking comments over the years; Emma Biggs for her inspirational rockism; Christine Rybek, Paul Furness and the Beauville contingent for explaining the true import of 'Bobby Brown'; John McMillan and Vinksu Chandrasekhar for the discography; the Leeds Jazz Committee (Dave Hatfield for lending me his magazine archive; 'Rhythm' in Chapter 9 is for Bill White); the tape-swappers Jack Collier, Steve Feigenbaum, Stuart Lester, Robert Taylor, Eric Ziarko; the many musicians whose remarks have illuminated Zappa for me: Chris Atton, Andy Blake, Stuart Edge, Billy Jenkins, Mike Jennings, Jan Kopinski, Tommy Mars, Orphy Robinson, Clark Rundell, Steve Swallow, Chad Wackermann, Alan Wilkinson; the many non-musicians who have done the same: Ina Dittke, Jane Dixon, Jackie Fournel, Melody Nalson, Everton Savage, Laurie Staff, Spencer Streeter, Anne Thoday, Simon Thompson, my brother Oliver; the classical commentators David Osmond-Smith and Max Paddison; Vanessa Bridge for saying 'stuff Roland Barthes and the primacy of the text – go to LA and talk to him!'; the people in LA who made my trip there so grand: Frank (of course), Gail, Bobby Plotnik, Gerry Fialka, PK, Matt Groening, Johnny 'Guitar' Watson; Richard Cook for bringing me overground as a writer and for editorial wisdom; Andrew Cowan, Simon Prentis, Mark Sinker, Gary Steel, Ian Watson and Geoff Wills for helpful nit-picking; my publisher Jeremy Beale for good humour and patience; Jane Williams for opening up a whole spectrum of modern music, and occasionally (when the words stop) admitting Zappa's brilliant; my father, Bill, for suggesting possibilities for Zappa's character-seal on *Zoot Allures*; my mother, Kay, for helping to transcribe the German words to 'Ya Hozna'; the idea of this book is to open the barn-door rather than say the last word, *Our Exagmination* rather than the Loeb edition, so all praise to jwcurry and Jonathan Jones for arriving at the last hour and making me believe this is a field others will plough.

PREFACE

The siren of the springs of guilty song –
Let us take her on the incandescent wax
Striated with nuances, nervosities
That we are heir to
Hart Crane[1]

WHY MARX, WHY FREUD

This book has its origin in writings that appeared in various avant-garde periodicals of the early 1980s under the pseudonym Out To Lunch.[2] Frank Zappa's work was used simultaneously to analyse and denigrate the achievements of Western literature, from the romantics through to Henry James, a method that went under the name *the negative dialectics of poodle play*. Though written in a manner likely to attract the attentions of *literati* rather than rock fans, the first paragraph of the opening salvo – 'Frank Zappa: The Negative Dialectics of Poodle Play Part One' – still for me summarizes the joys and terrors of analysing Zappa and his art.

> In writing about Zappa I'm going to engage at certain ratios inside the gearbox of accepted rationality because I don't want to write myself

---

[1]Hart Crane, 'For The Marriage of Faustus and Helen', 1926, *The Complete Poems and Selected Letters*, ed. Brom Weber, 1966, p. 31.
[2]Out To Lunch, 'Frank Zappa: The Negative Dialectics of Poodle Play Part One', *A Vision Very Like Reality*, ed. Peter Ackroyd, Ian Patterson, Nick Totton, December 1979; 'Frank Zappa: The Negative Dialectics of Poodle Play Part Two', *Reality Studios*, ed. Ken Edwards, Vol. 5, Nos. 1–4,1983; 'Erogenous Sewage: Poodle Play Explores the Work of Hart Crane', *Heretic*, ed. Paul Brown, Vol. 1, No. 2, 1980; 'Out to Another Lunch Party: Plato's transcendental sofa grounded in material hide by revelations concerning frightened phallicism, spatial screaming and nasal spores', *Equofinality*, ed. John Wilkinson, Rod Mengham, No. 2, 1982; *So Much Plotted Freedom: The cost of employing the language of fetishized domination – poodle play explores the sex economy of Henry James' lingo jingo*, Reality Studios, Occasional Paper, No. 6, 1987; 'Secret Hungers in Horace', *Horace Whom I Hated So*, ed. Harry Gilonis, 1992; *Secret Hungers in Horace: The Negative Dialectics of Poodle Play Performs a Psychoanalgesis on Horace*, Form Books, Occasional Paper, No. 1, 1993, available from Form Books, 42a Lowden Road, Herne Hill, London SE24 OBH.

into impressionism and art for art's sake; freewheeling is constrained by the necessity of forever travelling downhill. On the other hand I hate the tedious mountaineer's blatant preoccupation with self-justification, when language becomes apologetic it is already corrupt[3] and the language of Zappology is no exception. The discoveries of the Zappographer must not be left to warp in the waters of religion so that, as cane, they can be twisted into the tricky baskets in which they collect coined morality. Rather, these discoveries must be used to relieve the inflamed areolae of stomach-churning anxiety which disapproval spreads around even our most secret pleasure spots. Direct application of the salve, though, merely stalls the engine, like the fan belt which shrank and got shorter.[4] As in psychoanalysis, the aim is to summon a cure from within, not to initiate fencing with moral strictures, but unlike the domesticated perversions of psychiatry, Zappography doesn't envisage a welcome return to the universal overdrive of the 2–4–6–8 motorway conveyor belt. Double declutching for all we're worth, we throw all locomotive intentions to the winds, and if the whole caboodle falls to bits then it wasn't worth patching up anyway. Not that I'm going to take any crap about the 'risk' involved in writing, you can always cross things out. The whole process is enacted in microscosm each time one Zappa theme proves its worth, anyway: day by day, significance and confidence reco-agulate. Facing the inevitable pressures for justification head-on is all wrong, but that doesn't say we don't get there in the end, or that I haven't pulled it off before. I prefer rear entry and physical occupation of the enemy from within. Primary strategy resides in grasping the cheapest irrelevancies, structures which afford no possibility of analogy, like teeth. But even before the perpetration of that heavy-handed stroke of wit, poodle continuity beckons. It's an irrelevance still cheaper because its dull reliability begins to ape the concerned cognitions of the gearbox beneath the bonnet.[5]

The original went on to compare Zappa's 'Cheepnis'[6] to Samuel Taylor Coleridge's 'Kubla Khan' – but general readers would no doubt benefit from some kind of preamble.[7]

Besides being concerned with Frank Zappa and his records and concerts and videos, the negative dialectics of poodle play also seek to apply the insights of Karl Marx and Sigmund Freud. Supposedly superseded by the post-everything schools of

[3]Theodor Adorno and Max Horkheimer, *The Dialectic of Enlightenment*, 1944, p. 219.
[4]Frank Zappa, 'Florentine Pogen', *One Size Fits All*, 1975.
[5]Out To Lunch, 'Frank Zappa: The Negative Dialectics of Poodle Play Part One', *A Vision Very Like Reality*, ed. Peter Ackroyd, Ian Patterson, Nick Totton, December 1979, p. 22. These words also provided the text for a concerto for reader, orchestra and electric guitar by Simon Fell, *Four Slices of Zappa*, 1992.
[6]Frank Zappa 'Cheepnis', *Roxy & Elsewhere*, 1974.
[7]A preamble provided by the rest of this preface and the next five chapters. Readers wishing to skip ahead to the heart of the matter may turn to the discussion of 'pants' in the section entitled '*Roxy & Elsewhere*' in Chapter 5: Bizarre to DiscReet.

thought,[8] their ideas continue to burn bright, perhaps because what they talked about – capitalism and the family – are still with us. Though often said to be incompatible, Marx and Freud share crucial characteristics: materialism, hostility to religion, dogged insistence on the ability of human reason to grasp and change both the world and the mind. In his own unbookish way, Zappa holds to a similar belief in reason, a refusal to allow social norms to compromise a vision of how things could be. Marx wished to foment the political self-consciousness of the working class; Freud's slogan 'where id was ego shall be' shows a commitment to consciousness far removed from the Nietzschean pessimism of his Parisian inheritors. In unravelling the mysteries of the commodity and of the unconscious, Marx and Freud are frequently condemned by those who defend the current order – but far from damning their theories, to me this indicates an untruth in the way things are run.

If anyone involved in mass culture seems to point to an untruth in the way things are run, it would be Frank Zappa. Obstinate, irreducible, oppositional, his music presents a continual disjunct, a permanent dada. His explicit politics – loyalty to the family unit and the honest dealings of the small business – are as far from radical psychoanalysis or Marxism as you could imagine, yet it is precisely because he does not deliver back such philosophical precepts on the level of *representation* that his music provides convincing grist for radical thought. Zappa has produced a miscegenation of high and low elements that puts the rhetoric of Pop Art and postmodernism to shame.

Zappa's belief in knowledge as a blow against oppression is illustrated by this exchange with a born-again Christian during the US Senate hearing on 'porn rock'. You could tell how heartfelt his words were by an uncharacteristic tremor in his voice.

BORN-AGAIN CHRISTIAN: Some of those things are not normal sexual relations.

FZ: It doesn't mean you have to *do* them. Information doesn't kill you . . .

---

[8]The term postmodernism is notoriously vague, but was usefully summarized by Anna Copeland thus: 'A reaction to intellectual traditions that attempt to explain the world using universal concepts such as Freudian models of the personality, Marxist theories of economics, or the cause-and-effect explanations used by historians, postmodernism sees life in the late twentieth century as a series of disconnected events, a smorgasbord of narratives or discourses that compete for attention.' 'Two Cultures: A Reader's Guide', *Omni*, Vol. 16, No. 2, November 1993, p. 44. It is postmodernism of this ilk that poodle play opposes (along with Alex Callinicos; see his *Against Postmodernism: A Marxist Critique*, 1989).

BAC: They're too young to know the difference.

FZ: Children learn the difference by receiving information which they can store and sort with your help as a parent. If you don't let them know about this stuff they'll grow up and be ignorant.

BAC: I would rather have them ignorant of some things. [*Applause.*]

FZ: Anyone who would rather have their children be ignorant is making a mistake – because then they can be victims.[9]

The collapse of communism in Eastern Europe has led to the demise of state socialism as a viable ideology for the liberal middle class. As the vacuum this has created is filled with a whole panoply of new age irrationalisms, Zappa's appeal to reason is as unusual as it is timely.

OR ANY ART AT ALL?

In an interview in *Telos*, the American quarterly of Frankfurt School Marxism, Frank Zappa was asked whether he saw a distinction between high art and low art. He replied: 'Or any art at all?'[10]

Blurring the distinction between art and life has been an American activity since at least Walt Whitman, voicing unease with the honoured yet insulated status granted art in that society. It explains the seemingly contradictory combination of discipline and accident in Zappa's music. 'This has to be the tape with *all* the right notes in it',[11] coupled with 'what the fuck'.[12] Accident marks the entry of the real into his design. Like a Surrealist portraying a devastated Europe *before* the outbreak of the Second World War,[13] Zappa mixes in elements of the real world so that his art becomes microcosmic. Analysis bodies forth real information about the world, its past *and* its future. Not since James Joyce has anyone tried to raze the boundary between art and life with such productive zeal.

To talk of art begs the question of its definition. To the Marxist,

---

[9]Senate Hearing on 'Porn Rock', 1985.

[10]*Telos*, Spring 1991, No. 87, interview with Florindo Volpacchio, pp. 124–36. Thanks to Matthew Caygill for telling me about this.

[11]Frank Zappa preamble to 'Bebop Tango (of the Old Jazzmen's Church)', *Roxy & Elsewhere*, 1974.

[12]Sleeve note to Frank Zappa, 'The Sheik Yerbouti Tango', *Sheik Yerbouti*, 1979. Now elevated to the status of a minor philosophy in a recent interview: *Zappa!* (a supplement from the publishers of *Keyboard and Guitar Player*), ed. Don Menn, 1992, p. 64. Here it is expressed as a combination of 'when' and 'what the fuck' (where 'when' could be interpreted as entailing the 'right notes').

[13]Max Ernst, *Europe After the Rain*, 1933.

art is the bourgeoisie's *halfway house* – midway between the religious pageant of feudalism and the permanent re-creation of everyday life that would characterize post-commodity society. Before the advent of the bourgeois class, artworks – tales of adventure, occasional portraits, scores for lutes and viols – were not invested with the personal meaning given art by the romantics. If you had metaphysical quandaries, anxiety about the place your individual soul had in the cosmic scheme of things, you consulted a specialist: the priest. Religion had a monopoly on such expertise, castigating as heresy direct reference to the Bible (or to God). In 1789 the French Revolution made it plain how religion propped the old order: in its revolutionary phase the bourgeoisie wanted none of the old hierarchies of feudalism and faith. They demanded a rationalist world picture. Who now to plumb the depths of the soul, gauge the pulse of the 'inner' life? The poets and painters stepped in.

Art was the replacement for religion, a repository for values 'higher' than those of making money. The reactionary implications of this kind of idealism can be read off (in degraded form) from the triumph of Senator Paula Hawkins when she asked Zappa a question about profit at the US Senate.

PH: Do you make a profit from these rock records?
FZ: Yes.
PH: Thank you. I think that statement tells a story to the Committee.[14]

While the record industry offered to censor itself in exchange for legislation that would bring in income by taxing blank tapes, an artist who says he makes a profit is pilloried. The very statement that should align Zappa with the economic interests of the American ruling class is held up as proof of his worthlessness as an artist and his moral bankruptcy as a citizen.

Such statements are apt to draw equal condemnation from the left as they too moralize against commitment to the profit motive. Left aesthetics have suffered a decay since the days when Leon Trotsky corresponded with André Breton about the revolutionary implications of surrealism. The negative dialectics of poodle play has no time for so-called Marxist critiques of art which merely tail-end the prescriptive high-mindedness of the liberal bourgeoisie. To like art under capitalism is to revel in contradiction; the only other option is a lifetime of reading books on Percy

---

[14]Senate Hearing on 'Porn Rock', 1985.

Shelley.[15] To the sneers of those who baulk at poodle play's combination of Leninist politics and Zappology,[16] negative dialectics makes this point: Zappa's art, though necessarily underpinned by a petit-bourgeois belief in cottage-industry economics, is just as much part of a protest against the divisions of capitalist society as the music of Charlie Parker or Kurt Weill. Those who reduce Marxism to morality – a set of shibboleths which separate us from the rest – have ruined dialectics as much as they have prevented any understanding of the culture industry. These are all the same curmudgeons who said the left should ignore punk.

Art is not simply a representation of aspirations to be judged as worthy or not. It is itself a material process. This creates problems for the idea of art as a repository for 'higher', so-called non-material values. During the nineteenth century, its own technical development threw it into crisis. As the romantics squeezed more and more personal expression out of the old forms – chromaticism and dissonance in music, symbolism in poetry, pictures about painting – they extended the material scope of art, but lost it its audience. In the 1910s and 1920s artistic modernism presaged a new era in which representation was no longer required because humanity was actively reconstructing the world – the promise of the Russian revolution. Casimir Malevich's *White on White* was an object in the world itself, not a window on a world beyond the antagonism of self and society. Society was now the gallery in which art was to operate. As the revolutionary gains of 1917 were rolled back, such refusals of the divisions of capitalist society were no longer welcome. In the West, the distance between modern artworks and the lives of the mass of the population were held up as evidence of mass stupidity; under communism they were banned altogether.

Stalin's counter-revolution suppressed workers' power in the name of 'socialist' ideology and instituted Socialist Realism, a return to nineteenth-century forms with a proviso as to content. Modernism became the bad conscience of his regime. Just as Stalin purged the entire personnel of the Bolshevik central committee, abstract artists were persecuted and confined to insane asylums. Unsurprisingly, the United States saw that it could promote

---

[15]This remark is directed at Paul Foot and the Lukacsian social-realist cabal who monopolize cultural criticism in *Socialist Review*, the monthly magazine of the Socialist Workers Party.
[16]These remarks are directed at the anarcho-bohemian cabal who run the Termite Club, the monthly showcase for free improvisation in Leeds.

abstract art in the name of freedom and enterprise. When Jasper Johns exhibited American flags in art galleries, a patriotic gesture that could not really have been made more blatantly, his action was explained by Clement Greenberg as a further step in a mysterious discussion of the flatness of the picture plane, a dialectic that pretended to bypass cold-war politics altogether. A Jasper Johns retrospective at London's Hayward Gallery in 1991 – at the height of the Gulf War – was sponsored by Texaco, one of the American oil companies whose profits were threatened by Saddam Hussein's annexation of Kuwait. Such political observations, which challenge the transcendent status of art in society, exceed the frame of American art ideology – including that of postmodernism.[17] Zappa's 'or any art at all' also serves to free him from such obfuscations.

The need of the dealers for new waves of artists to promote, and artists' dissatisfaction with a commodity system that could not deliver the promises of modernism, led to the instant obsolescence that characterized post-war Western art styles. Art became a schizophrenic danger zone, a contradictory mish-mash of retro-religion and avant-denial. As commentators sought to find in art the 'balancing' humanity of a system geared only to the rationalization of profit, it disappeared before their eyes into the archaic hocus-pocus of religion (T. S. Eliot, Bob Dylan, Arvo Pärt) or the self-cancelling cryptograms of modernism (Samuel Beckett, John Cage, Joseph Beuys). In keeping faith with modernism, in recognizing art's inability to deliver its message in a commodity culture, artists found themselves involved in permanent paradox, a guerrilla warfare of subterfuge and denial. Hence the cultural establishment's preference for the classics produced during the heroic phase of the bourgeoisie: Shakespeare, Beethoven, Rembrandt. Recycling the old serves to hide the worrying fact that modern capitalist society can only produce authentic art by vaunting social flaws, resulting in an obsession with the past that postmodernism, with its enthusiastic consumption of filtered mass culture under the name of high art, has done little to mollify.

Frank Zappa's pursuit of modernism is intuitive rather than theoretical, in keeping with the fact that music and art are concrete philosophy – sensually embodied thinking about the world. *Them or Us (The Book)*, his 'answer' to questions about conceptual continuity, is prefaced with a disclaimer.

---

[17]See the discussion of Hans Haacke in Fredric Jameson, *Postmodernism, or, The Cultural Logic of Late Capitalism*, 1991, p. 159.

This cheesy little home-made book was prepared for the amusement of people who already enjoy Zappa Music. It is not for intellectuals or other dead people.[18]

Some fans take this hostility to systemized thought as a prerequisite for understanding Zappa, which would make a project like the current one pointless. Faced with the musical philistinism of the 'educated' classes, this is indeed tempting. However, it lets the custodians of high culture off the hook, allowing them to dismiss Zappa as a rock-cult eccentric. In fact, Zappa has an awareness of the historical role of art, and a vision of his own place in it, that is as clear-sighted as it is materialist.

Zappa has long declared an interest in the possibilities of classical music. After discovering the existence of an eighteenth-century composer named Francesco Zappa, he released an album called *Francesco* of the eighteenth-century Zappa's scores realized on computer. He was under no illusions, though, that the Baroque represented some golden age of musical creativity. As David Ocker pointed out in his sleeve-note, the eighteenth-century Zappa 'found honest employment sawing away while noblemen ate dinner'.[19]

Zappa expanded on the issue in *The Real Frank Zappa Book*:

All of the *norms*, as practiced during the olden days, came into being because *the guys who paid the bills* wanted the *'tunes'* they were buying to *'sound a certain way.'*

The king said: *'I'll chop off your head unless it sounds like this.'* The pope said: *'I'll rip out your fingernails unless it sounds like this.'* The duke or somebody else might have said it another way – and it's the same today: *'Your song won't get played on the radio unless it sounds like this.'* People who think that classical music is somehow more *elevated* than *'radio music'* should take a look at the *forms* involved – and at who's paying the bills.[20]

Zappa's use of scores has nothing in common with the petit-bourgeois daydreams of pre-industrial harmony that underlie twentieth-century consumption of classical music (and rock neo-classicism from Meatloaf to Michael Nyman).

In common with other figures in the American 'inventor' tradition – Buckminster Fuller, Charles Ives, Harry Partch, John

---

[18]Frank Zappa, *Them or Us (The Book)*, 1984.
[19]Frank Zappa, *Francesco*, 1984.
[20]Frank Zappa, with Peter Occhiogrosso, *The Real Frank Zappa Book*, 1989, pp. 186–7. Note that at the level of typescript itself – the overuse of emphases – Zappa offends the protocols of literary good manners.

Cage – Zappa's ideas have a *kooky*, crackpot, homemade feel, but because of his attention to the facts of his matter (and his impatience with liberal justifications) his insights are abetted by radical philosophers and avant-garde artists operating in very different circumstances. De Sade and Wyndham Lewis traced parallel trajectories. What follows examines the more recent manifestation of such ideas in Jacques Attali and the Situationist International, though it is really Marx and Freud (and the way their ideas were applied to music by Theodor Adorno) who are uniquely capable of gauging the decimating ferocity of Zappa's art.

WHY JACQUES ATTALI (A LITTLE)

Zappa's appraisal of the record industry as a business geared to making profits[21] shows he has no illusions in the fads and follies of the rock press. Its sole reason for existence is to make a case for the significance of buying records. Jacques Attali has talked of the necessity for the record industry to spend money stimulating demand because the effect of mass production (his term is 'repetition') is precisely to diminish the unique moment that music is to be valued for (which he calls 'ritual').

> Fetishized as a commodity, music is illustrative of the evolution of our entire society: deritualize a social form, repress an activity of the body, specialize its practice, sell it as a spectacle, generalize its consumption, then see to it that it is stockpiled until it loses its meaning.[22]

Despite Attali's claims to novelty,[23] this is actually Marxist theory. Attali is registering the impact on culture of exchange in a commodity system. A similar argument was developed by Walter Benjamin,[24] pointing out that mass production destroys the 'aura' of the work of art. Unlike Attali, though, Benjamin does not say

---

[21]For a trenchant slice of Zappa's views on the record industry, censorship, global politics, etc., read *The Real Frank Zappa Book*, written with Peter Occhiogrosso, 1989, brought out in response to a number of unauthorized books about Zappa that appeared at the end of the 80s. For a punchy, readable account of Zappa's explicit intentions you couldn't do better – for this reason *The Negative Dialectics of Poodle Play* is not concerned to relate Zappa's declared views. Instead, I want to examine his art and see what it tells us, placing it in the larger context of the history of avant-garde art, its relationship to class struggle ('high' versus 'low') and to investigate the unconscious structures of the work. *The Real Frank Zappa Book* has obviated the excuse for any more rock-bio cash-ins.

[22]Jacques Attali, *Noise*, 1977, trs. Brian Massumi, 1985, p. 5.

[23]'I believe this hypothesis is new', p. 30.

[24]Walter Benjamin, 'The Work of Art in the Age of Mechanical Reproduction', 1936, *Illuminations*, trs. Harry Zohn, 1968.

he is 'superseding' Marx, a claim Attali subsequently put into action by involvement with François Mitterrand's catastrophic association of socialism with attacks on the standard of living of the French working class – which ushered in the rise of LePen's Front National.

Nevertheless, Attali's formula is useful. Zappa pays acute attention to these themes, foregrounding fetishization ('Penguin in Bondage'), empty ritual ('Bogus Pomp'), body functions ('Why Does It Hurt When I Pee'), showbiz (*Thing-Fish*), mass production ('A Little Green Rosetta') and loss of meaning through repetition ('Teen-age Wind'). The grotesque 'extremes' of Zappa's imagination are really no more than a response to a commodity system that treats people as things, with all the vocabulary of race and slavery the American experience supplies.

The use of the term 'spectacle' is the key to the energy of Attali's concepts: he is evidently one child of 1968 who did not throw away his situationist tracts. The spectacle was both the Situationist International's analytical tool and their enemy: the sum total of media life – TV, radio, magazines, politics, rockshows, religion – that lives life for you. By criticizing the way successful so-called 'Subversives' (Surrealists, socialist architects, 'Marxist' film-makers, painter-rebels) merely contributed to the spectacle, basking in its rewards of fame and money while they replaced people's everyday creativity by their exploits, the SI developed strategies that resembled those of revolutionary politics: supporting unofficial strikes, perpetrating protests at religion and war that resulted in action rather than applause. Steeped in what un-Stalinized Marxism they could find (which included Henri Lefebvre and Herbert Marcuse and their vision of a left-wing Freud[25]) the SI developed a telling cultural rhetoric that has informed (and/or anticipated) every radical artistic development since. It is therefore naive to be surprised that Attali's concepts should be 'answered' by the rise of punk rock[26] – Jacques Attali and Malcolm McLaren were both using situationist ideas, but at the academic and rock 'n' roll 'levels' respectively (though such splits – or specializations – constitute betrayals of situationist lore). Because they deal with what capitalism does to people, the horror of living

[25]Though Guy Debord's partiality for Georg Lukacs, despite the latter's uneasy compromise with Czech Stalinism, indicates a satisfaction with totalizing abstraction impossible in either revolutionary socialism or Frankfurt School negative dialectics.

[26]As were afterwordist Susan McClary in the 1985 edition of *Noise* and Mark Sinker reviewing her *Feminine Endings* in *The Wire*, No. 96, February 1992.

beings in thrall to the accumulation of things, the themes of Attali and punk are also those of Zappa: sexual slavery, bodies, machines, commodity-fetishism, product, death, libidinal investment in atrocity – what Attali theorises as *sacrifice*: the repressed violence or unspoken crime that guarantees the social.

THE SITUATIONIST INTERNATIONAL AND FRANK ZAPPA

The most recent writer to bring discussion of the SI into rock-talk is Greil Marcus, with his archaeology of the situationist substratum to punk, *Lipstick Traces*.[27] Marcus sifts through the conflicting ideas of Surrealists, Lettrists and Situationists with a tone of blithe wonder, never once resorting to opinion or argument. As only an American could, he finds a way to convert these prickly, aggressive, electric ideas (precisely designed, as Adorno described modern art, to be 'unpleasurable in the commodity sense') into gold-crumbed morsels of consumption. It's a good read. Despite this recuperation, reflected in the use of the word 'situationist' all over the rock press, such theory was originally explosive, a critique that could talk art and politics in the same breath. It is not just punk and Attali – all the best ideas in cultural criticism, from the new art history (Tim Clarke was a member of the British wing) to avant-garde literature (Jeremy Prynne, Iain Sinclair), have been fired by their theses (only camel dung finds more applications). A powerful indication that only Marxist concepts are capable of conveying the bacillus of revolution.

In the vacuum opened up by the revolutionary moment of May 1968, the SI was not good because it was extreme, nihilistic and cool (though it was), or because its members wrote slogans down their ties (though they did), but because they had a Marxist analysis that had no truck with the Stalinism of either the Communist Party or the Maoists. This gets forgotten. They failed to swing the striking workers and occupying students away from the leadership of the CP and the reformist left, who proceeded to deliver the revolution to de Gaulle and the CRS riot police on a plate. They hadn't learned from Lenin the need to build a

---

[27]Greil Marcus, *Lipstick Traces: A Secret History of the Twentieth Century*, 1989.

revolutionary party rooted in the working class: they failed. This also gets forgotten.

However, unlike the sad grouplets of situationist 'followers' who deposit their diatribes against everything under the sun to wilt in sundry left-wing bookshops, the SI were *not* anarchists or romantic individualists. They understood the nature of the state and the importance of the workers' councils; they had a realistic view of the balance of class forces. Unlike Sartre, they saw through the Third Worldism of Fidel Castro and Mao;[28] unlike the Red Brigades they opposed terrorism as inconducive to mass activity;[29] unlike the Communist Party they saw the crucial need for unity between workers and students.[30] Because of this their views on Zappa are worth recording. In 1967 Raoul Vaneigem had this to say:

> The only way to produce a brief aesthetic outburst is to take a momentary lead in the spectacle of artistic decomposition: David Hockney, Frank Zappa, Andy Warhol, Pop Art and Reggae can be bought at random in chain stores. To talk about a modern work of art lasting would be like trying to discourse on the eternal values of Standard Oil.[31]

The idea of the 'lasting' work of art reveals an uncharacteristic aestheticism, though the way Vaneigem's book becomes mired in purist incantations – repeated *ad nauseam* – does show an idealist tendency. The list of names exhibits the crudeness of the SI's emphasis on consumption (a crudeness which postmodernism, despite a different slant, repeats). The boom years of the 50s were hard times for revolutionaries: capitalism seemed to be delivering everything it promised. The situationist critique of consumption – slogans which pointed out that anything that could be bought wasn't worth having, their sheer disgust with the ad-world of happy nuclear families – was a sneeringly definitive goodbye to the 50s and subsequently much plundered: from 'radical' art magazines like *Re/Search* to the Church of the Subgenius, Devo and advertising itself (the retro-50s chic of recent Brylcreem ads, for example). In Lancaster, California, Captain Beefheart and Frank

---

[28]'Geopolitics Of Hibernation', *Internationale Situationniste*, #7, April 1962, trs. Ken Knabb, *Situationist International Anthology*, p. 76.

[29]'Bad Days Will End', *Internationale Situationniste*, #7, April 1962, trs. Ken Knabb, *Situationist International Anthology*, p. 83.

[30]'Address to Revolutionaries of Algeria and of all Countries', *Internationale Situationniste*, #10, March 1966, trs. Ken Knabb, *Situationist International Anthology*, p. 151.

[31]Raoul Vaneigem, *The Revolution of Everyday Life*, 1967, p. 106.

Zappa were also plotting counter-measures to post-war ad-world conformism.

However, though criticizing consumption does mean that even a booming economy won't leave you content, it also means that the target is always the *same*. Vaneigem's cynicism becomes trite and blinkering. The availability of reggae in the stores is not random, it depends on a number of factors: the degree of racism in the record industry, the presence of indigenous West Indians in the area, their morale, the outreach of their culture, and so on. In dismissing reggae along with Warhol, Vaneigem forgets that music can also be the lifeblood of the community, the grapevine, the solace, a source of strength and of resistance. Of course, the only way to distinguish between different consumers is to look at their relationship to the means of production, which means looking at them as workers and not as consumers at all. The SI only developed such a focus on the working class once the 1968 general strike had already started. Despite their much-vaunted 'fraterniza-tions' (sharing a bottle of wine with some pickets in front of a photographer), it was then too late for the SI's revolutionary ideas to influence the course of struggle.

Vaneigem's anti-consumerism is nevertheless preferable to postmodernist celebration of the 'mix-and-match multiplicity of the market', which somehow forgets the *solvency* required to enter the new Garden of Eden.[32] The SI liked to foment the special glamour capitalism needs to compete in the market, and then point out that you can get *that* without buying anything at all. Fine as a strategy for people involved in creating marketable images, it relies on an economic boom to which it can run as a subversive undercurrent. Likewise, punk found that it could momentarily take a lead in the late 70s readjustment of the rock market by setting aflame the straw figures of 60s idealism. But both the SI and punk rely on riding a surge necessary to the development of consumer capitalism. As the rock boom of the 60s ran adrift into the corporate rock and disco of the 70s and punk into the MTV-dominated inanity of the 80s, it seems that it is not quite such a simple matter to fill the chain stores with 'substitutes' for revolu-tion. In a recession, the SI's rhetoric seems hopelessly misplaced: the real threat is of streamlined consumption without critical rip-ples at all. No space for the critique to scream in.

---

[32]A point excellently made by Sadie Plant, *The Most Radical Gesture: The Situationist International in a Postmodern Age*, 1992.

Vaneigem is attacking the enemy he knows: the purveyors of high art who market the avant-garde, art which is precisely designed to resist such marketing. The 1950s and 1960s witnessed a barrage of heretical anti-art ideas from which the visual arts have still not recovered. Of these heretical ideas the SI's were the purest, the most violent, the funniest and the best. They took Adorno's belief in the unexchangeable to a new level.

> Whereas in the real world all particulars are fungible, art protests against fungibility by holding up images of what reality itself might be like, if it were emancipated from the patterns of identification imposed on it. By the same token, art – the *imago* of the unexchangeable – verges on ideology because it makes us believe there are things in the world that are not for exchange. On behalf of the unexchangeable, art must awaken a critical consciousness toward the world of exchangeable things.[33]

However, like Adorno pronouncing judgement on radio music, the SI spoke from the position of bourgeois high art: they could see the mass market only as a degradation of the uniqueness of the high-art object, relentlessly vilifying those artists who peddled degraded wares. They became an international watch-dog committee, preventing the economic exploitation of anti-art: if someone in Rome was selling canvases by the yard as a critique of the way abstract expressionists turned their 'suffering' into money, they would disrupt anyone trying to pull the stunt again elsewhere. Because the idea of art irradiates the whole of society, such subversive ideas have enormous resonance, but without class consciousness they begin to replicate aristocratic disdain for the marketplace – 'You bought it in a shop? Oh, what a terrible job.'[34] The idea of the SI denouncing the Rasta buying a Big Youth album is palpably absurd.

Adorno's ideas work best in close dialectical association with Walter Benjamin's. Alongside Adorno's insistence that the artwork cannot embrace the market and survive, you need Benjamin's vision of the new materialism in the mass audience that is no longer mystified by the special uniqueness of the work of art, its 'aura' (itself a secular version of religious mystery): the horror-film audience that talk technically of how tension is built;[35] the

---

[33]Theodor Adorno, *Aesthetic Theory*, 1968, trs. C. Lenhardt, 1984, p. 123.
[34]Michael Flanders and Donald Swann, 'Song of Reproduction', *At the Drop of a Hat*, 1957, Parlophone PMC1033.
[35]Illustrated by the lines 'Imagine/throwing away the avalanche/so early in the movie' in 'Fantasy', Frank O'Hara, *Lunch Poems*, 1964, p. 73. This poem proposes a quite different reading of *Apostrophe (')* from that found below.

practical considerations about the depth of the bass sound in a dub twelve-inch or a house CD. In listing Zappa and reggae alongside Warhol and Hockney as merely 'leading the spectacle of decomposition', Vaneigem is echoing Adorno at his most mandarin, unaware of the manner in which class struggle manifests itself in music: the commercial arena as a battlefield, a war waged between musicians, record companies and audiences over money and use-value. Does the fucker *groove*? It is a materialist question none of the tedious debates about Morrissey or Madonna as pop icons ever address. Much to the annoyance of the pop journalists who would reduce everything to their moralistic chat, there *is* use-value in music. Vaneigem is so disgusted with the spectacle that to him it's all commercial shit, a pile of meaningless commodities to be opposed with his repetitive rhetoric of 'lived life' and the 'all-conquering imagination'. Such phrases become merely the purist incantations of the professional outsider. Vaneigem fails to grasp that a James Brown record is a material asset.

It is a bit like the argument about postmodernism. In opposing the return to old forms in classical music – symphony orchestras, tonality – the modernist is accused of inconsistency in liking, say, David Murray and his 1980s synthesis of free jazz with swing.[36] In fact the accusation of inconsistency stems from a similar idealism to Vaneigem's: thinking in abstractions that obscure the social facts. The reversion to tonality in classical music is designed to roll back the discoveries made at Darmstadt in the 1950s and 1960s, discoveries which could not be disputed by scholarly musical analysis (hence the prestige of Stockhausen and Boulez and Berio in academia) but which alienated consumers (empty concert halls). However much the argument for 'more accessible' music is phrased in demagogic populism ('multi-culturalism versus serialist élitism'), it in fact sides with middle-class use of classical music as a reassuring cement for social identity, a daydream of late aristocratic order and early bourgeois heroism which can only now be rehashed as kitsch. New tonality adopts irrationalism rather than face the consequences of form (which also explains the newfound respect for religion among its adherents).

Materialist analysis, on the other hand, does not judge art against immutable abstractions, but relates art to its historical role. The blues and ragtime and swing are the inventions of an

---

[36]At least by the Blake scholar Dr Susan Matthews, to whom the next three paragraphs are affectionately dedicated.

oppressed people, forms inimical to bourgeois mastery. The truth of the music may be bound up in maintaining ethnic specificity against commercial and academic homogenization rather than pursuing some necessary evolution. Abstract judgements about 'forward' and 'backward' (for example, condemning John Lee Hooker as reactionary because he is still playing the blues) are inappropriate. The black musician's use of the blues does not have the same meaning as a classical musician's use of sonata form. In the same way, talk of a white European composer's 'roots', borrowed from black nationalist jargon, has a racist taint (even if W. E. B. DuBois himself derived his idea of black pride from German philosophical traditions that fed into racial theory). As Lenin showed in his discussion of nationalism, one idea can have different political consequences depending on the global role (imperialist or colonized) of the nation in question.[37] Idealist criticism, which judges according to an inert set of abstract ideas (e.g. 'consumption' versus 'non-consumption'), regularly makes disastrous blunders.

The success of feminism in cultural studies has led to the terms 'sexist' or 'non-sexist' replacing the moral categories of 'improving' or 'corrupting' traditionally used by Matthew Arnold and F. R. Leavis. This might seem to ground aesthetic distinctions in social rather than moral concepts. However, when used outside a concrete understanding of musical form, the terms merely elaborate another idealism, susceptible – like all idealisms – to blatant contradiction. When Chris Blackford wishes to praise Van Der Graaf Generator in the radical music publication *Rubberneck*, he claims Peter Hammill's upper-class vocals are 'untainted by blues-derived misogyny'.[38] Susan McClary, on the other hand, says 'There are no white equivalents of Bessie Smith or Aretha Franklin – women who sing powerfully of both the spiritual and the erotic without the punitive, misogynist frame of European culture.'[39]

Both Blackford and McClary justify their tastes by reference to a moral system that transcends both the art and society they deal with; and contradict each other completely. Despite both being members of the 'anti-sexist' camp, Blackford's typically English 'anti-rockist' contempt for the blues is contradicted by

[37]V. I. Lenin, 'Critical Remarks on the National Question', *Prosveshcheniye*, Nos. 10, 11, 12, November – December 1913, *Collected Works*, 1951, Vol. 20, pp. 17–51.
[38]Chris Blackford, 'Notes from the Underground', *Rubberneck*, 10/11 April 1992, p. 5.
[39]Susan McClary, *Feminine Endings*, 1991, p. 153.

McClary, writing in America, where black studies have forced a certain amount of critical respect for the form.

Negative dialectics, on the other hand, views artistic forms as sedimented content: 'analysing them is the same as becoming conscious of the immanent history stored up in them'.[40] Instead of reducing artworks to mere examples of abstract ideas, it traces their material provenance. Of course, this means that critical 'judgement' must ultimately relate to a global political vision, an engagement which is anathema to liberalism, which thinks that only commitment to certain pre-selected 'ideas' separates the saved from the damned. Political support for the struggle for black emancipation in the States means that the use of rags by avant-garde musicians like David Murray or Henry Threadgill or Buell Neidlinger is understood as racial solidarity rather than retreat to outmoded institutions (and in the case of the neo-conservatism of Wynton Marsalis, perhaps not – these things can be resolved only by the listening ear).

Vaneigem puts an abstraction – condemnation of consumption – before the social context in which things occur. He seems utterly unaware of the need to score a good record for Saturday night's party. Far from being consumed 'at random' in chainstores, Zappa's presence in the marketplace has been a struggle, an epic achievement. Although Zappa started out as a self-taught composer with a background in serial composition, his decision to 'reach an audience' did not involve suppressing the logic of his material for something that would appeal to middle-class concert-goers. He also wanted to 'kill ugly radio',[41] to challenge pop anaemia with R&B. Despite the contentions of postmodern theory, class antagonism still persists. There is not simply one music that evenly goes from 'simple' to 'complex': different musical forms have their own dynamics. Zappa saw his way to using the materialism of the mass audience, its hunger for new effects and shock; a way to harness that dynamic to his avant-garde commitment to new sounds.

---

[40]Theodor Adorno, *Aesthetic Theory*, 1968, trs. C. Lenhardt, 1984, p. 126.
[41]A slogan that appeared inside the gatefold sleeve of *Absolutely Free*, 1967.

ANTI-SPIRIT

Zappa is concerned to compose music with the materials at hand – 'Just give me some *stuff*, and I'll organize it for you. That's what I do'[42] – but because his intentions are anti-ideological, the results glitter with suggestive information about the society we live in. The usual method used by artists to gain attention is to claim access to a higher or purer or more 'emotional' realm, making themselves careerists of the 'spirit'. Particularly repellent examples would be 'new age' composers like Alfred Schnittke and John Tavener, but all sorts of quite likeable artists wax suddenly secretive and sentimental about what they perceive as their 'talent'. Such big, bland, mystifying concepts are quite simply an insult to the variety and multiplicity and weirdness of the material world we live in. Zappa parallels the classical composer Pierre Boulez in his excitement with what is actually there, rather than with the vagaries of mysticism and piety.[43]

Defining himself as an *escaped* (rather than ex-) Catholic, Zappa could transform even church experiences with his materialist empiricism. At his grandmother's funeral

> The choir was singing, and I could see from the way that the candle flames were wavering, that they were responding to the sound waves coming from the choir. That was when I realized that sound, music, had a physical presence and that it could move the air around.[44]

Zappa's music and concepts make the head spin and the imagination conflagrate, but there is no recourse to drug culture or religion or engineered images of desirable lifestyle. He declares he is a capitalist – and, as with Duke Ellington, it is impossible to imagine him achieving the results he has without building a business around his music – but his materialism gives his music objectivity and science.

In his appearance as a video host on TV in 1985, Zappa was asked to explain his creativity.

> KATHRYN KINLEY: Where d'you get the inspiration for your satirical lyrics?
> FZ: I read them off the teleprompter.[45]

---

[42]Frank Zappa, with Peter Occhiogrosso, *The Real Frank Zappa Book*, 1989, p. 139.
[43]It has been gratifying to see them work together. See '*The Perfect Stranger*', in Chapter 10: Orchestras and Broadway.
[44]From the book of interviews *Once a Catholic*, reprinted in *Society Pages*, No. 44, March 1989.
[45]*Radio1990*, 1985.

Zappa answers the question by delivering a perfect example of his satire. He is inspired by the prospect of interrupting the smooth flow of the media charade. For this reason a Marxist can gain insights about capitalism from Zappa's music that are denied by romantic notions of the expressive artist in even such bold political pop figures as Billy Bragg or Sinéad O'Connor. This Marxism needs, though, to be more than a form of agitated Fabianism: it must use Walter Benjamin and the SI and Attali to understand what commodity-exchange has done to culture. It must reapply Marx.

In a sense, Zappa's initial idea was remarkably simple.

> The Mothers' project was carefully planned some eighteen months before it actually got off the ground. I had been looking for the right people for a long time. I was in advertising before I got into – ha ha – show business, and I'd done a little motivational research. One of the laws of economics is that if there is a demand, somebody ought to supply that demand, and they'll get rich. I composed a composite, gap-filling product to plug most of the gaps between so-called serious music and so-called popular music.[46]

Although he uses the rhetoric of the marketeer, Zappa's intention to realize music exceeded mere money-making 'cleverness'. He talks about a commercial niche but found a philosophical one. Zappa wrestles with the 'gap' between serious and popular and in so doing creates an art that addresses the issue of class. Other attempts to 'bridge' the gap have been a sorry tale of sentimentality, delusory wish-fulfilment and snobbery: Zappa's materialist focus on technical matters creates a real 'plug', livid with the confrontations and problematics of realizing a transcendent totality in a fractured world.

When Allan Bloom wrote in *The Closing of the American Mind* that he wanted an art that was 'noble, delicate and sublime', Zappa was asked by *New Perspectives Quarterly* to reply. He pointed out 'This is not a noble, delicate and sublime country. This is a mess run by criminals. Performers who are doing the crude, vulgar, repulsive things Bloom doesn't enjoy are only commenting on that fact.'[47]

It is the admixture of the real in Zappa's art that makes it exceptionally stimulating as an object of contemplation.

[46]Frank Zappa, spring 1968, quoted by Pete Frame, 'The No. 53, Earliest Days of the Just Another Band from LA', *ZigZag*, June 1975, p. 23.
[47]Frank Zappa, 'On Junk Food for the Soul', *New Perspectives Quarterly*, reprinted in *Society Pages*, No. 43, December 1988, p. 12.

Social documentation and underclass resistance

Zappa's father told him this about history when he was a kid: 'All the old history was written for the amusement of the ruling classes. The lower classes couldn't read, and their rulers didn't care about remembering what happened to them.'[48]

Accused frequently of triviality by rock writers, Zappa ripostes that his task is *social documentation*. Given the abysmal catalogue of rock's grappling with the larger issues – the Who on mental health, ELP on Armaggedon, Sting on the Russians – you would have thought critics would be grateful for a little local materialism. Apparently not. Underlying Zappa's gigantic ambition – the symphonies, the films, the scores for the Ensemble InterContemporain, the total 'project/object' – is a vitriolic underclass resentment. The statement he attributes to his father (also evident in David Ocker's sleeve notes to *Francesco*) evinces a distrust of pre-industrial 'civilization' that is as realistic as it is subversive: why indeed should the music of eighteenth-century aristocrats please us when our antecedents were living in abominable poverty and dying of dysentery at the age of twenty-two? The stunted daydreams of the classical-music listener – who sits on a Louis Quinze chair and 'appreciates' Haydn – provide for Zappa just as intense an image of sterility and repression as they do for Theodor Adorno (see 'Evelyn a Modified Dog' and 'Sofa' from *One Size Fits All*).

'Wet T-Shirt Nite', 'Magdalena', 'Bobby Brown', 'Teenage Prostitute' and 'Lonesome Cowboy Burt' are all about people and places the 'educated' person does not want to know. Where upwardly mobile rock music (Mike Oldfield, David Byrne, Laurie Anderson) cloaks its simple beats in the chic 'austerity' of modern art (tennis shoes, haircuts, repetition, etc.), Zappa seems intent on thrusting something unpleasant on you.

You mean I'm going to justify Zappa's worst excesses, all the humourless sexist crap? Sure.

---

[48]Frank Zappa, with Peter Occhiogrosso, *The Real Frank Zappa Book*, 1989, p. 200.

ALCHEMY

Zappa releases in the Zappologist what has been repressed in Western culture since the advent of rationalism. The medieval alchemist could read nature in the same way that he read Aristotle or the Bible: what mattered was not the accuracy of various positive assertions (an accuracy provable by recourse to empirical experiments) but an esoteric gloss that could reveal a hidden order beneath both nature and the writings of the revered texts. Rationalism exploded the myth that such an order existed and established procedures for testing what could be given public credence. Like many artists faced with the impersonal world-picture of bourgeois natural science, Zappa has invented a private system of references, a language in whose articulation he can play a more active role.

However, in deriving the elements of this private universe from modern life, where the environment is thoroughly artificial and manufactured, the elements contain sedimented social information that react in his crucible in unpredictable ways. The result is that the Zappologist's response to Zappa's themes in the external world – staring into the spooky interiors of poodle parlours, tearing off a post-it marked 'While You Were Out', reading the 'Crush All Boxes' sign on the garbage truck – is not an irrational imposition of abstract mystical schema on the natural world but a surrealist coup, a reading-off of the hidden dreams of everyday life. Despite his professional involvement in music and the music business, with all its temptations to special status and art-ideology flatulence, Zappa always directs his attention to the mind of the average person.[49] That it is frequently the *unconscious* aspect of that person's mind makes his art uniquely democratic, a *Finnegans Wake* in records. In Zappa, truth – blunt, banal, everyday – is *always* stranger than fiction.

TIMELESSNESS

One aspect of Zappa's work that makes it very hard to fit into the format of the 'rock biography' is how closely modelled the project/object is on the unconscious. Joyce scholars find it difficult

---

[49]It is significant that 'Strictly Genteel', the finale from *200 Motels*, which also (in an instrumental version) closes the 12-disc series *You Can't Do That on Stage Anymore*, includes the words 'God bless the mind of the man in the street.'

to expound a sentence of *Finnegans Wake* without referring back to *Ulysses* and *Dubliners*. They even find that they cannot really explicate early works without looking at subsequent exfoliations of germ ideas. It is just like that with Zappa. He relates this in the language of science.

> It's a universe of rates. You have molecular rates. You have large-scale rates. You have the expansion-of-the-universe rate. You have the rate of atomic decay. You have the rate of ageing. You have a world of rates. So, it's a world of rates and rates are time. Just so you really understand it, the rate is the difference between when it starts and when it ends. That's the rate. These are cycles. Now, that brings us back to the Big Note. A note is a cycle. A cycle is the way it goes up, the way it goes down. That's one cycle. You know it's pretty consistent the way I look at stuff. The other stuff that you have to realize is time doesn't start here and end over there. Everything happens at the same time.[50]

This is not mysticism, but a version of Einstein's relativity theory, principles that even Einstein admitted were not really imaginable. Freud, too, registered a problem with the historical (or biographical) idea of time.

> It is highly probable that there is no question at all of their being any direct function of time in forgetting. In the case of *repressed* memory-traces it can be demonstrated that they undergo no alteration even in the course of the longest period of time. The unconscious is quite timeless. The most important as well as the strangest characteristic of psychical fixation is that all impressions are preserved, not only in the same form in which they were first received, but also in all the forms which they have adopted in their further developments. This is a state of affairs which cannot be illustrated by comparison with another sphere.[51]

If Freud had not approached art via the individual psyche – his hopeless attempts to psychoanalyse the 'genius' Leonardo da Vinci – he would have found an ideal illustration of the timelessness of the unconscious in the sphere of art (though in 1907 the full-blown modernist presentation of timelessness was only prefigured in late-romantic disintegration: Mallarmé, Mahler, Henry James). If he had written half a century later, he would have found another illustration in relativity.

This psychoanalytical accuracy causes problems for the Zappo-

[50]Interview, 21–22 October 1988, by Bob Marshall, Dr Carolyn Dean and Gerald Fialka, quoted by Matt Galaher in his column 'Statistical Density' in *T'Mershi Duween*, No. 18, April 1991, p. 25. The *T'Mershi Duween* fanzine is available from 96a Cowlishaw Road, Hunter's Bar, Sheffield S11 8XH, England.
[51]Sigmund Freud, *Psychopathology of Everyday Life*, 1901 (added 1907), trs. Alan Tyson, 1960, p. 339nl.

grapher, who finds exposition of one album track ineluctably leads to explication of clusters of symptoms which streak the surface of the entire œuvre. It is this that has made album reviews – which place the latest Zappa opus in the context of releases by the Stones and Cher and Guns N' Roses – so absolutely inadequate, especially given the average rock writer's hostility to the hermeticism that characterizes modern art. Technical advances in recording, changing circumstances of musician personnel and status, battles with record labels – all these add up to a history of sorts, but the actual artworks expound a conceptual continuity that is essentially timeless. As the philosopher declares to Greggery Peccary, 'Time is an affliction',[52] a theme worked out explicitly in *Them Or Us (The Book)*. In what follows, a loosely chronological account frequently deviates into exposition of static themes – generally at the point when the theme has broken out in some unavoidably overt manner. Spotty but unashamed, the negative dialectics of poodle play proceeds undaunted.

---

[52]Frank Zappa, 'Greggery Peccary', *Studio Tan*, 1978.

CHAPTER 1
ORIGINS

EARLY DAYS

Frank Vincent Zappa was born on 21 December 1940 in Baltimore, Maryland. His father, Frank Vincent Zappa Senior, was born in Partinico in Sicily and emigrated to America as a child. His mother, Rose, was first-generation American: her father came from Naples and her mother was French and Sicilian. Frank Junior was the oldest child, with two younger bothers, Bobby and Carl, and a sister, Candy. The parents did not teach the children Italian, though they used it as a secret language to speak about money. In *The Real Frank Zappa Book* Zappa ascribes this need to hide their Italian backgrounds to the side taken by Italy in the Second World War. He mocks their contempt for 'hillbillies' and their insistence on sending him to an Italian dentist. He grew up in the Army housing facility in Edgewood, Maryland.

Frank Senior is a graduate of the University of North Carolina at Chapel Hill. He worked his way through college as a barber. His only musical instrument was what Zappa calls 'stroller' guitar. He was employed as a meteorologist at the Edgewood Arsenal, a job which Zappa reckons had to do with the manufacture of poison gas. There were tanks of mustard gas within a mile of the housing project and everybody had a personal gas mask in case of accidents. His father earned extra money by guinea-pig work – experiments that meant he wore patches on his skin. Working for the defence industry entailed all kinds of bureaucratic restrictions which impeded the family's socialization.

On *Freak Out!* Zappa's 'biographical trivia' included these words: 'When I was eleven years old I was 5ft 7 with hairy legs, pimples and a mustache ... for some strange reason they'd never let me be the captain of the softball team.'[1]

He expanded the point to Michael Gray

> We had two problems. One was the Security Clearance; the other was the fact that my father was born in Sicily and my mother was first-generation, from Italian and French parents. And most of the places we lived, anybody that was not one hundred percent all-white American was a threat to the community, y'know? And being associated with somebody of foreign parentage made it tough for me in school, and made it tough on them. There was that whole aspect of American life. And I never did understand it.[2]

The Zappas also moved house a great deal. They spent a brief period in Florida, which improved Frank's health, then returned to Edgewood. Shortly after that, in 1950, the family moved to Monterey on the West Coast, where Frank Senior had attained a position teaching metallurgy at the Naval Postgraduate School. They stayed there for three years. At the age of twelve Frank Junior became interested in percussion and took a summer school with a teacher called Keith McKillop, learning the rudiments of Scottish pipe-band drumming (the same basis used by many jazz drummers).

> They had all these little kids about eleven or twelve years old lined up in this room. You didn't have drums, you had these boards – not pads, but a plank laid across some chairs – and everybody stood in front of this plank and went *rattlety-tat* on it. I didn't have an actual drum until I was fourteen or fifteen, and all my practising had been done in my bedroom on top of this bureau – which happened to be a nice piece of furniture at one time, but some perverted Italian had painted it green, and the top of it was all scabbed off from me beating it with the sticks. Finally my mum got me a drum and allowed me to practise out in the garage – just one snare drum.[3]

It is Frank Zappa's developed sense of rhythm that has made it possible for him to create music that is effectively a third stream between classical and rock, so this background in percussion is highly significant.[4]

In 1953 they moved to Pomona, where Frank Senior pursued

---

[1]Frank Zappa, *Freak Out!*, 1966.
[2]Michael Gray, *Mother! is the Story of Frank Zappa*, 1985, p. 11.
[3]Steve Rosen, 'Frank Zappa', *Rock Guitarist*, 1977, reprinted in *Society Pages*, No. 26, July 1985, p. 20.
[4]I'd like to thank Orphy Robinson for his comments on drummer Ken Hyder which opened my eyes to the Scottish rudiment in sophisticated rhythmic extension – see *The Wire*, No. 63, April 1989.

metallurgy at Convair, and a year later to San Diego, where he worked on the Atlas missile. This nomadic lifestyle made it hard for the kids to make friends. The experience turned up in 'Ned the Mumbler', part of Zappa's rock 'n' roll opera, *I Was a Teenage Maltshop*, that CBS Television turned down in 1964:

> I'm new at your high school
> No teenage girl to call my name
> I'm new at your high school
> No teenage girl to call my name
> Just because my daddy done work for the government
> I've changed schools until it's a crying shame
>
> I'm just a-mumbling through your school yard
> Wishing someone knew my name
> I'm just a-mumbling through your school yard
> Wishing someone knew my name
> Lord know I need some friendship until it hurts me
> Why can't these people feel my pain?[5]

Although it is a humorous version of downhome blues – and gradually livens up into rock 'n' roll as Ned decides to show off to the girls – there is something very moving about Zappa's ragged delivery and the rough-necked, repetitive guitar. The sense of exclusion from mainstream American culture runs deep in Zappa: more than any explicit politics, it sources the subversive thrust of his art. The sleeve notes to Zappa's début, *Freak Out!*, their combination of protest and bitterness, their paradoxical reverse-psychology 'no commercial potential', so suited Swamp Dogg (the politicized songwriting persona of black soul producer Jerry Williams Jnr) that he lifted them wholesale for his first album, *Total Destruction to Your Mind*.[6]

Once relocated to the West Coast, Zappa, with his non-Anglo background, found fellow spirits in Mexican 'Pachucos' and shared their enthusiasm for black music. The reason that Zappa and the Mothers achieved the most authentic R&B sound of any of the white 60s rock groups was not down to musical virtuosity so much as to sympathy with the attitude of West Coast R&B: the splice of hurt, nihilism and celebration that characterizes the music

---

[5]Frank Zappa, 'Ned the Mumbler', *I Was a Teenage Maltshop* – part of the projected ten-record set, *The History and Collected Improvisations of the Mothers of Invention*. It was aired on Australian radio in 1975 and subsequently appeared scattered across the 'Mystery Discs' that came with *The Old Masters Box One* and *Two* and the *You Can't Do That on Stage Anymore* series. 'Ned the Mumbler' has not yet seen licit release.
[6]Swamp Dogg, *Total Destruction to Your Mind*, 1971, Canyon LP7706.

of Richard Berry, Big Jay McNeely and Johnny 'Guitar' Watson. Zappa played drums in a high-school R&B band called the Ramblers; he did not pick up the guitar until he was twenty-one.

> We used to go over to this Minister's house because his son was a piano player and I would sit in the living room with a pair of pots and a pair of sticks trying to get a shuffle going while Stewart Congden, which was his name, was plonking on the piano.[7]

In 1956 they moved to Lancaster, California, in the Mojave Desert near Palmdale. Frank Senior worked at Edwards Air Force Base, while Zappa attended Antelope Valley High School.

EDGARD VARÈSE

The early history of twentieth-century classical music is still subject to intense debate. The argument of modernists like Pierre Boulez, founder of IRCAM (Institut de Recherche et de Coordination Acoustique/Musique) and pre-eminent composer and theorist in France, is that certain key figures – Arnold Schoenberg, Anton Webern, Igor Stravinsky, Edgard Varèse – made technical innovations that augmented the musical vocabulary available to composers. Their legacy was further extended by the Darmstadt composers of the 50s and 60s – Boulez himself, Karlheinz Stockhausen, Luciano Berio. The proponents of postmodernism, on the other hand – composers like Steve Reich, Philip Glass and feminist theorists like Susan McClary – argue something completely different, saying that these innovations were perverse and unnatural, and that the true task of twentieth-century composition is to open up the Western classical tradition to world and pop music.

It is interesting to place Frank Zappa and his third stream in the context of this debate. In 1953, utterly ignorant of post-tonal classical music, he read an article in *Look* magazine about a record store owner named Sam Goody.

> A feature saying what a great guy Sam Goody was because he was such an exciting merchandiser and he could sell anything, he could sell any kind of record. And to give an example of what a great merchandiser he was, it said that he was even able to sell an album called *Ionisation* which had a bunch of drums banging, and it described the album in very negative terms. When I read that, I thought it sounded exactly like

---

[7]Quoted in John Colbert, 'Frank Zappa', *Musicians Only*, 28 January 1980, p. 15.

the kind of album that I wanted to hear because I had been playing drums since I was twelve. So I went looking for the album . . .[8]

Interestingly enough, as well as the idea of an all-percussion record, it was the saleable/unsaleable paradox of modern art that fired Zappa's imagination. He is responding to the same things that Adorno addresses.

> The social content of works of art sometimes rests precisely in the *protest* against social reception, particularly in relation to conventional and hardened forms of consciousness. From a certain historical threshold, which could be located about the middle of the nineteenth century, this is the general rule with autonomous creations. A sociology of art which neglected this fact would become just a technique in the service of those agencies which want to calculate how to get customers.[9]

The way Zappa actually found 'Ionisation' also provides an insight into his musical direction. He had been looking through the sale rack of R&B singles in a hi-fi store in La Mesa and was about to buy a couple of Joe Houston records.

Like many of the key figures in West Coast R&B, Houston came from Austin, Texas. He played raucous, big-toned tenor saxophone and in 1953 had a regional hit with 'Cornbread & Cabbage'. In 1955 he sold a million copies of 'All Night Long', the tune by Johnny Otis which also provided the chorus for 'Advance Romance' on *Bongo Fury* (recorded, incidentally, live in Austin, Texas). This kind of no-holds-barred small group swing was the other important input to Zappa's music and mythology, but on that day he put back the Houston singles when he saw something in the LP bin.

> I noticed a strange-looking black-and-white album with a guy on it who had frizzy gray hair and looked like a mad scientist. I thought it was great that a mad scientist had finally made a record, so I picked it up – and there it was, the record with 'Ionisation' on it.[10]

He got it cheap because they'd been using it to demonstrate hi-fi with. 'I took it home, put it on, and I loved it as soon as I heard it.'[11]

This response contradicts the postmodernist/minimalist

---

[8]John Diliberto and Kimberly Haas, 'Frank Zappa on Edgard Varèse', *Down Beat*, November 1981, p. 22.
[9]Theodor Adorno, 'Theses on the Sociology of Art', 1967, trs. B. Trench in *Working Papers in Cultural Studies*, No. 2, Spring 1972, p. 127.
[10]Frank Zappa, with Peter Occhiogrosso, *The Real Frank Zappa Book*, 1989, p. 31.
[11]John Diliberto and Kimberly Haas, 'Frank Zappa on Edgard Varèse', *Down Beat*, November 1981, p. 22.

argument that avant-garde music is unnatural and élitist. Varèse's *attitude* – described in 1924 by London's *Evening News* as 'Bolshevism in music'[12] – struck something in Zappa. Hans Richter, a participant in Zurich Dada during the First World War who developed an abstract visual 'music' on film, drew a direct line from Futurism to Varèse.

> The Futurists had already introduced the idea of provocation into art and practised it in their own performances. As an art it was called Bruitism, and was later given musical stature by Edgard Varèse, who followed up Russolo's discoveries in the field of noise-music, which was one of the basic contributions made by Futurism to modern music. In 1911 Russolo had built a noise-organ on which he could conjure up all the distracting sounds of everyday existence – the same sounds that Varèse later used as musical elements . . . Bruitism was taken up by the Cabaret Voltaire and gained a good deal from the furious momentum of the new movement: upwards and downwards, left and right, inwards (the groan) and outwards (the roar).[13]

This is a different version of Varèse from that of Pierre Boulez, who emphasizes his formal innovations. Richter reads off Varèse's creativity from his skill in fomenting social provocation. The conflict between these two positions – the academy versus romanticism – has been circulated since the mid-50s as the conflict between classical music and rock.

To the Marxist, who puts no transcendent value on any particular cultural rhetoric in bourgeois society, these two positions are merely sides of the same coin. Boulez himself learned crucial lessons from hearing Antonin Artaud's improvised emulation of Noh theatre – screams and non-player's percussion in an assault on the limits of radio theatre. Technical innovation is only ever possible in the teeth of social opposition, since art is not about building castles in the air but organizing socially symbolic acts. Only this can explain the formal inventiveness of socially transgressive movements, from the huge overhauls achieved by the revolutionary art of the 20s and 60s to the fascination exerted by the musical continuity in punk or performance art like Birdyak or Sergei Kuryokhin's Pop Mechanics – and the sudden dearth of artistic merit when these operations fail to question social limits. The technical freedom of Varèse, which allowed him to deal with sound in the manner of the abstract painter, balancing and

[12]*Evening News*, 31 July 1924, quoted Fernand Ouellette, *Edgard Varèse*, 1966, trs. Derek Coltman, 1973, p. 79.
[13]Hans Richter, *Dada – Art and Anti-Art*, 1964, p. 19.

contrasting blocks of sound, is a product of his Dada-Futurist social programme.

Varèse is as aware as Stravinsky of the excitement of a crashing pulse, but offsets unrelated rhythms, making the admixture a matter of textural collage. Distracted by the vocal icing on Zappa's music, people frequently fail to listen to it as *sound*: his weird abuttals of genre in fact work like extensions of Varèse's contrasting sonic blocks. Zappa's technical finesse in creating these shocks via orchestral scores and the multi-track recording studio should not obscure the political and social indignation which guides him. It is precisely because music is a materialist phenomenon, a symbolic response to social conditions, that R&B and Varèse can contribute to a single composer's music. Indeed, it is by grappling with the social totality, instead of serving the class layer it is by convention condemned to, that musical form evolves. Just as Boulez and his interest in the Second Viennese School after the Second World War were a reaction to nationalist parochialism and produced the huge strides of Darmstadt serialism, so the great moments in black music – James Brown, Marvin Gaye, Jimi Hendrix – arrived when its protagonists attempted global statements. Zappa could relate to R&B and Darmstadt because he understood that they both protested the sterility of the cold-war 50s, its chauvinism and its nuclear family and its sexual repression. Social critique was the key to his formal transcendence of idiom: a key without which would-be fusion is as lost and self-deluding as the progressive rock of the 70s or the minimalist commercialism of today.

For his fifteenth birthday Zappa got to make a long-distance phone-call to Edgard Varèse (he guessed rightly that Varèse would live in Greenwich Village and obtained the number from New York information). Varèse was away, working with Iannis Xenakis on *Le poème électronique* for the World's Fair in Brussels. Zappa spoke to his wife, Louise, and had a brief chat with Varèse later on. While staying with his aunt Mary in Baltimore in 1957, Zappa tried to arrange a visit; Varèse was again leaving for Europe, but wrote a letter, which Zappa keeps in a frame.

VII 12th/57

Dear Mr Zappa

I am sorry not to be able to grant you your request. I am leaving for
Europe next week and will be gone until next spring. I am hoping

however to see you on my return.
With best wishes.

Sincerely,
Edgard Varèse[14]

ANTELOPE VALLEY HIGH SCHOOL

Zappa has a practical attitude towards artistic materials that establishes links to Dada and modernist methodology. While at Antelope High School he was enrolled in an art class as a way of dealing with his 'difficult' attitude. He took a ten-minute length of film, wiped off the emulsion and painted it himself – then projected the results while musicians played his scores.[15] This bluntly experimental attitude characterizes all kinds of moments in his work, a version of his willingness to transgress taboos of social behaviour. He later deployed his band members and their foibles with the same mixture of cynicism and rapt attention he gave that piece of film.

Although remembered by Vice-Principal Ernest Tosi as 'forerunner' of the beatniks because of his sideburns and moustache (Tosi was named 'favourite confrontation with authority' in Zappa's answer to the United Mutations questionnaire), Zappa's uncompromising attitude earned him the respect of his teachers. To Tosi's surprise, after serving detention and being given a lift home, Zappa invited him into the Zappa home. His band director Mr Ballard and Tosi listened to *Freak Out!* and heard only Frank's 'beautiful music' rather than the rude words (which they concluded must be there to 'sell the album'). His English teacher asked him to score a cowboy film. The school superintendent, Dr Knapp, appears on the cover of *We're Only in It for the Money.* The cultural terrorism of *Freak Out!* was metaphorical rather than literal.

WEBERN AND STRAVINSKY

Zappa brought a copy of 'Angel in My Life' to Mr Kavelman, the band instructor at Mission Bay High School, and asked him what

---

[14]David Walley, *No Commercial Potential*, 1972, p. 29.
[15]Ibid., p. 22.

made it so good – 'parallel fourths' came the reply.[16] Kavelman also told him about twelve-tone music and Anton Webern. The latter became a favourite. Webern's sparse, glancing music, which associates musical events via intense consideration of the contrasting timbre of particular instruments, was closer to Zappa's preoccupations than the other music of the Second Viennese School (Arnold Schoenberg's linear stringency or Alban Berg's Mahlerian emotionalism). He found a record by Webern on the West Coast jazz label Dial, with a cover by David Stone Martin (the artist who defined the 'look' of late 40s/early 50s jazz – a cartoon version of Joan Miró, all thin wiry lines and ovals).

Zappa was brewing his own version of West Coast hip, adopting both its disregard for conventional boundaries and its proclivity for baroque complexity. Parallel figures might be Philip K. Dick, who combined a passion for classical music with a career writing pulp science fiction, or Phil Lesh, bass player with the Grateful Dead, who finances modern orchestral compositions. Zappa himself always denies any 'scene' apart from his immediate family and the musicians he employs, but the magisterial scale of his interests and art is nevertheless quintessentially West Coast. In New York, by comparison, it is all *angst*, individual ego, competition.

Igor Stravinsky's *Rite of Spring* was a revelation for Zappa. Though he later remarked that Stravinsky was really only a bigger, better version of Rimsky-Korsakov, Stravinsky's pounding rythms give rock composer another key to orchestration: where Varèse achieves shock, Stravinsky achieves splendour. The rich textures of *Hot Rats* owe a lot to Stravinsky (and to Rimsky-Korsakov). 'Igor's Boogie' on *Burnt Weeny Sandwich* is a nod to Stravinsky (as well as punning the composer's first name with that of Dr Frankenstein's henchman). 'Transylvania Boogie' on *Chunga's Revenge* relates rock to Béla Bartók (he was born in Transylvania and made field trips there to transcribe gypsy tunes) by adopting an East European peasant beat. Both Bartók and Stravinsky learned from folk music, and an element of European folk in string jazz – Western Swing, Joe Venuti, Stephane Grappelli, Stuff Smith, Ray Nance – meant that swing and classical music do have some common sources. The development of R&B was the result of paring down the swing orchestra and using electricity (bass and

---

[16]Frank Zappa, with Peter Occhiogrosso, *The Real Frank Zappa Book*, 1989, p. 34.

electric guitar) to make up for reduced forces: Johnny Otis is called the 'Godfather of R&B' because he pioneered this development. Zappa found violinists Sugarcane Harris and Jean-Luc Ponty and L. Shankar especially useful: they represented traditions of playing that contained elements of folk, classical, jazz and blues. The ambivalence of the violin as a genre-defined instrument was useful to Zappa's third stream.

The independent use of the same elements elsewhere appears to confirm the logic of Zappa's use of strings. Pinski Zoo, the Nottingham-based electric improvising outfit, combine leader Jan Kopinski's interest in Polish folk and classical music with funk. In Pinski Zoo 7 they add cello, viola and sax to their quartet and stress a Bohemian peasant wildness that is reminiscent of Zappa. Universal Congress Of, despite coming from LA, seem unaware of Zappa's music and yet they have recorded a track called 'Igor's Blues'[17] that both musically and in the title echoes Zappa's interests. Both Pinski Zoo and UCO derive their music more from Ornette Coleman than Zappa (via Ian Underwood, Ornette Coleman was a hidden influence on *Hot Rats*), but what is interesting is the manner in which the need for propulsive rhythm and harmonic interest has them using similar elements in Stravinsky. Zappa saw something in Stravinsky's exotic 'Eastern' barbarity that corresponded with elements of R&B.

R&B

R&B was enjoyed by Zappa in the company of high-school buddy Don Van Vliet (later Captain Beefheart), playing scratchy ex-jukebox singles into the night: electric downhome blues by Lightnin' Slim and Slim Harpo on the Excello label, West Coast R&B from Clarence 'Gatemouth' Brown, Johnny 'Guitar' Watson, Chuck Higgins, Joe Houston, Don and Dewey, the Chicago urban blues of Howlin' Wolf and Muddy Waters, doowop by the Spaniels, Nutmegs, Paragons and Orchids. This early immersion in what was then forbidden territory for whites, and the pair's subcultural surrealism – Beefheart's light blue Oldsmobile had a homemade werewolf-head sculpture built into the steering wheel – later allowed Beefheart and Zappa to ride the rock wave with music

---

[17]Universal Congress Of, 'Igor's Blues', *Prosperous and Qualified*, 1988, SST 180.

that was more than amped-up rock 'n' roll or collegiate blues. The notion of a genuine underground – which explains Zappa's early enthusiasm for the freaks, his contempt for flower power, and his ambivalent relationship to the rock industry in the late 70s and the 80s – was initiated by recognition of the emotional force of black R&B: its *reality*. Although anathema to postmodernism (and Jacques Derrida's insistence that there is nothing outside the text), such distinctions are the low-culture equivalent to arguments that philosophical speculation alone cannot dissolve the realities of capitalist exploitation and class. The refutation of idealism requires the distinction not only between Stalinism and Bolshevism but also between Pat Boone and Little Richard.

Unlike the nostalgia fostered by films such as *American Graffiti*, which refer to a homogenized experience 'we' are all meant to have lived through, Zappa's enthusiasm for black R&B puts him in conflict with mainstream society and its sanitized versions of that music. He didn't even like Elvis.

> The only record of Elvis I ever liked was 'Baby Let's Play House'. I was fantastically offended when he did 'Hound Dog' in '56, because I had the original record by Willie Mae Thornton and I said, '*How* could anybody do that?' Anybody who bought that Elvis record was missing out because they'd obviously never even heard Willie Mae Thornton's. See, they didn't play black records on the major radio stations. The only way you could hear the sort of music that I fell in love with was to pick up some scratchy station from a million miles away, or else go down to the juke-box record dump, something like that, where you could find these unusual labels – Peacock, or Excello, things like that. So most of the kids I went to school with had no idea and no knowledge of that kind of music. The only thing they knew about rock 'n' roll was when some white person decided they were going to, ah, memorialize on one of them R&B records. I mean, it's been said before but it's true – Pat Boone singing Little Richard numbers was an absolutely disgusting phenomenon.[18]

> Well, you know, you sit around and you intellectualize about these records, but during the Fifties I was in school and it was *real*. When those records came out I listened to 'em and I said, 'Yeah – they're really tellin' me somethin'.'[19]

To listen to these 50s records – those of Guitar Slim, Johnny 'Guitar' Watson, Richard Berry – Zappa's conclusion is hard to resist. Of course, blues 'authenticity' later became an ideological

[18]Michael Gray, *Mother! is the Story of Frank Zappa*, 1985, p. 23.
[19]Ibid., p. 20.

ball-and-chain every bit as oppressive as the junior-Sinatra moves of white pop'n'rollers like Fabian and Gene Pitney. It is Zappa's skill in negotiating these paradoxes that make his music so special. However, dialectics is not mere agnosticism, and it is impossible to understand Zappa's art without recognizing his critical stance, his appeal to sexual and social facts. He does have an idea of material reality: it explains both his delight in social documentation and his insistence on rigorous formal innovation, the mix of trivial poop and abstraction that has so effectively postponed serious critical attention. R&B provided both a musical foundation and a sociological slant, bass lines and horn-arrangements as well as a vision of music as the revenge-of-the-underdog on American middle-class values.

Zappa's contempt for the rock industry that grew up in the 70s also stems from his taste of the everyday creativity that surfaced in 50s R&B. Commerce had not yet intervened, assigning tasks to professionals and reducing fans to passive, paying customers.

> The people who went to see these bands *really* loved them. These weren't 'rock shows' put on by 'promoters' – instead there were girl gangs who would rent the hall, hire the band, hang the crepe paper, and sell the tickets. (The first gig I ever played – the one where I forgot my drumsticks – was sponsored by one of them, the 'BLUE VELVETS'.)[20]

Zappa's contribution to the Pomona College radio station when he was an R&B disc jockey (preserved by Zappa on tape and aired on Australian radio in 1975) had some of the 'here are three chords – go and form a band' ethos of punk fanzines like *Sniffin' Glue*.

> Here's another thing that you can do on the piano if you have one around, if you get tired of playing 'Home on the Range' by Colors – you have to learn two different kinds of backgrounds, you can do them both in the key of C and you'll be all right. The first one is like this [plays background for 'Night Owl'] that one's pretty easy to master and there's another which isn't too tricky either [plays a variant]. Now those backgrounds, those two backgrounds, will work for – oh I think it's a total of fifteen thousand different rock 'n' roll songs that you can all sing at parties.[21]

Zappa then segues into 'Charva', a delightfully dreary adolescent love-song that includes the lines

---

[20]Frank Zappa, with Peter Occhiogrosso, *The Real Frank Zappa Book*, 1989, p. 44.
[21]'This appeared on the 'Mystery Disc' in *The Old Masters Box One* and is talked about by Zappa in Michael Gray, *Mother! is the Story of Frank Zappa*, 1985, p. 32.

Charva, I loved you, I loved you through and through
I loved you since in grammar school when we were sniffing glue.[22]

Small wonder that Alternative TV, the punk band led by *Sniffin'*
Glue's editor Mark Perry, did such an authoritative version of
Zappa's 'Why Don't You Do Me Right?':[23] they were both talking
about the same drugs. Perry probably learned that glue-sniffing
was cool from the Ramones, but then the Ramones derived their
'gabba gabba hey' routine from *Freaks*, the movie that gave its
name to the cult Zappa adhered to (and which Zappa listed as his
favourite film in his answer to the United Mutations questionnaire:
Tod Browning's masterpiece, banned for thirty years, still constitutes a benchmark for art that would resist American normalcy).

Still on the subject of under-age intoxication, while at high
school Zappa formed a band called the Black-Outs, named after
some members of the group drank peppermint schnapps and
passed out. Zappa claims that it was the only R&B band in the
Mojave Desert at the time: 'Three of the guys (Johnny Franklin,
Carter Franklin and Wayne Lyles) were black, the Salazar brothers
were Mexican and Terry Wimberly represented the other
oppressed peoples of the earth.'[24]

Zappa was keenly aware of the social distinctions in the area.
Lancaster was a boom town due to employment at Edwards Air
Force Base (where Frank Senior worked), but the local alfalfa
farmers and feed-store owners held the new arrivals – mainly
Mexicans from the south and blacks from Texas – in contempt. A
Black-Outs gig planned at Sun Village in 1957, organized by a
local record-store owner, upset those in charge. Zappa was arrested
for vagrancy, but much to the cops' dismay, was extracted in
time for the gig. There was a big turnout of black school kids and
Motorhead's dance 'The Bug' went down a storm. Threatened by
a racist contingent of white high-school kids, the integrated band
were relieved to be backed up by the locals. Sun Village was
celebrated in *Roxy & Elsewhere* – Johnny Franklin is name-
checked. The 'Stumbler' in the song is someone who was famous
for dancing in front of the juke-box. Zappa was invited home by
the Stumbler and was impressed to find a large, brand-new

---

[22]'Mystery Disc', *The Old Masters Box One*, 1985.
[23]'Why Don't You Do Right' originally appeared as the B-side of the Big Leg Emma single
(Verve, 1967). It has now been included in the CD reissue of *Absolutely Free*. Alternative TV's
cover may be heard on *Live at Rat Club '77*, 1977, Crystal CLP001, and *The Image Has
Cracked*, 1977, Deptford Fun City D1P01.
[24]Frank Zappa, with Peter Occhiogrosso, *The Real Frank Zappa Book*, 1989, p. 45.

Magnavox stereo with a copy of Stravinsky's *Firebird Suite* on the turntable. Zappa wasn't the only genre-transgressive in the neighbourhood.

You can hear the Black-Outs being introduced at the Village Inn by an impromptu drunk-masquerading-as-MC on the first 'Mystery Disc'.[25] Then they play a song in the heartfelt yet humorous vein generic to West Coast R&B. The singer was also a stand-in.

> She was this huge lady, who wore white socks rolled down over her shoes and sang like a man. She's got a baritone voice and she's singing an old blues song called 'Steal Away' with the group – and, incidentally, with Motorhead on sax. He didn't have the first idea of how to play sax![26]

Although R&B seemed 'real' in comparison with lounge-music, West Coast R&B had an appealingly light touch. 'The West Coast music had a sense of humour, but the stuff from the East Coast was kinda desperate. Group music was brought to California music by black people from Texas, so it developed a different aura.'[27]

West Coast R&B legends Johnny 'Guitar' Watson and Sugarcane Harris provide some of the best moments of Zappa's music ('Andy', 'Willie the Pimp') precisely because Zappa's mix of heaviness and frenzy is so close to the music they pioneered. Another Hollywood-out-of-Texas musician was of course Little Richard, the ultimate experience in transvestism and R&B hysteria: 'I didn't want to sing the blues like some old black guy – I wanted to scream like a white lady!'

This remark encapsulates the social defiance contained in the first wave of R&B. There was also the sublimely *stupid-sounding* Richard Berry, whose boorishness conceals a fine-pitched dada. Zappa said in 1975

> Without getting the credit for it he made so much of what happened in R&B possible and so many people wouldn't have been there at all without him. He was one of the most important secret sources behind West Coast R&B in the 50s – and now he's walking around trying to get a contract.[28]

When Kevin Ayers said that Johnny Rotten was the most exciting voice since Little Richard's, and all the punk bands started playing

---

[25]'Mystery Disc', *The Old Masters Box One*, 1985.
[26]Quoted in Michael Gray, *Mother! is the Story of Frank Zappa*, 1985, p. 34.
[27]Ibid., p. 20.
[28]Ibid., p. 22.

Berry's 'Louie Louie', rock reconnected to the spark that originally inspired Zappa: the absurdist mind-fuck of R&B. By the late 70s Zappa was too occluded in his private enterprise to notice such continuities and he dismissed punk as a fad. It was Iggy Pop – another exponent of 'Louie Louie' and an intensity that transcends the categories of the absurd and the sublime – who received the 'godfather of punk' title. Nevertheless, Zappa's attitude has always been an extension of the transcendent idiocy of the 'Louie Louie' riff – the revolutionary heart of rock.[29]

STRAIGHTNESS

Zappa graduated from Antelope Valley High School on Friday, 13 June 1958. As he has often pointed out, he had not actually earned sufficient units, but they were glad to be shot of him anyway. He enrolled at Antelope Valley Junior College in order to meet girls ('You know there's no loose nook so I figured, "Let's be practical, lad", so I enrolled'[30]), but that scarcely lasted a semester, although he benefited from a special course in harmony taught by a Mr Russell. In the spring of 1959, the Zappas moved to Claremont, California. Frank left to live in Los Angeles, the Echo Park district, where he attempted to make a living writing movie scores, including that for *Run Home Slow*, a cowboy movie written by his English teacher at Antelope Valley High School, Don Cerveris. The producer, Tim Sullivan, went into debt when the star had a miscarriage on the third day of shooting. The project was scrapped for a few years. Lack of suitable food brought on an attack of ulcers and Zappa returned home in 1960. He attended Chaffey Junior College in Alto Loma, again 'for the express purpose of meeting girls',[31] and, along with a harmony course taught by a Miss Holly, he met Kay Sherman. Within a year they got married, and dropped out of school, though he also attended a composition course at Pomona High School. The marriage lasted five years. Sherman was working as a secretary for the First National Bank of Ontario, while Zappa went to work for Nile Running Greeting Cards.

In Claremont I was doing advertising work for trade magazines relating

[29] A point well made by Nick Tosches, *Unsung Heroes of Rock 'n' Roll*, 1984.
[30] Quoted in David Walley, *No Commercial Potential*, 1972, p. 32.
[31] Frank Zappa, with Peter Occhiogrosso, *The Real Frank Zappa Book*, 1989, p. 39.

to those greetings cards. And I was designing greeting cards. And I was making silk-screens for them. I could have run the place single-handed. My training in school, aside from the music things that I was doing on my own, was mainly in art. I supported myself part-time from working in commercial art. That's why my album covers were so good later on – not because I did them, Cal Schenkel has always done them – but I was very aware of the potency of that side of things. I really like it too. I still have a scrap book collection of some of those greetings cards and stuff.[32]

Their line consisted mostly of silk-screened greetings, designed for elderly women who liked flowers. I worked in the silk-screen department and, after a while, wound up designing a few of the floral horrors myself.

Then came a part-time job writing copy and designing ads for local businesses, including a few *beauties* for the First National Bank of Ontario, California. I also had short stints as a window dresser and a jewelry salesman and – the worst one – I sold *Collier's Encyclopedia*, door to door. That was truly wretched – but at least I got an inside look at how that shit is done.[33]

Such appreciation of hard sell entered into Zappa's art both as satire and practice. Like Philip K. Dick, who outdoes every sci-fi fantasist by concentration on the everyday concerns of the small businessman, Zappa outhips the hip by concentration on the straight.

At around the same time he played guitar in an integrated lounge band called Joe Perrino and the Mellotones at Tommy Sandi's Club Sahara in San Bernardino. They were allowed one up-tempo number a night, which was invariably a twist: 'It was quite a change from blues to hum-strum sitting on a stool wearing a white tux coat, your hair greased back . . . it was not too swift.'[34]

Another involvement was music for a film called *The World's Greatest Sinner*, a vehicle for Tim Carey. Zappa's score was played in 1960 by amateurs and semi-professionals gathered together by the music teacher at Pomona High School: fifty-two musicians, two microphones, mixed down to mono in a mobile studio in a track outside the Chaffey Junior College Little Theater. The credit ran: The Pomona Valley Symphony Orchestra conducted by Fred E. Graff. For the rock 'n' roll sections Zappa played guitar, Kenny Burgen saxophone, Doug Rost rhythm guitar and Al Surratt drums. 'Rancid' was Zappa's description of the recording con-

---

[32]Quoted in Michael Gray, *Mother! is the Story of Frank Zappa*, 1985, p. 27.
[33]Frank Zappa, with Peter Occhiogrosso, *The Real Frank Zappa Book*, 1989, p. 40
[34]Quoted in David Walley, *No Commercial Potential*, 1972, p. 33.

recording conditions.[35] Dominique Chevalier called the film 'fifth rate,'[36] but the Cramps, ever connoisseurs of American B-culture, put the film in their top ten.

LUX INTERIOR: This is one of the greatest rockabilly movies ever made. It stars this guy called Timothy Carey who is just unbelievable. He works for an insurance company and one day he walks into work and says, 'I've just had it with this job.' Then he says, 'Everybody listen to me. I've talked to Mr Simpson and he says you've all got the day off.' So he sends all the employees home. Then the boss walks in and says, 'What the hell happened', and he says, 'I quit' [laughs]. As he walks home from the insurance company he sees this great rock 'n' roll band playing and he gets this idea that he's going to be a rock 'n' roll star. He becomes a rockabilly star, buys a suit and changes his name to God Hilliard.

IVY RORSCHACH: It was made in 1961 and Frank Zappa did the music.

LUX INTERIOR: You won't believe his performances. He just starts shaking and his hair falls down . . . He must have watched Jerry Lee Lewis or something. He starts rolling around on the stage, he's just shaking all over. It's a live performance and he's smashing his guitar, he's really beating on it real loud. If you get a chance to see *The World's Greatest Sinner*, it'll just change your life. Wow![37]

Although Zappa now gives the impression that his involvement was minimal, the eleven minutes of the soundtrack on the *Serious Music* bootleg indicates a close parallel to the cartoon-style narration he used for *Greggery Peccary*. The part of Satan was played by Paul Frees.

[*Horse neighs. Rock band plays 'The World's Greatest Sinner' theme as an instrumental, followed by an orchestral overture.*]

SATAN: Oh yes, this is the place where a simple average American family lives. There's Clarence, my boy, just like any other male – the only difference is, he wants to be God.

[*Horse neighs.*]

SATAN: And that's coming right out of the horse's mouth. There's Edna, his loving wife and her brood, following Clarence to the very end – she had no choice. Alonzo, the gardener, Clarence's faithful friend, astute in the art of picking weeds.

[*Orchestra plays theme that later became 'Semi-fraudulent/Direct-from-Hollywood Overture' on* 200 Motels.]

They all want to get into the act, including myself. Oh boy, that Clarence, my greatest possibility since the apple incident – don't let me down, Clarence, don't let me down, boy, whatever you do.

CLARENCE: C'mon, followers!

[35]Ibid.
[36]Dominique Chevalier, *Viva! Zappa*, 1985, p. 8.
[37]Quoted by Ian Johnston, *The Wild Wild World of the Cramps*, 1990, pp. 119–20.

SATAN: Now, go, Clarence, go! Go! Go!
[*March music, fanfares, drum rolls.*]
CLARENCE: My name is God Hilliard! Follow me to every nook and corner of the United States!
SATAN: God – listen to them. It's fantastic! The best seat in my household is reserved for you, but you must keep up this high score. A representative will call on you to ensure your greatest hour yet to come. In other words, Clarence – go to hell! [*Laughs demonically. Dramatic chords followed by romantic flutes and strings.*]
GIRL: [*Softly*] God! I love you.
[*Heavy-breathing, more romantic music, birdsong, long section of orchestral music.*]

The integration of words and music in film soundtracks – much more artificially realized than most movie-goers are aware – is in fact a form of *musique concrète*. Walter Murch, who wound up working with Don Preston on the soundtrack of *Apocalypse Now*, started out as a devotee of Pierre Henri 'and those guys in France'.[38] 'Effects' music in films – designed to instil anxiety and fear or to accompany violence – are where most non-specialists first encounter twentieth-century classical innovations. Zappa's experience with *The World's Greatest Sinner* was grist to the mill. The sleeve of *Hot Rats* called it a 'movie for your ears' and the freedoms of *Lumpy Gravy* and *We're Only in It for the Money* learn from the effective dislocations of film. The speed and violence of film montage is generally far in advance of what people are prepared to accept in the concert hall. In the 1980s it became evident that John Zorn also learned from film – his Naked City albums use a continuity that comes straight out of Japanese monster movie soundtracks. *The World's Greatest Sinner* also played with themes – sexual repression and submission to authority, heaven and hell, temptation and ambition, Sadean amorality – that reappear in 'The Torture Never Stops' and 'Titties & Beer'.

STUDIO Z

With a pitch on music so unusual – an enthusiasm for both the twentieth-century avant-garde and R&B subculture – Zappa needed a recording studio. Live work did not allow room for experiment: then (as now) bands that got work played cover versions. An electronics hobbyist called Paul Buff ran a studio in

---

[38]Quoted by John Rockwell, *All American Music*, 1983, p. 155.

Cucamonga, California ('a blotch on a map, represented by the intersection of Route 66 with Archibald Avenue'[39]). The first most Zappa fans heard of this obscure start was in 1975 with the nostalgic song 'Cucamonga',[40] along with mentions on the concurrent bootleg *Confidential* (later *Metal Man Has Hornet's Wings*). The source of most of this bootleg was an Australian radio show presented by Captain Beefheart and Zappa in 1975, where the duo reminisced and joked as they played tracks off *Bongo Fury*, archive Cucamonga recordings and jammed 'Orange Claw Hammer' live in the studio.[41]

Paul Buff learned electronics while in the Marines with the intention of founding a studio. On discharge he set up Pal Recording Studio at 8040 Archibald Avenue. He built a mixing console housed in an old 40s dressing-table and constructed a five-track tape-recorder – at a time when most records were still being issued in mono. Only Les Paul, the electric guitar and overdub pioneer, had more tracks (eight). Buff played all the instruments and hawked his demos round Hollywood – Capitol, Del-Fi, Dot and Original Sound.

In 1963 Paul Buff's 'Tijuana Surf', a novelty instrumental in the 'cretin simple' style of organ classics like 'Rinky Dink' (Dave 'Baby' Cortez, 1962), reached number one in Mexico on Art Laboe's Original Sound label. Ostensibly played by the Hollywood Persuaders, the B-side featured Zappa playing some scorching guitar in a Johnny 'Guitar' Watson/Guitar Slim vein. Whereas the celebrated guitarists of the white blues boom favoured B.B. King's stringy expressiveness, Zappa plays thick-textured notes with particular attention to rocking his rhythm against the pounding mass-saxophones created by Buff's overdubbage. For good measure he overdubs stinging grace notes over the lead's distortions on the out-chorus, working the contrasting *tempi* like a tenor sax over a riffing horn section. Coruscating stuff, an indication that Zappa could hear a parallel violence in Varèse and R&B. It was called 'Grunion Run' and was celebrated twelve years later by appearing as a star in the vacuum cleaner constellation Coma Bernice on *One Size Fits All*. With some incredulity, Zappa mentions that he even got some royalties off it.

[39]Frank Zappa, with Peter Occhiogrosso, *The Real Frank Zappa Book*, 1989, p. 42.
[40]Frank Zappa, *Bongo Fury*, 1975.
[41]Some of this material was subsequently issued as part of 'Mystery Disc', *The Old Masters Box One*, 1985.

Buff and Zappa also leased recordings to the obscure Vigah label, supplying them with their first single: 'The Big Surfer' by Brian Lord & the Midnighters (Vigah 001). It featured a San Bernardino disc jockey impersonating President Kennedy judging a dance contest: a satirical messing of the boundary line between the spectacle of bourgeois politics and showbiz trivia that flowered as 'Wet T-Shirt Nite'.[42] Capitol Records bought the master but declined to issue it because of its punch-line about Medgar Evers, who had been killed in the meantime. Other releases at this time included 'How's Your Bird' by Baby Ray & the Ferns for Bob Keene's Del-fi label, a novelty sung by Ray Collins in falsetto, and 'Ned & Nelda' (Vigah 002), which took off on 'Hey Paula', the saccharine love duet by Paul and Paula. The B-Side was 'The World's Greatest Sinner', a two-minute R&B version of the movie.

> He's the world's greatest sinner
> As a sinner he's a winner
> He ain't no beginner
> He's just terrible! Too much!

Zappa unleashed a rocking guitar break that confirms his debt to Johnny 'Guitar' Watson: by 1963 his carving style was indeed well rehearsed.

Another single recorded at Studio Z was 'Dear Jeepers'/'Letter From Jeepers', which featured a local TV horror host called Bob Guy. Horror was a subculture that thrived on the reversal of all-American values. Count Dracula concludes: 'I must close now. The sun is coming up and I must return to the crypt'[43] – an interesting remark for a Californian TV personality. The Cramps named an album – *Stay Sick!* – after the catch-phrase of Ghoulardi, who graduated from DJ to TV horror host in the Cleveland area in 1963. In 1981 they had Vampira – star of *Plan 9 from Outer Space* and mid-50s TV horror host – climb out of a coffin on stage.[44] Like splatter movies now, horror was a genre with a great attraction for misfits.

Zappa's interest in classical music leads some critics to suspect him of upwardly mobile snobbery.

His *Perfect Stranger* is kind of great – he knows his Varèse, his Stravinsky – but his use of it, his presentation, his contextualization is just

---

[42]Frank Zappa, *Joe's Garage Act I*, 1979.
[43]Bob Guy, 'Dear Jeepers', *Cucamonga Years*, 1991.
[44]Ian Johnston, *The Wild Wild World of the Cramps*, 1990, p. 70.

so craven (no 'only in it for the money' jabs at the sacred cows of seriousness).[45]

Actually, Zappa's disgust with the Beatles (*Sgt. Pepper* being the target of his *We're Only in It for the Money* record sleeve) sprang from their adoption of the raggle-taggle bohemianism of San Francisco flower power, rather than mandarin hatred for mass culture. Distracted by Zappa's respect for cutting-edge classicism (which actually implies an Adornoite contempt for middle-class concert-culture), people forget that his pulp-roots are as extensive as such trash-hounds as the Cramps. Maybe with a little more sci-fi and a little less gore, Zappa's B-culture connoisseurship parallels the Cramps beyond an interest in early 60s TV horror hosts – both have covered André Williams' 'Bacon Fat'[46] and both applaud Jackie and the Starlites' 'Valerie'.[47] A surprising coincidence for those who see Zappa as some kind of progressive rock élitist.

Another single produced by Zappa was by Lowell George, who had a band called the Factory with guitarist Warren Klien, bassist Martin Kibbee and drummer Richie Hayward (with whom he subsequently formed Little Feat). Zappa did a 'fantastic job'[48] recording 'Lightnin'-Rod Man' for them, Lowell George's vocal a cartoon version of Mick Jagger and without doubt their finest moment (a subsequent release documents a 1966–9 evolution from joss-stick psychedelia to proto-Feat country-rock[49]). George also spent two months as lead singer in the Standells (whose 'Dirty Water' is now considered a 60s punk classic after appearing on the first *Nuggets* collection), joining the Mothers briefly in 1969.

In 1963 *Run Home Slow* was finally made – starring Mercedes McCambridge – and the soundtrack recorded. The theme opens the first 'Mystery Disc' and is a passable cowboy-film overture: galloping drums and trumpets bursting with sunrise optimism. With hindsight, one can see that its use of impressionist harmonies is a little unusual for hack film music in the early 60s. Zappa bought a new electric guitar with the proceeds, and took over Pal

---

[45]Mark Sinker, 'Outlines', *The Wire*, June 1992.
[46]Frank Zappa, 'Bacon Fat', *Our Man in Nirvana*, 8 November 1968, *Beat the Boots #2*, 1992, and *Broadway the Hard Way* (CD only), 1990; the Cramps 'Bacon Fat' live at Leeds University, 22 May 1984.
[47]Frank Zappa, 'Valarie', *Burnt Weeny Sandwich*, 1970; Lux and Ivy played the original on Kid Jensen's *Collector's Choice* on Radio 1 in 1984. See Ian Johnston, *The Wild Wild World of the Cramps*, 1990, p. 85.
[48]Lowell George, quoted by Andy Childs, 'The Exploits of Lowell George', *ZigZag*, No. 50, March 1975, p. 23.
[49]Lowell George and the Factory, *Lightnin'-Rod Man*, 1993, Edsel/Demon EDCD377.

Records from Buff, also buying $5,000-worth of old movie sets. He christened it Studio Z, painting the name on the door and 'Record your band' and '$13.50 per hour' on the front – all in the proto-psychedelic lettering he had presumably learned at Nile Greeting Cards (it was also used on the cover of *Absolutely Free*). The contract with Buff listed the equipment.

1 SHURE BROS. MICROPHONE	$ 30.00
2 ELECTRO VOICE £664 MICROPHONES	50.00
1 ELECTRO VOICE £654 MICROPHONE	35.00
1 OMEGA CONDENSOR MICROPHONE	80.00
5 MICROPHONE STANDS AND BOOM ARMS	57.00
1 15" KARLSON SPEAKER ENCLOSURE	35.00
1 12" SPEAKER ENCLOSURE	10.00
1 15" ELECTRO VOICE LS 15 SPEAKER	20.00
2 12" CALRAD SPEAKERS	20.00
1 12" UNIVERSAL SPEAKER	20.00
ASSORTED HIGH FREQUENCY SPEAKERS	10.00
3 POWER AMPLIFIERS (70watt, 30watt, 18watt)	100.00
1 PRESTO TAPE RECORDER (WITH HEADS & AMPLIFIER)	200.00
1 HAMMOND ECHO UNIT	40.00
1 REC O CUT RECORD CUTTING MACHINE	250.00
1 REC O CUT TONE ARM	10.00
2 VIKING TAPE RECORDING AMPLIFIERS	50.00
1 STEINWAY UPRIGHT PIANO	150.00
1 DESK	20.00
1 KOSS HEADSET	15.00
1 ELECTRIC HEATER	10.00
TOTAL	$1212.00[50]

Zappa taped the opening night party, and edited highlights appear on the first 'Mystery Disc'.

At the party was Beefheart, a guy named Bob Narcisso, Ray Collins, Motorhead, Beefheart's little girlfriend Laurie, another guy who used to play drums in our band, Al Ceraeff. I think that was about it. It was the night I took possession of Studio Z, and we just went into the studio and turned on the tape recorder and so I've got tapes of Captain Beefheart singing 'Night Owl' and Ray Collins singing 'Louie Louie'

---

[50]This document and others – rejection letters from Dot and CBS Television, press cuttings from 1962, layed-out and embellished by Cal Schenkel – surfaced in the booklet that accompanied the ten-record *The Collected History and Improvisations of the Mothers of Invention*, a bootleg box-set issued by Toad Hall's Rare Records in Australia. It was subsequently plundered for *Frank Zappa and the Mothers*, a collection of cuttings put out by Babylon Books in Manchester in the late 1970s and finally found official release with *Beat the Boots #2*, 1992.

and then we'd get a background going and be fucking around and making up lyrics on top of that.[51]

It is from tapes like these that Zappa selects the moments of time that build up his compositions, frequently pinpointing phrases or noises whose significance remains opaque for years. Hence the rumbles of dissatisfaction from people who feel they have been used: Beefheart claims that most of Zappa's ideas came from verbal improvisations he didn't even know he was taping. Years before the sampler made copyright an issue, Zappa was constructing collages of other people's sounds, hoarding the specific immediacy of people's spontaneity on tape. It was a procedure familiar to literary modernism – the inclusion of laundry lists and 'quoshed quotatoes' in *Finnegans Wake*, William Burroughs's fold-in – but unknown in music outside the little-known practice of *musique concrète* (although the manner in which Duke Ellington deployed the sound of individual musicians in his compositions is a pre-electronic anticipation of such cut-and-paste). Now that juxtaposition has become an accepted part of pop – the KLF are admired rather than criticized for recycling Tammy Wynette and Elvis – Zappa's 'rip-offs' appear in a new light. Pierre Boulez maintains that musical modernism lags behind its counterparts in painting and literature: certainly the stress on 'originality', an emphasis on the consistency of the individual psyche modelled on bourgeois property rights, is remarkably tenacious in rock ideology. It is an intrusion of Leavisite critical values that distorts the real dynamics of rock music, and fails completely to understand the blues, whose 'floating lyrics' (phrases common to hundreds of singers) are more effective than any of the self-consciously original couplets of singer-songwriters. With his tape montage and ringmaster tactics Zappa neatly sidesteps the paltry restrictions of individualism, producing epic abstractions that digest segments of the real world far beyond the reach of 'self-expression'.

Zappa moved into Studio Z shortly after his marriage to Kay Sherman ended, 'beginning a life of obsessive overdubbage – nonstop, twelve hours a day'. Like William Burroughs after the loss of his wife, Joan, Zappa saw this disruption of conventional domesticity as the start of his art: he made great play of it in the 'biographical trivia' section of *Freak Out!*. Motorhead Sherwood, dancer with the Black-Outs and later roadie and then baritone

---

[51]Michael Gray, *Mother! is the Story of Frank Zappa*, 1985, p. 32.

player in the Mothers, moved in and helped procure food. Unlimited access to a multi-track tape-recorder at this early stage in his career gave Zappa crucial experience. Performance is a great problem for avant-garde composers, who need to hear their music played if they are to evolve. Beethoven famously composed on into his deafness, but he was not abstractly sketching ideal compositions – some musicologists credit the thick texture of late works like the *Grosse Fuge* to his attempts to produce music he could feel through his body. He certainly thundered through his pieces on the piano however little he could hear. Theorists like Milton Babbitt can give the impression that modern composition is an arcane branch of higher mathematics. Opponents of 'difficult' modern music frequently claim that scored complexities are imperceptible. However, despite the rhetoric of Darmstadt serialism, which claims that it expands the parameters of musical logic outside human control, nothing has ever been achieved by garret composers who cannot hear their ideas realized. Maths is not music. Serialism expanded the repertory of sound available to the modern composer – but its techniques are not ends in themselves. Rather, they are a means of *foregrounding timbre*. Modernist music attempts to face the specificity of sound in a manner that is quite different from the traditional subordination of instrumental sound to abstractions of metre and pitch. As Pierre Boulez argues:

> You don't lose the substance, really, of a symphony by Mozart or by Beethoven if you play it in piano four hands – you have the main things. Of course, with the instruments you have a richness which adds to that, but does not add to the intrinsic value. You add a value, but if you take that out, the substance of the music is there. But now – and that's already begun in Schoenberg, with for instance, Opus 16 which is called *Farben*. If you reduce that to the piano, you take quite a lot out of it: you deteriorate the piece. Not only do you take something away, but you take something essential away from it. The mixture of rhythm and timbre is *with* the pitch and forms an amalgam which is absolutely unique, and if you take away a component then the music goes away also. Mallarmé said once, 'When I am speaking about a flower, I am speaking of something which is absent of any bouquet.' And that's true. When you write a note, a pitch is a symbol.[52]

Zappa often points out that it was Varèse's difficulties in achieving performances of his works that explains why he stopped composing for twenty-five years: 'He stopped composing pretty much

---

[52]Pierre Boulez in an interview with the author at the Maida Vale BBC Studios, 18 November 1990, written up in *The Wire*, No. 84, February 1991.

around 1940 because nobody would play his music and he couldn't earn a living.'[53]

Zappa was interested in written composition before he played an instrument.

> I was always interested in art. I used to practice, when I was a kid, drawing dollar bills. A lot of kids do that, I'm sure. Cal Schenkel was so good at it, he drew a five dollar bill one time and passed it. He bought his high school lunch with it. I'd never seen music on paper. What I had seen had been orchestra parts they give you in high school, beginner stuff. Then I saw a score. It just looked so wonderful – the very idea that this graphic representation, when translated into sound waves through the efforts of craftsmen would result in music. I said, Hey I gotta do this! So I got a ruler, I went out and bought some music paper, and I just started drawing. I didn't know what the fuck I was doing, but I could look at it. Then I went around looking for people who could play it, to find out what it would sound like. That's how I started out.[54]

Alchemy was a science directed at turning base metal into gold. Zappa views composition as similarly magical: tiny symbols that could signify big events – from free lunch to a symphony. Zappa's first score, 'Mice', was a solo for snare drum: 'Because I used to play snare drum in a school orchestra and we had a year-end competition where you go play your little solo.'[55]

After reading up on the theory he wrote some serial music in 1958 – but was disappointed when he heard it played: 'I didn't like it. I knew the serial integrity was there but nobody else was going to hear the mathematics that went into it.'[56]

The scores were discreetly discarded.[57] Paul Buff's multi-track recording studio was the means to actually hearing his creations, as was the 'instant composition' of improvising on electric guitar. The dialectic of improvisation/tape-transcription/composition has always been one of Zappa's methods: and that went for speech and documentary recordings as well as music. Like the pioneers of *musique concrète*, everything is grist to the mill.

> Once I learned to use the studio equipment I would sit there twelve hours at a time and play all the instruments myself onto the tape and

[53]Frank Zappa, 'On Edgard Varèse', *Down Beat*, November 1981, p. 22.
[54]Quoted by Michael Bloom, 'Interview with the Composer', *Trouser Press*, February 1980.
[55]Quoted in John Colbert, 'Frank Zappa', *Musicians Only*, 28 January 1980, p. 15.
[56]Quoted in David Walley, *No Commercial Potential*, 1972, p. 28.
[57]Although 'Waltz for Guitar' appeared thirty-four years later in *Zappa!* (a supplement from the publishers of *Keyboard and Guitar Player*), ed. Don Menn, 1992, p. 72, Zappa describing it as 'kind of short and boring' (p. 65).

I'd practise what I was going to do later when I got into a bigger studio. It was a lab for me.[58]

Compositions used as vehicles for the Mothers of Invention were prototyped at Studio Z. 'Toads of the Short Forest', which emerged on *Weasels Ripped My Flesh*, was originally played on overtracked guitars. Zappa experimented with speeded-up tape – 'Speed Freak Boogie' – and the kind of arhythmic juxtapositions that he later termed xenochrony. The intense pungency of Zappa's melodies was ready-formed by 1964, as was his burstingly brittle, inventive R&B guitar. He also learned to splice tape and to document practically anything. Playing a rehearsal tape on the Australian radio show – the Mothers of Invention fooling around with 'Rock Around the Clock' and improvising a song about sandwiches (Ray Collins in sublime form) – Zappa commented 'there's some old trapped air for you', which is an excellent image for the way in which recordings can evoke a whole ambience.

> From the tape you can really get back to how the whole thing was. You can just feel the atmosphere in that place. And it just happens to be a stereo tape so you can hear some room tone and the *old air* that was hanging there.[59]

The hours spent at Studio Z provided the basis for Zappa's devastating use of recording technology over the next three decades, his alchemical experiments with the power and suggestion of recorded sound. When he splices tape he is splicing not just sounds but whole environments.

To support himself during this lean period, Zappa played guitar in a combo that included Les Papp on drums and Paul Woods on bass. They played at all kinds of insalubrious joints, including the Sinners & Saints on Holt Boulevard in Ontario, California.

> Picture the scene – we were playing 'In the Midnight Hour' to an audience of Mexican laborers, entertained by four go-go girls in black net stockings ... I was wearing striped shirts – unheard of to a population that thrives on the white short-sleeved t-shirt because that's what you wore to work.[60]

They called themselves the Muthers.

Zappa recorded with Captain Beefheart as the Soots: 'Cheryl's Canon', Little Richard's 'Slippin' and Slidin' ' and 'Metal Man Has

[58]Quoted in Michael Gray, *Mother! is the Story of Frank Zappa*, 1985, p. 33.
[59]Ibid., p. 34.
[60]Quoted in David Walley, *No Commercial Potential*, 1972, p. 37.

Won His Wings'. To achieve a reasonable recording balance on the latter, Beefheart was put into the hall and improvised the words by reading out graffiti: the results were an amazing sort of proto-metal, using a generic descending blues riff that later surfaced as 'Top of the Stack' by James Brown.[61] Towards the end of 1963 Zappa started his own publishing company, operated from his home address of 314 West G Street, Ontario, California, calling it Aleatory Music (a Darmstadt reference that was no doubt lost on the record companies, agencies and television stations he submitted material to). The Rec O Cut lathe could manufacture acetate pressings, useful as a means of standing out from the usual spools of tape that inundated the record labels. Dot Records was sent 'Any Way the Wind Blows', an instrumental version of 'Take Your Clothes Off When You Dance' that featured suave jazz trumpet and 'Slippin' and 'Slidin' ',[62] to no avail. The rejection letter was the source of the famous 'no commercial potential' quote that graced the *Freak Out!* inner sleeve.

September 19, 1963

> Dear Mr Zappa:
> Let me thank you for submitting your material to Dot Records for recording consideration. This material has been carefully reviewed and while it does have merit, we do not feel strongly enough about its commercial potential to give you any assurance of a recording. It is, therefore, being returned to you.
> Please accept our sincere thanks for thinking of Dot Records and let me wish you every success.
> Milt Rogers
> Artists and Repertoire

In retrospect Zappa and Beefheart were mightily amused that Milt Rogers, justifying his rejection of the demos on the telephone, explained that it was 'because the guitar is distorted' – the Soots had merely arrived half a decade too early. Jerry Moss (the M to Herb Alpert's A of A&M Records) also told Beefheart that he could not possibly release his 'Electricity' because 'it wouldn't be good for my daughter'. Zappa's subsequent success allowed him

---

[61]James Brown, 'Top of the Stack', *It's a Mother*, 1969, King KSD1063.
[62]No doubt this is the reason why in 1976, when I asked Jeremy Prynne what he thought of Captain Beefheart, he said he thought he sounded like Little Richard. Ignorant of R. W. Penniman (and associating him with the dreaded Cliff Eponymous) I replied, 'No, like Howlin' Wolf, surely.' Though Beefheart's vocal grain derives from Chester Burnett, various mannerisms – his end-of-line falsetto squeak, for example – do indeed derive from Little Richard. Respect due to Home for Dinner for this early insight.

to sneer at Alpert and Moss just as the Sex Pistols did on 'EMI' – which Johnny Rotten concluded with a disgusted ' . . . and A-&-M . . .' Seems that whichever wave of rock is involved, Herb Alpert cannot win.

I Was a Teenage Maltshop

I Was a Teenage Maltshop was a 'heck of a little teenage opera',[63] a forerunner of the *Captain Beefheart vs. the Grunt People* movie project. It featured Beefheart speaking in his best pantomime accents, adopting the same mixture of condescension and tease that later led to Zappa being called 'Uncle Frank' in the rock press. As connoisseurs of R&B, any approach to teen 'culture' could only be tongue-in-cheek.

> It was the idea of an old man who has a daughter Nelda who was a cheerleader. The old man has a recording studio that hasn't hit and there's an evil landlord who's going to foreclose on him. So there's this group that comes in with a teenage hero that goes to the high school called Med the Mungler [*sic*], a teenage Lone Ranger. It was just a fantasy-type thing with rock 'n' roll music on it. [64]

The lyrics to 'Ned the Mumbler' (see above) indicate some kind of self-portrait, which maybe explains why years later Ike Willis's references to Tonto and 'Hi-ho Silver!' tickled Frank so much.[65]

Joseph Landis, the producer of the Repertoire Workshop at KNXT, a CBS TV station, rejected Zappa's treatment in December 1964, remaining 'unconvinced that the outline submitted can insure a quality show', though he did assure Zappa that he felt he had 'a great deal of imagination and talent'.[66] The tied-with-string continuity of *I Was a Teenage Maltshop* recurs in all of Zappa's major projects: from *200 Motels* to *Thing-Fish*, it's all really been one remake of *I Was a Teenage Maltshop*. This is like James Joyce, whose vast seventeen-year epic *Finnegans Wake* could just as well have been an episode in his first collection of short stories, *Dubliners*.

---

[63]Captain Beefheart introducing 'I Was a Teenage Maltshop', from 'Mystery Disc', *The Old Masters Box One*, 1985.
[64]Quoted in Michael Gray, *Mother! is the Story of Frank Zappa*, 1985, p. 33.
[65]Frank Zappa, *You Can't Do That on Stage Anymore Vol. 3*, 1989. Of course, it is Johnny 'Guitar' Watson who wrote the definitive Lone Ranger song: 'I Don't Want to be a Lone Ranger', *I Don't Want to be Alone, Stranger*, 1975, Fantasy F9484.
[66]Quoted in Michael Gray, *Mother! is the Story of Frank Zappa*, 1985, p. 33.

TANK C

Brushes with the law are eye-openers, giving those at the receiving end a personal experience no amount of political theory can supply. It took Miles Davis twenty-two years to document his famous beating and arrest outside Birdland (in *You're Under Arrest*, 1981), but the incident sparked a distrust of authority that lasted a lifetime. The plan to make *Captain Beefheart vs. the Grunt People* had been reported in the local press, including the *Ontario Daily Report*. Zappa built his own 'implausible' rocket ship inside Studio Z, using a job lot of flats he bought from the bankrupt F. K. Rockett Studios for a knock-down price of $50. He painted the scenery himself, all loopy psychedelic writing and cartoon-style nuts, bolts and dials. Towards the nose of the rocket in one photograph appears the inscription 'tear along dotted line', as if the whole thing had been built from instructions on the back of a cereal packet.[67]

Zappa's relatively long hair and the fact that Studio Z was a refuge for two white women and a black baby – who used to play on the sidewalk in front of the studio in view of those attending the Holy Roller church opposite – marked them out for persecution. That the authorities made it an obscenity rap indicated a prurience at the heart of cultural conservatism that Zappa goaded mercilessly for the rest of his career.

According to David Walley, Zappa had been approached while performing with the Muthers at the Sinners & Saints by a member of the San Bernardino police, asking if he would like to make training films for the vice squad. Zappa immediately thought in Pop Art/documentary/Warhol-esque terms.

> It was a great chance to do something interesting for the education of those people. I thought to myself, 'Now look, those guys are always going around and busting those weirdos and they treat 'em bad but that's probably because they don't understand. They don't know that these people they're arresting are really people.'[68]

This spirit of co-operation changed when the vice squad set up Zappa for a bust. They drilled a hole in the wall of Studio Z and watched for several weeks. Detective Willis of the San Bernardino vice squad first approached Zappa to audition for a part in the

---

[67]See photograph in Frank Zappa, with Peter Occhiogrosso, *The Real Frank Zappa Book*, 1989, p. 54.
[68]David Walley, *No Commercial Potential*, 1972, pp. 37–8.

29

film (that of Senator Gurney, 'the asshole'[69]). Willis then turned up disguised as a used-car salesman, asking Zappa to manufacture a porn flick 'for the boys', describing a list of the different sex acts to be included. The conversation was relayed via a wristwatch bug to a truck parked outside.

Zappa offered him a film for $300, an audio tape for $100. Willis accepted the latter.

> That evening, I manufactured the tape with the help of one of the girls – about half an hour's worth of bogus grunts and squeaky bedsprings. There was no actual sex involved. I stayed up all night to edit out the laughs and then added some background music – a complete production.[70]

As he handed over the results, Zappa and the girl, Lorraine Belcher, were arrested in a flurry of flashbulbs and news-reporters' questions. Zappa's father needed a bank loan to secure bail on them. They could not afford to fight this clear case of 'entrapment' (illegal in American law), so they pleaded guilty. In his private chambers the judge listened to the tape and roared with laughter, berating Zappa for being caught by Willis, the local cop known for harassment of homosexuals in public toilets, but nevertheless gave him a six-month sentence with all but ten days suspended. The days were served out in Tank C in San Bernardino County Jail. Like many first-timers, Zappa was shocked by the trivial nature of the crimes that could lead to imprisonment: 'There was a Mexican kid in there, about nineteen years old, who had been locked up for three weeks, awaiting *extradition to Beverly Hills* on a *jaywalking ticket*.'[71]

According to Zappa, the prison in Lancaster had been comfortable ('they gave you pancakes in the morning'[72]). In comparison, conditions in San Bernardino were appalling: one shower for forty-four men, cockroaches in the food, 140 degrees of heat, lights left on all night. Zappa says he has seen nothing to change his opinion of the Californian penal system. The imagery of incarceration, mixed in with that of wartime concentration camps, surfaces again and again in his work. The San Bernardino jail was memorialized in 'San Ber'dino' on *One Size Fits All*.

---

[69]Zappa seems to have it in for the Gurneys, however spelt: 'Brown Shoes Don't Make It' contains the line 'Gotta meet the Guerneys / And a dozen gray attorneys', *Absolutely Free*, 1967.
[70]Frank Zappa, with Peter Occhiogrosso, *The Real Frank Zappa Book*, 1989, p. 56.
[71]Ibid., p. 59.
[72]Ibid.

> They got some dark green air
> 'N you can choke all day[73]

Incarceration, claustrophobia, asphyxiation, poison gas, gas masks: a recurring cluster of images in Zappa's work that spells out a disturbing message about the freedoms allowed the citizens of social democracy. 'The Torture Never Stops' on *Zoot Allures* later spliced a sex-soundtrack with dungeon imagery: a guide to the repressions of Detective Willis.

THE SOUL GIANTS

Zappa had met singer Ray Collins before he set up Studio Z. In 1963 they wrote 'Memories of El Monte', a beautiful evocation of images from the doowop era. They contacted Cleve Duncan of the original Penguins and together with 'a bunch of guys from the car wash'[74] cut the song for Original Sound. In 1964 Collins was singing with the Soul Giants at a bar in Pomona called the Broadside. Davy Coronado was the leader and saxophonist, veteran R&B Mexican-American Roy Estrada played bass and Jimmy Carl Black – proud of his Cherokee heritage – played drums. 'A pretty decent bar band',[75] in Zappa's opinion. Zappa replaced their guitarist, Ray Hunt, after Hunt had a fight with Collins. They started playing Zappa's original material – a sure road to starvation. Davy Coronado quit to work in a bowling alley.

> He could play good but he was definitely into security. Security meant that you didn't play original material, you played what people asked for. You didn't say anything about it, you just played it because you were there to entertain people and if you did anything different from that it was possible that you wouldn't work. If you didn't work, you wouldn't eat, if you didn't eat it was no fun, so listen, What are you in the business for, why don't you guys play 'Midnight Hour' and enjoy it?[76]

Club owners wanted endless renditions of Sam the Sham's 'Wooly Bully', Richard Berry's 'Louie Louie' and Wilson Pickett's 'In the Midnight Hour'. It didn't help that the group began billing themselves as Captain Glasspack and the Magic Mufflers. The

---

[73]'San Ber'dino', *One Size Fits All*, 1975.
[74]Quoted in Michael Gray, *Mother! is the Story of Frank Zappa*, 1985, p. 29.
[75]Frank Zappa, with Peter Occhiogrosso, *The Real Frank Zappa Book*, 1989, p. 65.
[76]Quoted in David Walley *No Commercial Potential*, 1972, p. 42.

Beatles were all the rage, but that did not mean that the automatic association of original material and rock had yet been achieved. Rock music subsequently zeroed in on 'folk' integrity, despising the 'manufactured' stars who sang cover material (rock artists published with BMI not ASCAP), but that ideology did not wipe the board at once. Zappa notes with disgust that the Beatles craze simply meant that those without fringes, band uniforms and pretty faces got left in the cold. Bob Dylan was probably the key figure in making original material a viable commercial option for young musicians.

BOB DYLAN

Although Zappa was primarily inspired by black R&B and the classical avant-garde in terms of sound, Bob Dylan's early hits were a revelation from the point of view of marketing and politics.

> Dylan's 'Subterranean Homesick Blues' was a monster record. I heard that thing and I was jumping all over the car. And then when I heard the one after that, 'Like a Rolling Stone', I wanted to quit the music business because I felt that if this wins and it does what it's supposed to do, I don't need to do anything. It sold, but nobody responded to it the way they should have. They should have listened to that and said, 'Hey, that record got on the radio. Now wait a minute, we've got a chance to say something, you know? The radio is for us to use as a weapon.' It didn't happen right away, and I was a little disappointed. I figured, well shit, maybe it needs a little reinforcing.[77]

> I liked the lyrics to it because I felt they were fairly direct, and I was encouraged by the fact that the lyrics like that were on AM radio – and also by the fact that it was a *long* selection for AM radio. I said if this is on, if it's popular and it's selling, then it's setting up an important trend. But I didn't see it fulfilled in the way I'd hoped.[78]

You need to be aware of Zappa's initial enthusiasm to understand the sting of 'Flakes' on *Sheik Yerbouti*, where Adrian Belew puts on a Dylan voice to sing a 'protest song' about his car not being fixed on time, or Zappa's response when Dylan asked him to produce an album: in 1977 Dylan arrived unannounced at the log cabin in Laurel Canyon – 'in the freezing cold, with no coat and an open shirt' – and sat at the piano to play eleven songs (later to

---

[77]Ibid., p. 7.
[78]Quoted in Michael Gray, *Mother! is the Story of Frank Zappa* 1985, p. 49.

become *Infidels*). 'I said he should subcontract out the songs to Giorgio Moroder to do a complete synthesizer track and Dylan should play guitar and harmonica over the top. It would be fantastic!'[79]

By associating Dylan's music with the king of disco product, Zappa mocks Dylan's packaged 'humanity' – but they are the swipes of a fan betrayed (in *Joe's Garage* a disco beat symbolizes the punishment delivered to the individual by the record industry). Later developments notwithstanding, the effect of the first Bob Dylan was electric. His unashamedly untrained voice gave Jimi Hendrix the confidence to sing on his records. Despite Zappa's caustic remarks on 1960s LA's predilection for folk-rock over the blues, the abrasive real-guitar electric folk of Dylan's early hits – and his political lyrics – opened up a space for bands like the Mothers.

FREAKS

Zappa likes to focus on weirdness for its own sake, fashioning out of deviant behaviour icons of protest against the homogenized lifestyle of post-war America. He devotes three pages of *The Real Frank Zappa Book* to Crazy Jerry, who was addicted to electric shocks, and his mate Wild Bill the Mannequin Fucker.[80] This interest in the fringes of sanity bore artistic fruit with the Wild Man Fischer album. The freak phenomenon, though, was conscious counter-culture, an extension of beat bohemianism that has been eclipsed unduly by flower power. Unlike the hippies, whom he found conformist and stupid, Zappa was impressed by the freaks and *Freak Out!* aimed to put the movement on the map. Zappa later described the freaks.

> The origins of hippies as per San Francisco flower power Haight Ashbury is quite a different evolution from the LA freak movement of which I was a part. There was just a difference in the concept of it. I was never a hippie. I never bought the flower power ethic ... Most of the people in the LA freak scene around 1965 were getting their costumes together, dancing a lot. The real freaks weren't using any drugs at all. Then there were the weekenders who used to come in and stick anything in their mouth that they could find. And you were hearing about people

---

[79]Quoted in Dominique Chevalier, *Viva! Zappa*, 1985, p. 23.
[80]Frank Zappa, with Peter Occhiogrosso, *The Real Frank Zappa Book*, 1989, pp. 70–72.

freaking out on acid all over the place and it was quite colourful. Vito was the leader of the freak scene and Carl Franzoni was sort of like his lieutenant. Vito was about sixty-years-old and was married to a twenty-year-old ex-cheerleader, and they used to have this place down by Cantor's delicatessen and he would train people in how to be a freak.[81]

Vito was fifty-four. He made sculptures in his basement and taught sculpture too. He led a troupe of dancers: they would blag their way into gigs and shock everyone with their lack of inhibition. GTO Miss Pamela describes meeting him.

We saw Vito reclining on a rose-coloured velvet couch, surrounded by lavishly decorated people of all ages and races who seemed to be paying him homage. He had long, graying, uncombed hair and a ragtag beard that looked like it had been dipped in a bottle of glitter; he was wearing only a lace loincloth, and his chest had been painted like a peacock feather.[82]

She describes Vito's wife, Szou, suckling their three-year-old son Godot after he had danced nude on a table-top. Carl Franzoni, to whom 'Hungry Freaks' was dedicated, is described as 'an intensely unappealing guy in hand-painted red tights tweaking all the girls' bottoms'.[83] Pamela Zarubica was more charitable: 'The freak of all time – dressed in black tights and cape from head to foot and electric hair, with an undescribable goatee that rivalled only his tongue in length.'[84]

Sex of various descriptions – underage, public, multi-partner – was the great weapon in the war against middle America.

Vito invited a select few to come home with him to observe a tender fondling session. I had never witnessed two women in the heat of passion, so I dragged Sparky along to check it out. When we arrived at the pungent place, the moans had already started and we pressed through the oglers to Szou and Vito's tiny bedroom, which consisted of a doily-laden four-poster on which two tenderly young girls were tonguing each other to shriek city. It was such an odd occurrence; no one seemed to be getting off sexually by watching the pubescent girls, but everyone was silently observing the scene as if it were part of their necessary training by the headmaster, Vito. (Except for Karl, who was making no attempt to control his ecstasy.) One of the girls on the four-poster was only twelve years, and a few months later Vito was deported to Tahiti for this very situation, and many more just like it.[85]

[81]Quoted in Michael Gray, *Mother! is the Story of Frank Zappa*, 1985, p. 42.
[82]Pamela Des Barres, *I'm with the Band – Confessions of a Groupie*, 1991, p. 49.
[83]Ibid., p. 50.
[84]Quoted in Michael Gray, *Mother! is the Story of Frank Zappa*, 1985, p. 43.
[85]Pamela Des Barres, *I'm with the Band – Confessions of a Groupie*, 1991, p. 80.

The accidental death of Godot (he 'fell through a skylight during a wacky photo session on the roof'[86]) adds to the impression that Vito and Franzoni were living perilously close to madness.

The freaks were characterized by Miss Pamela as 'postbop, prepop',[87] a transitional culture between the beats and the hippies. The freak personnel merged with that of aspirant Hollywood *glitterati*. Lenny Bruce's funeral, for example, was addressed by Phil Spector with Miss Pamela, Dennis Hopper and Frank Zappa in attendance. It was the same scene that produced the Monkees, an innovative TV series whose spin-off chart success obscured its considerable merits. People were shocked when Zappa said that the Monkees – a byword for crass opportunism – were the best-sounding band in LA: he pointed out that they could afford good equipment.

Zappa's log-cabin home, which he moved into in 1968, was an inheritance from the freaks. Originally built by movie star Tom Mix, it first housed Carl Franzoni's commune. According to Miss Pamela,

> Frank Zappa wanted to live in the log cabin, and I guess he had clout with the mad-as-a-hatter landlady, because Carl and the girls were ousted from the basement and forced to seek accommodation elsewhere.[88]

Some commentators see this as symbolic of Zappa's exploitation of freak culture, but it's probably true that without Zappa the exploits of Carl Franzoni would have been swallowed by history long ago. Zappa talks with incredulity about the unquestioning nature of early 60s mass culture before the freaks arrived.

> Most of the stuff that I did between '65 and '69 was directed toward an audience that was accustomed to accepting everything that was handed to them. I mean *completely*. It was amazing: politically, musically, socially – everything. Somebody would just hand it to them and they wouldn't question it. It was my campaign in those days to do things that would shake people out of that complacency, or that ignorance, and make them question things.[89]

---

[86]Ibid., p. 57.
[87]Ibid., p. 51.
[88]Ibid., p. 88.
[89]Quoted in Michael Gray, *Mother! is the Story of Frank Zappa*, 1985, p. 50.

HERB COHEN

Zappa has always been explicit about the business side of his art, which is probably why he is often accused of being 'motivated by money'. Led Zeppelin, by contrast, are said to grant sessions with journalists and photographers on two conditions: there must be no mention of royalties due blues artists whose songs they used, and there must be no photographs showing their manager with the band. No besuited fat slob to be seen with the gods of cool. The rock aristocracy's suppression of economic realities was undone by punk, which brought up issues of management and cash like never before (like Zappa, Malcolm McLaren is frequently damned as a 'materialist' – in fact his saving grace). It is hard to recall the condescension of pre-punk rock-gods towards matters of finance. Zappa was never like that: management and record contracts feature heavily in his conceptual continuity.

Herb Cohen was introduced to Zappa by Mark Cheka, a pop artist from NY's East Village who had expressed some interest in managing the Mothers. They worked jointly for a while, but Cohen soon took over, managing the Mothers and Zappa until a series of lawsuits in the late 70s. Born in New York in 1933, Cohen joined the merchant marines in 1950. He worked in Mexico as a deckhand and fireman and was briefly involved in the Marine Cooks and Stewards Union. While serving in the army in San Francisco he began living with a folk-singer named Odetta and promoted Pete Seeger and the Weavers at the height of their persecution by Senator McCarthy as 'communists'. Cohen studied history at college, but his life experiences could not tally with the academic version ('they were just fucking lying'[90]). In 1956 he opened a club called the Purple Onion, promoting folk singers like Sonny Terry and Brownie McGhee and the Austrian singer Theodore Bikel, whom he subsequently managed (which explains Bikel's unlikely participation in *200 Motels*). In 1957 he opened a club called the Unicorn on Sunset Strip, a site next door to the Whisky-a-Go-Go to be. The folk and coffee-house boom of the late 50s – part of the general thaw in anti-communist paranoia – was underway. Cohen went on to greater success with the Cosmo Alley, where he promoted Lenny Bruce. Bruce's outspoken routines and Cohen's flair for publicity attracted lawsuits like flies

---

[90]Quoted in David Walley, *No Commercial Potential*, 1972, p. 48.

and Cohen took time off in the Near East and Africa, gun-running (he supported Lumumba while his competitors supported Moise Tschombe). In the early 60s he managed the Modern Folk Quartet and singer Judy Henske (which explains the appearance of Henske on Zappa's label Straight in 1969). Experienced, anti-authoritarian, obsessed with deals ('business is interesting, otherwise you get bored, there's nothing else to do'[91]), he was the ideal manager for a group like the Mothers. There's nothing like a lawsuit to sour relations, but his frequent name-checks on albums – including his photo on the Bizarre label's dust-sleeves and his portrait on the back cover of *Overnite Sensation* – show that for a while Zappa thought so too.

TOM WILSON

Zappa landed a record deal because of the insight of one of the producers at MGM, Tom Wilson. Though Zappa claims it was all a misunderstanding because Wilson saw the Mothers play their 'big boogie number' at the Whisky-a-Go-Go and assumed they were a blues band, Wilson's track record suggests otherwise. One of the first black Harvard graduates (economics, 1954), he had an ear for ground-breaking music. He produced the only encounter between Cecil Taylor and John Coltrane (*Coltrane Time*, 1958), then went on to record Simon and Garfunkel, the Animals, Country Joe and the Fish, Bob Dylan (*The Times They are-a Changin'* and *Bringing It All Back Home*, where Dylan went electric and upset the folk purists, and *Blonde on Blonde*), Richie Havens, Fraternity of Man, Nico and the Velvet Underground (*White Light/White Heat*), as well as *Freak Out!*, *Absolutely Free* and *We're Only in It for the Money*, appearing on the cover of the latter. Apparently, being into drugs helped him to relate to 60s rock artists (Zappa claims he was on LSD when 'Monster Magnet' was recorded). Wilson's role as a producer was to buffer the company accountants and the artists, something he evidently excelled at (what is now called an 'executive producer' rather than a hands-on, engineering one). Without Wilson's 'big mistake' (and he had plenty of opportunities to sever his support) Zappa might never have made it on to vinyl.

---

[91]Ibid., p. 49.

MGM/Verve refused to issue records by a band whose name was evidently a contraction of 'motherfuckers', so the Mothers became the Mothers of Invention – 'out of necessity', as Zappa says.[92] The new name encapsulated Zappa's critique of notions of freedom, a materialist rebuttal of idealism that weaves through his work like a black thread. As Arnold Schoenberg said: 'Art does not arise out of ability but rather out of necessity.'[93]

The Mothers consisted of the Soul Giants – Collins, Estrada and Black – plus the brilliant guitarist Elliot Ingber, who later flowered as Winged Eeel Fingerling with Captain Beefheart. Drawing upon his knowledge of marketing, Zappa made sure that MGM/Verve did not relegate the Mothers of Invention to the margins.

> We wouldn't have sold any records if we had left it up to the company. They figured we were odd-ball. One shot novelty-a-go-go. But we weren't. We had to show them ways that they could make money on the product. From the beginning it was hard to convince them of what we were talking about. We had to make them understand. First of all, I wanted to take the advertising account. Later they gave me most of it to do.
>
> MGM had no idea of merchandising in the underground press, and in certain periodicals that might tend to be left-wing, hippie-oriented, anything that didn't look like establishment media. We went after a peculiar audience – appealing to the curiosity of people who had some curiosity about things.[94]

According to the trade paper *Record World*, MGM were certainly trying to publicize the Mothers: 'MGM Goes Way Out on *Freak Out!* New York-MGM is massing a major promotional campaign, already well underway, to boom their new *freak-out* musical pactees, the Mothers of Invention.'[95]

An inter-office memo from Jack Maher to Mort Nasatir at

---

[92]Frank Zappa, with Peter Occhiogrosso, *The Real Frank Zappa Book*, 1989, p. 78. Talking on Nigel Leigh's documentary for the *Late Show* (BBC2, 11 March 1993, previewed in the *Guardian*, 10 March), Zappa said their name was a musicianly boast of technical excellence, an explanation in keeping with Zappa's new-found respectability in the 90s – the term's status as the most extreme swear word in black subculture suggests an alternative motivation. It was, for example, the name chosen by a group of New York anarchists inspired by SI texts. By *Fillmore East June 1971*, Zappa was able to drop 'of Invention'.
[93]Arnold Schoenberg, *Probleme Des Kunstunterrichts*, 1911. Quoted by Theodor Adorno, *Philosophy of Modern Music*, 1948, trs. Anne Mitchell and Wesley Blomster, 1973, p. 41.
[94]Quoted in Michael Gray, *Mother! is the Story of Frank Zappa*, 1985, p. 26.
[95]*Record World*, 9 July 1966, quoted in Michael Gray, *Mother! is the Story of Frank Zappa*, 1985, p. 64.

MGM makes clear that Zappa's ability to talk in terms of 'product' made an impression.

August 28, 1967
   One of the better ideas Herb Cohen and Frank Zappa have come up with since they invented advertising is the use of the billboard on the Sunset Strip.
   I have contracted with Grant Advertising to use this billboard for the months of October and November. The price is $3,200 for both months. The billboard will feature all of the Mothers of Invention albums from *Freak Out!* to *We're Only in It for the Money.*[96]

When accused of producing more commercial music later in his career, Zappa riposted that he had always had hopes: he thought *Freak Out!* would be a hit.[97] James Dillon (one of the leading lights in British classical music's embattled 'new complexity') maintains that Zappa could have been a great composer, but was sidetracked into rock music for commercial reasons.[98] This is to ignore the special dialectical relationship with commerce that makes Zappa's music so interesting, the value of having someone with a Frankfurt School aesthetic (someone who understands the fascistic tendencies of the culture industry) operating within the system. To wish that Zappa would stick to 'straight' music assumes that high-art music is unideological, unvitiated by its role in guaranteeing a 'higher realm' for hierachical society, in providing a mirror for middle-class self-esteem.

   Nor will Zappa's œuvre fit the classic rock schema of early creativity followed by sell-out and conformism, however much people try and pin him to that cross. The very notion of the sell-out tells us as much about those who accuse as the artists being denigrated. Spiritual investment in individual artists is inevitably followed by disappointment, as art and product appear at the end of the rainbow, rather than the hoped-for transformation of everyday life. As Zappa unfurls his petit-bourgeois politics over the decades, one has to recognize it was always there. For all its hairy packaging and 'no commercial potential' declarations, the songs on *Freak Out!* were as commercial as Zappa could make them. Compared to the heavy R&B of the Muthers at the Sinners & Saints (preserved on the 'Mystery Disc' of *The Old Masters*

[96]Quoted in Michael Gray, *Mother! is the Story of Frank Zappa*, 1985, pp. 26–7.
[97]Quoted by Chris Salewicz, 'OK Frank Let It Roll . . . The Frank Zzzzzzappa Snore-In', *New Musical Express*, 5 March 1977.
[98]An opinion relayed to me by the composer David Aldridge, who himself reckons that Zappa is one of the few who can 'both have his cake and eat it'.

Box One), the approach is melodic, inflated, popular in the current style. The soundtrack of the film *Mondo Hollywood* – a titillating 'documentary' of the LA freak scene made in 1965 which was going to feature the Mothers before Herb Cohen got them cut by demanding too much money – is close: clanging pop/rock brashly spiffed up with horns and strings, Nancy Sinatra-type arrangements rather than rocking R&B.

Today, though, *Mondo Hollywood* sounds like a showbiz response to rock, overblown and outdated. *Freak Out!* is still fascinating – not because it represents some purist alternative, but because it uses commercialism against itself. Zappa was still capable of off-the-leash, socking R&B (and showed this on 'Trouble Every Day'), but he was too fascinated by contradiction to restrict himself to that base. The leering threat of *Freak Out!*, a terrorizing hint that something unspeakably filthy is going on, was brilliantly co-ordinated with the cover graphics and liner notes: it was designed to catch the interest of anyone as jaded as Zappa with the conformist rigmarole of high school. A record of 'well-played' blues and avant-garde composition could not achieve the miasma of defilement achieved by perverting innocent pop.

> Forget about the Senior Prom and go to the library and **educate yourself** if you've got any guts. Some of you like **pep rallies** and plastic robots who tell you what to read. Forget I mentioned it. **This song has no message.** Rise for the flag salute.[99]

MGM saw the record's sales potential and reacted accordingly. *Record World* reported:

> Bud Hayden, exec in charge of album pushing, and Tom Wilson, who produced the two-records-for-the-price-of-one introductory package 'Freak-Out!' have already been to see distribs in a number of markets who have been extremely receptive, and the MGM men are readying a further push for this week's MGM meetings.
>
> Jigsaw puzzles of the album cover have been sent out to tease interest.[100]

The Mothers played in Hawaii and San Francisco and appeared on Robin Seymour's 'Swingin' Time' TV show on 19 July ('the switchboard was flooded with viewers either saying the Mothers were great or awful,' said Art Cevri, the talent co-ordinator) and on Dave Prince's 'Club 1270' on 23 July. On 29 July, as a fund-

[99]Note on 'Hungry Freaks, Daddy', *Freak Out!*, 1966.
[100]*Record World*, 9 July 1966, quoted in Michael Gray, *Mother! is the Story of Frank Zappa*, 1985, p. 64.

raiser for the *Los Angeles Free Press*, Zappa organized GUAMBO, the Great Underground Arts Masked Ball and Orgy. A poster, drawn in the greetings card/psychedelic style Zappa would use for *Absolutely Free*, ran: 'Filmmakers! Bring your own work and show it yourself. Poets arise!' A small warning hints at the kind of social taboos that were being broken. 'Warning: our lawyers say we can't admit total nudes to a public dance.'

The concert included what the *Los Angeles Free Press* reviewer called 'five short haired American Federation of Musician types in black suits, white shirts and black ties'[101] playing Zappa's scores alongside the Mothers. The gig lost money. Herb Cohen also organized concerts at the Shrine Auditorium in Santa Monica alongside bands like the West Coast Experimental Pop Art Band, the Mugwumps, the Factory and Count Five. The latter's 'Psychotic Reaction' became a greatly prized example of 60s punk.

A formative influence on 70s punk was *Nuggets*, the collection of 60s garage-band singles put together by critic and guitarist Lenny Kaye. Over the 80s, interest in the brief US mid-60s explosion of white high-school bands led to the discovery that Kaye was only skimming the surface: there were thousands of these raucous, dumb/clever outfits who learned the joys of R&B from the Beatles and Stones (*Nuggets* has become a series, along with an imitator named *Pebbles*). Although Zappa was an R&B connoisseur, and the Soul Giants had paid their dues in the clubs, many of the tunes on *Freak Out!* would not be out of place on *Nuggets*. Later on, with the recruitment of Sugarcane Harris and Johnny 'Guitar' Watson, Zappa would emulate more rootsy fare. The Mothers were a 60s punk band. If the Mothers had released *Freak Out!* and then sunk without trace, they would be honoured today as punk precursors. Punk was about discovering the despised and ignored – with Zappa playing world tours in the late 1970s, it did not seem appropriate to 'discover' his back catalogue (though ATV did cover 'Why Don't You Do Me Right').

The first song on *Freak Out!*, 'Hungry Freaks, Daddy', celebrates Carl Orestes Franzoni and the 'left behinds of the great society'. Its cavernous riff, a variant of that used by the Rolling Stones for '(I Can't Get No) Satisfaction', occupies a central role in the song in a like manner. When the guitar solo arrives, it is played in double-time, a device that made the Kingsmen's cover

---

[101]Quoted by David Walley, *No Commercial Potential*, 1972, p. 67.

of 'Louie Louie' so arresting. The twanging, aircraft-hangar sound (another punk feature) is abetted by snarling, well-peeved vocals from Ray Collins and Zappa. Despite the rampant, spiralling violence of the guitar solo, the arrangement – vibes, fanfares – is sheer *Mondo Hollywood*. Financial constraints meant that the horn charts were played on a kazoo, which gives the song a rubbishing, offensive edge.

Like jazz, rock has a peculiar relationship to Tin Pan Alley. Blues and folk were adopted in order to rid music of sentimentality and inauthenticity, but necessities of organizing the material for the culture industry – repeatable performances, hit songs – meant learning from the Gershwins and Cole Porter. Paul McCartney was particularly astute in this regard, writing melodies that were straight out of Broadway. West Coast R&B related to Hollywood via its 'sepia Sinatras': Nat King Cole, Charles Brown, Young John Watson (before he took up the guitar, Johnny 'Guitar' Watson played piano, cutting a devastating cocktail record for Chess[102]). The blues weight in these voices takes on the meretricious harmonies of Tin Pan Alley to great effect. Zappa hated lounge work and lounge music, but could not avoid the legacy of Sinatra when it came to his singers: the doowop voices he so admired frequently aspired to the butter-won't-melt vowel-sounds of Sinatra.

On 'Ain't Got No Heart' and 'How Could I Be Such a Fool,' Ray Collins sounds eerily like Jim Morrison. Those who see the Mothers as a Californian version of the Bonzo Dog Band might interpret this is as 'parody', but it was recorded a year before Morrison's début with the Doors. Zappa knew Morrison socially – and disapproved of his dope-smoking, calling him the 'spoilt high-school type'[103] – but Morrison was not well known enough in 1966 to merit satire. It is more a case of parallel development. Ray Collins's singing on these songs – narcissistic, portentous, petulant – does to Sinatra what James Dean did to Humphrey Bogart, replacing adult suss with an adolescent sneer. It nevertheless remains closer to Tin Pan Alley than to R&B. Morrison had

---

[102]Johnny 'Guitar' Watson, *I Cried for You*, 1962, Chess LPS4056, reissued in 1977 as *Getting Down with Johnny 'Guitar' Watson*, CA4056 (Watson does not play a note of guitar on it), to cash in on the success of *Ain't That a Bitch*, with a distasteful cover showing a nude model straddling a guitar. In 1989 Chess reissued it on CD (CDCHESS1020) and it has appeared on innumerable fly-by-night labels. 'Just the sort of stuff I like' John Jack of Cadillac Distribution. Probably the best release in the history of recorded sound.
[103]Quoted in Michael Gray, *Mother! is the Story of Frank Zappa*, 1985, p. 53.

trouble relating his light voice to the heavyweight blues he admired, and did so by using Sinatra-like posturing, the vocalist as actor rather than singer. Collins is doing the same thing, though because he is performing Zappa's music the whole performance is at the brink of collapsing into the ridiculous: nihilistic laughter edges every move. The Doors kept the frame in place, making records with the clarity of movie-makers. The need for structure had the Doors clinging to old forms: hearing José Feliciano put 'Light My Fire' right in the middle of the road is a chastening experience for those enamoured of the Doors and their high-school rebellion. Only Iggy Pop and the Stooges managed to take rock beyond the adolescent mind-set without using irony.

Freak Out! uses irony: tons of it. There's so much irony it is practically the stuff of which the music is made. The liner notes are full of self-deprecating remarks: 'Motherly Love' is 'trivial poop', 'Any Way the Wind Blows' is 'trivial nonsense'. 'Go Cry on Somebody Else's Shoulder' is 'very greasy. You should not listen to it. You should wear it on your hair.' 'Any Way the Wind Blows' is included because 'in a nutshell, kids, it is . . . how shall I say it? . . . it is intellectually and emotionally ACCESSIBLE for you. Hah! Maybe it is even right down your alley!'

'Ain't Got No Heart' is a rejection song, initiating the long line in not-love songs that gets Zappa into trouble with feminists. In the notes, Zappa calls the song 'a summary of my feelings in social-sexual relationships', but with his marriage to Gail Sloatman (which continued happily to his death) such not-love songs did not cease. Zappa claims that love songs are bad for mental health, manufacturing ideals that cannot possibly be fulfilled: 'Ain't Got No Heart' is not so much a summary of Zappa's personal feelings as a deliberate upending of love-song clichés. Zappa has said that he believes in real love, not the Madison Avenue kind, a statement that immediately recognizes the commercial colonization of private life that makes certain moves taboo to rebel art. 'How Could I Be Such a Fool' has technical sleeve notes about its use of time signatures. It is

> based on a modified **nanigo** rhythm. We call it a **Motown Waltz**. It stays in 3/4 time throughout, but shifts in the action occur from section to section. As an American teenager (**as an American**), this means **nothing** to you. (I always wondered if I could write a love song.)

Zappa is trying to educate his listeners in the *representational* nature of pop music, the fact that it is a construct, not real life. Pop's musical and emotional constraints (compared to either classical music or R&B) mean that these ambitions result in tension: the distance between Zappa's ideas and the forms to hand can be resolved only in absurdity. The lyrics are frequently a series of clichés that do not add up.

> How could I be such a fool
> How could I believe all those lies you told me ...
> But there will come a time and you'll regret the way
> You treated me as if I was a fool and didn't know
> The many times you lied about your love for me

Is the narrator a fool or not? In salvaging some kind of dignity for himself he ties himself in logical knots. It is procedures like these, attempts to make conventional song form self-destruct – rather than the woman-hatred he has been accused of – that explain the frequency of not-love songs in Zappa.

In many ways the love-song symbolizes the singer's relationship to his audience: in romancing the loved one the singer expresses an attitude towards the consumer. Zappa's offensiveness in this regard, no doubt abetted by a lack of regard for feminist arguments (a lack of regard which probably does make him sexist in terms of liberal debate), enables him to produce desecrations of the usual postures, desecrations unparallelled in pop. Zappa's not-love songs are part of his formal deconstruction.

> Why should I throw away the groovy life I lead?
> Cos baby what you got is sure ain't what I need.[104]

Even in 1966 the word 'groovy' hangs in the song with quotes round it, emphasizing the manner in which the white speaker has hijacked a black word (an unease Simon and Garfunkel framed for ever with 'Feelin' Groovy'). Zappa's songs are possibilities for feeling, not statements: he is a ringmaster, not a singer-songwriter. This explains his readiness to use other singers, part of his strategy in achieving an ambivalent resonance for so-called self-expression.

'You're Probably Wondering Why I'm Here' expressed with nervy bluntness the paradox of art in a commodity society.

> But maybe that's not for me to say
> They only pay me here to play
> You're probably wondering why I'm here
> And so am I, so am I

---

[104]'I Ain't Got No Heart to Give Away', *Freak Out!*, 1966.

'Not that it'll make a heck of a lot of difference to ya,' says Zappa at the end. The song has the net effect of a play by Alfred Jarry or Eugène Ionesco. A 'Relevant Quotes' section in the sleeve-notes includes one from David Anderle: 'I find your approach to music to be commensurate with the major motivational forces exemplified most manifestly in the "tragi-comic" aspects of the "theatre of the absurd".'

Samuel Beckett, whom the critics categorized as 'theatre of the absurd' along with Jarry and Ionesco, was for Adorno the paragon of literary modernism. Adorno's disgust with the streamlining of music for profit, the hit songs of the culture industry, precluded the idea that anyone could take such an idea on board and still work within the industry. Of course, there are still people who shelter in their well-upholstered havens from the 'vulgarity' of the mass media, but increasingly they find that in their isolation they cannot understand the moves of contemporary high art itself, ending up as the dupes of the subsection of the culture industry that recycles artworks from the past. Adorno was not one of these: the power of his analysis is derived from an unflinching vision of the social totality (or rather a totality which he could view only as precisely antisocial, administered and oppressive). Keeping a critical consciousness alive in the marketplace, an explicit degra-dation amidst the graded racks of available product: the project initiated by *Freak Out!*. This may have been deemed impossible by Adorno, but then he deemed workers' politics impossible too.

There are other signs of continuity between high-art modern-ism and the Mothers of Invention besides the reference to the theatre of the absurd. The most important was the quotation from Edgard Varèse: 'The present-day composer refuses to die!' This was from the manifesto of the International Composers' Guild, a group set up by Varèse at the Liberty Club on New York's East 40th Street on 31 May 1921. In July 1921 they issued a statement:

> The composer is the only one of the creators today who is denied direct contact with the public. When his work is done he is thrust aside, and the interpreter enters, not to try to understand but impertinently to judge it. Not finding in it any trace of the conventions to which he is accustomed, he banishes it from his programs, denouncing it as incoher-ent and unintelligible.
>
> In every other field, the creator comes into some form of direct contact with his public. The poet and novelist enjoy the medium of the printed page; the painter and sculptor, the open doors of the gallery;

the dramatist, the free scope of a stage. The composer must depend upon an intermediary, the interpreter.

It is true that in response to public demand, our official organizations occasionally place on their programs a new work surrounded by established names. But such a work is carefully chosen from the most timid and anaemic of contemporary production, leaving absolutely unheard the composers who represent the true spirit of our time.

Dying is the privilege of the weary. The present day composers refuse to die. They have realized the necessity of banding together and fighting for the right of the individual to secure a fair and free presentation of his work. It is out of such a collective will that the International Composers' Guild was born.

The aim of the International Composers' Guild is to centralize the works of the day, to group them in programs intelligently and organically constructed, and, with the disinterested help of singers and instrumentalists, to present those works in such a way as to reveal their fundamental spirit. The International Composers' Guild refuses to admit any limitation, either of volition or of action. The International Composers' Guild disapproves of all 'isms'; denies the existence of schools; recognizes only the individual.[105]

This concerns economic survival for the composer rather than aesthetic principle, which explains its stress on the individual (composers and musicians never like being assigned to schools as it does not advance their careers; it is individual fame that brings in gigs). Zappa took this individualism to its conclusion and altered the plural 'present day composers' to the singular.

EDGARD VARÈSE[106]

In literature, even unbendingly anti-commodified language has finally to recognize the objective force of the culture industry. The hard surface of Wyndham Lewis and Samuel Beckett, with their last-outpost refusal of a social dialectic, could only reasonably be extended in the pulp-pulsations of William Burroughs, who brought social conflict – the struggles of the dispossessed, gayness, the drug economy – into the text. Classical music, in contrast, might seem to be a haven for Adorno's powerless yet unbowed spirit of refusal. The fact that Brian Ferneyhough can still create authentic works which are an extension of Schoenberg means that

---

[105]Quoted by Fernand Ouellette, *Edgard Varèse*, 1966, trs. Derek Coltman, 1968, p. 66.
[106]This section constitutes a *theoretical diversion* from the rock-bio bits preceding – you can skip this, but be warned: *this is the shape of jazz to come.*

we are not yet finished with the claims of an utterly autonomous art. However, when Frank Zappa picked on Edgard Varèse as the presiding genius of *Freak Out!* he was picking up another strand of modernism.

In his *Philosophy of Modern Music*, Theodor Adorno approaches the problem of music in a commodity society by contrasting Igor Stravinsky with Arnold Schoenberg. Adorno's attention to the detail of the score, an analysis that treats of music and society in rapid stroboscopic alternation, enables him to articulate with precision the wider issues which were concentrated in the heated controversy between the two composers' camps. Schoenberg's twelve-tone technique, as a fully worked-out elimination of the traces of tonality left in 'free tonality', took the logical approach to the ruptions of what had hitherto been read off as expressive emotionalism, a stringent process akin to Freudian psychoanalysis: instead of 'subjectivity' we are suddenly threatened by science. Adorno compares dissonance to the revelations of the unconscious in the malfunctions of rational discourse. It is 'the vehicle of meaning for all those factors which have fallen victim to the taboo of order. Dissonance is responsible for the censored sex drive.'[107]

Like the Bolshevik emphasis on strikes and class struggle, twelve-tone concentrates on moments of rupture, making a deliberate discipline of aspects which tonal music uses as a titillatory sprinkling. It does not 'abandon' the notion of the suffering subject with the facile radicalism of the followers of John Cage. This laid the Second Viennese School open to the charge of indulgence.

> Among the arguments which would attempt to relegate the disquieting phenomenon of Schoenberg into the past of Romanticism and individualism (in order to be able to serve the operations of modern collectives with a better conscience), the most widely spread is the one which brands him as an '*espressivo*' composer and his music as an 'exaggeration' of a decayed mode of expression.[108]

Such relegation is suitable for the peculiarly English philistinism which says that Freud was overly concerned with the 'individual' and Marx 'too intellectual'. Worse, a sinister ideological alliance between bourgeois respectability (which doesn't like to feel its

[107]Theodor Adorno, *Philosophy of Modern Music*, 1948, trs. Anne Mitchell and Wesley Blomster, 1973, pp. 124–5.
[108]Ibid., p. 38. An argument put to me by Jeremy Prynne, who affected amazement that I should be taken in by Schoenberg's 'schmaltz', an opening shot in his on-going support for what he calls 'systems' music.

teeth grating) and postmodernist musicology also threatens to relegate the Second Viennese School and Edgard Varèse to the dustbin of history. Susan McClary's *Feminine Endings* is one of the best expressions of this argument (she also wrote the post-word to the Minnesota University Press translation of *Bruits* by Jacques Attali).

In 1963 Zappa presented some of his avant-garde classical compositions to an audience at Mount St Mary's College. When asked to explain his attitude towards the 'classics' (Beethoven and Bach) he said he didn't 'listen to tonal classical music at all'. Zappa did not pursue his experiments with serialism in the 50s and his music is post-tonal rather than strictly atonal (there are keys, and maybe several at once, but also all kinds of untempered sonic events). In what follows Susan McClary attacks 'atonality' but what she really means to reject is all the disturbance brought to classical music by the Second Viennese School – which is precisely where Zappa starts.

McClary and postmodernism

Susan McClary sees climactic musical expression as orgasmic, male-centred and sexist. She welcomes the victory of minimalism as a less oppressive ethic. Modernism in music, along with all its uncool unpostmodern heaving about, is dismissed as the dying gasp of Eurocentric romanticism. Getting rid of the subject, getting rid of the pain; it sounds suspiciously like Althusserian academics and their erasure of Marx's bothersome stress on subjectivity and class struggle. To her credit, McClary unfurls devastating sexual-reductionist accounts of Beethoven's Ninth and Bizet's *Carmen*, showing how both enact Vladimir Propp's narrative (male order/ female challenge/re-establishment of male order, a schema that also characterizes, for example, 50s westerns). Then McClary suddenly drops everything in order to embrace minimalism and the 'new' tonality. This is particularly strange when she has just demon-strated how crucial twelve-tone technique might be in the abolition of the binary dualisms that keep the feminine in music 'other' and inferior. She pinpoints a key argument of Schoenberg's.

> For *Theory of Harmony* is in large measure an attempt at imagining a musical language that could eschew binarism, whether they be major/

minor, consonance/dissonance, or masculine/feminine . . . he goes on to express his longing for a musical discourse that is, like the angels, 'asexual' . . . an exceptionally brave, if tortured, intellectual agenda.[109]

Schoenberg's dialectic promises a genuine symbolic supersession of the polarities that keep women down, but McClary suddenly switches her argument to castigation of the modern: 'The turn from late Romantic hysteria and popular music to the refuge of rigorous Modernism is a gesture partly informed by the desire to remasculinize the discourse.'[110]

There is a certain amount of truth in this. When the Futurists and Wyndham Lewis call for truth and hardness in art, an end to the frilly veils of Victorian domesticity, their terms betray classic castration-complex sexism. McClary acknowledges that Schoenberg's modernism challenges the binary oppositions according to which such sexism articulates itself, but instead of pursuing this dialectical critique she adopts postmodern orthodoxy and attacks modernism as an outbreak of male aggression. Like any other good liberal, she abandons her attempt to think beyond the reified categories of class society and starts arguing that we must simply stress the *good* (i.e. the soft, the repetitive, the unthrusting, the female) at the expense of the *bad* (i.e. the hard, the teleological, the phallic, the male).[111]

McClary claims that her female students prefer soothing 'clockwork' minimal music to climactic 'male' music. This of course is to read off a feminist agenda from what may merely be another instance of oppression (does the fact that most women would rather read *Hello* than *Spare Rib* prove that the former is more feminist?). McClary's case hinges on what you do in bed. She is convinced that the model of the sexual climax is inherently anti-female. Of course, the so-called sublimity of the climax in classical music reflects the low opinion of the body that characterizes a sexist culture. Her analyses of Beethoven and Bizet are subversive of the respect for the 'masters' that makes commercial classical music magazines so reactionary. But it is one thing to degrade the classics by reducing the sublime to a grunting phallic

---

[109]Susan McClary, *Feminine Endings*, 1991, p. 12.
[110]Ibid., p. 18.
[111]The similarity of her argument with that of Stephen Heath in *The Sexual Fix* (1982) would be uncanny if it were not so predictable. They both quote Adrienne Rich, of course (why not Denise Riley, who grapples with such issues without preaching?). For a polemic against Stephen Heath's binary moralism, see Out To Lunch, *So Much Plotted Freedom*, Reality Studios Occasional Paper, No. 6, 1987, pp. 30–34.

spurt (a procedure dear to poodle play), another to start being prescriptive about what kinds of sex we are meant to enjoy.

It is not an easy argument, since we are dealing with a matter capitalism condemns to a weird combination of domestic privacy and commercial exploitation: sexual knowledge. The clinical study of sexual arousal has always been problematic, from the persecution of Wilhelm Reich through to the controversies surrounding Masters and Johnson. McClary is adept at the rhetoric that makes any disagreement hinge on embarrassing personal revelations or indefensible claims.[112] The feminist doxa on the 'sexism' of pornography reinforces the silence that surrounds the physical reality of sex (though there are signs that the S&M dykes want to bust this particular restriction). Examples of climactic female sexuality available in the public domain – Sister Sledge's 'Reach Your Peak',[113] Bow Wow Wow's 'Sexy Eiffel Towers',[114] Lydia Lunch[115] – are easily dismissed as products of a male-domininated music industry. The one conclusive piece of evidence I could use to prove my case is necessarily private, an indication of the social power and paranoia that surrounds these issues. It is a tape-letter I received from a girlfriend, where she brings herself to orgasm while describing her actions. It works remarkably like another piece of music that also started life as a tape-letter, in which guitarist Derek Bailey reads, to his own improvised accompaniment, a monologue from *Guitar Player* magazine in which Henry Kaiser describes how he composed 'Sugaki for Conlon' on the Synclavier.[116] In both, tension is achieved because the listener is waiting for the finish throughout: it is this tension that makes the details jarring and vital. In Bailey's tape, as you ache to hear that Kaiser has finished his Synclavier piece, guitar note deviations become ever more poignant and pointed: like foreplay in relationship to orgasm, waiting makes every detail glow with energy. In moral condemnation of such a structuring device (in postmodernism nothing is quite so damning as the category 'modern', which combines old-fashioned, naff, sexist and boring in one useful blast), McClary repeats exactly the suppression of the body she

---

[112]Issues which meant that the following section has been withdrawn and reinserted many times.
[113]Sister Sledge, 'Reach Your Peak', 1980, Atlantic/Cotillion K11477.
[114]Bow Wow Wow, 'Sexy Eiffel Towers', *Your Cassette Pet*, 1980 EMI WOW1.
[115]*Passim.*
[116]Derek Bailey, 'In My Studio', *The Aerial*, Vol. 5, Spring 1993, CD magazine available from: PO Box 15118, Santa Fe, NM 87506, USA. The piece of music whose construction Bailey is describing is Henry Kaiser, 'Sugaki for Conlon', *Devil in the Drain*, 1989, SST Records SST118. Derek Bailey's records are available from Incus, 14 Downs Road, London E5 8DS, England.

condemns in classical music criticism. Though she says all the right things about Bessie Smith, McClary's strictures would banish all Smith's accompanists (and every important jazz player) from the postmodern tableau. Starting out from admirably progressive ideals, McClary finishes by asserting the moral superiority of her academic, middle-class culture. The vocabulary is updated, but this is the same old litany that, since the dawn of the century, has condemned black music as excessively 'sensual'.

Female sexuality as perfectly represented by Steve Reich's 'clockwork' rhythms is a fantasy that could flourish only in an American music college. The idea that wanting something to finish is merely a male hang-up (endemic in postmodern theory, with its attack on Marxism as goal-oriented, teleological and oppressive) also has damning symbolic implications for those who want an end to capitalism, the real source of the oppressions McClary wishes to oppose.

During 'In My Studio', Bailey reads Kaiser talking about some clarinet samples 'given to me by Frank Zappa', which shows how difficult conceptual continuity is to avoid (even if you wanted to). Zappa has always been fascinated by aural documentation of sex, from the Cucamonga sex-tape to the heavy breathing of 'Help, I'm a Rock'[117] and the pumpkin on 'Call Any Vegetable',[118] through to Bunk Gardner's bed-recordings.[119] With 'The Torture Never Stops',[120] Zappa used an extended soundtrack of a woman's orgasmic moans, providing verbal imagery that would probably confirm McClary's worst suspicions. It appears to finish in her orgasm or death. The rock paper *Sounds* described 'The Torture Never Stops' as an 'audio snuff movie'. This very offensiveness makes it a *problem* – a site of controversy – where *Carmen's* parallel trajectory is celebrated as high tragedy. Zappa traces precisely the structures McClary objects to, but he is not dressing up his personal libido as the transcendent sublime *à la* Bizet. McClary's refusal of musical modernism is part of her belief that music represent nice ideas rather than tell us about the world or steel us to face the world – or ourselves.

The pre-eminent musical theorist of modernism is Theodor Adorno. McClary uses his ideas to destroy Beethoven and Bizet;

[117]Frank Zappa, *Freak Out!*, 1966.
[118]Frank Zappa, *Absolutely Free*, 1967.
[119]Frank Zappa, 'Right There', 1968, *You Can't Do That on Stage Anymore Vol. 5*, 1992.
[120]Frank Zappa, *Zoot Allures*, 1976.

once that is done she dispatches him by pointing out some racist and sexist tropes in his texts, using the anachronistic sniffiness liberals often use to avoid the consequences of revolutionary writings (very like the idiots who call Marx anti-Semitic). The feminist current McClary swims in actually derives in no small measure from Adorno and *The Dialectic of Enlightenment*'s thoughts on de Sade. McClary cannot grasp that for Adorno twelve-tone is revolutionary because it refuses to underwrite tonality's re-enactment of the existing social order: the very order that perpetuates racism and sexism. Indeed, in celebrating postmodernism and its unashamed spirit of eclecticism, its lack of 'thrust' and intensity, she is actually at work 'defending' the commercial order of the day. It is like Beatrix Campbell condemning 'macho' behaviour on miners' picket lines: resistance to an exploitative system is condemned for creating 'noise'. Musical modernism is damned as yet another manifestation of 'male' egotism and violence.

If you confine orchestral music to tonality it is true that its climaxes are insufferable (as the film scores of John Williams demonstrate), but that is to put the argument the wrong way round. With minimalism we simply have tonality *without* thrust and, spared of the insufferable, we die of boredom. Minimalism is bourgeois music with a conscience, and, as with the political hegemony of liberalism in rock – Sting, Peter Gabriel, Tracy Chapman – conscience does not seem to interrupt the flow of commerce at all. In fact, it seems to be the ideal lubricant. It is simply too convenient that the currently newsworthy proponents of new music – Laurie Anderson, Diamanda Galas, Steve Reich – are suddenly at the forefront of deconstructing the sexuality of capitalism and saving the world. Galas 'heralds a new moment in the history of musical representation'[121] because she brings back the body into music: but what have Bessie Smith, Cassandra Wilson and Crystal Waters been doing all this time? As with its infatuation with prettied-up ethnic musics, postmodernism becomes a way of applauding the entry into high art of forms better delivered in less rarified zones. Meanwhile, high-class commercialism is given a special seal of approval as somehow anti-élitist and democratic. Musical works which dramatize the contradictions of free art in an unfree society are abandoned as old-fashioned (and unlikely to generate commercial sponsorship or

---

[121]Susan McClary, *Feminine Endings*, 1991, p. 111.

CD sales). Postmodernism has to suppress atonal music because it remains a site of resistance to commodification. The corporations are long inured to the sight of Andy Warhol 'desecrating' their values, and the Saatchis patronize Jeff Koons with gusto: but they are not going to sit still for Michael Finnissy or Leroy Jenkins.

Max Paddison has pointed out how quickly Gyorgy Ligeti's knotted chords could be reharnessed for the culture industry (Ennio Morricone using them for a 'battle scene'), a recuperation for representative purposes that destroys their ability to shake the reified tokens of musical communication, bust through the collusive skin of reference, shock us into listening to *sound*. Certainly, it would be the sheerest sentimentality to imagine that there is any art that in itself can constitute a replacement for politics (it would, for a start, deny that the emancipation of the working class is the act of the working class). Avant-garde music can be recuperated as sound effects (which explains why a frequent response to avant-garde music is that it 'sounds like a scary film') but that does not transform it into easily commodifiable great art. Pierre Boulez has (or had) a central position in the French cultural establishment, but the music of IRCAM is not making the record companies any money. Despite the prestige of Schoenberg and Stockhausen, their music still empties the house at parties. Visual images are recuperated as signs of the famous name (the nihilism of silk-screened art mass-production is quickly subsumed to – it's a Warhol!), whereas music is a physical *experience*. Naming music does not break its spell, it cannot be shrunk down to a trademark, passed around as illustration. Or at least, though this is precisely what has happened to tonal classical music, they haven't yet found a way of packaging Schoenberg for consumption in the manner of Picasso and Warhol. Unlike its spectacular success in drawing the critical sting from modern painting, marketing has not solved the problem of modern music: which is why it remains a privileged site for the creation of genuinely critical art.

McClary goes from her Monteverdi concerts to the latest Philip Glass production without surrendering her postmodernist principles. Atonality becomes the leper excluded from the postmodern feast. Following on from this is the real danger that modernism in classical music will simply become eclipsed, just like modernism in literature. Literature can still be produced in editions of 200 copies and circulated to interested parties around the world: music requires a scoop of social labour power (either congealed, in terms of the investment required for innovative electronic music, or living, in terms of paid musicians) to be actualized at all.

Before the victory of the postmodernist argument in American universities, state-funded modernism provided the classical institutions with problems, if hardly with solutions: its scope was dented by social constraints. The greatest works came in the late-60s when social movements seemed to promise new ears and new audiences. At least the taboo on tonality prevented the wall-to-wall kitsch currently on display. Only through the purgatorial logic of atonality can classical technique offer its discoveries to those in other realms. Precisely because Yes and Emerson, Lake and Palmer and Michael Nyman plunder tonal musics their classical rock reverts to the pompous Englishness – overstuffed, heroic and imperialist – of Holst and Elgar, suffocating the vulgar spark of rock 'n' roll on the way. Adorno's advocacy is clear about this. He does not see twelve-tone as a prescriptive necessity (as did the pre-minimal musical academy in America), instead seeing *emancipation* from it as the music of the future, 'through the amalgamation and absorption of twelve-tone technique by free composition – by assumption of its rules through the spontaneity of the critical ear'.[122]

Though Adorno would never admit it, jazz for him being a byword for light-music commodification of high-art values, this is precisely the trajectory of black American jazz: its progressive discovery of blue notes, its flowering in free jazz and improvisation. Like Robert Rauschenberg, who began his career in 1953 by exhibiting the white canvases he had painted two years before, showing he was using Piet Mondrian's (narrowly avoided) conclusion as a premise, Zappa *starts* with the conclusions of the European avant-garde. Like Mondrian, though, Zappa found in black music the ideal somersault from bleached-out high-art purity: his own *Broadway Boogie Woogies*.

Adorno defines Schoenberg by contrast with Stravinsky, initiating a dialectic that takes us beyond his personal taste. Pierre Boulez is critical of the way Adorno ignores Schoenberg's own retreats into neo-classicism, explaining this blind spot as mere prejudice, the result of his Viennese background. Nevertheless, Adorno's attack on Stravinsky as an *external* composer may be developed into an alternative to Second Viennese School

[122]Theodor Adorno, *Philosophy of Modern Music*, 1948, trs. Anne Mitchell and Wesley Blomster, 1973, p. 115.

54

subjectivism, and one which is equally critical of tradition and authority. In *Philosophy of Modern Music*, Adorno refers back to the Sirens myth he and Horkheimer had made central to *The Dialectic of Enlightenment*. Stravinsky's music is, he argues, the very opposite of the song of the Sirens. In order to survive in 'civilized' society people must – like Odysseus – block their ears to the music that speaks of the realities of love and death, dominate inner nature in order to dominate others. Stravinsky's music, on the other hand, 'attracts all those who wish to rid themselves of their ego, because it stands in the way of their egoistic interest within the total composition of commanded collectivization.'[123]

The pounding of the percussion in *The Rite of Spring* reduces the audience to passive obedience as the ballet enacts the ritual sacrifice of an adolescent girl.

> As an individual, she reflects nothing but the unconscious and coinciden-
> tal reflex of pain: her solo dance – like all the others, in its inner
> organization a collective dance, a round dance – is void of any dialectics
> of the general and specific. Authenticity is gained surreptitiously through
> the denial of the subjective pole.[124]

The audience enjoys the sacrifice as a sadomasochistic self-annihilation by the subject: 'Just as the magician on the stage of the vaudeville theatre causes the beautiful girl to disappear, so the subject in *Sacre* vanishes.'[125] This elimination of the subject leads to a cynical musical attitude, in which the remnants of past styles may be recycled and rearranged in an arbitrary and meaningless way, the inelectable logic of Western music towards atonality thrown over in favour of something humorous, crowd-pleasing and commercial. Neo-classicism, in returning to the eminently saleable distortions provided by the straitjacket of archaic forms, was not, though, simply a matter of selling out: Stravinsky 'ritualized the selling-out itself'.[126] In so enthusiastically enumerating Stravinsky's sins, Adorno gives Stravinsky a lurid appeal, making him susceptible to applause as satire and cultural degradation. His *danse macabre* becomes a possible response to a commodity society, an industry that defines music as money-making. It is as if Adorno is anticipating *Chunga's Revenge* and the mutant vacuum cleaner's depraved abandon, the surreal dimension of an entire audience

---

[123]Ibid., p. 197.
[124]Ibid., p. 159.
[125]Ibid., p. 158.
[126]Ibid., p. 171n25.

shouting 'dynamo, dynamo' during 'Dinah-Moe Humm': the enthronement of the mechanical factor indeed.

The imbalance of power between artist and audience in rock-arena shows is like an extension of the themes Adorno adumbrates in Stravinsky, but Adorno's words glitter with the poetry of menace in the way commercial rock doesn't. Despite Jimmy Page's alleged interest in whips, commercial rock is never quite able to deliver the sheer *evil* such an imbalance promises. Led Zeppelin at Earls Court Stadium in 1975 was characterized by the kind of impersonal boredom one has at the cinema, only relieved by a folky section where the boys jammed on acoustic guitars. Like Adorno's resonant images of Stravinsky's demoniacal sadism, Zappa's heavy metal pastiches ('Magic Fingers', 'Bamboozled by Love'), even his songs of C&W callousness ('Harder Than Your Husband') seem to pack the inhumanity the form promises but never quite delivers. Zappa's music is in many ways the complete enactment of Adorno's every horror, a wild crushing of subjectivity in mountains of reified trash, but the scientific aspect of his research, its keen sense of sound as socially coded information, voices what (according to Adorno) Schoenberg snatched from Wagner, namely 'the promise contained in the age-old protest of music: the promise of a life without fear'.[127]

Adorno repeatedly denounced the positivists' version of music sociology that used audience questionnaires to gauge the meaning of music, rather than analysis of the construction of the music itself. Unlike McClary, Adorno understands the dialectics of the commodity too well to criticize Stravinsky for any supposed 'effect' his music might have on people.

> Fascism, which literally sets out to liquidate liberal culture – along with its supporting critics – is for this reason unable to bear the expression of barbarism . . . In the Third Reich – with its astronomical sacrifice of human beings – *Le sacre du printemps* could never have been performed. Whoever dared to acknowledge the barbarism directly in practice within the ideology of the movement fell from grace.[128]

Adorno seems unaware that Mussolini actually welcomed Stravinsky to fascist Italy: 'I don't believe that anyone venerates Mussolini more than I,' Stravinsky told the music critic of *La Tribuna* after

---

[127]Theodor Adorno, *In Search of Wagner*, 1938, trs. Rodney Livingstone, 1981, p. 156.
[128]Theodor Adorno, *Philosophy of Modern Music*, 1948, trs. Anne Mitchell and Wesley Blomster, 1973, p. 147.

meeting Il Duce in Rome in 1925.[129] Until the alliance with Germany and the anti-Semitic edicts of 1939, the problems artists experienced under Mussolini more nearly resembled those suffered under Stalin – 'directives about art for the masses, art for the people'.[130] However, Adorno's point still stands: there is no direct connection between the symbolic enactment of violence in art and political oppression. While the Jews were being herded into the ghettos and concentration camps, the German nation watched uplifting films about gloriously disciplined demonstrations and bouncing Aryan babies. While their air force carpet-bombed Iraq, the US population were not all watching *Driller Killer.*

Jorg Buttgereit, director of the horror films *Nekromantik* and *Nekromantik 2*, made a similar point when accused of social irresponsibility: 'In the nazi era in Germany there were no horror movies to teach them how to murder people.'[131] In so far as Stravinsky does what Adorno accuses him of, he is a perpetrator of scathing acts of social commentary, though the ritual sacrifice at the heart of *The Rite of Spring* is in fact a well-kept secret. It is precisely awareness of this horror that Zappa brings out in his music. Part 1 of 'Return of the Son of Monster Magnet', the instrumental outrage that occupies side four of *Freak Out!*, is titled 'Ritual Dance of the Child-Killer'.

The running conflict between Adorno and Walter Benjamin over Brecht concerns precisely the relative evaluation of artistic objectivity. Adorno posits the expression of the suffering subject as the only possible location for artistic resistance, whereas Benjamin appreciates Brecht's epic collapse of so-called artistic values into the bright, bold shapes of political debate. What Adorno appears incapable of appreciating is an art that, instead of distilling the pure spirit of subjective expression, should purposely construct learning mazes with the materials to hand.

Art does not only have to crystallize social truth; it can also be used to generate the conditions necessary for crystallizing truth. When Benjamin theorized the progressive aspect of film he talked about the technically informed hunger for new material effect that characterized the film audience: social truth as a by-product of the artwork. The Adorno/Benjamin debate will continue so long

[129]Quoted by Harvey Sachs, *Music in Fascist Italy*, 1987, p. 168.
[130]Gianandrea Gavazzeni, quoted by Harvey Sachs, *Music in Fascist Italy*, 1987, p. 162.
[131]Jorg Buttgereit, quoted by Robert Leedham, 'Deadly Earnest', *Guardian*, 1 June 1992, p. 36.

as the divide persists between commodity and labour (art and politics), but it is also the only debate that makes sense. Everything in Adorno's criticism of Stravinsky hits the mark, but that is not to say that an objective (epic) aesthetic could not *pursue* Stravinsky's insistence on musical effect and thereby produce a resistant praxis.

Stravinsky *is* flawed and the flaw is connected to the features Adorno perceived. The problem was that Stravinsky did not know what was happening in *The Rite of Spring*. He therefore could not develop the diabolical, analytical aspects of his *danse macabre* round the fetishized character of his musical production. This would have meant an interest in commercial music that went beyond his borrowings from jazz. Stravinsky was applauded as a 'great' composer, and therefore thought he occupied the exalted position which, as Adorno argued, rightfully belonged to Schoenberg. Instead of developing the cardboard constructivism of *A Soldier's Tale*, the cartoon-like juxtaposition of simplistic and tarnished elements, he attempted to repay the establishment's accolades with musical depth. This explains the ponderous religiosity of his later works (before his late conversion to twelve-tone), full of boring bourgeois 'profundity', devoid of the wild nihilism that marked his early works. After *Symphony of Psalms* the next stop is the much-patronized 'piety' of Alfred Schnittke: the straitened imagination required to supply bourgeois art with its required 'masterpieces'.

Adorno finds in Stravinsky's best pieces a perpetration of all the evil in the world. He quivers at Stravinsky's grotesques as if the percussion's hammer-blows were being physically received. He quivered in identical fashion at the 'violence' of Tom and Jerry, at the 'unfeelingness' of the 'mechanical' syncopation of jazz. He remains utterly committed to Schoenberg's extension of the subjectivity of European compositional tradition. Incapable as he is of dealing with artistic objectivity at any level, he cannot think what these things might sound like to someone *outside* the tradition. He is in danger of becoming as much of a dualist as McClary – supporting one artistic symptom versus another as if art could change the world. In the end, Adorno's reification of expression as the one true way led to such dislocation with modern experience that his arguments become laughable, the cantankerous bigotry of the uncomprehending mandarin (to read Adorno on sunbathing[132] is like inhaling laughing gas). His politics likewise developed an almost smug refusal of action, a refusal couched in paradoxes that lack the explosive contradictions of his earlier formulations.[133] No wonder the Dadaists had a sign reading 'Death to expressionism!' at the First International Dada Fair exhibition held in Berlin in 1920.[134]

Walter Benjamin realized that artists must seize the opportunities opened up by this objectivity, this idiot freedom with tarnished materials enforced at every turn by advertising and film and radio, or perish. Adorno *understands* what is happening, but he is mesmerized with horror, he cannot act or even conceive of action. He was the literary critic so mortified by Samuel Beckett's last fizzle that he cannot read the joke on a Christmas cracker.

Adorno mentions Varèse only once.

> The modern aspect of Stravinsky is that element which he himself can no longer bear: his aversion, actually, to the total syntax of music. All his followers – with the possible exception of Edgard Varèse – are completely void of this sensitivity.[135]

This possible exception became the key to Zappa's integration of fetishized musical moments – the trash of the music industry – into his compositional dialectic. Varèse eliminated Stravinsky's return to the old forms, his neo-classicism, seeking to create music that would balance sound against sound in the manner of abstract art. Stravinsky laid a nylon net-curtain of bogus primeval mythology across his mechanical constructions: Varèse tore it away. Zappa reintroduced it as a degraded plastic remnant, explicit references to the manufactured Disneyland which Stravinsky–Korsakov passed off as true enchantment.

Zappa is one of the few composers to have grasped that Varèse's music could be the key to transcending musical genre, a symbolic refusal of the social restrictions they embody. Varèse showed how the orchestra could be organized to contrast musical materials, opening the ear to the marimba, woodblocks and drums: the instruments of Africa. Hall Overton, the third-stream composer who worked with Thelonious Monk and taught jazz drummer Joe

---

[132]Theodor Adorno, 'Free Time', ed. J. M. Bernstein, *The Culture Industry*, 1991, p. 165.
[133]See 'Resignation', ed. J. M. Berstein, *The Culture Industry*, 1991, pp. 171–5.
[134]As reconstructed at the John Heartfield exhibition, Barbican Art Gallery, London, 1992. See *John Heartfield*, ed. Peter Pachnicke and Klaus Honne, 1992.
[135]Theodor Adorno, *Philosophy of Modern Music*, 1948, trs. Anne Mitchell and Wesley Blomster, 1973, p. 153.

Chambers,[136] pursued Varèsian logic. Overton's *Pulsations* (1972) is a dialogue between jazz instrumental sound which imbues sonority with stance and Varèsian constructivism: it also sounds remarkably like Zappa, an indication that Zappa's quest is far from idiosyncratic. Charlie Parker talked to Edgard Varèse about the possibility of lessons,[137] but his death in 1955 prevented it. Eric Dolphy's *Out To Lunch* (Blue Note, 1964) was the record Bird would have made if he had survived to study with Varèse: a crucial combination of jazz and Futurism. Again, its similarity to Zappa's music indicates a common use of Varèse in transcending the limitations of genre.

Varèse drew the lessons from Stravinsky's externalizing montage of degraded materials and created an entire music of external events. The attitude towards the musical material is indeed sadistic, but in pulverizing the elements they glow as in an alchemist's cauldron. In contrasting external blocks of sound Varèse finds an expressiveness that is different from Second Viennese School anguish, a delight in transmutation that constitutes a utopian vision of work, tied in completely with the aspirations of the 20s: Mondrian, Malevich, proletarian revolution.

As with Mondrian and Malevich in painting, it is not possible to reproduce that moment after the rivers of blood poured on the twentieth century by American imperialism and Stalinism. Likewise, notwithstanding the elegaic, displeasing truth of atonality to postmodern ears, Second Viennese extensions are not enough to answer the crimes of twentieth-century history. The taboo on tonality still stands, as does Varèse's materialist aesthetic of productive labour, but in the interim the gap between high-art consciousness and the victims of the culture industry became a gulf. In the arena of visual art, the pop-artists sought to address this, but only compounded the problem: their search for the 'popular' merely repeated the contempt commercial graphic design has for the consumer. Roy Lichtenstein's 'Whaaam!' did not grasp the subcultural dynamic of comics, but sentimentalized a freeze-frame memory of adolescence as folkloric Americana – *American Graffiti* for the gallery. Under capitalism, visual imagery is an

[136]See Nat Hentoff, sleeve note to Bobby Hutcherson, *Components*, 1965, Blue Note 84213. This extraordinary record, which contains a whole side of compositions by Joe Chambers, is highly germane to the Varèse/Zappa issue. Steve Chambers (Joe's brother) is described in the notes as 'a *very* modern classical composer' – which, along with his being black, probably explains why his compositions appear to have sunk without trace.
[137]Ross Russell, *Bird Lives*, 1972, p. 342.

institutionalized specialization, it could not just be scooped from the streets.

Music, though, is a social necessity: the most exploited people in the history of capitalism produced the blues. Black music became the left-out that gave art-music the lie. Here was an aesthetic dynamic that actually did come from underneath (everything that 30s Communist Party sentimentality about miners' folk-songs failed to deliver). The blues swallows at one gulp the subjective/objective debate of 'twelve-tone versus Varèse' as the improvisations of the player become vinylized, facts of style. Black music uniquely exploited the ability of recording to reify individual timbre, the twist-point of contingency as art, producing a form that could engage dialectically with the culture industry, a dialectic the classical tradition finds impossible to pursue. Classical composers who seek populism without learning the lessons of black music find themselves in religion or schmaltz or military brass bands.

THE POLITICS OF *FREAK OUT!*

As well as everything else – its ironic use of show arrangements, its tribute to *The Rite of Spring*, its theatre-of-the-absurd affront – *Freak Out!* also has an acute grasp of race relations. 'Trouble Every Day' is a Dylanesque protest which emulates Dylan's virtuosity with rhymes:

> Unless your uncle owns a store
> You know that five in every four
> Won't amount to nothing more
> Than watch the rats go across the floor
> And make up songs about being poor
> *Blow your harmonica, son*

The sardonic reference to the blues in the last line perfectly encapsulates Zappa's ambivalence towards self-expression. The phrase later resurfaced on 'Didja Get Any Onya' on *Weasels Ripped My Flesh* as pig-like snorks accompanied parlour piano. 'Trouble Every Day' deals with the Watts riots with a directness hitherto unknown in pop (even Dylan's early songs tended to be poetic and diffuse, a vagueness he found useful when he reinterpreted them as religious statements during his Christian period). Zappa keeps the form at arm's length, just as he acknowledges his racial and political distance from the rioters.

> And he said it served them right
> Because a few of them were white
> It's the same across the nation
> Black and white discrimination[138]

From these lines it might look as if Zappa is adopting liberal 'impartiality' (which, given the reality of black racial oppression in the States, is a form of racism), but the song goes on to develop a commentary on the riots that acknowledges the economic basis of oppression. It knows which side it is on. Zappa manages to combine anger and self-defence in a highly memorable formulation.

> You know people I ain't black
> But there's a whole lot of times
> I wish I could say I ain't white[139]

This scrupulous attention to racial attitudes runs parallel to Zappa's iconic use of blues cliché. It saves him from the flatulence of, say, John Mayall trying to 'sing the blues'. Zappa's politics – rationalist and cautious – never had the kick-out-the-jams absoluteness of the Panthers (Black or White) or the Situationists. *Freak Out!*, though, has just the kind of urgency and vitriol to foment such expectations: revolutionary art purveyed by a non-revolutionary. Student radicals were disappointed in his later pronouncements, but close attention to these show that, from *Freak Out!* to 'Porn Wars', his line has been remarkably consistent. Only those who sentimentalize art as a form of politics could fail to notice this. Poodle play luckily takes its political lessons from the symbolic resonance of Zappa's art in the hierarchies of capitalist culture rather than from his interviews.

An important aspect of *Freak Out!* was gaining the respect of various session players (listed on the sleeve as 'The Mothers' Auxiliary'), proving to them that this rock 'n' roll guitarist was capable of writing music that required skill. Lowell George made some revealing comments.

Frank was a very demanding man to work for. He wrote some great charts. There was this big joke. All these session players in Los Angeles, who were very accomplished, were going to a Mothers of Invention

---

[138]Frank Zappa, 'Trouble Every Day', *Freak Out!*, 1966.
[139]Ibid.

session, and they thought it was a big laugh and so they dressed funny. They wore Bermuda shorts, and put tennis shoes on the wrong feet and stuff. And they got to the session and the charts were so hard they couldn't play them. It scared them to death, and they all came out of there saying, 'this guy's no slouch'. And it changed everybody's attitude at that point.[140]

Zappa made important contacts. Johnny Rotella (woodwinds) later played on both *Lumpy Gravy* and *The Grand Wazoo* and Jerome Kessler electrified his cello for the Wazoo tour in 1972. Benjamin Barrett was celebrated as the contractor 'Ben-Hur Barrett' in the story for *The Grand Wazoo*; trombonist Ken Shroyer later took up this role. Zappa had proved himself to the session fraternity – precisely the kind of musicians who could combine the score-reading and improvised trenchancy he needed for his particular third stream.

SPORTS

'Trouble Every Day' is about watching the Watts riots, events filtered through the TV stations' commercial competition. Sports are mentioned as an indicator of the untrustworthiness of the medium.

> You can cool it you can heat it
> 'Cause baby I don't need it
> An' take your TV tube and eat it
> An' all that phony stuff on sports
> An' all the unconfirmed reports
> You know I've watched that rotten box
> Until my head began to hurt
> From checkin' out the way the newsmen say they get the dirt
> Before the guys on channel so-and-so
> An' further they assert . . .[141]

Recorded in 1974, *Apostrophe*'s 'Excentrifugal Forz' was a sci-fi rewrite of 'Trouble Every Day'. It also recalled the fantasy rocket ship of Studio Z: domestic TV sets as portholes on to the world outside, TV sport as the epitome of alienation.

> The clouds are really cheap
> The way I seen 'em thru the ports
> Of which there is about a dozen

[140]Quoted by Andy Childs, 'The Exploits of Lowell George', *ZigZag*, March 1975, No. 50, p. 26.
[141]Frank Zappa, 'Trouble Every Day', *Freak Out!*, 1966.

On the base of my resorz
You'd never think I'd have too many
As I've never cared for sporz[142]

Zappa's 'biographical trivia' on the sleeve of *Freak Out!* mentions that 'they' would never let him become captain of the softball team. Whether or not this is apocryphal, it is a perfect symbol of his outsider status. When asked to describe his dream girl by Michael Vosse in 1966, Zappa gave out an interesting list of don'ts that starts with sport: 'No interest whatsoever in sports, sunshine, deodorant, lipstick, chewing gum, carbon tetrachloride, television, ice cream ... none of that stuff!'

In England, supporting football has long been an outlet for working-class youth, usually factional and self-defeating. Despite the late 80s cross-fertilization of rave culture and football (which showed that exploitation by the right is not inevitable), it was no surprise to see the neo-nazi Aryan Brotherhood manage to instigate a race riot against Lebanese immigrants by English football fans attending the Swedish European Championships in 1992.[143] The spectacle disempowers the spectator, who can find themselves again only through violence, the one time the media pay attention to the fans rather than the players. From a game played with abandon on the streets of nineteenth-century towns, suspending normal business for days at a stretch, football has become a commodity supplied by specialists.

> Football fans took to the Alcester streets following England's win in the World Cup. Six people started an impromptu football game at the traffic lights in Station Road, watched by more supporters. But their game came to a premature end when local beat officers confiscated the ball and the crowd went home.[144]

This enforced powerlessness has meant that sport has generally been a preserve of the right, from conformity at school to the nationalistic ritual of the Olympic Games. Adorno's description of the way in which the culture industry reduces everything to sport makes Zappa's rejection highly charged (as well as anticipating by twenty years TV's adoption of the game-show/competition format for every conceivable subject – including elections).

> Sport itself is not play but ritual in which the subjected celebrate their

[142]Frank Zappa, 'Excentrifugal Forz', *Apostrophe (')*, 1974.
[143]*Guardian*, 15 June 1992.
[144]*Alcester Chronicle*, 4 July 1990, quoted by Sadie Plant, *The Most Radical Gesture – The Situationist International in a Postmodern Age*, 1992, p. 68.

subjection... The passion for sport, in which the masters of mass culture sense the real mass basis of their dictatorial power, is grounded in this fact. One can play the master by inflicting the original pain upon oneself and others again through a kind of compulsive repetition... This is the school for that integration which finally succeeded politically in transforming the powerless into a band of applauding hooligans. One is allowed to inflict pain according to the rules, one is maltreated according to the rules and the rule checks strength in order to vindicate weakness as strength: the screen heroes enjoy being tortured on film. The rules of the game resemble those of the market, equal chances and fair play for all, but only as the struggle of all against all.[145]

Adorno's abstract critique works like a political psychoanalysis of Zappa's disdain. If you fall short of Adorno's concept of the hurt done to subjectivity by the mass media in capitalism, then the violence and venom of Zappa's art remains opaque, his perceptions merely idiosyncratic and nasty. The close-tracking of Adorno's ideas by Zappa's un-bookish art also demonstrates the lack of arbitrariness in the Frankfurter, the accuracy of his protest.

In sport, spectators accept limits in order to 'enjoy' the results, denying precisely the boundless promise of true pleasure. Zappa's insistence on open play – dismissed as 'self-indulgence' by the curmudgeons of the rock press, who reduce all music to sport (competition for chart placings) – is a site of resistance to the way capitalism can only understand anything as a means to making profit. In the short story 'SPQR',[146] sci-fi writer Kim Newman envisages a society in which sport, soap opera and news have become seamless, a story which updates the Adornoite vision (as only arts marginal to the liberal mainstream – SF, comics, Cambridge poetry, hardcore – seem able to do). Zappa's rejection of sport is a token of his rejection of what the Situationists called the spectacle.

The hypnotism of the spectacle replaces lived life with passive observation of the activities of the famous and successful, which are turned into 'objective fact' as undeniable and unchangeable as the stars. This hypnotism is precisely Zappa's target. Unlike the tabloids, Zappa's trivia (an aspect continually decried in record reviews) does not supply details about the generally known, but realizes the surrealist spark in specificity: it declares war on the pseudo-science of sport, the way in which sports commentators

[145]Theodor Adorno, 'The Schema of Mass Culture', ed. J. M. Bernstein, The Culture Industry, 1991, p. 77.
[146]Kim Newman, 'SPQR', Interzone, May 1992.

turn play into something homogenized, global and abstract. With its sad calibration, its world records and expertise, sport is the epitome of the spectacle, the reduction of the variety of life to a single measure. The dada journal *Jeder Mann Sein Eigener Fussball* (everyone their own football) provided a catchword in 1917 Berlin, precisely demolishing the oppression of sport, its conversion of play into competition. James Joyce gave it an extra twist: 'each man his own goaldkeeper',[147] making it a slogan for the downfall of the exchange economy. Zappa's attitude to sport is a key to understanding his dadaistic assault on the spectacle.

COMMERCIAL OR WHAT?

Freak Out! presents commercial music with a joke on itself. Questioning the self-evidence of musical merit pops the consumer out of passivity, forces the listener to make decisions, to resolve to 'like' this stuff as a protest against alienation rather than because it's certifiably 'good'. The tracks on *Freak Out!* which are not in pop/R&B format – 'Help, I'm a Rock' and 'Return of the Son of Monster Magnet' – suffer if they are characterized as 'avant-garde classical compositions' sneaked on to a pop record. 'Help, I'm a Rock' might benefit from knowledge of contemporary experiments with vocal interaction by Karlheinz Stockhausen and Luciano Berio, but only because these composers asked audiences to sit still for the hitherto-perceived-as-unlistenable. *Freak Out!* did not present 'difficult' music that required study and contemplation, but a processed collage of moments of spontaneity. Though a masterpiece of editing, 'Monster Magnet' was also 'what *freaks* sound like when you turn them loose in a recording studio at one o'clock in the morning on $500 worth of rented percussion equipment', what people can sound like when they are transforming themselves. There are only a few records which manage to sound utterly brilliant, yet also give you the feeling that everyone can do it: it's the promise of pop, in which social documentary and art fuse in a single flash.[148]

'Help, I'm a Rock' includes an amateur teen-party doowop

---

[147]James Joyce, *Finnegans Wake*, 1949, p. 129–31.
[148]Other examples: Richard Berry's 'Louie Louie', Little Richard's 'Rip It Up', Lonnie Donegan's 'Rock Island Line', the first Beatles' singles, Anthony Braxton's *This Time*, the Sex Pistols, the Adverts' 'One Chord Wonders', the Mekons' 'Never Been in a Riot', the Honkies' *What Can We Do to Prevent the Advance of the Desert?*.

workout on the line 'it can't happen here', as cities are named that might 'freak out' next. Released as a single, it was given a 'miss' by *Juke Box Jury*, the BBC's pop TV show hosted by David Jacobs. It documents both the freaks' breathless optimism and their global ambition. The Mothers of Invention managed to preserve this sense of real-life-as-art until their break-up in 1969. Those who proclaim Zappa 'finished' after that are asking for something no professional musician can deliver: the long-term perpetuation of a historical moment. What makes Zappa's later work special is that it recognizes its *distance* from the transformation of everyday life. Rather than circulating a fraudulent husk in the usual manner, it works the culture industry with a knowing sneer.

Luciano Berio sought an *événement* spontaneity that parallels 'Help, I'm a Rock' in *Laborintus 2* (written between 1963 and 1965). On the 1971 recording the soprano's closing question, elated and unselfconscious, has a parallel this-time resonance to the voices of Suzy Creamcheese[149] and Dale Bozzio.[150] The sleeve note of *Laborintus 2* talks of Berio 'discovering sounds, phrases, effects of all kinds which have permitted him to venture further and further into areas which so far have been thought impermissible or impossible for the human voice'.[151] Working closely with the singer Cathy Berberian, Berio expanded the parameters of allowable art-music vocalese, experimenting with spontaneity, recording (the cut-up *Thema* [*Omaggio a Joyce*], 1958) and direction via scores. Using similar methods, Zappa foregrounds precisely the issue of the 'permissible', and orgasmic female breathing supplies a rhythm to 'Help, I'm a Rock' and flits through the mix of 'Monster Magnet'. This might be read off as revenge for Detective Willis's frame-up, making freely available in the record shops the same sounds that had got Zappa and Lorraine Belcher arrested.

> At one point in the trial, the judge took me and the girl into his private chambers, along with all the lawyers, listened to the tape and started laughing. It *was* funny – and nowhere near as bizarre as the vocal noises eventually released on side four of the *Freak Out!* album.[152]

However, the close-tracking of Zappa's 'pornographic' endeavour and 'avant-garde' vocal sounds indicates the social repression

[149]Frank Zappa, *Freak Out!*, 1966; *Uncle Meat*, 1969.
[150]Frank Zappa, *Joe's Garage Act I*, 1979.
[151]Jacques Meunier sleeve note, Luciano Berio, *Laborintus 2*, 1971, RCA Red Seal SB6848.
[152]Frank Zappa, with Peter Occhiogrosso, *The Real Frank Zappa Book*, 1989, p. 58.

behind Western art-music's traditional 'training' of the voice. Although Zappa continually anticipates the procedures of the high-art avant-garde, this is not the self-conscious transgression of Andy Warhol with the Velvet Underground. Zappa's social intent rides in front of his aesthetic practice, and although he manages to evade the high/low dichotomy better than anyone else, this is because his content bypasses formal limits. Zappa transcends the split between Anton Webern and Muddy Waters because he grasps that both are aspects of a single social totality, hence equally useful for a negative critique. This is why his music is not some postmodern hybrid, but reeks its own singular pungency.

'Help, I'm a Rock' is dedicated to Elvis Presley. It uses a monotonous dead beat, heavily played on bass and drums, the Mothers gibbering and gabbling Pachuco obscenities all over the stereo mix. The lack of musical progression is admirably suited to its title, as if the Mothers are protesting about the restrictive nature of the music they have chosen. As the lyric turns to 'Help, I'm a Cop', it also becomes a satire on social stasis, musical repetition as an unendurable prison. It is hard to make such a one-note vamp work, but it proves to be an excellent hold-all for verbal and instrumental spontaneity, leaving a dub-like space for words and notes to hang in (reduction of music to this kind of unitary simplicity is rare: Sun Ra's 'Rocket No 9',[153] PiL's 'Fodderstompf',[154] Craig Harris's 'Sound Sketches'[155] are other examples). The repetitions build tension, all bass twang and drum reverb and then (at 2.01) there is one of Zappa's hallucinatory shocks, a few bars of guitar feedback and muffled screams spliced in from an utterly different ambience. A similar moment happens on 'Who are the Brain Police?'. Although the upfront recording of bass and drums has been unreal and the voices intrude from bizarre places, the space we are listening to, this repeated beat, has been very firmly indicated: the sudden smear of another continuity, a headlong rush of squeezed sound, is disorienting – the more so because the regular rhythm returns, slightly more wound-up. Ever since romanticism, surprise has been one of music's legitimate ends, though the sheer effectiveness of Zappa's surprises means he is often relegated to the humoresque (a tradition that might com-

[153] As played by Ramsey McLean and the Survivors, *New Orleans Music: Jump Jazz*, 1986, Core COCD9.00916.
[154] Public Image Limited, *Public Image*, 1978, Virgin V2114.
[155] Craig Harris and Tailgaters Tales, *Shelter*, 1987, JMT 870008.

comprise composers like Erik Satie, William Walton, Carla Bley, Willem Breuker, Judith Weir and Django Bates). However, the term is shock rather than surprise, because Zappa's evocation of context is so single-minded: we are utterly *on the rug* Zappa pulls, not applauding coy somersaults over the safety net of a recognizable genre. The big sonic lesson for this came from Varèse's careful and dramatic choice of contrasting timbres – but there was also a low-art precedent for such time-space bogglement.

LORD BUCKLEY

Richard Buckley, born in Stockton, California in 1907, was a half-Cherokee lumberjack who developed a line in jazz-jive comedy that established him as a stand-up comic at Chicago's Suzi Q Nite Club in the 40s. His Church of the Living Swing included belly-dancers, nudity and routines like 'The Bad Rapping of the Marquis de Sade'. Wearing a crown or pith helmet, his crash collision between English aristocrat and hipspeak needs to be heard to be believed. In 1969 Zappa released his *A Most Immaculately Hip Aristocrat* on the Straight label.[156] Despite rumours that he died after being beaten up by indignant black Muslims in New York City in 1960, where his use of black argot had been mistaken for racial abuse, his death was recorded as the result of prolonged alcohol and drug abuse.

Lord Buckley's surrealist boptalk was a prime influence on both Frank Zappa and Captain Beefheart (who adopted a similar persona on *I Was a Teenage Maltshop*). Buckley takes you on a verbal trip, summoning forth a stream of images with illustrative mouth-noises and expostulations that precede events in the story, achieving utterly unexpected changes of tone and pace. He would work himself into a frenzy of excitement but keep his wit poised to deliver a hallucinogenic twist. Although Zappa learned a lot about tension and surprise from Varèse, Lord Buckley taught him about the use of timing and imagery in speech, not just in his monologues (*Apostrophe (')*, *Greggery Peccary* and the introduction to 'Muffin Man' on *Bongo Fury*) but also in music, both via tape-slice (*We're Only in It for the Money*) and scores ('Punky's Whips'). Towards the end of 'Help, I'm a Rock' (7.26) someone

---

[156]Lord Buckley, *A Most Immaculately Hip Aristocrat*, 1969, Straight STS1054.

69

says, 'No no no no no ... man you guys are really safe, everything's cold', verbal derailment straight out of a Lord Buckley
routine.

MUSIQUE CONCRÈTE

The white-blur moment in 'Help, I'm a Rock' is not, though, a
comedy routine: its use of the possibilities of tape more nearly
resembles *musique concrète*. This was a term coined by Pierre
Schaeffer in France in 1948 to describe realizing avant-garde music
on a tape-recorder (the latter a product of the high-pressure technological competition of the war years). Schaeffer wanted to distinguish his art from electronic music, which used purely synthetic
sounds. He was interested in the original provenance of his
material, producing aural collages that are a musical equivalent to
the *merzbau* of Kurt Schwitters. This approach informed *We're
Only in It for the Money*.

> All the music heard on this album was composed, arranged and
> scientifically mutilated by Frank Zappa (with the exception of a little
> bit of surf music). None of these sounds are generated electronically ...
> they are all the product of electronically altering the sounds of
> NORMAL instruments.[157]

Such distinctions were important to those informed of the avant-
garde schools of the 50s. In 1958 Varèse, with the assistance of
Iannis Xenakis, created *Le poème électronique*. This mixed purely
electronic and documentary sound, and since then all tape-music
has been called electronic, whatever its sound sources. *Musique
concrète* is reserved for the music of Schaeffer and his collaborators
like Pierre Henry. Close to surrealism in their emphasis on social
and sexual issues, *musique concrète* lives on in the work of Conrad
Boehmer and Luc Ferrari, though of course the availability of the
sampler has made such procedures ubiquitous. The ascendancy of
the classical tendency at Darmstadt – Stockhausen and Boulez and
their disinterest in 'found' materials, their need to make all their
music a willed exfoliation of the genius of the individual composer
(a sensible economic move in a system geared to recognizing such
entities) – meant that *musique concrète* is now seen as a minor
aberration in the onward march of Western art music.

---

[157]Sleeve note, Frank Zappa, *We're Only in It for the Money*, 1968.

Zappa's later xenochrony and Synclavier pieces perpetuate the patchworked time that *musique concrète* originally pioneered with the simple expedient of taking a razor blade to the recording tape itself. Disrespect for the usual procedures, a fascination for the physical aspect of the medium, had already been demonstrated when Zappa wiped the emulsion off ciné film for his art performance at Antelope High. 'Help, I'm a Rock' and *We're Only in It for the Money* retain some of the manic energy of Schaeffer's early cut-ups, made all the more disruptive by the fact that their use on a pop record is so unexpected. This sudden intrusion of the material medium into the signifying arena resembles the manner in which sexual desire returns us from words to the body, a connection made by the sexual whoops and cries in *Monster Magnet* (even the handclapping starts sounding like sexual smacks). Zappa pursued *musique concrète*'s eroticism of presence into a social critique of repression, making the music so immediate, so ludicrous and filthy, that it sites itself beyond the pale of 'serious' music criticism – though Conrad Boehmer seems headed in a similar direction.[158]

Towards the close of 'Help, I'm a Rock' Zappa sings 'who could imagine? . . .', and the music cuts into a cluster played on woodwinds. Sounds that belong in a Darmstadt *étude* suddenly have a surreal intensity. 'Return of the Son of Monster Magnet (Unfinished Ballet in Two Tableaux)' combines monster-movie traditions and tape-recorders in its title and comprises two parts: 'Ritual Dance of the Child-Killer', which associates the ritual sacrifice of the young virgin in *The Rite of Spring* with Suzy Creamcheese's loss of innocence, and 'Nullis Pretii (No Commercial Potential)'. Suzy Creamcheese, an example of unliberated maidenhead whom Zappa questions about her 'development', was played by Jeannie Vassoir. When Zappa asks, 'Suzy Creamcheese, honey, what's got into ya?', his intimate, father-confessor voice lures the listener into a false security that makes the eruption of siren, drums and screams still more frightening. It is the kind of shock exploited by Hollywood horror in *Carrie* and *The Exorcist*, the anxiety that beneath the surface of the controlled, civilized, tamed body lies absolute terror. Horror films and thrillers frequently use avant-garde musical devices the mass audience would never sit still for in the concert hall: by placing such music in a blatantly sexual drama, one of fear and repression, Zappa seeks to

---

[158]Conrad Boehmer, *Apocalips Cum Figuren*, 1987.

restore its visceral impact. The electronics, twittering over the drums like agitated bats (best appreciated on the CD), deliver stinging notes at the edge of hearing. As the drum 'freak-out' disintegrates into Zappa saying 'America's wonderful', there is a bleak section of reverb, windswept and industrial (an aural equivalent to William Burroughs's repeated figure of 'vacant lots'), renewed vocal gibber, and a snappy rhythmic invocation of Suzy Creamcheese, driven by clacking spoons. This section is then replayed at double speed, overdubbed with atonal piano, giving a curiously classical formality to the album's ending. This dance-of-the-demons is actually music; its ability to evoke fear and distress not so much evil intent as a mark of our repression.

PERSONAL MYSTIQUE

Freak Out! also developed Zappa's personal mystique. On the cover he looks inscrutably peculiar, wearing the mangy fur coat that caused Pamela Zarubica to dub him 'Omar' (after Omar Sharif). He is described in the sleeve notes as only occasionally attending Mothers concerts (a complete fabrication):

> His performances in person with the group are rare. His personality is so repellent that it's best he stay away . . . for the sake of impressionable minds who might not be prepared to cope with him. When he does show up he performs on guitar. Sometimes he sings. Sometimes he talks to the audience. Sometimes there is trouble.

The threat of violence being precisely the scam that got everyone going with punk ten years later. Rock-lore conventionally celebrates Zappa for just two things: first, eating a shit on stage and second, a poster that showed him, naked, sitting on a toilet. He has always denied eating the shit on stage (he begins *The Real Frank Zappa Book* by denying it) and the poster was apparently a bootleg operation using a photo taken by an uncontracted photographer in a London hotel. People seem to need some biographical weirdness to explain why Zappa's music should be so strange, and scatology fits the bill. The 'international groupie' Dr G repeated such rumours in *Oz*.

> I'd think twice about balling him because Ed Sanders told me that he has the same perversion as Tyrone Power on *Hollywood Babylon* and somebody else told me he's a shit fancier! How do you get that together

for Godsake? I don't really believe it. It's probably meant to frighten off all but the brave and resourceful.[159]

Unlikely though it is, the rumour has a symbolic appropriateness: materialism and scatology are close associates. Freud drew parallels between economic calculation and anal retention; Norman O. Brown reads off the Protestant work ethic of accumulation from Martin Luther's bowel problems; for Gustave Courbet, the socialist French painter of the early nineteenth century, weight and a sense of mass were a criticism of airy aristocratic art: he frequently placed large brown lumps in the foreground of his paintings. In *Uncle Meat*, 'The Voice of Cheese' (Pamela Zarubica) extends Zappa's mystique by talking about his 'groupie status' and refers to his house 'what had your shit all over'.[160]

Zappa has the ability to create a paranoia of prurience, a fear that he is referring to experiences which are denied the straight folk. That is, of course, precisely what drugs are used for, but their use tends to diminish the concrete capability of the artist – hence Zappa's contempt. Drug-oriented art, from the corny sub-*art nouveau* of fantasy graphics to the country-rock meanderings of the Grateful Dead, has always been dilute and sprawling. Zappa's mystique is thoroughly his creation, part of his output macrostructure and of his revenge. When Pamela Miller (Miss Pamela of the GTO's) first visited the Zappas, she was amazed that anything was normal.

> Gail came out of the kitchen and I tried not to stare. She asked us all if we would like a cup of tea; oh, it was so civilized. The whole setup instantly changed my mind about domesticity: You could be a rebel, a profound thinker, and a rock and roll maniac and still eat breakfast, lunch, and dinner, have a baby, and drink a nice cup of tea with your friends.[161]

Likewise, Zappa's hostility to drugs caused puzzlement to those who associated drugs with subversion. Ralph Gleason, the jazz critic who embraced hippiedom with open arms, was floundering when he reviewed *Freak Out!*.

> Hollywood hippies full of contrivance, tricks and packaging; a kind of Sunset Boulevard version of the Fugs. They are really indoor Muscle

---

[159]Dr G, quoted by Germaine Greer, 'The Universal Tonguebath: A Groupie's Vision', *Oz*, 19 March 1969, p. 47.
[160]'Our Bizarre Relationship', *Uncle Meat*, 1969.
[161]Pamela Des Barres, *I'm with the Band – Confessions of a Groupie*, 1987, p. 90.

73

Beach habitués whose idea of a hip lyric is to mention LSD or pot three times in eight bars.[162]

It seemed much easier to explain *Freak Out!* by reference to drugs than to account for the cultural implications of someone wanting to splice Pierre Schaeffer with 'Louie Louie'. In the October *LA Free Press* Zappa published a statement carefully disassociating the Mothers from Carl Franzoni's advocacy of drugs.

> Carl Franzoni is not a member of the Mothers of Invention. Nor does he claim to be. But, for the most part, we as a group agree with him in his plea for a sane drug policy (basically stick it up your ass and fly to the moon). We, as a group, do not recommend, verily we repudiate any animal/mineral/vegetable/synthetic substance, vehicle and/or procedure which might tend to reduce the body, mind or spirit of an individual (any true individual) to a state of sub-awareness or insensitivity. We are here to turn you loose not turn you on. Turn *yourself* on. The sort of high you really want is a spiritual high and you are bullshitting yourself if you trust any chemical and/or agricultural short cut to do it for you. You can't be busted yet for awareness. Maintain your aristocratic coolness.[163]

But Gleason is right on one account: though Zappa has no time for drug-users, he is always very informed about the detail of drug consumption, this being one of the key terms of hip in twentieth-century subculture. Zappa's mystique centres on the idea of arcane knowledge:

> Don't never try to look behind my eyes
> You don't wanna know what they have seen[164]

And the hostility to drugs in no way implies ignorance of their rituals and effects, as is shown by songs like 'Pygmy Twylyte' and 'Cocaine Decisions', and the in-concert intros to 'Dupree's Paradise'.

MGM/Verve set up a tour to promote *Freak Out!* and the Mothers played in Washington, DC, Detroit and Dallas. They reported sales of 30,000 units: royalties (60 or 70 cents per album) did not cover the 'twenty-five or thirty thousand dollars'[165] MGM had spent on the recording session. MGM/Verve therefore allocated a budget of $11,000 for its successor (Zappa claims that many more records were sold by back-door methods

[162]Michael Gray, *Mother! is the Story of Frank Zappa*, 1985, p. 63.
[163]*Los Angeles Free Press*, 7 October 1966.
[164]'A Token of My Extreme', *Joe's Garage Acts II and III*, 1979. This song, with Captain Beefheart on vocals, frequently opened performances by the 1975 band.
[165]Frank Zappa, with Peter Occhiogrosso, *The Real Frank Zappa Book*, 1989, p. 78.

and unaccounted for). Ever concerned about technical excellence, Zappa has dismissed the results, but *Absolutely Free* is an amazing record. Traditionally, rock bands use up their first set of songs with their first album and therefore face a crisis of creativity with their second album, but this was not a problem for the Mothers. Zappa expanded the line-up. Don Preston (keyboards), Bunk Gardner (saxophones) and Billy Mundi (drums) joined and Motorhead was promoted to a 'sort of' member (the list of band members had his name in smaller type). Bunk Gardner and his trumpet-playing brother Buzz (subsequently inducted into the Mothers for the 1969 US Spring tour) were jazz players. In the late 50s they had appeared regularly with André Hodeir at St Germain-des-Près.

Don Preston

Born in Flint, Michigan, on 21 September 1932, Donald Ward Preston was crucial in helping Zappa develop the Soul Giants from an R&B combo into the improvising electric chamber orchestra he needed in order to realize his musical ambitions. Preston's father was resident composer for the Detroit Symphony Orchestra.

> I was affected early on by Boulez, Xenakis, Penderecki. That's what I listened to more than anything, more than jazz. I was listening to Lennie Tristano, Lee Konitz, Miles. But my ear was always trying to get something new.[166]

Preston played jazz piano, and sat in with the best. In the early 50s he played with Elvin Jones, subsequently the drummer in John Coltrane's classic quartet.

> Jones was only about eighteen himself. He had total independence – nobody could figure out why his members didn't try to follow one another. Unbelievable. The only challenge was, 'Oh there's a white guy coming. (*Rapid count off*) One, two, one two three four . . .' When they found out I could play those fast tempos, then they sort of let up on me.

Preston played bass for flautist Herbie Mann. He was always interested in musical innovation, and recalls chewing out John

---

[166]Quoted by Josef Woodard, 'Don Preston: Synthesizer from Apocalypse Now to Zappa', *Down Beat*, August 1987, pp. 25–7. Subsequent quotes all from this source.

Coltrane for playing in the same realm for too long (to have nudged both Coltrane and Zappa towards musical freedom must make Preston some kind of *eminence grise* for twentieth-century music). In the late 50s he moved to LA, catching Ornette Coleman at Georgia Lee's Caprice, and toured with Nat King Cole, in the latter's stand-up crooner phase. He had met Paul Bley in Florida in 1955 and linked up with him on the West Coast. After a spell with the AHA (Aesthetic Harmony Assemblage), Preston ran a club for experimental music in the Silverlake area. Participants included big band leader and trumpeter Don Ellis, saxophonist Bunk Gardner and Frank Zappa. When he recruited Preston and Gardner to the Mothers, Zappa commented: 'I'd known Don and Bunk several years before . . . we used to play experimental music a long time ago – we got together in garages and went through some very abstract charts – just to entertain ourselves, you know.'[167]

Preston's version ran:

I said, 'Hey, I have a group. We play improvisational music. Why don't you come sit in with us.' He said, 'Sure, okay.' We were improvising to films of microscopic life: he had some real unusual films. The first time, I couldn't believe it; here's this real strange looking guy with long hair and a beard. He looked like Rasputin. After I found out who he was, I let him in the house.

Zappa and Preston auditioned – unsuccessfully – for a jazz gig together. Not to be left out of conceptual continuity, microscopic pond-life appears on the inner sleeve of the Wild Man Fischer album. Zappa's dialectic between populism and the experimental meant that Preston failed his first audition to join the Mothers.

I auditioned and Frank said 'I'm sorry, Don, you don't know anything about rock 'n' roll' – which I didn't. I never even played it and hardly ever listened to it. After that, I got a bunch of jobs in rock bands.

The apprenticeship served its purpose and Don Preston joined the Mothers in 1967. The time spent improvising to films of pond-life did not go wasted.

I had been doing all the avant-garde-type music prior to that, and when we got in the band, that's what we'd do, especially when we got Bunk Gardner in the band. I'd been doing that stuff for years, so when we did it onstage, we were right home.

---

[167]Quoted by Pete Frame, 'Mothers: The Earliest Days of the Just Another Band from LA', *ZigZag*, No. 53, June 1975, p. 23.

The free improvisations of the Mothers – frequently directed by Zappa with 'secret' gestures, a procedure later known as conduction (used in the 80s by figures like John Zorn and Butch Morris in New York and Mick Beck in Sheffield) – produced some of the most extraordinary music of the twentieth century (best documented on *Weasels Ripped My Flesh*). It begs the vexed question of creativity and authorship, especially vexed in this context because of the subsequent lawsuits between Zappa and his original band (who later toured as the Grandmothers, denouncing Zappa's 'rip-offs' at every opportunity). On the CD release of *Absolutely Free* Zappa went so far as to omit the band photograph and credits for the musicians. Eugene Chadbourne, who worked with Jimmy Carl Black, recorded an Islamic-Country protest song about the issue, 'The Man Who Made Off with the Money'. The sleeve note runs

> A group of embittered ex-sidemen of the legendary Saudi-Arabian band-leader Crank Zapatalist get together to moan and groan about how things could have worked out differently for them. An example of the 'fuss' or 'bitch' song popular with the Islamic country and western movement.[168]

Chadbourne's irony prevents us from concluding that he takes the Grandmothers' complaints at face value. In taking experimental music to market, providing an influx of money where traditionally there is so little to be had, Zappa was bound to take a lot of flak. With the Mothers Don Preston played some really extraordinary music – he has innovative mini-moog solos on *Live at Fillmore East* ('Lonesome Electric Turkey') and on the title tracks of both *Waka/Jawaka* and *The Grand Wazoo* – and has gone on to grace dance (Meredith Monk's *The Visit from Bob Smith*), jazz (John Carter's *Fields* series), soundtracks (*Apocalypse Now*) and avant-rock (the 1979 Michael Mantler/Carla Bley band had Preston playing in a Mothers vein) with his middle-tech keyboards. The extra exposure granted by a place in the Mothers was helpful.

> As far as becoming popular, I was somehow oblivious to it. It happened so gradually that I wasn't really aware of it until much later. There were certain times when I'd look out into the audience and think 'that's incredible'. There would be little flashes, but most of the time I was too busy trying to play the music.

---

[168]Eugene Chadbourne, *Country Music in the World of Islam*, 1990, Fundamental Records SAVE80.

Zappa's music has been affected by his post-70s employment of technically skilled musicians who lack the character of innovators like Don Preston; like many ageing composers – including Boulez and Stockhausen – he has gone for total control rather than pursuing the necessary dialectic of his first efforts. No doubt the original Mothers could not have played the boggling perversions of 'Sinister Footwear' or 'Ship Arriving Too Late to Save a Drowning Witch', but Don Preston's background and subsequent interests are an important reminder that Zappa's music is not created in isolation (a common mistake of Zappaphiles). Zappa absorbed Preston and Gardner's post-Stockhausen improvisations into the procedure of his art: you can actually hear Preston's mini-moog bubbling fifteen years later in the Synclavier pieces of *Jazz from Hell*. Accident and technology, genre-transgression and abstraction are the stock-in-trade of the avant-garde: what makes Zappa's project special is the action of these devices on the marketable – it makes his music more ambitious. Outside the art ghetto there is more to play with.

ABSOLUTELY FREE

Freak Out! at least contained one disc of conventional-sounding pop songs. On first listen *Absolutely Free* sounds like a free-form collage of wacked weirdos howling and joking at random (a veritable 'Sunset Boulevard version of the Fugs'). Now that the Mothers had established the freak image it could be used as a stalking horse for ideas that would not fit pop formats. It is Zappa's refusal to supply substantial, usable music – toe-tapping rock 'n' roll, heavy rock, lilting songs – that offends regular rock fans (who make an exception for *Hot Rats*). However, unlike equivalent albums by the Bonzo Dog Band or Cheech and Chong, there is a musical core that reveals itself on repeated listenings. Don Preston recalls that 'most of the songs were recorded in 4-bar sections, each section requiring about fifty or sixty takes – indeed, some of the less sectionalized songs took about 100 takes'.[169]

The opener, 'Plastic People', continues the line of attack from

---

[169]Quoted by Julian Colbeck, *Zappa: A Biography*, 1987, p. 53.

Freak Out!. 'You're Probably Wondering Why I'm Here' had the lines

> Plastic boots and plastic hat
> And you think you are where it's at.[170]

'Who are the Brain Police?' found a more sinister meaning for plastic.

> What will you do when the label comes off
> And the plastic's all melted
> And the chrome is too soft?[171]

This is straight out of Philip K. Dick's paranoid-schizophrenic vision of people as automata or 'simulacra'. The original 'Plastic People' went

> Plastic People
> You gotta go
> They've got no balls
> They've got no roots[172]

In using black R&B, the Mothers – just like the Stones – used male sexuality to criticize what they considered to be false social codes. When Zappa described one of the Mothers' first appearances on TV (a teenage dance show in Dallas) he is keen to mention Carl Franzoni's large testicles.

> The high point of the performance was Carl Franzoni, our 'go-go boy'. He was wearing ballet tights, *frugging violently*. Carl has testicles which are bigger than a breadbox. Much bigger than a breadbox. The look on the faces of the Baptist teens experiencing *their grandeur* is a treasured memory.[173]

However, when 'Plastic People' arrived on vinyl with *Absolutely Free*, it necessarily gave such notions of authenticity a touch of irony. Zappa still used the classic dumbness of the chords of 'Louie Louie', but embedded in a more complex arrangement. It starts with a drum roll announcing the president of the United States, who can only say 'Fellow Americans' before he starts singing the chords to 'Louie Louie' – 'Doot, Doot, Doot . . .' He's been sick, we are told, his wife is going to bring him some chicken soup. It

---

[170]Frank Zappa, 'You're Probably Wondering Why I'm Here', *Freak Out!*, 1966.
[171]Frank Zappa, 'Who are the Brain Police?', *Freak Out!* 1966.
[172]Frank Zappa, 'Plastic People', from 'Mystery Disc', *The Old Masters Box One*, 1985.
[173]Frank Zappa, with Peter Occhiogrosso, *The Real Frank Zappa Book*, 1989, p. 80.

is as if the subcultural junk of American lowlife has become contagious, even the president has it.

Since the onset of Aids, disease imagery has proliferated everywhere – viruses attack computers, pornography infects the population – but it is but the latest version of an old theme. Nineteenth-century sanitary reformers couched their proposals to Parliament in terms that linked disease with social unrest; Lenin and Trotsky talked of the 'bacillus' of revolution. Fashions – hairstyles, clothes, dance crazes – sweep through the population like diseases. 'Packard Goose' from *Joe's Garage* accuses the music press of

> Selling punk like some kind of new English disease[174]

and *Apostrophe (')* has Zappa leer in his best adman tones:

> Out thru the night and the whisperin' breezes
> To the place where they keep the imaginary diseases
> This has to be the disease for you
> Now scientists call this disease bromodrosis
> But us regular folks who wear tennis shoes
> Or the occasional python boot
> Know this exquisite little inconvenience as . . .
> STINK-FOOT![175]

Zappa always keeps alive a trembling ambivalence about cultural value, a contradictory posture that offends the guardians of high-culture just as it disappoints the proponents of pop.[176] For its ability to threaten hierarchy and cultural value, the idiocy of pop culture is celebrated: but because Zappa has an almost situationist sensitivity to the moment where lived resistance is turned into commodities, he cannot go along with the way *Rolling Stone*, for example, seeks to elevate pop into a culture, a canon like those of great literature and painting. Just as advertising invents 'imaginary' diseases for its pharmaceutical products to 'cure', so pop foments 'imaginary' desires. However, there is no safe haven from this pulsating, all-consuming process: the disease has infected the president and we are not immune either. The song commemorated a confrontation between the freaks and the law, a police siege of a venue called 'Pandora's Box'.

> Take a day and walk around
> Watch the Nazis run your town

---

[174]Frank Zappa, 'Packard Goose', *Joe's Garage Acts II and III*, 1979.
[175]Frank Zappa, 'Stink-Foot', *Apostrophe (')*, 1974.
[176]For example, Mark Sinker on Zappa's 'contempt for rock', *The Wire*, No. 10, June 1990.

> Then go home and check yourself
> You think we're singing 'bout someone else[177]

Zappa's satire revolves through 360 degrees; there is no way to stay out of the line of fire. Zappa's 'protest' song about 'plastic people' of course only reaches the consumer by being pressed on plastic: the song's fast-cutting montage of different voices and recording spaces would have been impossible in a live performance (though Zappa characteristically attempted this with 'Brown Shoes Don't Make It' on *Tinsel Town Rebellion* in 1981). Plastic, like the 'fast 'n bulbous jelly' of *Trout Mask Replica* and *Uncle Meat*, the 'UDT – Undifferentiated Tissue' of *The Grand Wazoo* and the 'slime' of *Overnite Sensation*, is an image for the way commodity exchange makes everything equal to everything else. Pioneeringly described by Marx in the first pages of *Capital* (where he talks of the 'magical' act by which money can find equivalence between a coat and yards of linen), this process finds an ideal symbol in the infinitely variable nature of plastic.

> Me see a neon moon above
> I searched for years I found no love
> I'm sure that love will never be
> A product of plasticity[178]

'Plastic People' interleaves the pumping chords of 'Louie Louie' (a tirade against the singer's girlfriend for using cosmetics) with presidential hypocrisy ('I know it's hard to defend an unpopular policy every once in a while') and fear of surveillance ('There's this guy from the CIA and he's creepin' around Laurel Canyon'). These muttered lines of speech, utterly without velocity, traverse the song in the way sections of 'smooth' time alternate with 'striated' time in the music of Pierre Boulez. It is Zappa's discovery that the vectors of excitement used in pop music may be arranged in a similar manner to Varèse's 'blocks of sound'.[179] The hallucinatory shocks that litter a Zappa record, moments that suspend the music's momentum, defy expectation in a way that makes the listener reflect on how music is used to manipulate. The song disintegrates into gibberish, some of which anticipates the next song: 'a prune is not a vegetable/cabbage is a vegetable'.

---

[177]Frank Zappa, 'Plastic People', *Absolutely Free*, 1967.
[178]Ibid.
[179]Varèse talked about 'blocks of sound' to the *New York Times* in 1936. See Ferdnand Ouellette, *Edgard Varèse*, 1966, trs. Derek Coltman, 1968, p. 84.

'The Duke of Prunes', a tune recycled from the *Run Home Slow* soundtrack, has been supplied with surrealist lyrics that replace the moon/June rhymes of pop with June/prune nonsense. The declaration of undying love is mocked by spoken asides.

The love I have for you will never end (well, maybe)

Zappa says, 'this is the exciting part – just like the Supremes, see the way it builds up' and the Mothers parody 'Baby Love', singing it as 'cheesy love'.

'Call Any Vegetable' is introduced by Zappa. 'This is a song about vegetables, they keep you regular, they're real good for you . . .', a scatological reminder that works against the metaphorical use of the term 'vegetable' (the message is that freaks should attempt to communicate with their straight neighbours). In the transcription accompanying the CD release, Flo & Eddie's word mutation from *Just Another Band from LA* (substituting 'joint' for 'hand' in the lines 'standing there shiny and proud by your side / holding your hand . . .') has surfaced: Zappa probably played the song with them more often than he did with the original Mothers.

The title of 'Invocation and Ritual Dance of the Young Pumpkin', like part one of *Freak Out!*'s 'Monster Magnet', echoes *The Rite of Spring*, whose theme is played on 'The Duke of Prunes' as a wind figure, to be taken up by an inane 'la-de-la-de-lah' vocal. The music takes off into a storming guitar/soprano sax duet over a single chord vamp ending with a parody of female orgasm.

Oh no! Can you see them responding? the
pumpkin is breathing hard . . . h-h-h-h
h-h-h-H-H-H-H-H-H-H-H – H – HHHHHHHHHHHHHH!
(what a pumpkin!)

A woman lurking behind Zappa on the innerfold is labelled 'MY PUMPKIN' and he listed 'Gail Pumpkin' as 'fave rave' on his United Mutations questionnaire. The sexual act, during which the human species encounters at some level an unmediated animality, is the end of the plastic charade. Of course, any representation of sex is achieved through the use of artificial codes, and it is the way in which sex makes these codes seem artificial and unworkable that explains Zappa's emphasis on sex. Songs like 'Baby Love' recycle the romantic clichés that are the soundtrack of the transition from high school to marriage, a transition Zappa is at pains to interrupt.

'Brown Shoes Don't Make It', Zappa's celebrated attack on repression, is the climax of side two of the LP, which is a sequence of songs that operates like a suite. 'America Drinks' is a deconstruction of a cocktail-bar ballad. By slowing its pace but keeping the drummer playing a regular swing 'ten-to-ten' on the cymbal, the Mothers can interject all kinds of bilious comments; 'Status Back Baby' satirizes the conformist high-school rat-race, contrasting the cheerleader-type banality of its theme (introduced by a whistle) with a heavy guitar section; 'Uncle Bernie's Farm' attacks the war-toys that are promoted at Christmas and compares authority and parents to robot simulacra: the paranoid vision of the world as an assemblage of artificial objects.

> There's a little plastic 'CONGRESS'
> There's a 'NATION' you can buy
>
> There's a doll that looks like daddy
> (He's a funny little man . . .
> Push a button and ask for money:
> There's a dollar in his hand!)[180]

'Son of Suzy Creamcheese' is an update on the Creamcheese saga. Having frequented Cantor's, the delicatessen where Vito held court, she has now discovered drugs and politics.

> Blew your mind with too much kool-aid
> Yeah, yeah, yeah
> Took my stash and left me lonely
>
> Vito said she split for Berkeley
> Yeah, yeah, yeah
> Protest marching styrofoam[181]

The certainty that explicit political protest is just another facet of the spectacle (styrofoam being a kind of plastic) underlies Zappa's repudiation of collective political action throughout his career. 'Join the march and eat my starch,' he said, introducing the march from *Greggery Peccary* in 1973. For Zappa politics is always a matter for the individual, which is why, despite his vision of the corruption of American institutions and his awareness of the way the media serve the government and its marketing of, say, the Gulf War, Zappa's political actions – running for president, telling us

---

[180]Frank Zappa, 'Uncle Bernie's Farm', *Absolutely Free*, 1967.
[181]Frank Zappa, 'Son of Suzy Creamcheese', *Absolutely Free*, 1967.

to register to vote – are so inadequate. Like Adorno (whose inspirational, oppositional ideas were betrayed by his political position on campus in 1968), Zappa's art requires commentary that will reveal a political unconscious at odds with his explicit pronouncements. The paradox is that his materialism continually deconstructs the 'individual' into its component impulses, revealing these as socially reproduced and unfree, and destroying the idea of the autonomous individual on which his petit-bourgeois politics is founded.

'Brown Shoes Don't Make It' is a case in point. It draws a Reichian parallel between repression and authoritarian government.

> A world of secret hungers,
> Perverting the men who make your laws
> Every desire is hidden away
> In a drawer, in a desk
> By a naugahyde chair[182]

The drawer contains pornography (in 'Dirty Love' the words go: 'Give me your dirty love / Just like the tacky little pamphlet / In your daddy's bottom drawer'[183]). The tune for these lines is like one of those used by Kurt Weill to suspend Brecht's shocking denunciations before the moral gaze of the listener. Further on, the arbitrary nature of the atonal writing stresses the arbitrary nature of the words, which seem to outline the listener's psychic resistance: prurience as a shaping force, the images moulding themselves like a negative cast of guilt and desire.

> We see in the back of the city hall mind
> The dream of a girl about thirteen
> Off with her clothes and into a bed
> Where she tickles his fancy all night long[184]

Zappa proposes a cultural politics: the explosion of sexual freedom will topple the powers-that-be. As it dawned on him that it wasn't going to work, the stress on sexuality became instead a satirical slant, a litmus test on the freedoms of his audience and his society. His obscenities could be harmless only in a world free of corruption: enunciation of themes excluded from polite discourse becomes denunciation of power and its hypocrisy.

---

[182]Frank Zappa, 'Brown Shoes Don't Make It', *Absolutely Free*, 1967.
[183]Frank Zappa, 'Dirty Love', *Overnite Sensation*, 1973.
[184]Frank Zappa, 'Brown Shoes Don't Make It', *Absolutely Free*, 1967.

The closing 'America Drinks & Goes Home', a reprise of 'America Drinks', re-creates the lounge ambience that Zappa so hated when he was playing with Joe Perrino and the Mellotones in 1960. Crooner and brush-drum jazz combo struggle to be heard over a chaos of drunken revelry and cash registers (which, of course, were meticulously arranged and overdubbed). The tune artfully evokes Tin Pan Alley, the circular melody inducing a claustrophobic sense of arrested development.

> We rehearsed the crowd noises. The talk track itself which is underplayed there, is funny because they're saying things like 'I got a new Mustang' and the girls are saying 'Sally, will you go with me to the bathroom?' you know that stuff . . . the crowd mumble was carefully programmed, like choreographed. Then on top of that, which you can't even hear, there's a fight going on. We had a crowd separated in two rooms . . . We had Bunk trying to pick up girls. You know, 'What's a girl like you doing in a place like this?' . . . And meanwhile the chicks tell this guy to fuck off because he's coming on too strong, you know: 'What kind of girls do you think we are?' . . . And it's all happening in there, but you can't listen to it all. You've got to have it on ten tracks so you can walk around the room and see where it's all coming from. Those things are so carefully constructed that it breaks my heart that people don't dig into them and see all the levels that I put into them.[185]

The crowd noise becomes an indecipherable riot behind the jazz combo, but the same phrases occur in *Fillmore East* and 'Dancing Fool', icons of the sexual hysteria of a fucked-up America. Despite targeting the kind of music and venue good freaks would never frequent, the satirical content veers round to confront the listener, as in 'You're Probably Wondering Why I'm Here'. As Ray Collins says 'goodnight', it is as if Zappa is asking if the record itself is going to become merely another generation's backdrop to a night of desperate non-communication.

MGM/Verve caused delays over the slogan 'War means work for all' in Zappa's collage, eventually printing it in half-tone, making it illegible in the CD release (the words appear over the US flag beneath the atom-bomb explosion on the back cover). They also refused to print the lyrics. Zappa responded by making them available by mail order, along with a 'freak map', a guide to underground LA originally published in the *Los Angeles Free Press*. This was a pop version of situationist psychogeography.

Out front, the newcomer to Freakdom must know that in the rapidly

---

[185]Quoted by Frank Kofsky, *Jazz and Pop*, October 1967.

changing 'hot action' that locations can cool off instantly (especially under police pressure) and places that once were happening become parking lots or hardware stores or whatever you can dream of that's worse.[186]

In *The Broken Bubble*, one of Philip K. Dick's posthumously published mainstream novels, an adult is horrified to hear how a young couple are harassed by the police. It is set in 1965.

> Now, he thought, he was saying 'they'. He was thinking as Art and Rachael were thinking: in terms of the unyielding 'they'. But to him 'they' would not be adults; they would be – what? He pondered, drawn into this despite himself. Looney Luke, perhaps. Or Ted Haynes. Or, for that matter, anyone and everyone.
>
> But nobody was keeping him out of restaurants. Nobody had halted him at night and shoved him against a wall. So it was in his mind; it was not real. For these kids it was real enough. The good people talk about civil rights, the protection of minority groups. And then they passed a curfew.[187]

There is hardly a 'good-time' Louis Jordan or Bessie Smith song that does not end in a police raid; scares about 'juvenile delinquents' extended to white youth treatment the black minority had suffered for decades. Dick's words brilliantly record the dawning realization that the liberal consensus may not look like that for some parts of the population. Zappa's political consciousness, already informed by his overnight arrest in Lancaster and his imprisonment in San Bernardino, escalated as he saw people picked up by the police for no other reason than the length of their hair. In the freak map a photograph shows someone being set upon by three cops. The legend runs 'All I wanted was a pastrami' (the cop has a speech bubble: 'Silence fool'). It could be a situationist graphic.

> Cantor's Fairfax Restaurant is the top freako watering hole and social HQ, scene of more blatant Gestapo practices than the peaceful natives care to recollect, it is a good place to go as soon as you arrive in town. If a black bus (or two) pulls up in front and you see your fellows, brethren and kinfolk being loaded into them (as if it were off to Auschwitz) do something normal . . .

Zappa's next record focused on these images of repression, but awareness of the extremes the bourgeois state will stoop to in times of crisis runs right through Zappa's work.

[186]*Los Angeles Free Press*, 11 November 1966, pp. 8–9.
[187]Philip K. Dick, *The Broken Bubble*, Paladin, 1988, p. 16.

CHAPTER 2
FREAKDOM AND THE HIPPIES

NEW YORK

Work was thin on the West Coast. In late November 1966 the
Mothers secured a two-week run in New York, at the Balloon
Farm (a venue rumoured to have been named by Bob Dylan) at
23 St Mark's Place. According to Julian Colbeck, they played New
Year's Eve there with Allen Ginsberg, the Fugs and Andy Warhol
in the front row. In January 1967 the Mothers played for two
weeks in Montreal. A brief trip to LA proved fruitless, and they
returned to New York at Easter and began a two-shows-a-night
residency at the 300-seater Garrick Theater on Bleecker Street.
During the same period Andy Warhol was promoting the Velvet
Underground at St Mark's Place, calling it his Exploding Plastic
Inevitable (like Zappa, Warhol saw an unstoppable dynamic in
American consumer culture). Zappa endorsed Panther organs and
Hagstrom guitars for Merson/Unicord in order to secure equipment and called his show *Pigs & Repugnant*. Pop-art happenings,
the result of Black Mountain School experimentation hitting the
media, were big news: Zappa encouraged such goings-on. At
the height of hippie/military tension (a marine had been murdered
in the Village that week – rumours were that soldiers were out
looking for revenge) Zappa had three Marines rip apart a doll onstage, pretending it was a 'gook'. 'I thanked them and, with quiet
musical accompaniment, showed the ruined parts of the doll to
the audience. Nobody was laughing.'[1]

Ray Collins would massage a stuffed giraffe. Its tail became
erect and the audience was sprayed with whipped cream piped
through its anus. Salamis sailed down to the stage on wires. It
was Zappa's own Cabaret Voltaire, and each eye-witness account

---

[1]Frank Zappa, with Peter Occhiogrosso, *The Real Frank Zappa Book*, 1989, p. 94.

reveals themes that crop up later. Zappa had a plan for a side of beef rotting in a gallows-cum-shower unit with a curtain consisting of the American flag, which would be whipped away, sending clouds of flies into the audience.[2] Daily reports of Vietnam casualties in the papers made such extremities appear quite legitimate. Jimi Hendrix was playing at the Café-a-Go-Go opposite and sat in a few times, perhaps his first taste of the wah-wah pedal. In late June the Mothers played at a Community Defense Budget benefit with Allen Ginsberg, The Fugs and Moondog, the blind street performer whose music sounds like a naïve version of Sun Ra.

Zappa had done the artwork for *Absolutely Free* himself, brushing New York soot off the copy, but when he heard that the other act's ex-boyfriend was an artist, he got him over from Philadelphia with his portfolio. This started his long-term association with Cal Schenkel, who moved into the Zappas' New York apartment. 'Cal Schenkel, talented boy artist from Philadelphia, whose main fetish was his unusual love for eggs and his ability to pile dirty dishes in the kitchen until there wasn't any room for people.'[3] In his *We're Only in It for the Money* montage Schenkel can be seen hugging a carton of a dozen eggs. When the Mothers moved back west, Schenkel was installed in one wing of Zappa's log cabin. Motorhead Sherwood picked up a 'strange girlfriend'[4] who also came out west – she turned out to be Joni Mitchell. Before leaving for a European tour Zappa married Gail, who was nine months' pregnant with Moon. The 1967 New York period was also productive in terms of recordings: *Lumpy Gravy* was recorded in February at Apostolic Studios and *We're Only in It for the Money* at Mayfair and Apostolic between August and October, interrupted by the European tour. By then, Zappa had recruited a new Mother.

IAN UNDERWOOD

The story of Ian Underwood's induction is recounted in his own words on *Uncle Meat*, one of the slices of behind-the-scenes documentary that segue many of the tracks. Having established the

[2]Ibid., p. 93.
[3]Pamela Zarubica, quoted by Michael Gray, *Mother! is the Story of Frank Zappa*, 1985, p. 78.
[4]Michael Gray, *Mother! is the Story of Frank Zappa*, 1985, p. 73.

Mothers as the ugliest, hairiest, heaviest group in the world, they could now welcome some light relief: someone willing to call himself the 'straight' member of the group. Like Don Preston and Bunk Gardner, he had experience of classical music and jazz, essential attributes for the new music that Zappa wanted to play. *We're Only in It for the Money* represented the crest of the Mothers as inflammatory socio-sexual commentators: what followed were albums that were to stretch the boundaries of rock 'n' roll to the point of starting off (albeit unwillingly) a whole new genre: art rock.

Ian Underwood was born in New York City on 22 May 1939 and raised in Rye, a well-to-do suburb on Long Island. His father was an executive for Republic Steel. At the age of five he discovered Beethoven and started piano lessons. In 1953, inspired by bebop, he took up alto and tenor saxophones, flute and clarinet. He attended Choate Prep School in Wallingford, Connecticut, with bassist Steve Swallow, later to make his name with Carla Bley. Underwood later said: 'We'd get up at three o'clock in the morning and sneak down to the basement of the chapel. He'd play bass and I'd play alto sax until six in the morning, crawling back to bed when the sun rose.'[5] Both he and Swallow attended Yale, again sharing their musical enthusiasms.

> We'd drive down to New York and listen to Ornette's trio play in the Village until four in the morning, then drive all the way back to school with no sleep at all. I would say that for the next four years, Ornette Coleman was a major influence on my thinking.

At the final concert of the 1959 summer school at Lenox, Massachusetts, Ian Underwood played alongside Ornette in the Herb Pomeroy Ensemble.[6] Underwood graduated from Yale in 1961 with a BA in composition and from Berkeley with a Masters in 1966. Initially, following parental advice, he studied electrical engineering and mathematics, but when his sister took him to the Garrick and he heard the Mothers he knew this music was what he wanted to play.

> I never listen to the radio, nor was I up on any pop or rock groups at all. I didn't know anything about Zappa or the Mothers, who was in it, what it was, or what they did.

---

[5]Quoted by Lee Underwood, 'Ian Underwood: Free Lance Energizer', *Down Beat*, 19 May 1977, pp. 18–20. Subsequent quotes all from this source.
[6]*Lenox School of Jazz Concert 1959*, Royal Jazz RJD CD513. Thanks to Ian Watson for this information.

The moment I heard them, however, I knew Zappa's music was the closest thing to what really interested me then – that combination of Stravinsky, blues, Hindemith, goofy lyrics, Ornette Coleman, corny jokes and Stockhausen. That's exactly what I liked: complex music with bizarre humour.

Zappa gave him some keyboard music to play (reading was not one of Don Preston's strong points) and Underwood passed the audition. Apart from providing the butt of jokes about being 'wholesome' (his description on *We're Only in It for the Money*), Underwood's ability to read and play many instruments was invaluable for the complex orchestrations of *Uncle Meat*, and *Hot Rats* was essentially an Underwood/Zappa duo album. In *The Jazz Book* Joachim Berendt (who warmly applauds Zappa's music) says that Underwood is not a 'convincing soloist in the jazz sense',[7] but actually his raw blatancy is perfect for Zappa's music, his rasp evoking all kinds of images (industrial vacuum cleaners, gypsy rituals, nasal sadism) that became part of conceptual continuity. In September 1973 he left the Mothers, having recorded on *Overnite Sensation*, and toured since February. Like Don Preston, he benefited from the early access to hardware Zappa's rock-scale budgets made possible, and went on to studio and film work using synthesizers. His (live) Arp synthesizer contributions to Freddie Hubbard's *High Energy*[8] were promising, but his subsequent involvements have been less cutting-edge than Preston's (for example, the band Ambrosia, the kind of laid-back soporific that gives the West Coast a bad name, was a low point).

LUMPY GRAVY

Lumpy Gravy is a provocative and puzzling record, one that refuses to 'add up'. Some parts can only be described as avant-garde classical, but in the midst of twanging electronics, *musique concrète* interference, stoned dialogue, boogaloo drums and eerily twee arrangements of jolly melodies, it is hard to listen to these scores in terms of flutes and violins and castanets. It is Zappa's utopian disregard for genre (and the social limits genres imply) that is peculiarly disorienting. His ear for instrumental timbre is as strong as anything classical music has to offer between Varèse

[7]Joachim Berendt, *The Jazz Book*, 1973, p. 220.
[8]Freddie Hubbard, *High Energy*, 1974, CBS 80478.

and Giacinto Scelsi, yet the setting is such that it defies high-brow analysis. When addressing the American Society of University Composers in 1984, Zappa mentioned that composers have to eat, and that 'mostly what they eat is brown and lumpy',[9] which gives a characteristically scatological twist to the title of his brown-sleeved album.

The opening words, spoken in a dumb slur, sound as about as aesthetically enthused as a concert promoter selling a hotdog concession: 'The way I see it, Barry, this should be a very dynamite show.' This ambivalence towards the musical and verbal material permeates the whole record. The absence of a governing semantic system allows a free combination of elements. The effect, though, is to be distinguished from the free play of images supposedly characteristic of 'postmodern' art. Achille Bonito-Oliva talks of the 'mildness' of postmodernism's run-through of incompatible styles[10] and Fredric Jameson notes that this 'results from the abstention of the art object to address and hector you for ideological purposes'.[11]

Zappa's music does not – any more than the work of Marcel Duchamp or Casimir Malevich – serve to illustrate a prior conception of society. However, to set up a choice between postmodern art (which reduces everything to a trivial stream of images) and propaganda (which is also trivial, since it is merely an add-on to a preconceived politics) is false: the point is to draw attention to the material provenance of the elements.

In 1962 Theodor Adorno wrote: 'Entertainment music no longer does anything but confirm, repeat and reinforce the psychological debasement ultimately wrought in people by the way society is set up.'[12] It was a similar awareness that led Zappa to fashion an art that could work like an invert-virus, operating with the very tools he wished to destroy.

> I am trying to use the weapons of a disoriented and unhappy society against itself. The Mothers of Invention are designed to come in the back door and kill you while you're sleeping. One of our main, short range objectives is to do away with the Top Forty broadcasting format because it is basically wrong, unethical and unmusical.[13]

---

[9]ASUC, 4 April 1984, transcribed in *Society Pages*, No. 25, April 1985, p. 7.
[10]Achille Bonito-Oliva, *The International Transavantgarde*, 1982, p. 24.
[11]Fredric Jameson, *Postmodernism, Or, The Cultural Logic of Late Capitalism*, 1991, p. 175.
[12]Theodor Adorno, *Introduction to the Sociology of Music*, 1962, p. 225.
[13]Quoted by Robert Shelton, *New York Times*, 25 December 1967.

Lumpy Gravy pans across the sound sources available in twentieth-century society, but does not produce a decorative postmodern cascade. By abutting various modes of representation it seeks to dramatize their shortcomings, create dissatisfaction with limits.

Wyndham Lewis, the artist and writer who instigated Vorticism, London's version of the avant-garde currents that swept Rome, Zurich, Paris and Moscow during the years before the Russian Revolution, developed a prose style that compares to Zappa's music. His fierce intolerance of bourgeois liberalism finds many parallels with Zappa (though growing up an Italian-American meant that Zappa is spared Lewis's racist and colonial prejudices, giving Zappa a left rather than a right inflection). In describing Lewis's language, Fredric Jameson defines a collage methodology of greater critical severity than PoMo's warm shower of *imageoiserie*.

> The satire-collage is the form taken by artificial epic in the degraded world of commodity production and of the mass media: it is artificial epic whose raw materials have become spurious and inauthentic, monumental gesture replaced by the cultural junk of industrial capitalism. So it is that the most authentic realization of the epic voice in modern times – an ideal of many centuries of western culture – yields not some decorative and beautiful pastiche, but the most jarring and energetic mimesis of the mechanical, and breathes a passionate revulsion for the standardized manipulations of contemporary existence.[14]

Jameson's words can serve to describe Zappa's concatenation of cultural elements. As Gary Steel said to Zappa when interviewing him for the New Zealand *Listener*, his output is 'a heck of a thing to comprehend'. Zappa agreed.

> That's the point, though. The problem is that very few people even have the nerve to say what you just said. It is a *heck* of a thing to comprehend. It's a miracle if somebody can follow all of it, because that would mean that they would either have had to have done a lot of research to find out what all those lyrics mean, and/or have listened to a wide variety of different ethnic music and classical music and different kinds of blues stuff that I've listened to throughout my life.[15]

In the same interview he went on to give a typical example of the kind of detail he means: 'For example, the ending notes on the *Stage* version of 'Strictly Genteel',[16] that was the Hawaiian

---

[14]Fredric Jameson, 'Wyndham Lewis As Futurist', *Hudson Review*, 1973/4, p. 325. An essay superior in its insights to Jameson's book on Wyndham Lewis, *Fables of Aggression*, 1978.
[15]Gary Steel, 'The Father of Invention', *Listener*, 22 April 1991, pp. 32–3.
[16]'Strictly Genteel', 1981, *You Can't Do That on Stage Anymore Vol. 6*, 1992.

Punch commercial featuring Donny and Marie Osmond. That was so esoteric. That was on in 1980.'[17]

In more extreme cases of irritation with the press he has said it is simply impossible to interpret his work. Steel, though, drew him out by reminding him of his immediate response to *Ionisation* at the age of twelve. Surely fans can have that kind of unmediated response to Zappa's music?

> Most of them have. The ones that just really crave it, maybe just because it touches them in a weird emotional way or a weird intellectual way that they don't understand what it is but they like it. It's a bit like eating a sausage: you don't know what's in it, you probably shouldn't know what's in there; but if it tastes good, well there you go.[18]

He goes on to summon up the same image of a junk sculpture used by Jameson.

> Let's say I build a junk sculpture. You don't know what the pieces are or where they come from, but if the sculpture works when it's done, who gives a fuck? You don't have to know that's Donny and Marie.[19]

This is an important principle and connects Zappa to the progressive aspect of modernist collage. In *The Waste Land* T. S. Eliot hijacked such techniques, but attempted to restrict his borrowings from some known canon of 'great' literature, a terroristic élitism practised against the unschooled reader. Like Wyndham Lewis, Zappa does not have any qualms about the source of his vectors of excitement: the net result is a grating, contradictory work which mocks artists tied to single genres, those incapable of surviving without a nurturing context.

However, Zappa is not devoid of a concept of the unconscious, and is therefore less at the mercy of Lewis's limited (and reactionary) set of psychic figures. Unlike the strident castration complex that marched Lewis along the path of male chauvinism, class rule and ultimately Fascism, Zappa experiments with the unconscious imagery of his art, a procedure that brings him closer to Joyce. *Lumpy Gravy* is unique in Zappa's discography, because it presents us with his set of resonant ideas – the raw poetic substructure – before it has been worked into a set of songs. In some ways the record operates like an imagist blueprint for *Money*. Not that this makes it any more accessible. Joycean scholars were

[17]'Way Down in New Zealand: FZ Talks to Gary Steel, 5 December 1990, Part 2', *T'Mershi Duween*, No. 21, September 1991, p. 15.
[18]Ibid., p. 16.
[19]Ibid., p. 18.

amazed that the original manuscript for *Finnegans Wake* (published as *Scribbledehobble*), despite its relatively plain English, was actually less easy to follow than the mangled verbiage of the finished work. Something like *Lumpy Gravy*'s cluster of resonant symbols works beneath every one of Zappa's albums, but nowhere else are they so blatant. If you are not going to take pleasure in tracing them, there is precious little to enjoy – which may explain why it is a favourite for Zappologists and unpopular with everyone else.

As well as introducing rubbish-epic, twentieth-century modernism also broke with the rational shell that romanticism provided to protect its libidinal associations, exposing the kernel of unsocial, personal ideas that charge words for the poet. An insult to the bourgeois, who would like to see rationality rewarded in art just as it is supposed to be in business, *Finnegans Wake* acts as an eruption of the associative, infantile, repressed thoughts that actually determine word choice in 'respectable' poets like William Wordsworth and Samuel Taylor Coleridge. In extreme forms of modernism, these associations replace representation as guarantees of continuity, leading to the occluded 'private' work. However, because of the colonization of the unconscious by the culture industry, such opaque art is frequently more social than its detractors – both conservative and postmodern – imagine. When one goes beneath the surface of Coleridge's poetry (to his notebooks, for example) the words read like modern poetry – or the movement of images in *Lumpy Gravy*.

Reo = reor probably an obsolete Latin word, and res the second person singular of the Present Indicative – If so, it is the Iliad of Spinozo-Kantian, Kanto-Fichtian, Fichto-Schellingian Revival of Plato-Plotino-Proclian Idealism in a Nutshell *from* a Lilliput Hazel. Res = thou art thinking. – Even so our "Thing": id est, thinking or think'd. Think, Thank, Tank = Reservoir of what has been *thinged* – Denken, Danken – I forget the German for Tank/The, Them, This, These, Thence, Thick, Thing, Thong, Thou, may all be Hocus-pocused by metaphysical Etymology into Brothers and Sisters – with many a Cousin-German/All little Miss Thetas, the ● being a Circle, with the Kentron [*Kentrum*], or central Point, creating the circumference & both together the infinite Radii/ – the Central point is primary Consciousness = living Action; the circumference = secondary Consciousness <or Consc: in the common sense of the word> and the passing to and fro from the one to the other Thought, Things, necessary Possibilities, contingent Realities / = Father, Son, Holy Ghost/the Tо Ον, Ο Λογος, η ΣοΦια / – The ● is I which is the articulated Breath drawn inward, the Ο is the same sent outward, the ⊜ or Theta expresses the synthesis and coinstantaneous reciprocation of the two Acts, the Dualism of *Thought* by *Distinctions*, the Unity of *Thing* by Indivisibility/[20]

Like Hans Richter's 'inwards (the groan) and outwards (the roar)',[21] or even the Cabbalah's En Sof (the primal breath of being)[22] which donated the Sofa theme to *One Size Fits All*, Coleridge's dialectic of the breathing body underlies *Lumpy Gravy*. Private webs of verbal association echo each other as they begin to descry the material body.

Lumpy Gravy was coupled with *We're Only in It for the Money* by speech bubbles that asked if they were parts one and two of the same set. The style of *musique concrète* is similar and there is even a little music in common ('Mother People' on *Money* is suddenly interrupted – the needle sounds as if it is being ripped across the grooves – to land in the cowboy-pastoral section that follows the words 'I don't think I can go through this again' on *Lumpy Gravy*). Despite these links, *Lumpy Gravy* works in an utterly different way. *Money*'s complete lyric sheet and extensive sleeve note directions give the listener a framework (even if the data overload is such that most people are still quite baffled). The track listing on *Lumpy Gravy* just consists of 'Part One' and 'Part Two' for the album's two sides.

The engineer on the record – Gary Kellgren – has complained that the tapes were in a complete mess when delivered by Capitol's engineers (MGM/Verve insisted that Capitol could not have an individual contract with Zappa). Some people use this to 'explain' its broken continuity, but Zappa would not cite it as his favourite record if it were really a product of record-company sabotage. The dislocations are quite deliberate.

What follows is a blow-by-blow account of the record, trans-

---

[20]Samuel Taylor Coleridge, *The Notebooks*, Vol. 2, 1804–1808, ed. Kathleen Coburn, 1962, #2784, 1 January 1806.
[21]Hans Richter, *Dada: Art and Anti-Art*, 1964, p. 19.
[22]Rabbi Ben Zion Bokser, *From the World of the Cabbalah: The Philosophy of Rabbi Judah Loew of Prague*, 1957, p. 4. An act as fundamental as breathing has always offered mystics and poets opportunity for speculation. In a competitive exchange economy, inhalation is associated with 'take/buy', exhalation with 'give/sell' – hence Captian Beefheart's question, 'Must the breathing pay for those who breathe in 'n don't / Breathe out?', 'Petrified Forest', *Lick My Decals Off, Baby*, 1970, Reprise K44244. In this connection, breathing relates to the alpha and omega of the Jewish mystics, a trope that reoccurs with unerring frequency as writers theorize the body. See, for example, 'take: "ah"; give: "o" ' in Rod Mengham, 'Review: Jeremy Prynne, *Word Order*, 1989', *Parataxis: Modernism and Modern Writing*, No. 2, Summer 1992, p. 40 (*Parataxis* is available from Drew Milne School of English and American Studies, Arts Building, University of Sussex, Falmer, Brighton, East Sussex BN1 9QN, England).

cribing its dialogues and key phrases (a task that has not been done before, to my knowledge), but it should be remembered that these float in the repetitive, timeless space of the record's listening life, rather than being reduced (as here) to a linear narrative, with all the moral conclusiveness that implies. The last words on the album are

M: 'Cause round things are ... are boring.

This is followed by a longish silence – then the speaker exhales, perhaps blowing a ring of smoke. The album concludes with an instrumental version of 'Take Your Clothes Off When You Dance' from *Money* – cheesy electric organ, bright rhythm guitars, a moronically happy snare figure, a la-la-la chorus of speeded-up falsettos (a Munchkin version of the Swingle Singers). When they finally modulate, and Zappa's characteristic bent guitar notes supply some relief, the song is faded. As the review in *Rolling Stone* said, it could have been played by the Ventures.[23] The record is opened in similar style, with a tune that subsequently resurfaced as 'Bwana Dik' on *Fillmore East June 1971*. The circular tunes of pop are boring, but so is the process of listening to records (round things themselves), whatever music they contain. The phrase later appeared on the starmap on the back of *One Size Fits All*, as if to say that the circular (terrestrial) view of the heavens is boring. On that album, ants are boring beneath the surface of Hollywood, causing it to collapse. Round things are cyclical and imply repetition, which, according to Jacques Attali, 'produces less and less use-value ... meaning degenerates, like a mould worn out from overuse'.[24]

This theme is taken up in the film *200 Motels*, with its moulded-resin stage props and the duplication of the groupies (by Flo & Eddie in drag and the dummies-on-strings) – and further still in 'Dinah-Moe Humm'. As Attali points out, 'No organized society can exist without structuring differences at its core. No market economy can develop without erasing those differences in mass production.'[25]

Mass-production condemns workers to repetitive labour but simultaneously ushers in the possibility of a world of material plenty, leading to political questions about the need for inequality.

[23]Jim Miller, 'Lumpy Gravy', *Rolling Stone*, 22 June 1968.
[24]Jacques Attali, *Noise*, 1977, trs. Brian Massumi, 1985, p. 42.
[25]Ibid., p. 5.

The meaning that 'degenerates' is respect for authority and the star: the tarnish of a binful of unwanted Michael Jackson albums. As a phrase, 'round things are boring' sums up both the oppressive and subversive aspects of capitalist production. Likewise (in common with rock 'n' roll itself), the record *Lumpy Gravy* is disposable, plastic, mass-produced, but also an agent of anti-authoritarian consciousness. Like Coleridge's theta (which could picture a record), the phrase combines opposites.

Burnt Weeny Sandwich subsequently reused the idea of 'sandwiching' extrapolated composition between banal slices of pop. *Lumpy Gravy* has some ravishing sections in a post-Varèse classical vein, but classical critics (if they encounter the record at all) are immediately alienated by the banality of the opening and closing themes, as well as other outbreaks of American vulgarity that disfigure the orchestral surface.

A beautiful arrangement of 'Oh No' (a tune which appeared with words on *Weasels Ripped My Flesh*, 1971, and *Roxy & Elsewhere*, 1975) is interrupted by *musique concrète* similar to the scrofulous effects that riddle *Money*. 'Oh No' is later reprised in the middle of one of Motorhead's interminable monologues about jobs and cars and girls. Listened to with ears trained by lyrics subsequently associated with the tune ('Oh no, I don't believe it . . .'), the music immediately casts doubts on the truth of what Motorhead is saying. 'The Air' performs a similar function when it appears after Jimmy Carl Black's diatribe about pay on *Uncle Meat*.

In keeping with the notion of providing a 'dynamite show', a voice suggests 'a bit of nostalgia for the old folks' and is answered by a bass riff. We cannot tell if this is futuristic parody of the music we like, or if this music is really out of date. Vocal gibber, electronic farts, atonal piano clusters, throbbing contrabassoon: the context for listening is in shreds. When the dialogue comes, avant-garde instrumentation becomes film music, setting a mood of foreboding, yet the words never add up either. Improvised by some GTO's and other guests according to Zappa's directions, the words are as wittily distrustful of their speakers' existential basis as any late Samuel Beckett text.

F1: I'm advocating dark clothes.
F2: If I'm not alone – how long have I been asleep?
F1: As long as I have.
F2: Did you ever live in a drum?

F3: No.
F2: Well then you aren't me.
F1: I only dreamt I lived in a drum, ever since it got dark.
F2: Dreaming is hard.
F3: Yeah, but with nothing over your head?
F1: No, just light over my head, and underneath too.
F2: I don't think I could take it without anything over my head.
F3: Uh-oh, I couldn't either.
F2: Why don't you go out and see what's out there?
F1: Well, I don't know if that's what's out there.
F2: That's a thought.
F1: But still you can say, darker and darker. I don't know what the outside of this thing looks like at all.
M1: I do. It's dark and murky.
M2: How do you get your water so dark?
M1: Because I'm paranoid. I'm very paranoid. And the water in my washing machine turns dark out of sympathy.
M2: Out of sympathy?
M1: Yes.
M2: Where can I get that?
M1: At your local drugstore.
M2: How much?
M1: It's from Kansas.

Which segues into a frenzy of speeded-up Dixieland trumpets. Existential poetry or biting satire of mumbling dopeheads? It is similar to the conundrums raised by Philip K. Dick's drug-addled dialogue in *Through a Scanner Darkly*: the mental somersault you have to perform when you realize the trusted narrator is mad.

Pieces of superbly crafted *musique concrète* that would hold their own with Pierre Henri and Luc Ferrari pile straight into rubbishing two-chord-trick twelve-bar rock 'n' roll. A sample from Motorhead's monologue appears ahead of time, twisted by tape vari-speed: 'Good bread, because I was making $2.71 an hour'. Despite the premonition of late-1980s techniques like sampling, there is nothing postmodern about this play with representation. Unlike the singers Luciano Berio uses in *Laborintus 2*, Motorhead's history and character burn through – grit in the flutter. His rootless switching of jobs and cars and girls becomes the lived equivalent of the fast cuts at the editing board.

MOTORHEAD: I worked in a cheesy newspaper company for a while, but that was terrible, I wasn't making enough money to build anything.
CHORUS: Louie Louie.
MOTORHEAD: [*Echo on*] Then I worked in a printing company and a couple of gas stations, oh at the gas station where I was working...

my brother had just gotten married, he'd bought a new car and his
wife was having a kid and all this miserable stuff and he needed a job
so I gave him a job at the gas station, from which I was fired because
– y'know he was gonna work there. And he had his car in the rack
and he was lubin' and changin' tyres and everything all the time and
so he got fired [*Fade in chatter on right speaker*] because he was
goofin' off, man, he just kept takin' parts and workin' on his car day
and night, so he lost that one and went to work on another gas
station. He took that one, so he could feed the kids an' that and I
went to work in an aircraft company, I was building these planes,
I worked on the XB70, I was the last welder on there. It was pretty
good bread because I was makin' $2.71 an hour, makin' a hundred
and a quarter a week and it was good enough money to be workin'
on, so I got myself an Oldsmobile, a groovy Olds, but I was going
with this chick at the time and by the time I got the Olds running
decently she went out and tore up the engine and the trans, her and
her girlfriend got in there and booze it up and tear up the seats, ripped
the seats completely out, so I got a '56 Olds, which was this one
chick's I was going with and we used to drive that all over the place
and finally she got rid of that, and I got another pick-up . . .

This has some of the deadpan compulsion of Robert Altman or
those avant-gardists who document American vulgarity in endless
videos.

The documentary impulse extends to listing the entire fifty-
one-piece orchestra by name: these included many of the best
session musicians of the day, including jazz drummer Shelly
Manne and John Guerin, who subsequently drummed on *Hot
Rats*. Other notables include vibes player Vic Feldman, the English
expatriate cool jazz legend, Mother Bunk Gardner and trombonist
Ken Shroyer, contractor for *The Grand Wazoo* session and mini-
tour. As a flute section dies into studio chatter we hear a musician
say, 'I don't think I can go through this again.' The effect of this
phrase is almost subliminal, inducing a wave of exhaustion that
fits exactly the musical tone, a reminder that Zappa had studied
advertising psychology when working for the greetings-card firm
(a later song of his mentions Vance Packard, author of *The Hidden
Persuaders*, the celebrated 50s exposé of advertising methods[26]).

The great achievement of *Lumpy Gravy* is to place orchestral
effects – evocative cowboy-film romanticism, Varèse-type blocks-
of-sound avant-garde, experimental tape music (splices, *musique
concrète*, speed-ups) – in a new context, freeing them from the
pall of art music that reserves so much musical exploration for a

---

[26]'Packard Goose', *Joes's Garage Acts II and III*, 1979.

high-brow élite (even when the nearest comparisons would have to be Gyorgy Ligeti or music by the Association for the Advancement of Creative Musicians). After the long discussion of Motorhead's conflict with the bogeymen, they fall asleep: the plucked strings and irrationally scored percussion seem to depict their dreams. The score echoes their speech rhythms and in a way the music does indeed parallel dreamwork: the pursuit of thought without words. The discussion itself is full of punning deviations ('hard back', 'pick up sticks'). Although these can be dismissed as 'stoned' nonsense, extraneous meanings are being generated by attention to the sound material itself, a function of dreamthoughts as registered by both Freud and Joyce.

PIG: Babaabaaa.
M1: There it went again, a little pig with wings.
M2: I hear you've been having trouble with pigs and ponies.
FZ: What about us? Don't we get any?
M3: Just the opposite.
FI: We don't get any . . .
M4: That's very distraught, man.
FI: We don't get any because we're otherwise.
M1: Everything in the universe is made of one element, which is a note – a single note. Atoms are really vibrations, you know, which are extensions of THE BIG NOTE. Everything's one note, everything, even the ponies. The note however is the ultimate power, however the pigs don't know that, the ponies don't know that.
FI: You mean just we know that?
M1: Right.
  [Musique concrète *including Mothers plus guitar solo played on a transistor radio.*]
M2: 'Merry go round! Merry go round! dootdootdootdoot!' And they call that doing their thing.
M3: Oh yeah? *That's* what doing your thing is?
M1: The thing is to put a motor in yourself.
MOTORHEAD: Arf! Arf!! Teeth out there and I had to attack them. I had to fight back and like hit 'em and hit 'em and kick 'em and kick 'em.
M1: Did they get on top of you?
MOTORHEAD: No, I fought so back, so hard back.
M2: Hardback?
MOTORHEAD: White.
M1: White?
MOTORHEAD: Yeah, white ugliness.
M1: Did it have teeth?
MOTORHEAD: There was two bogeymen on the side of the block entrance, I had to kick, I had to fight, I had four or five bogeymen in front of me.

M1: Maybe he could turn it, Motorhead could maybe . . .

M2: Paah!

M1: I heard those ponies were really vicious.

MOTORHEAD: I know they're vicious, but . . .

M1: There's claws – they get on top of you and they just tear you apart.

MOTORHEAD: I know, scars over here, see, scars right here.

M1: Teeth to live. Was it white? You sure it wasn't black . . .

MOTORHEAD: I think they were white but I was too scared to n-n . . .

M1: Or gold or something?

MOTORHEAD: I was too scared to n-n-notice their physical appearance. They were attacking me!

M1: They were? What were they doing to you?

MOTORHEAD: They were surrounding me, there were yells, they were attacking me and I had to fight back, fight and fight back, and pick up sticks . . .

M1: Pick-up-sticks?

MOTORHEAD: Yes, pick up sticks.

M1: I used to play that game, pick-up-sticks.

MOTORHEAD: Me too, did you ever play that game?

M1: Yeah! That was funny!

[*Laughter*]

M1: Anyway, back to the horse – or the pony. Anyway . . .

MOTORHEAD: Pony . . .

M1: President . . .

MOTORHEAD: Pope or something – something out there's dangerous.

MOTORHEAD: Could be a cigar or something.

M1: A cigar?

M2: A cigar, man, you insane? C'mon!

MOTORHEAD: No, no. I remember when I was . . . no I don't remember . . .

M1: That was before the days of the horses.

MOTORHEAD: Before the days of the . . . ponies, bogeymen, what's out there?

M1: Then there was . . . what was it there?

MOTORHEAD: No pimples?

M1: No.

MOTORHEAD: Sure?

M1: Positively.

MOTORHEAD: You had to have them – you've got one right on your nose right now [*Laughter*] – scratching them.

M1: I'm getting tired, we should go to sleep. I just hope he comes back. I think I'll pray for him.

M2: I think I'll join you.

MOTORHEAD: You do yours and I'll do mine.

[*Laughter*]

MOTORHEAD: And we'll hope for the best.

M1: That's Motorhead!

M2: Now I lay me down to sleep – Amen.
MI: Amen.

The exchange 'white ugliness / did it have teeth?' is a fantastic moment of Lord Buckley-style surrealism – also touching on dental continuity, a structuring obsession throughout Zappa's project-object.

Lumpy Gravy's discussion about music sets off other themes that occur throughout Zappa's works, pursuing an interest in materialist physics – relativity, quantum theory – that generates greater poetic resonance than the mystical twaddle favoured by his hippie contemporaries. Whether Zappa puts his own words in the mouths of his speakers or extrapolates from random discussions, the dialogues are pregnant with his later preoccupations. A simultaneous ejaculation of the word 'kangaroos' points to some kind of scripting. In many ways, it is a false debate, similar to the fruitless attempts to separate the contributions of Duke Ellington – as a composer – from his collaborators. Lord Buckley, Captain Beefheart, even Kim Fowley extemporized magical moments into the air – the point was that Zappa acted on them.

> MI: I think I can explain about how the pigs' music works.
> F: Well this should be interesting.
> MI: Remember how they make music with a very dense light – and remember about the smoke standing still and how they really get uptight when you try to move the smoke?
> F: Right.
> M2: Yeah.
> MI: I think the music in that dense light is probably what makes the smoke stand still. Any sort of motion has this effect on the ponies' manes, you know, that thing on their neck. As soon as the pony's mane starts to get good in the back any sort of, like, motion – especially of smoke or gas – begins to make the ends split.
> M2: That's the basis of all their nationalism – like, if they can't salute[27] the smoke every morning when they get up . . .
> MI: Yes. It's a vicious circle – you got it.

The last remark, left hanging in the air by a return to the orchestra and the 'King Kong' theme, connects to the 'round things are boring' phrase: political reaction seen as the mute reflection of the repetitions of work.

Jimmy Carl Black, credited as part of the 'chorus' on the sleeve, says: 'Drums are too noisy when you've got no corners to hide in.'

---

[27] R. D. Cook hears this as 'salute', although I have always heard it as 'solute', meaning 'dissolve'.

This puts the drummer in the same relationship to the music he plays as alienated wage slaves to the products they produce.

After a beautifully placed evocation of the washing-machine/dark-light debate (the phrase 'envelops the bath-tub') there is an astonishing stretch of composition. A line played on a horn, followed by rattling strings and percussion: the drums pound in, introducing interplay with the winds and strings somewhere between Stravinsky's *A Soldier's Tale* and a Gunther Schuller/Eric Dolphy third-stream collaboration. The piece climaxes with dramatic solo violin playing a few restricted notes, against which winds and percussion abrupt. Then the voice says: ' 'Cause round things are ... are boring [*Silence ... exhalation*]', leading into the sublimely vacuous surf-rock arrangement of 'Take Your Clothes Off When You Dance' that ends the record.

When set down on paper, the sequence of *Lumpy Gravy*'s words, from existential quandary (the dark/light discussion) to examination of the cash nexus (sympathy from Kansas), wage labour (Motorhead's monologue) and social violence (perhaps racism – the colour of Motorhead's assailants is important), ending in theoretical clarity (the way the pig's music works) and a self-cancelling consciousness of the uselessness of art (round things are boring – equivalent to Zappa's 'throw the record away'[28]) suggests a programme, but this impression is a product of examining a written transcription. The experience of the record is of a revolving set of fragmentary moments. Jonathan Jones takes Zappa's description on the cover ('a curiously inconsistent piece which started out to be a ballet and probably didn't make it') as applicable to all Zappa's music.[29]. Despite the beautiful cluster of images around breath, round things, repetition, dark/light, finding these requires work on the part of the listener: a poetic coherence that can only be recollected in tranquillity. The record itself is a series of jarring shocks, fulfilling perfectly the idea rubbish-epic Jameson finds in Wyndham Lewis's prose and its 'revulsion for the standardized manipulations' of the culture industry.

Lumpy Gravy extruded the audio-concerns of the European avant-garde into an area of crossover the classical composers treated as taboo. When they peeked at vulgar existence from their ivory tower, they did so with the strawberry-tinted glasses of

---

[28]'Little Green Rosetta', *Joe's Garage Acts II and III*, 1979.
[29]Jonathan Jones, 'A World of Secret Hungers', *Eonta*, Vol. 2, No. 2, July/August 1993. *Eonta* is published from 27 Alexandra Road, Wimbledon, London SW19 7JZ, England.

Maoism[30] or other theoretical headsets that filtered out the working class or rock 'n' roll (usually both). *Lumpy Gravy*, Zappa's blueprint for a dialectic between rock 'n' roll's lived immediacy and classical music's outward-bound orchestration, went utterly unheeded in the state-funded corrals of classical value. No wonder that neo-minimalism, with its postmodernist rhetoric of 'facing rock and world music' (and its hidden agenda of making classical music a fully profitable – and privatized – concern), has outflanked the serialists of academia and become the order of the day.

Precisely because of its multivalency – cult-rock totem, pop-art happening, comedy record, avant-garde symphony, paranoid prophecy, fold-in masterpiece – *Lumpy Gravy* has long been relegated to the category of 'harmless indulgence'. Its manifold innovations and unparallelled scope speak otherwise. It reached 159 in the US album charts (for one week).

EUROPE

In mid-August 1967 Zappa visited London to raise some interest in the Mothers' forthcoming European tour. Despite his later contempt for England and its rock press, Zappa has always recognized London's key role in creating publicity for the European media. Zappa appeared on the cover of *Melody Maker* wearing a dress and a padded bra, his hair in bunches. Perpetuating the impression of anarchic disorganization hinted at by *Freak Out!*'s statement that Zappa's in-person performances with the Mothers were rare, Zappa announced: 'We'll come into London about a week before the concert to do some promotion and things. I may bring six, eight or fifteen Mothers with me – it just depends upon how many cats want to come to England.'[31]

His drag act provoked a useful quantity of indignant readers' letters in the 9 September issue. Zappa bought a bowler hat, had the Mothers filmed outside Buckingham Palace (a still showed up on the *Hot Rats* inside cover), went to the Marquee to see the Crazy World of Arthur Brown and met Pete Townshend of the Who. They continued on to the Speakeasy, where Zappa talked

---

[30]A reference to Cornelius Cardew and the decline of a promising avant-garde composer into patronizing tea-room music and political moralism.
[31]'Meet a Mother!', *Melody Maker*, 26 August 1967, p.1.

to Noel Redding, Jimi Hendrix and Jeff Beck. In his column in *International Times*,[32] John Peel, at that time playing tracks from *Absolutely Free* on his Radio London show, *The Perfumed Garden*, reported a Speakeasy showing of the Buckingham Palace footage (a location also used by the Sex Pistols when they signed to A&M). A rough mix of *We're Only in It for the Money* was used as the soundtrack.

Zappa's distance from the London counter-culture was illustrated by an incident at the Roundhouse related by Pamela Zarubica.

> On the way out some typical type came running up to Frank seemingly to shake his hand. Instead, he placed a small object in it which I immediately recognized to be hash. I should have grabbed it and marched out the door, but all these people were standing around waiting to see what Frank would do. He just looked down at the hash and said, 'What is it?' ... The numbers of freaks stood around in complete shock, trying to figure out how the freak of them all could not only not want the hash but not even know what it was.[33]

Zappa's ability to lord it in a drug culture he wanted no part of has always been one of the paradoxes of hippiedom. On 23 September the Mothers of Invention played at the Royal Albert Hall. The band consisted of Ray Collins (vocals), Bunk Gardner (sax), Don Preston (keyboards), Roy Estrada (bass), Jimmy Carl Black (drums), Billy Mundi (drums) and Ian Underwood (sax and keyboards), assisted by nine members of the London Philharmonic Orchestra. Don Preston played 'Louie Louie' on the 'mighty majestic Albert Hall pipe organ' (as described by Zappa on *Uncle Meat*), symbolizing everything Zappa wanted to say about traditional European values. The orchestral musicians played scores and blew raspberries on cue. The *Sunday Mirror* reported: 'It was probably the weirdest, hippiest, most psychedelic – frankly, way out – happening that London has endured since it started swinging.'[34]

Pamela Zarubica, flown in to play the part of Suzy Creamcheese, was pictured arm-in-arm with Zappa and two bunches of flowers. The tour continued on to Amsterdam and Copenhagen. Zappa and Tom Wilson flew to Italy to investigate the possibility of scoring Jane Fonda and Roger Vadim's *Barbarella*, but the

[32]John Peel, *International Times*, 31 August–13 September 1967.
[33]Pamela Zarubica, quoted in Michael Gray, *Mother! is the Story of Frank Zappa*, 1985, p. 83.
[34]Bernard McElwaine, 'Mothers Stun 'Em', *Sunday Mirror*, 24 September 1967.

collaboration came to nothing. On the way to Gothenburg Zappa fell ill with food poisoning, but managed to avoid cancelling any dates (he left the stage during the televised Stockholm concert). Back in Copenhagen they needed to borrow John Mayall's equipment to replace lost gear. On to Lund, then back to New York.

WE'RE ONLY IN IT FOR THE MONEY

As capitalism has developed, artists have become increasingly sensitive to the effects of economic exploitation on their art. Mass-production makes artworks consumable on a scale hitherto undreamt of, but at the cost of transforming the art into commodities whose circulation benefits the system – both financially (by generating profits) and ideologically (by creating the illusion that this is the only way things can be). All the significant art movements of the twentieth century have attempted to deal with this dilemma. *Freak Out!* used pop songs and advertising techniques to broadcast the message of freaking out, which meant to centre creativity in one's own activity.

> On a personal level, *Freaking Out* is a process whereby an individual casts off outmoded and restricting standards of thinking, dress and social etiquette in order to express CREATIVELY his relationship to the environment and the social structure as a whole. Less perceptive individuals have referred to us who have chosen this way of acting and FEELING as '*Freaks*', hence the term: *Freaking Out*. On a collective level, when any number of '*Freaks*' gather and express themselves creatively through music or dance, for example, it is generally referred to as a *FREAK OUT*. The participants, already emancipated from our national *social slavery*, dressed in their most inspired apparel, realize as a group whatever potential they possess for *free expression*. We would like to encourage everyone who HEARS this music to join us . . . become a member of *The United Mutations . . . FREAK OUT!*[35]

In some ways this merely uses sociological terms to restate the manner in which black music uses the recording industry to disseminate an involving culture, one that defies the alienation implicated in buying music impressed on pieces of plastic. Black music challenges the traditional antinomy of Western philosophy between the particular and the general, between physical participation and universal objectivity: hence its central significance in

---

[35]Frank Zappa, *Freak Out!*, 1966, sleevenote.

any understanding of what capitalism has done to culture. That post-war mass music can articulate the subject (something Adorno never dreamt) is intimately bound up with the emancipation of blacks in the United States, and saws at one of the central planks of capitalist ideology in that country: racism.

It is not only the strength of the blues form in co-ordinating individualized timbre and a common pattern which explains black pre-eminence as a basis for pop, but also its long history of using recording in a creative, dialectical way – a spur to spontaneity rather than its opposite. Freaks felt sufficiently alienated from American normality to believe that they need only behave in a new way and the old system would crumble. Like the rock 'n' roll of the mid-50s, the prospect of the mass of the population adopting a black cultural perspective terrified the authorities. Politically informed by the years of the civil rights movement and the protests against the Vietnam War, freakdom represented something still more subversive than rock 'n' roll. The measures taken against the movement – the police harassment, the notorious siege outside Pandora's Box – seemed only to confirm the political importance of what they were doing. The history of Zappa's output shows this utopian hope refracted through the exigencies of capitalist production. Forever chastised by the rock press for his 'cynical' outlook, it must be remembered what consumer culture falls short of in Zappa's view: total transformation.

Freak Out!, with its jangling pop songs and anti-high-school provocations, represents a cunning synthesis of commercial and subversive signals, but it did not have to compete with dilutions of the theme. The enemy was Madison Avenue, vacuous pop, bands who did not say 'fuck' on stage. *Absolutely Free* continued the same line of attack on all things plastic and conformist. But by *We're Only in It for the Money* Zappa had recognized the 'counter-culture' had itself become a commodity, a new conformism. The record played out his critique by counterposing freakdom to the hippies.

The distinction between surface and truth becomes peculiarly problematic in commercial culture. You can trace the origins of Philip K. Dick's problem with the reality of social life (which represents existence to him, which is why he is more politically interesting than the existentialists) to the duplicity of sales talk. In Anglophone culture, it was William Blake who first registered the way in which religion – now a host of free-floating, competitive ideologies rather than a unified social system – had become undermined by commodity exchange.

> Once meek, and in a perilous path,
> The just man kept his course along
> The vale of death . . .
> Till the villain left the paths of ease
> To walk in perilous paths, and drive
> The just man into barren climes.[36]

The cult of the gothic, which flaunts the trappings of 'evil' in a society in which false piety commits monstrosities, was another response to these developments, creating literary figures – Frankenstein, Dracula – which persist in the B-culture admired by Zappa and the Cramps. Zappa would return to these vital, populist forms at a later date: what concerned him in 1967 was the growth of flower power, which seemed to embody freak ideas and yet betrayed them.

Of course, to some he was just being a spoilsport.

> This was the greatest send up (or down) of pop music, of the audience, America and the group themselves I've ever witnessed. As musicians they were fantastically good and the act professionally presented. But frankly, what's the point? An entire concert of biting ridicule, both verbal and musical – however well done – is just a bore.[37]

The symbol of long hair was hopelessly vague. For example, the letters complaining about Zappa's drag cover photograph in *Melody Maker* all denounced – *flower power*!

> Frank Zappa must be joking! Lipstick and handbag were all that were missing, or do *MM* readers fancy him as he is? What a pathetic state the pop scene has got to when you have to look like him to sell records. Flower power is only another craze started up by the Yanks and as usual our gullible fans and groups have fallen for it. Thank God for Tom Jones.
>
> E. H. Tull, Abingdon, Berks[38]

Of course, flower power was itself a mixture of elements. While in New York Zappa had played a benefit with Allen Ginsberg, whose reliance on dubious Indian gurus, mantras and floral wreaths were meant to propagate rabid homosexual subversion,

---

[36]William Blake, *The Marriage of Heaven and Hell*, 1790, p. 2.
[37]Review of the Mothers at the Royal Albert Hall (23 September 1967), *New Musical Express*, 30 September 1967.
[38]*Melody Maker*, 9 September 1967, quoted by Michael Gray, *Mother! is the Story of Frank Zappa*, 1985, pp. 81–2.

revolution and free love. You can probably blame Ginsberg for a lot – the man whose great 'subversive' poem *Howl* begins with the sentimental élitism of the phrase 'the best minds of my generation' – but it needs to be remembered how selective the media are. Ginsberg's relentless celebration of the beauty of anal sex and revolution never seemed to crop up in definitions of flower power. Likewise, the achievements of Thelonious Monk and Charlie Parker are in no way invalidated by the bebop 'hep' fad of 1948.

However, there were failings at the heart of the hippie mentality that led to its easy co-option by the record industry. The hippies' accommodation to class society was expressed in their idealism, which recycled one of the basic tenets of middle-class ideology: the belief that true values are above commerce, above the here-and-now of material society. Unlike rock 'n' roll, this meant that its relation to a mass audience could only be hypocritical. It explains why hippie bands were invariably photographed in the countryside: the 'non-commercial' (as opposed to Zappa's anti-commercial) floats outside time in idealized nature. By contrast, *Absolutely Free* depicted a cartoon cityscape blocked with traffic.

Zappa has mentioned how disappointed he was with the music of the San Francisco scene, and it is easy to see why: its anthemic, folk-based meanderings had little relationship to either R&B or Edgard Varèse. Jefferson Airplane, the Grateful Dead, the Quicksilver Messenger Service provided a kind of pastel wallpaper to the hippie lifestyle. Even the ever generous Charlie Gillett mentions how such bands never 'fulfilled their promise'.[39] Compared to them, even the Doors sound shocking. Part of the hippie ethos was a hazy contempt for 'product': this entailed lifestyle soundtracks without great aesthetic ambitions. Everyone was only too happy to hear Jerry Garcia plunking away as they rolled their joints. These bands were explicitly pro-drugs, which directly contradicted what Zappa felt was a freak principle (though of course there *had* been plenty of drug-taking in LA). Most of all it was the philosophy that offended Zappa: in engaging with it he worked out a species of materialism, a defence of secular imagination and real-time capability that is truly inspiring (unless of course you are a hippie or an idealist, in which case he just bursts your

---

[39]Charlie Gillett, *The Sound of the City*, 1970, p. 357.

109

balloon). His assessment of the San Francisco bands jazz critic Ralph J. Gleason raved about was deadly and accurate:

> People think that San Francisco rock is supposed to be cosmic value and all that, but it is manufactured music and manufactured music is worthless ... I was expecting wonders and miracles and what I heard was a bunch of white blues bands that didn't sound as funky as my little band in high school.[40]

Zappa's materialist ear cuts through the incense-smog of ideology with the bruising logic of the blues. In pop journalism – which prides itself on revolving the imponderables of fashion – such an attitude was never going to be popular.

'Who Needs the Peace Corps?' numbers the accoutrements of the hippie lifestyle with withering accuracy:

> I will buy some beads and then perhaps a leather band to go around my head, some feathers and bells and a book of Indian lore. I will ask the Chamber of Commerce how to get to Haight Street and smoke an awful lot of dope. I will wander around barefoot. I will have a psychedelic gleam in my eye at all times. I will love everyone. I will love the police as they kick the shit out of me on the street.[41]

The last sentence was cut (among others) by MGM prior to release. The song segues into 'Concentration Moon', which is about the second World War internment camps rumour had it the government were readying to contain the hippie/anti-war movement. 'Mom and Dad' chillingly evokes the Kent State University killings a year *before* they happened. Although one can criticize Zappa's politics, he at least had an idea of the forces arranged against the protestors. The dopey music of San Francisco evades precisely this sense of *limits*, of conflict.

> I'm completely stoned
> I'm hippy & I'm trippy
> I'm a gypsy on my own[42]

This is a highly charged insult, criticizing the whole history of bourgeois bohemianism since the nineteenth century. Gypsy life only makes sense as the mode of existence of a nomadic *tribe*: a solitary 'gypsy' is meaningless.

The song 'Absolutely Free' attacks psychedelia for its idealist

---

[40]Quoted by Jerry Hopkins, 'Frank Zappa', *Rolling Stone*, 1968, reprinted in *Society Pages*. No. 42, October 1988, p. 16.
[41]Zappa's spoken conclusion to 'Who Needs the Peace Corps?', *We're Only in It for the Money*, 1967.
[42]'Who Needs the Peace Corps?', *We're Only in It for the Money*, 1967.

mystification. You hear Suzy Creamcheese (played by Pamela Zarubica) say, 'I won't do publicity balling for you anymore', and then Zappa explains the meaning of 'discorporate': 'The first word of this song is discorporate. It means – to leave your body.'

Deliberately meaningless psychedelic lyrics ('Cloudless / Starless') end up in a list of the names of the deer-team from 'Rudolf the Red-Nosed Reindeer'. Like hallucinogenic drugs that bring on cartoon images (as Captain Beefheart said about acid, 'I can paint better than that'), such 'freedom' is shown to be as limited and predictable as America's most hackneyed seasonal jingle. For good measure, the slogan 'flower power sucks' (again a victim to record company censorship) interrupts the song, as well as the absurdist word 'boin-n-n-n-n-g' (later developed as a figure for unfreedom in *Roxy & Elswhere* and *Zoot Allures*). The final couplet

> You'll be absolutely free
> Only if you want to be

implies that you will descend to this level of hippie inanity only if you wish to. The word 'want' reminds us that psychedelic imagery, in leaving the material body behind, also represses carnal desire. Zappa always finds in the body the imagery required for his songs, a practice that critics condemn as 'trivializing' and 'schoolboy', but has more to do with his polemic against idealism. Pamela Zarubica's comment about 'publicity balling' points out the physical – and sexual – reality behind the façade of 'discorporation'. According to Zarubica, Zappa engineered her seduction of Tom Wilson in order to facilitate the original MGM/Verve deal.[43]

The FBI's case against payola was used to bring down key figures in 50s rock 'n' roll, but as Fredric Dannen has shown, the flower-power boom simply allowed the gangsters who control US radio play to regroup.[44] Hippie other-worldliness was a perfect front, the usual middle-class cultural hypocrisy applied to a movement that promised the opposite: the entry of R&B materialism on to the stage of mainstream American life.

More than any other of Zappa's albums, *Money* is about the physical nature of a vinyl record, and therefore its effectiveness is

---

[43] Michael Gray, *Mother! is the Story of Frank Zappa*, 1985, p. 53. According to Zappa (interview with the author, 25 October 1993), this is Zarubica's fantasy: Tom Wilson was so popular with groupies that he was not susceptible to this species of influence.
[44] Fredric Dannen, *Hit Men*, 1990.

diminished in the CD (quite apart from the re-recording of bass and drum parts, replacing the original brittleness with post-digital luxury, a 'creative' decision by Zappa resulting from the physical deterioration of the two-track master: rather than remix from the eight-track he decided to re-record – in response to a barrage of complaints, though, he plans a remix for purists[45]). Twice there is a violent gouging sound as the needle seems to run off the grooves. In 'Mother People' it ends up playing some gentle music from *Lumpy Gravy*. At the conclusion of 'Nasal Retentive Calliope Music' the listener is promised some pounding surf rock, which is actually the introduction to 'Heavies', recorded at Studio Z and released on Original Sound as a single by the Rotations in 1964.[46] The way Zappa's 1967 *musique concrète* integrates with the novelty 'surf' effect is seamless (one more example of the way in which Zappa degrades the art status of various sounds). However, just as the beat gets going, the needle is shoved across the grooves to 'Let's Make the Water Turn Black', another song in the mockingly 'light' style that characterizes *Money*'s songs – Byrds-type strummed guitars and idiot falsettos. The same thing happens to the psychedelic heaven promised by the electric guitar that concludes 'Are You Hung Up?' – the listener is plunged without warning into one of the Mothers' teasing ditties. This need to play with the listener's craving for excitement is Zappa's forte: it is why many people hate his music, but for those who are interested in becoming conscious of their own impulses, it is invaluable.

In a section of the sleeve-notes headed 'instructions for the use of this material' Zappa tells listeners to read Franz Kafka's short story 'In the Penal Colony' before listening to the album. Viewed in the light of Kafka's story, *Money* becomes even more unsettling. Writing in 1919, Kafka tells the tale of the 'explorer' who visits an unspecified penal colony maintained in the Tropics by the French. He is shown a punishment device that, using

---

[45]See William Ruhlman, 'Frank Zappa: Moving on to Phase Three', *Goldmine*, 27 January 1989, reprinted in *Society Pages*, No. 44, March 1989, p. 12. 'The original two-track mix was virtually unplayable. Let's define tracks – the master tracks were eight-track originally, in some instances twelve-track. They could've been remixed from scratch with the addition of nothing else, but the original two-track masters had deteriorated: you could see through the tape. So if you're going to go to the extreme of remixing it, why not stick another set of bass and drums on it? But I have since that time purchased a piece of digital equipment [Sonic Solutions] which may make it possible – if I've ever got enough strength to do it – to reconstitute the albums from safeties and other bits and pieces, like leftover mixes from that period, that would contain no overdubs. So it's possible they could be reconstructed' Frank Zappa to the author, 26 October 1993 (see 'Tuesday', Epilogue: Going to Meet the Man).
[46]Frank Zappa, *Cucamonga Years – The Early Works of Frank Zappa (1962–1964)*.

complex steam-age machinery, carves an appropriate message in the body of the culprit before dumping his corpse into a grave that has been dug at the side. The details are peculiarly disgusting – the victim's clothes are thrown into the grave before him and

> the short needle sprays a jet of water to wash away the blood and keep the inscription clear. Blood and water together are then conducted here through small runnels into the main runnel and down a waste-pipe into the grave.[47]

The prisoner is going to have the words 'HONOUR THY SUPERIORS' gouged into him as punishment for having threatened a commanding officer. He neither understands French, nor the nature of his crime. According to the officer, who is obsessed with the aesthetic logic of the machine, prisoners develop a beatific expression of comprehension after six hours, as their bodies recognize the inscription. The officer shows the original designs to the explorer, but he cannot read them.

> 'Yes,' said the officer with a laugh, putting the paper away again, 'it's no calligraphy for school children. It needs to be studied closely. I'm quite sure that in the end you would understand it too. Of course, the script can't be a simple one; it's not supposed to kill a man straight off, but only after an interval of, on an average, twelve hours; the turning-point is reckoned to come at the sixth hour. So there have to be lots and lots of flourishes around the actual script; the script itself runs round the body only in a narrow girdle; the rest of the body is reserved for the embellishments.'[48]

It is as if the machine is printing a banknote, or some kind of certificate, signalling Kafka's horror of the archaic, bureaucratic trappings of administered society. The machine is also an allegory of art – especially Kafka's art, with its continual deviations and 'embellishments'.

A new regime at the penal colony is, however, unsympathetic to this mode of execution, and, failing to convince the explorer of its necessity, the officer becomes convinced that its use will be discontinued. He climbs in it himself, programming it to cut 'BE JUST' into him. The machine breaks up as it stabs him to death, sending cog wheels rolling out across the sunbaked sand. It's an extraordinary and powerful text, with a strong current of anxiety about homosexual penetration (the prisoner must strip before

---

[47]Franz Kafka, 'In the Penal Settlement', 1919, *Metamorphosis and Other Stories*, trs. Willa and Edwin Muir, 1961, p. 177.
[48]Ibid., p. 178.

stepping into the machine). In predicting the horrors of Ausch-witz, it confirms the characterization of fascism as the visitation of the methods of imperialism on the indigenous working class. Its images of ritualized punishment have the sour, haunting quality that characterizes memory of bad dreams.

Money was the first record to feature the Bizarre logo (which in 1969, with the move from Verve to Reprise, became the name of a fully fledged label, releasing Mothers of Invention records alongside its sister company, Straight). Dust-covers from that period showed Zappa and Cohen in a studio with a quote from the American constitution concerning freedom of speech: 'We make records that are a little different. We present musical and sociological material which the important record companies would probably not allow you to hear. Just what the world needs... another record company.' The logo used a nineteenth-century engraving of a bizarre-looking vacuum pump, part of Schenkel's library of dated commercial imagery. It seems likely that it repre-sents Kafka's machine: Zappa's art is also meant to work like that. Zappa concludes his instructions for listening with: '6. At the end of the piece, the name of YOUR CRIME will be carved on your back.'

The officer's description of the machine is reminiscent of the processes involved in cutting a record.

> It consists, as you see, of three parts. In the course of time each of these parts has acquired a kind of popular nickname. The lower one is called the 'Bed', the upper one the 'Designer', and this one here in the middle that moves up and down is called the 'Harrow'.[49]

Zappologist Jonathan Jones makes an apt comparison of Kafka's machine to the mechanics of recording itself.

> What is this apparatus but a vast recording device? Kafka's phrase 'the performance' increases the power of the apparatus, as it simultaneously inscribes and reproduces, punishment and entertainment produced of the same needling movement. 'The Megaphone of Destiny' is not pro-gramme music in the tradition of the *Pastoral Symphony*. It should be heard in the context of the rest of the album, prepared for by the cuts and lacerations that constitute the songs themselves – the speeded-up fragments, gibbers, manic laughs and screams. This is where the force of Kafka's story is to be located, and the ripping sound of the stylus as it is yanked across the grooves enacts a physical and psychical damage. The turntable is metamorphosed into a stage, a theatre of cruelty, for the measured violence implicit in recording.[50]

[49]Ibid., p. 171.
[50]Jonathan Jones, 'A World of Secret Hungers', *Eonta*, Vol. 2, No. 2, July/August 1993.

Money begins with a series of vocal 'er' sounds, underscored by a tape-looped, grating bass. It is as if someone cannot decide what to say. *Finnegans Wake* and psychoanalysis both associate stuttering with guilt, the punishment inflicted by social and moral codes for private thoughts. Like William Burroughs, Zappa is fascinated by the institutions that use the split between public and private domains in order to exert power: the Church, the judiciary and censorship lobbies. Technological innovations like photography, sound-recording and video have made it possible to cross the boundary between private and public in a way that begs all sorts of questions about social control. Zappa's experience in Cucamonga with the sex tape, and his awareness of police surveillance, add to the aura of danger surrounding taped sound. The original Mothers had a song about police spies.

> The kids are freaking out
> Everybody's going nuts
> The heat's out every night
> To call them names and kick their butts
>
> Well, every time you turn around
> You'll see some joker staring back
> He's got a secret tape recorder
> And a camera in a sack
>
> Pretending that he's just another
> Of the kiddies freaking out
> But they pay him off in acid
> 'Cos he's a downtown talent scout
>
> He's got your name, he's got your face
> He's got your ex-old lady's place
> He's here to see what's going down
> And he don't believe the things he's found[51]

The importance of taped conversations went public with Watergate, but in 1967 *Money* was already riddled with such technoparanoia. A male voice asks, 'Are you hung up?' over and over again of a nonplussed female, who giggles and says she can't understand. In 60s-speak to be hung up was to be anxious about sex and the body: the record itself has the pent-up aggression of the sexually predatory male. The voice of engineer Gary Kellgren, swirling with multiple echo, threatens to make the tapes 'blank – empty – space . . . I know he's sitting in there in the control room

---

[51]'The Downtown Talent Scout', 1965, *You Can't Do That on Stage Anymore Vol. 5*, 1992.

now, listening to everything I say. But I really don't care. Hello, Frank Zappa...'

Pamela Zarubica is taped talking to her sister Vicki about their father sending the FBI to look for her. Jones quite rightly points out how, by making himself the organizing intelligence, Zappa creates a 'travesty of power'. This is a theme that was developed in the film *200 Motels* ('we've got to do it before Zappa finds out and steals it and makes us do it in the movie') and in *Joe's Garage* (where Zappa is 'The Central Scrutinizer', enforcing 'all the laws that haven't been passed yet'). Power over representation is power over people; the limits drawn by the censors actually shape our ideas of what is possible, what is pleasure, of what is illicit. Zappa's sudden shifts of register between private and public are designed to make us question the iron rules of decorum that organize our world for us, to dramatize the artificial nature of morality.

In developing this critique he encountered the constraints of censorship himself. 'Harry You're a Beast' had a chorus of 'Don't come in me, in me', which had to be censored by playing it backwards. 'Shut your fucking mouth about the length of my hair' was cut out and appended backwards at the end of side one (this was pointed out in the lyric sheet). This imitated the fun and games of the 'backwards' message at the end of 'Day in the Life''s final chord on *Sgt. Pepper*, but the issues were more controversial. MGM got so paranoid that the innocent lines

> And I still remember Mama with her apron & her pad
> Feeding all the boys at Ed's Cafe

were also cut. Zappa's first inkling of this was when the record was played during the presentation of an award in Holland – he promptly gave the award away to a music paper in protest. Apparently they thought mama's 'pad' was a sanitary towel: Zappa is always caustic about their 'sick' minds, but the misunderstanding is a tribute to the power of *Money* to suggest the unthinkable, to act as a confessional for associations: their crime was indeed carved on their backs.

'What's the Ugliest Part of Your Body' has been cited as the first sign of Zappa's male chauvinism.

> I'm gonna tell you the way it is
> And I'm not gonna be kind or easy
> Your whole attitude stinks, I say
> And the life you lead is completely empty

You paint your head
Your mind is dead
You don't even know what I just said
THAT'S YOU: AMERICAN WOMANHOOD![52]

The aggression that runs right through Zappa's lyrics manifests itself frequently in his coverage of sexual matters in a particularly repellent kind of male chauvinism. In his earlier lyrics this could be masked as political comment, but later, as his focus shifts from American womanhood to the groupies hanging round Laurel Canyon, it becomes obvious that while the men, even the straight men, are people with a potential for redemption, women are objects, the ugliest part of whose bodies are their minds.[53]

Karl Dallas would be correct if Zappa was a singer-songwriter whose lyrics are presented as self-expression. Precisely because he presents us with a 'travesty of power', the real issue is the exposure of band-members' private lives on stage, a corollary to their exposure as musicians, shifting the acceptable boundaries of (public) musical technique and (private) personal behaviour in order to reveal these distinctions as arbitrary. If the lifestyle of rock stars is not conducive to respect for women, Zappa is not going to present us with something cleaned up and ideal. In *Money* the political statements – the denunciations of 'American Womanhood' and the older generation in general – storm out of the paranoid texture like desperate pleas. These were the most directly political statements Zappa made until *Broadway the Hard Way* twenty years later. Audience reactions; his characterization as a hippie and drug-user by the music press; his experiences with student revolutionaries (who thought his politics was like theirs): all led him to downplay explicit political statements. His later stance as rock's blue comedian, however, concealed an art that was just as attentive to social issues: you just had to work it out for yourself.

What's the ugliest
Part of your body?
What's the ugliest
Part of your body?
Some say your nose
Some say your toes
But I think it's
YOUR MIND[54]

[52]Frank Zappa, 'Harry You're a Beast', *We're Only in It for the Money*, 1967.
[53]Karl Dallas, 'What Did You Do in the Revolution, Dada?', *Let It Rock*, June 1975, pp. 34–6.
[54]'What's the Ugliest Part of Your Body?', *We're Only in It for the Money*, 1967.

This is not just addressed to women. It is an assault on the whole philosophical and religious history of the West that has condemned the body and the appetites and *women* to a lower sphere, the Platonic and Christian emphasis on the ideal that was Adorno's target in *The Dialectic of Enlightenment*.

> In man's denigration of his own body, nature takes revenge for the fact that man has reduced nature to an object for domination, raw material. The compulsive urge to cruelty and destruction springs from the organic displacement of the relationship between the mind and the body.[55]

The concluding instrumental on *Money*, 'The Chrome Plated Megaphone of Destiny', is an astonishing piece of *musique concrète*. Zappa's atonal score concentrates on the reverberant *sound* of the piano in a manner unsurpassed until Tristan Murail's *Territoires de l'oubli* in 1977.[56] It used Ian Underwood's classical keyboard skills to great effect. The integration of acoustic and electronic elements is seamless: the sounds produced by Underwood are treated with the same attention to timbre as all the rest of the music on *Money*. Just because Zappa is writing a score does not mean he abandons his sensitivity to the specific gravity of recorded sound. Speeded-up laughter and notes struck from inside the piano all pursue each other with a unique energy. Compared to this, the celebrated final chord of 'Day In The Life' on *Sgt. Pepper* was naïve and showy: mere beginners' stuff.

It was also advanced technically at a time when audio equipment was going through a period of rapid development.

> The percussive-type noises, the thing that sounds like little squirts and explosions, was done by using a box that we built called the Apostolic Vlorch Injector. It was a litle box this big with three buttons on it. The console at the studio where we used to work, Apostolic, was unique. In the 60s the audio science was growing, and people were trying all kinds of different things, and there was a lot of non-standard equipment around. This particular console didn't have a stereo fader; it had three master faders – a separate fader for the left, the centre and the right, so you could fade out the centre and leave the left and right, or whatever. So these three buttons on the box corresponded to the three master faders, and you could play it rhythmically.
>
> The input to the box would be any sound source cranked up to the level of gross square-wave distortion. Any noise. You'd crank it up só that if it was printed on a piece of tape, you couldn't stand to listen to it. It would be trashed to distortion. But as short little bits you'd get

[55]Theodor Adorno and Max Horkheimer, *Dialectic of Enlightenment*, 1961, pp. 9–10.
[56]Tristan Murail, *Allégories/Vues aériennes/Territoires de l'oubli*, 1990, Accord 200842.

very complex, technicolor noise. When you hit the button and open up a little window of time, the structure of the distortion was a complex waveform, and that's where the bumpy, crunchy stuff comes from.

Then we had some backwards tape and tape slowed down and speeded up with the VSO (variable speed oscillator), and were using parts of recordings of ethnic instruments. There's a tamboura in there, a koto in there someplace. Some filtered tapes of industrial noises, horses, all collaged together. I started doing that in 1962, before I had a record contract. I just experimented in this little studio they had, so I was well into *musique concrète* techniques before I made a record.[57]

'The Chrome Plated Megaphone of Destiny' was named after the voicebox that makes dolls squeak when squeezed, frequently placed between the legs. When the young child is given a doll, this is the first place that is examined – to give much needed information about where human beings came from and where they are going. Meeting a chrome-plated megaphone suggests a weird destiny that only Zappa's music could be equal to. The title is an example of sexual materialism providing more genuine poetry than any amount of drug-tinged mysticism: an important point in 1967.

The cover of *Money* became Cal Schenkel's most celebrated piece of work: a parody of *Sgt. Pepper*. Peter Blake's collage of pop personalities is replaced by a strange and disturbing pantheon with cancelled eyes: Lyndon B. Johnson, viewed as a war criminal by the anti-war movement, appears twice; Elvis is holding snakes, one of the accessories of Southern religious mania; the girl from the *International Times* logo watches a mechanical man drink a glass of water. The Beatles were attending a burial of their old image: compared to the Mothers' jumble-sale dresses their Carnaby Street military chic looks hopelessly twee. Where the Beatles spelt their name in neat rows of tulips, 'Mothers' is written in carrots, tomatoes and ruptured water melons. Schenkel himself crouches next to a TV aerial and a six-pack of beer – symbols of middle-aged inertia. Zappa stands over a cancelled bust of Beethoven, his right foot seemingly extended in a ludicrous boot.[58] Instead of Madame Tussaud's careful waxworks Schenkel has fashioned grotesque dummies of Zappa, Black, Mundi, Preston and Underwood. A plastic doll in the dummy's lap and a toy robot at its feet repeat the theme of mechanical humanity. Near one of Titian's Popes a Christmas tree sprouts up, symbol of

[57]Quoted by Rick Davies, 'Father of Invention', *Music Technology*, February 1987, pp. 48–9.
[58]See 'Zomby Woof', *Overnite Sensation*, 1973.

everything false and conformist in American family life. Producer Tom Wilson is wearing nothing underneath his high-school sweater and is holding his left nipple. Behind Zappa a pregnant Gail poses in an uncharacteristically dowdy dress and Jimi Hendrix holds a cut-out of a small girl (Herbie Cohen's daughter Lisa), satirizing racist paranoia about black sexuality threatening family values. *Money* reached number 32 in the UK pop chart during the summer of 1968.

BACK TO LA

Although *Money* was finished in October, release was delayed until January 1968 while EMI prevaricated about *Money*'s cover (solved by issuing the gatefold in reverse). In November 1967 Zappa appeared in both the Monkees' TV series and *Head*, their feature film directed by Bob Rafaelson. *Head* also had its problems with the entertainment status quo, with release being delayed two years. Its treatment of the Monkees as a pop product was provocatively cynical ('The money's in, we're made of tin, we're here to give you more!'[59] the band recite at the start) and the soundtrack album, beginning with its doped-out voices reciting the word 'head' repeatedly over a collage of media inanity, and its habit of intercutting songs with snatches of dialogue, bears more than a passing resemblance to *Money*. The film has Zappa in the role of critic, leading a cow – the Monkees owe it to the youth of America to practise their instruments more, he explains. He was there to add to the intellectual weight of the film: 'They're trying to make a heavy of me,' he complained.[60] Zappa himself had cultivated a high-powered mystique, but as soon as he felt constrained by it – and the ideas of cosmic seriousness brought about by the marketing of 'progressive rock' – he would gleefully emphasize his taste for provocative vulgarity.

In December 1967 Arthur Tripp, who had spent two years as percussionist with the Cincinnati Orchestra, was inducted into the Mothers, an invaluable aid in realizing the increasingly tricky metrics of Zappa's scores. Tripp had read an article on Zappa that mentioned his interest in Stravinsky and Varèse and heard from engineer Richard Kunc that the Mothers were looking for a drum-

[59]The Monkees, 'Ditty Diego', *Head*, 1969.
[60]Michael Gray, *Mother! is the Story of Frank Zappa*, 1985, p. 87.

mer to replace Billy Mundi (Mundi had left to play drums in the Elektra label's house band, which issued records under the name Rhinoceros; he later played on Bob Dylan's album *New Morning*). Art Tripp said: 'For years Frank had had lots of percussion ideas that no one could play, and obviously from my background it was comparatively simple, I'd just make up a chart, or Frank would, and I'd learn it by heart.'[61]

The Mothers played weekend concerts at the New York Town Hall during December 1967 and continued working at Apostolic until February 1968 on tracks that would become *Uncle Meat* and *Cruising with Ruben & the Jets*. In February the Mothers played at the National Academy of Recording Arts and Sciences in New York. Zappa expressed a disgust with the industry that has not mellowed over the years.

> All year long you people manufacture this crap, and one night of the year you're going to listen to it! . . . Your whole affair is nothing more than a lot of pompous hokum, and we're going to approach you on your own level.[62]

In June 1968 the Zappas returned to California, moving into the spacious log cabin whose bowling alley Carl Franzoni had been living in. Cal Schenkel set up an art department in one wing. Other new residents included Zappa's secretary, Pauline Butcher, road manager (and sometime industrial vacuum cleaner) Dick Barber and Motorhead Sherwood. Christine Frka, the costumier who founded the GTO's and appeared on the cover of *Hot Rats*, had been living in a closet in the basement: she endeared herself by doing housework and taking care of the eight-month-old Moon and was employed as her 'governess'. Pamela Miller (later a GTO) commented, 'This was a very enviable job for an eighteen-year-old wack-job from San Pedro in 1968',[63] and Miller herself used the contact in order to make visits. In the same month the Mothers played a return concert at the Shrine Auditorium: absence and record releases had built up their following and they played to an audience of 7,000. The trip East had established the Mothers as a leading voice in the counter-culture. Perverse as ever, Zappa's next release was a tribute to the 50s.

[61]Julian Colbeck, *Zappa: A Biography*, 1987, p. 82.
[62]Quoted by Sue C. Clark, 'Mothers' Lament', *Rolling Stone*, 27 April 1968.
[63]Pamela Des Barres, *I'm with the Band – Confessions of a Groupie*, 1987, p. 91.

By the end of the 60s the Mothers were playing to a new audience of teens to whom the music of the 50s meant very little. As the promise of 60s counter-culture receded in the ensuing decade, rock reverted to the temporary teen experience it had been before, something fans leave behind as they grow older (or ossify as nostalgia). *Ruben & the Jets* was both a reminder of pre-60s limitations and a warning of things to come.

It pulled into focus a whole area of soft rock 'n' roll, or doowop, unknown in England (where rock musicians like Cliff Richard and Tommy Steele sweetened rock 'n' roll by reverting to music hall or Tin Pan Alley). Interviews with Zappa had him praising bands and songs the English music press had never heard of. The blues boom had ensured that everyone knew the Chicago blues of Howlin' Wolf and Muddy Waters; people were less informed about West Coast R&B; doowop was a closed book. Doowop was street corner music, a secular version of the black gospel quartets that produced such devastatingly emotional vocal music in the 30s and 40s. However, doowop's popularity reflected the enhanced economic status of 50s teenagers and spoke for a generation, crossing race lines: Italian, Puerto Rican, Jewish and downtrodden white youth were involved too. As a group music it shrugged off the hard-bitten individualism of the blues, ravishing the ear with skyward harmonies that spoke directly to adolescent desire and aspiration.

The Mothers' attitude towards doowop was complex, and *Ruben & the Jets* registered every ambivalence. On the back of the album, in a gold frame on a pink background, Zappa is shown as a short-haired teenager (though Schenkel has pencilled in a proto-Zappa moustache), a 'Grade-A-High-School-Prom-Heart-Throb' as the celebrated groupie Dr G put it to Germaine Greer.[64] There is a spoof biography that runs through 50s obsessions – cars, girls, Richie Valens records – and reports that Ruben has left the band because he needed time to fix the car so he could take his girl to a drive-in. A sleeve note inside says the album contains 'greasy love songs & cretin simplicity', but 'we really like this music': a paradox surprisingly few commentators have been able to accept. Further confusion is provided because songs from *Freak*

---

[64] *Oz*, No. 19, March 1969, p. 47.

Out! – 'You Didn't Try to Call Me', 'How Could I Be Such a Fool', 'Anyway the Wind Blows' and, most disturbingly, the existential angst of 'I'm Not Satisfied' – are all reworked as drooling 50s numbers.

Zappa had space to extend his harmonic and metrical fantasies elsewhere (in *Uncle Meat*), so the record concentrates on the limitations of the song format – simple chords, rhythmic repetition, banal words – rather than trying for the virtuosities that characterize some doowop records. As with punk in the 70s, the early 50s fashion for doowop had seen thousands of bands forming, and frequently a one-off record deal could reveal astonishing street-honed ingenuity. Talking in 1975, Zappa mentioned two songs he liked.

> 'Can I Come Over Tonight' – the Velours. Any musicologist that can find that record and listen to the bass singer ... he's singing quintuplets and septuplets ... 'Let's Start All Over Again' – the Paragons. Also prototypical and it has the unmitigated audacity to have the most moronic piano section I ever heard on any record – and it repeats it often enough to convince me that it's deliberate.[65]

Ruben develops 'deliberate dumbness' on an epic scale. The effect is the kind of suspension of meaning that minimalism is meant to achieve. Because there is no overt musical development to follow, the attention drifts between the (finely separated) levels of the mix with some of the grateful disorientation of listening to dub or house. It predicted the way in which Kraftwerk and Devo would use machine-like regularity to make pop strange and alien. The polished musical surface and pleading voices set up a brittle surface, tense with repression.

Claustrophobia and the inability to breathe – recurrent symbols of repression in Zappa – crop up twice. The singer complains that his girlfriend has thrown his clothes out on the street

> right on top of some dog waste ... and my best white shirts with the Mr B. collar laying all over the front lawn. Where's my cuff links? Lemme back in dere. *Dere?*
> Huffa puffa. Huffa puffa.
> There's no room to breathe in here.
> That's alright honey. You can come out the closet now.[66]

The 'Mr B. collar' refers to shirts patented by Billy Eckstine,

---

[65]Quoted by Giovanni Dadomo, 'Frank Zappa Talks of Faves, Raves and Composers in Their Graves', *Let It Rock*, June 1975, p. 38.
[66]'Later That Night', *Cruising with Ruben & the Jets*, 1968.

bandleader, balladeer and trumpeter, who devised a method of buttoning that would give his neck room to swell (a necessity for trumpet-players) without popping the top button. A neat symbol: the restrictions of decorum encountering the swelling of flesh. The proximity of 'dog waste' and 'huffa puffa' points to 'Dog Breath' on *Uncle Meat*. Although supposedly exchanges in some romantic quarrel, Zappa's 'there's no room to breathe in here' resonates as a direct comment on the restrictions of the music.

The final song has the singer committing suicide.

> If you decide to leave me, it's all over
> I tried to make you happy
> I gave you all my love
> There's nothing left for me to do but cry
> Ooo, oo-ooo, ooo, oo-ooo, ooo, oo-ooo
> Stuff up the cracks, turn on the gas
> I'm gonna take my life. (Stuff 'em up)[67]

After these words you can hear the hissing of the gas. The connection between repression and gas was later used in 'San Ber'dino' and 'Wind up Workin' in a Gas Station', extending its scope to judicial incarceration and genocide.

Zappa called *Ruben* his 'neo-classical' album, referring to Stravinsky's return to older forms after the fireworks of *The Rite of Spring* (a retreat denounced by Theodor Adorno). Zappa's neo-classicism is not, though, being proposed as the next step, the only road: it is a diversion. This is evident in the two guitar features. 'You Didn't Try to Call Me' has a stinging guitar solo, which starts to rock the relentless piano triplets. The final 'Stuff up the Cracks' works towards an electric blow-out, all distortion and wah-wah: the harpsichords and one-chord drone suddenly sound incongruously like the Mothers at full tilt. The guitar playing pushes the music out of its circular triteness, a flash of linear development, history, freedom: all the more poignant after the rest of the record's suffocating limitations.

Cal Schenkel's artwork expertly expressed the contradictions between the Mothers' freak sophistication and their continuing affection for the rock 'n' roll of their youth. In *Time out of Joint* Philip K. Dick depicted a cheery idyll of post-war Americana, only to have it split at the seams to reveal a stage set designed to humour an intuitive genius (his well-being is necessary for the

---

[67]'Stuff up the Cracks', *Cruising with Ruben & the Jets*, 1968.

inter-planetary war effort). Schenkel reproduces a similar anxiety in his gatefold sleeve. A photograph of the Mothers breaks jaggedly to reveal constellations of machinery, printed circuits, industrial plumbing. Any 'humanity' this mass-produced artwork communicates is *constructed*: the flesh that clothes these bones is an illusion. Although the singing is far too authentic to count as 'parody' – Ray Collins is a consummate lead and Roy Estrada's falsetto amazingly accomplished – there is nevertheless a sense of unreality that is genuinely distressing.

The chilling mindlessness at the bottom of *Ruben*'s music is a death-rattle, the hollow clatter of skeletons clacking in the wind. Common not just to *Ruben* but to *Uncle Meat* and other music Zappa produced in 1969, these sounds may be heard by rattling the handle of a toothbrush against the teeth (this almost exactly reproduces the sound of Art Tripp's percussion). You are hearing a sound which could be made with the same materials long after your death: throats that sing, tongues that talk, palms that clap all pass away – teeth remain. Recorded using the same multi-track capability as *Uncle Meat* (the Mothers discussed recording the songs in mono with fake 45rpm crackle, but decided against the idea), the same rattling percussion underlies *Ruben*, a sinister reminder of the mechanics of representation – to which Schenkel's artwork is the perfect analogue.

This alienating effect is lessened in the CD issue due to re-recording of bass and drum tracks. Roy Estrada's broad, solid, 'dumb' electric bass, without what Zappa called '1980s transience and top end',[68] was replaced by Arthur Barrow's expressive upright. 'Real' drums have replaced the echoing 'snats' of the original multi-tracks: artificial drums gave the music a tinny, inhuman feel and tied it back to *Uncle Meat*. This is probably the CD re-release most regretted by fans, but Zappa had no hesitation in 'improving' the sound. As his own concept of 'trapped air' recognizes, recording preserves more aspects than imitations – however 'authentic' in intention – can replicate. Maybe it's better just to enjoy Art Barrow's undeniably beautiful playing. The exponential increase in playing ability – younger players seem to hear extra possibilities in the finest interstices of the older generation's beat – means that retro is actually impossible (take jazz, for example: none of the 'neo-classical' bassists, however skilled,

---

[68]Quoted by William Ruhlman, 'Frank Zappa: Moving on to Phase Three', *Goldmine*, 27 January 1989.

has managed to reproduce the majesty that was Paul Chambers, the new players are working in an era whose time-sense is too fast to play that simply with equal conviction). Zappa accused those who regretted the change of fetishism.

> Bass and drums added was not a solution to the tape problem. The tape problem had to be dealt with with a remix, no matter what. The idea of putting digitally recorded bass and drums on to those tracks was a creative decision that I made because I've always thought that... we were just trapped into that level of technical quality because that's the way the world was then ... The problem with people who are collectors and purists and stuff like that is, their regard is not for the music, it is for some imaginary intrinsic value of vinyl and cardboard. People who demand to have the original release of this, that and the other thing in the original wrapper and all that stuff, that's fetishism. And I think that's fine, if you want to be a fetishist and have that kind of a hobby. But it is a type of attitude that I don't share when it comes to re-releasing the material. I think that the material should have a chance to sound as good as you can make it sound, given the technical tools that are at your disposal.[69]

Still involved in the production of music, Zappa obviously resents those who 'freeze' his back catalogue to its original technical limitations. However, when those limitations have a poetic aroma one regrets seeing them abolished – and, as with *Money*, he has talked of releasing an 'original' mix to please the grumblers.

In the light of the musical liberties of *Uncle Meat*, the repetitions of *Ruben*, instead of signifying groovy rock 'n' roll, become threatening and mechanical. This deathly quality is more a comment on nostalgia than on the musical forms themselves (doowop continued to be an inspiration for Zappa). In later songs – 'Dinah-Moe Humm', 'Teen-age Wind' – repetition is used as a contradictory symbol: libidinal energy revolved into stasis. Long before 1973, when the film *American Graffiti* gave 50s rock 'n' roll a new vogue, *Ruben* delineated the pleasures and perils of nostalgia.

The cover has a Schenkel cartoon of the band wearing 50s clothes, snatting their fingers and sporting dog-like snouts. A science fiction story in the booklet that accompanied *Uncle Meat* explained that the snouts were designed to accommodate the extra brain cells required for Uncle Meat's 'vocal drone mechanism'. They are under his control, part of his plan for world domination.

---

[69]Ibid.

126

Swaying titanically, snatting immense white-gloved fingers & lip-syncing their latest hit, Ruben & the Jets prepare to destroy everything that contemporary civilization stands for.
The crowd is hypnotized. They begin to writhe & quiver & huddle closer together. The moon & the stars come out. Brightly colored crepe paper streamers descend from the buildings all around. Men & women hug each other close & begin to dance in the street (super teenage 1950 style). Zoom in on a couple as they kiss & dance . . . dissolve through distortion glass to a dream-sequence of 1950s drive-ins, make-out parties, high schools, the Korean War & 'I Like Ike', intercut with the titanic Ruben & the Jets: brain-snouts flopping in slow motion.

It reads like William Burroughs, and for a reason: Zappa is also playing with the way in which life and memory (and hence subjectivity) are mediated by the culture industry. On *Roxy & Elsewhere* Zappa joked about Richard Nixon attempting to turn back the clock to a previous decade.[70] *Ruben* provokes the paranoid fear that the freedoms of the 1960s may be insubstantial, a matter of shifting scenery. This insight is diametrically opposed to the smugly superior indulgence applied to 50s naïvety by *American Graffiti* and the rock 'n' roll hits packages that came in its wake. The strength of Zappa's art has always been its ability to trash the cultural products that affirm the position of the spectator. It is politically progressive in the grain of its production: hence its high standing among people who are far to the left of Zappa in terms of explicit politics. *Ruben & the Jets* was released in August 1968.

'THE ORACLE HAS IT ALL PSYCHED OUT'

On 28 June 1968 *Life Magazine* published Zappa's account of the history of rock, titled 'The Oracle Has It All Psyched Out'.[71] In it Zappa was more relaxed and benign about rock culture than usual: given the chance to give his own account, there was less need to use shock tactics to blow away the shibboleths that serve the industry. One section is a two-part questionnaire that asks questions about various items of subcultural folklore in the 50s and then the 60s: like *Ruben*, it mocked the counter-culture by comparing its moves and grooves to the disdained pre-hippie legacy, but it also registered what was for Zappa genuine progress.

---

[70]Preamble to 'Bebop Tango', *Roxy & Elsewhere*, 1975.
[71]Reprinted in Dominique Chevalier, *Viva! Zappa*, 1985, pp. 92–8.

Society was very repressed, sexually, and dancing was a desperate attempt to get a little physical contact with the opposite sex. Free love, groupies, the Plaster Casters of Chicago and such variants, and the GTO's of Laurel Canyon didn't exist then.[72]

Zappa explains that as a teenager he liked only black R&B, but admits that the film *Rock Around the Clock* was still a real revelation. Never mind that Bill Haley was a tubby, middle-aged exponent of Western swing with an absurd kiss-curl.

In cruddy little teen-age rooms, across America, kids had been huddling around old radios and cheap record players listening to the 'dirty' music of their life style. ('Go in your room if you wanna listen to that crap . . . and turn the volume all the way down'.) But in the theater watching *Blackboard Jungle*, they couldn't tell you to turn it down. I didn't care if Bill Haley was white or sincere . . . he was playing the Teen-Age National Anthem and it was so LOUD I was jumping up and down. *Blackboard Jungle*, not even considering the story line which had the old people winning in the end, represented a strange sort of 'endorsement' of the teen-age cause: 'They have made a movie about us, therefore, we exist . . .'[73]

This attention to context is a model of materialist analysis. So often cultural debate (is Bill Haley any good?) gets mired in unreconcilable assertions because it presumes to discuss some ideal artwork, ignoring the situation in which it is perceived. In the classical world Pierre Boulez pays a similar amount of attention to the material facts of sound: the shape of concert halls, the possible combinations of instruments. Zappa then continues *Lumpy Gravy*'s speculations about the possible effects of music in a universe made of vibrations. He enters the realm of fantasy, but not without leaving a material base. His quotes from Hal Zeiger, one of the first rock promoters of the 50s, present a practical entrepreneurial view of rock 'n' roll that is a million miles from the mythology that sustains US rock culture.

Zappa explains the evolution from the basic rock 'n' roll beat (4/4 with a stress on 2 and 4 plus triplet fills: 'ya-da-da ya-da-da ya-da-da ya-da-da-womp') as bound up with improvements in studio and recording techniques. Early R&B could not be recorded with anything more hard-hitting than brush drums (the clean sound and boggling complexity of hip hop beats as developed with 80s technology bears this out). He bemoans white covers of

---

[72]Frank Zappa, quoted in Dominique Chevalier, *Viva! Zappa*, 1985 p. 92.
[73]Ibid., p. 94.

R&B songs that 'cleaned up' the words and the use of strings to make songs acceptable. In this context, the Beatles were a good thing.

> White rock, overproduced and shiny, nearly slickened itself to death. (Remember Fats Domino with '*Strings*'?) The music was slumping a bit. Was this to be the end of rock? Were we doomed to a new era of country & western tunes, smothered in vaseline? Then, just in the nick of time, Beatlemania. New hope.[74]

In *Twilight of the Gods* Wilfrid Mellers made a brave but unconvincing effort to explain the artistry of the Beatles in formal terms. Zappa explains it in terms of sex – Elvis was too greasy and sullen, the Beatles were huggable and cute – introducing a sociological dimension which, as Susan McClary has demonstrated, can also gain insights into classical music denied to purely 'formal' analysis. Zappa is optimistic about the way that the audience is broadening its musical outlook and he is grateful for groupies. The piece ends with an uncharacteristic description of the rock experience – about being drunk and listening to a wild version of 'Green Onions' played by a local rock 'n' roll combo (Ruben & the Jets) – that sounds like another generation's experience of punk rock or acid house. It ends with a question: 'Is a force this powerful to be overlooked by a society that needs all the friends it can get?'

In the 70s, the greater intellectual credence given pop led to incursions of classical pretension that resulted in the bombast and kitsch of 'progressive rock' (the Nice, ELP, Pink Floyd, Genesis). In the 80s, postmodernism provided an ideology for classical music to imitate the (so-called) simplicities of pop (Reich, Glass, Nyman, Adams). Both these movements have been heralded as solutions to the pop-classical class divide when in fact they merely provided the soundtrack to a lifestyle elevated 'above' popular culture. Zappa understands rock as an *experience* in the context of social existence. His extensions of the form recognize that fact. Rather than gratifying the wish to transcend society, his aesthetic is one of sociological materialism: social limits are played out in the processes of the music itself.

---

[74]Ibid., p. 96.

POLITICS

The Mothers of Invention were the most politically potent musical force since the collaborations of Bertolt Brecht with Kurt Weill. Their radical, up-to-date response to the sinister aspects of mass society rivalled that of the Situationists – and they connected to rock 'n' roll (the SI was always a bunch of *literati*, however gratifyingly pissed off). In May 1968, with the independent action of the students and workers in Paris, Europe was rediscovering the revolutionary tradition of the 1920s. This tradition had been all but extinguished during the preceding forty years: by Nazism and the counter-revolution of Stalin, by a world war fought in terms of bourgeois 'democracy' versus fascism, and finally by a post-war boom that seemed to show capitalism delivering the goods. In these conditions of burgeoning militancy Zappa's music was bound to attract attention from the new left.

On 9 September 1968 the Mothers played in Munich, billed as 'Total Music Theatre' (a phrase which incongruously joins Brecht to Wagner). In October, at the Berlin gig, there was trouble. Left-wing students wanted the Mothers to make some sort of statement against capitalism. According to Zappa, they asked him to lead the audience out to a nearby Allied Forces building and burn it down. He refused, pointing out that if they did something like that the CIA would wipe them out before they left the country.[75] Forced by local police to carry on with the concert (despite a barrage of tomatoes), all ended in uproar as the students stormed the stage. Zappa wrote 'Holiday in Berlin' to commemorate the event. It was issued on *Burnt Weeny Sandwich* as an instrumental, but the Flo & Eddie band sang it with words.

> Look at all the Germans
> Watch them follow orders
> See them think they're doing something
> Groovy in the street
> See the student leader
> He's a rebel prophet
> He's fucked-up, he's still a Nazi
> Like his Mum and Dad
>
> We played for a night in Berlin
> That afternoon we set up our shit and rehearsed
> Half a dozen phony student rebels in the hall

---

[75]Julian Colbeck, *Zappa: A Biography*, 1987, p. 88.

Came to see if I could find a way to help them all
'What is your desire?'
'Help us start a fire
In the Allied Centre
Round the corner down the street'

And then we began to play
A bunch of punks arose from the crowd
Student rebels with flags of red
Began to chant 'Ho Chi Minh
Ho Ho Ho Chi Minh'
Threw tomatoes
And the next thing we knew we were under siege[76]

In 1969 Zappa was asked to give a lecture at the London School of Economics, then a fertile source of new left ideas and agitation. Zappa condemned demonstrations as impractical. The men should cut their hair and take over the city councils – 'infiltrate the establishment'. The women should assert 'slot power' – seduce and maybe marry establishment figures and industrialists, thereby 'exerting a profound influence'.[77] The audience was not impressed and called him variously 'naïve' and 'the Bob Hope of rock 'n' roll'. From Zappa's rock perspective, revolution was simply that year's flower power, and he was as cynical about this fashion as much as the last. With the *Double White* album the Beatles showed how easy it was for Haight Ashbury chic to move on to street-fighting (though attention to the lyrics of 'Revolution' showed that the Beatles actually rejected the message their images implied). In the late 60s Theodor Adorno also condemned the student movement, even though many of its leading lights were applying his own ideas. Like Zappa, Adorno interpreted revolutionary agitation as another 'pseudo-activity' inculcated by the culture industry. Zappa's politics were condemned as 'naïve', but in some ways his position reflects the oversophistication of the Frankfurt School as well. In the night of paranoia all cats are CIA agents.

In 'The Oracle Has It All Psyched Out' Zappa had reiterated the Reichian analysis of society that had informed 'Brown Shoes Don't Make It': 'A lot of things wrong with society today are directly attributable to the fact that the people who make the laws are sexually maladjusted.'[78] It was a brave attempt to keep together a coherent radical politics in a time when the issues being raised

---

[76]'Holiday in Berlin', *Freaks & Motherfuckers*, 1991.
[77]Quoted by Mike Bourne, 'An Interview with Frank Zappa', *Down Beat*, 1971, p. 38.
[78]Michael Gray, *Mother! is the Story of Frank Zappa*, 1985, p. 92.

– war, black power, feminism, the existence of capitalism itself – went far beyond the 'revenge on the parents' of rock 'n' roll and the freaks. Since then, Zappa's stress on sexual freedom has become a satirical touchstone that, while landing him in trouble with the feminists (and hence with the whole American liberal establishment), has also put him into conflict with the PMRC, the cultural wing of the new right in the 1980s.

According to Michael Gray, Pamela Zarubica (Suzy Creamcheese) parted company with Zappa because he proved himself unwilling to shoulder the full gamut of his political responsibilities. She had sensed this even at the end of the 1967 European tour.

> That night, Pam and Frank stayed up late talking. Pam was struck by how frightened Zappa was of the weight he had successfully placed on his own shoulders: 'He was scared and he wasn't ready to leave the times we had in Europe.' Her reaction was unsympathetic: 'Why how dare you be scared you motherfucker, I mean I gave up a lot just to come and go with you because you were the one who knew how democracy could work and who could be President, and now when the responsibility is yours and all these people look to you for the answers you realize it isn't an easy job, that you're tired and that it could cost you more than your security.'[79]

After *Ruben* was released Zarubica deserted Zappa. Summing up her feelings, Gray says: 'She'd thought he was going to change the world, but she found he'd postponed that project.'[80]

In 1979 Zappa has the protagonist of *Joe's Garage* play an 'imaginary guitar solo' in order to assuage his feelings at the way he has been maltreated by society. In providing such a huge, co-ordinated œuvre that encourages obsessive, paranoid speculation about meaning, Zappa almost seems to provide a retreat for the victims of capitalism. It is a world away from the raw polemic of Crass or Napalm Death or even Charlie Haden's Liberation Music Orchestra. However, it needs to be pointed out that Zappa's guitar solos are *not* imaginary: his business practice has enabled him to keep his radical, critical art afloat in the market. The achievement of substantial art under capitalism entails running it like a business. Small-press lyric poetry, by contrast, with its minimal capital investment, is much freer of economics – but also, in being com-

---

[79]Ibid., p. 86.
[80]Ibid., p. 93.

mercially invisible, closer to an 'imaginary' guitar solo. As Zappa said in 1981:

> Without money I can't make records and I can't do my art, because every piece of equipment I use costs money. Most of what I earn goes right back into the work which I do. The only thing that money means to me is whether or not I will have enough to do my next project.
>
> If you're a poet you don't need any equipment, but if you make records, you need a lot of other stuff, and nobody gives it to me.[81]

It is evident that Zappa's experience as an *employer* – of band members, graphic artists, orchestral musicians – leads him to think in 'boss' terms (his hostility to trade unions, for example). However, for those social determinists who think that economics is inevitably reflected in ideology, his music presents an anomaly: why should he bother with moves that are so obviously uncommercial if he is merely a capitalist swine? The answer is to be found in the relationship of music to truth (a romantic idea that postmodernism seeks to bury). Zappa may not recommend revolutionary politics, but in producing music that is truthful to the social forces it embodies – perpetuating the tradition Adorno identified in Western art music – his art actually refuses to countenance any other kind of activity. Unlike most consumer culture it does not confirm anyone's lifestyle, enhance a direction towards the future considered in terms of capitalism's specializations and separations. In its unblinking grasp of the totality of society – reflected in the strenuous eclecticism of diverse socio-musical material – it refuses to affirm the social order.

To the urgencies of political action all culture appears as a distraction, especially that which talks in terms of protest and change. It should be borne in mind how political movements reserve their most acrid rhetoric for those whose ideas only just fall short of their own. The contradictions in Zappa's position were brought out forcefully when he was interviewed for Canadian TV in 1980. Asked why it was that people generally assumed – despite the facts – that anyone as off-the-wall as Zappa must be on drugs, he replied:

> People are just not accustomed to excellence – they're not trained to it, y'know, because when you go to school . . . they teach you just enough to be a slug in a factory and do your job so you can take home your pay check and consume some other stuff that somebody else makes.[82]

---

[81]Quoted in Dominique Chevalier, *Viva! Zappa*, 1985, p. 26.
[82]Frank Zappa, *New Music City TV*, Canadian TV, 1980.

The next question was, 'Do you have any friends?' and he replied:

I don't have any friends because I have so many employees – if you're the boss you'll never have a friend because whenever somebody works for somebody else they can't really like them because he's the boss and make no doubt about it, I'm the boss of these guys. I run the show. I sign the checks, there it is, that's what I do. If you have a friend in the ordinary sense of the word, what have you got? Somebody who thinks they can borrow money from you.[83]

At the same time that Zappa protests at the social consequences of treating people as employees and consumers, he declares that this is precisely how he deals with his associates. Although involved in a cash nexus that reduces people to 'slugs', Zappa nevertheless refuses to accommodate the opinions that provide bosses with a common ideology: unlike the right, he does not applaud obedient workers and conformist consumers as models of American citizenship. Zappa is a capitalist who hates ideology, a genuine spanner in the works.

Zappa can steer his way through such contradictions only by refusing to entertain such analytical concepts as 'right and left' and 'capitalist and worker'. This refusal to leave the area of the concrete and think in abstractions brings back dividends as art: as Adorno's *Aesthetic Theory* makes clear, it is precisely art's refusal to subsume the particular under general ideas that constitutes its protest. When Vaclav Havel invited Zappa to visit post-communist Czechoslovakia – to a tumultuous welcome at Prague airport – Zappa started talking about running for president. However, within weeks, Zappa had been demoted from his official position as 'cultural liaison officer'. Visiting US senators – some of whom had clashed with Zappa at hearings on censorship – must have told Havel to break relations with this maverick. Havel and his country simply did not have the clout to offend the US. As Zappa burned his fingers in his attempts at nurturing free enterprise in Eastern Europe, it became clear that his politics are valuable as iconographic rupture rather than as practical intervention.

[83]Ibid.

UNCLE MEAT

In *Money,* Zappa developed an explicit politics by criticizing rock culture. The events of 1968, though, went beyond either the idea of a revolt against the older generation, or even a critique of that revolt. This struggle threatened to end the social system in which Zappa's music operated. At a loss to communicate to those involved, he returned to his strength: his ability to organize sound. The Situationists, who attacked the separation of art and politics as surrender to the separations of bourgeois society, never succeeded in intervening in musical debates: they never recruited any musicians or composers.[84]. While it was easy to point to the recuperation of literary intellectuals in academic and administrative roles, and of visual artists as suppliers of commodities, music's social function has never been so susceptible to definition. 'Basically this is an instrumental album', read the sleeve note: *Uncle Meat*'s music made many points Zappa's political vocabulary was too unformed to articulate.

The cover of *Uncle Meat* consists of an exceptional Cal Schenkel collage. Although it has an abstract beauty and sense of movement to rival the *merzbau* of Kurt Schwitters, it is its presence as a record sleeve amongst others that crucially realizes its iconic blasphemies. In the middle, a photograph glued to some hardboard shows a forefinger and thumb pulling back an old man's lips. The white hairs of his moustache curl over the mouth. The teeth have been crayoned yellow and you can make out the glint of a gold tooth. A complete dental array is provided by the addition of a photograph of disembodied teeth next to the 'living' ones. The back cover shows a skull stamped with the number 1348 (the year of the Black Death in Europe), looking like some Auschwitz relic, along with polarized photographs of the musicians with their names scrawled underneath. Art Tripp, Ray Collins and Don Preston have X-ray slides of teeth glued by their portraits. Inside the gatefold sleeve, there is a dentist's X-ray machine, along with a girl in an old-fashioned dress sitting in a dentist's chair. These images derive from pre-war commercial literature (updating Max Ernst's use of Victorian engravings in the 30s). Schenkel used

---

[84]The composer Walter Olmo was a member of the International Movement for an Imaginist Bauhaus during its four-year existence (1953–7), but was expelled from the SI as early as the second conference (25/6 January 1958), unable to defend himself against Guy Debord's denunciations. See Stewart Home, *The Assault on Culture: Utopian Currents from Lettrisme to Class War,* 1991, p. 32.

similar material in the gatefold of *Lumpy Gravy* (a couple dancing), *Ruben & the Jets* and *An Evening with Wild Man Fischer*. The name 'George' appears on the back cover, but with no photograph. It refers to Lowell George, who was playing with the Mothers at that time, before he and Estrada left to form Little Feat. Named by Jimmy Carl Black (according to one story), with two ex-Mothers and a Mothers auditionee, Bill Payne,[85] Little Feat illustrated the creativity of the musicians gravitating towards Zappa. They went on to become the greatest country-funk band in the history of rock. Lowell did not actually play on *Uncle Meat*, but his name was necessary for dental continuity.

Zappa's œuvre in fact begins with teeth: those of the 'Hungry Freaks' of *Freak Out!*. The original cover of *We're Only in It for the Money* shows the Mothers against a yellow background (a picture, omitted in the CD release, which imitated the inner gatefold of *Sgt. Pepper*). Surrounded by the Mothers in bouffant wigs, gold lamé stockings and jumble-sale dresses, gazing out with the doleful look of animals dressed for the circus, Zappa, his lip lifted in a quizzical sneer, bares his teeth and asks, 'Is this phase one of *Lumpy Gravy*?' (on the back of *Lumpy Gravy*, dressed in top hat and conductor's tuxedo, giving his best waiter's smile of mock servility, he asks, 'Is this phase two of *We're Only in It for the Money*?'). 'Lumpy gravy' was a catchword from a TV commercial for Aloma Linda Gravy Quick: lumps were something every good conformist American housewife should avoid. As Suzy Creamcheese says on *Uncle Meat*, 'The first thing that attracted me to the Mothers' music was the fact that they played for twenty minutes and everyone was hissing and booing and falling off the dance floor.'[86] Nowhere was this reverse psychology better applied than on the cover of *Uncle Meat*.

In 'The Oracle Has It All Psyched Out' Zappa pointed out that the marketing of the lovable, huggable, mop-top Beatles provided the fans with 'kissable close-ups' (enlarged views of their idols' lips, teeth and gums).[87] Besides the photographs making up a (half-living/half-dead) set of teeth, the collage on the cover of *Uncle Meat* includes five real teeth stuck in among mouldy fragments of food, spashes of paint, blobs of sealing wax and other

---

[85]According to Lowell George, interviewed by Andy Childs, 'The Exploits of Lowell George', *ZigZag*, No. 50, March 1975, p. 26.
[86]Frank Zappa, 'Voice of the Cheese', *Uncle Meat*, 1969.
[87]'The Oracle Has It All Psyched Out', reprinted in Dominique Chevalier, *Viva! Zappa*, 1985, p. 93.

136

detritus. Despite the revolutionary chic of the graphics on the songsheet, the *Double White* album included large colour photographs of each Beatle's face. Working like an anti-serum to such marketing ploys, Cal Schenkel's collage makes out the Mothers' music, in the commodity-as-substitute-for-boyfriend sense exploited by the Beatles, to be about as pleasurable as kissing a rotten corpse. Like the absurd idea of finding a rubber tyre 'tasty',[88] libidinal investment in articles of consumption is parodied as necrophilia or fetishism: the sexual allure of objects.

Lowell George enters dental continuity because of his part in a semi-improvised pantomime.

> The albums I'm featured on most prominently haven't been released yet. There was a ten-album set in the works – one side had me as a German border-guard interviewing each of the band members, asking them about the condition of their gold fillings and things like that.[89]

This points to the reduction of the human body to an object by the Nazis, the notorious piles of gold teeth removed from victims' mouths before they were sent to the gas chambers. That this is not merely an historical outrage is shown by the fact that the banks that handled such loot are still in operation today.[90] That human beings are not composed of pure spirit is of course emphasized by using *Meat* as a name. On the cover another hand holds what appears to be a camera seen from the point of view of the photographer, forefinger poised to release the shutter: the record is allowing us to take a picture. By showing the consequences of reducing people to objects, an objectification that results from a system that treats human labour – and hence human life – as a commodity (not just a blight introduced by the sex industry, as feminism would have us believe), the record allows us to see through the processes of modern society, to take documentary (X-ray) pictures of what we see.

The grubby fingers that pull away the lips of the old Jew in

---

[88]See the back cover to Frank Zappa, *Burnt Weeny Sandwich*, 1970.
[89]*Sound*, 31 August 1974. This has now been released ('German Lunch', 1969, *You Can't Do That on Stage Anymore Vol. 5*, 1992), though the gold teeth section is missing. Thanks to Mårten Sund for supplying me with the uncut original. The name Zappa chose for the piece (there is nothing about lunch in the original) seems particularly resonant.
[90]According to the Simon Wiesenthal Centre for Holocaust Studies, Hermann Abs, executive of the Deutsche Bank at the time that the SS cashed in gold and jewellery plundered from extermination-camp victims, was appointed by the Pope to look into the Banco Ambrosiano affair (director Roberto Calvi was found hanging from Blackfriars Bridge in London), *Searchlight*, No. 92, February 1983, p. 8.

order to see if there is gold worth preserving before he is extermi-
nated, extracting the element of exchange value before the subject
is disposed of, finds an analogy in the X-ray machine, which also
sees past lips and cheek to the teeth. The kiss, which is done
with the lips, is central to romance: the music of *Uncle Meat* is
determinedly anti-romantic. The 'Uncle Meat' theme itself, a dazzling yet vacuous ditty whose notes have the urgency of a march
combined with the unpredictable intervals of serial music,
announces an entire album of music that seems designed to deflate
romantic intoxication, clear the air ('they really get uptight when
you try and move the gas'[91]). The use of harpsichord instead of
piano adds a tinny anti-romanticism parallel to the badly tuned
player-pianos Conlon Nancarrow uses for his dada run-throughs
of impossible Bach and boogie.

There were childhood experiences of dentistry and sinus treatment which Zappa called on in developing his imagery.

> Along with my earaches and asthma, I had sinus trouble. There was
> some 'new treatment' for this ailment being discussed. It involved
> stuffing *radium* into your sinus. (Have you ever heard of this?) My
> parents took me to see *yet another Italian doctor*, and, although I didn't
> know what they were going to do to me, it didn't sound like it was
> going to be *too much fun*. The doctor had a long wire thing – maybe a
> foot or more, and on the end was a pellet of radium. He stuffed it up
> my nose and into my sinus cavities on both sides. (I should probably
> check to see if my handkerchief is glowing in the dark.)[92]

A horror and fascination for the structures beneath the face continually recur in Zappa, a counterpart to his interest in musical
and social processes operating beneath the surface of convention.
When Screamin' Jay Hawkins performed,

> before he would even appear on stage, he would always send out a pair
> of chattering teeth that would click from one end of the stage to the
> other. Then he would leap from the shadows of the stage and scare hell
> out of the audience.[93]

The sound of chattering teeth inspires fear because it is the sound
of skeletons talking, as well as the involuntary response to sub-
zero temperatures and fear. It clears the gas, the 'no room to
breathe' that characterizes social transactions within the terms of

---

[91]*Lumpy Gravy*, 1968.
[92]Frank Zappa, with Peter Occhiogrosso, *The Real Frank Zappa Book*, 1989, p. 20.
[93]Michael Ochs, 'A Forward Look into the Past', *Encyclopedia of Pop, Rock and Soul*, ed. Irwin
Stambler, 1974, p. 8.

oppressive ideology: 'The gasp of surprise which accompanies the experience of the unusual becomes its name.'[94] The use of shock in Zappa – a version of the redeeming strategy at the heart of all gothic, from Mary Shelley to George Romero – is an attempt to make people name things themselves, to register their own experience rather than merely learn names from the experience of others.

There is a sinister political dimension to the destruction of the veils of liberal myth. Early twentieth-century intellectuals who did not heed Leon Trotsky imagined that fascism could usher in a more 'truthful' society, less veiled by liberal sentimentality: F. T. Marinetti, T. S. Eliot, Ezra Pound, D. H. Lawrence, W. B. Yeats, Wyndham Lewis. The list of anti-Semites and out-and-out fascists among the heroes of modernism should prevent anyone from imagining that artistic modernism is a stand-alone life-guide. Amongst the modernists James Joyce almost single-handedly fought these tendencies by basing *Ulysses* on a Jew's view of Ireland, and then with the scurrilous, demotic subversion of *Finnegans Wake*. However, despite Filippo Marinetti's espousal of the fascist cause, Benito Mussolini did not repay him by sponsoring Futurism in the arts. The fascists favoured neo-classicism, reviving precisely the features of the Roman past that the Futurists wanted to destroy (particularly evident in architecture). Because fascism represents a compromise between the masses' desire for change and respect for the laws of private property, it ultimately returns to petit-bourgeois culture at its most archaic and mystifying.

Mussolini was well received by the Italian intelligentsia; composers – including a few modernist ones – gratefully accepted his stipends.[95] Both Schoenberg and Stravinsky were performed in Italy in the 30s. However, with the outbreak of the Second World War and the alliance with Germany in 1939, anti-Semitic edicts meant that Second Viennese School atonality was branded as the musical wing of the international Jewish-Bolshevik conspiracy. Modernism became the scapegoat of a regime looking for a way to assuage working-class indignation at what they could not understand without challenging the conditions of incomprehension.

Ezra Pound was so impressed with Mussolini that he went to live in Italy, ruining his postwar career by making notorious propaganda broadcasts on behalf of the fascist state. Like the

---

[94]Theodor Adorno and Max Horkheimer, *The Dialectic of Enlightenment*, 1946, p. 15.
[95]A strategy well documented in Harvey Sachs, *Music in Fascist Italy*, 1987, p. 163.

Futurists, Pound was also an opponent of romanticism. He saw all modern musical developments as further examples of romantic 'degeneracy' and was particularly incensed by music whose structure is not self-evident (he therefore lost touch with the musical avant-garde). Instead, he rediscovered the early eighteenth-century composer Antonio Vivaldi and proposed a return to such 'noble' simplicity. The post-war 'rediscovery' of Vivaldi was prefigured by Pound's championing of 'authentically Italian' and 'non-Semitic' values during his years as a spokesman for fascist Italy.[96]

Uncle Meat – in common with Kurt Weill and Conlon Nancarrow – is important because it attacks romanticism without falling into either élitism or archaism (interesting to note that Weill was a communist and Nancarrow fought the fascists in Spain). It X-rays modern society – just as it does the Mothers' teeth – in order to show the horrifying processes beneath, but it does not sentimentalize such processes and in so doing validate them. Wyndham Lewis and the Futurists wound themselves up into such hatred for the hypocrisy of the liberal bourgeoisie that they became blatantly reactionary (a similar twist fuelled Oi! in the early 1980s). When Valentine de Saint-Pont wrote

WE MUST STRIP LUST OF ALL SENTIMENTAL VEILS THAT DISFIGURE IT[97]

there was the very genuine danger that such insistence on *what is* would turn to glorification of sexism and war (as it did with Marinetti). *Uncle Meat* demolishes the pretensions of romanticism, but not by extinguishing its utopian hope for a better state of things. It desecrates consumer myths of pretty kissable pop stars, but it also provides information about society and documents the place the Mothers occupy in it. It seeks to replace the confected image of the Beatles with the dynamism and activity of a group of people acting and performing in real time: stretched by Zappa's compositions, soloing on stage and arguing about money. Zappa's documentation of the Mothers is so various because his project is not only about the technically competent carrying out musical specifications, but the creation of situations conducive to social insight. On stage, in the street, on the bus – everything was

---

[96]See 'Chapter 4: The Rapallo Years 1928–1941', *Ezra Pound and Music: The Complete Criticism*, ed. R. Murray Schafer, 1978.
[97]'Futurist Manifesto of Lust 1913', ed. Umberto Apollonio, *Futurist Manifestos*, 1974, p. 73.

important. With the Mothers, Zappa made fantastically inventive use of one of the great assets of rock: lived life as art. The images Zappa deploys are so suggestive that his work needs to be magnified for true appreciation – that is, discussed in a 'high-art' context (though the fact that the Futurists and James Joyce are now considered to be 'high art' is actually a mark of the failure of the social movements whose ideas they precipitated). To gauge precisely the anti-ideological success of *Uncle Meat*, though, it also makes sense to bring in some contemporary pop material for comparative purposes. No one ever got anywhere talking about modern art who did not mention the Electric Prunes.

The air	BLACK THOUGHT
Escaping from your mouth	FLASHING THOUGHTS
The hair	EXPLOSIVENESS
Escaping from your nose	POSSESSIVENESS
My heart	COLORED LIGHTS
Escaping from the scraping	FIVE MULTI-FACETED
And the shaping	WEIRDLY CONNECTED
Of the draping	TWELVE ARMS
. . . The air	ONE EYE
Escaping from your pits	ONE MIND
The hair	ONE DIRECTION
Escaping from my teeth	PRUNES, PITS, STEMS
My hand[98]	SHOCKING ELECTRIC[99]

The first text is the beginning of 'The Air' on *Uncle Meat*. It breaks in on a discussion of money (Jimmy Carl Black has just said: 'I'm not living very extravagant, I can tell you for sure'), undermining Black's position, because it reduces his words to the physical act of breath. In a radio broadcast of *Uncle Meat* before the record's final edit, Black goes on to ask 'Is that thing on?' and Zappa replies 'No . . . (*pause*) . . . it doesn't matter.'

   M1: Mmm. My lips are getting heavy.
   M2: I can't tell when you're telling the truth.
   M3: I'm not.
   M2: How do I know anything you've said to me is . . .
   M3: You don't.[100]

The paranoia inflicted by documentation becomes part of the artwork, a scrupulous reflexiveness that looks ahead to the political significance of tapes in the Watergate conspiracy. When Pink Floyd

---

[98]'The Air', *Uncle Meat*, 1969.
[99]Sleeve note on Electric Prunes, *Underground*, 1967.
[100]End of 'Electric Aunt Jemima', *Uncle Meat*, 1969.

made *Wish You Were Here* in 1975, they talked of using tapes of the band discussing the problem of alienation from audiences, but bottled out. The kind of escapism they supply could not survive such documentary rigour. It is a mark of how ambivalent Zappa's music itself is that it can integrate so well with speech and documents: everything is approached as construct, there is no artistic meta-language, no all-enveloping explanation, though the resulting 'paranoid listener'[101] invariably seeks to provide one.

The Electric Prunes text is from a sleeve note by Barbara Harris for *Underground*, an album of 'psychedelic' rock from 1967 (all Davey Jones-style lisped vocals and surf rhythms). It appears just above an advertisement for the Electric Prunes Appreciation Society, 'because "Fan Club" sounds undernourished'. This was part of the imperialist nostalgia favoured by the commercialized drug culture: the music-hall loquaciousness of 'Mr Kite'; high-mod Edwardian clothes; I Was Lord Kitchener's Valet (a boutique on Carnaby Street); droopy moustaches; album titles like the Jefferson Airplane's *After Bathing at Baxters* or *The Laurel Canyon Ballet Company* (the GTO's original name before Zappa's suggestion). Despite the fact that the Electric Prunes were no more than a Monkees-style exploitation of the 'underground' tag, the 'surrealism' of 'prunes, pits, stems' cannot coexist with the straightforward idea of the 'fan club'. 'The Air' has not got the Prunes' hard-sell breathlessness, but it uses much the same vocabulary – 'armpits' as a transgressive thrill, for example – and 'Duke of Prunes' also played on the scatological possibilities of references to 'prunes'. On *You Can't Do That on Stage Anymore Vol. 5* Zappa includes a piece called 'My Head?', which is a spoken-word document: 'the result of the MOI attempting to assume some sort of mutant cluster-fuck pose'.[102] The Mothers were physically adopting the 'weirdly connected/twelve legs/one eye' group aesthetic proposed in Barbara Harris's sleeve note.

Zappa was using the same motifs as the Electric Prunes, but his ideas go beyond the mild surrealism of 'prunes, pits and stems' into a constellation of teeth, reification and Nazism that delves into the implications of commodity fetishism. The status of teeth as hinge-point of organic and inorganic makes them peculiarly incandescent in poetic experimentation that dramatizes the horror of commodification, the incursion of product on flesh. As with canine

---

[101]I am indebted to Jonathan Jones for this coinage.
[102]Frank Zappa, note to 'My Head?', 1969, *You Can't Do That on Stage Anymore Vol. 5*, 1992.

continuity, the dental stimulus reaches an apogee with *Overnite Sensation*, where condensation and displacement make manifest many themes which until then have been merely latent: 'Montana' is a song about dental floss.

'Nine Types of Industrial Pollution' is a long speeded-up guitar solo (a technique developed at Cucamonga, most notably with 'Speed Freak Boogie'), Art Tripp and guest percussionist Ruth Komanoff supplying a clockwork universe within which the guitar coils and jumps like a liquid spring. Zappa's melodic invention is astonishing. Particularly impressive is the refusal of any realistic ambience for the recording: the sleeve notes stressed the number of tracks that could be built up on the board at the Apostolic and there is no attempt to use it to reproduce a credible sound-space. Speeded-up vocals increase the sense of unreality (a classical soprano, Nelcy Walker, was also used, her 'legitimate' voicings adding to the bizarre mix of registers). The whole record feels like a laboratory product.

'Dog Breath in the Year of the Plague' is one of Zappa's great melodies (now available as a splendid orchestral score and recorded by the Ensemble Modern[103]). The snatting drum tracks that gave such a brittle, weird feel to *Ruben & the Jets* allow all kinds of chronic hiccups and sleights-of-hand. Just as the asymmetric ostinatos to 'The Legend of the Golden Arches' and 'Pound for a Brown on the Bus' generate complex irrational structures, the hallucinogenic effects rely a great deal on illusory simplicity. Vocals are used to replace musical processes: the extraordinary snore that ends the allegro section of 'Golden Arches'; the word 'fade' that finishes 'Pound for a Brown on the Bus'. Different recording spaces – Suzy Creamcheese's raps interspersed with violent 'snorks'; meticulous overdubs; live chaos and a song that mentions smuggling tapes ('The Air') – emphasize the record's status as piebald documentary, but the sense of 'underground' creativity and optimism makes it utterly coherent. 'Zolar Czakl', 'Project X' and 'We Can Shoot You' are gems of *musique concrète*.

'Pound for a Brown' proved a durable vehicle for soloing throughout the 70s and 80s, appearing as an orchestral version as late as 1993.[104] Zappa described the genesis of the song at the Albert Hall concert in London in 1969. The 'brown out' – showing

---

[103]Frank Zappa, *The Yellow Shark*, 1993.
[104]Ibid.

the bared backside – was a custom among surfers on the West Coast.

> Also known as a 'Brown', and also known as 'Mooning' on the East Coast, and there are innumerable variations on this procedure. If you brown out against a wire screen it's called 'The Chipped Beef', and if you do it against a plate glass window at the delicatessen it's 'The Pressed Ham'.[105]

On the way from the airport to the hotel Jimmy Carl Black bet Bunk Gardner a pound he would not brown out on the bus – which Gardner immediately did.

> This piece of music is *program music* because it tells little stories with pictures that go along with the different parts of the music to evoke realistic scenes in your imagination. This is an inferior kind of music designed for audiences who can't stand listening to music, but need pictures, and it was invented here in Europe a long time ago. The first part of the piece has the simulated effect of London traffic. We do this ingeniously by using actual *horns* which you squeeze with your hands and they go 'ooga'. The next thing that happens is a jolly little theme which gives the impression that the Mothers of Invention love to go around the countryside in a bus with big windows, followed by another abstruse section that simulates the conversation on the bus, the calculation of the monetary difference and this leads up to a throbbing and otherwise surging climax wherein the pants come off and the buns are revealed, followed by some great rocking out and instrumental improvisation for about the next twenty minutes. Or something.[106]

Zappa's explanation both belittles the status of the work of art and suggests the worrying idea that we are all living in an unreal, cartoon world.

Uncle Meat was hugely influential and provided the basic forms for much European art-rock. However, though bands like Henry Cow adopted the careful orchestration of tunes like 'The Uncle Meat Variations', they missed the rock power of 'King Kong' and the explosive disorder of 'God Bless America' or 'Louie Louie'. 'Electric Aunt Jemima' was professedly written about a miniature Standall amplifier, but the regressive wordplay of the lyrics is directed to the black nanny on the label of the brand-name maple syrup. At the time Zappa explained the obscurity of his lyrics – which relates to the hermetic nature of modern poetry from Mallarmé onwards – by referring to an early conversation with Captain Beefheart, where they discussed

---

[105]Frank Zappa, Royal Albert Hall, 1969, transcribed in *Society Pages*, No. 20, May 1984, p. 13.
[106]Ibid., p. 14.

the problems of lyrics in the music we were being fed on the radio. I always felt that the music I grew up with, except for the R&B, was just horrible and I didn't want to be subjected to it and I wished that I'd had something better to choose from. But I couldn't get anything better so we were talking about this and I said, 'Well I'm going to do this' and Don says 'Well I'm going to do that' and I said, 'OK, well let's go do that.'[107]

Supplying the underground with this vast cornucopia of music was as political an act as the finger-pointing of *Money*. According to a note above the transcribed lyrics inside the gatefold: 'The words to the songs on this album were scientifically prepared from a random series of syllables, dreams, neuroses and private jokes that nobody except the members of the band ever laugh at.'

Dreams, neuroses and jokes (as well as the 'random syllables' of slips of the tongue, a theme later taken up on *Joe's Garage*[108]) are classic loci of the unconscious in the Freudian schema. Zappa seems to be painting a picture of the Mothers' thoughts when asleep: the only periods of wakefulness are 'God Bless America' at the Whiskey-a-Go-Go, and 'Louie Louie' played on the Albert Hall pipe organ. The images played with are resolutely pre-hippie, a backwash of 50s subcultural totems.

A booklet included with *Uncle Meat* contained a science-fiction story and a film storyboard. Both developed the theme of vegetable mutation. In the first Ruben & the Jets are drugged by Uncle Meat, using techniques reminiscent of Zappa's radium 'treatment' for his sinus complaint.

> Each victim is given a blast from a nasal mist squeezer . . . He explains that the human skull (a hard bone) doesn't really leave room for the type of tissue growth the victims will experience here, and the enlarged brain will extend through the sinus cavity into the noses of the group. This area has been softened by the nasal mist and will reshape itself to accommodate the extra brain cells. He throws a switch. Under the posters, the noses have become erect.[109]

This explains the nose snouts on the cover of *Ruben & the Jets*. Amplifying the sound of a 1939 Chevrolet causes the plants beneath to grow beanstalk-style, lifting them to outer space. In the storyboard a decadent senate orders the army to exterminate an evolved vegetable (looking very like Frank Zappa) who 'knew

---

[107]Frank Zappa, interviewed by Barry Miles, *International Times*, No. 63, 29 August–11 September 1969, p. 20.
[108]Frank Zappa, 'Dong Work for Uda', *Joe's Garage Acts II and III*, 1979.
[109]Frank Zappa story in booklet accompanying *Uncle Meat*, 1969.

too much'. Both stories equate sexual development (the awakening of desire at puberty) with power and knowledge that threaten the status quo.

Doll's foot and giraffe graphics perpetuate the themes of the Garrick Theater happenings. A woman uses the doll's foot as a vibrator, exclaiming 'zorch stroking fast 'n bulbous'. A note points out that 'fast 'n bulbous jelly' was invented by Don Vliet (it is part of an exchange between Captain Beefheart and the Mascara Snake on *Trout Mask Replica*): on the cover of the booklet it threatens the Mothers in the form of a 1939 Chevrolet, and 'attacks the Vatican' on the reverse. The jelly replicates the Mount Rushmore carvings of the United States presidents. A peculiarly American threat, fast 'n bulbous jelly is an intuitive image for consumer-oriented capitalism, portraying its peculiar ability to give sex appeal to objects and to make everything equivalent to everything else. A diagram of the doll foot as a 'young rifle' indicates its sinister integration with the military-industrial complex. The Mothers' relationship to this force is ambiguous, as represented by their *alter egos*, Ruben & the Jets (promotional packs of the latter were sent out with tubes of hair gel and instructions on achieving a 'jelly roll'[110]).

> The difference between us
> Is not very far
> Cruising for burgers
> In daddy's new car
> My phony freedom card
> Brings to me
> Instantly
> ECSTASY[111]

The *Uncle Meat* film included semi-improvised sketches in the manner later used for *200 Motels*, with Don Preston claiming that moving a sock from one side to another could make all the difference between something being 'underground' and being 'highly commercial', as well as Phyllis Altenhouse beating Aynsley Dunbar with a toilet brush and Zappa and Preston failing to persuade her to take off her clothes. On the CD release, dialogue from the film is used as filler on the second disc.

The last twenty minutes of the *Uncle Meat* album are an extended workout on 'King Kong'. As with *Freak Out!*, this

---

[110]Julian Colbeck, *Zappa: A Biography*, 1987, p. 87.
[111]'Cruising for Burgers', *Uncle Meat*, 1969.

makes the fourth side of the double album an extended musical *tour de force* (a recurring habit). Like many of Zappa's blowing vehicles, 'King Kong' benefits from its single-chord 'drone'. Unhampered by the jazz restriction of 'going through the changes', the Mothers proved that they were one of the great blowing outfits of all time. The tune's 3/8 time signature and eccentric intervals provoke brilliant solos from Don Preston and Bunk Gardner; even Motorhead's lumpen outburst is a treat. The final exchanges between Zappa and Underwood point ahead to their collaboration on *Hot Rats*. 'King Kong' showed that Zappa had something missing from nearly every act marketed as fusion in the next decade: the key to combining rock excitement and extended musical event.

STRAIGHT

The new deal negotiated with Reprise – the West Coast label set up by Frank Sinatra and now owned by Warner Brothers – allowed for two labels: Bizarre and Straight. The burgeoning success of the underground made it possible to stretch the rules about what was deemed commercial, and during this period Zappa brought a number of unusual projects to fruition.

One of the more elaborate projects was a double album for Wild Man Fischer, issued on Bizarre in 1968.[112] Larry Fischer had been committed to mental institutions in 1963 and 1965. In 1968 he was singing songs for a dime on Sunset Strip. They are the kind of songs people make up in the bath; simple, repetitive themes with no development or narrative structure: disturbingly like pop songs in fact. Zappa recorded Fischer talking and singing both at Sunset Sound and in the basement of the log cabin. He also had Dick Kunc record Fischer at work selling songs on the street. As with *Uncle Meat*, Art Tripp overdubbed percussion at Sunset, an embellishment which turns the first side of the album into an extraordinary suite. Some songs – 'Merry-Go-Round', 'The Taster', 'Serrano Beach' and 'Circle' – are given full backing tracks, but most of them are acapella. Fischer was obsessed with pop, and he proved capable of producing interesting songs long after his involvement with Zappa, when he recorded the singles 'Go to

---

[112]Wild Man Fischer, *An Evening with*, 1968, Bizarre/Reprise RS6332.

Rhino Records' and 'Don't be a Singer' and an album for Rhino (the West Coast independent who also picked up the original Mothers of Invention working as the Grandmothers).

Zappa presents Fischer as sociological documentary. In an era when the Beatles had broken through to mass consciousness precisely because of their ability to be ordinary – breaking with the idea of skilled interpreters performing professionally written material (the Broadway catalogue used by Frank Sinatra and finally adopted by Elvis) – it is fascinating to see what happens when an album makes a 'star' out of someone who has no evident musical skill whatsoever. The conclusion to side one has Kim Fowley (who was credited with 'hypophone' on *Freak Out!*) improvise messianic prophecies to piano accompaniment by Rodney Bingenheimer: Wild Man Fischer will sweep the board, Elvis and the Beatles are trembling in their shoes. Fowley's stream of consciousness makes Fischer's eccentricities seem almost benign. Charles Manson, another hustler on the narrow line between love-happening organizer and pimp, talked (and still talks) similar stuff. Zappa was lucky to get Fowley rather than Manson. Manson had been looking for a record deal: the house in which he murdered Sharon Tate in August 1969 – just up the road from the log cabin – had previously been occupied by Terry Melcher, a record producer who backed out of a record deal with him. Fowley's subsequent involvements – poor solo albums (*I'm Bad*, 1972; *International Heroes*, 1973) and managing the Runaways – have been less interesting.

The inner gatefold includes a diagram by Fischer that shows three levels. At the bottom are Chubby Checker, Ricky Nelson, Fabian, the Everly Brothers and Wild Man Fischer 'before he met Frank Zappa'. In the middle is Johnny Cash and Wild Man Fischer 'after he met Frank Zappa'. At the top is Wild Man Fischer 'after you hear this album', above even the Beatles – who are saying 'hello down there' to the rest (the Rolling Stones, Dylan, Elvis, Donovan, Tiny Tim, the Mothers, the Monkees, the Who, the Cream, Mozart and Jimi Hendrix). The status of pop is not about its inherent worth or meaning but the fact of its being on vinyl: people's ability to purchase it and hear it. This addresses the issue of power in a very direct way.

Music as a commodity – records – requires that people work in order to pay for them. Fischer's 'madness' was to sing songs himself, making song a disruption of work rather than its comple-

148

ment: 'I'd say I'm a relaxed sort of person. I would say I'm a normal person. It's just our society under capitalism says you cannot do that shit all the time. And I do it all the time.'[113]

Fischer's transgressions shows how the marketing of music cements the current social order, but also how the need for excitement (Fowley jokes about the imitators that will arise – for the Puerto Rican market, Wild Man Rodriguez who has 'boogaloo drums on his records') makes the record companies focus on everyday creativity, giving the special status of their stars the lie. If the definition of avant-garde art is the special action that can throw light on the workings of the mass-culture industry, *An Evening with Wild Man Fischer* abundantly qualifies.

Naked Angels[114] and *Lucille Has Messed My Mind Up*[115] were releases on Straight by multi-instrumentalist Jeff Simmons. The first was a film soundtrack album, a sequence of instrumentals that combined melody and fuzz guitar: heavy, psychedelicized surf-rock. Zappa produced *Lucille* under the name La Marr Bruister, wrote the title track (to appear on *Joe's Garage Act I* in 1979), co-wrote 'Wonderful Wino' (to appear on *Zoot Allures* in 1976) and played lead guitar on two tracks. Jeff Simmons was in the Mothers at the time of *200 Motels* and left under a cloud (his ambitions to form a 'heavy' group were satirized in Cal Schenkel's brilliant animation 'Dental Hygiene Dilemma' and the attitude of the rest of the band to him can be examined on *Playground Psychotics*), but returned to play rhythm guitar on *Waka/Jawaka* and clown about with Napoleon Murphy Brock on *Roxy & Elsewhere*.

Playing bass, piano, organ and accordion and singing in a style similar to that of Jack Bruce with Cream, Simmons presented a brace of strong, harmonically sophisticated songs that have some of the explosive multi-hued impact of the Jimi Hendrix Experience. Craig Tarwater plays excellent B.B. King-style blues guitar (he wound up working in the studios and selling tuition videos in the back pages of *Guitar Player*[116]). It explored a vein of mutant, psychedelic R&B that has had regrettably few successors: most rock this musically accomplished tends towards the jazz-rock limbo of Steely Dan (or the AOR of Blood, Sweat and Tears); the

[113]Quoted by Michael Ross, 'Wild Man Fischer', *ZigZag*, No. 20, June 1971, p. 25.
[114]Jeff Simmons, *Naked Angels*, 1969, Straight STS1056.
[115]Jeff Simmons, *Lucille Has Messed My Mind Up*, 1968, Straight STS1057.
[116]At least he was in *Guitar Player*, November 1991.

Velvet Underground's folk drones proved an easier model for most would-be 'psychedelic' teenage bands. Only Sundae Times, an Experience-type trio put together by Eddy Grant in the early 70s,[117] and the first record by cyberdelic new wavers Chrome[118] enter the same territory. 'Appian Way' and 'Madame du Barry', about the eighteenth-century hostess, display literary interests unusual in pop and 'I'm in the Music Business' has some great lines.

> I'm in the music business
> Future looking doubtful
> Lying in the dirt
> Supposed to go to law school
> Music business – bound to be my downfall
> Hair down to my shoulders
> I need a sandwich . . .
> Running out of money, crazy going hungry
> Gotta get a part in a skin flick
> Running out of money, gotta put a mask on . . .
> Gotta take my clothes off, try and play some bebop
> . . . Then they rolled the cameras
> Gave me forty dollars for a cock shot

Despite such felicities, Zappa's title tune still comes off best: a rocking, pleading ballad in the manner of *Chunga's Revenge*'s 'Sharleena', with a classic horn arrangement played by a multi-tracked Ian Underwood. After his Zappa involvements were over, Simmons vanished: a shame, because Simmons's songwriting and ecstatic, jazzy singing are quite unique.

The next release on Straight came from the GTO's: *Permanent Damage*,[119] The album documented the female angle at a time of sexual 'liberation' that had not yet been brought to account by feminism. As explained on ' . . .Who's Jim Sox?', GTO stands for Girls Together 'Often, Only, Occasionally, Organically, Outrageously. All those O's'. Centred on the Zappas' log cabin in Laurel Canyon, most of the GTO's had found each other by attending Vito's parties. Pamela Zarubica cordially hated them: 'A group of freaky dressing, hard-narcotics-loving young girls who feign lesbianism as their thing.'[120]

'Lesbianism' served to titillate their (male) sexual targets and

[117]Sundae Times, *Us Colored Kids*, 1969, Joy/President JOYS159.
[118]Chrome, *The Visitation*, 1977, Siren DE1000.
[119]The GTO's, *Permanent Damage*, 1969, Straight STS1059.
[120]Quoted in Michael Gray, *Mother! is the Story of Frank Zappa*, 1985, p. 92.

to deflect unwanted overtures by the likes of Vito and Carl Franzoni, but they did not actually practise it. According to Pamela Miller (who called herself Miss Pamela at the time), Miss Lucy and Miss Sandra (who married Cal Schenkel and had a daughter called Raven) kept lists of pop stars on the walls of the vault in the basement of the log cabin they inhabited: names were struck off as the girls scored. Christine Frka explained the 'Miss' phenomenon in a sleeve note: 'The GTO's are Misses. They miss out on a lot of things they see, so they must do them theirselves.'

Courtesans to the male rock aristocracy could call on 'heavy friends': accomplices on the album included Rod Stewart, Jeff Beck and Nicky Hopkins. Lowell George wrote, arranged and produced 'Do Me in Once' and 'I Have a Paintbrush', while Don Preston provided music for 'TV Lives'. The main musical heritage appears to be cheerleading, but the mismatch between this and their topics – stuffed bras, Captain Beefheart's shoes, triangular relationships, male groupies like Rodney Bingenheimer (the BTOs – Boys Together Often – were actually bi-sexual[121]) – produces a gripping musical grotesque, aided by some of Zappa's finest *cinéma verité* splices. Lowell George was less enthusiastic.

> We did a GTO's session once which was real fun – even if the production wasn't top drawer, because there were no real singers in the GTO's, they were performers rather than singers – but that was the original Little Feat on those GTO's songs: Russ Titelman on guitar, Ry Cooder and me, and I go back to those two cuts we did, and I gasp and cringe. They are hell-on-earth.[122]

Despite misgivings by musicians involved, *Permanent Damage* is a good record to play to people arguing the Dworkinite line that 60s sexual liberation was only an excuse for outrageous male chauvinism. There are elements the subsequent generalizing of anti-racist politics would probably avoid: the guying of 'cones' (coons) and their pick-up lines seems to be the inevitable result of groupie equation of social standing with commercial success (Hendrix being the only black rock star); although 'the blues' were universally honoured, young blacks were not part of the 'scene'. The record ends on a touching note as Miss Pamela tries to explain to one of the Plaster Casters of Chicago (their collection of casts of pop-star erections – including Jimi Hendrix and Noel Redding,

---

[121]Pamela Des Barres, *I'm with the Band – Confessions of a Groupie*, 1987, p. 108.
[122]Quoted by Paul Kendall, 'Little Feat', *ZigZag*, No. 63, August 1976, p. 14.

though Eric Clapton and Zappa did not 'volunteer'[123] – currently belongs to Herb Cohen) that her 'fave rave' is not actually a pop-star.

Permanent Damage shows that fan fantasy is frequently more creative than the 'art' that inspires their worship (like Jimmy Sommerville talking about the pleasures of teeny-bopper hysteria for David Essex: the music is incidental to the excuse for a riot). Crossing the boundary between art and life in a way that still causes a disapproving shudder to pass through polite society, the GTO's managed to cut a great 60s record. Pamela Miller's 'confessions of a groupie' book, *I'm with the Band*, shows that the GTO's pursued hedonism with discernment and anti-authoritarian wit. According to Zappa, other 'groupie papers' (diaries kept by those involved) were still better.[124] The groupie phenomenon was a subject of much discussion at the time and received Zappa's wholehearted seal of approval.

> These girls, who devote their lives to pop music, feel they owe something to it, so they make the ultimate gesture of worship, human sacrifice. They offer their bodies to the music or its nearest personal representative, the pop musician. These girls are everywhere. It is one of the most amazingly beautiful products of the sexual revolution.[125]

In a social system that – for reasons of maintaining capitalist profitability – cannot come up with anything better than the family for reproduction of the next generation, the promise of boundless sex is never going to be unequivocally in the interests of women. On the other hand, it is inevitably an issue around which utopian dreams (and their commercial betrayal) are bound to revolve. The ethics of the scene documented by the GTO's seemed to reside somewhere between the innocent promiscuity of youth 'before settling down' to downright procurement and exploitation. *Permanent Damage* has the advantage of allowing the women involved in the 60s 'free-love revolution' to make their voices heard. Not until punk did women contribute such a subversive undermining of the shibboleths of rock culture: the GTO's seem to be enjoying themselves, and this reduction of the personalities of the great rock gods to fuckable objects significantly degrades their mystique.

Another two releases were spoken word albums: *The Berkeley*

[123]Frank Zappa, with Peter Occhiogrosso, *The Real Frank Zappa Book*, 1989, p. 105.
[124]Ibid., p. 104.
[125]Reprinted in Dominique Chevalier, *Viva! Zappa*, 1985, p. 96.

Concert by Lenny Bruce[126] and *An Immaculately Hip Aristocrat*, a club set recorded by Lord Buckley in 1965.[127] Adverts for the former pointed out that Zappa had selected the concert,[128] but a further selling point was that it was unedited (the first uncut Bruce performance according to *Rolling Stone*[129]) so there was little room for Zappa's production skills. In spring 1968 Zappa had plans for a Broadway show.

> This summer I'd like to present a show on Broadway. It's a musical science-fiction horror story based on the Lenny Bruce trials. He was a friend of mine . . . he was a saint. What the Big Machine of America did to Lenny Bruce was pretty disgusting – it ranks with civil rights as one of the big pimples on the face of American culture . . . but nobody will ever really find out about it, I guess.[130]

Zappa was right. Even in the concert Zappa chose, it is hard to find anything to laugh at today, despite Bruce's high-standing among the cognoscenti of the time. The routines are so reliant on concepts of 'in' and 'out', as well as 'hip' argot and contemporary racial brickbats, that they remain largely impenetrable. The Lord Buckley album is a different matter. It is not helped by being recorded live – laughter and applause often seem embarrassingly overdone, as if people feel they ought to laugh if they were not to be thought 'square' – but it still has many moments of genuine word-flip magic. 'Governor Slugwell' is an inspired attack on the Californian political establishment. 'The Raven' shows the links between Zappa's subcultural roots and the literary gothic of Edgar Allan Poe. Recorded in 1956, 'The Bad Rapping of the Marquis de Sade' sounds like the beatnik ur-text for such B-culture monuments as *The Rocky Horror Show*, 'The Torture Never Stops' and *Thing-Fish*.

Straight also gave Zappa the opportunity to record an album for Captain Beefheart: the epochal double album *Trout Mask Replica*.[131] Although Beefheart later claimed that Zappa's involvement was nil and that he simply fell asleep at the control board, it

[126]Lenny Bruce, *The Berkeley Concert*, 1968, Bizarre 63629, later issued on Transatlantic TRA195D in April 1969.
[127]Lord Buckley, *An Immaculately Hip Aristocrat*, 1968, Straight STS1054.
[128]Oz, No. 20, April 1969, p. 39.
[129]Ronald Hayes, '*Berkeley Concert* review', *Rolling Stone*, 5 April 1969.
[130]Quoted in Pete Frame, 'Mothers: The Earliest Days of the Just Another Band from LA', *ZigZag*, No. 53, June 1975, p. 23.
[131]Captain Beefheart and the Magic Band, *Trout Mask Replica*, 1969, Straight STS1053.

seems no accident that this Zappa production is also Beefheart's masterpiece. According to Herb Cohen:

When we did the album with him, Frank said, 'Hey, let's go into the studio and you rehearse the group and we'll put down exactly what you want.' It was the first album he ever made where he had total control of everything that went down.[132]

Previous records – *Safe As Milk, Mirror Man, Strictly Personal* – had been in a quaint, jangling, pentatonic R&B style that occupied the exotic end of the white blues spectrum. With *Trout Mask Replica* Beefheart went right off that dial.

Captain Beefheart's voice was a flabbergasting version of Howlin' Wolf. Though it lacked the sheer growling intensity of the Wolf, it had a range and depth and variety which is unsurpassed. There was also a playfulness with registers and postures and accents which bears comparison to Lord Buckley. The music of *Trout Mask*, reputedly written at the piano in a single eight-hour stretch, took Howlin' Wolf's music – deceptively simple rhythmic figures that pound against each other – into what sounds at first like complete cacophany. *Trout Mask* is the only record ever made for which no other music is suitable 'preparation' (neither Beefheart's own nor any other). The critical cliché is 'a fusion of free jazz and Delta blues' (a description first coined by Zappa), but there is a brutal attack in the guitars and bass that is beyond either. Familiarity with the record reveals a plaintive lyricism and an artistic coherence that is utterly assured: 'experimental' it is not. Bootlegged live versions of the tunes show that there is no improvisation: they are played note for note to Beefheart's specifications.

Like *Money* and *Uncle Meat*, 'Dachau Blues' used images of the nazi death camps to hold up warnings for current social developments. The CD release includes the lyrics (some of the best of which get lost in Beefheart's expressive vowel twists).

Dachau blues, Dachau blues those poor Jews
The world can't forget that misery
'n the young ones now beggin' the old ones please
t' stop bein' madmen
'fore they have to tell their children
'bout the burnin' back in World War Three's
War One was balls 'n powder 'n blood 'n snow
War Two rained death 'n showers 'n skeletons

---

[132]Quoted in Michael Gray, *Mother! is the Story of Frank Zappa*, 1985, p. 123.

> Danced 'n screamin' 'n dyin' in the ovens
> Cough 'n smoke 'n dyin' by the dozens [133]

The power of these songs gives the lie to those who believe only an in-bred culture can give birth to authentic statements. Don Van Vliet's adolescent obsession with R&B brought forth poetry framed in a black idiom – itself, it should be recalled, an improvised version of a foreign language – that makes disjuncture and play-acting central to the picture. 'The Blimp' combined a recitation of Beefheart's words by Antennae Jimmy Semens over the telephone with a vamp recorded by the Mothers at Columbia University in New York, now issued as 'Charles Ives'.[134] The sense of magic is palpable as Frank Zappa chuckles and says he thinks 'there is enough on the tape to use it as it is for the album'. According to Zappa, Beefheart insisted that

> the cymbals have pieces of corrugated cardboard mounted on them (like mutes), and that circular pieces of cardboard be laid over the drum heads, so Drumbo wound up flogging stuff that went 'thump! boomph! doof!'[135]

One of the reasons Trout Mask makes for such difficult first-time listening is this rawness of instrumental sound. Later albums developed atmospheres – the marimba–drenched Afro-ethnicity of Lick My Decals Off Baby, the high-tech future-soul of Clear Spot, the weird guitar-sleaze of The Spotlight Kid – but Trout Mask maintains an attack that promises music that is no more than its own sounds. Apart from Ornette Coleman's harmolodics with Prime Time (actually an independent development of Ornette's earlier style and one that relies on collective improvisation), attempts to replicate the music of Trout Mask have been unsuccessful. In the heyday of punk Wire and the Fall emulated its emphasis on brute playing, but at the cost of introducing a certain puritan drabness. Certainly Trout Mask is far from the 'poet bellowing over a racket' that many anarcho-art-rock bands seem to think it is.

Like Sun Ra's Arkestra, Magic Band members all lived in the same house at the time (Zappa wanted to record the album there on Dick Kunc's Uher portable tape-recorder, but Beefheart wanted a 'real' recording studio) and this social experimentation may explain the unmediated nature of their music. Beefheart later

---

[133]Captain Beefheart, 'Dachau Blues', Trout Mask Replica, 1969, Straight STS1053.
[134]Frank Zappa, 'Charles Ives', You Can't Do That on Stage Anymore Vol. 5, 1992.
[135]Frank Zappa, with Peter Occhiogrosso, The Real Frank Zappa Book, 1989, p. 52.

objected to being marketed as a 'freak' alongside Wild Man Fischer and Alice Cooper, but the photograph of the band on the back cover shows individuals who are well beyond conformist drug-culture 'weirdness'. They are standing in front of greenery, Ed Caraeff's photo making use of sun-ring lens effects, much like any hippie band, except hippies generally choose open 'untouched' nature, not urban back gardens. It takes a moment to notice the (unlisted) Drumbo, wearing punk slit-eye shades, standing below the bridge the rest of the band are standing on. Beefheart is holding a table lamp with a denuded wire frame, the flex dangling down past Drumbo/John French's head. The resonance could be Dylan's 'trying like a flame in the sun'[136] – indicating that human art is nothing next to nature – but it also refers to electricity, title of the most important song on *Safe As Milk*, and crucial ingredient for the sound of the Magic Band. Beefheart has a strong line in nature mysticism, but it is the wide range of Beefheart's imagery, its inclusive take on urban squalor as well as fishing-holiday idylls, whalebone corsets as well as the whale's song, that makes his poetry surreal rather than merely escapist.

Zappa's satirical and degraded vision is to some people the very opposite of Beefheart's 'childlike' charm, but he proved to be the one producer who could document the full range of Beefheart's vision. The Situationists noted that surrealism lost its critical edge when it started believing the mysticism and irrationality it plays with. The British surrealism of Henry Moore and John Cowper Powys – astrology and archaism rather than psychoanalysis and revolution – has always been tame compared to its continental models. Correcting this tendency in Beefheart, emphasizing the material conditions of recording and playing, Zappa managed to incubate his finest album.

Other releases on Straight included Judy Henske and Jerry Yester,[137] Tim Buckley[138] and Tim Dawe[139] – Herb Cohen folk contacts – and three records by Vincent Furnier, better known as Alice Cooper.[140] None of these were exceptional. Henske and

---

[136]Bob Dylan, 'It's All Over Now Baby Blue', *Bringing it all Back Home*, 1965, Columbia, CS9128.
[137]Judy Henske and Jerry Yester, *Farewell Aldebaran*, 1969, Straight STS1052; *Rosebud*, Straight/Reprise RS6426.
[138]Tim Buckley, *Blue Afternoon*, 1969, Straight STS1060; *Starsailor*, 1969, Straight STS1064; *Greetings from LA*, 1971, Straight/Reprise RS2631.
[139]Tim Dawe, *Penrod*, 1969, Straight STS1058.
[140]Alice Cooper, *Pretties for You*, 1969, Straight STS1051; *Easy Action*, 1970, Straight STS1061; *Love It to Death*, 1971, Straight STS1065.

Yester invented an excruciating species of neo-medieval folk psychedelia, while Tim Buckley attempted to apply Coltrane's harmonic expansion to a limited folk-rock idea of melody. Alice Cooper played hard rock laced with 'atrocities' that reduced the Mothers' surrealism to cabaret entertainment. According to Zappa, Cooper's relationship with Christine Frka furnished him with most of his ideas. There was also *Acapella* by the Persuasions,[141] a black vocal group keeping alive doowop's tradition of unaccompanied singing. It was a live concert and included a spirited version of the Olympics' 'The Bounce'.

As well as the founding of Bizarre and Straight and the issue of a sampler, *Zappéd*,[142] 1969 saw the release of Zappa's 'solo' album *Hot Rats*. It harnessed some of the important musicians on the West Coast.

DON 'SUGARCANE' HARRIS

Don Bowman Harris was born on 18 June 1938 in Pasadena, California, and was one of the prime movers in the California R&B scene. Classically trained on violin and piano by 'an old Russian Jew by the name of Abraham Goldfarb',[143] he listened to gospel at first and came later to R&B and modern jazz. While at John Muir High School he formed a doowop group called the Squires: Harris on piano, Dewey Terry on guitar. They had a regional hit with 'Sindy' in 1955. It almost broke nationally when Alan Freed played it on the radio. In 1957 they left the Squires to form a group called Don and Dewey. They recorded for Specialty, the label that discovered Little Richard, a similar-sounding high-energy R&B. As with many many black songwriters, white cover bands sold many more records than they did. Dale and Grace had a hit with 'Leavin' It All Up to You' in 1964, a cleaned-up version without the devastating majesty of Harris's ahead-of-its-time soul singing. The Righteous Brothers apparently swiped their act wholesale.

Harris decided to use his classical training in an R&B context. First of all, the violin needed amplifying. The way he did this perfectly evokes the raw and soulful sound he achieves:

[141]The Persuasions, *Acapella*, 1970, Straight STS1062.
[142]Various, *Zappéd*, 1969, Bizarre/Reprise PRO368.
[143]Quoted by Ray Townley, 'Sugarcane . . . Got Da Blues', *Down Beat*, 9 May 1974, p. 13.

I took a cartridge off a record player, taped the crystal to the wood of my violin, attached a shielded wire, and plugged it into an amp![144] It was before Diamon came out with a pickup mike, around '63.[145]

Don and Dewey recorded with violin once – a searing cover of Joe Liggins's 'Pink Champagne' – but Specialty released it only in the wake of Harris's violin playing on *Hot Rats*. Sonny Bono (of Sonny and Cher) recorded Harris playing violin on Rush Records: 'Soul Motion'. When Zappa played it on the radio,[146] segued from the UK Subs' 'I Live in a Car', he was amazed to find that listening to it with headphones allowed him to discern a barely audible horn section. Zappa found Don Harris by hunting the LA waterfront district for the Johnny Otis Roadshow, the recently resurrected vehicle for the Godfather of R&B. Born of Greek immigrants (Otis is a contraction of Veliotes) in 1921, Johnny Otis became black by cultural adoption, marrying a black woman called Phyllis and leading a black swing band in the 40s. Buddy Holly was not the first white to play Harlem's Apollo; Johnny Otis was. He discovered a whole roster of R&B talent (including Esther Philips, Jackie Wilson, Hank Ballard and Little Sylvia, who wound up setting up the 80s rap label Sugarhill) and pioneered the postwar paring down of the big band into a small electric combo that ushered in R&B. Zappa copied his trademark moustache from Johnny Otis – a significant homage.[147] The Kent album credited to Snatch and the Poontangs was actually by Otis and points to the roots of Zappa's obscenities in the R&B underground and the African tradition of the 'signifying monkey'. Otis's book *Tell It to the Lambs* (1965) also showed a highly developed racial and political consciousness. Otis had been out of the scene for a while, but re-emerged with *Cold Shot*[148] – its direct, funky drive has much in common with *Hot Rats* and the Mothers when in R&B mode. Otis also produced an outstanding R&B/soul album for Harris called *Sugarcane*[149] with funky psychedelic songs and ambitious instrumental workouts called 'Funk and Wagner' and 'Take It All Off'. Well into John Coltrane and drugs (he had his

---

[144]Jim Dawson, sleevenote, Don and Dewey, *Bim Bam*, 1985, Ace CH151.
[145]Quoted by Ray Townley, 'Sugarcane . . . Got Da Blues', *Down Beat*, 9 May 1974, p. 39.
[146]Frank Zappa, *Star Special*, BBC Radio 1, 27 January 1980.
[147]'Nobody's ever asked me,' he said to Michael Bloom. 'I thought it looked so good on bluesman Johnny Otis, so I grew it.' 'Interview with the Composer', *Trouser Press*, February 1980.
[148]Johnny Otis Show, *Cold Shot*, 1969, Kent KST534.
[149]Don 'Sugarcane' Harris, *Sugarcane*, 1969, Epic E30027.

Down Beat interviewer sharing joints), Sugarcane made the cultural transition from R&B to hippiedom with no difficulty.

Once Zappa 'rediscovered' Don Harris for *Hot Rats*, John Mayall obtained his services for recordings and tours. Sugarcane Harris was a great success in Europe.

> It's funny, man, the response I get in Europe as compared to over here. They'll scream and shout so much that I can't get off the stage. I guess they're familar with the violin. In fact, violin is a very European instrument. And hearing it played so differently, it's a gas to them. They say, 'Wow, the things that can be done with the violin!' And it opens up the field for a whole lot of other violinists.[150]

Ornette Coleman makes a similar point when asked why he often uses white bass players – the European thing for strings. Sugarcane can relate to the most recent musical developments, as was shown by his contributions to the great LA punkharmolodic band Tupelo Chain Sex in the 80s. Despite his early 70s success, Sugarcane's dislike of being on the road has consigned him to obscurity. It's a shame, because there are not many musicians who can combine a classical background, gospel singing, electronics, R&B and extended post-Trane modal jazz in a single blast.

HOT RATS

Zappa's solo album *Hot Rats* was basically a collaboration with Ian Underwood. Recorded entirely on the West Coast between August and September 1969 (at three studios: Whitney, TTG and Sunset, where Art Tripp had overdubbed percussion for *Uncle Meat* and the Wild Man Fischer albums), its fulsome, real-time sound was a different universe from the dadaistic surprises of *Uncle Meat*. Underwood's 'organus maximus' supplied a glossy, powerhouse drive that is reminiscent of the swinging jazz of organists like Jimmy McGriff and Shirley Scott. Big, professional production gave Zappa's eccentric tunes a new glamour and the record raised a lot of interest. Whereas *Uncle Meat* appealed to European avant-rock musicians, *Hot Rats* showed jazz and studio players how rock excitement could be used to showcase chops. Without Zappa's purposefully eccentric melodies and fine ear for fresh instrumental combinations, such 'fusion' became as over-

---

[150]Quoted by Ray Townley, 'Sugarcane ... Got Da Blues', *Down Beat*, 9 May 1974, p. 13.

blown as progressive rock (it ended up as the academic definition of jazz, the MOR soundtrack for TV and film and anyone from Berklee School). Tom Scott, whose ubiquitous studio and film work came close to defining the commercial sound of the 70s, was evidently impressed by *Hot Rats*. In the sleeve notes to *Rural Still Life*[151] he declares that 'the Mothers is my favorite rock and roll group' and names a song 'Freak In'. He uses the same drummer – John Guerin – as Zappa used on *Hot Rats* and his saxophone catches the 'cartoon jazz' rawness of Ian Underwood's playing. On *Tom Cat*[152] he went one better and got in bassist Max Bennett as well as Guerin (and used the same graphics artist – David B. McMacken – Zappa had used for *200 Motels* and *Overnite Sensation*). When people say that *Hot Rats* sounds like TV themes they are probably hearing back an echo that, via Tom Scott, was sounded by Zappa in the first place. Of course, Zappa was defining something that was already in the air. Roger Kellaway (who, like George Duke, had spent time with the seminal Don Ellis big band) recorded some proto-*Hot Rats* rock-jazz as early as 1967, with *Spirit Feel* (produced by Richard Bock)[153] and a collective of West Coast sessioneers called Spontaneous Combustion produced *Come and Stick Your Head in* in 1968.[154] As the percussionist Gary Coleman – who participated in a Zappa concert at LA's Shrine Auditorium – noted:

> In general the idea was to combine jazz and rock, but rather than have them occur one after the other in juxtaposition, to try and get *both* of them going in layers. Maybe there's a little influence from Charles Ives or Zappa and the Mothers, but the basic idea was a collage type of effect. When we did all this in early 1968 I hadn't heard Frank's new group, and I was surprised when I did hear it, because it's very similar.[155]

The rock heaviness in these early rock-jazz experiments, though attractive, tends to a kind of rugged stasis – *Hot Rats* managed to create a sense of movement. Zappa's music did not come from nowhere: it solved musical problems posed by 'chops with long hair'.

Like the tale of eating shit on stage, the idea that *Hot Rats* is

---

[151]Tom Scott, *Rural Still Life*, 1969, Impulse! AS9171.
[152]Tom Scott and the LA Express, *Tom Cat*, 1974, Ode 77029.
[153]Roger Kellaway featuring Tom Scott, *Spirit Feel*, 1967, Liberty LBS83061E.
[154]Spontaneous Combustion, *Come and Stick Your Head in*, Flying Dutchman FDS102.
[155]Quoted by Frank Kofsky, sleeve note, Spontaneous Combustion, *Come and Stick Your Head in*, Flying Dutchman FDS102.

Zappa's only 'good' album is one of the few 'facts' about Zappa to have penetrated rock consciousness, especially in England (as Zappa notes in his book[156]). Lester Bangs, whose insistence on 'real-rock' virtues often expressed itself in hostility to Zappa, praised its lack of 'self-indulgence' in Rolling Stone.[157] Apart from the professional, straight-ahead sound, the attraction lies in the lack of interruptions: no musique concrète, no live chaos, no Suzy Creamcheese, no nonsense. Although uncredited, Johnny Otis was in on the sessions, exhorting and playing tambourine, and there is a rocking R&B-roadshow lilt to the beat. 'Peaches en Regalia' showcases the parodic pomposity that later informed tunes like 'Penis Dimension' and 'Regyptian Strut'. There is a lot of cunning multi-tracking – the CD issue restored some embellishments vinyl could not cope with – but the overall effect also has some of the seamless quality of West Coast cool jazz.

'Willie the Pimp' itself is based on a classic blues riff, though one that requires crisp execution (as Aynsley Dunbar proved with his dismal cover version[158]). Zappa overtracks rattle-and-chain percussion, but these are not like Art Tripp's Dadaistic clockwork; they contribute to the groove. Max Bennett – veteran of the Stan Kenton orchestra – plays fluid walking bass (Bennett played on every track apart from 'Peaches' which used Johnny Otis's son Shuggie). Zappa's guitar solo – making maximum use of wah-wah – was his best-recorded showcase so far. You can hear him make mistakes and then incorporate the erroneous directions in his line:[159] cutting-edge stuff. 'Son of Mr Green Genes', a version of Uncle Meat's 'Mr Green Genes' (on the lines of monster movies like Son of Godzilla), speeds up the riff and cooks. 'Little Umbrellas' has delightful acoustic bass from Max Bennett and a mysterious, intricate score that hides all kinds of wilful Nancarrowisms in its loping swing. Those used to the way Zappa writes for voices can hear a splenetic wit in the contrasting textures given succeeding choruses.

'The Gumbo Variations' locks a timeless stop–go funk bass-riff with a cymbal-heavy drum figure from Paul Humphrey. Zappa carefully exposes the different instruments by having some lay out at key moments (something that the lazy solo sequence in hum-

[156]Frank Zappa, with Peter Occhiogrosso, The Real Frank Zappa Book, 1989, p. 109.
[157]Lester Bangs, 'Hot Rats review', Rolling Stone, 7 March 1970.
[158]Aynsley Dunbar, Blue Whale, 1969, Charly CR30142.
[159]I'd like to thank Mike Laurence for suggesting this idea to me back in 1975.

drum jazz rarely delivers). Ian Underwood's strangled, flat-but-funky tenor rasps are a highpoint, full of the mutant-industrial-vacuum-cleaner-round-a-campfire sound later used on *Chunga's Revenge* (Beefheart is holding up a domestic model on the inner sleeve). Sugarcane Harris's solo shows how sophisticated this R&B player is, his thick, scraped tone an equivalent to John Coltrane's sheets of sound. The jazz term 'cooking' – coined to describe building up a rhythmic sweat – could have been made to describe the climaxes on *Hot Rats*: Harris's violin and Underwood's organ actually sound like bubbling saucepans and whistling pressure-cookers.

'It Must be a Camel' is another of Zappa's tunes whose floating harmonies bring him into the orbit of John Carisi and cool jazz. Jean-Luc Ponty's break (too short to be deemed a solo), ushered in with some intricate Varèse-like percussion from Zappa, has his instantly recognizable sound, as if the violin notes are melting and running down the music: a taste of collaborations to come.

Hot Rats is full of evident virtuosity and clear climactic solos: the workouts on 'Willie the Pimp' and 'The Gumbo Variations' may not go on surprising the listener after twenty years in the manner of *Uncle Meat*, but to those unused to the tendency of modern art towards hermetic form, it is a treat. Everything is recorded and played at full tilt: this lack of reticence and denial made it popular (*Money*, it should be remembered, goaded listeners with promises of heavy rock, only to mock them). There is humour in the arch manner in which tunes and arrangements introduce strange chasms into the music, but the beat does not let up. Released in 1970, it got to 99 in the American charts. Zappa pronounced it 'another flop'.[160] The album was dedicated to Dweezil, born to the Zappas in late 1969.

THE MOTHERS SPLIT

In late 1969 Zappa officially disbanded the Mothers. Announced over dinner after the Canadian tour, the split so surprised Art Tripp he 'almost threw up'.[161] It was a matter of economics: Zappa had been guaranteeing the Mothers a regular income and he did

[160]Frank Zappa, with Peter Occhiogrosso, *The Real Frank Zappa Book*, 1989, p. 109.
[161]Julian Colbeck, *Zappa: A Biography*, 1987, p. 107.

not want the expense any more. Band members would be re-employed for specific projects. Roy Estrada and Art Tripp wound up in Captain Beefheart's Magic Band under the names Orejon and Ed Marimba. Although he was in his anti-Zappa phase, saying things he later retracted, Beefheart made some interesting points (and puns).

> You see, Art Tripp was in music college for eight years. And when he got out and found that he was just cutting up cadavers, when he realized that he was just being an Igor for Frank Zappa, I guess it was quite a shock to him, to come from music college and realize that all they're doing is paying homage to people that aren't living. I'm interested in who's living.[162]

Estrada also joined Lowell George's Little Feat. Jimmy Carl Black formed a band named after one of his sons – Geronimo Black – playing the kind of heavy soul-R&B the Soul Giants had originally adopted.[163] Bunk Gardner played reeds and their slide guitarist Denny Walley joined the Mothers in 1975. Zappa performed live a few times with Don Harris and Ian Underwood, billing the group as Hot Rats, including a much-bootlegged show at the Olympic Auditorium. To replace Art Tripp, Zappa called up Billy Mundi and Aynsley Dunbar, John Mayall's drummer, whom he had met in Belgium. Max Bennett played bass. *Hot Rats* showed everyone what Zappa could achieve without his first group: he was looking for musicians who could develop this new music. Two of these were Jean-Luc Ponty and George Duke, both of whom came from the world of jazz.

JEAN-LUC PONTY

Jean-Luc Ponty was born in Avranches, France, on 29 September 1942. His family were musicians and he left school at thirteen to devote himself to violin six hours a day. He studied violin at the Paris Conservatoire and won top awards, but was also attracted to jazz; many of the pre-eminent bop players, including Bud Powell, Kenny Clarke, Johnny Griffin and Dexter Gordon, were living in Paris in the late 50s. He started playing jazz on clarinet and tenor saxophone, which may explain the way his violin seems

---

[162]Captain Beefheart, quoted by Ben Edmonds, 'The Answer is Blowing in the Wind: More Kites', *Zigzag*, No. 14, August 1970, p. 38.
[163]Geronimo Black, *Geronimo Black*, 1972, Uni UNLS127.

to breathe like a reed instrument. However, in order to achieve the facility to jam with the likes of Bud Powell he switched to violin, putting to use his accumulated years of study. Stephane Grappelli was of course the primary influence, but he later listened to Stuff Smith, then Miles and Coltrane. A recording in 1963 with drummer Daniel Humair and bassist Henri Texier[164] shows someone who has definitely graduated from copying Grappelli, and he is already playing his distinctive long, drooping lines. He later recorded with German keyboardist Wolfgang Dauner; both bop[165] and free.[166] He also participated in a series of *Violin Summits* organized by the German jazz critic Joachim Berendt. It was during a tour of the States in 1969 that he met up with George Duke and Frank Zappa. After he left Zappa in 1973 – in acrimonious circumstances that mean that Ponty is the only musician for whom Zappa has no good words to say at all – Ponty played on two records for John McLaughlin's Mahavishnu Orchestra and then released *On the Wings of Music*.[167] Like many of the musicians seeking to capitalize on the exposure Zappa had given them, it emptied out musical statement in place of predictable virtuosity: a shame, because Ponty's technique was second to none and his playing had great character.

GEORGE DUKE

Born in San Rafael, California, on 12 January 1946, George Duke imbibed jazz as part of his upbringing: his mother took him to see Duke Ellington when he was four. At seven he was playing gospel piano and Les McCann tunes, acknowledging Miles Davis's early 50s turn towards soulful roots. He studied piano and trombone at high school and received a bachelor's in composition from San Francisco Conservatory in 1967 and a master's from California State University. He had a residency at the Half Note club in San Francisco between 1965 and 1967. In the late 60s he led his own vocal group, which he called the Third Wave and also backed such jazz luminaries as Dizzy Gillespie, Bobby Hutcherson (who played vibes on Eric Dolphy's *Out To Lunch*) and Harold Land,

[164]Jef Gilson/Jean-Luc Ponty/Jean-Louis Chautemps, *Œil Vision*, 1964, Spalax SPX6836.
[165]Jean-Luc Ponty, *Sunday Walk*, 1967, MOS/BASF BAP5070.
[166]Wolfgang Dauner, *Free Action*, 1967, MPS CRM624.
[167]Jean-Luc Ponty, *On the Wings of Music*, 1974, Atlantic 18138.

the West Coast tenor player. His 1966 album *Presented by the Jazz Workshop*[168] has the MOR-tinged quality of a lot of West Coast jazz, with Latin rhythms and easy flugelhorn (played by David Simmons), but you can already hear the distinctive Duke keyboard style: rich improvisations rooted in a kind of smiling, benign funk. In 1968 he toured with Don Ellis, who introduced him to electronic keyboards. Duke first played with Jean-Luc Ponty at an LA nightclub after hearing a record of his and plying him with letters and tapes.

> When we started playing at Donte's neither of us had heard the other, yet we got so excited with each other's playing we didn't want to stop. It was a once-a-lifetime feeling. Jean-Luc heard things in my playing that inspired him and often I wanted to simply lay back completely, and just listen to that violin wail.[169]

Duke's style is evidently derived from McCoy Tyner, adopting the full chords and harmonic expansion of Coltrane's pianist, and this suited Ponty's Traneish violin. They both were keen to 'rock out' (relate to the heavy rock music that was happening all round them), so it was hardly surprising they got on well. The music they made together is exciting, a kind of rock-jazz with a much more spontaneous feel than what later emerged as 'jazz-rock'. On *Live in Los Angeles*[170] they play with a linear suaveness that is different from the blocky integrity of the original Mothers, but which Zappa adopted when he started using Duke and Ponty (especially evident on *Overnite Sensation*). Ponty appears to quote 'King Kong' in his solos on 'Foosh' and 'Contact' and Duke seems to quote from his solos on *The Grand Wazoo*, but that is of course Zappa's knack of making everything his musicians play seem utterly his own. After joining the Mothers for a tour in 1970, Duke went to work for Cannonball Adderley (1971–2). His predecessor in the great soul-jazz combo was Joe Zawinul; after an important spell with the Mothers (1972–5), George Duke was to follow Zawinul into the technical (and economic) stratosphere of fusion.

At first Duke had problems relating to Zappa's requirements. An early rehearsal required him to play triad triplets: he was

---

[168]George Duke, *Presented by the Jazz Workshop 1966 of San Francisco*, MPS JS077.
[169]Quoted by Philip Elwood, sleeve-note on Jean-Luc Ponty with the George Duke Trio, *Live in Los Angeles*, 1969, Sunset Records SLS50232.
[170]Jean-Luc Ponty with the George Duke Trio, *Live in Los Angeles*, 1969, Sunset Records SLS50232.

disgusted ('I mean, I'm from jazz!'[171]), but later appreciated this lesson in non-self-seriousness. George Duke played keyboards in an edition of the Mothers that has become an acknowledged favourite: his combination of harmonic education, blues, funk feel and good humour was ideal. Zappa commented:

> I don't think I was playing that well there, but it was real easy to play with George, especially, because he's such a great musician and you can always count on him to play something musical behind you. It's not just a matter of having a keyboard player to blast his way through and be obnoxious during somebody else's solo. George would always seem to support whoever was doing a solo, whether it was Napoleon, me, or whoever. I don't always get the same sensation from other accompanists I've worked with since that time.[172]

While still with Zappa, Duke recorded for the German MPS label, a species of 'funny funk' that predicted much 80s M-Base 'innovation', and then stretched out into P-Funk and fuzak, becoming ubiquitous as an arranger and producer. He was prominent in organizing the band for the Mandela release concert in 1990 and contributed a track to *Tutu*, the late-period Miles Davis masterpiece.[173] Triad piano triplets seem to have been a way out of the jazz ghetto.

KING KONG

Ponty and Duke were big news on the West Coast. Gerald Wilson, the noted arranger for Duke Ellington in the late 40s, featured both on his *Eternal Equinox*;[174] the title-track, appropriately enough, was John Coltrane's 'Equinox'. Engineer Richard Bock played Zappa acetates of Jean-Luc's playing. Zappa jammed with Duke and Ponty at Thee Experience in Los Angeles in September and got Ponty to add his distinctive notes to 'It Must be a Camel' on *Hot Rats*. The duo were considered saleable, recording six albums in quick succession. Zappa suggested a project and, under Ponty's name, managed to realize some pretty advanced compositions on the record *King Kong*.[175] Despite naming the main

---

[171]Quoted by Steve Metalitz, 'An Underexposed Mother', *Down Beat*, 7 November 1974, p. 43.
[172]Quoted by Bill Milkowski, 'Frank Zappa: Guitar Player', *Down Beat*, February 1983, p. 16.
[173]Miles Davis, 'Backyard Ritual', *Tutu*, 1986, Warners 925490.
[174]Gerald Wilson, *Eternal Equinox*, World Pacific ST20160. Many thanks to Richard Cook for this £2 bargain.
[175]Jean-Luc Ponty, *King Kong*, 1970, Liberty LBS83375.

section 'Music for Electric Violin and Low Budget Orchestra' after his request for a ninety-seven-piece orchestra was turned down, things were not too bad economically. Buell Neidlinger, the bass player who made his name with Cecil Taylor, was flown in from Boston as 'the only man I can think of who could play the bass part on the long piece' (evidently beyond the rock capabilities of Jeff Simmons). Notorious for his abrasive outspokenness as a white proponent of the 'black revolution in jazz', one awaits the Zappa–Neidlinger dressing-room tapes with impatience. A tentet conducted by Ian Underwood played behind Ponty. It starts out with a section derived from the 'marching' music of Stravinsky's *Soldier's Tale*, Donald Christlieb's bassoon tackling the characteristically irregular ostinato. Zappa takes flourishes and descensions to ridiculous extremes and orchestrates moments like those he achieved with electric instruments on 'Eric Dolphy Memorial Barbecue'.[176] 'Duke of Prunes' provides the main theme for the first set of variations, and as with 'Idiot Bastard Son' on side one, its sick, wasting melody is ideal for Ponty's sound. Both composer and player seem to be wreaking revenge on the tonal conformity of the academy. With hindsight, undistracted by cartoon dazzle, the listener can identify many of the ideas of 'The Adventures of Greggery Peccary'. Patches of chaos are beautifully orchestrated, typical Zappa-moments that transcend the distinction between avant-garde abstraction and humorous sound effects (the humour of 'America Drinks and Goes Home' is made still broader with a musical rush-to-the-toilet joke). 'The Legend of the Golden Arches' from *Uncle Meat* sounds still more like Stravinsky in this arrangement. Where Stravinsky's jazz pieces are often held back by the classical pusillanimity of his interpreters, Zappa makes use of the extra-classical abilities of his musicians, especially George Duke's groovy, Fats Wallerish piano, which romps into Zappa's strange harmonies with keyboard-professor glee.

'King Kong', 'Idiot Bastard Son' and 'Twenty Small Cigars' are given jazz arrangements, with a snorting Underwood tenor solo on the first and debonair outings by Ernie Watts on the others. Sleeve notes were by a bemused Leonard Feather, giving us the charming incongruity of someone trying to view a Zappa recording session as a 'jazz date'. He shores up Zappa's credibility

---

[176] *Weasels Ripped My Flesh*, 1969.

by having him mention bassoonist Don Christlieb's track record interpreting Karlheinz Stockhausen. On Ponty's 'How Would You Like to Have a Head Like That' Zappa guests on guitar, using such a processed sound that, despite quoting a few licks from his 'Willie the Pimp' solo, he sounds as if he is on another planet from the musos in the studio.

Burnt Weeny Sandwich

Burnt Weeny Sandwich marked a return to the more ponderous sound of the Mothers of Invention. There are no credits, but a photograph inside the inner gatefold shows the Mothers at work on stage: Bunk Gardner on bass clarinet, soprano, alto and baritone saxophones, Ian Underwood on alto, Don Preston on keyboards, Billy Mundi and Art Tripp on percussion, Jimmy Carl Black carrying a doll (the bass player is turning his back, but it is probably Roy Estrada). The cover montage by Cal Schenkel perpetuates the organic–inorganic anxieties of *Uncle Meat* by nailing motor parts and cogwheels next to dummy hands (which have the same red-varnished nails as the hand which enters the frame just below the M of Mothers on *We're Only in It for the Money*). A nail and dripped red paint inevitably recall the crucified Christ, though here it is not wood the suffering subject is nailed to but a machine. On the reverse Ian Underwood bites a rubber tyre, exclaiming, 'God! this *is* a tasty little sucker!', extending the blasphemy by recalling communion. Teeth bouncing back from their prey, art resistant to ingestion: teeth again a symbol for the uncommercial commodity, the undesirable desire. Within the gatefold, photographs are arranged by John Williams as a complex series of thought bubbles, a visual equivalent to the hallucinatory way Zappa's mixing focuses on the thoughts of different participants (Williams used the technique again for *Joe's Garage* in 1979). In a frenzied blur of soprano playing, Bunk Gardner is thinking of Black, Estrada and Zappa listening to the playback; behind them is a picture of a white woman sucking a black woman's nipple, perhaps a psychoanalysis of a jazz saxophonist's thoughts while playing.[177] However, Gardner's playing is merely being thought (or remembered) by Don Preston. Just as dreams-within-dreams

---

[177]Cropped in the CD booklet.

do not become any less 'real' or intense, the thoughts-within-thoughts of the graphics imply no hierarchies.

The serious/trivial contrast of *Uncle Meat/Ruben* here surfaces as a sandwich: the record places complex music between 'appetizing' tracks: 'WPLJ' and 'Valarie'. 'WPLJ', a song in praise of white port and lemon juice, was sung by Zappa and Lowell George.[178] It was a cover of a single by the Four Deuces (the B-side, 'Love Lies Limp' was also sung by Lowell George and appeared on *You Can't Do That on Stage Anymore Vol. 5*). 'Valarie' was a brokenhearted ballad, a precursor of 'Lucille Has Messed My Mind Up'. Both were a far cry from the *heaviness* expected of the Mothers. 'Igor's Boogie' ushered in a suite of music that has some of the mocking quality of *Uncle Meat*, though the reverberant 'real-time' sound makes the music both cruder and more powerful. 'Theme from Burnt Weeny Sandwich' is faded in and out to abstract sound effects which dramatically contrast close-miked abrasion with the public sound of the band: the full presence of the Mothers and Zappa's guitar reduced to one sound among many. 'Holiday in Berlin' appears as an instrumental, its tipsy voicings bringing out an apt cabaret flavour. Zappa's riposte to the students is contained in an answer to a heckler complaining about the uniforms of the security guards attempting to return the audience to their seats: 'everyone in this room is wearing a uniform and don't kid yourself', which produces gasps of acclaim from the crowd. As pointed out in the sleevenote to *200 Motels*, 'Holiday in Berlin, Full Blown' later became 'Semi-Fraudulent/Direct-from-Hollywood Overture' on *200 Motels*. Listeners familiar with the vocal version have the usual inability to disentangle the tune from memories of its words. Zappa's woodwind arrangement has Underwood's alto solo sleazing over the bierkeller flutes and clarinets to maximum drunken effect. Rather than thinking along academic lines (vertical harmony versus horizontal rhythm) Zappa is contrasting each as timbre in the manner of Varèse: the dull thunder of the bass guitar and the dead beat of the drums separate out from the 'melody' instruments in the most intriguing way. In his solo Zappa strums up and down the mode like a bouzouki player, one of the most pungent statements of his claustrophobic melancholy. 'Aybe Sea' (a maritime title to set by 'The Purple Lagoon', 'The Ocean is the Ultimate Solution', 'Flam Bay' and 'Naval Aviation in Art') is

---

[178]According to George, interviewed by Andy Childs, 'The Exploits of Lowell George', *ZigZag*, No. 50, March 1975, p. 24.

closely worked and shows Zappa's debt to Conlon Nancarrow, a flamenco flamboyance in the guitar adding Mexican heat. The piano conclusion makes full use of Underwood's Mozartian lightness of touch, a haunting moment to compare with Walter Gieseking playing Debussy.

On the record, side two gratifyingly carried on with Underwood's playing (on the CD the two tracks merge into one). 'Little House I Used to Live in' – perhaps a counterblast to Frank Sinatra's patriotic 'The House I Live in' – is an arrangement of a tune originally played by the Mothers as 'Return of the Hunchback Duke'. It is difficult to explain to people appalled at Zappa's vulgarity the peculiar pleasure of being reminded of Flo & Eddie's rumbustious 'mud shark' routine when hearing these beautiful chords. The offensiveness seems a small thing to suffer compared to the exhilarating *incongruity* of the project/object, an incongruity doubly effective because it is less Zappa's problem than a feature of the watertight compartments in which we are told to live. Social satire at the level of the notes themselves.

Sugarcane Harris soars in for a majestic solo. Sugarcane plays with absolute conviction across Zappa's arrangement, the kind of across-the-spectrum intensity that led to Coltrane dispensing with everything but drums on *Interstellar Space*[179] and saxophonist Evan Parker to perform unaccompanied. Frank Zappa's closing organ solo milks the instrument's bagpipe possibilities against a pipe-band beat. 'Valarie' eschews the histrionics of the original by Jackie and the Starlites (where the singer bursts into tears), providing a conclusion both stately and sonorous.

WEASELS RIPPED MY FLESH

Burnt Weeny Sandwich showed what the Mothers could achieve playing a set of compositions in the studio at one time: *Weasels* was a collage of the Mothers in concert and in studios from all over, a brilliant and complex record, a 'sampler' for the fabled twelve-record set, *The History & Collected Improvisations of the Mothers of Invention* that finally became the *You Can't Do That*

[179]John Coltrane, *Interstellar Space*, 1967, Impulse GRP11102.

on Stage Anymore series.[180] The title of *Weasels* was borrowed from a cover story in *Man's Life* magazine for September 1956, showing a man knee-deep in a swamp, fighting a pack of weasels.[181] The cover of the record, one of Zappa's most striking concepts, was executed by Neon Park. Best known for his work for Little Feat, it was the *Weasels* cover that first impressed Lowell George.

> He was hitching one afternoon, and a friend of mine picked him up on one of the sidestreets of Hollywood. He cruised over to my house and I met the man, because I admired his cover of *Weasels Ripped My Flesh*. I mean . . . an electric weasel . . . whatever next![182]

Neon Park uses blocky oilpaints with a deadpan ugliness reminiscent of René Magritte. His epic detachment is particularly suitable for grandiose statements about the banal (such as his *City Lights* cover for Dr John[183]): *Weasels* was his masterpiece.

Uncle Meat had played with the idea of a materialism that would see through the flesh to teeth and the skull. In Park's painting a smiling, Brylcreemed salesman-type rips open his face with an electric-razor/weasel (which looks terrified) as if to lay bare his teeth. It is a shocking image, one used by Trotsky when talking of the horrors of the First World War:

> It was as if a man, to prove that his pipes for breathing and swallowing were in order, had begun to cut his throat with a razor in front of a mirror.[184]

Public Image Limited had a story about a man who shaved himself to death in the tabloid satire that accompanied their first single 'Public Image'.[185] Eliding the idea of social conformity and danger, the detourned shave is the perfect image for those who believe that regular 'virtues' – cleanliness, conformity, patriotism – are the most murderous virtues of all.

Much of the music on *Weasels* was cued by Zappa's hand signals. As Lowell George joked on 'German Lunch',[186] the

---

[180]The projected album titles were: *Before the Beginning, The Cucamonga Era, Show and Tell, What Does It All Mean, Rustic Protrusion, Several Boogie, The Merely Entertaining Mothers of Invention Record, The Heavy Business Record, Soup and Old Clothes, Hotel Dixie, The Orange County Lumber Truck* and *The Weasel Music*, Jerry Hopkins, 'Mothers' Day Has Finally Come', *Rolling Stone*, 18 October 1969.
[181]*Society Pages*, No. 7, 30 September 1991, p. 53.
[182]Lowell George, quoted by Paul Kendall, 'Little Feat', *ZigZag*, No. 63, August 1976, pp. 11–12.
[183]Dr John, *City Lights*, 1978, Horizon A&M SP732.
[184]Leon Trotsky, *My Life: An Attempt at an Autobiography*, 1929, trs. Joseph Hansen, 1971, p. 602.
[185]Public Image Ltd, 'Public Image', 1978, Virgin VS228.
[186]Frank Zappa, *You Can't Do That on Stage Anymore Vol. 5*, 1991.

Mothers were very *disciplined* (at this point they all erupt with a 'poo-err!' which is very like their stage antics). The idea of abstract vocalese was central to dada. James Joyce's polyglot *Finnegans Wake*, though syntactically based on English/Irish, used a freedom derived from dada experiments like Hugo Ball's 'jolifanto bambla ô falli bambla', a response to the humour of international misunderstandings in a Zurich overrun with refugees (Joyce was impressed that a request for orange squash was interpreted by a waiter as 'life is rubbish' – '*Leben ist Quatsch*'). As national differences erupted into the horrors of the First World War, technically advanced art experimented with non-specific linguistics. The masterpiece of such sound-poetry was written by Kurt Schwitters: his *Ursonate* was presented at the Bauhaus in 1924.[187] The Mothers' experiments in pure voice theatre encode a similar optimism: internationalist, new, revolutionary.

The opening track continues the (oft-submerged) discussion of authoritarianism that flows through Zappa's work. In 'German Lunch' George played the part of a German customs officer: here he uses the same accent to say,

> Years ago in Germany when I was a very small boy, there was a lot of people standing around on ze corners, asking questions – why are you standing on the corner? acting ze way you act, looking like you look? why'd you looked at me? zey asked me . . .[188]

He seems to be referring to the Nazis and their xenophobia.[189] One of the Mothers starts up a wonderfully irrelevant atonal operatic bawl and Lowell's muttering is lost in the music. With a title track consisting of two minutes of painful feedback, *Weasels*, like all Zappa's records, plays with the idea of inflicting rubbish on the audience. The 1984 'Broadway' spectacular *Thing-Fish* had a chorus of Mammy-Nuns who piss on the audience; 'D'ja get any on ya down dere?' asks Thing-Fish.[190] This phrase is used as the title for the opening track of *Weasels*: 'Didja Get Any Onya'. The CD has an extended version, including a section of 'Charles Ives',[191] but the great moment is the segue into Little Richard's 'Directly from My Heart to You', where the Mothers' abstract play with voice and instruments suddenly coalesces as rock-solid

---

[187]Expertly performed by Eberhard Blum, *Ursonate*, 1992, Hat Hut CD6109.
[188]Frank Zappa, 'Didja Get Any Onya', *Weasels Ripped My Flesh*, 1969.
[189]I'd like to thank Andrew Blake for suggesting this idea to me back in 1974.
[190]Frank Zappa, 'The Mammy Nuns', *Thing-Fish*, 1984.
[191]Frank Zappa, *You Can't Do That on Stage Anymore Vol. 5*, 1991.

172

R&B – a feat achieved since only by Last Exit. Don Harris sings and plays on this devastating tract of soul: the contrast with the music before it, combined with its authentic grit, is a bravura demonstration of Zappa's ability to slice and dice genre. No other white rock band got close to this weighty blues feel.

'Prelude to the Afternoon of a Sexually Aroused Gas Mask' simultaneously nods to Debussy and Zappa's childhood memories of the gas masks the family had to keep at the ready in case of spillage from the tanks of mustard gas at Edgewood Arsenal. The introduction has a bruising sense of sonic event, Varèse-style 'objective' processes unfolding in outer space. The Mothers caterwaul with a finesse honed by singing falsetto doowop. On *Stage Vol. 5* Ian Underwood played Mozart to 'snorks' supplied by Dick Barber; here Motorhead snorks over discreet lounge organ. Zappa uses his sardonic phrase from 'Trouble Everyday' – 'blow your harmonica, son' – as if this abuttal of sophistication and crudeness approximates to the blues. 'Toads of the Short Forest' was a tune pioneered at Studio Z.[192] Here, Zappa points out the various time signatures being played and describes Ian Underwood's alto as 'blowing its nose'. This willingness to characterize as *physical* the sounds that many in jazz were associating with transcendent spirituality, the saxophone outreach of John Coltrane, Pharoah Sanders and Albert Ayler,[193] is characteristic. The same impulse led to the major critiques of scientology in *One Size Fits All* and of John Coltrane's interpreters in *Zoot Allures*. 'Get a Little' ends side one with some relaxed, business-as-usual guitar.

'Eric Dolphy Memorial Barbecue', a studio cut, is one of Zappa's most exciting pieces of music. Apart from the Jimi Hendrix Experience, no one else has used the sound of rock instruments with such a fresh ear for surprise, such a sensitivity to the timbral weight of cymbals and toms and bass and guitars. 'Oh No' included the lines

Oh no I don't believe it
You say that you think you know the meaning of love
You say love is all we need
You say with your love you can change

---

[192]Played by Zappa on his Australian radio show in 1975.
[193]Also of course, Archie Shepp, though his talk tended to politics rather than the cosmos. He was also the only one to play with Zappa – Frank Zappa, 'Let's Move to Cleveland – Solos 1984' *You Can't Do That on Stage Anymore Vol. 4*, 1991.

All of the fools, all of the hate
I think you're probably out to lunch[194]

Before the Sex Pistols made this Americanism current with 'Pretty Vacant' in 1977, the phrase 'out to lunch' sounded quite lunatic – unless the listener discovered the existence of the classic record by Eric Dolphy.[195] In the same way that Zappa could open the rock listener's ear to Varèse, Zappa's use of Dolphy enabled his fans to discover jazz.

Originally from the West Coast, Eric Dolphy came up with Chico Hamilton in the late 1950s, playing his cool cocktail of Latin rhythms and jazz. Dolphy's velocity and technique were the next step from Charlie Parker, especially impressive as he played so many instruments: alto, flute and bass clarinet (his technique on the latter still makes even the best current proponents sound under-practised). Migrating to New York, he became a member of John Coltrane's band (his Bird-derived rhythmic stringency evidently fascinated the tenor player), and recorded with the pianist Andrew Hill. In 1964 Dolphy cut a record that sounds like the kind of music Charlie Parker might have recorded if he had worked with Varèse. He called it *Out To Lunch*.

It is an apt title, because the music, with its metric disassociation, in which the players' lines revolve round each other with some of the freedom of Alexander Calder's mobiles, has a kind of controlled lunacy about it, as if the conscious mind is on vacation. By comparison, Cecil Taylor's hard-edge modernism, by cutting all metric ties in favour of pulse and emphasis, is more straightforward. The combination of time and abstraction makes for surreal jazz: it also freed the percussionist to create percussive events on the level of Varèse (this was probably happening in bebop with Kenny Clarke's 'bombs', but recording technology was such that it is difficult to hear bebop drummers in terms of Varèse's futuristic universe). Vibes player Bobby Hutcherson adopted Thelonious Monk's out-of-time funk, revelling in the extra freedom from harmony granted by a less chordal instrument (*Out To Lunch*'s opener, 'Hat and Beard', was a tribute to Monk). Modernist space, improvisation and funk: *Out To Lunch* addressed precisely the issues Zappa was working at. Both Dolphy and Zappa wished to transcend the black/classical divide, a divide that uses racism

---

[194]Frank Zappa, 'Oh No', *Weasels Ripped My Flesh*, 1969.
[195]Eric Dolphy, *Out To Lunch*, 1964, Blue Note 84163.

174

to confirm a more fundamental split: that between heart and head, between body and soul, the metaphysical polarities perpetuated in a social system that relies on the divison of labour. The aesthetic issues ran in parallel because of a shared social attitude – art's utopian promise of an undivided world.

More concretely, Zappa learned from *Out To Lunch* how to set a soloist in a conducive instrumental environment. Sal Marquez's trumpet solo on 'Big Swifty'[196] emulates Freddie Hubbard's combination of wholesome hard bop propulsion and wiggling Ornette-ish quandaries;[197] on 'Echidna's Arf' and 'Don't You Ever Wash That Thing'[198] Ruth Underwood played very like Bobby Hutcherson.

'Dwarf Nebula Processional & Dwarf Nebula' is a slice of mocking gnome music spliced to *musique concrète* blits and blats from the Apostolic sessions for *Money*. Its combination of comedy and abstraction again comes close to the spirit of *Out To Lunch*. The last tune on that album, 'Straight Up and Down', reminded Dolphy of 'a drunk walking'.[199] It was emulated by 'America Drinks and Goes Home' on *King Kong*, which 'suggests a bunch of drunks leaning up against a wall', according to Zappa.[200]

Although short, 'Oh No' is the key song to *Weasels*. Its remarkable Weill-on-Broadway melody is sung with consummate sincerity and grace by Ray Collins. As well as mentioning Dolphy's album, the words directly challenge the shibboleths of the love generation.

> Oh no I don't believe it
> You say that you think you know the meaning of love
> Do you really think it can be told?
> You say that you really know
> I think you should check it again
> How can you say what you believe will be the key
> To a world of love?
> All your love – will it save me?
> All your love – will it save the world
> From what we can't understand?
> Oh no I don't believe it
>
> And in your dreams

---

[196]Frank Zappa, *Waka/Jawaka*, 1972.
[197]Though in interview Zappa denied any such intention; talking of the solo he said, 'I had no control over that', interview with the author, 23 October 1993.
[198]Frank Zappa, *Roxy & Elsewhere*, 1975.
[199]Quoted by A. B. Spellman, sleeve note, Eric Dolphy, *Out To Lunch*, 1964, Blue Note 84163.
[200]Quoted by Leonard Feather, sleeve note, Jean-Luc Ponty, *King Kong*, 1970, Liberty LBS83375.

You can see yourself
As a prophet
Saving the world
The words from your lips
I just can't believe you are such
A fool[201]

The words 'Do you really think it can be told?' echo the *Freak Out!* sleeve note, 'I always wondered if I could write a love song.' In interviews Zappa has said that he believes in 'real love', but hates the Madison Avenue version: he is aware of how easily representation of moral values disguises hypocrisy. 'Love' is a value everyone will agree on, so it is useless as a critical concept – the very title of 'Oh No' asserts this negative dialectic. 'Will it save the world from what we can't understand?' is the characteristic challenge of radical Freudianism as it insists on the need to explore the unconscious, to articulate urges rather than smother them in well-meaning pieties. It is the question the gay S&M movement asks of feminism and its condemnation of pornography.

The last words of 'Oh No' segue into a driving Mothers instrumental: 'The Orange County Lumber Truck'. On *Roxy and Elsewhere*, 'Son of Orange County' has Napoleon Murphy Brock sing the last seven lines of 'Oh No', with Zappa using the Richard Nixon quote 'I am not a crook' to give it a political twist. Naming the 'Oh No' jam on *Weasels* after Orange County – Nixon's conservative power base – was uncannily prescient. After three minutes of heavy playing the sound is cut, there is mocking laughter and the listener is plunged into the *Weasels* title track, two minutes of blood-curdling feedback recorded in Birmingham, England. When it is over, Zappa is careful to let us hear the audience shouting for more: his music may lacerate just like the weasel-razor (or Kafka's machine), but it also engages our desires.

[201]Frank Zappa, 'Oh No', *Weasels Ripped My Flesh*, 1969.

CHAPTER 3
GLAM ROCK AND THE MARKET

THE MOTHERS IN 1970

Ernest Fleischman, the LA Philharmonic's executive director, expressed an interest in playing some of Zappa's scores. This led to the formation of a temporary Mothers as the organizers did not think that a straight orchestral show could fill UCLA's Pauley Pavilion – 11,000 seats (though Zappa claimed the gate on the day was 14,000). The concert was held on 15 May 1970, conducted by Zubin Mehta, one of four 'Contempo Seventy' concerts. It was a sell out. Mel Powell, serial composer and Dean of the School of Music at Cal Arts, withdrew his piece – *Immobiles 1–4* – in protest at this incursion of pop. Unabashed, Zappa did his best to make the audience relax, with statements like 'Hit it, Zubin!' He also did his parody of Jim Morrison's oedipal drama 'The End'.[1] George Duke played keyboards and Jeff Simmons played bass. Simmons was another reason for Art Tripp's move to Beefheart: the ex-Cincinnati percussionist was unlikely to warm to an aspirant rock star who said of the orchestral musician, 'Those dudes are really out of it, man. It's like working with people from another planet.'[2] Without Contraries, no progression.[3]

Zappa now juggled his musicians, and Don Preston and George Duke and Ian Underwood became interchangeable. Both Ponty and Duke shine on 'King Kong' and Duke dusted off his trombone for 'Penis Dimension'.[4] Duke's funky keyboards add a new slant to 'Pound for a Brown', contrasting with Underwood's cool organ.[5] The new streamlined velocity made Zappa's eccentric tunes

---

[1]According to *Disc and Music Echo*, 30 May 1970. This routine later appeared as 'Tiny Sick Tears', 1969, *You Can't Do That on Stage Anymore Vol. 4*, 1991.
[2]*Time*, 1 June 1970.
[3]William Blake, *The Marriage of Heaven and Hell*, 1790, p. 3.
[4]Frank Zappa, *Disconnected Synapses*, 1970, *Beat the Boots #2*, 1992.
[5]Frank Zappa, *Tengo Na' Minchia Tanta*, June 1971, *Beat the Boots #2*, 1992.

and guitar playing still more piquant. For vocalists, Zappa needed a new element.

THE TURTLES

With the decline of the social movements associated with the counter-culture – the defeat of the Parisian students and workers in 1968, the ebb of the anti-war and black power movements that had rocked the ruling class in the States – underground rock found itself in a strange situation. The herald of social change, it found itself being used to shift product and cement the consumerist order. One response was to keep up the show of bombast and revolt, but astutely milk the market (Led Zeppelin were merely the first of a queue of bands to do so), the other to use irony and self-confessed 'decadence' to rid rock of its now preposterous ambition (beautifully achieved by T Rex with Marc Bolan's revamp of Chuck Berry-type rock 'n' roll). Zappa, as ever, revelled in the contradictions.

Mark Volman and Howard Kaylan attended the concert at the Pauley Pavilion and visited Zappa backstage, saying that the Turtles had split and that they would like to work with him. *Freak Out!* had included a quote from 'a noted LA disk jockey' (whose name was Lord Tim[6]): 'I'd like to clean you boys up a bit and mold you. I believe I could make you as big as the *Turtles*.'

A high-school band from south LA, the Turtles began as message-oriented folk band called the Crossfires, playing a weekend residency at Reb Foster's Rebellaire Club on Manhattan Beach (just south of Santa Monica). Along with two former distributors for Liberty Records, Foster formed the label White Whale. Changing their name to the Turtles, the Crossfires were their first signing. Their big break was a slot opening for Herman's Hermits at the massive Rose Bowl in Pasadena. In early 1966 they followed the Byrds into the charts with a Dylan cover, 'It Ain't Me Babe'. Synonymous with airy, melodic chart-fodder, they represented everything the Mothers growled at. In early 1967 they had a massive hit with 'Happy Together', a song of rousing pop inanity. A certain satirical strain can be marked in their output towards the late 60s (on the single 'Sound Asleep' the 'zzzzz' after the

[6] According to Frank Zappa, interviewed by Michael Goldberg, 'Frank & Moon', *Creem*, Vol. 14, No. 6, November 1982.

words 'keeping my mind on you' sounds more like jerking off than snores): they were evidently discovering long hair and drugs. Working with Zappa would allow them to shake off their twee image. For Zappa, contemptuous of the elevated cultural niche rock was aspiring to, the symbolism of working with the diametrical 'opposite' of the underground was a too good to miss (rather like Malcolm McLaren forming the 'sun, sea and piracy' pop band Bow Wow Wow after the proletarian realism of the Sex Pistols). They also had extremely good falsetto voices.

Volman and Kaylan named themselves after two Turtles roadies, the Phlorescent Leech and Eddie, and became perfect glam rock stars to put under the microscope. The Flo & Eddie edition of the Mothers was designed to expose backstage events at precisely the time when rock was turning into a patronizing spectacle of cosmic proportions. Whereas the original Mothers were presented as some kind of alternative – a band of genuine freaks who would improvise 'genuine' atonal piano backstage – Flo & Eddie were presented as sweaty, horny pop stars whose main interest was getting laid. It marked the first of the series of provocations that has caused fans and critics to part company with Zappa's 'project/object'. With hindsight it can be seen that much of the 'surrealness' of the Mothers was in fact an orchestration of their everyday lives: their Chicano subculture, though, gave them a mysterious exoticism that Flo & Eddie's vulgarities completely lacked. What Flo & Eddie had, though, was a guileless energy that has its own charm – particularly to those fans who, arriving later, did not have the chance to feel 'betrayed'.

Aware of such criticisms, Zappa defended himself live on the radio when talking to Martin Perlich in 1972.

> Unfortunately some people have a peculiar attitude towards things of a glandular nature connected to things of a musical nature and they say, Well, music is so far as here and glands are way down there. We can't really get them together and they're hypocritical and then they turn around and a group that comes in and doesn't sing overtly about those things but *couches* their language a little bit and does it with a little choreography, they think that's great and that's real rock 'n' roll and I maintain there's no difference, we were just honest enough to go out there and say, This is this and that's that and here you are and respond to it and the response to it was, I'm hip but of course I am offended.[7]

The attack on people who denigrate the body (glands) at the

[7]Frank Zappa, *Leatherette* (a scrappy bootleg with bits of *Läther* and some interview filler).

expense of the mind (music) is part of Zappa's sexual materialism, his refusal of Platonic and Christian idealism. Using Flo & Eddie to do this was a masterstroke. It is interesting how appropriate and suggestive is Zappa's conversational imagery. A group that 'couches' their language evokes the sofa of the suburban drawing room: his orchestration of the band's backstage antics were designed to trash such comfortable illusions. There was also the sofa routine, famously available on the early bootleg *Pootface Boogie*, but now in the public domain thanks to the *Beat the Boots #2*, in which Mark Volman acted the primal cosmic maroon sofa, a theme later taken up in 1975 with *One Size Fits All*.

Zappa was particularly excited with their ability to sing harmony. He explained that he did not mind cutting down on the original Mothers' spontaneous interactions (spontaneity was restricted to guitar solos in 'Wino Man', 'You Didn't Try to Call Me' and 'Call Any Vegetable' and band solos in 'King Kong'), because he could now hear his tunes properly.

> For the first time the melodic content of those songs can come out – 'cause I was never a good singer, and Ray Collins, at the time he was the lead singer, was not very fond of harmonizing with anybody else. So we couldn't get into any of the stuff that we're doing now: the three and four part vocals, which I enjoy doing. I don't mind singing those same songs over and over again.[8]

Howard Kaylan, though, felt that he and Volman contributed commercial appeal to Zappa's music.

> Frank tried for a long time with just his music, but now, through his music plus the acting and dialogue, he's creating his environment and, as a result, he's reaching a larger audience. He felt it was silly to have just a small band of committed, active followers when, by changing his approach just a bit, he could attract a larger audience. Then, when they're not looking, he can give them what he wanted to play in the first place. As well as keeping most of the hardcore Mothers' audience that he already had, Frank has now got a larger, younger following; when Mark and I joined the group we were playing 2,000 seater halls, but now we're selling out places with a capacity of 10,000.[9]

As the heady days of rock counter-culture receded into the past it became obvious that rock was again a temporary cultural phase associated with adolescence. It was Zappa's ability to relate to that audience throughout the 70s and 80s that ensured that, whatever

---

[8]Quoted by Mike Bourne, 'An Interview with Frank Zappa', *Down Beat*, 1971, p. 36.
[9]Howard Kaylan, *ZigZag*, No. 25, July 1972, p. 15.

the difficulties he encountered in terms of corporate promotion and distribution, his music still kept a connection to the marketplace: precisely the situation required for his ambivalent, contradictory art to flourish.

CHUNGA'S REVENGE

Chunga's Revenge was the record that introduced Volman and Kaylan. Billed as a Frank Zappa album, each track had its own line-up. Half the songs read 'with THE PHLORESCENT LEECH & EDDIE (vocals)' in upper case. Aynsley Dunbar played drums throughout, except on 'The Clap', an excellent piece of clattering 'dental' percussion overtracked by Zappa himself (venereal disease and vagina dentata – subjects he would return to) and 'Twenty Small Cigars'. As well as their usual instruments Ian Underwood played guitar, Sugarcane Harris played organ, George Duke played trombone. Max Bennett played bass on the jazzier numbers, Jeff Simmons on the rock ones.

'Transylvania Boogie' provided a vampiric vamp for some of Zappa's most Eastern-sounding guitar. The title referred to the homeland of Dracula, but also that of Béla Bartók. Born in Nagyszentmiklos on the Hungarian side of the border with Romania, in 1881, Bartók pioneered the study of folk-music, especially that of his homeland, where the majority of the musicians are gypsies. It is possible to trace gypsy music and dance back to religious cults in Egypt and India: Bartók provides a crucial model for composers seeking to break out of the limitations of the Western tradition. The complex time-signature and Dunbar's shimmering cymbals are exotically bohemian, though there is a distinctly sci-fi flavour to Zappa's wah-wah guitar sound. The mid-section has him plucking irrational runs with some of Nancarrow's delirium: he builds to a peak note and then moves into an irresistible boogie, Underwood's organ grooving behind, Dunbar contributing a new fluency.

The title tune furthers the gypsy theme, with Ian Underwood's wah-wah alto saxophone caste as the 'mutant gypsy industrial vacuum cleaner' illustrated in Schenkel's magnificent gatefold illustration. In *Money* Zappa had mocked the neophyte hippie's attempts to be 'a gypsy on his own'; as usual Zappa is sensitive to the implications of borrowing culture. Since the nineteenth-century fad for gypsies (well illustrated by Bizet's *Carmen*) they have come to represent everything that is erotically alluring about non-Western culture (the term bohemian actually means gypsy). Far from pretending that *Chunga's Revenge* is giving us unmediated 'natural' vitality, Schenkel places the dancing vacuum cleaner in a recording studio.[10] He could have been illustrating a point of Adorno's.

> In an effort to preserve a feeling of contrast to contemporary streamlining, culture is still permitted to drive about in a kind of gypsy wagon; the gypsy wagons, however, roll about secretly in a monstrous hall, a fact which they do not themselves notice.[11]

The claustrophobia of Zappa's guitar on 'Chunga's Revenge' perfectly expresses this idea. 'Twenty Small Cigars', one of Zappa's subversive slices of cocktail jazz, seems to have been recorded at the *Hot Rats* sessions. Too gentle for inclusion on that album, it has some beautiful playing from Max Bennett on double bass and John Guerin on brush drums. 'The Nancy and Mary Music' used audience shouting as a textural element and George Duke doing 'vocal drum imitations', carrying on the tradition of the Mothers' free-form vocalese. In his electric piano showcase Duke demonstrates that he is fully on top of Zappa's freaky-funk concept, winding up with some excellent atonalities.

As noted by Zappa on the sleeve, the vocal tunes 'preview' the story from *200 Motels*: 'Road Ladies' was about groupies and 'Rudy Wants to Buy Yez a Drink' denounced musicians union bureaucrats. 'Tell Me You Love Me' and 'Would You Go All the Way' were vehicles for Flo & Eddie's hysterical falsettos. The words of the latter mix monster movies, cinema gropes and the sexual frustration of American servicemen, themes returned to on *Roxy & Elsewhere* with 'Cheepnis' and the appearance of Brenda – who had been stripping at the Edwards Air Force Base – in the 'Bebop Tango' dance contest. 'Sharleena' is a slow, swinging,

---

[10]The studio could be seen as a mobile situated *inside* a wood, as the moon can be seen looming over some straggly pines at the end of a forest track. More likely, though, both moon and trees are simply a painted backdrop (cf. 'zeroes/someone painted' in *The Torture Never Stops*, the flats of *200 Motels*, or Zappa's statement 'where the illusion becomes too expensive to maintain they will just take down the scenery' – see below 'The output macrostructure', Chapter 5: Bizarre to DiscReet). The idea that such bohemian rhapsody is confined to the studio agrees with Gail Zappa's description of the painting: 'If you look in the artwork, there's the vacuum cleaner dancing around in the studio, a gypsy dancer', interview with the author, 28 October 1993.
[11]Theodor Adorno, 'Culture and Administration', 1978, trs. Wesley Blomster, *The Culture Industry*, ed. J. M. Bernstein, 1991, p. 102.

tear-stained ballad in the vein of the Starlites' 'Valerie': Jeff Simmons proves himself a nimble and sensitive bass player and George Duke finds a highly original, vocalized growl sound for his organ. Ian Underwood's grand piano stylings over the multitracked horns are truly splendid. *Chunga's Revenge* is generally dismissed as 'transitional',[12] but for those plugged into the project/object it hits many musical and conceptual targets. The jazz bible *Down Beat* recognized as much and in December 1970 made Zappa Pop Musician of the Year.

200 MOTELS

Financed by United Artists to the tune of half a million dollars, *200 Motels* was shot using innovative video technology at Pinewood Studios in England with the Royal Philharmonic Orchestra and a Mothers consisting of Flo & Eddie, Ian Underwood, George Duke, Aynsley Dunbar, Jimmy Carl Black and the bassist Jim Pons (another ex-Turtle). Jeff Simmons quit half-way through and was replaced by Martin Lickert, Ringo Starr's chauffeur. Ruth Komanoff, the classically trained percussionist who had played on *Uncle Meat*, appeared as Ruth Underwood (she had married Ian in the meantime). Theodore Bikel, the Austrian folk singer managed by Herbie Cohen, was the uniformed MC, Ringo Starr played Larry the Dwarf and Keith Moon a nun and trainee groupie. Motorhead Sherwood appeared in a love duet with Dick Barber in his vacuum-cleaner outfit. Don Preston continued the monster routine he had started in the *Uncle Meat* film, concocting and swigging vile foamy liquids (a monster movie version of the effects of beer). The groupies were played by Lucy Offerall (GTO Miss Lucy) and Janet Ferguson. Pamela Miller played the Rock and Roll Interviewer. Tony Palmer, who had told Herb Cohen about the video technology, was to have done the mixing but Zappa took over. Palmer reacted by writing an article in the *Sunday Observer* colour supplement that described the whole venture as decadent rock chaos.

He missed the point. Zappa is aware that all sound is ideology: meaninglessness is strictly impossible. In fermenting the situations of *200 Motels* Zappa carefully constructed a suggestive

---

[12]For example, Dominique Chevalier, *Viva! Zappa*, 1985, p. 65.

scrapheap. Jeremy Prynne described the agenda of *200 Motels*
when he wrote

> Rubbish is
> pertinent; essential; the
> most intricate presence in
> our entire culture; the
> ultimate sexual point of the whole place turned
> into a model question.[13]

200 Motels was shot in seven days after only five days of rehearsal:
Pamela Miller commented 'the movie seemed to be over in seconds
because Frank was using videotape'.[14] It was filmed on four simultaneously running video cameras. One third of the 320-page script
was never shot. A device that could cast resin copies of real
objects was used to create 'obviously fake' props, reminiscent of
the plasterwork household objects pop-artist Claes Oldenburg
sold from an art gallery in his *Store Days* project. In one scene,
Flo & Eddie, dressed up like the two groupie protagonists, move
in sequence between dummies of the groupies. This satirizes
Hollywood 'entertainment' and its fondness for formation dancing, the grotesque tendency to standardization in mass culture.
The words to 'A Nun Suit Painted on Some Old Boxes' list the
usual requirements made of music: 'Some old melodies', *'four-
four'*, 'aura' (these derive from a routine that had the Mothers
arguing about musical progress[15]). All elements which mass-production makes problematic.

> That which withers in the age of mechanical reproduction is the aura of
> the work of art ... the technique of reproduction detaches the repro-
> duced object of tradition ... the instant the criterion of authenticity
> ceases to be applicable to artistic reproduction, the total function of art
> is reversed. Instead of being based on ritual, it begins to be based on
> another practice – politics.[16]

200 Motels is about the destruction of meaning involved in

[13]Jeremy Prynne, 'L'Extase de M. Poher', *Brass*, 1971, p. 23.
[14]Pamela Des Barres, *I'm with the Band – Confessions of a Groupie*, 1987, p. 218.
[15]Frank Zappa, 'Don Interrupts', 28 October 1968, 'Mystery Disc', *The Old Masters Box Two*,
1987. The routine also surfaces in the *Uncle Meat* film and as 'Progress?', 1968, *Ahead of Their
Time*, 1993.
[16]Walter Benjamin, 'The Work of Art in the Age of Mechanical Reproduction', 1936, *Illuminations*, trs. Harry Zohn, 1968, pp. 215–18.

repetition:[17] the disorientation of touring where every motel and city and venue merges into a single blur. It is evident that we never leave the physical space of the studio. The flimsiness of the sets acts like a pointer to the shoddiness of life in the real world. The Royal Philharmonic Orchestra is housed in a concentration camp, with lookout towers and barbed wire, picking up the theme of incarceration and extermination which threads its way through Zappa's work. 'Arbeit Macht Frei' was set in wrought-iron letters over the entrance to Auschwitz; 'Work liberates us all' is written up over the entrance to the *200 Motels* camp. As Adorno said, 'All post-Auschwitz culture, including its urgent critique, is garbage.'[18] Just before 'Magic Fingers' explodes on to the soundtrack Ringo Starr – dressed up to look like Frank Zappa – explains:

> Many of these musicians study for years, learning to play the violin, for instance, only to be rewarded with a humdrum job in the fourth row of a symphonic string section. That's why the Government have constructed, at great expense, this Experimental Reorientation Facility, to find a way perhaps to retrain these useless old musicians with their brown fiddles and little horns, give them a trade, a reason to exist in the modern world, a chance of a happier, more productive life. Some will enter the military, some will learn shorthand and some will disappear in the middle of the night on a special train they're sending in. It's the only way, really, to bring about the final solution to the Orchestra Question. I am sure that many of us realize that a pop group can earn a vast amount of money compared to these other kinds of musicians. That's why the Special Government Agencies for Mass Response Programming and Psychological Stultification prefer to treat them in a more subtle manner. They know, just as many of you vigilant and thoroughly upstanding citizens have discovered for yourselves: the power of pop music to corrupt and putrify the minds of world youth are virtually limitless.

To put such a speech in the mouth of a Beatle has a special resonance. The satire is ambivalent. In 1971, defending himself against accusations of sarcasm and cynicism, he talked in disbelieving tones of the usual manipulation at rock concerts.

> I wish that the audience would understand that by not giving them any special treatment, by not bending over backwards to do something on their behalf, they're being treated as *adults*, and being given the benefit

---

[17]In many ways the case made for the subversive use of repetition in Andy Warhol can be applied directly to Zappa. The way radical interpreters are challenged by Warhol's own actions is highly reminiscent of the acrobatics of poodle play. See Peter Gidal, *Andy Warhol – films and paintings – The Factory Years*, 1971.

[18]Theodor Adorno, *Negative Dialectics*, 1966, trs. E.B. Ashton, 1973, p. 367.

of the doubt. You know I think it's really pandering to the lowest common denominator in the audience to go out there and just . . . I don't know how to describe it, what most groups do.[19]

The Mothers are in the camp too: it portrays the limits to art and free creativity under capitalism. At the end the credits are scrolled over accountant paperwork for the film. In its production *200 Motels* was constrained by the tormenting calipers of time and money, but instead of letting them pinch him, Zappa uses them to tweeze us: the constraints of the film are used as a metaphor for *our* own everyday lives. He challenges us to see our own activities as meaningless banter in fake bars, policed by guards making sure we lead a 'productive' existence.

Zappa also developed his personal mystique: having Ringo Starr in a Zappa costume means that audiences immediately alert themselves to Zappa's 'real' appearances with whispers of 'that's him!' At the introduction Ringo is asked by Rance Muhammitz if he was forced by a 'crazy person to insert a mysterious imported lamp into the reproductive orifice of a lady harpist . . . would you do it?' 'Yes!' shouts Ringo. Towards the end of the film Howard Kaylan denounces this 'crazy person'.

> He's making me do all this, ladies and gentlemen! I wouldn't be doing it if it weren't for this. You notice all this material I've been glancing over toward my left? Well I'll tell you the reason for that, ladies and gentlemen: HE is over there, HE is over on the left, HE is the guy that is making me do all this shit, right over there! Now, all through this movie, every time we've been on stage, I've had to look there in that direction, right? You saw it, you know! Well, that's 'cause HE is over there and I gotta watch him for signs, he jumps up and down like a jackass. I can't even believe the guy sometimes! But, we gotta watch him, after all, we said, it's Frank's movie: now, we're THE MOTHERS, but it's still Frank's movie, he rented the studio, had all these cheesy sets built – it's so *moche*![20]

There is a scene in the movie where the Mothers are being bugged by Larry the Dwarf (dressed as Zappa). They are trying to revive Jeff (played by Martin Lickert): 'we've got to get him back to normal before Zappa finds out and steals it and makes him do it in the movie!' Flo & Eddie joke about credits for 'special material' (which they did eventually receive). The film's finale is mixed with a close-up of Zappa's brown eye. This is the theme

[19]Quoted by Mike Bourne, 'An Interview with Frank Zappa', *Down Beat*, 1971, p. 36.
[20]Frank Zappa, 'Strictly Genteel', *200 Motels*, 1971.

that was taken up later on with the Central Scrutinizer in *Joe's Garage*: the artist as all powerful mediator, shaping reality like God. In the context of *200 Motels*, with its fake sets and cheap gags, the status of this exalted figure is dubious: a parody of power. The implosion of meaning this triggers throws us back to the non-represented reality of the lives of the participants, and to our lives too. As with any pop-art happening, in rubbish the incursions of the real.

When Rance Muhammitz asks the groupies if they will trade what lies behind the curtain for what Howard Kaylan has in his pants we get a glimpse of what lies behind the curtain: a Nazi in uniform. This is the Reichian idea that sexual repression lies at the root of fascist psychology. The turmoil of *200 Motels*, its play with the elements available in the five days, indeed makes of rubbish 'the/ultimate sexual point of the whole place turned/into a model question'.[21] Building junk sculpture out of the banal sleaze around him, Zappa made of *200 Motels* a social microcosm: it turns work and sex, limits and desire into specific questions unresolvable in abstract moral terms. The chaos and competition of life on the road becomes a metaphor for capitalism: people reduced to puppets within a schema they cannot understand. *Playground Psychotics*,[22] a double album of music and documentary recordings of the Flo & Eddie band issued in 1992, shows how close to the reality of touring *200 Motels* actually cleaves.[23]

The double album *200 Motels*, released by United Artists, was the first time Zappa was able to put his symphonic ideas on show (score pages were proudly displayed in the accompanying booklet). 'This Town is a Sealed Tuna Sandwich', in which the Mothers explore a dead mid-western town, has some of the tawdry power of Brecht/Weill's *Mahagonie City*. It was a chance for absurdist opera: 'A Nun Suit Painted on Some Old Boxes' is a definitive parody of post-*Pierrot Lunaire* atonal writing for soprano. The Top Score Singers soprano's trained enunciation of 'stumpy grey teeth' and 'dental floss' is truly bizarre. The words achieve surreal provocation equal to the music's insane intervals – something distinctly lacking in the tame literary texts used by even the best Darmstadt composers. The segue into 'Magic Fingers', a heavy *tour de force* with a devastating live-on-film guitar solo by

[21]Jeremy Prynne, 'L'Extase de M. Poher', *Brass*, 1971, p. 23.
[22]Frank Zappa, *Playground Psychotics*, 1992.
[23]See 'Playground Psychotics', Chapter 13: Webern vs. Televangelism.

Zappa, is the sort of contrast no other twentieth-century musical force has been able to achieve. An animation designed by Cal Schenkel and executed by Charles Swenson has a score ('Dental Hygiene Dilemma') that walks a tightrope between Tex Avery and Krystof Penderecki. In it an angel and a devil (who says 'bollocks' to peace and love – six years before the Sex Pistols) battle for Jeff Simmons's soul. The devil wants him to dump Zappa's 'comedy music' and play commercial heavy rock. The soundtrack album of *200 Motels* was delayed until the completion of the film, so that it appeared after the first live showcase for the Flo & Eddie band, *Fillmore East.*

After the filming,[24] the Mothers – along with the Royal Philharmonic and the Kings Singers – were scheduled to appear at the Royal Albert Hall on Monday, 8 February, a gambit in order to pay the RPO scale for rehearsals for *200 Motels*, as rehearsals for a recording session without a live performance have to be paid at full recording rates. The concert was cancelled by Albert Hall manager Marion Herrod due to 'lyrical obscenity'. Zappa offered to rewrite the lyrics but was turned down. He made the most of the publicity, holding a press conference outside the locked building with banners reading 'Albert Hall cancels concert claims obscenity'. *Time Out* criticized the apathy of the audience collecting their refunds and printed a 'Penis Dimension' badge to wear at the next Albert Hall concert.[25] The *Daily Telegraph* printed an editorial saying 'nobody will much regret the cancellation' (putting the description 'concert' between quotes). Zappa sued the Albert Hall. The proceedings became a celebrated court case in 1975 and the subject of some entertaining pages in *The Real Frank Zappa Book.*[26] It was admitted that Zappa was capable of altering the lyrics in the time available after Zappa took a mere five minutes to come up with new lines for 'Shove It Right In'. As Mick Farren reported in *New Musical Express:*

> Zappa started to render. The results were startling. Lines came out like: 'The places that she goes / Are filled with guys from Pudsey / Waiting for a chance / To buy her Sudsy'.
> This was the moment, reading in deadpan voice, when Zappa the witness came closest to Zappa the performer. The judge, however, seemed confused.
> 'Pudsey?'

---

[24]Not before, as Michael Gray has it in *Mother! is the Story of Frank Zappa*, 1985, p. 104.
[25]'Penis Dimension Meets the Fathers of Convention', *Time Out*, 21 February 1971, pp. 17–22.
[26]Frank Zappa, with Peter Occhiogrosso, *The Real Frank Zappa Book*, 1989, pp. 120–37.

Zappa's counsel attempted to help.
'Pudsey. Yorkshire, m'lud. It's produced some fine cricketers, I believe.'[27]

Despite such droll humour, the establishment closed ranks against this counter-cultural purveyor of filth and Zappa lost the case.

FILLMORE EAST JUNE 1971

There were enough cuts from the *Hot Rats* sessions on *Chunga's Revenge* to satisfy Zappa's 'alternative' music fans: *Fillmore East June 1971* raised the first mutterings of discontent. Whereas 'Little House I Used to Live in' was an extended instrumental work-out on *Burnt Weeny Sandwich*, it now became the introduction to a routine in which Flo and Eddie told the story of the use of live fish in the sex act, rock folklore that originated with the Vanilla Fudge – 'The Mud Shark'. 'Bwana Dik' portrayed the musicians' secret thoughts: as Zappa explained in court during the Albert Hall trial, 'Bwana' is what the 'guy with the box on his shoulder' calls the white man in jungle-movies – it means boss.

> In every band there is some member of the band who, during the course of the touring, gets the opportunity to entertain more girls than the other members of the band. It is like winning a contest. If we carry this concept to a ridiculous extreme, this person could be awarded the *title* of 'Bwana Dik'. The song deals with the fact that each in his own way, each member of the group, secretly believes he is 'Bwana Dik' and the song attempts to show how foolish this is.[28]

Continuing the tradition of jolting 'rocking-out' expectations, the record originally broke the big guitar solo on 'Willie the Pimp' between the two sides. 'Peaches en Regalia' makes maximum use of Flo & Eddie's vocals: they had no problem relating to its intricate absurdities. There was no George Duke, and Bob Harris was drafted in as a third keyboard player besides Underwood and Preston. The latter had a delirious mini-moog feature on 'Lonesome Electric Turkey'. Aynsley Dunbar's drums – a sophisticated version of Keith Moon's 'hit everything' mania – are excellent throughout, especially on the 'hit single' 'Tears Began to Fall'.[29]

---

[27]Mick Farren, 'What is a Groupie? Asked His Lordship', *New Musical Express*, 26 April 1975, p. 28.
[28]Frank Zappa, with Peter Occhiogrosso, *The Real Frank Zappa Book*, 1989, pp. 124–5.
[29]Mothers of Invention, *Tears Began to Fall*, 1971, Reprise K14100.

On the single release, credited for some reason to Billy Dexter rather than Frank Zappa, Zappa's introduction to the song is uncut[30] and the flip side is a blistering guitar solo named 'Junior Mintz Boogie', evidently recorded live at the same concerts as the album.

With *Fillmore East* Zappa debuted the ambivalent crowd-pleasing which has allowed him to survive twenty years of audience miscomprehension. Over the years, you can hear a world-weariness creep into his onstage voice along with the adoption of sarcastic standard showbiz greetings and phrases. To some, the mere presence of these tics cancels any value in the music – to others, it merely adds another layer to the project/object. Those who, goaded by Zappa's tone and subject matter, dismissed *Fillmore East* as mere pop music, make a big mistake: it is still incredibly disciplined, with virtuosic setting of words, highly creative arrangements and playing, all delivered with explosive energy. It is doubtful if he could have tapped this energy if he had not written about subjects so close to the hearts of his musicians and singers. The fact that it is two *men* having such upfront sexual negotiations with each other adds to the shock (though one of them is 'acting' a female groupie). The joke is that this was real rock opera, but its enthusiastic vulgarity meant that 'critical' opinion ignored its technical achievements in favour of such overblown nonsense as *Tommy* and *Tales of Topographic Oceans*. At a time when the great commercial ploy was to deny interest in the 'commercial' single charts (a tendency Zappa had pioneered), the routine has the groupies insisting that the salivating rock stars play 'Happy Together', the Turtles idiotic hit (which they do, with great gusto).

> There was one groupie I write about on the *Fillmore* album who wouldn't fuck the guy unless he sang her his hit single first. That's a true story. It happened to the two guys in the Turtles who were in the band with me at the time. She wanted them to sing 'Happy Together'. And they did; you know, because why not?[31]

Fillmore East's raw rock sound also dismayed those who saw some kind of higher moral value in violins and bassoons. It is in fact

---

[30]A symbolic moment in my own initiation to Zappography was when, attempting to find out if the single was a different version from that on *Fillmore East*, Danny Houston asked me if I could remember if Zappa introduces the song on the album. We both laughed and I realized he was not, after all, a trainspotter.

[31]'20 Questions: Frank and Moon Unit Zappa', *Playboy*, November 1982, p. 217.

the *absurdity* of such quaint instruments that attracts Zappa, not any perceived superiority in classical instrumentation. With *Fillmore East* Zappa trashed the pretensions of rock to herald a new era. He has been in trouble for that ever since – especially among those whose careers are bound up with insistence on rock's edifying aspects. The music, though, was great. On 7 August another live gig was recorded, subsequently released as *Just Another Band from LA*.

DISASTERS

John Lennon and Yoko Ono guested at one of the *Fillmore* concerts. Over an Italian meal, Lennon and Zappa agreed to give each other full rights to the music. Lennon issued the results as one record of the *Some Time in New York City* double album,[32] in a reproduction of the *Fillmore East* sleeve with scribbled amendments in red felt-tip. Zappa was not pleased at the renaming of 'King Kong' as 'Scumbag' and the consequent loss of royalties. The onstage Lennon was evidently respectful of Zappa's political and underground credentials, but Zappa took umbrage at the shoddy mix by Phil Spector and the suppression of Flo & Eddie's vocal (apparently they were singing 'Put Yoko in a scumbag'). Yoko's artless screaming during Zappa's solo is irritatingly egotistic and unmusical. When Zappa released these performances himself[33] the sound was much improved and Yoko Ono's banshee wailing is now framed by the Mothers in full improvisational splendour.

The winter of 1971 was a catalogue of disasters. On 4 December 1971,[34] when the Mothers were playing at the Montreux Casino in Geneva, fire broke out during the start of Don Preston's solo on 'King Kong'. Preston stopped playing and Mark Volman joked 'fire! . . . Arthur Brown in person!' Zappa said firmly, 'If you will just calmly go towards the exit, ladies and gentlemen.' There were luckily no casualties, though the explosion of the heating system did blow some people through the windows. The event may be listened to – an audience recording – on *Swiss*

[32]John and Yoko Plastic Ono Band/Elephant's Memory, *Some Time in New York City*, 1972, Apple PCSP716.
[33]Frank Zappa, *Playground Psychotics*, 1992.
[34]Not 4 November 1972, as David Walley has it in *No Commercial Potential*, revised edition, 1980, p. 159.

Cheese/Fire![35] The whole venue was burned to the ground and £25,000 worth of equipment lost (a solitary cowbell was rescued from the cinders). Watching the fire across the lake, Deep Purple commemorated the occasion with their song 'Smoke on the Water'. The Mothers voted to continue the tour but disaster struck again. On 10 December, claiming that Zappa had 'made eyes at his girlfriend', a man called Trevor Howell pushed Zappa off the stage into the orchestra pit at the Rainbow. Zappa was knocked unconscious, received cuts on his face and head, a broken rib, a fractured leg and a paralysed arm. Howell was let out on bail and so Zappa's Harley Street clinic required a twenty-four-hour bodyguard. Zappa was in a wheelchair for the better part of a year: the leg healed shorter than the other, something referred to later in both 'Zomby Woof'[36] and 'Dancin' Fool'.[37] His crushed larynx led to the deeper voice of *Overnite Sensation*. The band broke up and Zappa's next three albums were produced from his wheelchair.

JUST ANOTHER BAND FROM LA

Originally released in March 1972, *Just Another Band from LA* documented a single night at Pauley Pavilion, UCLA, in 1971, when the Mothers performed a suite of songs and the epic 'Billy the Mountain'. 'Billy the Mountain' is full of images that register only because they trigger clichés: advertising jingles ('a large El Dorado Cadillac leased from Bob Spreene "Where the freeways meet in Downey!" '); cartoon images (Ethel the tree 'creaked a little bit, and some old birds flew off of her'); musicals (as the tornado approaches Howard Kaylan becomes Dorothy in *The Wizard of Oz* shouting 'Toto, Toto'); film frames ('when the phone rang in the secret briefcase, a strong masculine hand with a Dudley Do-Right wristwatch and flexy bracelet grabbed it and answered in a deep, calmly assured voice').

Like *200 Motels*, it invites dismissal as a pile of random rubbish, but is actually a very cunning and complex construct. What seems to be a purely surreal pronouncement by Zappa, 'the philosophical

---

[35]Frank Zappa, *Swiss Cheese/Fire!*, *Beat the Boots #2*, 1992.
[36]Frank Zappa, 'Zomby Woof', *Overnite Sensation*, 1973.
[37]Frank Zappa, 'Dancin' Fool', *Sheik Yerbouti*, 1979.

significance of a frozen beef pie'[38] actually refers to the origins of Studebacher Hoch – a conglomerate portrait of establishment political whizzkids like Richard Nixon and John Masnanian: 'He was born next to the beef pies, underneath Joni Mitchell's autographed picture, right beside Elliott Roberts's big bank book, next to the boat where Crosby flushed away all his stash.'[39]

This notion of the importance of trivia has been taken up by chaos theory (though its popularity is really to do with the way the 'butterfly effect' gives a 'scientific' explanation to the way dreams charge insignificant objects with affective power). It also relates to the importance of trivial detail in detective fiction. 'Idiot Bastard Son' on *Money* and Quentin Robert De Nameland's crab-grass baby in *Thing-Fish* both explore Chandlerish themes of illegitimacy, power and corruption. Genetic mixing, itself a surrender to chance recombination of DNA, provides a subtext to this association of trivial detail and meaning. In exploring the complexities of the motivation of those in power, the paranoid political observer – particularly prevalent in the US, where the left is so weak – ends up with a rubbish-pile of incidental detail. Billy the Mountain, loosely associated both with the youth revolution (the fact that he is wanted for draft evasion gets a cheer from the audience) and the San Andreas faultline, is a subversive power that ignores such minutiae: he simply swallows Studebacher Hoch.

One Size Fits All extended the resonant political symbolism of 'Billy the Mountain': a geological cross-section of the faultline appears on the cover and Flo & Eddie's verbal free associations appear on the star map. Studebacher Hoch's method of flight – spreading Aunt Jemima maple syrup on his crotch and using the wing-power of accumulated flies to levitate his phone booth – recalls the side of rotting meat Zappa wanted to have in a shower cubicle at the Garrick Theater (it could even be a satire on electoralism, along the lines of 'eat shit – ten million flies can't be wrong'). Unlistenable for most non-fans, 'Billy the Mountain' is super-rich in conceptual continuity.

Side two of the album demonstrated the power and velocity of this edition of the Mothers in a five-song suite. 'Call Any Vegetable' is an action-packed burst, with a raw Zappa solo to rival that of *200 Motels*'s 'Magic Fingers'. 'Eddie, are You Kidding?' documents regional TV advertising and has Mark Volman declare,

---

[38]Frank Zappa, 'Billy the Mountain', *Just Another Band from LA*, 1972.
[39]Ibid.

'These pants I'm wearing are double knit. They stretch in all the right places', which gives a phallic dimension to the phrase 'one size fits all'. 'Magdalena' was the true story of a girl molested by her father, the same father–daughter eroticism that 'Brown Shoes Don't Make It' found at the heart of conservative morality.

The cover of *Just Another Band* had a message (for a change, this has been enlarged rather than cropped in the CD release): 'Any visual similarity between the cover of this and the *Uncle Meat* illustrated booklet (not to mention Ruben & the Jets) is thoroughly intentional and contains 4 secret clues.'

The Mothers are shown driving the purple-jelly Chevy that was 'attacking the Vatican' on the back of the *Uncle Meat* booklet. Zappa has a flopping dog-snout. He is lying horizontally across the backseat – his leg, complete with plaster cast, emerges on the other side, his toes snapping a 'snat' like the Jets on the cover of *Ruben*. The picture is superimposed on a burger painted by Sherm Thompson. In 1973 Ruben Guevara formed a rock 'n' roll revival band called Ruben & the Jets. Their first album[40] was produced by Zappa. The inner gatefold shows the band eating in a Tex-Mex diner: this picture was superimposed on one of the burgers on the table.

There was resentment towards Flo & Eddie for the manner in which they badmouthed Zappa to further their own careers (they signed a deal with Reprise, taking Preston, Pons and Dunbar along with them).

> The means by which they chose to promote their careers at my expense, while I was sitting in a wheelchair trying to help them get a job and a record contract, I believe to be despicable and will always think so, even though I regard Howard as a fine singer and Mark as a great tambourine player and fat person.[41]

In Schenkel's illustration Zappa is 'taking the backseat': his head looks like a glove puppet manipulated by Howard Kaylan – who is driving. Zappa's only form of expression appears to be his guitar, which is bursting out of the roof of the car as if it is his erect penis. The secret message appears to be that Zappa has lost control of the Mothers: they are now 'just another band from LA', as ordinary as junk food. All this is entirely mythical ('Billy the Mountain' was almost totally scored and required great discipline

---

[40]Ruben & the Jets, *For Real*, 1973, Mercury 1–659.
[41]Cherry Ripe, 'Frank Zappa Has No Underwear', *New Musical Express*, 17 April 1976.

in performance), as even a cursory listen to the return-to-the-Turtles pop of Flo & Eddie's solo records will attest. But it was a chance for Zappa to pin the era of groupie routines and onstage comedy to Volman and Kaylan: his next project was in a very different vein.

CHAPTER 4
MUSIC MUSIC

WAKA/JAWAKA: HOT RATS

Working from his wheelchair, Zappa began writing music for a new album. Ostensibly a follow-up to *Hot Rats*, its only common feature lay in being another personal, non-group project: the music was quite different. Recorded at Paramount Studios in LA 'under the thoughtful supervision of Marshall Brevitz', Zappa used trombonist Ken Shroyer to find first-class session players, as he had done when organizing the sessions for *Lumpy Gravy*. *200 Motels* had combined rock and classical music by contrasting them in their two extremes: *Waka/Jawaka* invented a new genre between the two. Contemporary reviewers called it jazz, but though it used jazz players and fusion sonorities, the method used to shape the (largely unscored) playing was quite different. Rock critics were not impressed. Charles Shaar Murray wrote:

> Another big downer ... It sounded like the work of a man who's just broken his leg, is held down by leg-irons, whose entire band has just walked out on him, and is feeling utterly pissed off about the whole thing.[1]

In contrast, jazz critic Joachim Berendt saw *Waka/Jawaka* and its successor as the 'culmination point'[2] of Zappa's music. Zappa's ability to project his ideas through diametrically opposed musical styles has made critical reception neither easy nor loyal.

'Big Swifty' occupied the whole of side one. The title comes from *Greggery Peccary*, the name of the advertising agency Peccary works for. The phrase suggests the streamlined polish of the music, the way it slides on to the next idea before you have fully grasped the first. The band sounds larger than its six pieces due

---

[1]Charles Shaar Murray, 'Soundz', *Oz*, No. 46, January–February 1973, p. 36.
[2]Joachim Berendt, *The Jazz Book*, 1976, p. 363.

to overdubbing and unconventional instrumental combinations. The opening bars abut a series of ideas in quick succession, each idea using contrasting instrumentation. The tension this builds is suddenly evaporated in a precipitous space of chimes and bleeps, a cartoonish version of the *Bitches Brew* cauldron. George Duke comes in with his warm, funky 'ring-modulated and echo-plexed electric piano', Aynsley Dunbar mining a rich seam of beats and fills. Bass player is session man Alex Dmochowski, billed as Erroneous. Texan trumpeter Sal Marquez uses a mute; his playing has a Spanish flavour. Zappa manages to make the instruments accelerate and decelerate in different time zones: his guitar winds up tension and Marquez releases it. The mid-section exchange between guitar and bass sounds like John McLaughlin's alone-in-space-guitar, mocking his existentialist pose with sly wit. The way Tony Duran's slide guitar solo drags against the ensemble's swing has a unique, crazy grace, notes stretching like putty.

In the last four minutes the theme is introduced, confirming intervals that the soloists have been hinting for some time. The line is actually a Zappa guitar solo transcribed by Marquez and arranged for multitracked trumpets. It catches Zappa's characteristic unforced tricksiness (a result of phrasing based on speech rhythms rather than academic subdivisions). It maintains the unreal atmosphere of Zappa's evocations – pungent, but somehow illusory. There is delightful mockery in the repetition of some restricted 'Batman' notes (compare the still more deliberate 'loop' on 'The Beltway Bandits'[3]) which returns the variations to the basic fanfare.

The flickering sensitivity of the musicians – Duke's groovy organ, Dunbar's stream of inventive fills, Marquez's chirruping trumpet – has some of the timeless feel of contemporary jazz-rock by Miles Davis. Zappa was talking appreciatively of *Nefertiti* at the time, but the music is different: his harmonic sequences are far too zany, the musical events too tightly packed. Although Miles and Teo Macero had been making records by editing together endless studio sessions, Zappa's use of the multi-track was in a different league: he is controlling every event. 'Big Swifty' was also played by the *The Grand Wazoo* and *Roxy & Elsewhere* bands.[4] There it was basically a vehicle for solos,

---

[3]Frank Zappa, 'The Beltway Bandits', *Jazz from Hell*, 1986.
[4]Frank Zappa, 'Big Swifty', 12 December 1973, *You Can't Do That on Stage Anymore Vol. 1*, 1988.

preserving only the intricate introduction and the transcribed solo (by 1974 it had been reduced to a sign-off theme[5]), indicating how many of the felicities on the record were the results of carefully selected improvisation and studio mixing.

'Your Mouth' is in the vein of songs that culminated in 'Bamboozled By Love', shocking cameos of male jealousy. The singing by Chris Peterson and Marquez makes so free with the vowels that, in the absence of a lyric sheet, it seems best to reprint the words from the *Plastic People Songbook* (which was corrected in Zappa's hand).

Your mouth is your religion
You put your faith in a hole like that?
You put your trust and [your] belief
Above your jaw, and no relief
Have I found

I heard your story when you come home
You said you went to see your sister last night
Well, you might lose a bunch of teeth
And find a funeral wreath
While you're laying in the ground
All alone

So tell me where are you coming from
With all them lines
As you stumble in at breakin' of the day
Where are you comin' from, my shot-gun say
Because he just might want to blow you away
'cause he just might want to blow you away

An evil woman can make you cry
If you believe her every time she lies
Well, you can be a big fool
If she makes you lose your cool, and so
I've got me some advice you should try

Just let her talk a little
Just let her talk a little more
Just . . . just let her talk a little more
And when she runs out of words
Just say the same thing that I told you before:

---

[5]Frank Zappa, 'Big Swifty', 22 September 1974, *You Can't Do That on Stage Anymore Vol. 2*, 1988.

> So tell me where are you coming from
> With all them lines
> As you stumble in at breakin' of the day
> Where are you comin' from, my shot-gun say
> Because he just might want to blow you away
> 'cause he just might want to blow you away[6]

In the absence of a band whose folklore he could orchestrate Zappa constructs a song out of C&W clichés. In the early 70s the West Coast was awash with a back-to-roots movement. Miss Pamela setting her sights on Waylon Jennings in *I'm with the Band* is a revealing indication of the new status of country in the rock milieu.[7] In one photograph in Miller's book the GTO's are standing arm-in-arm with the Flying Burrito Brothers. On the left, by Miss Christine, is 'Sneaky Pete' Kleinow, whose pedal steel guitar Zappa featured on the next track, 'It Just Might be a One-Shot Deal'. The talk of funeral wreaths and shotguns served as a reminder of the backward *mores* of rural idiocy at a time when the laidback country sound was becoming a craze – Kleinow was not only playing with Little Feat, but with Stevie Wonder, John Lennon, Linda Ronstadt and the Bee Gees (not that contemporary reviewers got the point: *Melody Maker* referred to 'unintelligible Scottish vocals').

'It Just Might be a One-Shot Deal' is similarly opaque, a tale of strange hallucinations sung by Marquez and Janet Ferguson (the tough-minded groupie in *200 Motels*). Jeff Simmons's Hawaiian guitar sets up a dreamy smoothness worthy of Steely Dan, but with the words

> But you should be diggin' it
> While it's happening
> 'cause it just might be
> A one-shot deal[8]

the tune derails into an aural nightmare. Such a device puts Sneaky Pete's pedal steel virtuosity in a strange light, his shiny, snaking notes suddenly aberrant and strange. His solo abruptly terminates: one of Zappa's typical shocks. Though played in real time rather than achieved with a splice, it again sounds as if the music has started to run backwards. Zappa's facetious

---

[6]Frank Zappa, *Plastic People Songbook Corrected Copy*, ed. Carl Weissner, 1977 (an edition of 2,001), pp. 306–8.
[7]Pamela Des Barres, *I'm with the Band – Confessions of a Groupie*, 1987, pp. 185–6.
[8]Frank Zappa, *Plastic People Songbook Corrected Copy*, ed. Carl Weissner, 1977, p. 310.

And see if he's brought along
A little bag for you, rant[9]

introduces 'Waka/Jawaka'. A distant cousin of Ravel's *Bolero*, it keeps up a fraudulent fanfare splendour until the last three minutes, when the arrangement is proudly peeled back to reveal Aynsley Dunbar's truly impressive simultaneous rhythms. Don Preston takes a mini-moog solo, all suggestive wriggles and gurgling runs. Zappa's guitar solo is not the one Marquez transcribed for 'Big Swifty' but it is in a similar vein, with stretched arpeggios and 'rocking-riff' quotes: the idea of it being a horn line effects the way we listen to it. It is often said that soloing is 'instant composition', but *Waka/Jawaka* brings that home in the same forceful manner as Ornette Coleman's plunder of his soloing back catalogue for tunes. The horns – Sal Marquez (trumpet), Bill Byers and Ken Shroyer (trombone and baritone horn), Mike Altschul (flute and reeds), Joel Peskin (tenor sax) – remained on board for the next album, as did the Dmochowski/Dunbar rhythm section. Having discovered these clever, pliable, sparky musicians Zappa was not going to leave it at that.

The cover of *Waka/Jawaka* was an idea of Sal Marquez's realized by Marvin Mattelson: a sink with two taps, one marked 'hot', the other 'rats'. On the reverse (omitted in the CD release) Zappa sits outside a garden summerhouse wearing an ill-fitting jumper and red jeans, sunlight filtering through rafters, the smell of old paint and sun-warmed wood. Behind him to his right, slipping down and nearly invisible beneath the dusty mesh of a ventilation window, is a reproduction of a nineteenth-century oil painting of a nude woman (perhaps a harem picture by Jean-Auguste Dominic Ingres). This may be the same woman's head that appears, enlarged so that the screened colour dots are showing, beneath the 'Mothers' thought bubble on the cover of *Burnt Weeny Sandwich*. It certainly has a similar resonance: a palimpsest of femininity. A pot plant to Zappa's right is labelled 'ARALIA ELEGATISSMA'. Both indicate something less stringently ugly than previous covers, as do the wickerwork stool and flowered wallpaper on the wall in the summerhouse. As against the brutal X-rayed teeth of *Uncle Meat*, these elements of femininity – as well as the song 'Your Mouth', which is about talk and belief –

---

[9]Frank Zappa, *Plastic People Songbook Corrected Copy*, ed. Carl Weissner, 1977, p. 312, though R.D. Cook suggests 'and' for 'rant', in which case 'Waka/Jawaka' is the splendid conclusion to the pusher's cornucopia.

indicate a lightened tone. This is not to claim conscious intention on the part of Zappa and Cal Schenkel (who designed the package), but these aspects of the photograph generate a 'mood' which would affect its choice. The music itself, in whatever twisted and deliberately illusionistic a way, seems more willing to play with conventional enchantment than previous records.

THE GRAND WAZOO

The idea of *The Grand Wazoo* is a poetic extension of the pungent yet fraudulent-sounding evocations of Zappa's melodies and solos. As with *Uncle Meat*, a short story accompanied the album. It has Stu (Uncle Meat's first name, and an apt description of the simmered eclecticism of the music) 'fumbling through a stack of books, records, newspaper clippings, religious pamphlets and campaign buttons' before he throws a switch and creates 'a life-size, minutely detailed, historically inaccurate, somewhat perverted illusionary replica of ANCIENT ROME or something'.[10]

The Grand Wazoo's music describes the political events of this pseudopolis. Like Larry the Dwarf composing in *200 Motels*, using spilt coffee and random bursts of sound from a transistor radio as inspirations, this creation of a spurious totality out of ill-assorted elements is an analogue of Zappa's own methods: what Fredric Jameson calls junk epic.[11] The tongue-in-cheek 'splendour' of *Waka/Jawaka* has become an entire concept.

The notion of irony was introduced into Western music at the turn of the century, when modernism made all use of music for evocation seem suspect. Gustav Mahler managed to save the romantic symphony by letting its emotional vectors tear the fabric of the music apart: the instrumentation that allows him to express heroic surges of feeling is pursued to its own demise in preposterous exaggeration. Kurt Weill recycled the martyred self-pity of the hit song by using irony to give it a mocking, confrontational edge. As introduced to Hollywood by middle European composers fleeing Nazism and the Second World War, late romantic music was all but ready to turn sour, and only a small tweak was required to make the music Miklos Rosza wrote for Hollywood epics sound absurdist and cheap. Sun Ra used irony to allow his Arkestra to

---

[10]Frank Zappa, sleeve note, *The Grand Wazoo*, 1972.
[11]Fredric Jameson, 'Wyndham Lewis As Futurist', *Hudson Review*, 1973/4, p. 325.

play with Hollywood enchantment without becoming enslaved to it. When critics claim to hear the 'influence' of Mahler, Weill and Ra in *The Grand Wazoo* they are registering its similarly ambivalent attitude towards the evocation of grandeur: for reasons of personal alienation, political commitment and racial oppression they could not endorse the music of power. Zappa's use of irony stems from all three considerations.

It was when describing the true meaning of 'zircon-encrusted tweezers' that Frank Zappa brought together the ideas that underlie the parodic splendour of *The Grand Wazoo*. They are first mentioned in 'Dinah-Moe Humm' (it is the tweezers that cause Dinah to shout 'that's it' and reach orgasm). Zappa describes zirkon, imitation diamonds favoured by Fats Domino and country stars, as figuring 'fake grandeur'. 'Zircon-encrusted tweezers' would be fake grandeur that is also sexually arousing. The tune of 'Sealed Tuna Sandwich',[12] a Weill-like celebration of the tawdriness of the American city, was later used in the orchestral piece 'Bogus Pomp'.[13] Operating at the interface between personal feeling and public pronouncement, musical power in Zappa is forever sexual, splendid and fraudulent.

'For Calvin (and his Next Two Hitch-hikers)' is the only vocal, telling the story of two hitch-hikers who disappeared from the backseat of Calvin Schenkel's car, leaving behind nothing but sandwich crumbs. A sense of mystery is created by Sal Marquez and Janet Ferguson singing in the same obscure manner as they did on *Waka/Jawaka*. Don Preston's mini-moog sounds more weirdly electronic than ever in the mainly acoustic context and Bill Byers and Ken Shroyer play some humorously vocalized trombone. As he did on *King Kong*, Zappa scores music that implodes with the sense of surreal decomposition that characterized the *musique concrète* of *Money*.

'The Grand Wazoo' begins as a light shuffle, Zappa playing a slippery solo on acoustic, Aynsley Dunbar's fluidity contributing to a sense of sunny ease. Tony Duran's bottleneck solo catches at the beat in the same perverse way as his playing on *Waka/Jawaka*. As the rhythm becomes stronger, Bill Byers's trombone solo recalls Freddie Hubbard's work on *Out To Lunch*: confident, hard bop riffs in a bizarre context. Sal Marquez plays his trumpet with a

[12] Frank Zappa, 'Sealed Tuna Sandwich', *200 Motels*, 1971.
[13] Frank Zappa, 'Bogus Pomp', *Orchestral Favourites*, 1976, and *London Symphony Orchestra Vol. II*, 1987.

mute, a long solo full of vocalized emphases and humorous fidgets. The relation of the band's pattering polyrhythms to the solo line is quite unprecedented: the forward propulsion is reminiscent of rock but it has the finely divided rhythmic grid of jazz. Don Preston's mini-moog leads back into the theme, replete with characteristically splendid marimbas doubling the melody.

'The Grand Wazoo' was originally part of the science-fiction musical comedy *Hunchentoot*, there called 'Think It Over', 'sung by an industrial knight who is fanatically religious about the future, to initiate his supporters who are meditating under the influence of Alpha Waves'.[14]

> If something gets in your way
> Just think it over . . .
> And . . . it will fall down, etc.[15]

This is materialist satire in the vein of 'Cosmik Debris'[16] (where the mystery man claims to have 'the dust of the Grand Wazoo') or 'The Meek Shall Inherit Nothing'.[17] All three songs mock cults that exploit idealist wish-fulfilment. The phrase 'The Grand Wazoo' was meant to evoke some ridiculous Rotarian or Masonic club in which ordinary businessmen dress themselves in archaic costumes and perform weird rituals. Although Zappa was accused of deserting rock 'n' roll and 'message' music with the chamber jazz of *The Grand Wazoo*, his social commentary is as germane to the music as ever.

In the story accompanying *The Grand Wazoo* Zappa details the life of Emperor Cletus Awreetus-Awrightus. The name derives from a catch-phrase of Big Joe Turner's who, fronting a big band with a cardboard loudhailer (before amplification, the only mechanism a big band 'shouter' would have to make himself heard), would sing 'Well, all right then! All reet then! All root then!' The part of the Emperor Cletus was played by underrated West Coast tenor saxophonist Ernie Watts, whose subsequent claims to fame have included the sax solo on the flip side of 'You're the One That I Want' by John Travolta and Olivia Newton-John[18] and recording and touring with Charlie Haden in Quartet West.[19] His

---

[14]Dominique Chevalier, *Viva! Zappa*, 1985, p. 113.
[15]Ibid.
[16]Frank Zappa, 'Cosmik Debris', *Apostrophe (')*, 1974.
[17]Frank Zappa, 'The Meek Shall Inherit Nothing', *You are What You is*, 1981.
[18]John Travolta and Olivia Newton-John, 'You're the One That I Want', 1978, RSO 006 7.
[19]Charlie Haden, *Quartet West*, 1989, Verve 831673.

gruff, snorting solo on 'Cletus Awreetus-Awrightus' becomes in Zappa's story the exhortations of a dubious tyrant, a figure remarkably like that of the Bailiff in Wyndham Lewis's *Human Age* trilogy.[20] The theme's pomposity is guyed by Zappa's 'la-la-la' vocal. What is interesting about Zappa's mythologizing is that it postdates his musical ideas: the idea of tarnished splendour is a corollary of musical decisions about the authenticity of evocation, gauging the resonance of clichés. Far from reducing the music to mere illustration of literary ideas (a problem that bedevils both rock 'concept' albums, poetry-jazz experimentation and contemporary opera), the music itself generates conceptual absurdities.

When Pierre Boulez is asked for a visual image that might help a listener new to his music, he generally questions the helpfulness of such an idea, but does have one favourite: his music could be seen as an aquarium of bright tropical fish darting about in unpredictable ways. In 'Eat That Question' Zappa provides a humorous image for the tendency of free jazz and fusion to deconstruct tempo and harmony into the free interaction of small sounds. In a burlesque of feeding Christians to the lions, the 'solution' to the problem of Questions (individuals who don't like music) is a literal one: a tank of undifferentiated tissue.

> The wagon contains a giant aquarium sort of thing, in which we see writhing an impressive amount of UDT (UnDifferentiated Tissue), a symbolic accumulation of all the statistical errors and failed attempts of this empire's scientific community. The union people go away, as they always do, and, after receiving a series of congratulations, awards, business cards, and fund donations, hold a board meeting off to the side, wherein it is unanimously decided to provide an ultimate solution for the QUESTIONS. The solution itself is released when a high guitar twang shatters the glass of the UDT tank. It burbles and fumes for a few moments, finally gulping them all down. A hush falls over the arena as the vapors dissipate and the pit orchestra makes a triumphal reprise of the opening figure.

The idea of such a 'final solution' is echoed in the presence of some books on Uncle Meat's shelves: *The Rise and Fall of the Third Reich* and *Arms of Krupp (Condensed)*. UnDifferentiated Tissue derives from *Naked Lunch*, a debt Zappa acknowledged by

---

[20]Wyndham Lewis, *The Human Age: The Childermass, Monstre Gai, Malign Fiesta*, 1928. Quite apart from Fredric Jameson's 'junk-epic' observations, the figure of the Bailiff – who grows his nose on purpose, 'I feed it with fine nasal fodder imported from my sweated plantations' (*The Childermass*, p. 272) – is very similar to Emperor Cletus and Ruben. Both satirize the public persona as a phallic grotesque.

reading out a section that included a reference to UDT, 'The Talking Asshole', at a gathering of New York *literati* including Patti Smith, Allen Ginsberg and William Burroughs himself (who told Zappa that he had got the idea for the talking asshole from the ventriloquist scene in *Dead of Night*).[21]

In the CD release, 'Calvin' and 'The Grand Wazoo' have changed places, but in both the last three tunes shine with the playing of George Duke on electric piano. His 'UDT' discord breaks into Zappa's wah-wah guitar solo with an impressive mixture of both comedy and musical invention. The electric piano was relatively new. Joe Zawinul had pioneered its use with Cannonball Adderley and Miles Davis before forming Weather Report for the express purpose of exploring electronic sounds. The idea of the 'funky Emperor' relies upon Duke's playing, as it combines a groove with a chordal richness that suggests barbaric splendours. 'Blessed Relief', a short piece with some beautiful, lazy solos from Marquez and Duke is well named: an indication of how agitated the preceding music has been. Duke's awareness of McCoy Tyner's interrogative chord sequences keep it from being anodyne. Zappa's closing acoustic solo represents some of his most restful yet imaginative playing on record.

In the story Emperor Cletus and his musical army oppose the forces of Mediocrates of Pedestrium, who are similarly armed except that they are heavy on strings and vocals.

> By means of a small-but-powerful portable transmitter, the combined forces of Mediocrates proceed to croon, strut, blither, and bloop a suspiciously accessible barrage of DITTIES into the air-waves in an attempt to anaesthetize the decent townspeople into drooling submission.
>
> Cletus 'n the Army Awreetus defend their turf by marching to a nearby hummock and playing a shuffle.[22]

This humorous ending – bathos after the epic feast and the emergency of the attack – is also a comment on the absurdity of art as a political force.

The pot plant that appeared to Zappa's right on the back cover of *Waka/Jawaka* makes a reappearance in Schenkel's painting of Uncle Meat in his laboratory. This time it is labelled 'ECU DAMP PUCKERED RICTUS'. 'ECU' is a film script direction for

[21] Michael Brenna, 'The Talking Asshole As Read in Public by Frank Zappa', *Society Pages*, No. 14, February 1983, pp. 28–9.
[22] Sleeve note, Frank Zappa, *The Grand Wazoo*, 1972.

Meat, which indicate a desire to X-ray through the blandishments of conventional music, *The Grand Wazoo* works like a close-up of West Coast cool arrangements, with all their romanticism and superficial prettiness.

Zappa put a Grand Wazoo band on the road, an eight-date tour with a similar instrumentation to the album. Dave Parlato replaced Dmochowski on bass and Jim Gordon replaced Dunbar. Ian Underwood replaced Duke and Preston. Jerry Kessler was brought in on electric cello, Jay Migliori and Ray Reed on woodwinds, Tom Malone and Glen Ferris on brass, Tom Raney on vibes. Important new members were trombonist Bruce Fowler and Ruth Underwood, heavy talents who were crucial to the success of the Grand Wazoo live band and Zappa's music for the next four years. The band debuted at the Hollywood Bowl on 10 September 1972, left for Europe on 13 September (Berlin, London, La Haye), then played in New York and Boston and returned to LA on 25 September. Pieces were long, with ample room for solos (no vocals) and Zappa conducting what amounted to a small orchestra. According to programme notes that appeared in a Warner Brothers promotional bulletin,[23] the repertoire included 'Big Swifty', 'Calvin', 'The Grand Wazoo', 'New Brown Clouds' and the march from *Greggery Peccary* (an interesting demonstration of how music frequently dismissed as 'trivial' because of Zappa's cartoon narration could provide challenges for his least rock-oriented band). 'Approximate' was a piece that specified rhythms but not pitch, resulting in some truly exciting cacophony.[24] 'Low Budget Dog Meat' segued the written parts of 'Music for Electric Violin and Low Budget Orchestra', 'Dog Breath' and 'Uncle Meat' and 'Variant Processional March' previewed the theme that became 'Regyptian Strut' (*Sleep Dirt*). Although not mentioned in the tour notes, 'Penis Dimension' also made a regular appearance.

At the gigs Zappa would joke his way through the extensive soundchecking necessary for temperature-sensitive woodwinds and revel in the anti-rock nature of the enterprise.

Thanks to Shroyer's irreproachable diplomacy, The Wazoo has probably

---

[23]Reprise Circular, Vol. 4, No. 40, 9 October 1972, reprinted in Dominique Chevalier, *Viva! Zappa*, 1985, pp. 110–15.

[24]'It later turned up combined with 'The Purple Lagoon', *Zappa in New York*, 1977, and it can be heard in its solitary splendour on *You Can't Do That on Stage Anymore Vol. 2*, 1988, and *Vol. 4*, 1991.

Thanks to Shroyer's irreproachable diplomacy, The Wazoo has probably earned its place in the Rock and Roll Hall of Fame, for the simple reason that it is the only 'new' group in rock history which has known from the start that it will not be as successful as The Beatles, and has also known throughout its history the exact time and place that it will split up: after the Boston show, in the dressing room, on September 24.[25]

Zappa promised to tour the band again next summer if the tour was 'anything other than a financial catastrophe', but in the event found himself bored by the band's muso attitude. He did not enjoy the company of musicians whose idea of relaxation was playing chess.[26] Although Zappa uses scores and reading musicians, he also likes the stimulation of outgoing personalities, musicians prepared to perform both on and offstage. This meant the formation of a new band. Bassist Dave Parlato was not available. Trombonist Bruce Fowler suggested his brother Tom, who passed the audition. George Duke and Jean-Luc Ponty were required for their skill in handling electric lead instruments. Sal Marquez played on *Overnite Sensation* and on the 1973 US and Australian tours, but left under a cloud[27]. On drums Zappa brought in Ralph Humphrey. Although there was a lot of continuity between this new band and old ones in terms of live playing, the new album – heavy on vocals and rock-funk panache – was a startling change of direction after the 'music music' of *Waka/Jawaka* and *The Grand Wazoo*.

---

[25]Reprise Circular, Vol. 4, No. 40, 9 October 1972, reprinted in Dominique Chevalier, *Viva! Zappa*, 1985, p. 110.
[26]Quoted by Cherry Ripe, 'Frank Zappa Has No Underwear', *New Musical Express*, 17 April 1976.
[27]According to Zappa (*Musician*, February 1994), Marquez was sacked for asking for *per diem* payments on top of his salary; Zappologist Geoff Wills takes the term for a lay-off from playing in the sleevenotes to Sal Marquez album (*One For Dewey*, 1992, GRP 96782) – 'relaxing on this scene and that' – as a euphemism for involvement with drugs, something unlikely to please Zappa either.

CHAPTER 5
BIZARRE TO DISCREET

his reverse makes a virtue of necessity while his obverse mars a mother
by invention
    James Joyce[1]

ART ROCK MEETS ANTI-ART

In 1973, with the release of *Overnite Sensation*, Frank Zappa
mortally offended his art-rock supporters. No matter that the title
did not refer to commercial success but to the practice of fucking
grapefruits engaged in by tour drivers on long night trips (a suitably inviting specimen appears on the cover, running with erogenous slime and marked 'roadies delite'). Absence of instrumentals,
glossy production and lewd vocals – talked close to the microphone in the manner of TV advertisements, using Zappa's new
low voice – all indicated something alien, shiny and unsettling. It
was like asking for *Rolling Stone* and getting *Playboy* (in 1973
these felt like very different consumer guides). The conclusion was
that Zappa had sold out, gone commercial, joined the other side.

The change of label name from Bizarre to DiscReet was ostensibly to relate to JVC Discrete quadrophonic methods (*Overnite
Sensation* was originally released in the short-lived format). Herb
Cohen maintained that things had not changed, though he did
admit that 'Bizarre fitted a different era, it fitted the 60s'.[2] The
resonance of the word 'discreet' is summed up in Norman Mailer's
description of J.F. Kennedy.

> He learned too much and too early that victory goes to the discreet,
> that one does not speak one's opinion, that ideally one does not even

---

[1]James Joyce, *Finnegans Wake*, 1946, p. 133, 32–3.
[2]Quoted by Pete Erskine, 'Meet Discreet', source unknown.

develop one's opinion. For a man with opinion is less free to move with the turn of power.[3]

The Bizarre logo made its last appearance on the cover of *The Grand Wazoo*, a petrified urn on a column being toppled by the Mediocrites of Pedestrium, an excellent image for the state of the counter-culture. DiscReet's logo combined business-like simplicity with a sinister, retro-50s 'streamlined' look. The words of 'Fifty-Fifty' on *Overnite Sensation*

> I figure the odds be fifty-fifty
> I just might have some thing to say
> *To my friends*[4]

deny any overt message, implying that the audience will have to supply half the meaning. 'Montana', a C&W tale of growing dental floss, seemed to be pretty much a statement of ignoring public issues, Zappa resolving to 'cultiver mon jardin' ('moving to Montana', in US political jargon, means to retire). Bizarre to DiscReet looked like a retreat.

Interestingly enough, Fredric Jameson traces the origins of postmodernism to 1973.

> It is my sense that both levels in question, infrastructure and superstructures – the economic system and the cultural 'structure of feeling' – somehow crystallized in the great shock of the crises of 1973 (the oil crisis, the end of the international gold standard, for all intents and purposes the end of the great wave of 'wars of national liberation' and the beginning of the end of traditional communism), which, now the dust clouds have rolled away, disclose the existence, already in place, of a strange new landscape . . .[5]

Jameson's postmodernism argues for a watershed in bourgeois ideology, a new situation in which the connection between images and their referents have been severed, but his choice of date shows that the background to this is the fading of the hopes of May 1968, the beginning of the right-wing backlash represented by the electoral victories of Ronald Reagan and Margaret Thatcher. Veteran revolutionary Tony Cliff has pointed out that when certain Bolsheviks despaired of victory after the defeat of 1905, some of them turned to writing pornography: certainly *Overnite Sensation*

---

[3]Norman Mailer, *The Presidential Papers*, 1963, p. 7. Zappa's intention was to combine a word for record ('disc') with an arcane R&B expression ('reet!' as in 'all reety all righty'); 'it was certainly not meant to be a label for musical circumspectitude' (interview, 26 October 1993).
[4]Frank Zappa, 'Fifty-Fifty', *Overnite Sensation*, 1973.
[5]Fredric Jameson, *Postmodernism, Or, The Cultural Logic of Late Capitalism*, 1991, pp. xx-xxi.

and 'Dinah-Moe Humm' can be read as that kind of surrender to the existent structures of desire. In 1973 the coup in Chile, in which Allende's elected government was toppled by the machinations of ITT and the CIA, resulting in General Pinochet's blood-soaked dictatorship, marked the first stirrings of post-Vietnam US imperialism (wary of committing troops to the field all the way up to the Gulf War of 1990/91). *Overnite Sensation*, in all its neon-lit brashness, was an atrocity committed on a counter-culture now revealed as hypocritical and collusive. *Overnite Sensation* declared bankrupt the consumer-defined movement that at one time thought it could overturn governments and stop wars: explicit trash for the market, mechanical sex-substitutes on the display racks. Actually predicting many of the shock tactics of punk (a more generalized assault on the hypocrisies of 60s counter-culture), art rock it was not.

The ideology of English art rock is contradictory, antagonistic to America and capitalism, yet finding in rock 'n' roll the key term in loosening the grip of the European cultural heritage. The pioneers of English underground rock were the Soft Machine. Their first albums, all heavy riffs and anti-commercial raggedness, sound like a bunch of musos playing at being the Mothers of Invention (in a tramshed). Charming stuff, if technically limited and abominably recorded. While Emerson, Lake and Palmer, Genesis and Yes provided the spectacle of 'challenging' rock (in truth, music-college exercises of naïvety that would be laughable if they hadn't obscured so much other music by their commercial success), the Softs, Egg, National Health, Henry Cow and Lol Coxhill developed a music – termed 'Canterbury Rock' by the press – that by its very reticence gave the lie to such empty grandeur. Quietistic middle-class music that, in common with the little-press poetry of the time by Andrew Crozier, achieved results by acknowledging limits just where progressive rock failed to. It was not just an English phenomenon – in France Marc Hollander was producing very similar music.[6] To these musicians, Zappa's turn to commercial vulgarity on *Overnite Sensation* was a crime.

The carefully layered multi-tracks of *Uncle Meat* have a tinny 'bed-sit' quality that was much valued by the British avant-garde. However, commitment to art rock was not on the agenda for Zappa. He dismissed it as 'Classical Rock – real intellectual with

---

[6] Marc Hollander, *Ak Sak Ma Boul: Onze Danses pour Combattre la Migraine*, 1977, Crammed Discs CRAM011.

ugly chords and the beat's no good'.[7] Zappa's detachment showed in 'Cucamonga', a song from 1975 about his early days[8] which gently parodies Egg.[9] In that song Stravinsky-like rhythms and breathless sincerity have now become mere tokens of youthful optimism, pigments in a palette flushed of value. This style is as much an empty vessel as the nihilistic blues of 'Muffin Man'.

For English art-rockers Henry Cow, *Uncle Meat's* Stravinsky-derived thinness and variegated instrumentation, the hallucinogenic changes of pace and timbre, were rejections of commercialism. Updating the Softs' translation for the 1970s, Henry Cow used the tricky time signatures and dada melodies of *Uncle Meat*, developing a homely, relective music at odds with the pompous commercialism progressive rock had become. The intricate twists and turns of *Waka/Jawaka* and *The Grand Wazoo* were interpreted as heroic blows against the industry. *Henry Cow* (1973) and *Unrest* (1974) infused Zappa's relentless defiance-to-expectations with English pastoral, a tradition carried on into the 80s and 90s by Martin Archer with Bass Tone Trap and the Hornweb Saxophone Quartet. Growing awareness of studio techniques allowed them to emulate the glossy clarity of *Waka/Jawaka*. The handwritten details on the back of the first album – neatly inscribed in then fashionable Rotring pen – demonstrate Henry Cow's horror of product impersonality. Here critique of the commodity blends into middle-class tastefulness: superior product on a caring label. The history of Virgin Records is a salutary lesson in how capitalism co-opts so-called alternatives into another choice in the homogeneous shopping mall.

The commercial brashness of *Overnite Sensation* was a shock these purveyors of little-England craftsmanship could do without. With the mid-70s radical press awash with talk of ley lines, alternative technology and growing cabbages in your back garden, a whole catalogue of petit-bougeois daydreams it took punk to clear away, Zappa's new record looked like a Coca-Cola can at an exhibition of studio pottery. Pop Art to the max.

---

[7] *International Times*, No. 115, 1971.
[8] 'Cucamonga', *Bongo Fury*, 1975.
[9] Specifically, 'Cucamonga' is a dead ringer for Egg 'A Visit to Newport Hospital', *The Polite Force*, 1970, Deram SML1074. Zappa has declared he has no knowledge of Egg (interview with the author, 27 October 1993), which makes this similarity still more intriguing.

ROCK INCORPORATION

The fact that the dominant language in the States is English confers a spurious transparency to Anglo-American communications. Americans greet English disdain for commercialism with particular incredulity (usually the disdain itself is such an unlikely confusion between proletarian resistance and aristocratic snobbery that it *is* hard to credit). Zappa might appear on British television in 1968 and declare that 'we must stop America before it scarfs up the world and shits all over us' but the music he played – a piece of improvised rock 'n' roll with Roy Estrada singing 'oh, in the sky!'[10] in falsetto – was precisely the American stupidity that is the bedrock of Zappa's art.

The danger is the neatness of identifications. Critics complained about the 'insistent, almost depressingly professional backing'[11] on *Overnite Sensation*'s 'Dinah-Moe Humm' as if amateurishness were a guarantee of authenticity (and the Beatles had not yet released a record). The ideology of 'alternative' art has always been stumped by its fetishism of form, plumping for this or that external characteristic as the mark of virtue. In terms of the multi-valency of signs in the real world, it is like trying to paint your toenails while wearing seven-league boots.

Adhering to musical forms and audience possibilities which had been colonized by the market, the counter-culture was reduced to moral rather than aesthetic criteria. In a press release in 1978, promoting a set of 'alternative' rock bands drawn from all over Europe, Rock In Opposition characterized Henry Cow in these terms:

> They are the only politically and musically progressive group in the country who have managed to surface and survive (for nine years now). The only person who has covered the same ground as they have is Frank Zappa and he was finished long ago. Henry Cow are still at it.[12]

At what exactly? The music is pleasantly oddball, but really only a soft-focus version of Mothers instrumentals. The belief in alternative rock – given the heightened political climate of punk, which by 1978 required Rock Against Racism and 2-Tone – is merely hippie tears in spilt milk. Punk at least recognized that the

---

[10]Not 'who is that guy?' as originally thought – a correction made by Zappa (interview with the author, 27 October 1993).
[11]Arthur Schmidt, '*Over-Nite Sensation*', *Rolling Stone*, 20 December 1973.
[12]Quoted by Kenneth Ansell, 'Rock in Opposition', *Impetus*, No. 7, 1978, p. 282.

commercialization of progressive rock by the likes of Led Zeppelin and Genesis was a fact of life. No amount of special pleading could resuscitate the good old days when Ginger Baker and Mitch Mitchell were plugged into the spirit of Elvin Jones. The individual musicians of Henry Cow gravitated towards the avant-garde of free improvisation, leaving behind their populist daydreams. Of course, musicians should not be judged by the ideologues who make use of them: Fred Frith and Tim Hodgkinson in particular created important music in the following decades. Frith finally wound up playing punk – twelve years later – from scores provided by John Zorn in Naked City, Zorn's zigzag between abstraction and commercial suss being distinctly Zappa-like (and because he started out fifteen years later, distinctly different too). Drummer Chris Cutler founded Recommended Records (later These Records), which has provided a continuous source of 'anti-commercial' music of varying degrees of merit for the last ten years[13]

It is important to recognize what had happened to the rock music of the 'underground' in the years between the Mothers of Invention and *Overnite Sensation*: its incorporation into an industry as tightly sewn-up as pre-rock 'n' roll Tin Pan Alley. As Marc Eliot puts it: 'Far from the threat that political and social critics would have it seem, rock and roll has become the corporate spine of American entertainment.'[14]

FZ AND PUNK

The dazzling banality of *Overnite Sensation*, its leering sex-in-two-dimensions, is an atrocity committed on the counter-culture – several years before punk. It is worth dwelling on the disgust of the art-rockers with what looked to them like Zappa's sell-out. Confusing art with politics, Rock In Opposition's cottage-industry values result in bad versions of both: providing us with the art we 'ought' to like for its encoded ideology. Despite the mumblings of the hippies-who-refuse-to-die, Zappa's 'alternative rock' phase finished because that possibility died in the real world: the consumers failed to make a revolution (again). What remained for someone with access to the machine was to produce what Theodor

---

[13]These Records operates from 387 Wandsworth Road, London SW8 2JL. Ring up for a catalogue (071–622–9934).
[14]Marc Eliot, *Rockonomics*, 1989, p. 201.

Adorno called prisms: crystallizations along the unconscious webs that are used to create values and to communicate, or *art* as it is called. We are used to the avant-garde encoding such data. Zappa's achievement is to paint with the vibrant clutter of commercialism.

Rejected by the hippies, Zappa found no favour with the punks either. If you survey the writings of Charles Shaar Murray[15] from *Oz* and *Creem* to *New Musical Express*, it is evident that it was not just the art-rockers who did not like the change from Bizarre to DiscReet. Murray is evidently a Mothers fan – his writings are loaded with quotes from Mothers of Invention records. The word 'punk', which he used liberally from 1971 onwards, actually derived from Zappa: 'Hey Punk' from *We're Only in It for the Money* parodied the Leaves' 'Hey Joe', the song immortalized by Hendrix.

Like Henry Cow, Murray parted company with Zappa around the time of *Overnite Sensation* – not because Zappa was deserting musical abstraction for rock 'n' roll, but because he was no longer street-cred. Disgusted by the party which Reprise records organized to celebrate the entry of *Apostrophe (')* into the top ten – a lavish £30,000 occasion in tune with early 70s record-industry PR budgets – Murray denounced all Zappa as a sell-out, his music mere 'chic debris'.[16] These sentiments reached a happy climax in the *NME*-sponsored punk explosion, but failed to explain how Zappa in particular was able to keep delivering albums that astonished and disgusted in equal measure.

OVERNITE SENSATION

Because rock operates in the mass market it invites sociological rather than aesthetic critique. From the point of view of the punk frontline, Zappa's late 1979 concerts at the Hammersmith Odeon – five performances in four days and no empty seats – seemed irrelevant, but the artefacts of style wars have a tendency to cast strange shadows on to the future. Now *Overnite Sensation* towers over the patchy output of the Clash like Philip K. Dick over John Wyndham.

Murray described the 'phase of Zappa's work that commenced with *Overnite Sensation*' as 'a fairly zingy little combo

[15]Conveniently collected as *Shots from the Hip*, 1991.
[16]*New Musical Express*, 5 October 1974, *Shots from the Hip*, 1991, pp. 61–7.

experiment with funk riffs and heavy metal textures and whimsical little songs with little appreciable ideas content and a tetch of elementary word play'.[17] From where Murray sits – a commitment to basic rock values that can see the common links between Muddy Waters, the Stones, Dr Feelgood and the Sex Pistols – this assessment is just fine, but for folks with a sense of the trajectory of Western civilization, it is inadequate. To build a surrealist documentary of modern life, one that challenges *Finnegans Wake* for scale, complexity and breadth of reference, and explicitly site it in the marketplace is cultural outrage of the highest order. It is a blow to hierarchies of value that moralism, no matter how well intentioned, can never achieve, because moralism relies on a notion of the few who are saved percolating truth to the damned below.

What the rock journalists did achieve – no enemy like a disciple betrayed – was utter contempt for Zappa from new-wave fans. This was part of punk's appeal, of course: wiping the slate clean, 'no Elvis, Beatles or the Rolling Stones in 1977'. It enabled many people to approach rock who had previously been put off by the stench of hippie ideology, setting up a spectacular divide that provided the entire frame of reference for 80s rock-talk. Despite the brilliant anti-hippie polemic of *We're Only in It for the Money*, Zappa was consigned to the old-wave dumper, creating immense problems for the Zappologist who refused to die: every fan-contact turned out to be a hippie dinosaur. It is still like that today. When *T'Mershi Duween* asked its readers to vote on what else they listened to in November 1991 the only post-punk band listed was the Fall.[18] By the late 70s, reviews and interviews with Zappa in the English rock press (which adopted punk wholesale) became nothing but an uncomprehending barrage of insults.

---

[17]*New Musical Express*, 'One Size Fits All', 19 July 1975.
[18]The list ran: 'Captain Beefheart, Peter Hammill/Van Der Graaf Generator, Fripp/Eno/King Crimson, Pink Floyd, the Beatles, Neil Young, Jimi Hendrix, Grateful Dead, Led Zeppelin, Miles Davis, Talking Heads, Jethro Tull, the Canterbury Scene bands, Yes, Van Morrison, Magma, Steve Vai, Stravinsky, the Fall, Richard Thompson and Henry Cow', *T'Mershi Duween*, No. 23, January 1992, p. 17. Such a characterization of the Zappa constituency is so depressing a little Theodor Adorno is in order: 'In the empirical sociology of culture, which tends to start out from reactions rather than from what is reacted to, the *ordo rerum* is ideologically twisted into the *ordo idearum*: in art, being precedes consciousness in so far as the structures in which the social force has been objectified are closer to the essence than the reflexes to them, the immediate social modes of the receivers' behaviour,' Theodor Adorno, *Introduction to the Sociology of Music*, 1962, trs. E. B. Ashton, 1976, p. 202. In other words, the Zappologist is not to be deterred by fan demography.

PUNK AS REAGANOMICS

There is an element of truth in the characterization of punk as preparation for Reaganomics and Thatcherism. The Ramones started out as quite explicitly right-wing, Joey Ramone saying he regretted not being old enough to go and fight in Vietnam. British punk rode the power of the form while infusing it with leftist politics. By stressing live gigs in small venues, DIY values, politics, kicking the National Front, the rock press echoed the situationist disdain for art as consumption of commodities ('The real fans aren't buying the single,' said Malcolm McLaren proudly after the release of 'Anarchy in the UK'). However, if you are not actually putting up the barricades and holding de Gaulle to ransom – in fact you are looking at successive Tory electoral victories – this iconoclasm begins to look more like puritanism than the SI's 'all power to the imagination'.

John Peel characterized Zappa's project as 'building dungeons in the sky',[19] while the punks condemned Zappa for having twenty-minute saxophone solos (just as Rock In Opposition condemned him for *not* having twenty-minute saxophone solos). The utter nonsense of the 'concept album' and the grandiose vacuity of progressive rock were enough to make any substantial use of the industry seem worthless. However, as Adorno says:

> One of the contradictions of musical life is this: its bad side, the commodity character, is most concentrated in the very sphere which absorbes so much productive vigour that the uncorrupted part, the part that is true in itself, will also be made susceptible by reduced power of realization, a lack of precision, a sensual threadbareness.[20]

It is the contention of this book that Zappa made the game worth the candle: the dungeons in the sky were worth the stadium rock gigs, the endless 'Dinah-Moe Humm' encores.

THE OUTPUT MACROSTRUCTURE

Reputedly a memo to Warners Brothers sales excecutives, *International Times* in 1971 printed a communiqué by Zappa in which he made the following remarks:

---

[19]On a lift he gave me when hitch-hiking from Cambridge to London some time in 1976, for which I thank him.
[20]Theodor Adorno, *Introduction to the Sociology of Music*, 1962, trs. E. B. Ashton, 1976, pp. 124–5.

Perhaps the most unique aspect of the Mothers' work is the *conceptual continuity* of the group's *output macrostructure*. There is, and always has been, a conscious control of thematic and structural elements flowing through each album, live performance and interview.

Do you know about Earth Works? Imagine the decades and the pile of stuff on them subjected to *extensive long-range conceptual landscape modification*. Houses, Offices. People live there and work there. Imagine that *you* could be living there and working there and not even know it. Whether you can imagine it or not, that's what the deal is.[21]

The heavens roll up like a scroll: the apocalyptic vision of seeing reality as artifice. What terrified medieval piety has, since the industrial revolution, become the average experience, because we do indeed live in an environment shaped by humans: even the toilers of the soil (especially the toilers of the soil, in fact) are affected by the global market in rice. The hand from the sky in the Holiday Inn window on the cover of *Overnite Sensation* promotes, like Philip K. Dick's *Time out of Joint*, a vision of reality as a mere stage set. The hand is either fixing or extinguishing a streetlamp: we are living on a model landscape and all the clouds are merely Zeppelins, the sun's heat a confection of mirrors and magnifying lenses. The proximity of Hollywood and Disneyland – with their townscape replicas, the physical reproduction of reality in pursuit of illusion – exerts a strong pull on both Dick and Zappa.

These ideas parallel certain types of schizophrenic vision. The alienation they register, seeing the environment we live in as artificial, actually recognizes a truth. Zappa and Dick provide us with a surrealist documentary of life in capitalism, where an environment created by human beings is deemed natural and inevitable by what Marx called 'ideology': the set of ideas that justify rule by the capitalist class. Zappa gives this paranoid vision a political twist when he says:

> The illusion of freedom will continue as long as it's profitable to continue the illusion. At the point where the illusion becomes too expensive to maintain they will just take down the scenery, they will pull back the curtains, they will move the tables and chairs out of the way, and you will see the brick wall at the back of the theatre.[22]

When Zappa sings 'I'm the Slime' on *Overnite Sensation* he was

---

[21]*International Times*, No. 115, 1971.
[22]Quoted by Jim Ladd, 'Zappa on Air', *Nuggets*, No. 7, April/May 1977, p. 17.

reviled for merely satirizing the 'easy target' of television,[23] but it is better than that because the record *is* the slime, not an alternative. On the cover the TV set shows Zappa baring his teeth in a threatening leer as slime droozles off from the screen: there is no haven in alternative art, no margin for spectators, just margarine (or mahjuh-rene) for one and all.[24] Surprisingly enough, it nevertheless delivers more chew for the analysts of avant-garde art than the carefully embroidered artefacts of non-commercialism.

Such talk reiterates the paradoxes of Pop Art, but Zappa's albums are not safely graded at the Tate. The memo continued:

> What we sound like is more than what we sound like. We are part of the *project/object*. The *project/object* (maybe you like *event/organism* better) incorporates any available visual medium, consciousness of all participants (including audience), all perceptual differences, God (as energy), The Big Note (as universal basic building material), and other things. We make a special art in an environment hostile to dreamers.
>
> What I'm trying to describe is the type of attention given to each lyric, melody, arrangement, improvisation, the sequence of these elements in the album, the cover art which is an extension of the musical material, the choice of what is recorded, released, and/or performed during a concert, the continuity or contrasts of material album to album etc etc etc . . . all of these detail aspects are part of the Big Structure or the Main Body of Work. The smaller details comprise not only the contents of the Main Body of Work but, because of the chronology of execution, give it a 'shape' in the abstract sense.[25]

The themes and images which connect and articulate this structure are deliberately chosen from a peripheral detritus of cultural symbols and clichés. Zappa described the riff of 'Tryin' to Grow a Chin'[26] as 'archetypally stupid' and has talked about how his songs are built up of cultural icons: 'It contains codified information not only about the American way of life but it contains codified information about psychological processes which are common here, too, in Europe.'[27] You cannot read Zappa's songs off as 'self-expression'; they concatenate verbal and musical licks into *merzbau* monstrosities. When these licks are encountered in the 'real' world they have a weird aura: Zappa has successfully demonstrated how artificial is the culture around us, a surrealist coup.[28]

---

[23] Zappa 'lashes out – hold on to your social consciences – at television,' Arthur Schmidt, 'Overnite Sensation', *Rolling Stone*, 20 December 1973.

[24] Jeremy Prynne, 4 January 1980, in response to Out To Lunch *1–2–3–4*, 1978.

[25] *International Times*, No. 115, 1971.

[26] *Sheik Yerbouti*, 1979.

[27] Quoted by Karl Dallas, 'Carry on Composing', *Melody Maker*, 28 January 1978.

[28] Poodle coincidences, for example, constitute a whole sub-genre in Zappography.

This alchemy has an objective element in that Zappa's crystallizations refract social truths beyond his special control: all is not predigested and arranged. In interpreting the way the cultural icons interact, the Zappographer inevitably confronts actual society rather than merely Zappa's particular confection. Art as the mirror of nature – Zappa contends that his art reverses that traditional relation ('imagine that *you* could be living there'). Such is the experimental catalysis of these signs in his work that the fusions become prophetic: the world outside the album appears to ape his themes. In the cover to *Overnite Sensation* the inverted letters of the mirror (the message about recycling on the crumpled beer can) appear on *our* side of the mantelpiece: we become a reflection of Zappa's art.

The choice of cover artist is interesting. David B. McMacken's airbrushed collations were also used for the cover and poster for *200 Motels*. Whereas Cal Schenkel's collages have a Schwitters-like beauty alongside their disgust-entertainment, this is the world of the graphic design studio. The cluttered motel scene was entirely directed by Zappa. A doll's foot kicking a chair refers to a roadie who kicked over a chair in a tantrum, there is the roadie-abused grapefruit, a briefcase plastered with Mothers stage passes.

HALLUCINATORY TRIVIA, OR THE ABSTRACTIONS OF MINUTIAE

One of Zappa's concerns has always been the documentation of trivia, finding in the accurate delineation of mass-produced banality a surrealism more pungent than heroic self-expression. Over the bed is a print by Brittini depicting a closed Venetian blind. According to Zappa, Brittini's prints may be found in motels all over the US, screwed into the walls in case you might steal them. The reduction of art – supposedly the window on a better world – to such an image, a mass-produced denial of vision, is the kind of strategy one associates with the satirical avant-garde. Here it is simply business as usual.[29]

A giant fire extinguisher is embossed with the word Perellis,

---

[29] Also the *alter ego* of Mårten Sund, for many years editor of Norway's Zappa-fanzine *Society Pages* and chief honcho of Mind Expanding Records, who had a hit in 1981 with Beranek's 'Balls & Calls', in which he states that 'all men have desirable balls' – which is, according to Paul Hession, 'a contentious statement'.

the name of the Mothers' road manager (Marty Perellis is credited with 'otherwise' on *Overnite Sensation* and 'abuse (unwarranted)' on *One Size Fits All*). Its nozzle is held by a double-headed man (laughing/frowning like the masks of comedy/tragedy) and is issuing a small gob of foam. In the bathroom there is an 'Ultra Clean' aerosol and a dirty hand-towel. The juice running from the grapefruit is causing a multimeter to flash. The slime from the TV set is pouring up on to the table, dissolving a map of Florida and ending in what appears to be a giant ring-pull from a beer can. As in a dream, all these extraneous details repeat the same idea of phallic ejaculation.

These details do not tally with any possible reality the mirror might be reflecting. The whole cover is a painting in a frame, with a plaque indicating title, painter and date. The frame itself is a riot of sexual detail – shark-toothed faces bite on tongues (or is it faeces?); corncobs thrust up anuses; heads upturn to drink urine; cracked doll-faces; monsters with bound lips: Hieronymous Bosch modelled in jello. To the right a couple stare out, looking like pleased voyeurs. The frame itself is a hallucination – you can see a wah-wah pedal, complete with DiscReet thunderflash, through the bottom left corner. The lead illogically merges into another electronic unit, other switches and knobs unrealistically scaled. The whole thing is a dream. Manager Herb Cohen is seen pushing up through the studio floor like a drill or the vacuum tube of an amplifier; an arm materializes out of a medical textbook – red for arteries, blue for veins – and pulls a cigarette out of the mirror.

A dream is an overnight sensation and *Overnite Sensation* is a dream. Recall the note on *Uncle Meat* which said that the words 'were scientifically prepared from a random series of syllables, dreams, neuroses & private jokes' – all Freudian sites of the unconscious. The garish vulgarity of *Overnite Sensation* means that it has not gained the careful psychoanalysis granted, say, *Finnegans Wake*, but beneath the superficial gloss Zappa is performing all kinds of operations – shifting letters, secret puns, strange combinations – characteristic of the unconscious.

Overnite Sensation opens with 'Camarillo Brillo', a cartoon sketch of sex with a hippie mama, registering how ghost-like alternative culture had become by 1973.

> And so she wanderered
> Through the door-way

Just like a shadow from the tomb . . .
She stripped away
Her rancid poncho
An' laid out naked by the door
We did it till we were unconcho
An' it was useless anymore[30]

There is an idiot bounce to the tune that revels in its triviality:
a negative image of what had been lost more powerful than
the strenuously embattled rock of 'survivors' like Neil Young.
Its commercial vacuity acknowledges the alienation of the
rock market. Adorno remarked: 'Novelty songs have always
existed on a contempt for meaning which, as predecessors and
successors of psychonalysis, they reduce to a monotony of sexual
symbolism.'[31]
In 1978 Zappa referred to

the type of psychological information conveyed by basic geometric
patterns in advertising layouts, the triangle being a very simplistic surro-
gate replica of a female pubic region, or the way in which they compute
that a circle resembles a breast. These are all factors which they actually
deal with on the advertising agency concept level, you know. They have
people who charge you a fortune per hour to analyse the motivational
aspect of layouts. You can intuitively combine these things to convey
information that is not in the written text itself or in the illustration.
It's the same thing in music.[32]

During the fade-out of 'Camarillo Brillo' she is asked if the poncho
is Mexican or one bought from the Sears & Roebuck mail-order
catalogue (a running joke that appears in 'Cosmik Debris' on
Apostrophe (') as well).

She said she was
A Magic Mama
And she could throw a mean Tarot
And carried on without a comma
That she was someone I should know[33]

Rhyming poncho with the unconscious and mama with a comma
is to perform verbal alchemy that both parallels and mocks hippie
magic. A poncho is a circle of cloth with a hole in the middle, a
material zero: a comma omitted recalls an apostrophe. The idea
of a sign that denies its own meaning has a special resonance

[30]Frank Zappa, 'Camarillo Brillo', Overnite Sensation, 1973.
[31]Theodor Adorno and Max Horkheimer, The Dialectic of Enlightenment, 1944, p. 138.
[32]Quoted by Karl Dallas, 'Carry on Composing', Melody Maker, 28 January 1978, p. 8.
[33]Frank Zappa, 'Camarillo Brillo', Overnite Sensation, 1973.

(Zappa has mentioned how useful he found Zen when shaking off his Catholicism). Along with the ejaculatory phalluses of the cover there are also abstracted vaginas: a gigantic floating doughnut, the ring-pull, the grapefruit. The doughnut evokes denial – don't, do-nothin'. This apparatus of hints and half-meanings floats through *Overnite Sensation* like a miasma. 'Camarillo Brillo' is a song of surrender to the meaningless domain of sexuality, a discussion of the philosophical implications of materialism that continues in *Apostrophe (')*.

This interest in punctuation is a literary version of the care needed to write scores, itself a practice that arose to a fine art alongside the emergence of the bourgeois class. The anal retention of the accountant, the concentration on minutiae coupled with paranoic mistrust of everybody else, is the secret soul of capitalism. In music, improvisatory residues were finally abolished in the nineteenth century (apart from some organ playing in Catholic churches). Computer programming, which is really a branch of accountancy (most non-military programmers earn their living in creating and/or maintaining accounting, stock control or sales order processing software), reached musical composition with the invention of the Synclavier, an obsession of Zappa's since the mid-80s. The dialectic between discipline and chaos in Zappa is derived from a self-conscious extension of capitalist logic, a play with the nihilistic violence that lies behind repression. William Blake's 'heaven in a grain of sand' is often taken to be an otherworldly vision of the microcosmos: in fact it is better understood in the light of Marx's *Capital*, which unfurls a whole theory of history from consideration of the most banal item of market capitalism, the commodity. Zappa's attention to detail both celebrates and mocks the accountant's vision. This care underlay the Mothers of Invention albums, but becomes an evident structural principle in the DiscReet era.

Zappa found in Bruce Bickford, an artist who works by freeze-framing models in clay, someone with a parallel combination of extreme meticulousness and shocking invention. In the video *Dub Room Special* there is a telling moment during the lyrical guitar solo to 'Inca Roads': Zappa's fingers moving over the strings are punned with images of someone moving papers at a desk and then a whole office at work. In finding the least likely visual counterpart to the music, the images – created by Bickford but mixed by Zappa – begin to psychoanalyse the anal retention in Zappa's note choices, linking to the frequent associations of daydreams and work in Zappa's songs: 'Little Green Rosetta',[34] 'No Not Now',[35] 'While You Were Out'.[36]

In 'Dirty Love' Zappa says that he will 'put you in a coma / With some dirty love', eliding the missing comma of 'Camarillo Brillo' with sexual ecstasy (just as *Apostrophe (')* turns out to be orgasm). One more letter change and you have the first four letters of 'Camarillo'. There is a famous Charlie Parker tune called 'Relaxin' at Camarillo' that followed his rest cure there occasioned by heroin addiction. Comma/coma/Camarillo – Zappa's instinct for suggestive wordplay has the same dizzying intimation of infinity as that of James Joyce.

Spelling margarine

Performances of 'St Alphonso's Pancake Breakfast' on the 1973 tour included a section where Zappa free-associated according to the initial letters of margarine (spelt mar-juh-rene). In Australia the 'm . . . under these circumstances could stand for *marsupial*', the 'r for *rebus*'. The hyphen 'could be used by a very desperate stenographer for purposes of sexual gratification'. In Sydney someone in the audience lit a firework. Zappa very expertly paused midsong, called on security to remove the culprit, no doubt not wishing to relive his memories of the fire at Geneva in 1971, and then used the routine to both vent his wrath and reassure his audience:

> where I stole the mar-juh-rene . . . and here's exactly how I did it. Groping my way, I proceeded into St Alphonso's pantry and located by the mere sensitivity of my fingers themselves the box containing the mysterious mar-juh-rene. And I took out a bit of it and rubbed it on my right eye, I pumped the mystery and the majesty of the mar-juh-rene, and I said the 'm' of the mystery mar-juh-rene must stand for *moron*, which is the kind of person who lights fireworks in a crowded room, and the 'a' of mar-juh-reen stands for *asshole*, as if moron was not a good enough word to describe the motherfucker and 'r' in this case stands for *rat*, which is also what that guy is for lighting fireworks in this room and there is a hyphen, ladies and gentlemen, 'm-a-r-hyphen' and the hyphen should be stuffed up his ass, 'm-a-r-hyphen-j' and 'j' is for *juvenile hall*, which is where they would send him if they caught him in Los Angeles and 'u' is for *unguentene*, which is a remedy for

[34]Frank Zappa, *Joe's Garage Acts II & III*, 1979.
[35]Frank Zappa, *Ship Arriving Too Late to Save a Drowning Witch*, 1984.
[36]Frank Zappa, *Shut Up 'N Play Yer Guitar*, 1981.

burns which might be used for a potential victim of his stupidity over there, folks, and then-then (*stutters*) de-ded-de there's an 'h' which stands for *hot*, which it would have been if it would have got on you and then there's another hyphen 'm-a-r-hyphen-j-u-h-hyphen'. This hyphen, this second hyphen, this delightful hyphen – you should stuff that one up his ass again too because one's not enough, they're small, and then there's another 'r' which should be for *religion* – a person like that needs true religion, don't you think? or a girl named *Romona*, either way – maybe a little of both, to lay down and pray with him, and then there's an 'e' 'm-a-r-hyphen-j-u-h-hyphen-r-e' it's a very long 'e', that 'e' stands for *ejaculation*, which is what that thing was doing over there and then there's an 'n' which stands for *nude*, which is how everyone should sleep when they get home, of course it is, and then there's another 'e' on the end of that – 'm-a-r-hyphen-j-u-h-hyphen-r-e-n-e-to-the-enth-degree-n' – a little tiny weenie dwindling 'e' which shall go *undisclosed* tonight simply because . . .[37]

This piece of structured verbal improvisation, with its blind grop-ing among foodstuffs, looks forward to 'Dangerous Kitchen'.[38] Its reference to 'juvenile hall' looks back to 1956, when Zappa himself was almost incarcerated for experimenting with explosives, an incident he had recounted on the radio three months before:

Well, folks, I hate to tell you about this, but I used to be a juvenile delinquent. I was always doing all kinds of terrible things in school. I was at high school in San Diego. It was the night of the full moon and it happened to be open-house night at school. I have had an interest in chemistry since I was about six years old when I first learned how to make gunpowder and I was experimenting with explosives and fireworks and various forms of ornamental flames for a bunch of years. That one night me and another guy decided that we were going to do something amusing for the parents of the place called Mission Bay High School in San Diego. So we mixed up a potion – I won't give you the formula – what it did was, if you lit it, it made an enormous white flaring flame about four feet high from about a two ounce quantity and left a horrible black sludge and smelled bad all at the same time. Sort of an ideal vandal preparation. I had a quart mayonnaise jar full of it which I'd concealed in the sleeve of my leather jacket and me and this other guy hitch-hiked down to this school and the first stop was the cafeteria where we gathered up a bunch of paper cups and split up a certain amount of this material between various other juvenile-delinquent-type agents going, Hey let's go set some fires. Well, anyway, I got thrown out of school for that and they almost stuck me in juvie but fortunately I was going to be moving away from that area within a matter of weeks and the probation guy was Italian and my mother went down there and gave him a couple of weeps and I escaped and moved to Lancaster, California,

[37]From 'St Alphonso's Pancake Breakfast', Sydney, Australia, 26 June 1973.
[38]'Dangerous Kitchen', *The Man from Utopia*, 1983.

which is in the middle of the desert. While I was there I had a lot of trouble relating to the teachers and pretty much the rest of the student body at that place.[39]

This incident also appears in *The Real Frank Zappa Book*,[40] where he gives the formula (evidently reasoning that juvenile-delinquent pyromaniacs are less likely to read a book than listen to the radio). Apart from giving a good example of conceptual continuity going both forward and back – relating to the fundamental timelessness of the unconscious – the comment that the miscreant deserves two hyphens 'because they're small' reveals the symbolic nature of Zappa's aggression (in the same way that the information about Zappa's own scrape with juvenile hall reveals some kind of sympathy with the offender). This concern with minutiae and an ability to connect themes together is virtuosic but also banal, because it is the way dreams and the unconscious work. Like Joyce, Zappa mixes his own life into his work until separation is impossible.

Zappa's extemporization on mah-juh-rene follows procedures used by surrealists with their automatic writing and by modernist poets when they concatenate verbal stimulants to the unconscious. It also parallels hermetic traditions in European thought that concentrate on the material linguistic make-up of key terms. The 'Teutonic theosopher' Jacob Boehme (1575–1624), a mystic cobbler who lived in Gorlitz, irritated the religious authorities with his idea of God's truth residing in every human being (hence making the church otiose). He expounded the meaning of *mercurius* in a manner that can be compared to Zappa.

> Understand aright the manner of the existence of this *Mercurius*. The word MER, is first strong, tart, harsh attraction; for in that word (or syllable *Mer*) expressed by the tongue, you understand that it jarreth proceeding from the harshness, and you understand also, that the bitter sting or prickle is in it; for the word MER is harsh and trembling, and every syllable is formed or framed from its power or virtue and expresseth whatsoever the power or virtue doth or suffereth. You [may] understand that the syllable CU signifieth the rubbing or unquieteness of the sting or prickle, which maketh that the harshness is not at peace, but boileth and riseth up; for that syllable thrusteth itself forth with the breath from the heart, out of the mouth. It is done thus also in the virtue or power of the *prima materia* in the spirit, but the syllable CU having

---

[39]Radio interview with Mark Christopher, Arlington, Texas, March 1973.
[40]'The End of My Scientific Career', Frank Zappa, with Peter Occhiogrosso, *The Real Frank Zappa Book*, 1989, p. 27.

so strong a pressure from the heart, and yet is so presently snatched up by the syllable RI, and the whole sense or meaning is changed into it; this signifieth and is the bitter prickly wheel in the generating, which vexeth and whirleth itself as swiftly as a thought. The syllable US signifieth the swift fire-flash, that the *materia*, or matter, kindleth in the fierce whirling between the harshness and the bitterness in the swift wheel; where you may very plainly understand in the word, how the harshness is terrified, and how the power or virtue in the word sinketh down, or falleth back again upon the heart, and becometh very feeble and thin: Yet the sting or prickle with the whirling wheel, continueth in the flash, and goeth forth through the teeth out of the mouth; where then the spirit hisseth like a fire akindling, and returning back again strengtheneth itself in word.[41]

Boehme is applying a stringent micrological analysis of the body's involvement in pronunciation whereas Zappa skates on the free association of initial letters, but both insist on the relevance of the specific material of a word. Boehme registered the first tremors of the bourgeoisie's discovery of personal aesthetic response. He was avidly read by both William Blake and Samuel Coleridge. The former turned Boehme's intense descriptions of transformative essences into proto-psychoanalytic characterization of psychic forces; the latter mocked Boehme's wordplay but learned from it to construct the private linguistic cosmogeny which underlies his poetic effects. Mercury to margarine traces the distance between Jacob Boehme and Frank Zappa: from alchemy as metaphorical insight to chemistry as organized mass (food) production. Zappa nevertheless still uses Boehme's strategic wordplay to resist the curmudgeons who would reduce language to a system of means rather than an end in itself.[42]

CONCEPTUAL CONTINUITY AND THE FANS

Zappa's rhetoric of 'conceptual continuity' causes both creative speculation and intense disappointment among the fans. For example, David Pilcher wrote to the Zappa fanzine *T'Mershi Duween*[43] with connections he had found with the science-fiction writer Kurt Vonnegut Jnr: in *Slapstick Or Lonesome No More* (1976) there are characters named Vera Chipmunk-5 Zappa and

[41] *Jacob Boehme: Essential Readings*, ed. Robin Waterfield, 1989, pp. 85–6.
[42] See also Jeremy Prynne, *Stars, Tigers and the Shape of Words*, 1993.
[43] *T'Mershi Duween* is available from Fred Tomsett, 96a Cowlishaw Road, Hunters Bar, Sheffield S11 8XH, England (SAE for details).

Lee Razorclam-13 Zappa; in *Palm Sunday* (1981) it is revealed that '(1) He chainsmokes Pall Mall cigarettes (Zappa will only smoke Pall Mall or Winston). (2) He owns a "small shaggy dog named Pumpkin who is always barking". Getting spooky, eh?' The spookiness is caused by the fact that in 1981 Zappa called his record label Barking Pumpkin Records. Pilcher continues: 'On the back of the hardback edition of his most recent novel, *Bluebeard* (1987), the photograph of Vonnegut is not a million miles away from the front of *Jazz from Hell*. In fact, it could almost be a picture of an older incarnation of Frank! . . .'[44]

Such obsessive tracking of clues and signs is a neurotic response to mass culture: the transformation of consumer into collector. Traditionally, the collector's joy-in-the-object is a mark of high-art appreciation. Mass-marketed products are rarely catalogued with the high-definition zeal that has second-hand book dealers describing glue-marks on specific volumes in the catalogue.[45] But they are sometimes. In this, Zappology approaches the world of *Record Collector* magazine, in which mass-market objects aspire to art status, sprouting Benjamin-type auras. Completism, a rock word that describes the attempt to define your universe by collecting *every* release by a chosen artist, is usually an excuse used by collectors to justify their purchase of overpriced dross; but it can also be a species of materialism. In directing attention to the material evidence – the hardback edition of Vonnegut, the cover of *Jazz from Hell* – Pilcher diverts attention from the ideology of the 'author' to the objects themselves. Of course, it is possible to continually look for the arbiter of meaning in the author himself. In this guise, interpretation becomes merely *another* set of interviews, as if the streams of interviews Zappa has conducted since his career began could be the 'key' to his work (if so, why bother with the records at all? Go straight to the horse's mouth!) whereas in fact they merely serve to 'significantly complicate'[46] the project-object.

One of the shibboleths of structuralist criticism as propounded by Roland Barthes is that analysis must focus on the *text*. Critics

[44]*T'Mershi Duween*, No. 15, September 1990, p. 19.
[45]Antiquarian book dealers are ubiquitous. Two book dealers with the necessary combination of aesthetic suss and anal retention are Peter Riley (modern poetry), 27 Sturton Street, Cambridge CB1 2QG, England, and jwcurry (Zappa and avant-garde writing), Room 302, Books, 1357 Lansdowne Avenue, Toronto, Ontario M6H 3Z9, Canada (write for catalogues).
[46]Blurb by Carol Christ on the back cover of Eve Kosovsky Sedgwick, *Between Men: English Literature and Male Homosocial Desire*, 1985.

point out how a sentimental image of 'Van Gogh the madman' limits the possible meanings of Van Gogh's paintings, obstructing an objective materialist analysis of the art itself: everything is made to illustrate a mythical notion of 'personality'. Likewise, Freudian psychoanalysis insists that people do not necessarily understand the full repercussions of what they are saying. It is no use simply consulting the artist to find out what the art 'means'. This also recognizes that art becomes a commodity: once launched on to the market, an artwork is beyond the artist's control, and may be put to all kinds of uses. Art is just as much an example of alienated labour as any other product under capitalism. The methods of both Freud and Marx question the idea that art may be explained by referring to the conscious intention of the artist.

As befits the hagiographic nature of fanzines, the editors of *Society Pages* ceaselessly quiz Zappa about the 'meaning' of every puzzling feature. However, although in the short term this appears to 'clear up' nagging doubts, this actually merely accumulates further versions, further complexities. Zappa has said on TV that Barking Pumpkin was named for Gail and the bad cough she got from smoking Marlboros, but the resonance of the name does not stop there.[47] Pumpkin is a nickname for Gail, certainly, but the logo has a Halloween pumpkin barking at a cat (which replies 'Holy shit!', transcribed in Chinese characters[48]). It fits with Zappa's schema to have a symbol of pagan residues shocking a respectable domestic animal. The negative dialectics of poodle play ferrets out these meanings quite without regard to the yay-saying of the source.

Some fans suffer irredeemable disappointment when they realize the artwork will not suddenly resolve into a whole picture as Zappa promised.

For years, I have passionately 'consumed' vast quantities of Frank's material, absorbing as much as possible, in the vague hope that one day

---

[47]Frank Zappa talking to Kathryn Kinley, *Radio1990*, 31 October 1985. One rumour was that Barking Pumpkin referred to Gail Zappa's farting; the TV statement may be a 'cleaned-up' explanation, or on the other hand another example of the popular propensity to find scatological themes in Zappa. Either way, the more data the less we understand. *Society Pages* frequently gets close to the artwork-as-crossword-puzzle approach that nearly killed my interest in *Finnegans Wake* (e.g. William York Tindall, *A Guide to Finnegans Wake*, 1974). Microscopic attention to detail certainly generates interesting material, but by ignoring the *why* of art it can easily kill what Zappa terms the 'chuckle in the laugh', 'Way Down in New Zealand: FZ Talks to Gary Steel, 5 December 1990, Part 2', *T'Mershi Duween*, No. 21, September 1991, p. 17.

[48]According to Simon Prentis, this would read strangely to a Chinese reader – along the lines of 'sacred excrement' – because although the words stand for 'holy' and 'shit' there is no such expression in Chinese. Letter to the author, 21 December 1993.

I might come to recognize his legendary 'Conceptual Continuity'. Finally, after all this time listening to the material and fondling and fetishing the record sleeves, I think ... the theories were developed as a way of manipulating the music business (whom Frank has been playing games with from the outset), into believing that Frank is on a higher plane than the rest of the music industry, and should therefore be given greater consideration (i.e. coverage and publicity)... Frank *is* bullshitting.[49]

'Conceptual continuity' may well serve as a term for an underlying substratum of associations that anyone uses over the years in order to express themselves – the network of meanings revealed, say, in Samuel Taylor Coleridge's notebooks, which show irrational attachment to words that appear at key points in his poems – but what makes Zappa's use of it modernist is that he brings this substratum to consciousness. You cannot approach Zappa as you would André Gide or Sting, absorbing their art and imagining some rounded human personality. You must deal with it as you would *Finnegans Wake*, actively tracing images and connections as they emerge on the material surface. This is modern art you cannot approach in the old way.

EXPLICIT POODLE CONTINUITY

The lyrics for 'I'm the Slime' feature virtuosic repeated rhymes in the manner of the early Bob Dylan and a silvery, tweaked electric guitar sound that flickers like a TV image. Particularly telling is the couplet

> And you will do as you are told
> Until the rights to you are sold[50]

a paranoid vision of advertising that has the advantage of summing up very accurately what goes on when TV stations sell prime-time commercial slots. One idea was to feature extracts from Richard Nixon's Watergate speech, but this was dropped.[51] 'Dirty Love' explicitly introduces a poodle for the first time. It's a lust song:

> Give me
> Your dirty love

---

[49]Dirk Manuel, 'Conceptual Continuity: Is Frank Zappa Bullshitting', *T'Mershi Duween*, No. 12, May 1990, pp. 10–11.
[50]Frank Zappa, 'I'm the Slime', *Overnite Sensation*, 1973.
[51]Michael Wale, 'The Charge of the Wale Brigade', *ZigZag*, No. 33, March 1973, p. 35.

Like some tacky little pamphlet
In your daddy's bottom drawer[52]

In 'Brown Shoes Don't Make It' mention had been made of pornography:

A world of secret hungers
Perverting the men who make your laws
Every desire is hidden away
In a drawer in a desk by a Naugahyde chair[53]

In 1967 Zappa used Reichian arguments to connect sexual repression with moralistic, right-wing behaviour. In 1968 Leroi Jones touched on similar themes:

Reich has written about the repression of sexuality in the white man, and how this blocking of natural emission and other violent energies causes cancer and madness or white Americans. And this sexual energy is a dirtiness, which always threatens the 'order' i.e. 'rationalism', the a-human, a-sexual social order the white man seeks with all his energies to uphold.[54]

When Frank Zappa was playing at the Hammersmith Odeon in 1979 he noticed a baby in the arms of one of the aisle dancers. After saying he hoped the baby wouldn't get dropped on the head, he added that listening to the words to of the next song might help the baby 'grow up straight':[55] the band went into 'Dirty Love'. On *Overnite Sensation*, the demand for 'dirty love' is delivered with a paradoxical leer that implies offence rather than liberation.

I'll ignore your cheap aroma
And your little-bo-peep diploma
I'll just put you in a coma
With some dirty love[56]

The mention of the diploma evinces the same hostility towards women in higher education as 'The Illinois Enema Bandit'. The net effect is a high-tech jazz-rock rewrite of Iggy Pop's primal 'Now I Wanna be Your Dog':

Give me
Your dirty love
The way your mama

[52]Frank Zappa, 'Dirty Love', *Overnite Sensation*, 1973.
[53]Frank Zappa, 'Brown Shoes Don't Make It', *Absolutely Free*, 1967.
[54]Leroi Jones, *Home: Social Essays*, 1968 p. 33.
[55]Hammersmith Odeon, London, 19 February 1979.
[56]Frank Zappa, 'Dirty Love', *Overnite Sensation*, 1973.

Make that nasty poodle chew . . .
THE POODLE BITES!
(*Come on, Frenchie*)
THE POODLE CHEWS IT!
(*Snap It*)[57]

Dogs seem to be a noted feature of pop subversion from Iggy to George Clinton ('Why must I do that? Why must I chase the cat?/Nothing but the dog in me'[58]) and Malcolm McLaren with Bow Wow Wow. But the association of dogs and sex has a longer history than that, an undercurrent that shows how accurately Zappa selects his cultural icons.

As far back as the seventeenth century, the servility of the domesticated dog had a sexual charge. In *Venice Preserv'd, or, A Plot Discover'd*, Thomas Otway has an old senator called Antonio entreat Aquilina to treat him like a dog:

> now I am under the table, kick again – kick
> harder – harder yet, bough waugh waugh, waugh,
> bough – 'odd, I'le have a snap at thy shins – bough waugh
> waugh, waugh, bough – 'odd she kicks bravely.[59]

She obliges and whips him – with the words 'here's the discipline'.[60] In *Dialectic of Enlightenment* Theodor Adorno and Max Horkheimer find in de Sade a key to understanding why Western rationality punishes sexuality: instinctual urges are a residual site of nature, something rationality sees as an enemy. As the most common domestic animal, the dog readily becomes a symbol for such repressed nature.

JOHN RUSKIN AND DINAH-THE-DOG

'Dinah-Moe Humm' was a song that celebrated the efficacy of discipline in achieving sexual arousal. On 11 November 1847 John Ruskin wrote to his fiancée Euphemia comparing himself to her dog Dinah.

> If she should be sad – what *shall* I do – And – if she should *not* – what shall I do – either – how shall I ever tell her my gladness – Oh – my own love – what shall I do indeed – I shall not be able to speak a word

---

[57]Ibid.
[58]George Clinton, 'Atomic Dog', from the album *Computer Games*, 1982, Capitol STI2246.
[59]Thomas Otway, *Venice Preserv'd, or, A Plot Discover'd*, 1682, III, i, 122–7.
[60]Ibid., III, i, 137.

– I shall be running round you – and kneeling to you – and holding up my hands to you as Dinah does her paws – speechless – I shan't do it as well as Dinah though – I shall be clumsy and mute – at once perfectly oppressed with delight – if you speak to me I shall not know what you say – you will have to pat me – and point to something for me to fetch and carry for you – or make me lie down on the rug and be quiet – or send me out of the room until I promise to be a good dog; and when you let me in again – I shall be *worse* – What *shall* I do?[61]

This is an unconscious sexual fantasy: the room is – euphemistically – Euphemia's womb, with Ruskin's 'dog' slipping in and out like a penis. It is a Victorian premonition of doggie sex in both Iggy Pop and Frank Zappa. On the fade-out to 'Dirty Love' you hear Zappa say 'two paws stickin' up', which connects audience applause to canine servility. To hear an entire audience join in 'Dinah-Moe Humm''s chorus of 'dynamo, dynamo' is a chilling reminder of the mechanics of sexual stupidity. So offended was the author by Zappa's insistence on playing the song as the encore throughout 1978 that he interrupted a rendition in Newcastle on 13 February 1979:

FZ: Would y'all like some more-a?

OUT TO LUNCH: No! Fuck off!

FZ: On the floor-a. And how about you fauna?

OTL: No! Piss off!

FZ: This is the second part where you get to do something stupid.

OTL: Play something else stupid! We're sick of this fucking song you big fool!

FZ: Keep playing on down behind me boys – I hear a native. [*Laughter*]

OTL: Right! I'm sick of this song.

FZ: Come on, louder. I want to hear what that guy said.

OTL: I'm sick of this song. Play me something else. Play me – ah – the Smegmates!

OUT OF GAS: The Smegmates!

FZ: What did he say?

AUDIENCE: Can't hear you.

OTL: I am fucking sick of it, this is it. I'm going to make a stand here! [*Stands up*] Zappa! Listen to me, Zappa!

FZ: To talk to me you've got to talk like this. I'm from America, we all talk this way. This is bullshit. We needed to give you the opportunity to say something like that because we know it's a lot of hot air. [*Applause*]. You can all sing along because we're going back to the beginning of the song.

OTL: Fuckin' hell. [*Band starts song, then stops*]

FZ: Theoretically we share the same language. Therefore it should come

[61]John Ruskin, *The Order of Release*, ed. Admiral Sir William James, GCB, 1947, pp. 50–51. I am indebted to Emma Biggs for showing me this passage.

as no surprise to you that when I say you're going to sing 'Dinah-d-i-n-a-hyphen-moe-m-o-e' when I aim the microphone toward you you will know I am not pulling your chain. Now hear this. This is enforced audience participation – it's the American way.

OTL: Sure is. They're all doing it, the stupid fuckers.

FZ: Dinah-Moe!

AUDIENCE: Dinah-Moe!

FZ: Dinah-Moe!

AUDIENCE: Dinah-Moe!

OTL: Hang on to that for a bit, I have to find another cassette.

FZ: Yes, it's almost as if each and every one of you were alive. I've experienced cardboard cutouts of English people for the last week or so but I'm telling you – you guys look the best to me. [*Applause*] So let's get along with it folks. You have – by virtue of the fact that you endeavoured to act stupid along with me – you have earned one more stupid song. The name of the song is 'Camarillo Brillo' . . .

Zappa's showbiz cynicism here rubbed the idealistic punkrocker up the wrong way, though it should be noted that most of the audience had probably not OD'd on live encores of 'Dinah-Moe Humm' from swapped cassettes. In retrospect what one appreciates is the unerring suggestiveness of Zappa's motifs, and of course it was the endless touring of the late 70s that kept the project viable. Like Stravinsky, 'Dinah-Moe Humm' 'thoroughly ritualized the selling-out itself, indeed even its relation to consumer goods. He performs a *danse macabre* round its fetish character.'[62]

Punk – and Out To Lunch's heckling – reflect an Adornoite/situationist impatience with Stravinskian compromise. What cannot be denied, though, is the accuracy of Zappa's delineation of hit-song stupidity.

The fact that Euphemia's dog should be called Dinah is exactly the kind of inexplicable coincidence that dazzles the Zappologist. In the preface to *The Real Frank Zappa Book* Zappa pointed out:

the epigraphs at the heads of chapters (publishers *love* those little things) were researched and inserted by Peter [Occhiogrosso] – I mention this because I wouldn't want anybody to think I sat around reading Flaubert, Twitchell and Shakespeare all day.[63]

So it is unlikely that Zappa is pursuing a deliberate desecration of Ruskin, doyen of all things pious and Victorian – but his deployment of Dinah in 'Dinah-Moe Humm' certainly puts Ruskin in a new light.

62Theodor Adorno, *The Philosophy of Modern Music*, 1948, trs. Anne Mitchell and Wesley Blomster, 1973, p. 171 n25.
63Frank Zappa, with Peter Occhiogrosso, *The Real Frank Zappa Book*, 1989, p. 10.

In 'Dinah-Moe Humm' Dinah bets the narrator he cannot make her come. He only wins the bet when her sister Dora 'gets *nekkid*' and asks for it:

> 'Till Dinah-Moe finally
> Did give in
> But I told her
> All she really needed
> Was some discipline[64]

It certainly sounds like that is what Ruskin – in his persona as Dinah-the-dog – would have liked from Euphemia. To religion's exploitation of masochism Zappa counters an absurdist parade of S&M insignia.

Canine servility

In dramatizing the efficacy of domination in achieving sexual arousal Zappa questions the 'self-evident' media myth that sexuality resides in sex objects – to which a lustful response is 'natural'. From de Sade to Pat Califia recognition of the erotic possibilities of power has always been associated with disrespect for authority. As a symbol of craven servility the poodle has an eminent history. Since the eighteenth century it has been used frequently in politics (in the late 1970s the left picketed Shirley Williams with signs that read 'SDP – NATO's poodle'). Henry James, always attentive to the sexual charge of metaphor, wrote: 'Lord, how she would bully him, how she would "squeeze" him, in such a case! The worst of it would be that – such was his amiable, peace-loving nature – he should obey like a showman's poodle.'[65]

The use of poodles as performing animals actually stems from their unusual intelligence. Poodles were introduced into England from Germany as hunting dogs. The name derives from the German word for lake – *pudel* – as they were used as retrievers for ducks shot over water (the standard poodle cut has a mane, originally to aid buoyancy). However, the discovery that their woolly fur could be used to sustain sculptural effects consigned them to ornamental use at an early date. Pampered and obedient, they became a symbol of nature tramelled, disciplined,

---

[64]Frank Zappa, 'Dinah-Moe Humm', *Overnite Sensation*, 1973.

[65]Henry James, *The Princess Casamassima*, 1886, p. 448. See also Out To Lunch, *So Much Plotted Freedom*, Reality Studios Occasional Paper, No. 6, 1987.

domesticated. When Gary McFarland wanted to invoke spiritual death in *America the Beautiful*, his album of music protesting the despoliation of the countryside, he called the third movement 'Suburbia – Two Poodles and a Plastic Jesus'.[66] Jeff Koons, who installed a poodle in polychromed wood next to a penetration shot that emphasized the proximity of asshole and vagina, was completely correct, if not startlingly original.[67]

In 'Camarillo Brillo' they 'did it till we were unconcho', sex used as a critique of rationality. This is a standard romantic procedure given new trappings. Romanticism – the movement that sought to round out the bourgeoisie's view of the world by providing a secular treatment of matters hitherto considered sacred – was keen to deny the centrality of reason to creativity. Again, the poodle appears. Samuel Taylor Coleridge argued in *The Friend* that 'Understanding and Experience* may exist without Reason.' The footnote indicated by the asterisk runs: 'Of this no-one would feel inclined to doubt, who had seen the poodledog...'[68]

Possibly Dora is simply the other orifice, 'all she really needed / Was some discipline' referring to the connection between anality and masochism: attention to Dora stimulates Dinah.

ANTI-CONSUMERISM

Poodles seemed to arrive with *Overnite Sensation*, but they had been around in latent form before. Zappa is making use of a continuity that underpins earlier albums. Dissatisfied with the desultory manner in which Jack Anesh had arranged the photographs for *Freak Out!*, Zappa designed the sleeve of *Absolutely Free* himself. A dog collar appears on an advertising hoarding above a street filled with banal and busy cartoon cars, a view of the city that reappears in many guises – from the 'traffic music' of 'Pound for a Brown' to the toytown of 'City of Tiny Lites' and the car chase in 'Greggery Peccary' – a paranoid vision of the world as cheap illusion. The dog collar is accompanied by the slogan 'BUY A FYDO fits swell', which later evolved into the album title *One Size Fits All*. Other signs read 'Buy!',

---

[66]Gary McFarland, *America the Beautiful*, 1968, Skye Recording SK8.
[67]'Poodle', 1991, and 'Ilona's Asshole', 1991, *Jeff Koons*, catalogue of exhibition at San Francisco Museum of Modern Art, 10 July–3 October 1993, plates 54 and 57.
[68]Samuel Taylor Coleridge, *The Friend: A Weekly Paper*, 1809–18, p. 156.

'Crombly Crombly and buy some', 'War means work for all' and 'Move your goods with patriotic sell!' Pets and their attendant paraphernalia are symbols of unnecessary consumerism. In the live version of 'Call Any Vegetable', originally a call for the Hollywood freaks to spread the word to straight America, the Mothers had a routine designed to satirize the consumerism of the so-called counter-culture. Poodles head the list.

> FZ: A lot of people don't bother about their friends in the vegetable kingdom. They think, what can I say? Sometimes they think, where can I go?
> HK: Where can I go to get my poodle clipped in Burbank?
> MV: At *Ralph's Vegetarian Poodle Clipping*.
> HK: Where can I go to get organic Vaseline?
> MV: At *Bobby Ray's Swahili Restaurant*.
> HK: Where can I go to get my jeans embroidered?
> MV: At *Jeans North*, where nothing fits.
> HK: Where can I go to get my zipper repaired?
> MV: Who gives a fuck anyway?
> HK: Where can I go to get my speakers fixed? Where can I go to get my exit lights?
> FZ: Questions, questions, questions, flooding into the mind of the concerned young person today.[69]

Another hoarding on the *Absolutely Free* cover reads: 'You must buy this album, top 40 radio will never ever play it – buy this thing.' Zappa has the wit to extend his satire to himself, an element lacking in the righteous tirades against consumer society by groups like Jefferson Airplane. A similar point was made by Jamie Reid when he reproduced his satire of the ad family from Chris Gray's collection of SI texts, *Leaving the Twentieth Century*, on the back of the pic sleeve of 'Holidays in the Sun' by the Sex Pistols. The family are depicted at breakfast labelled 'nice middle-aged man', 'nice furniture', 'nice little girl' etc. – Reid added 'nice sleeve' at the bottom. The ironies of anti-consumerist art.

Beneath the dog collar ('copper safety lines shown in phantom') one can make out graffiti – the names Benny, Martha, Ruben, Joe and Steve grouped around a 'pachuco cross' (a cross with three dashes above it, symbolizing the Trinity, tattooed on the back of the hand where thumb and forefinger join – see God's hand on the cover of *One Size Fits All*). The biography of Ruben Sano on *Ruben & the Jets* concluded with the statement: 'Ruben has three dogs. Benny, Baby & Martha.' Priests in dog collars, dog

---

[69]Frank Zappa, 'Call Any Vegetable', *Just Another Band from LA*, 1971.

names round a cross: Zappa is making the God/doG reversal beloved of blasphemers. As these references in *Absolutely Free* and *Just Another Band from LA* show, dog continuity did not arrive with *Overnite Sensation*, but it did become overt – inescapable.

DREAM THOUGHTS AND DENTAL FLOSS

In the innerfold of *Lumpy Gravy* someone with dog-ears exclaims 'curses!' because the compiler of the chorus personnel listing has been told to 'omit last names'. The same character later appeared as part of the decadent rabble on the cover of *Tinsel Town Rebellion*. On the cover of *Ruben & the Jets* the band sport dog-snouts (necessary to accommodate the brain growth stimulated by Uncle Meat's 'vocal drone mechanism'). The song 'Dog Breath' (*Uncle Meat* and *Just Another Band from LA*) is about being 'on the sniff',[70] cruising in a car looking for members of the opposite sex. In *200 Motels* there is a scene in which the musicians line up like racing greyhounds in start-cages before rushing off to chase the groupies: dogs and low desires.

But it is only after *Overnite Sensation* that we are invited to follow such themes. In the film-treatment in the booklet that accompanies *Uncle Meat* we are told: 'It is quiet except for a little light wind. We are travelling across the wasteland towards a huge hydro-electric dam. Dynamo hum increases as we near it.' *Overnite Sensation*'s 'Dinah-Moe Humm' constructs retro-continuity.

Overnite Sensation makes an epistemological break with the Bizarre period: unconscious continuities are brought to the surface whilst overt 'counter-cultural' protests are suppressed. Poodles emerge as an explicit theme whereas before they had only been present in cryptic details, like the trivial fragments of memory – what Freud called 'day's residues' – which are used by repressed and unconscious wishful impulses to construct the latent dream content (which is again condensed and displaced and censored before making its manifest appearance). In dreams, actions and objects of the most complete triviality (such as toothpicks or bandages or labels) can become endowed with great affective

---

[70] A quaint term used in Manchester in the mid-80s for being on the look-out for sex.

power: it is exactly this sensation that the Zappologist undergoes when examining Bizarre records for evidence of DiscReet themes.

In *Overnite Sensation* dental floss follows dynamo hum in becoming the subject of an entire song. *200 Motels* had already mentioned it:

CHORUS: Some old melodies!
SOPRANO: *Four-four!* An aura!
CHORUS: An areola!
SOPRANO: Pink gums! Stumpy gray teeth! Dental floss ... GETS ME HOT!
CHORUS: Mmmmmmmmmm!
SOPRANO: Wanna watch a dental hygiene movie?[71]

In the film, this question is followed by the whirring of a projector and an animation by Cal Schenkel showing Donald Duck as a dental care adviser. On the record, the question segues into 'Magic Fingers', Zappa's heavy-rock masterpiece, which ends with Howard Kaylan describing in detail his erotic projects for a groupie he has dragged back to his hotel room – activities that include taking off her clothes, making her pose with a plastic chair and an old guitar strap, doing a wee-wee in her hair and beating her with a pair of tennis shoes he got from Jeff Beck. Before the struggle between devil and angel over Jeff Simmons's soul we see a photograph of Zappa's face – his lips open and his teeth dance. The 'dental hygiene dilemma' is anxiety about sin: Zappa's response, explicitly documented in 'Titties & Beer',[72] when he outwits the devil by his enthusiasm in selling his soul, is 'why not?' As Adorno said:

> The fact that Sade and Nietzsche insist on the *ratio* [bourgeois rationalism] more decisively even than logical positivism, implicitly liberates from its hiding place the Utopia contained in the Kantian notion of reason as in every great philosophy: the Utopia of a humanity which, itself no longer distorted, has no further need to distort.[73]

Freud was sure that dreams with a dental stimulus derive their motive force from the masturbatory desires of the pubertal period. This was because, unlike the other parts of the face,

> the one structure which affords no possibility of an analogy is teeth: and it is precisely the combination of similarity and dissimilarity which

---

[71]Frank Zappa, 'A Nun Suit Painted on Some Old Boxes', *200 Motels*, 1972.
[72]*Zappa in New York*, 1977.
[73]Theodor Adorno and Max Horkheimer, *The Dialectic of Enlightenment*, 1944, p. 119.

makes the teeth so appropriate for representational purposes when pressure is being exercised by sexual repression.[74]

Nose and mouth are too overtly phallic and vaginal, respectively, but the teeth can be a focus for masturbatory impulses. This sounds like an exegesis of 'Montana'.

> I might be movin' to Montana soon
> Just to raise me up a crop of
> Dental Floss . . .
> Movin' to Montana soon
> Gonna be a Dental Floss tycoon (yes I am)
> Movin' to Montana soon
> Gonna be a mennil-toss flykune[75]

In live performances, Zappa is wont to throw in the aside, 'whatever that means'. Perhaps it refers to Johnny 'Guitar' Watson, the black singer and multi-instrumentalist who frequently builds up whole songs by overdubs. Johnny Otis has joked on the radio with Watson about 'playing with himself'.[76] 'Guitar' Watson dresses in nothing but the sharpest clothes: a mental-toss fly coon? The title itself contains the name Onan (mONtANa), a biblical figure who was slain by the Lord for 'spilling his seed on the ground'[77] and, like the Marquis de Sade and Sacher Masoch, gave his name to a sexual impropriety that, until that time, had no name – onanism (after 'Onan' is removed from 'Montana' we are left with the letters MTA which, when read aloud, reveal the phrase 'empty, eh?' which could be a comment on these proceedings).

> I'm ridin' a small tiny hoss
> (His name is MIGHTY LITTLE)
> He's a tiny bit dinky
> To strap a blanket or saddle on anyway
> . . . By myself I wouldn't
> Have no Boss,
> But I'd be raisin' my lonely
> Dental Floss[78]

'Mighty little', a vehicle that can change its size, is distinctly

---

[74]Sigmund Freud, *The Interpretation of Dreams*, 1900, trs. James Strachey, 1953, p. 510.

[75]Frank Zappa, 'Montana', *Overnite Sensation*, 1973.

[76]Undated radio broadcast, Johnny 'Guitar' Watson, *The Gangster is Back*, 1976, Red Lightnin' RL0013.

[77]Genesis 38: 9. Progressive theologians argue that the Bible is taking a stand against *coitus interruptus* – a psychically harmful and ineffective form of contraception – rather than masturbation.

[78]Frank Zappa, 'Montana', *Overnite Sensation*, 1973.

phallic. 'Montana' is a song about the lonely pleasures of masturbation.

It also pushes the melody – as so often, derived from the rhythms of the words – through some uniquely perverse cavorts. Ruth Underwood's marimbas, which in concert supply the hallucinogenic 'gleaming tweezers' sound effect, are quite simply bravura. The words of *Overnite Sensation* often distract people from the music, which was played by what was probably Zappa's greatest band. Zappa recognized the special nature of this edition of the Mothers and devoted a whole double CD to it in the *You Can't Do That on Stage Anymore* series.[79]

Much of *Overnite Sensation* was recorded at Bolic Sound in Inglewood, Ike and Tina Turner's studio. Tina and the Ikettes sang backing vocals, but Ike Turner would not allow them to have a credit, so at the time of the release Zappa only talked about a 'possible' collaboration.[80] Later, he explained the situation to Simon Prentis.

> I wanted to put some back-up singers on the thing, and the road manager who was with us at the time checked into it and said, 'Well, why don't you just use the Ikettes?' I said, 'I can get the Ikettes?' And he said, 'Sure.' But you know what the gimmick was? We had to agree, Ike Turner insisted, that we pay these girls no more than $25 per song, because that's what he paid them. And no matter how many hours it took, I could not pay them any more than $25 per song per girl, including Tina.
>
> It was so difficult, that one part in the middle of the song 'Montana', that the three girls rehearsed it for a couple of days. Just that one section. You know the part that goes 'I'm pluckin' the ol' Dennil Floss . . .'? Right in the middle there. And – I can't remember her name, but one of the harmony singers – she got it first. She came out and sang her part and the other girls had to follow her track. Tina was so pleased that she was able to sing this thing that she went into the next studio where Ike was working and dragged him into the studio to hear the result of her labour. He listened to the tape and he goes, 'What is this shit?' and walked out.
>
> I don't know how she managed to stick with that guy for so long. He treated her terribly and she's a really nice lady. We were recording down there a Sunday. She wasn't involved with the session, but she came in on Sunday with a whole pot of stew that she brought for everyone working in the studio. Like out of nowhere, here's Tina Turner

---

[79]Frank Zappa, *You Can't Do That on Stage Anymore Vol. 2: The Helsinki Concert*, 1991.
[80]Michael Wale, 'Charge of the Wale Brigade', *ZigZag*, No. 33, March 1973, p. 36.

coming in with a rag on her head bringing a big pot of stew. It was kinda nice.[81]

The idea of the Ikettes singing the diabolical twists and turns of the 'Montana' chorus is an apt symbol of Zappa's music: extruded R&B indeed.

'ZOMBY WOOF'

Like *Uncle Meat* and *Ruben & the Jets* showing that the same sounds can shape both underground abstractions and 'cretin simplicity', the introduction to 'Zomby Woof' – ostensibly a lewd rocker – is as dizzyingly complex as anything on *Waka/Jawaka*. It uses brief sections of contrasting material that seem to give the musicians an obstacle course to cover, interleaving propulsive R&B horns with smarmy lite-jazz trumpet (and a complex, atonal tune). A typical adjuncture of contradictory elements. As usual, too, 'Zomby Woof' self-consciously perpetuates a tradition, this time in the line of threatening, demonic songs like 'The Wolf Is At Your Door' by Howlin' Wolf (he actually sings his own name so it sounds like 'woof', the *'reety-awrighty'* chorus refers to Joe Turner's routine). *Overnite Sensation* was mixed and originally released in quad (the step beyond stereo that never caught on). Ricky Lancelotti's voice was meant to swirl about the room. The Zomby Woof is a wraith-like incubus with a dog-bark built into his name. The woofer (as opposed to the tweeter) is the bass component of a loudspeaker: the song also comments on the sexual division of pitch.

Despite the frenzied pace of the music on 'Zomby Woof' the drummer hits the cymbals only once a bar, a measured beat where you would least expect it. Zappa's guitar solo is at his most twistingly organic, a writhing, arching mess of electricity; George Duke's keyboard is slitheringly loose and suggestive. The cartoon quality of the words might lead you to expect a simple-minded rock-out, but if you pay attention to the placement of the instruments in the solo, bass and drums keep popping up in unexpected places (just like the Woof!): a unique arrangement. Rock and jazz bands generally work towards their own special chemistry

[81]Quoted by Simon Prentis, 'Anything Anywhere Anytime for No Reason At All', *Society Pages*, No. 45, May 1989, p. 35.

intuitively: by contrast, Zappa is extremely deliberate. Each tune has a distinct content. His perverse directions chafe against the musicians' fantastic sense of swing. Duke uses a 'Superstition' clavinet bass for the re-entry of the vocal, while Jean-Luc Ponty's close-miked violin overlays his special taint.

George Duke's years of jazz experience gave a great lift to the solos.[82] His funky musicality added an ease to the music that was much missed in Zappa's bands of the 80s. Duke was also very amusing, as he proved in his famous 'finger-cymbal' routine, where he'd tell stories and joke about the band members and booger-bears. On the CD mix of Overnite Sensation, Tom Fowler's bass has been brought forward, a mixture of firm, round force and suppleness. On 'Montana' his 'country' bassline is astonishing. 'Fifty-Fifty' features the only solos: George Duke is gorgeous, rampagingly inventive; Jean-Luc Ponty's melting violin is the perfect aural equivalent of the slime Cal Schenkel has drawn over him on the inner sleeve; Zappa has begun his conquest of high-tech guitar *sound*, drenching his linear logic in sizzling effects.

A new discovery – made by Zappa in a bar in Hawaii – was saxophonist Napoleon Murphy Brock. Also a fantastic dancer, flautist and amazingly elastic singer, Brock's spontaneity and enthusiasm indelibly marked Zappa's music for the next few years.

APOSTROPHE (') AND KING LEAR

Apostrophe (') is Frank Zappa's *King Lear*, an absolute masterpiece – chillingly abstract, dizzyingly clever and extremely silly. The king/fool dialogue of *King Lear*, which famously equates ultimate realities with folly, is taken up as a dialogue between Zappa and his dog. The slick, meretricious humour of the record has of course meant that it has attracted no attention at all from even those postmoderns who claim to have transcended traditional divides between the high-minded and the frivolous.

There is a frozen, desolate landscape, a primal encounter that results in a blinding, a meditation on orgasm and time, refutation of Sri Chinmoy and Plato, political comment on the civil rights movement and satire on religion. Images used in *King Lear* coincide again and again with those of *Apostrophe (')*. In

[82]A point Zappa made to Bill Milkowski, 'Frank Zappa: Guitar Player', *Down Beat*, February 1983, p. 16.

Shakespeare's play Lear says 'Nothing will come of nothing',[83] initiating an obsessive series of references to nothingness, emptiness, absolute zero. 'Thou art an O without a figure,'[84] says the Fool. *Apostrophe (')* begins with a series of rhymes on 'O':

> Dreamed I was an Eskimo
> Frozen wind began to blow
> Under my boots 'n around my toe
> Frost had bit the ground below
> Was a hundred degrees below zero[85]

The narrator is Nanook. *Nanook of the North* was a pioneering documentary about an Eskimo made by Robert Flaherty in 1920. In 'Nanook Rubs It' Nanook blinds the fur trapper by rubbing his eyes with snow discoloured by dog urine. Blindness is also central to *King Lear*: Goneril proves her duplicity in saying she loves Lear 'dearer than eyesight'.[86] When Kent defends Cordelia, Lear responds with 'Out of my sight!'[87]. Gloucester's tragic blinding is a culmination of these metaphors.

In *Apostrophe (')* the philosophical dialogue with the dog is prompted by smell ('Stink-Foot'). Loss of sight and reliance on smell go together. In *King Lear* the Fool says:

> All that follow their noses are led by their eyes but blind men, and there's not a nose among twenty but can smell him that's stinking.[88]

Regan concludes Gloucester's blinding with the order:

> Go thrust him out the gates, and let him smell
> His way to Dover.[89]

Lear has the Fool remove his boots:

> Now, now, now, now.
> Pull off my boots; harder, harder – so.[90]

After a struggle to remove his own boots, Zappa has Fido fetch his slippers. In *King Lear*, Cornwall contrasts the foot (organ of domination) with the eye (organ of perception):

> See't thou never shall. Fellows, hold the chair

---

[83]William Shakespeare, *King Lear*, 1608, I, i, 90.
[84]Ibid., I, iv, 193.
[85]Frank Zappa, 'Don't Eat the Yellow Snow', *Apostrophe (')*, 1974.
[86]William Shakespeare *King Lear*, 1608, I, i, 55.
[87]Ibid., I, i, 157.
[88]Ibid., II, ii, 68–71.
[89]Ibid., III, vii, 93–4.
[90]Ibid., IV, vi, 172–3.

Blindness and feet: the two central principles of *Apostrophe (')*. Zappa's live performances of 'Stink-Foot' included a section of poodle discipline.

> FZ: Well, here Fido, here Fido. Bring the slippers little puppy ... Fido, I told you to bring me the slippers!
> F: Oh Frank, I was so stoned I couldn't keep them in my mouth.
> FZ: Fido, when a big person tells a little animal to bring the slippers and the little animal doesn't bring the slippers it means that the little animal can be punished to the full extent of Imperial law!
> F: No shit?
> FZ: Yes Fido, I must punish you.
> F: Hurt me, hurt me, hurt me.
> FZ: Very well then.[92]

King Lear also resounds with the philosphical implications of power and social domination.

> Truth's a dog must to kennel, he must be whipt out[93]
>
> Thou gav'st them the rod, and put'st down thine own breeches[94]
>
> Knowing nought (like dogs) but following[95]
>
> Thou hast seen a farmer's dog bark at a beggar?
> And the creature run from the cur?
> There thou mightst behold the great image of
> authority: a dog's obeyed in office.
> Thou rascal beadle, hold thy bloody hand!
> Why dost thou lash that whore?
> Strip thy own back,
> Thou hotly lusts to use her in that kind
> For which thou whip'st her[96]

Sado masochism and the obedience of the dog: instances of domination used as symbols from Shakespeare to Zappa. At St Alfonzo's Pancake Breakfast the handsome parish lady says: 'Why don't you treat me mean? (Hurt me, hurt me, hurt me, ooooooh!)'

When Lear goes from Goneril to Regan and back, his retinue is reduced from a hundred knights to fifty to twenty-five to none

---

[91]Ibid., II, vii, 67–8.
[92]This from the same concert as 'Black Napkins' on *Zoot Allures* and 'Ship Ahoy' on *Shut Up N' Play Yer Guitar*, Osaka, 3 February 1976.
[93]William Shakespeare, *King Lear*, 1608, I, iv, 111.
[94]Ibid., I, iv, 174.
[95]Ibid., II, ii, 80.
[96]Ibid., IV, vi, 154–61.

at all, an image of barter and diminishing returns. Nanook's mother tells him:

> Don't be a naughty Eskimo-wo-oh
> Save your money; don't go to the show[97]

The blasted heath of Lear and the frozen white wasteland of *Apostrophe (')* are the landscape of the world of exchange, degree zero of humanity and warmth. The psychoanalytic figure for loss is castration – which Freud connected to blinding.

Freud interprets the mutilation of the eyes in the Oedipal myth as castration (Oedipus blinded himself in shame after discovering he'd had sex with his mother). In *Lear* the Fool jokingly refers to castration:

> She that's a maid now and laughs at my departure
> Shall not be a maid long, unless *things* be cut shorter[98]

The tale of Nanook blinding the fur trapper is called 'Nanook Rubs It'. He rubs with 'a vigorous circular motion'. The reflexive and narcissistic nature of masturbation was given circular imagery in 'Disco Boy'.

> It's disco love tonight
> Make sure you look all right[99]

And blindness is of course the traditional punishment for masturbation:

> JOHNNY OTIS: Didn't your mama tell you you'd go blind doing that?
> And you said, Can't I just do it until I need glasses?[100]

It's not Nanook who is blinded, of course, but the fur trapper. However, since it is a dream, identity shifts between protagonists. During 'Nanook Rubs It' a voice says 'Here Fido . . . Here Fido', the chorus of 'St Alfonzo's Pancake Breakfast' contains the line, 'I brought you your snow shoes.' Everything freezes into a reflection of everything else. It is not a linear narrative so much as a cluster of symptoms. That they reflect those of *King Lear* at every juncture is not the result of literary references but of seeking imagery adequate to both the economic and psychoanalytical terrors of exchange society.

---

[97]Frank Zappa, 'Don't Eat the Yellow Snow', *Apostrophe (')*, 1974.
[98]William Shakespeare, *King Lear*, 1608, I, v, 5–2.
[99]Frank Zappa, *Zoot Allures*, 1976.
[100]Undated radio broadcast, Johnny 'Guitar' Watson, *The Gangster is Back*, 1976, Red Lightnin' RL0013.

'Excentrifugal Forz' is an abstracted 'Trouble Every Day' with genital protagonists.

> I'll watch him buff that
> Tiny ruby that he use
> He'll straighten up his turban
> An' eject a little ooze[101]

Besides its poetic images for clitoris and penis,[102] the words are dreamlike in their sci-fi denial of time:

> I'll fine out
> How the future is
> Because that's where he's been[103]

This seems to apply the slogan 'The future is female' – fucking as clairvoyancy, orgasm as future-flash – creating the next generation.

Freud connected the mechanics of genital sexuality to ice in a note in his interleaved copy of the 1904 edition of *The Psychopathology of Everyday Life*.

> From a dream of Ps it appears that ice is in fact a symbol by antithesis for an erection: i.e. something that becomes hard in the cold instead of – like the penis – in heat (excitation). The two antithetical concepts of sexuality and death are frequently linked through the idea that death makes things stiff.[104]

Apostrophe (') is set in the Arctic and is replete with masturbation and erection jokes. Zappa's measured delivery promises narrative, but the story never adds up: there's no moral, but instead a deadpan, facetious juggling of some of the heaviest themes in European culture. 'Stink-Foot', though, ups the tension, like a dreamer trying to think something through: we seem to get to the 'crux of the biscuit'. And indeed, with a little help from Theodor Adorno and Plato, we do.

POODLES AND PHILOSOPHY

In *Apostrophe (')* the assault on Plato takes the form of a talking-blues dialogue called 'Stink-Foot'. It was inspired by the TV commercial for Mennen foot-spray deodorant, in which a dog

---

[101]Frank Zappa, 'Excentrifugal Forz', *Apostrophe (')*, 1974.
[102]I'd like to thank Dr Mike Laurence for this insight.
[103]Frank Zappa, 'Excentrifugal Forz', *Apostrophe (')*, 1974.
[104]Sigmund Freud, *The Psychopathology of Everyday Life*, 1901, trs. Alan Tyson, 1960, p. 90nl.

keels over when his master takes his shoes off.[105] As Zappa remarked:

> If they think I have a fetish about dogs, they are sadly mistaken. It's not profound – it's entertainment. Poodles serve as a convenient mechanism for conveying certain philosophical ideas that might otherwise be more difficult.[106]

Phaedo is Plato's work on the immortality of the soul, and consists of an account of the death of Socrates by one of his favourite disciples, named Phaedo. On stage Frank Zappa had been introducing 'Dirty Love' with the following account of poodle genesis:

> In the beginning God made the light. Shortly thereafter, God made the Poodle. Now, as you might remember from your childhood, God was pretty good at making stuff a long time ago. His quality & His workmanship have gone down quite a bit (the Japanese have taken over where He left off), but when He originally constructed the Poodle it was a pretty sharp-looking dog. It had hair evenly distributed all over its charming small compact canine-type body (it looked good to me, how about you?). Then God made two big mistakes. The first one was called Man and the second was called Wo-Man. Wo-Man looked upon the Poodle & said to herself: 'Boy, I'd really like to fuck that dog, except for the fact that it's not *mod* enough for me'. Whereupon the Man trotted out immediately from the Garden of Eden and got a job & brought his pay cheque home to the Wo-man, who took the money away from him and went out and bought a pair of scissors. And she took these scissors & clipped upon the Poodle in these important areas: the Snout; the Thorax; the Medulla; the Managua; the Garnish (right here). And then she put the dog in a position that might be favourable to her impending erotic procedures. She set the dog up like this & laid down & put her legs up in the air like this & looked deep into the eyes of the aforementioned Poodle and said:

> > Give me
> > Your dirty love
> > Like you might surrender
> > To some dragon in your dreams[107]

In *The Dialectic of Enlightenment* Adorno connected the short-person entertainers of the absolutist court with the fashion for lapdogs. Talking of women in a society run by males, it is explained that they find an outlet in

---

[105]Julian Colbeck, *Zappa: A Biography*, 1987, p. 143.
[106]Frank Zappa, interview, *New Musical Express*, 17 April 1976.
[107]Frank Zappa, Munich, 14 February 1976. Official release of this text came from a performance at the Palladium, New York, 31 October 1977, 'The Poodle Lecture', *You Can't Do That on Stage Anymore Vol. 6*, 1992.

neo-Buddhism and in Pekingese dogs, whose distorted faces, today just as in old paintings, remind one of those jesters who were overtaken by the march of progress. The tiny dog's features, like the hunchback's clownish leaps, still display the mutilated lineaments of nature.[108]

Adorno is talking about a similar sense of horror to that evoked by the poodle. Adorno explains our reactions using a Freudian-Marxist gloss; Zappa intuitively assembles his themes according to his surrealistic-documentary aesthetic, but they are talking about the same matters. The clipped poodle and the dwarf (Evelyn the dog 'ponders the significance of short-person behavior' in *One Size Fits All*) both represent subjugated nature.

When Bubba (Zappa's road manager for the 1976 tour and also road manager for Tony Orlando and Dawn) lost at backgammon to Smothers, Zappa's seven-foot bodyguard, the wager he lost was his beard (if Smothers had lost he was to have stopped shaving his head). At a concert at Troy, New York, in 1976, Smothers shaved Bubba live onstage, an event that replaced the usual poodle lecture (which Zappa referred to as 'a speech on the origins of poodle seduction'). When asked how it felt to be shaved live onstage Bubba replied, 'I feel like a schmuck!', a Yiddish term for the circumcised foreskin. Just as Delilah unmanned Samson by cutting his hair, the poodle clip and ritual tonsure are analogues of castration.

Phaedo/Fido, seeking the hearthrug of domestic comfort and assurance of immortality, obediently fetches the slippers for his dose of 'consolation'. In being clipped, though, he learns something else: the actuality of loss, castration and mortality.

PHAEDO: You shall hear, for I was close to him on his right hand, seated on a sort of stool, and he on a couch which was a good deal higher. He stroked my head, and pressed the hair upon my neck – he had a way of teasing me about my hair, and then he said: Tomorrow [*This is Socrates talkin' now*], Phaedo, I suppose that these fair locks of yours will be severed.
Yes, Socrates, I suppose that they will, I replied.
Not so, if you will take my advice.
What shall I do with them? I said.
Today, he replied, and not tomorrow, if this argument dies and we cannot bring it to life again, you and I will both cut off our hair: and if I were you, and this argument got away from me, and I could not hold my ground against Simmias and Cebes, I would myself take an

[108]Theodor Adorno and Max Horkheimer, *The Dialectic of Enlightenment*, 1944, p. 251.

248

oath, like the Argives, not to let my hair grow any more until I had renewed the conflict and defeated them.

Yes, I said.[109]

In poodle play, as in a dream, symbols condense multiple meanings – contradictions coexist side by side. Fido is polymorphous perversity clipped and shorn to the genital level; Fido is mutilated nature constrained and clipped by civilization; Fido/Phaedo is a hopeful aspirant to belief in immortality who, his hopes dashed, severs his locks in mourning.

Heh-heh heh ... sick ...
Well then Fido got up off the floor an' he rolled over
An' he looked me straight in the eye
An' you know what he said?
Once upon a time
Somebody say to me
(*This is a dog talkin' now*)
What is your conceptual
Continuity
Well, I told him right then (*Fido said*)
It should be easy to see
The crux of the biscuit
Is the Apostrophe (')
Well, you know
The man who was talkin' to the dog
Looked at the dog an' he said:
(Sort of staring in disbelief)
'You can't say that!'
He said
'*IT DOESN'T, 'n YOU CAN'T!*
I WON'T, 'n IT DON'T!
IT HASN'T, IT ISN'T, IT EVEN AIN'T
'N IT SHOULDN'T ... IT COULDN'T
He told me *NO NO NO!*
I told him *YES YES YES!*
I said 'I do it all the time ...
Ain't this boogie a mess!'
THE POODLE BY-EE-ITES
THE POODLE CHEWS IT
THE POODLE BY-EE-ITES
THE POODLE CHEWS IT[110]

Amongst other dialogues, *Phaedo* was used by Erik Satie as the text for a cantata called *Socrate*, written in 1918 and performed at

---

[109]Plato, *Phaedo*, c. 400 BC, 89b–c.
[110]Frank Zappa, 'Stink-Foot', *Apostrophe (')*, 1974.

a Zappa festival called 'Zappa's Universe' in New York in November 1990 (Zappa was too ill to attend).[111] This is a possible 'real-time' connection between Zappa and Plato, since Zappa has long declared an interest in Erik Satie. The organizers followed *Socrate* in presenting Plato's hero in a positive light, even making comparisons between Socrates and Frank Zappa as men of integrity resisting the vulgar mass. The issue is further complicated by the fact that Satie's text omits the discussion of hair following the words, 'I suppose that these fair locks of yours will be severed.' It is therefore possible to read '*Tu feras couper ces beaux cheveux, n'est-ce pas?*' as 'Do have this lovely hair cut, won't you?' (which, for example, Stephen Firth's translation does[112]) – accurate enough if you do not know that in the original Socrates goes on to argue that, since the soul is immortal, his death should *not* cause Phaedo to cut his hair in mourning. There are many other philosophical issues which emphasize that Zappa is Plato's nemesis, not his ally.

MATERIALISM AND THE SOUL

Phaedo also includes arguments against treating the body as a lyre and the soul as harmony, based on a horror of corporal being.[113] The whole argument seeks to deny the body. *Phaedo* may be a founding text for European philosophy, but it is totally disagreeable to the sexual materialist. Phaedo loses his faith in Socrates's arguments, suffers a clipping and becomes Fido, the vulgar negation that lies at the heart of rock 'n' roll and revolution. The archaic doyen of countless generations of repressed and oppressing misogynistic old farts, the touchstone of all the élitist systems of the Western world, gets his just deserts on a record that got into the American top ten.

Nanook's 'vigorous circular motion' is 'destined to take the

---

[111]'Zappa's Universe' occurred at the Ritz in New York, 7–10 November 1991. It was written up in *Keyboard* by Robert L. Doerschuk, February 1992, pp. 96–110, and by Geoff Wills in *T'Mershi Duween*, No. 23, December 1991, p. 10, and was the subject of a special edition of *Society Pages*, No. 8, February 1992. The Fido/*Phaedo* connection was made by the negative dialectics of poodle play in 1979, in ignorance of Erik Satie's cantata. Zappa has declared his devotion to the works of Satie, so this provides a 'realistic' link between Plato and *Apostrophe (')*. Poodle play insists that the more absurd the connections are, the better they are: such documentation being gratifying rather than essential.
[112]Eric Satie, *Socrate*, 1990, Factory FACD356.
[113]See 'Lyres, mortality, repression of the body', Chapter 6: Guitars, for a treatment of this part of *Phaedo*.

place of the Mud Shark / In your mythology'.[114] When first introduced, the Mud Shark was a dance that was meant to 'sweep the ocean' (like the twist): where *Fillmore East June 1971* was a hit (i.e. Australia), Zappa turned the 'The Mud Shark' into a dance event. The famous twist was merely the most successful of a series of dances – the hucklebuck, the watusi, the funky chicken – which constituted commercial extrusions of traditional African ritual. In getting his audience to dance and be out to lunch on stage Zappa dramatizes the issues of getting people back into their bodies, refuting Plato's élitist idealism and denial of the body. After this degradation – which, passed along the global networks of the record industry, has indeed swept the ocean – it is doubtful that *Phaedo* can survive outside the academy as anything more than a footnote on which Zappographers bark their shins.

HAIR

Hair is the pre-eminent escutcheon of the counter-culture. In a society in which individuals appear to confront each other as atomized free agents, hairstyles constitute a kind of hotline to what authority regards as transgressive or incorporable at different moments. Unlike clothes, which are evidently manufactured, hair inscribes the social orientation of the wearer on the body itself. Unlike tattoos or nose-rings, it is a part of the body the individual cannot help making a social statement with.

> The bourgeois religion of art would like to keep art neatly apart from fashion. This is simply impossible. Ever since the aesthetic subject began to take a polemical stand against society and its objective spirit, it has maintained a secret link to that society through the medium of fashion.[115]

Miss Pamela of the GTO's begins her *Confessions* with an account of Elvis Presley's GI haircut.

> I get shivers whenever I see those old black-and-white films of Elvis getting shorn for Uncle Sam. When he rubs his hand over the stubs of his former blue-black mane, I get a twinge in my temples. In the glorious year of 1960, I was at the Reseda Theater with my parents, and I saw the famous army footage before the onslaught of *Psycho*. I don't know which was more horrifying. I hung on to my daddy's neck and inhaled the comforting familiarity of his drugstore aftershave and peeked

---

[114]Frank Zappa, 'Nanook Rubs It', *Apostrophe (')*, 1974.
[115]Theodor Adorno, *Aesthetic Theory*, 1970, trs. C. Lenhardt, 1984, p. 437.

through my fingers as Norman Bates did his dirty work, and the army barber his. I tried to believe that Elvis was doing his duty as an AMERI-CAN, but even at eleven years old, I realized his raunch had been considerably diminished.[116]

This text echoes the old biblical association of haircuts with castration (Samson and Delilah). Miss Pamela picks on a key historical moment for the haircut. After such blatant mobilization of castration themes in order to broadcast the taming of Elvis and the death of rock 'n' roll, there could be no doubt that the rock revolution and opposition to the war in Vietnam would be waged by the hairy. The equation of long hair and rebellion became a 60s shibboleth. According to David Walley, LA club owners were already refusing to book bands with short hair during the 1965 Beatles-boom. Zappa told the Mothers to grow theirs. Roy Estrada and Jimmy Carl Black, who lived in Santa Ana in Orange County, Richard Nixon's power base and notorious bastion of conservatism, and avoided the social consequences by spraying their hair into pompadours before returning home.[117] Long hair was about style as much as length. Miss Pamela tells a touching tale of her rejected greaser boyfriend, Bob Martine, attempting to transform James Dean into James Morrison.

> The next day he went out and bought some cord bell-bottoms that were way too short; he combed his precious pompadour down over his ears, and it stuck out on both sides like Bozo. I ached with compassion and cringed quietly.[118]

Ruben & the Jets included directions on achieving a perfect jelly roll, mockery of antiquated fashion moves that seemed simply surreal to a younger audience. Changes in hairstyle summed up the transition from rebellion against school and parents to a global denunciation of capitalism: from rock 'n' roll to the freak out.

As with everything else, punk turned the symbolism upside down: long hair was attacked as conformist and corrupt. By the late 80s, long-hair conformism had seeped through to the rest of the community: the economic and technocratic prestige of the hippie 'unix guru' meant that long hair became acceptable in a business environment (in a ponytail – Heaven 17 had predicted this in their cover to Penthouse and Pavement as early as 1981[119]).

[116]Pamela Des Barres, I'm with the Band – Confessions of a Groupie, 1987, p. 13.
[117]David Walley, No Commerical Potential, 1972, p. 53.
[118]Pamela Des Barres, I'm with the Band – Confessions of a Groupie, 1987, p. 42.
[119]Heaven 17, Penthouse and Pavement, 1981, Virgin V2208.

Like the phallus in the Lacanian version of Freud, the totemic object signifies only in a context and may therefore coin contradictions. Only those who believe styles and art objects carry significance as some intrinsic essence are surprised by the way in which they suddenly reverse their meanings.

Zappa has always been sensitive to the unstable nature of style-in-opposition, but his materialist attention to detail means that he does not propose a transcendental 'style-less' alternative (a sure route to ideological confusion). Frequently attacked for the 'triviality' of his subject matter, Zappa constructs his art from the debris of mass culture, the fetid flotsam bobbing in the wake of fashion's blinkered trajectory.

> Who cares if hair is long or short
> Or sprayed or partly grayed
> WE KNOW THAT HAIR AIN'T WHERE IT'S AT[120]

Zappa's 'nihilism', for which he was attacked in *Let It Rock* in 1975,[121] is in fact a refusal of binary ethics. This is the utopian aspect of musical innovation, which seeks to signify in its specificity the actuality of sound, rather than by making choices according to predefined categories, options that encode oppression. In his attitude towards the key 60s symbol of hair, Zappa works the same dialectic that led Arnold Schoenberg to question the traditional polarities of major and minor, theme and variation, legitimate key and chromaticism – the questioning that led to free atonality.[122]

MUSIC, NO WORDS, ORGASM VS. ANAL RETENTION

'Apostrophe' is also the name of the one instrumental track on *Apostrophe (')*, a jam between Zappa, bassist Jack Bruce and drummer Jim Gordon. The title is perhaps a nod to Thelonious Monk and his 'Epistrophy'. Julian Colbeck, who otherwise demonstrates a blithe enthusiasm for Zappa's DiscReet turnaround, is rude about this track ('throwaway'[123]), reporting that Zappa disclaimed it. Zappa has mentioned that Bruce is too 'busy' a bassist for him,

---

[120]Mothers of Invention, 'Take Your Clothes Off When You Dance', *We're Only in It for the Money*, 1968.
[121]Karl Dallas, 'What Did You Do in the Revolution, Dada?'*Let It Rock*, June 1975, pp. 33–6.
[122]Susan McClary, *Feminine Endings*, 1991, p. 12.
[123]Julian Colbeck, *Zappa: A Biography*, 1987, p. 143.

but its pivotal position in the album and its steamy sci-fi virtuosity make it too good to dismiss. As Colbeck points out, Zappa had always set 'a lot of store' by Cream. He described his early 60s combo with Paul Woods on bass and Les Papp on drums as 'close to an Eric Clapton-Cream-type-format'[124] and Eric Clapton's voice was used on *We're Only in It for the Money* where he was described as 'noted philosopher and guitarist with THE CREAM' in the sleeve-notes. Rightly so: Clapton, Bruce and Baker were ground-breaking on the level of the Jimi Hendrix Experience, bringing improvised spontaneity and electro-acoustic innovations to huge audiences. Only in retrospect, with Clapton's descent into easy-listening country-rock and the subsequent plundering of the 'heavy-rock' tag by waves of British hacks, has the legacy become tarnished. Like 'cream', 'boogie' means semen: 'I do it all the time... / Ain't this boogie a mess!' at the end of 'Stink-Foot' indicates a sexual climax to Fido's dialogue. The moment of orgasm is the unutterable extremity that is conventionally bracketed off from polite discourse: the crux of the biscuit is a musical tribute to Cream, guitar as godhead.[125] It was recorded at Electric Lady-land, the studio built by Hendrix, in December 1972.[126]

Even orgasm, though, is no release from property relations.

ERIC BUXTON: Is *Apostrophe (')* a concept?
FZ: Well, an apostrophe is that funny little thing, y'know, that dangles at the end of the word denoting...
EB: And it has a certain function.
FZ: Yeah. It has functions. It denotes ownership.
EB: Ownership. Okay. Is that what you were thinking of when you...
FZ: Yeah.[127]

Zappa usually phrases his critique of socialism in the conventional ideological manner, pointing out that in every language 'the first word after *Mama* that every kid learns to say is *Mine!*'.[128] Looked at from the Freudian perspective mama-to-mine is a summary of the castration complex, a development from undifferentiated polymorphous perversity to obsession with *that which you fear to lose*. Eric Buxton's 'okay' at Zappa's explanation of the 'mean-

[124]Michael Gray, *Mother! is the Story of Frank Zappa*, 1985, p. 33.
[125]There is a tendency for radical noise bands to make a similar guitar/God/sex equation: God, Godflesh, Prong etc.
[126]Michael Wale, 'Charge of the Wale Brigade', *ZigZag*, No. 33, March 1973, p. 36.
[127]Quoted by Den Simms, 'They're Doing the Interview of the Century, 22 December 1989, Part Two', *Society Pages USA*, No. 2, undated, p. 35.
[128]Frank Zappa, with Peter Occhiogrosso, *The Real Frank Zappa Book*, 1989, p. 330.

ing' of the title of the album documents the pitfall of hoping to solve Zappa's riddles by reference to the source. Grammatically speaking an apostrophe does *not* signify ownership, it signifies omission. In eliding the word 'has', though, it does mean ownership: 'Richard has toy' becomes 'Richard's toy'. By this logic, an existentialist could claim that an apostrophe stood for existence itself ('Richard's weird' means 'Richard is weird'); a rave-oriented pataphysician that it stands for 'an' or 'heste' ('M'c'r'). In the poetic clusters of *Apostrophe (')* ownership and fear of absence are punned together. Zappa's insistence on one use of the apostrophe points to his own interpretation, revealing the socio-economic basis of the record's production values.

As Nanook indulges his 'vigorous circular motion' he blinds the fur trapper who was 'strictly from commercial'. Rock 'n' roll is delinquent music that proposes immediate pleasure against the deferred gratification of school and work. Parental threats about the danger of sex suggest anal retention and restriction of spending (a Victorian term for orgasm).

> And my momma cried:
> *Nanook-a, no no*
> *Nanook-a, no no*
> *Don't be a naughty Eskimo-wo-oh*
> *Save your money; don't go to the show*[129]

Nanook is a thoroughly 'nought-y' Eskimo, with his opening lines about hundreds and zeros (and thirteen rhymes on 'O') and his interest in *circular motion*.

> Whereupon I proceeded to take that mitten full
> Of the deadly Yellow Snow Crystals
> And rub it all into his beady little eyes
> With a vigorous circular motion
> Hitherto unknown to the people in this area,
> But destined to take the place of THE MUD SHARK
> In your mythology
> Here it goes now . . .
> THE CIRCULAR MOTION . . . (rub it) . . .
>
> (Here Fido . . . Here Fido)

According to Norman O. Brown, revolutionary Freudian and psychoanalyst of the unconscious of capitalism, parental threats about sexuality cause regression from the genital to the anal stage,

---

[129]Frank Zappa, 'Don't Eat the Yellow Snow', *Apostrophe (')*, 1974.

a fascination with faeces that finds its sublimation in money-making and capital formation. Lutheran anality and the Protestant work ethic have always been partners. In order to cure his eyes after the encounter with Nanook, the fur trapper must trudge across the tundra, mile after mile, right down to the Parish of St Alphonzo ('patron saint of the smelt fishermen of Portuguese extraction', according to Zappa's concert versions) where he will regain his sight attending St Alphonzo's Pancake Breakfast and smearing margarine on to his eyes. Having suffered the traditional punishment for masturbation – blindness – the fur trapper meets someone involved in the mass production of pancakes. Work discipline and mass production surface in Zappa's work with unerring frequency.

'Father O'Blivion' is compressed religious satire. While he is 'whipping up the batter / For the pancakes of his flock', a leprechaun (another 'shortperson') strokes his smock, giving him an erection – he tops it off with a 'WOO WOO WOO'. He invites everyone to eat his come:

> They're so light 'n fluffy-white
> We'll raise a fortune by tonite
> They're so light 'n fluffy-brown
> They're the finest in the town[130]

Sucking cock is a favourite Zappa image for subjection – but being 'fluffy-brown' the pancakes are also faecal.

> Good morning, your Highness
> Ooo-ooo-ooo
> I brought you your snow shoe
> Ooo-ooo-ooo[131]

Alphonzo has made his congregation a servile Fido fetching his footwear. It is a typically Freudian conjunction: the fetish simultaneously consisting of phallus and faeces and foot. Henry James, who unconsciously traced many similar psychological conjunctions, relates the fetish to money.

> A man of decent feeling didn't thrust his money, a huge lump of it, in such a way, under a poor girl's nose – a girl whose poverty was, after a fashion, the very basis of her enjoyment of his hospitality – without seeing, logically, a responsibility attached.[132]

---

[130]Frank Zappa, 'Father O'Blivion', *Apostrophe (')*, 1974.
[131]Ibid.
[132]Henry James, *The Golden Bowl*, 1904, p. 173. See also Out to Lunch, *So Much Plotted Freedom*, Reality Studios Occasional Paper, No. 6, 1987.

It is a lump and hence excrement, it thrusts like a phallus, it is offensive to the nose and hence foot-like ('Your STINK FOOT puts a hurt on my nose,' says the narrator's girlfriend on *Apostrophe (')*). James is charting the same triple threat as Zappa, as well as touching on the unhappy fate of de Sade's Justine (another poor girl thrown on a man's 'hospitality'). In Henry James's excruciated syntax, successive interpolations between nose and responsibility subvert his overt argument, implying instead that it is the poor girl's responsibility to reciprocate the man's hospitality – by eating his excrement, sucking his cock and kissing his foot. In telling us what the decent man does *not* do he spins an erotic fable. Psychoanalysis notes that the greater the psychical expenditure on repression, the more forcibly what is repressed returns in unconscious forms: the master is horrified at Fido's assertion that 'the crux of the biscuit is the apostrophe' but replies in a volley of negations and apostrophes (or is it him? the dialogue becomes hopelessly confused in reported speech and conceptual parentheses).

The images of semen and excreta and footwear merely emphasize the fact that Father Vivian O'Blivion is raising a fortune by fleecing his flock. Live performances of the *Yellow Snow* suite segued into a song called 'Rollo', which explained where the money goes:

> To some asshole with a basket
> Where it goes we dare not ask it[133]

Like Henry James, Zappa is aware that the ultimate fetish is money, because in capitalism it is money that can make anything equal anything else, allowing the exploiters to cream off the surplus.

'Uncle Remus', written with George Duke, made direct political points. It asks if the black civil rights movement is 'movin' too slow'.

> We look pretty sharp in these clothes (*yes we do*)
> Unless we get sprayed with a hose
> It ain't bad in the day
> If they squirt it your way
> 'Cept in the winter, when it's froze
> An' it's hard if it hits
> On yer nose

---

[133]Frank Zappa, 'Rollo', see 'Don't Eat the Yellow Snow,' 1979, *You Can't Do That on Stage Anymore Vol. 1*, 1988.

> On yer nose
> Just keep yer nose
> To the grindstone, they say
> Will that redeem us,
> Uncle Remus . . . [134]

This witty account of the contemporary urban black lifestyle – and the water cannons used to quell riots and demonstrations – uses all the previous themes. Again, the notion of hard water has a phallic quotient, and also relates to the harsh truths of economic necessity. The grindstone, though, is not *enough*. The light, summery tune makes full use of Duke's post-McCoy Tyner romanticism to outline the redemptive nature of secular politics. It is a perfect fusion of political insight and song. The dialectic of hair symbolism is pursued by commenting on the abandonment of processed hairdos (achieved by wrapping up the hair in a [hair] do-rag) for the natural 'Afro' look.

> Can't wait till my Fro is full-grown
> I just throw 'way my Doo-Rag at home[135]

The arcane abbreviations relate to the mysteries of Korla Plankton's tiny ruby on 'Excentrifugal Forz' (itself a refracted version of the racial politics of 'More Trouble Every Day'). Even if their 'real' meanings do not register, there is something very evocative about these hermetic fragments of black culture, an encoded resistance to American homogeneity.

In 'Cosmik Debris' the Mystery Man claimed to have

> . . . the oil of Afro-dytee
> An' the dust of the Grand Wazoo[136]

Zappa's spelling of the Goddess Aphrodite emphasizes the African element in her name, precisely the element in Greek culture which classicists have always sought to deny (particularly vigorously in the 1890s and 1920s, high points of European racism). Zappa's enthusiasm for the historically 'dubious' in *The Grand Wazoo* took on board the cultural politics that informs Sun Ra's use of Egyptian motifs: a recognition of miscegenation, of culture as an in-mixing, an assault on the romantic model of perfection as chthonic purity. In 1974 Zappa was already registering an underground critique of Aryan-Ancient-Greece-as-unsullied-by-Africa,

---

[134]Frank Zappa, 'Uncle Remus', *Apostrophe* ('), 1974.
[135]Ibid.
[136]Frank Zappa, 'Cosmik Debris', *Apostrophe* ('), 1974.

a critique that Martin Bernal – after decades of research – brought above ground in 1987, showing that Greek civilization actually derived from a racially mixed ancient Egypt (mummy faces vary from brown to black).[137] That Africa returns later in the record as a *hairstyle* – one that manifested black consciousness – illustrates the profound way in which Zappa's refusal to be bound by cultural levels makes real connections across history to the most intimate personal issues. The pursuit of beauty, Aphrodite, 'black is beautiful' – all these are aspects of a single political issue: slavery and racism.

'Uncle Remus' continues

> I'll take a drive to
> BEVERLY HILLS
> Just before dawn
> An' knock the little jockeys
> Off the rich people's lawn[138]

This relates to the schizophrenic sense of a duplicate, toytown landscape that informs 'Cheepnis'.[139] The little jockey referred to is the racist garden ornament that portrays a negro stableboy, common in US white suburbia. The artist has a strange relationship to the ornamental appendages of the bourgeoisie. This anxiety was shown by one of David Hockney's boys when he stroked the stuffed moose's head in the film *A Bigger Splash*; by Robert McAlmon when his patroness refused to buy a portrait bust of him, saying he was no suitable companion for the 'high-bosomed girl eating grapes' in the library;[140] by Philip Marlowe, that unwilling lackey of the *haute bourgeoisie*, when he strikes up a relationship with 'a little painted Negro in white riding-breeches and a green jacket and a red cap'[141] outside his patroness's front door, imagining that they are equally victims of her wilful inaccessibility. The artist is himself an unnecessary piece of bric-à-brac, and Zappa is defending his patch by criticizing a politics that can only go so far as iconoclasm. As he later demonstrated by the use of a 'negrocious dialect',[142] politics which only operates at the level of the symbolic – tokenism – merely restricts the space in which art can operate, without achieving real benefits (or redeeming us).

---

[137]Martin Bernal, *Black Athena: The Afroasiatic Roots of Classical Civilization*, 1987.
[138]Frank Zappa, 'Uncle Remus', *Apostrophe (')*, 1974.
[139]Frank Zappa, 'Cheepnis', *Roxy and Elsewhere*, 1974.
[140]Robert McAlmon, *Being Geniuses Together*, 1938, p. 44.
[141]Raymond Chandler, *The High Window*, 1943, p. 5.
[142]Frank Zappa, *Them Or Us (The Book)*, 1984, p. 262.

Roxy & Elsewhere is an astonishing album in terms of sound, the burnished textures of real-time instrumentation given a rich, vibrant, percussion-heavy mix. *One Size Fits All* may have the edge on it in terms of architectonic multi-layered beauty, but the sound of the band was gorgeous, and the music was gorgeously caught. Like many of Zappa's masterpieces, it presents highly crafted and detailed work in the guise of chaos. 'Dummy Up' is a typical slice of the joking interplay that existed between Napoleon Murphy Brock and George Duke. 'Bebop Tango (of the Jazzman's Church)' – later presented as a 'serious composition' by the Ensemble Modern[143] – is one of the most outrageously difficult arrangements Zappa has ever concocted, but it nevertheless disintegrates into audience participation, onstage dancing and crowd-pleasing R&B. Zappa's verbal introductions, at the start of each of the four sides of the vinyl edition, are startling illustrations of his paradoxical wit.

The introduction to 'Penguin in Bondage' has Zappa describing his song without mentioning the sexual act, 'the procedure that I am circumlocuting at this present time in order to get this text on television', making sex, as in *Apostrophe (')*, the unmentionable absence around which the piece revolves. This absence finds a symbol in the circus imagery of the song itself.

> Lord, you must be havin' her jumpin' through a hoopa real fire
> With some Kleenex wrapped around a coat-hang wire[144]

Like the 'Camarillo brillo flamin' out along her head' (changed to 'Henna Brillo' in the vacuum cleaner on the *One Size Fits All* star map) and 'Ring of Fire', a C&W song the 1988 band prepared for Johnny Cash to guest on,[145] the flaming hoop is an image of the vagina. Laura Mulvey argued that 'fetishistic' gear (constricting leather and rubber garments, high-heeled shoes, corsets, suspenders, etc.) stimulates the male castration complex, brought into action by the fearful sight of a human being – woman – with no penis, by transforming the whole female body into a reassuring phallus; constriction and bondage ensure that the woman's body

---

[143]Frank Zappa, *The Yellow Shark*, 1993.
[144]Frank Zappa, 'Penguin in Bondage', *Roxy & Elsewhere*, 1974. This image originated in a stunt performed by the Flo & Eddie band. See sleeve note to 'Billy the Mountain', *Playground Psychotics*, 1992.
[145]Frank Zappa, *The Best Band You Never Heard in Your Life*, 1991.

takes on the correct smooth vertical shape.[146] 'Penguin in Bondage' plays on satirical fear of the terrible absence relieved by straps and bonds: a literal enactment of bourgeois property relations to shore up fear of losing everything.

The sound is highly flavoured and succulent, a special juicy texture achieved by George Duke's synths and the horn section. The word 'boy' in 'She's just like a penguin in bondage, boy' is pronounced 'boin-n-n-n-ng', which connects back to the absurdist interpolation on 'Absolutely Free' (*We're Only in It for the Money*). In his preamble Zappa points out with glee that bondage equipment may be purchased at a local drugstore 'but invariably at least in one of those fancy new shops that they advertise in the back pages of the free press'. As against the wishful thinking of flower power, Zappa asserts the mechanics of sex, indicating how arousal strums ready-made social structures. His cryptic phrase 'Knirps for moisture' refers to a brand of German umbrella.[147] Like the many references to rubber goods and leatherwear in Henry James,[148] this reference to a branded protection from water immediately invokes the world of sexually charged accoutrements. In asserting the pull of bondage, twanging the sexual apparatus that is there to twang (just like the punks after him), Zappa insists on the aspects of sexuality that tie it into the current relations of property, giving the lie to the idea that we can simply let it all hang out nature's way.

The Vorticist aesthetic, which insisted on rigidity and hardness, deployed phallic imagery in its pathic denigration of everything soft and wet and female. Gaudier Brzeska carved Ezra Pound's head as an ithyphallic monolith (a giant stone erection). In 'Enemy of the Stars' Wyndham Lewis sets the action at the Pole, calling it 'where Europe grows arctic, intense, human and universal'.[149] Sub-zero temperatures ensure stasis. The phallic imagination fears movement or friction because it may stimulate to orgasm: ejaculation means the loss of erection. 'They really get uptight when you try and move the smoke.'[150] A bare, hard, cold, isolated environment is preferred. In its denunciation of the Futurists'

[146]Laura Mulvey, 'On Allen Jones', *Spare Rib*, February 1973.
[147]The shock of encountering a rack of Knirps umbrellas in a respectable London menswear store was a memorable Zappological surrealist coup.
[148]See Out To Lunch, *So Much Plotted Freedom*, Reality Studios Occasional Paper, No. 6, 1987, p. 17.
[149]Wyndham Lewis, 'Enemy of the Stars', 1914, *Collected Poems and Plays*, ed. Alan Munton, 1979, p. 6.
[150]Frank Zappa, *Lumpy Gravy*, 1968.

predilection for speed and movement, Vorticism sought to preserve phallic stasis. No surprise that the flipside of Gary Glitter's 'I Didn't Know I Loved You (Till I Saw You Rock 'n' Roll)', an echoing football-stadium stomp amidst intimations of machine-style rigidity, should be called 'Hard On Me' (though only Freddie Mercury managed the trick of actually looking like an erect penis onstage, straining with engorgement – Gary Glitter was too plump).

Apostrophe (') was set in the Arctic, but it is in 'Penguin in Bondage' that Zappa provided the definitive description of this psychoscape.

> She's just like a Penguin in Bondage, boy
> Oh yeah, Oh yeah, Oh . . .
> Rennenhenninahenninninahen
> Howlin' over to some
> Antarticulated moon
>
> In the frostbite night
> With her flaps gone white
> Shriekin' as she spot the hoop across the room
>
> Lord you know it must be a Penguin bound down
> When you hear that terrible screamin' and there ain't no other
> Birds around
>
> Aw, you must be careful
> Not to leave her straps
> TOO LOOSE
>
> 'Cause she might just box yer dog
> She just might box yer doggie
> An' leave you a dried-up dog biscuit[151]

The fetishist keeps the woman bound because any movement might trigger his ejaculation: she arches her body towards the man, attempting to bring him off. If she is not tied tight enough she may enclose his penis in her vagina (box as in surround, as well as punch) and make him come. In *Apostrophe (')* the crux of the biscuit turned out to be the Cream-like music of the title track, an ejaculation ('ain't this boogie a mess!') – here the 'dried-up dog biscuit' is the deflated husk of post-orgasmic man.

'Cheepnis', ostensibly a film about monster movies, enacts a parental copulation for the benefit of the infantile voyeur, as Frunobulax (the name of the Zappas' pet dog) is lured towards

---

[151]Frank Zappa, 'Penguin in Bondage', *Roxy & Elsewhere*, 1974.

the cave where the National Guard hope to destroy it with napalm. 'Cheepnis' is the central point of performance, the whole rigmarole shorn of its pretentious adult trappings, displayed in all its weeny shortcomings and fearful wide-eyed curiosity. The child is frightened by the prospect of the father's penis.

> KEEP IT AWAY! DON'T LET THE POODLE BITE ME!
> WE CAN'T LET IT REPRODUCE! OH!
> SOMEBODY GET OUT THE PANTS![152]

So he invents the fantasy of a destructive vagina (the cave and napalm) to destroy this threat, a chemical version of *vagina dentata*. Zappa uses 'pants' to condense the notions dog-breath and trousers-cum-chastity-belt. Similarly, Coleridge's use of the word provides the possibility of gross extrapolation in 'Kubla Khan'.

> And from this chasm, with ceaseless turmoil seething,
> As if this earth in fast thick pants were breathing,
> A mighty fountain momently was forced[153]

The fake *chinoiserie* has much in common with Zappa's guitar orientalism: ersatz use of exotic cultures can allow the artist to escape the cage of tradition. 'Cheepnis' extends the awkward sexualizing of the landscape experienced when 'fast thick pants' is read as enclosing woolly underwear.

The back cover of *One Size Fits All* includes a cross-section of the earth's crust which shows the rift between the Pacific and American land plates: the San Andreas Fault that runs beneath Los Angeles. The diagram portrays the forces responsible for upending Beverly Hills, a literal analogy to Coleridge's dreamed geological outburst. Figuring class conflict, it is the faultline Superman is meant to have healed. Using the 'pathetic fallacy' beloved of the romantics, 'Kubla Khan' deploys landscape as a stage prop in the portrayal of some unutterable experience. 'Cheepnis' derides this artifice by reference to the techniques of B-feature monster movies.

> The jelly & paint on the 40 watt bulb
> They use when the slime droozle off
> The rumples & the wrinkles in the cardboard rock
> And the canvas of the cave is too soft[154]

---

[152]Frank Zappa, 'Cheepnis', *Roxy & Elsewhere*, 1974.
[153]Samuel Taylor Coleridge, 'Kubla Khan', *Christabel and Other Poems*, 1816.
[154]Frank Zappa, 'Cheepnis', *Roxy & Elsewhere*, 1974.

Monster movies are the present-day offspring of romantic tales of the unnatural. Zappa makes explicit the shoddiness of the illusion, as well as the crude sexual point around which the tawdry façades revolve.

Roxy & Elsewhere also includes 'Pygmy Twylyte', a forerunner of 'City of Tiny Lites', a song about the restricted experience of the drug user. It is refracted rock 'n' roll with a subdivided beat that slices up Napoleon Brock's elastic vocal into surreal subsections. 'Village of the Sun' was described by Zappa as a 'sentimental lyric'.[155] It is about Sun Village, a town where Zappa played R&B with the Black-Outs in the late 50s. Like 'Oh No' – also covered on *Roxy* as 'Son of Orange County' – its devious intervals were a beautiful showcase for Brock. 'More Trouble Every Day' was resurrected as a vehicle for a wonderful, spiralling guitar solo. 'Dummy Up' had Jeff Simmons corrupting Napoleon Brock and suggesting he smoke a high-school diploma stuffed with a gym sock belonging to Zappa's brother Carl. Its jammed good humour reflects the ease and looseness of the musical interaction between the members of this edition of the Mothers. Simmons finally offers Brock a college degree stuffed with absolutely nothing at all – as Zappa comments, 'you get nothing with a college degree' – and while Brock sings 'nothing, that's what I want' Zappa comes in with

A true Zen saying – nothing is what I want[156]

which refers back to the nihilism of *Apostrophe (')* and triggers a fluorescent piece of musical effect probably cued by a hand signal (like the 'poo-errs' of the original Mothers). In the midst of the horseplay the band is still capable of extremely disciplined playing.

'Echidna's Arf (of You)', named after an anteater in the LA zoo, and 'Don't You Ever Wash That Thing' were instrumentals that contain some of the best music Zappa has ever recorded. Perfect vehicles for the band's combination of improvising flair and tightness, the latter included a great trombone solo by Bruce Fowler, full of fantasy and invention, and some extraordinary post-*Lunch* percussion by Ruth Underwood. As on the whole album the two drummers, supplying funk (Chester Thompson) and reading accuracy (Ralph Humphrey), work together brilliantly, achieving one of the few worthwhile drum duets on record.

---

[155]Frank Zappa, with Peter Occhiogrosso, *The Real Frank Zappa Book*, 1989, p. 48.
[156]Frank Zappa, 'Dummy Up', *Roxy & Elsewhere*, 1974.

The way the guitar solo melts into the percussion break and the concluding chord sequence are staggering abutments of different atmospheres. On the CD release Zappa added a message: 'Register to vote. Sometimes you can be surprised that "the Universe works whether or not we understand it".'[157] A succinct statement of materialism. It also prefigures the title concept of the next album.

ONE SIZE FITS ALL

One Size Fits All is the jewel of the DiscReet period, a favourite among fans[158] if not among the public.[159] Its mix, rich and saturated and gleaming, is like a woven version of the sound-colours of *Roxy & Elsewhere*. In 1991 keyboardist Tommy Mars made some interesting observations about mixing on Zappa's records.

> The last few albums I don't care for. My favourite was Mark Pinske. He was a genius. For sonority, for fidelity, for resonance ... whenever he did mixing for Frank, it sounded great. I don't understand where his mixing with the thrust on it is lately, on the more recent albums. Things don't seem to have the fidelity. Even when you talk about an album like *One Size Fits All*, that seems to have more fidelity than the newer stuff.[160]

The search for greater control – over sonority and over his musicians – led to an artificial mix that may have lacked earlier beauties, but enabled the perpetration of absurdities real-time fidelity could not approach. *One Size Fits All* was credited to the Mothers of Invention and in a sense it is a last nod at the group ethic. Photographs of musicians disappeared from the album covers after *Roxy & Elsewhere* or became stage-props (Eddie Jobson is on the cover of *Zoot Allures* although he does not play on it).

After the streamlined simplicity of the artwork for *Apostrophe (')* and *Roxy & Elsewhere*, the cover revived the detail and complexity of pre-DiscReet releases. Cal Schenkel was responsible for the artwork. Instead of the painterly, hands-on style of the

---

[157]Frank Zappa, sleeve note, *Roxy & Elsewhere*, 1974; CD 1992 only.
[158]A poll held by *T'Mershi Duween*, No. 7, June 1989, made *One Size Fits All* a 'runaway winner'.
[159]Zappa's notes to 'Sofa' on *Zappa in New York*, 1977, advise people to check out *One Size Fits All*, 'since that album was not very popular'.
[160]Interview by Axel Wunsch and Aad Hoogesteger, *T'Mershi Duween*, No. 21, September 1991, p. 11.

Mothers of Invention graphics the design is clean and professional, but the allusions are dense enough to OD the conceptual continuity sleuth – there is even a hand adding scrubby, Schenkel-like painterliness (to illustrate the expansion of gases in an exploding star). Many of the remarks that follow have to do with details unavailable to CD consumers: the names of the stars, for example, are not legible on the CD booklet (even though, frustratingly, new star names have appeared). History occludes the very material that promises to give imagination a break. Like the politics of Lenin, though, this material is too good to sacrifice on the altar of the democracy of available product. What follows may illuminate material beyond consumer grasp, but it is poodle play's contention that a local insight is worth two in the bush.

On the back of *One Size Fits All* is a star map which renames stars and constellations according to low humour and in-jokes. The pivotal North Star has become 'ZIRCON the Nose Star', the nose of a beast called 'Ursula Minor'. Of the twenty-four images used for constellations only one had appeared on an album cover before: COMA BERNICE is the dancing industrial vacuum cleaner from *Chunga's Revenge*, named after the constellation Coma Berenices. The vacuum cleaner's hair contains the star Henna Brillo, a variant of *Overnite Sensation*'s 'Camarillo Brillo'. The tube of the vacuum cleaner is named DRANO (after the constellation Draco) and ends in two stars, Rascallion and Grunion, both names for onions. The B-side of the Hollywood Persuaders' 'Tijuana Surf' hit was 'El Grunion Run'. And so on: the canopy of the sky – named by Arabs, Romans and moderns with an arbitrariness that is typical of humanity's blithe imposition of words on things – becomes an extension of conceptual continuity.

The star Alpheratz is renamed Hotratz; stars in AGITTARIUS are named Ernie and Chunky, two participants in *The Grand Wazoo*; Leo Minor has become LEO LIMON and is pictured as a car (Leo Limon, the photographer for Zappa's first song book, is credited with 'chollo' on *Just Another Band from LA*, which has a car on the cover) with stars called Fan Belt (a reference to the song 'Florentine Pogen') and Abracaddabra (a premonition of 'Debra Kedabra' on *Bongo Fury*, the next album). VIRGIL is made up of some of the London tube map, including Charing Cross (now renamed Embankment) and Waterloo, two stops each side of the Thames used by visitors to the South Bank arts complex and the Festival Hall (where 'Prelude to the Afternoon of a

Sexually Aroused Gas Mask' was recorded for *Weasels Ripped My Flesh*). The map connects to parts of the New York and LA railway systems and mutates into a diagram of electronic circuits. Mark Spitz, Olympic swimmer and gold medallist, is a star in AQUARIUM. Free association supplies alternatives to the historic names. Although most references are too arcane for comprehension, the energy of the transpositions suggests some inexaustible fund of private myth, the clusters reading like surrealist poems: 'Necta/Misogynis/Arktourist' for DAVID BOOTES, 'Wizened/ Teflon/Serious' for CUNARD, 'Itinerary/Per Diem/Oedipus/ Enough' for REX BEGONIA. The necessary underground stations to reach the gig, per diem payments and an itinerary: the flotsam and jetsam of the musician's mind while on tour (Per Diem is also the name of the Emperor's roadie in *The Grand Wazoo*).

AROUND THE STAR MAP

Around the star-map appear the words: 'January/February/March/ July/Wednesday/August/Irwindale/2:30 in the afternoon/Sunday/ Walnut/A Puente/Funny cars/City of industry/Friday/Round things are boring' (the phrase from *Lumpy Gravy* is particularly resonant placed on a circular star map of the heavens). Performances of 'Billy the Mountain' featured a similar recitation of dates and images, recited while waiting for the phone to ring in Studebacher Hoch's briefcase (a Philip K. Dick-like anticipation of technology still decades in the future). At Stoneybrook University on 16 October 1971 it ran: 'Time passed/January/March/1943/ Capricorn/Your mother's Mustang/Easter Sunday/And then the phone rang in the secret briefcase', but none gets so close to the words on *One Size Fits All* as the one recorded on 7 August 1971 at UCLA (released as *Just Another Band from LA*): 'Time passes/January/February/March/July/Wednesday/August/ Irwindale/2:30 in the afternoon/Sunday/Monday/Funny cars/Walnut/ City of industry/Big John Masmanian/So when the phone rang in the secret briefcase'. Conceptual continuity is not about total control – as Zappa likes to hint – so much as a dialectical use of accident. Flo & Eddie are invited to free associate, but the psychic material revealed is put to work. Once when James Joyce was dictating part of *Work in Progress* (the work published as *Finnegans Wake*) to Samuel Beckett, someone knocked at the door. On reading back the transcript to Joyce, Beckett was queried as to an interpolation of the words 'come in' – Joyce had said it in reply to the knock; Beckett had thought it was part of the text. Joyce considered a moment, then said 'let it stand'. He had seen a way to incorporate this accidental moment into his design. Zappa's work is very much in this spirit, bouncing between chaos and highly disciplined carrying out of directions. As society has become more and more humanized (though not necessarily more humane), artists have found it more and more suggestive to incorporate accident: because every 'accidental' fragment embodies social meanings a vital social overview finds it can incorporate any old debris.

Billy the Mountain caused what Flo & Eddie call an '*Oh, Mein Papa!*' (a song sung by Eddie Fisher in the 50s – a pun on fissure[161]) 'in the earth's crust, right over the secret underground dumps, right near the Jack in the Box on Glenoaks where they keep the pools of old poison gas and obsolete germ bombs'.[162] In this context, the stream of free-associated images points mysteriously to some sinister and important event, with its cryptic codes and reference to a politician. 'Funny cars' and 'City of industry' evoke the cartoon streetscapes of the *Absolutely Free* cover, 'Pound for a Brown', *Greggery Peccary* and 'City of Tiny Lites', as well as Bruce Bickford's clay animations. But if conceptual continuity had a meaning only in relationship to itself it would not hold a lot of interest. The string of images gains from being embedded twice in obscure parts of the artwork, but its unsettling force really derives from its unguessable syntax. Fans tend to treat conceptual continuity as a crossword puzzle, seeking the 'correct solution'. However, it is precisely the sensation of scanning surface details for meaning and *not* finding it that is expressive. Despite Watergate, American society – especially the CIA and the military aspects alluded to in 'Billy The Mountain' – is opaque to those who observe it: modern life is actually like this.

> Art in general is like handwriting. Its works are hieroglyphs for which the code has been lost, and this loss is not accidental but constitutive of

---

[161]Thanks to *Society Pages* editor Den Simms for pointing this out in a letter dated 22 September 1992.
[162]Frank Zappa, *Just Another Band from LA*, 1971 – the recitation occurs at 12.50.

their essence as art works. Only *qua* handwriting, do they have a language, do they speak.[163]

On the back of the *One Size Fits All* record sleeve (omitted from the CD reissue) a note runs: 'A line from Musak and Dublin, the two main stars in Ursula Major ("The Big Dip") points directly to Crux Verbatim or "The Western Cross".' And sure enough it does, pointing to a constellation on the 'Ycleptic' (appropriately enough, the Ecliptic has become 'yclept' an archaic term for 'named' used in romantic and mock-romantic poetry) called CRUX (its constituent stars are: D Crux/Uvda/Madder). Musak and Dublin is a resonant opposition, the former representing the universalization of music in the space of the commodity, the latter an irrevocable reminder of local poignancy (where James Joyce set *Ulysses*, his tale of exile). An extension of both commercial generalization and modernist protest at universal exchange, Zappa's music is well represented as the Crux Verbatim: literal sound.

SOFA

The cover illustrates the tune 'Sofa' (present musically in two versions, with words and as an instrumental). It first featured in a routine performed by Flo & Eddie on the 1971 tour.[164] It was considered important enough to serve as the opening number of the whole twelve-CD *You Can't Do That on Stage Anymore* series.[165] In it Mark Volman (Eddie) asks Howard Kaylan (Flo) a riddle: he is portly, he is double-knit and he is maroon – what is he? The answer – a sofa. As Zappa put it in Rotterdam on 27 November 1971:

> Once upon a time, way back when the universe consisted of nothing more elaborate than Mark Volman trying to convince each and every member of this audience here tonight that he was nothing more, nothing less than a fat maroon sofa suspended in the midst of a vast sports arena.

[163]Theodor Adorno, *Aesthetic Theory*, 1968, trs. C. Lenhardt, 1984, p. 182.
[164]Although the NDOPP disclaims interest in bootlegs, considering them the flotsam of fleecing fans without access to the international FZ tape-swap co-operative, it must be admitted that the version of the sofa routine referred to below comes from 'Geef mij wat vloerbedekking onder deze vette zwevende sofa', an excerpt from the Rotterdam 1971 concert on the bootleg *Pootface Boogie*, an illegal issue of such antiquity (1974) that its cover consisted of inserts in the shrink wrap. It was bought under the impression it was official. The full routine may now be bought over the counter as *Swiss Cheese, 1971, Beat the Boots #2*, 1992.
[165]'Sofa #1', 10 December 1971, *You Can't Do That on Stage Anymore Vol. 1*, 1988.

The Cabbalah, the Jewish hermetic/mystical tradition, names the Infinite, the Boundless One, 'En Sof'.[166] Zappa continues:

A light shined down from heaven and who should appear but the good Lord Himself (and I'm sure you all know what he's like). And He hopped out there on the sky that day and he looked at the sofa and studied it momentarily and thought carefully to Himself, what would make this sofa even better if you had to tell an audience in Rotterdam about it? And so He came up with this little song.

Led by George Duke on trombone, Flo & Eddie sing 'Geef mij wat vloerbedekking onder deze vette zwevende sofa', Zappa's sole performance in Dutch.

Then they sing God's sofa song itself, described by Zappa as 'a formal address which would set forth in minute detail the rest of their future relationship.'

FZ: Now we hope you won't be offended by this, but in talking to the sofa for the contractual part of these obligations the Lord had to speak German [*party-poop whistle*] – you can sleep through this part.
MV: We do!
FZ: A light shines down from heaven, a dense ecumenical patina at the right hand of God's big sofa and the Lord was righteously pleased with the sofa, studied it again briefly, put his eye on his cigar one more time and decided the ideal thing to do that afternoon in the sky would be to amuse himself with the sofa, perhaps with his girlfriend and her assistant, a lovely little pig she uses whenever she makes special movies. So he went like this –
MV: Bring es zu mir, das kurte Mädchen.
FZ: He had an extremely small girlfriend and so he said, Bring unto me the short girl.
MV: Und Squat der Magisches Schwein.
FZ: And Squat the Magic Pig and the big light he liked to use and they were going to make a home movie.

Then Flo & Eddie sing 'Stick It Out', an invocation to bestiality of considerable obscenity (later sung in a disco version by Joe to the nuclear-powered sex robot Sy Borg in *Joe's Garage Act II*).

FZ: Sheets of fire, ladies and gentlemen, sheets of real fire . . . Well, the Lord caused the short girl to kneel and make mysterious gestures near the reproductive orifice of Squat the Magic Pig and likewise caused her to sing unto him in a pure soft voice and broadcasted the voice throughout his greatest new PA system and this is what she said, just a swingin' through the trees [*a phrase from 'Jungle Hop' by Don and Dewey*] . . . take it away!

---

[166]Rabbi Ben Zion Bokser, *From the World of the Cabbalah: The Philosophy of Rabbi Judah Loew of Prague*, 1957, p. 4.

MV: Magisches Schwein [*unintelligible German obscenities shouted at the top of Volman's voice*]...!!!

FZ: And basically translated that means, Fuck me swine until sparks shoot out and nebulas are revealed, along with sheets of fire, ladies and gentlemen ... sheets of [*unintelligible*] ... sheets of large fried ... a light shines down from heaven, an immense ecumenical bandana, at the right hand of God's big rhumba and his voice comes out in sheets of plywood and bales of old sports shirts ... and you'll be surprised to find out that all he's got to say is, *Beklekke nicht mein Sofa*, which means, Don't get no jizz on the sofa. It is time now for the bales of unmitigated imported zircon!

MV/HK: [*Sing the Sofa song in German.*]

According to Zappa, the title *One Size Fits All* 'means that the Universe is the one size – it fits all':[167] hence Volman, in his universe/sofa manifestation, saying, 'I stretch everywhere.' God's hand, complete with Pachuco cross tattoo, appears in the foreground of *One Size Fits All*'s cover, holding a cigar. We are witnessing His vision: a giant maroon sofa hovering in outer space. You can make out a coin embedded in the upholstery (the 'lost metal money' referred to in the song). To the right of Schenkel's painting hand a chalked note runs 'crab nebula goes here'. On the star map Cancer the Crab is represented by the pubic parasite (a theme of Suzy Creamcheese's on *Uncle Meat*): God's short girlfriend wants to be fucked until 'nebula are revealed' (recalling the 'Dwarf Nebula Processional March & Dwarf Nebula' from *Weasels Ripped My Flesh*). 'Evelyn' refers to 'shortperson' behaviour: a cluster of symptoms that bring together stunted growth and sex. Zappa's publishing company was called Munchkin Inc., after the dwarves in *The Wizard of Oz*, and in *200 Motels* Mark Volman refers to anxiety about 'munchkin tits' in 'Penis Dimension'; Ringo Starr plays a character called Larry the Dwarf. Stunted growth is repression – but it is also an illusion – because one size fits all.

THE COSMIC AND THE BANAL

Hands present the moon and put the spin on Saturn. There is the chrome dinette of the 'Sofa' song with stuffing torn from the chair's yellow seat, symbols of impoverished urban domesticity

---

[167]Frank Zappa, interviewed by Bob Marshall, Dr Carolyn Dean and Gerald Fialka, October 1988, quoted by Matt Galaher, 'Statistical Density: Extensive Long Range Landscape Modification', *T'Mershi Duween*, No. 18, April 1991, p. 25.

(in Philip K. Dick's *Mary and the Giant*, assembling chrome furniture is portrayed as the bleakest of dead-end jobs). Mercury is represented by a dime coin (which has Mercury's head on it). Antique diagrams reminiscent of da Vinci sketches illustrate the workings of Saturn as a system of gears lubricated by 'Sodium & Wasser', 'Sodium & Gommorah', 'Scotch & Sodium'. Like the star map, this vision – which crosses the cosmic and the banal, the sacred and the profane – has an unexpected charge.

In 1795 the English poet William Cowper wrote a mock-epic that began with the words 'I sing the sofa', deflating Homeric pretension by referring to the most banal item of bourgeois furniture. Zappa encoded it in his title: the initials of *One Size Fits All* are an anagram of sofa. The Wagnerian pomp of 'Sofa' and the use of German lyrics parodies the cosmic pretensions of German classical music, which Adorno described as 'enthroned upon the plush sofa of pseudo-romantic bathos'.[168] The motto 'Divan, Divan, weisst du wer ich bin?' appears engraved on a speech-scroll on the cover, a pun on the German word for a sofa and 'divine'. The sofa image perpetuates Zappa's criticism of the passivity induced by TV culture. To the technicians of mass culture who declare 'we live in a visual age' the sight of the sofa is shocking, because it reminds them where all the people who are watching TV actually are. 'Behind the cult of visuality there lurks the philistine cliché of the body that stretches out on a sofa while the soul soars to rarefied heights.'[169] Roland Barthes referred to 'the mystification which transforms petit-bourgeois culture into a *universal nature*'[170] and Karl Marx noted in 1848 'the bourgeoisie would transform the intoxicating "grace of God" into a sobering *legal title*, the rule of blue blood into the rule of white paper, the royal sun into a bourgeois astral lamp.'[171] By projecting the banality of bourgeois respectability on to the heavens, Zappa summons a special disgust.

Inside the gatefold sleeve the lyrics are printed in archaic script upon a crumpled paper background, with generous use of ampersands, giving it the appearance of an antique parchment (it may also be a reference to Jefferson Airplane's *Bark*, which used a similar paper-bag effect on its cover and had Grace Slick singing

---

[168]Theodor Adorno, *The Philosophy of Modern Music*, 1948, p. 130.
[169]Theodor Adorno, *Aesthetic Theory*, 1970, trs. C. Lenhardt, 1984, pp. 144–5.
[170]Roland Barthes, Preface, 1970, *Mythologies*, trs. Annette Lavers, 1972, p. 9.
[171]Karl Marx, 'The Counter-revolution in Berlin', 1848, *Revolutions of 1848*, trs. Paul Jackson, 1973, p. 179.

in German). On the cover the initials of the artists – CS and LL (Lyn Lascharo was credited with the sofa art) – appear over the date 1675 instead of 1975. The manner in which *One Size Fits All* addresses history is integral to its impact. 'Evelyn, a Modified Dog' is replete with the trappings of the bourgeois parlour.

> In the darkened room
> Where the chairs dismayed
> And the horrible curtains
> Muffled the rain
> She could hardly believe her eyes
> A curious breeze
> A garlic breath
> Which sounded like a snore
> Somewhere near the Steinway (or even from within)
> Had caused the doily fringe to waft & tremble in the gloom[172]

Its use of ampersands and its claustrophobic vision of domestic paraphernalia make it strongly reminiscent of a passage in William Blake's *Visions of the Daughters of Albion*.

> The moment of desire! The moment of desire! The virgin
> That pines for man shall awaken her womb to enormous joys
> In the secret shadow of her chamber: the youth shut up from
> The lustful joy shall forget to generate & create an amorous image
> In the shadows of his curtains and in the folds of his silent pillow.
> Are not these the places of religion, the rewards of continence,
> The self-enjoyings of self-denial? Why dost thou seek religion?
> Is it because acts are not lovely that thou seekest solitude
> Where the horrible darkness is impressed with reflections of desire?[173]

These lines are part of William Blake's polemic against Christian repression of sexuality. Though still taboo in polite society, talk of masturbation still seems peculiarly subversive of moral scares – as Zappa demonstrated in his Statement to Congress on 19 September 1985.[174] 'Evelyn' is about a dog's approach to the human sphere informed by both Kafka,[175] and Dick:[176] recited against the shabby genteel sound of a harpsichord there is a peculiar horror about its speculation about the meaning of music, reminiscent of repression's musings on sex. While the academic study of literature

---

[172]Frank Zappa, 'Evelyn, a Modified Dog', *One Size Fits All*, 1975.
[173]William Blake, *Visions of the Daughters of Albion*, 1793, lines 178–86, *The Poetical Works of William Blake*, ed. John Sampson, 1928, p. 291.
[174]Frank Zappa, with Peter Occhiogrosso, *The Real Frank Zappa Book*, 1989, p. 274.
[175]Franz Kafka, 'Investigations of a Dog', 1931, *Metamorphosis And Other Stories*, trs. Willa and Edwin Muir, 1961.
[176]Philip K. Dick, 'Roog', 1953, *Beyond Lies the Wub*, 1987.

serves to both innoculate Blake's politics and to denigrate Zappa's art, the negative dialectics of poodle play points out that both target the same oppression, and in remarkably similar terms.

Poodle play contends that deployment of cultural symbols entails a positioning *vis-à-vis* the entire momentum of human history. Parallel critiques will foment parallel artistic techniques; this is why Zappa resembles Blake. Commentators who restrict comparisons to 'influence' perpetuate a spurious idea of art as a species of pass-the-parcel, an élitist skate across the mass surface. Being materialist, though, poodle play cannot remain utterly uninterested in the facts and figures of who-read-who and who-saw-who.[177] 'Evelyn' was in fact probably inspired by the kind of titles the American artist Donald Roller Wilson gives his pictures. Wilson later supplied the cover art for three of Zappa's records.[178] Starting with paintings reminiscent of Magritte, Wilson added the lighting of Georges de la Tour and the translucent hyper-reality of Edward Hopper to produce highly charged grotesques. He gave each of them long titles that work like poems, always written in uppercase.

BLUE ROAST: ROLLED RUMP

THE SHADOW OF THE BONE IS CURVED;
IT FALLS ALONG THE FOLDS
OF DRAPES WHICH HANG BEHIND THE STEAMING JEANS[179]

Those familiar with the rock band Creaming Jesus will immediately register a religious taint to these words. Oil paint was first pioneered in order to give an astonishing presence to religious images; surrealist use of its power implies sensitivity to these historical nuances. Blake and Zappa also sense something atrocious in repression, a reminder of the disgust provoked by church vestments: impregnation with fraudulent meanings. Another Wilson title reads

SHIRLEY'S LAST SUPPER PRIOR TO HER RETURN FROM
   PARADISE
BEFORE HER ENTRANCE THROUGH THE GATE

---

[177]A similar point is made in criticizing Garrett Stewart in Jeremy Prynne, *Stars, Tigers and the Shapes of Words*, 1993, p. 21n96: 'refusal to countenance interpretative rank-ordering of relative probabilities, within social, historical and authorial frames as well as within the performance horizons of the text, amounts to assigning an ungraded *force de frappe* to both signal and noise equally'.

[178]Frank Zappa, *The Perfect Stranger*, 1984; *Them Or Us*, 1984; *Francesco Zappa*, 1984.

[179]*The Paintings of Donald Roller Wilson*, Introduction by Peter Frank, 1988, p. 36.

BETWEEN THE LEGS OF GLADYS
BEFORE THE CALL WHICH CAME–(PLACED BY HER HOST)

SHE PASSED A MAN WHO HAD TWO HEADS
WHO ALSO CAME THROUGH GLADYS
BUT, IN REVERSE–THE SON–(THE HOLY GHOST)[180]

Like the lines from Dylan Thomas Zappa read out during the poetry matinée at Hammersmith,[181] there is no question of plagiarism – not because Zappa adds in some irrelevant 'personal' ingredient to 'Evelyn' but because the material is recycled only for its use-value. Wilson's pun on host (domestic ritual and communion) runs parallel to Zappa's God and sofa routine. 'Evelyn' may have started as a musical tribute to the atmosphere of Donald Roller Wilson's pictures, but it serves to connect Zappa to the main river of anti-clerical polemic in both surrealism and its left-romantic precursors like Blake.

PEOPLE ARE SIMULACRA

Over the first chords of 'Andy' there are noises of dogs barking, perhaps played on a lion's roar (a greased string pulled through a resonant box, an instrument played by symphony percussionists). The net effect is one of terror, similar to that caused by the orchestral devices used by Richard Strauss in *Elektra* and *Salomé* (which run parallel to some of Varèse's innovations). In *Martian Time-Slip* by Philip K. Dick one protagonist has terrifying visions of people as mechanical marionettes, of reality as a flimsy façade:

> What had tormented him ever since the psychotic episode with the personnel manager at Corona Corporation was this: suppose it was not a hallucination? Suppose the so-called personnel manager was as he had seen him, an artificial construct, a machine... a glimpse of absolute reality, with the facade stripped away. And it was so crushing, so radical an idea, that it could not be meshed with his ordinary views. And the mental disturbance had come of that.[182]

Later, he ascribes the visions to 'A schizophrenic distrust. A collapse, he realized, of the ability to communicate'.[183] Dick is

---

[180]Ibid., p. 38.
[181]Frank Zappa, 'Don't Eat the Yellow Snow', 1979, *You Can't Do That on Stage Anymore Vol. 1*, 1988. See below 'Stage one', Chapter 12: Stageism, or, Issuing the *Œuvre*.
[182]Philip K. Dick, *Martian Time-Slip*, 1964, p. 70.
[183]Ibid., p. 205.

touching on a theme that runs right through European philosophy, a silver thread of fear: dread of the consequences of materialism. In Britain the civil war of the seventeenth century unleashed social movements and ideas that questioned all the old verities of God and king and state. When Thomas Hobbes wrote *Leviathan* in 1651, a tract in favour of authoritarian rule, he wanted to reason without recourse to either notions of spirit or to arguments culled from the Bible. He starts from a mechanical view of the body: 'For what is the *Heart*, but a *Spring*; and the *Nerves*, but so many *Strings*; and the *Joynts*, but so many *Wheeles*?'[184] That is the resonance of the cover of *One Size Fits All*: the universe as a giant clock, the human frame as an automaton – images that register the early stirrings of European rationalism. Hobbes actually argues less via empirical observation than via metaphor – rationality itself is accountancy ('as when a master of a family, in taking an account, casteth up the summs of all the bills of expence, into one sum'[185]); the state is a body, needing a sovereign just as a body requires a head; the body is a machine – but his images have a chilling undertow. Fascinated by the transactions that made his class money (*Leviathan* is dedicated to a *Mister* Francis Godolphin, a man with no feudal titles), Hobbes can see relations between people only as relations between things. What Dick stares at with so much horror is the bourgeoisie's real vision of the world, one that is conventionally cloaked in hypocritical talk of humanity and innerness, veils of degraded religion and 'culture' disguising the brutal mechanics. Zappa connects to the tradition that detects beneath bourgeois comfort a horrifying and exploitative system: petrol profits dependent on burning flesh in the Gulf.

Talking of the hypocrisy of bourgeois philosophy in *The Revolution of Everyday Life*, Raoul Vaneigem said: 'Humanism merely upholsters the machine of Kafka's "In The Penal Colony".'[186] As in *We're Only in It for the Money*, Kafka's torture machine is a presiding image in Vaneigem's *The Revolution of Everyday Life*. The lushness of orchestration on 'Sofa' pads Zappa's torture music, but the crimes are still carved on your back.

As objective standards and the rational division of labour come

---

[184]Thomas Hobbes, *Leviathan, or The Matter, Forme and Power of a Common-Wealth Ecclesiasti-call and Civill*, 1651, p. 85.
[185]Ibid., p. 112.
[186]Raoul Vaneigem, *The Revolution of Everyday Life*, 1967, p. 20.

to regulate daily life, innerness became a commodity peddled like any other.

> As the helplessness of the independent subject grew more pronounced, inwardness became a blatant ideology, a mock image of an inner realm in which the silent majority tries to get compensation for what it misses out on in society.[187]

In *The Dialectic of Enlightenment* Adorno and Horkheimer celebrate de Sade for his projection of bourgeois rationality into fantasies of cruelty and mass slaughter. For them it predicted the horrors of Auschwitz, which as Marxists they see as a logical product of capitalism rather than as some aberration. Zappa's insistence on a viewpoint shorn of sentimentality is similar to de Sade's. That such a viewpoint does not necessarily result in a progressive politics is illustrated by the case of Wyndham Lewis. From his reading of Charles Baudelaire and Henry Bergson, Lewis developed a theory of humour: what makes people laugh is human beings viewed as things, as machines. Dismissing any talk of innerness as humbug he insisted on an art constructed of externals, and developed a prose style to match. He chose as a literary 'opposite' James Joyce, whose interior monologue and evident interest in Freud he found repellent. Lewis wished to defend the conscious mind and accused Joyce of dissolving personal identity in the play of language. That Joyce's attention to language is actually a version of materialism – that psychoanalysis, too, deals with external, empirical evidence (jokes, dreams, neuroses, slips of the tongue), bypassing myths of morality and feeling – eluded him.

Impatient with the hypocrisies of morality, emphasizing the hard, external facts of the matter, Lewis represents one possible outcome of mechanical materialism. Adorno has pointed out that pure satire ends up as reaction because it insists on what *is*.[188] In his fury against the bourgeois bohemians – Virginia Woolf, Clive Bell and the Bloomsbury group – Lewis developed a virulent right-wing politics that resulted in him supporting Hitler and the Nazis. His artistic resentment came out fascist. You can see a similar ambivalence in Iggy Pop and punk, and when Zappa has been accused of racism, as in the controversy over 'Jewish Princess', he claims to be merely 'stating the facts'. His song about

---

[187] Theodor Adorno, *Aesthetic Theory*, 1968, trs. C. Lenhardt, 1984, pp. 144–5.
[188] Theodor Adorno, *Minima Moralia: Reflections from Damaged Life*, 1951, trs. E. F. N. Jephcott, 1974, Chapter 134, pp. 209–12.

racist delusions, 'You Are What You Is', is open to Adorno's charge of leaning to the right by emphasizing brute fact. However, Zappa and Iggy and punk are expressions of a culture that is at root anti-élitist. T.S. Eliot, W.B. Yeats, Ezra Pound and Wyndham Lewis (not to mention David Bowie and Morrissey) all show signs of sympathy with fascism because they do not break with the Platonic equation of power and knowledge. Their experience of what was true and beautiful coincides with an archaic, militarist view of social order. The political importance of Joyce's centring *Ulysses* on a Jew and, in *Finnegans Wake*, devaluing literature into a document of the unconscious, has been insufficiently stressed[189] – as has the stress on dumb rock 'n' roll in Iggy and Zappa.

MORALITY, INDIVIDUALISM, FASCISM

As rock was incorporated by the entertainment industry, stars like David Bowie and Michael Jackson began to flirt with authoritarian imagery: Bowie's notorious *sieg heil* of 1975; the footage of Jackson in military dress running with a regiment of cops, everyone in dark glasses (given a sinister twist by recalling that Mussolini and his entourage used to run at military inspections to 'give a sense of urgency'); Scorsese's vigilante lighter-versus-blacker gangfight video for 'Bad'. The glamour of the dictator seems appropriate to those whose art relies upon centralization on the single individual. Despite the economic pressure to use similar tropes, Zappa, though, still harbours a grudge against official society: he orchestrates a travesty of power, not its imitation. Ironically, the commercial marginalization that provokes this attitude is as much a product of his classical music aspirations as his low-rent aesthetic.

Unlike the fascist élitists of modernism like Lewis and Pound, Zappa does not maintain the fiction of the heroic individual, culture as something that needs protecting against the vulgar hordes (which it is why it is inappropriate to cast him as Socrates). Abolition of morality that holds on to individualism and hierarchy becomes simply reaction: 'He who holds fast the self and does away with theological concepts helps to justify the diabolical

---

[189]Honourable exceptions: Colin MacCabe, *James Joyce and the Revolution of the Word*, 1977, and Fredric Jameson.

positive, naked interest.'[190] Only by breaking with the idea of self and hierarchy can desire become free. This is illustrated by de Sade, who insists on equality, not because it is empirically 'true' but because it is an obstacle to dissolving the self in pleasure:

> No distinction is drawn among the individuals who comprise the Sodality; not that it holds all men equal in the eyes of Nature – a vulgar notion deriving from infirmity, want of logic, and false philosophy – but because it is persuaded and maintains that distinctions of any kind may have a detrimental influence upon the Sodality's pleasures and are certain sooner or later to spoil them.[191]

This is what the SI called 'radical subjectivity'. Unlike the neoconservative pessimists of the Parisian Nietzsche revival, who find in desire only a confirmation of the social order, it makes a case for desire as revolutionary. Unlikely as it may seem, Zappa – probably the last person to romanticize desire in terms of bathing it in attractive lights – has found a new democratic energy in his celebration of the degraded and obscene, a critique of hierarchies of value.

Finnegans Wake understood that to make use of avant-garde freedoms with language was to hurl literature into a pit of personal association that would make everybody's unconscious a work of art. Zappa understands that by collaging the detritus of social life he can achieve a finer delineation of unconscious processes than by defending a frame for pure expression. In so doing he has been persistently criticized for paying attention to trivia. Adorno talks as if he were already defending him:

> The superstitious belief that the greatness of philosophy lies in its grandiose aspects is a bad heritage of idealism – as though the quality of a painting depended on the sublimity of its subject matter. Great themes prove nothing about the greatness of insight. If, as Hegel argues, the whole is what is true, then it is so only if the force of the whole is absorbed into the knowledge of the particular.[192]

It is precisely by acute attention to the particular that Zappa lets the unconscious speak: realism so close-up that the results are fantastic, surreal, shocking.

Refusal of innerness is always the charge directed at materialism by the tender souls of idealism. It is ever the last stand of the

[190]Theodor Adorno, *Minima Moralia: Reflections from Damaged Life*, 1951, trs. E. F. N. Jephcott, 1974, Chapter 99, p. 154.
[191]Marquis de Sade, *Juliette*, 1797, trs. Austryn Wainhouse, 1968, p. 418.
[192]Theodor Adorno, *Prisms*, trs. S. and S. Weber, 1967, p. 62.

reactionary to bemoan materialism's ignorance of the 'inner life', when really what is missed is collusion in a class-based social bond. Zappa extends the tradition of bourgeois satirical materialism, that of Hobbes and Swift and de Sade and Lewis, into a rampant critique of cultural high-mindedness ('I may be vile and pernicious//But you can't look away'[193]), showing that its themes are in fact spattered all over the tacky and banal.

Lewis argued that: 'The condition of our enjoyment of vulgarity, discord, cheapness or noise is an unimpaired and keen disgust with it.'[194] His junk-epic prose, a literary precedent for Zappa's musical method, was meant to wall out the world, protecting the finer feelings within. Zappa unpeels the *bricolage* and turns it inside out. Instead of personal identity as the last citadel of human consciousness, an embattled, heroic, neo-medieval contempt for the masses milling at the castle gates, Zappa reads off innerness from the external facets of contemporary degradation: underdog surrealism with profound implications for the status of social criticism.

ANDY

'Andy' is a song about Andy Devine, the Hollywood B-movie cowboy actor. In its dramatically abutted levels, Zappa creates studio rock equivalent to Varèse's sound blocks, the consummate example of the external approach in early twentieth-century music. The words emphasize the theme of human consciousness as an innerness:

> Is there anything good inside of you
> If there is I really wanna know[195]

asks George Duke, his voice breathy against the microphone. The song seems to press on the skin of reality with a desperate urgency, as if the whole set is about to collapse and reveal the struts behind the movie fronts. It must be listened to in conjunction with the back-cover's apocalyptic image of the San Andreas faultline: as it swallows up Beverly Hills, the famous letters spelling out

---

[193]Frank Zappa, 'I'm the Slime', *Overnite Sensation*, 1973.
[194]Wyndham Lewis, 'Vorteces and Notes', *BLAST*, No. 1, 20 June 1914, p. 145.
[195]Frank Zappa, 'Andy', *One Size Fits All*, 1975.

Hollywood, Letraset men and the red hotels and green houses of Monopoly are toppling into the abyss.

Earth movement – which applies the historicization of Darwin and Marx to land, the economic basis of feudal faith in eternal values – has frequently been used for imagery of social upheaval. As Marx himself put it:

> The so-called revolutions of 1848 were but poor incidents – small fractures and fissures in the dry crust of European society. However, they denounced the abyss. Beneath the apparently solid surface they betrayed oceans of liquid matter, only needing expansion to rend into fragments continents of hard rock.[196]

To speak of reality as a 'thin crust' is to alert people to the fact that society is not immutable. This is the tangible achievement of Zappa, as much as it is that of Philip K. Dick. Less a matter of propagandizing for definite political positions, it destroys the first plank of bourgeois ideology: that nothing can be changed.

In Schenkel's design the earth's crust merges with the human skin: on the left is a geological cross-section, on the right veins and hair follicles. The disintegration of the surface of the landscape is also the disintegration of the hidebound, repressed personality. 'Andy' is an update of 'Call Any Vegetable', an attempt to communicate, to get beneath the skin. The voices of George Duke and Johnny 'Guitar' Watson embody innerness and outerness respectively. Whereas Duke's comfortable, warm, laughing voice invites us in, Watson's nasal, hard, shiningly linear singing is impermeable and brittle.[197] Duke and Watson alternate in a soft cop/hard cop routine, lining slabs of organ and guitar with contrasting vocal textures. In the instrumental interlude drums, bass, organ, guitar and percussion are introduced one at a time with the objective force of the tectonic plates of continental drift, until the tension snaps (at 3.18) and we glimpse an abyss of rattling bones. This

---

[196]Karl Marx, 'Speech at the Anniversary of the *People's Paper*', 1856, *Surveys from Exile*, trs. Paul Jackson, 1973, p. 299.
[197]Watson went on from the *One Size* sessions to create the extraordinary futuristic funk of *Ain't That a Bitch*. People who think that Edgard Varèse is in an opposite camp to dance music should try seguing 'Love That Will Not Die' from *Funk Beyond the Call of Duty*, 1977, with *Hyperprism*, 1923. Sirens, percussion, sci-fi offworld visions: the transition is seamless. Asked if Zappa had played him any Varèse, though, Watson replied: 'No, I never knew anything about Edgard Varèse until you just mentioned it, it's the first time I heard anything about it, I never knew where his inspiration came from, all I knew was, Jesus man, whoever he was digging was very classical and very heavy – that's all I knew! And his concept has always been so superb and he can incorporate all these different musics, man, no other but Zappa has been able to do that', interview with the author at Paramount Studios, 27 October 1993. Another of the bizarre coincidences that populate Zappa's universe.

moment is like Schenkel's machinery behind the surface of the Mothers in the innerfold of *Ruben & the Jets* or Dick's vision of the personnel manager as a simulacrum.

INNER AND OUTER

Outspoken S&M enthusiast Pat Califia has talked of the erotic charge of leather's impermeability,[198] Jacques Lacan of the reason for sexuality's stress on rims (mouth, eye, anus):[199] dramas of the inside and outside of the body.

> Andy de Vine
> Had a thong rind
> It was sublime
> But the wrong kind[200]

In 'Andy' Zappa faults the fake by reference to externals, a view of inner/outer that refuses the pious chicanery of transcendent innerness. This corresponds to the dialectic. Hegel found it in beauty (he subsequently demoted the aesthetic moment in his philosophical scheme – Hegel's art theory finds him at his most materialist): 'According to this conception we find as characteristic constituents of the beautiful an inward something, a content, and an external rind which possesses that content as its significance.'[201]

Adorno made a refusal of the acceptance of inside/outside central to his thought:

> the very opposition between knowledge which penetrates from without and that which bores from within becomes suspect to the dialectical method, which sees in it a symptom of precisely that reification which the dialectic is obliged to accuse.[202]

One Size Fits All is a musical realization of this dialectic. 'Inca Roads' mocks Von Daniken's appeal to flying saucers as agents of history (knowledge penetrating from without) while the depiction of ants eating the foundations of Hollywood on the back cover gives a new twist to 'round things are boring' (that which bores from within). Again and again, Zappa creates artworks that give material form to Adorno's imagery, a coincidence explained by

[198]Pat Califia, *ZG*, No. 1, 1979, p. 2.
[199]Jacques Lacan, *The Four Fundamental Concepts of Psychoanalysis*, 1964, p. 172.
[200]Frank Zappa, 'Andy', *One Size Fits All*, 1975.
[201]G.W.F. Hegel, *The Philosophy of Fine Art*, 1823–9, trs. F. Osmaston, 1920, para. xxxiii.
[202]Theodor Adorno, *Prisms*, trs. S. and S. Weber, 1967, p. 33.

how frequently both embed their materialist philosophy in the language of the body. 'Andy' cannot find meaning *within* Andy Devine but equally refuses to impose meaning from without. 'Inca Roads' dissolves talk of spaceships into sexual horseplay: in coitus a model of knowledge that transcends the opposition of penetration from without and being bored from within.

CHAPTER 6
GUITARS

Soot allours
James Joyce[1]

BONGO FURY

In the early 70s Captain Beefheart denounced Frank Zappa for attempting to market him as a 'freak'. This was a poor response to the unprecedented artistic freedom Zappa had given him for *Trout Mask Replica*, though it served to justify Beefheart's own moves towards the mainstream. In 1975 Captain Beefheart made his peace with Zappa and joined the Mothers. Beefheart always denies that his music is work: for him everything is play. Zappa, on the other hand, delights in responding to enquiries about his 'freaky' lifestyle by describing his gruelling work schedule. Beefheart accused him of a 'red-in-the-face, erection-at-all-times, nose-to-the-grindstone' work ethic. Zappa took up this idea in the phrase

> In the night of the iron sausage
> Where the torture never stops[2]

– the 'evil prince' could be a portrait of himself sweating over his mixing desk. The song was originally sung by Beefheart, using Howlin' Wolf's 'Smokestack Lightnin'' riff and announced as 'Why Doesn't Someone Get Him a Pepsi?' (a reference to Beefheart's teenage habit of shouting at his mother to bring him drinks).[3] On *Unconditionally Guaranteed*, a brilliant distillation of hypnotic pop generally dismissed as a sell-out, Beefheart sings:

[1]James Joyce, *Finnegans Wake*, 1939, p. 251, 27.
[2]Frank Zappa, 'The Torture Never Stops', *Zoot Allures*, 1976.
[3]'The Torture Never Stops', 1976, *You Can't Do That On Stage Anymore Vol. 4*, 1991.

She said, Baby, how long is your song?
I said, Baby, as long as you want it to be
She said, I've got all night long
So play me a happy love song . . .
Play me a long love song . . .
I'll play for you a melody
That goes on and on and on
Happy love song[4]

In contrast, in 'Fifty-Fifty' on *Overnite Sensation*, Frank Zappa
had Ricky Lancelotti sing:

Ain't gonna sing you no love song
How my heart is all sore
Will not beg your indulgence
'Cause you heard it before . . .
I have taken your time
I have sung you my song
Ain't no great revelation
But it wasn't too long[5]

Even during a period of hostility they were using each other's
concepts. They milk this contrast on *Bongo Fury*, Beefheart's wild
antagonism to conventional syntax set off by the smart, cartoon-
like wit of Zappa's preambles to '200 Years Old' and 'Muffin
Man'.

According to Zappa, Beefheart was difficult to work with.
Timing was a problem. He complained that his own voice was
never loud enough in the monitors. Zappa reckons that it was the
tension of his extreme vocalizing that closed up his ears. He found
the words difficult to remember.

The way he relates to language is unique, the way he brings my text to
life. Of course he has problems. He won't be separated from his sheets
of paper that have his words written on. He clings to them for dear
life.[6]

On tour he carried bags around full of drawings and poems,
causing regular crises when he mislaid them (his sleeve credit runs:
harp, vocals, shopping bags).

The cover of *Bongo Fury* shows Zappa and Beefheart sitting
in a squalid diner, cigarette butts and matches strewn on the floor.
Beefheart is wearing shoes but no socks, recalling the cover of

[4]Captain Beefheart, 'Happy Love Song', *Unconditionally Guaranteed*, 1972, Virgin V2015.
[5]Frank Zappa, 'Fifty-Fifty', *Overnite Sensation*, 1973.
[6]Quoted by Mick Farren, 'What is a Groupie? Asked His Lordship', *New Musical Express*, 26
April 1975, p. 29.

Archie Shepp's *Four for Trane*.[7] Zappa holds an unpleasant-looking ice-cream and looks up at the camera with an exasperated expression; Beefheart appears to be smiling but his eyes are hidden beneath his broad-brimmed hat. The back cover is a blow-up of a square of floor at their feet, a mottled brown that is perfect for the overall disgust and dismay of the material. Denny Walley, the slide guitarist from Geronimo Black, and drummer Terry Bozzio, from San Francisco and a band called Azteca, are the new musicians. After the majestic clarity of *One Size Fits All*, the sound is guitar-heavy, clotted and ugly. Beefheart's 'the music was dirt-like'[8] seems highly appropriate. 'Abracadabra' had appeared as the name of a star in the constellation Leo Limon on *One Size Fits All*; on *Bongo Fury* she has become a witch in the tradition of Camarillo Brillo. Both words and musical effects seem to bait Beefheart as if he were a performing bear: the lyrics are a torrent of subcultural detail whose origin no one could be expected to guess.

> Debra Kadabra
> Say she's a witch
> *Shit-ass Charlotte!*
> Ain't that a bitch?
> Debra Kadabra –
> Haw, that's rich!
> June, a rancher granny,
> Shook her wrinkled fanny
> Shoes are too tight and pointed
> Ankles sorta puffin' out
> Cause me to shout:
> Oh Debra Algebra Ebneezra Kadabra!
>
> Witch goddess of Lancashire Boulevard
> Cover my entire body with Avon Cologne
> And drive me to some relative's house in East LA
> (Just till my skin clears up)
> Turn it to Channel 13
> And make me watch the rubber tongue
> When it comes out
> Of the puffed & flabulent Mexican rubber-goods mask
> Next time they show the Brnokka
> Make me buy *The Flosser*
> Make me grow brainiac fingers

---

[7] John Coltrane – apparently dragged from his bed to the photo session – is sockless: Archie Shepp, *Four for Trane*, 1964, Impulse IMPL8049.
[8] Captain Beefheart, 'Sam with the Showing Scalp Flat Top', *Bongo Fury*, 1975 – though both R.D. Cook and Ian Watson prefer 'thud-like' (see below).

(But with more hair)
Make me kiss your turquoise jewellery
Emboss me
Rub the hot front part of my head
With rented unguents
Give me bas-relief!

Cast your dancing spell my way
I promise to go under it
Learn the Pachuco Hop
And let me twirl ya
Oh Debra Fauntleroy Magnesium Kadabra!
Take me with you . . .
Don't you want any a these?[9]

This documents more media trivia than anyone who does not live in Los Angeles can credit – the Flosser is a TV-advertised device to hold a length of dental floss, for instance – but the point is Beefheart's agonized reactions as the images whizz by. The reference to Avon Cologne – a predecessor of the carrier of the 'mystery disease' in *Thing-Fish* – was derived from a real-life incident.

> Don's mother, who sold Avon products door to door, had all this stuff from Avon stashed at the house, which everybody used. Y'know, it was free beauty aids. Don, being neurotic, and a bit of a narcissist, was quite prone to dumping any kind of beauty aid that he could find on to his body. He made the unfortunate mistake of taking some Avon cologne and putting it in his hair, one day, which made it start falling out. He also put some sort of Avon cream on his face, which made him break out in this giant rash. His face looked like an alligator. He was losing a great deal of status at the high school, and he moved out of our little desert community, Lancaster, where he went to school, and moved down to East LA to stay with his aunt for a while while he got his chops back together.[10]

This traumatic experience must explain Beefheart covering 'Grown So Ugly':[11] a literal analogue for the fascination with transformation and ugliness – and the way in which they interrogate social norms – in both Beefheart and Zappa. One section describes a Mexican science fiction film Van Vliet and Zappa used to watch, called *The Brainiac*.

> Oh God, it's one of the worst movies ever made and when the monster

[9]Frank Zappa, 'Debra Kadabra', *Bongo Fury*, 1975.
[10]Frank Zappa, quoted in 'Didja Know', *Society Pages*, No. 7, September 1991, p. 54.
[11]Captain Beefheart and the Magic Band, 'Grown So Ugly', *Safe As Milk*, 1967, Buddha BDS5001; also an experience of Danny Houston's while camping in New Zealand.

appears, not only is the monster cheap, he's got a rubber mask that you can see over the collar of the guy's jacket and rubber gloves that don't quite match up with the sleeves of his sport coat. When the monster appears there's this trumpet lick *that isn't scary*. It's not even out of tune, it's just exactly the wrong thing to put there . . . when you hear in the background DA-DA-DA-DA-DA-DAHH that's making fun of the stupid trumpet line.[12]

Beefheart's voice on 'shoes are too tight and pointed' becomes itself almost too tight to achieve utterance: his confusion and panic are painfully real. 'Give me bas-relief' is rewarded with a regular bass line and words about the pachuco hop, a dance Chuck Higgins immortalized in 1952 with an instrumental of that name.[13] This highly suggestive series of words and images – a routine lifted wholesale (and remarkably successfully) by the French surrealist poet and singer Jacques Higelin[14] – is in fact a stream of B-culture absurdities. Like a collage by Kurt Schwitters, it taps an energy from urban detritus that is more than the sum of its parts.

'Carolina Hardcore Ecstasy' is a sick tale of masochism, depicting a girl who likes being trampled. She ends up looking as if she had been 'blendered', her mouth 'extended'. Napoleon Murphy Brock's elastic singing seems quite disturbingly appropriate. There is a great soaring guitar solo that makes use of Terry Bozzio's storming cymbals, a feature of his playing Zappa frequently asked him to subdue.[15] The peculiarly organic textures Bozzio gets from his drums add to the sense of pummelling in the words.

'Sam with the Showing Scalp Flat Top' reinforces the atmosphere set up by the mottled brown cover and the sonic murkiness. It uses the adjectives 'black' and 'dark' repeatedly, with references to tobacco juice and fly-pecked doorways. An amputee whose 'hard dark ivory cup held saleable everyday pencils' anticipates the satire on bicentennial trash that follows ('Poofter's Froth Wyoming Plans Ahead'), whilst his trolley's 'dark hard dark rubber wheels' recall the black vinyl of the record itself.

> I used to fiddle with my back-feet music for a black onyx
> My entire room absorbed every echo
> The music was dirt-like
> The music was dirt-like

[12]Edwin Pouncey, 'To be Perfectly Frank', *Sounds*, 29 January 1983.
[13]Chuck Higgins, *Pachuko Hop*, 1983, Ace CH81.
[14]Jacques Higelin, *Mocador*, a live set that includes 'Paris New York, New York Paris' and 'Tête en l'air'. A tape given to me and Caroline by a driver when hitching out of Rennes, France, in 1983, after visiting noted Zappologist Jackie Fournel.
[15]Simon Braund, 'La Dolce Vita', *Rhythm*, July 1989, p. 44.

> I usually played such things as Roughneck 'n Dug
> Opaque melodies that would bug most people
> Music from the other side of the fence[16]

After he had pointed out Beefheart's affinity to Howlin' Wolf and the way Denny Walley's slide-guitar playing suited his style, Zappa was asked if he was moving towards a 'blues thing': 'Frank smiles and nods'.[17] 'Sam with the Showing Scalp Flat Top' is an intense summary of the elements of R&B that initially attracted both Zappa and Beefheart ('other side of the fence' is no metaphor). There is disagreement about the above transcript: some[18] insist that Beefheart says 'the music was thud-like'. The whole issue of Beefheart's pronunciation is highly intriguing. 'Entire room' is pronounced 'in tar room', an image perpetuated by the nicotine-stained hand, chipped teeth and black rubber cigarette-holder of 'Man with the Woman Head'. Indeed, jwcurry has pointed out that *mis*heard lyrics are an important part of the experience of a record, transcribing a chorus from 'The Mammy Nuns' to read like a sound-poem by Bob Cobbing.[19] In their enthusiasm for R&B, no doubt Zappa and Beefheart misunderstood many aspects of black culture, but they could nevertheless relate to it as *texture* (just as Varèse could relate to African percussion via *timbre*). In responding to Zappa's music as if it were abstract art, jwcurry points to the aspect that makes it special.

'Sam with the Showing Scalp Flat Top' is in fact one of a series of close-focus vignettes of Californian life which pepper *Bat Chain Puller*, the unreleased masterpiece Beefheart recorded at this time. Where Zappa's fascination with trivial detail is provocatively degrading, Beefheart achieves more traditional poetic moments (Zappa wanted him to improvise words, but Beefheart never felt comfortable enough on stage to do so). Beefheart's onomatopoeic pronunciations and weird emphases are everything that poetry and jazz – Kenneth Rexroth and the West Coast Beats – never quite achieved. As usual, rock 'n' roll actually solves technical problems raised by slumming fine art.

Beefheart's poem segues into 'Poofter's Froth Wyoming Plans

---

[16]Captain Beefheart, 'Sam with the Showing Scalp Flat Top', *Bongo Fury*, 1975.
[17]Quoted by Mick Farren, 'What is a Groupie? Asked His Lordship', *New Musical Express*, 26 April 1975, p. 29.
[18]Especially my editor, R.D. Cook.
[19]jwcurry, 'Grammatical Sabotage: Conversing with Frank Zappa's *Thing-Fish*', *Rampike*, Vol. 7, No. 2, 1991.

Ahead', a country tune which rubbishes the bicenntenial celebrations by listing all the souvenir trinkets that will appear.

> This is a *Buy-Cent-Any-All* salute –
> Two hundred years have gone *kaput*![20]

In '200 Years Old' Walley's guitar and Beefheart's double-tracked vocals indeed get into a 'blues thing'. America is 'too mean to grow a beard' (an accusation of immaturity that reoccurs with 'Tryin' to Grow a Chin' on *Sheik Yerbouti* and in 'The Massive Improve'lence' on *Thing-Fish*). Beefheart comments in an aside 'but not too mean to grow a *merde*'. This dirt-like 'music from the other side of the fence' is smeared with relish over the lily-white face of complacent bicentennial patriotism.

Captain Beefheart's presence prompts memories of early days in 'Cucamonga'. The stilted way the melody is spread across the beat with

> And as fate would have it
> Later on we got a chance to play[21]

is highly reminiscent of Egg's 'A Visit to Newport Hospital',[22] also a nostalgic tale of musical beginnings. The distinctive clavinet-drum doubling suggests direct parody. Beefheart's harp adds an unEgg-like sleaze that was also used to good effect on 'Find Her Finer'.[23]

'Advance Romance' extends the blues theme with beautifully massive slide-guitar assertions from Walley. Tom Fowler's dry, funky, astonishingly precise bass offsets the scummy looseness of the playing. After a juicy harp break from Beefheart, Zappa's solo is ushered in by George Duke joking about 'cold chicken'. The middle section recalls his Transylvanian style from *Chunga's Revenge*, provoking exclamations of 'long time!' and 'chicken was never like that!' from Duke. To a traditional R&B chorus of 'all night long', Zappa rocks away with a small-combo intensity and warmth which is highly unusual for him. The closing lines revive Potatohead Bobby from 'San Ber'dino',[24] as well as predicting the potatoheads of the Mammy Nuns in *Thing-Fish*. Bobby is standing

---

[20]Captain Beefheart, 'Poofter's Froth Wyoming Plans Ahead', *Bongo Fury*, 1975.
[21]Frank Zappa, 'Cucamonga', *Bongo Fury*, 1975.
[22]*The Polite Force*, 1970, Decca SML1074.
[23]Frank Zappa, *Zoot Allures*, 1976.
[24]*One Size Fits All*, 1975.

in the food-stamp line: physical deformity an analogue for the horror respectability feels for poverty.

'Man with the Woman Head' sounds like a grotesque from *Trout Mask Replica*, but Beefheart's closing line 'so this was a drive-in restaurant in Hollywood' places it as a realist response to the squalor of modern America. Zappa's 'Muffin Man' preamble introduces the Utility Muffin Research Kitchen – later the name of Zappa's home studio – and the kind of leering inanity brought to a fine art by the Central Scrutinizer on *Joe's Garage* (Zappa fluffs a line and then carries on with 'let's try that again': this from someone who thought nothing of abandoning thirty hours of mixing on *Overnite Sensation* and starting again from scratch). The way it cuts into Beefheart's evocative rhapsody is a chilling reminder of their different methods. Where Beefheart asserts subjectivity – however repulsive to norms of voice and image – Zappa skates on the superficial polish of commercial clichés, absurdist recitative backed by George Duke's eighteenth-century harpsichord.

No Birds

'Muffin Man' refers to the arctic degree zero of 'Penguin in Bondage' and *Apostrophe (')*.

> Girl you thought he was a man
> But he was a muffin
> He hung around till you found
> That he didn't know nothin'
> Girl you thought he was a man
> But he only was a puffin
> No cries is heard in the night
> As a result of him stuffin'[25]

Whether or not 'a puffin' is actually 'a-puffin'', the arctic bird is evoked, alongside the denial of song. As defined by Theodor Adorno, negative dialectics implies continual refutation of the tendency to think that the concept exhausts the thing conceived. It is also aware that denial of the concept does not abolish its power. This was termed 'negative capability' by the romantics, who discovered that to deny something in poetry was still to evoke it. Poetry is like Freud's unconscious or Beulah, Blake's

[25]Frank Zappa, 'Muffin Man', *Bongo Fury*, 1975.

land of dreams where there are no contradictions. The most famous example of negative capability – 'La Belle Dame sans Merci' by John Keats – links it to the terrifying female who can unleash orgasm and unman the man. She took the poet to her 'elfin grot' and 'sigh'd full sore', but he awoke

> On the cold hill's side.
> And this is why I sojourn here
> Alone and palely loitering
> Though the sedge is wither'd from the lake,
> And no birds sing.

The melancholy of these lines is triggered by the songbirds' absence, which is like the loss that makes up desire. The 1960s meaning of bird – female sex object – also resonates in these lines. When Fred Frith released an album of guitar solos intended to reduce rock music to its minimal component, he named the last track 'No Birds'.[26] On *Metal Box* PiL had a song called 'No Birds'.

> THIS COULD BE HEAVEN
> MILD MANNERED MEWS
> WELL-INTENTIONED RULES
> TO DIGNIFY A DAILY CODE[27]

This is the perfect peace of bourgeois wealth, where the individual is safe because completely absorbed into the grid of the social system. The violent strife of phallocentric romanticism has been left behind: the birds so absent they are only left in the title. As Keith Levene said at the time, John Lydon is not some tosser expressing his emotions; the loss of tension in the words, which have become documentary, is replaced by boosting the bass, copying the movement from blues to reggae (individual to collective).

Captain Beefheart denied birds too, in a poem that appeared on the back cover of *Mirror Man*.

> One nest rolls after another
> Until there are no longer any birds
> One tongue lashes another
> Until there are no words
> I love
> Sails
> No birds[28]

---

[26]Fred Frith, *Guitar Solos*, 1974, Virgin – thanks to R. D. Cook for pointing this out and to Mike Laurence for supplying a tape.
[27]PiL, 'No Birds', *Metal Box*, 1979, Virgin METAL1.
[28]Captain Beefheart and his Magic Band, *Mirror Man*, 1968, Buddah BDS5077.

This traces the extinction of conceptual thought in sexual arousal (like the French calling orgasm *'petit mort'*). All these themes occur in 'Penguin in Bondage'.

> Lord you know it must be a Penguin bound down
> When you hear that terrible screamin' and there ain't no other
> Birds around[29]

Mucking around with 'dried muffin remnants' – recorded sounds, dried-up remains of human activity – in the Utility Muffin Research Kitchen, Zappa himself is the muffin man. When he 'poots forth a quarter-ounce green rosette' on a 'dense but radiant muffin of his own design' he is putting the final touches on an album. Like poetry, like concepts, records are dead matter.

> No cries is heard in the night[30]

sums up the negative capability of recorded sound, its signal of absent activity. Zappa's huge, spiralling guitar solo on 'Muffin Man' and his closing 'goodnight Austin Texas, wherever you are' declare an empty grandeur – the Muffin Man is a cipher.

The net effect of Beefheart and Zappa's collaboration is not to project themselves as the centre of meaning, but to present the blues – recorded live in Texas where of course most LA blues musicians came from – as under-class vengeance on white America's complacency (Zappa's closing 'good night Austin Texas wherever you are!' signals that his affection for the place is musical rather than geographical). With Walley's slide and Zappa's solos on 'Carolina Hardcore Ecstasy' and 'Muffin Man', the guitar – abetted by Bozzio's turbulent drums – was becoming central to Zappa's increasingly them-or-us perspective.

Zappa subsequently created extra space for his guitar by paring down the band completely. He told Steve Rosen:

> with a larger group you have to play less – there are a lot of people waiting in line to play solos. That's one of the reasons I've got a smaller group now, because I happen to like to play solos ... I have some stuff to say, and I'm going to get out there and do it.[31]

So Zappa began edging towards guitars and rock, ending an era that many people felt combined the perfect balance of chops and character. George Duke told *Down Beat* in 1978:

[29]Frank Zappa, 'Penguin in Bondage', *Roxy & Elsewhere*, 1974.
[30]Frank Zappa, 'Muffin Man', *Bongo Fury*, 1975.
[31]Quoted by Steve Rosen, 'Frank Zappa', *Rock Guitarist*, 1977, reprinted in *Society Pages*, No. 26, July 1985, p. 23.

I can say in earnestness that if there was one band that stayed together I'd probably still be there because I felt very free – that was in the small group with Ruth Underwood, Tom Fowler, Chester Thompson, myself and Frank. That was an incredible band.

Duke had been recording his own albums: Zappa guested on *Feel*[32] (under the name Obdewl'l X, later used as a name for a Mammy Nun in *Thing-Fish*); *The Aura Will Prevail*[33] featured 'Echidna's Arf' and 'Uncle Remus'. *I Love the Blues She Heard My Cry* – with Ruth Underwood, the Fowlers and a wonderful on-the-porch blues sung with Johnny 'Guitar' Watson – gets nearest to the spirit of the Zappa band. Duke left to form a fusion band with Billy Cobham and John Scofield. Chester Thompson only played on the two studio tracks of *Bongo Fury*, and subsequently split for work with Duke and Genesis. A drummer in transition from jazz towards the funk of Clyde Stubblefield and Dennis Chambers, Thompson's contribution to Zappa's music was underrated by those who never saw this band live (his drumming is beautifully preserved on *Stage #2*, which is devoted to one gig by the *Roxy* band) and his qualities were revealed only when the immaculate close-focus jazz of *Studio Tan* appeared on CD with a proper credit in 1991. The Fowler Brothers – of whom there were more, including Walt Fowler, who played trumpet for Johnny 'Guitar' Watson – formed their own band.

In February 1976 Zappa toured with a quintet: Terry Bozzio – increasingly impressive as he filled every splinter of time with beats – Roy Estrada, Napoleon Murphy Brock and André Lewis, the brilliant soul synthesizer player who had been working with Johnny 'Guitar' Watson.[34] In the early 70s Lewis co-led a Sly Stone-style funk outfit featuring his wife Maxayn on vocals, recording for Warner Brothers.[35] One of the first movers in black music to recognize the value of Hendrix, Lewis's synthesizer work spurred Zappa into guitar-feedback outreach: it is difficult to imagine the extremities of Zappa's guitar coda to 'Zoot Allures' ('Duck Duck Down' on *Läther*, 'Ship Ahoy' on *Shut Up 'N Play Yer Guitar*) without Lewis's example. The three records Lewis cut

[32]George Duke, *Feel*, 1975, MPS 2122312–4.
[33]George Duke, *The Aura Will Prevail*, 1975, MPS 68025.
[34]Johnny 'Guitar' Watson, *Listen*, 1973, Fantasy/EMI 5C038–61279; *I Don't Want to be Alone, Stranger*, 1975, Fantasy F9484.
[35]Maxayn, *Maxayn*, 1972, Capricorn CP0103; *Bail out for Fun!*, 1974, Capricorn K57503.

for Motown after the Zappa tour as Mandré[36] were masterpieces of cyberfunk, years ahead of their time (some claim Zappa is playing on *Mandré* under the name Boondoxatron, but if so his playing is quite unrecognizable). On the first album 'Dirty Love' is done in the style of *Zoot Allures*, making the *Overnite Sensation* version sound positively wholesome. André Lewis's musical suites are the most convincing pieces of black symphonic pop since those of Marvin Gaye. He came to London with Johnny 'Guitar' in 1987,[37] but has since retired to Munich. It is a pity one of the *Stage* volumes was not the momentous Osaka concert that contributed 'Black Napkins' to *Zoot Allures*; this band was really something special.

LYRES, MORTALITY, REPRESSION OF THE BODY

The defeat of Plato's argument for the immortality of the soul and the consequent shearing of Fido's locks has already been described.[38] When Socrates's argument began in *Phaedo*, though, he first considered the idea that the soul is akin to the harmony of a lyre. If it is, then it will perish along with the material instrument, and the soul is not immortal. For Plato, the immortality of the soul is bound up with denigration of the body.

> We have already acknowledged that the soul, if she were a harmony, could never utter a note at variance with the tensions and relaxations and percussions and other affections of the strings out of which she is composed; she could only follow, she could not lead them.[39]

Socrates draws out the metaphysical consequences of the analogy while everyone tuts their disapproval: the idea of the soul following the body is simply disgraceful. His description of manipulating the strings of the lyre has a latent eroticism which relates to the way players view the electric guitar. 'I have to change the low E string *every* night, because I stressify on it. And even if I tried, man, it just won't stand the bending the following night. I bend those suckers, boy, to death.'[40]

---

[36]Mandré, *Mandré*, 1977, Motown STML12062; *Two*, 1978, Motown STML12084; *M3000*, 1979, Motown M917.
[37]Johnny 'Guitar' Watson, Town and Country Club, London, 17 June 1987.
[38]See 'Poodles and philosophy', Chapter 5: Bizarre to DiscReet.
[39]Plato, *Phaedo*, c. 400 BC, 94c.
[40]Johnny 'Guitar' Watson, interviewed by Jaz Obrecht, *Guitar Player*, February 1982.

Such an erotic charge, an audible result of physical manipulation, is not, according to Socrates, to be encouraged. The soul is like music, but it must come from on high (the music of the spheres), not from the individual body. Music as social ritual encodes power, and Plato's hierarchical view of society cannot countenance siting the source of music in the individual. In ancient Greece the lyre was used to accompany personal and sophisticated styles of poetry – Plato preferred the flute, which was associated with more earnest and didactic works. When Zappa, as a teenager, collected R&B records with guitar breaks instead of tenor saxophone solos, he was tapping into a form that seems designed to refute Plato's preferences. The guitar, of course, goes back to Africa, and Plato may simply be voicing prejudice against the lyre's origins. When Don Cherry showed his *doussn'gouni* (a hunter's six-string instrument from Mali) to John Lee Hooker in Paris one time, the latter looked at it and declared 'that's a guitar, man'.[41] The blues guitar is Plato's nemesis.

Socrates pursues his anti-body argument: 'It is characteristic of the philosopher to despise the body; his soul runs away from his body and desires to be alone and by itself.'[42]

The idea that the soul should be a chord struck from the body is therefore abhorrent. Socrates also argues that the idea of the soul as the harmony of the body would make impossible any distinction between 'good' and 'bad' souls, as a musical instrument is either in tune or completely inharmonious and useless. In defending this judgemental and punishing moral code Socrates set back the possibility of psychoanalysis a few thousand years. In a symbolic manner, every Zappa guitar solo denigrates the Platonic philosophical ideal. His guitar playing is imbued with an understanding of the plucked string and its intimations of sexual piquancy and existential mortality, an understanding which reached its apogee in *Zoot Allures*.

ULYSSES, TWANGS, DEATH

Horkheimer and Adorno take issue with *Phaedo*'s use of Homer (though they never explicitly mention Plato), developing a contrary argument that makes *The Dialectic of Enlightenment* one of

---

[41]Don Cherry, Riley Smith Hall, Leeds University, 10 October 1987.
[42]Plato, *Phaedo*, *c.* 400 BC, 65d.

the founding texts of radical twentieth-century philosophy. In *Phaedo* Plato praises Ulysses and contrasts his subjugation of lower nature to the (now discredited) metaphor of the soul being the harmony of the body's instrument. The notes of a lyre can never utter a note at variance with the physical situation of the strings, but Ulysses can control himself:

> Do we now not discover the soul to be doing the exact opposite – *leading* the elements of which he is believed to be composed; almost always opposing and coercing them in all sorts of ways throughout life, sometimes more violently with the pains of medicine and gymnastic; then again more gently; now threatening, now admonishing the desires, passions, fears, as if talking to a thing which is not itself, as Homer represents Ulysses doing in the words – 'He beat his breast, and thus reproached his heart: Endure, my heart; far worse hast thou endured!'[43]

In *The Dialectic of Enlightenment* Adorno and Horkheimer concentrate on one particular Homeric story, that of Ulysses and the Sirens. The Sirens were female bird-monsters who preyed on human flesh, singing songs of such allure that sailors swam to their island to be devoured. Ulysses wanted to hear their song, so he stopped his rowers' ears with wax and had himself bound to the mast – a scene depicted on many an amphora to be viewed in London's British Museum.

> However consciously alienated from nature he may be, he remains subject to it if he heeds its voice ... Ulysses recognizes the archaic superior power of the song even when, as a technically enlightened man, he has himself bound ... The Sirens have their own quality, but in primitive bourgeois history it is neutralized to become merely the wistful longing of the passer-by. Since Ulysses' successful-unsuccessful encounter with the Sirens all songs have been affected.[44]

Both the Mothers of Invention

> Mr America walk on by your schools that do not teach
> Mr America walk on by the minds that won't be reached[45]

and the Sex Pistols

> I am the antichrist
> I am an anarchist
> I don't know what I want

---

[43]Ibid., 94e.
[44]Theodor Adorno and Max Horkheimer, *The Dialectic of Enlightenment*, 1944, p. 59.
[45]Mothers of Invention, 'Hungry Freaks', *Freak Out!*, 1966.

> But I know how to get it
> I wanna destroy the passer-by[46]

began their recorded œuvre with affronts to the passer-by.

DEMOCRACY, THE CITIZEN, SELF-CONTROL

Athenian democracy revolved around discussion in public places and respect for the passer-by (unless you were a slave or a woman, in which case you did not count). Citizens were not connected together by their economic activities but by their entry as 'free' leisured agents, responsible and articulate individuals, on to the sunbaked pavements of the agora. The Athenians made a positive fetish of a social form that was later to become, with the decline of communist state-capitalist ideology, *the* mask for capitalist exploitation everywhere: social democracy. Here everyone has a vote to elect parliamentary representatives but no control over capital, the real taskmaster. Despite the petit-bourgeois nature of Zappa's explicit politics, his art is a symbolic protest against this situation.

In the capitalist world of exchange, music is an affront, a reminder of pleasure as an end in itself. Both freaks and punks interrupt the smooth flow of consumers on the street, the atomistic 'citizens' of Greek-style democracy, and propose that life be lived right here. The presence of this moment in pop music shows that the anti-exchange impulse is not confined to high art (in this sense Adorno falls short when he deals with what he calls 'radio music').

Adorno and Horkheimer find in the story of the Sirens a parable of repression: the initial crime that explains how man can subjugate and exploit. First, he must repress his own nature, his own responses to the body and sexuality.

> He just pulls through; struggle is his survival; and all the fame that he and the others win in the process serves merely to confirm that the title of hero is only gained at the price of abasement and mortification of the instinct for complete, universal and undivided happiness.[47]

---

[46]Sex Pistols, 'Anarchy in the UK', 26 November 1976, EMI 2566, as transcribed in *The Sex Pistols*, ed. Fred and Judy Vermorel, 1978, p. 27. R.D. Cook favours 'Ponsonby' instead of 'passer-by' and I have heard SWP members insist that it is in fact 'posh exploiters', but the Vermorels and Jon Savage, *England's Dreaming*, 1991, p. 253, remain more convincing than either. No accident that John Lydon's delivery should raise problems of interpretation not registered since Beefheart.

[47]Theodor Adorno and Max Horkheimer, *The Dialectic of Enlightenment*, 1944, p. 57.

The Dialectic of Enlightenment has been widely influential, providing both feminism (Angela Davis was taught by Adorno) and left-wing Freudianism with an inspirational text. If it is *repression* that causes oppression, then absolute freedom is a possibility.

The centrepiece of *Zoot Allures*, 'The Torture Never Stops', described by *Sounds* as an 'audio snuff movie', is so overtly offensive to feminist shibboleths that it may come as a surprise that it works the same themes as *Dialectic of Enlightenment* (though it should be recalled that Adorno and Horkhemer also included in *The Dialectic* a long – and enthusiastic – treatment of de Sade). Before feminism was co-opted to become yet another facet of liberal anxiety about what the working class is consuming, it actually asked questions about sexuality, class and exploitation. It is to that radical tradition Zappa contributes.

By astute punning of the exclamations of sexual pleasure and groans of torture, and verbal imagery which Disneyfies Gothic horror, Zappa concocts an arresting *mélange* designed to tweak the repressions of the passer-by. Other songs on the album interrogate the listener's libido with formats that copy the limitations of commercial pop rock and disco. As well as punning on the French expression '*zut alors!*', the title indicates the allure of 'zoot', a subcultural buzzword which surfaced most famously as a description for the exaggerated suits worn by black hipsters in the 40s – the zoot suit. The 'zoot-suit riots' in Los Angeles were said to be started by sailors' reactions to the way ghetto hipsters mocked wartime austerity by their extravagant use of material. It is close to the word 'soot' and therefore combines blackness, filth and the unknown into one word – as the epigraph at the top of this chapter indicates, for another famous scatologist the French expression suggested the idea that the allure of soot could *allow*.

The allure of zoot

Inside the gatefold sleeve of *Zappa in New York* (and still visible in the CD insert), the album that followed *Zoot Allures*, there is a photograph of the group onstage taken by Gail Zappa. The musicians aren't playing their instruments, but dancing or acknowledging applause. Careful examination[48] shows that Ruth

---

[48] I am indebted to Danny Houston for this observation.

Underwood has an enamel badge of the cover of *Zoot Allures* pinned to the right pocket on the seat of her jeans. Ray White – lead singer on 'The Legend of the Illinois Enema Bandit' – is holding her from behind by the waist. Given the Bandit's proclivities, he looks as if he is going to plug her from behind. The allure of zoot is the allure of anality, which connects to the death instinct. As Samuel Beckett says: 'Under its heather mask the quag allures, with an allurement not all mortals can resist. Then it swallows them up or the mist comes down.'[49]

In 'The Torture Never Stops' Zappa challenges us not to find the girl's squeals alluring. Arousal works like avant-garde instrumental practice, pushing instrument and player to extremes of pitch and audibility. The girl's screams sound like the 'out' saxophone playing of Archie Shepp or the scrapes and snaps of Siegfried Palm's cello when he is playing Iannis Xenakis or Isang Yun.[50]

Child psychoanalyst Melanie Klein drew a connection between the sadistic impulses of the child towards the mother and the child's desire for knowledge. During the latency period (which lasts from about the age of seven until puberty) the child represses 'anything that savours of search or interrogation or touches on the impulses she just manages to keep under control';[51] 'arithmetic and writing symbolized sadistic attacks upon her mother's body'.[52] This savour of search is the allure of zoot; the tang of twang. The initial 'Z' of *Zoot Allures* implies knowledge that goes right to the end of the alphabet. As Benedetto Croce puts it: 'From the compasses to the bistouri, and from that to the zither!'[53]

The zither, like the harp, has one tuning per string, merely awaiting the performer's finger stroke to release its twang. The title track 'Zoot Allures' has Lu Ann Neil on harp, the instrument of angels. The title puts 'Z' before 'A', a Satanic reversal like reciting the Lord's Prayer backwards. On the cover Zappa appears with his young accomplices – Patrick O'Hearn, Terry Bozzio and Eddie Jobson (neither O'Hearn nor Jabson play). Terry Bozzio's T-shirt reads 'Angels' (a reference to Punky Meadows's group Angel, later satirized in 'Punky's Whips' on *Zappa in New York*,

[49]Samuel Beckett, *Mercier and Camier*, 1946, trs. Samuel Beckett, 1974, p. 97.
[50]Siegfried Palm and Aloys Kontarsky, *Musik für Violoncell (und Klavier)*, 1975, Deutsche Grammophon 2530562.
[51]Melanie Klein, *The Psychoanalysis of Children*, 1932, p. 58.
[52]Ibid. p. 57.
[53]Benedetto Croce, *What is Living and What is Dead in the Philosophy of Hegel*, 1906, p. 3.

though the plural indicates that this is not a band T-shirt). Surrounded by guileless youth, Zappa, with long, bedgraggled hair, bulging crotch and defiantly wide flares (this was 1976) looks darkly demonic. On the back he is bending his knees as if to ease an incipient erection. The anti-classicism of the Celtic harp is enforced by a Chinese name seal on the cover and handwritten Japanese characters on the back.[54]

In 'The Torture Never Stops' Zappa returns to his old theme of the world's greatest sinner.

> He's the best of course of all the worst
> Some wrong been done he done it first[55]

The absolutely scurrilous sound of the guitar on this track comes from a fretless acoustic with Barcus-Berry pick-ups.

> I bought it for $75. The only restriction was that they had to take a chisel and some black paint and scratch off the word 'Acoustic' on the headpiece, because Acoustic didn't want anybody to know that they had made such a grievous error as to make a fretless guitar ... it's different than a regular guitar: you don't push the strings to bend them, you move them back and forth like violin-type vibrato, which is a funny movement to get used to.[56]

Seldom has the act of playing guitar been made to seem quite so physical and sexually suggestive. As the girl subject to 'recreational direction' makes a conclusive yelp, she sounds as if she has been trampled underfoot by the militaristic massed drums of 'Ms Pinky', a song about a *lonely person device* that costs $69.95: a rubber replica of a child's head, complete with (cock-size) open mouth lined with sponge and built-in vibrator, battery pack and two-speed motor. Sticking out of its neck is a nozzle with a

---

[54]The interpretation of the meaning of oriental name transliterations is highly ambiguous, given the multi-valency of Chinese characters. One session with my father revealed 'revolution is not my aim; bitterness', which sounded like a perfect summary of Zappa's position to me at the time. Simon Prentis has pointed out that the characters first appeared on the tickets for a concert at Kyoto University in 1976. Zappa took a great interest in them and learned to write them himself (the handwritten characters on the back cover are in his hand). Prentis's interpretation is as follows: 'The reading of the five (Chinese) characters from left to right (and it should be emphasized that this is the *Japanese* reading, as a Chinese reading would be different, and also depend on the particular region) is: FU RAN KU ZA(P) PA. Taking the surname first, the two characters mean "various" and "groups" ... The characters FU RAN KU which make up "Frank" mean, individually, "no", "confusion" and "suffering/distress" ... Thus the full meaning of the five characters can be expressed more colloquially as follows: "Without confusion or distress, through many groups", which is perhaps as fine a summary of the unfolding of conceptual continuity in Frank's work as one could wish for,' letter to the author, 21 December 1993.
[55]Frank Zappa, 'The Torture Never Stops', *Zoot Allures*, 1976.
[56]Steve Rosen, 'Frank Zappa', *Rock Guitarist*, 1977, reprinted in *Society Pages*, No. 26, July 1985, p. 20.

squeeze-bulb that makes the throat contract.[57] Unconcerned about offending feminists who wish to legislate about abuse of women in the mass media – and in the 80s to supply the Christian right with useful rhetoric – Zappa cannot be accused of glamorizing the receptacle for these impulses. The horror of *Zoot Allures* is anxiety, the self's fear of its own impulses.

In his *Aesthetic* Benedetto Croce saw 'an absolute limit at the disgusting and nauseating, which kills representation itself'.[58] Full of the disgusting, the nauseating and the downright shocking, Zappa's art does indeed kill representation. What we have is the consciously artificial deployment of cultural icons: the wall that 'weeps greenish drops', for example, is derived from Bartók's 1911 musical fantasy *Bluebeard's Castle*. The cartoon Gothic of 'The Torture Never Stops' is a series of self-proclaimed clichés that nevertheless pack huge emotive force.

'Black Napkins', a soaring Santana-style guitar solo over a two-chord vamp, is quite unlike anything Zappa had recorded before. At the UCLA orchestral concert in September 1975 he improvised an arrangement by telling the strings to play two chords in succession, and then played electric guitar over the top. Whereas previously his solos were marked by an obstinate resistance to the beat, this is straightforwardly rhapsodic. The title derives from a Thanksgiving dinner in Japan where the band were amazed to be given black table napkins. It was recorded live in Osaka. American pulp culture of the 50s frequently used supposed 'documentation' of Japanese war atrocities to indulge S&M scenarios. This helps explain the subsequent combination of *japono-iserie* and S&M in John Zorn (Georges Delerue's 'Contempt' on *Naked City*[59] is a dead ringer for 'Black Napkins', a neat illustration of the objectivity of both artists' concerns as there is no traceable influence either way). The intensity of 'Black Napkins', the straining clarity of the guitar's notes, copies the white-heat sting of orgasm as well as emulating a western notion of Japanese extremity. Although Zappa has abandoned the lumpy oppositional integrity of his solos with the Mothers, the deployment of commercial devices has a clarity and sense of purpose that makes it experimental.

[57]A full explanation may be heard on Frank Zappa, 'Lonely Person Devices', 1975, *You Can't Do That on Stage Anymore Vol. 6*, 1992.
[58]Benedetto Croce, *Aesthetic*, 1911, p. 58.
[59]John Zorn, *Naked City*, 1990, Elektra Nonesuch 7559–79238.

Max Ernst

This development corresponds to a phase in the career of the surrealist painter Max Ernst. For years he resisted illusionistic oil painting as the medium of the bourgeoisie, resorting instead to collage, montage, frottage – anything but standing to paint in the traditional manner. Suddenly in the late 1940s he began producing heavy oil paintings, gigantic imaginary landscapes of unwholesome decadence. He showed he was a great painter in the traditional sense, with a feeling for the lie of paint that resists photographic reproduction (nothing prepares the viewer for a confrontation with the originals). The surrealists had rejected Salvador Dali for his fascist politics, but also for his reliance on oil paint and traditional methods of representing space, his photographic realism. Max Ernst's use of oils was, though, no sell-out. He had suddenly found how to develop the 'why-not' of surrealism in a way that broke his own rules, but also delivered works of unsettling power. Where he differed from Dali was in his use of accident: 'decalcomania', the practice of squeezing paint under glass, suggested motives that he then extended and developed. Likewise Zappa. With *Overnite Sensation* he broke with alternative rock sentimentality about bed-sit recording quality; with 'Black Napkins' he abandons any scruples about pursuing the blatant aspect of the electric guitar's ability to soar. But he also introduced accident.

Utter control, utter chaos

Despite its mainstream direction, it is on *Zoot Allures* that Zappa introduces a technique called variously 'resynchronization'[60] and 'xenochronicity'[61] – taking parts played by musicians without reference to each other and combining them in a multi-track studio. On 'Friendly Little Finger' the guitar solo comes in playing to a totally different rhythm. The result is an exotic schizophrenia, but Zappa has made every sound so much his own that the result is not average chaos but highly individualized music. Just as the

---

[60]Sleeve note to 'Rubber Shirt', *Sheik Yerbouti*, 1979.
[61]Sleeve note to the promotional sampler for the *Shut Up 'N Play Yer Guitar* box set. I owe much of this passage to ideas resulting from discussions with the composer Simon Fell, whose *Compilation II*, 1991, Bruce's Fingers BF2, makes effective use of the technique. Bruce's Fingers may be contacted at 24 Chauntry Road, Haverhill CB9 8BE, England.

music seems to become completely rigid and formularized according to commercial dictates, the door opens on the utterly random. The paradox of serialism is that its total determination of elements eschews expression and generates chance events. Multi-tracking is a technology that gives the pop producer unprecedented control over the musicians (and explains the sterility of 80s pop that does not explicitly experiment with production techniques). Such heretical use of multi-tracking (Zappa has described the engineers' horror at what he wanted to do) parallels the movement from order to chaos in serialism.

Prince also uses the technique. The opening of *Parade* has Clare Fischer's orchestral overture come in at variance with the electric instruments[62] in a way that refers to the experience of hearing brass bands move about in the city. Most famously exploited by Charles Ives, the idea of simultaneous musics has been taken up by John Cage as well as Anthony Braxton and Henry Threadgill. Ornette Coleman's harmolodics takes the idea of simultaneous musics into the method of improvisation itself. All these are attempts to let art deal structurally with the complexity of modern life in a way that does not pretend to integrate them via the 'expressive' personality. At the end of 'Friendly Little Finger' what sounds like a Bavarian bierkeller barrel-organ starts up, playing the hymn 'Bringing in the Sheaves' (a Salvation Army-type intro suitable for 'Wino Man'). In *The Philosophy of Modern Music* Adorno talks of how Bach's religious organ music has been reduced to sounding like a hand-organ or hurdygurdy because society has suffered 'the enthronement of a mechanical factor as authority'.[63] The German input into disco – Giorgio Moroder, Kraftwerk – meant that alongside the sense of machinery there is also a dose of *lederhosen* inanity. In deploying the traditions of mechanized music – the hand-organ, the multi-track studio, disco – Zappa also points to their liberating effect, the freedom from human control, the possibility of undreamed-of combinations.

The sensitive listener – and any Adornoite (indeed, any human being) needs to be sensitive to traces of Auschwitz – is unsettled that the first song is titled 'Wind up Workin' in a Gas Station'. Ostensibly about the failure of higher education to provide graduates with jobs, there is a sinister sense that 'pumpin' the gas

[62]Prince, 'Christopher Tracy's Parade', *Parade*, 1986, Paisley Park 925365.
[63]Theodor Adorno, *The Philosophy of Modern Music*, 1948, trs. Anne Mitchell and Wesley Blomster, 1973, p. 145.

every night' might refer to gassing Jews. Inexplicably the chorus develops a German accent on 'Manny the Camper wants to buy some white... (FISH)' ('v's for 'w's).[64] Germanitude also arises via associations with Volkswagen camper-vans.[65] The absurdity of such connections is evident – unfortunately, as Freud was wont to say of the unconscious, that's how art works. The phrase 'You ought to know now all your education' hangs over the song like a challenge to listeners who might gag on what follows. Given the Japanese/German Second World War references and the overall miasma of concentration camp atrocity, the reference to pork in 'The Torture Never Stops' can only be described as tasteless:

> An evil price eats a steamin' pig in a chamber right near there
> He eats the snouts and the trotters first
> The loins and the groins is soon dispersed
> His carvin' style is well rehearsed
> He stands and shouts: 'All men be cursed!
> All men be cursed! All men be cursed!
> All men be cursed!'
> And disagree no-one durst[66]

The words are phrased in a deep-south nigger accent ('rehearsed' is 'rehoizt'), a practice which reached its ridiculous peak in *Thing-Fish*. If this doesn't derive from a Lenny Bruce routine it ought to: concentration camps and pork, orgasm and torture, it's a barrage of unpleasant reminders. Zappa credits himself as 'director of recreational activities' for the song on the sleeve: 'director of recreation' was Lenny Bruce's title at the Premier Hotel in 1951.[67] Yes indeed, tasteless to the max – but maybe these are aspects of history that are too often swept under the carpet. It is certainly more listenable than the Grateful Dead's contemporary opus 'The Music Never Stopped'.

---

[64]This transcription courtesy of Simon Prentis, who taped an interview about the words to *Zoot Allures* with Zappa in 1992 (letter to the author, 21 December 1993). I had previously heard 'man in the camper wants to buy some wine'; the appearance of a stereotypical Jewish foodstuff, though, actually encourages a gas-chamber reading.

[65]Connections cemented by Eugene Chadbourne's collaborations with a band called Camper Van Beethoven and later on with Jimmy Carl Black (including a tour with the latter in England, June 1993).

[66]Frank Zappa, 'The Torture Never Stops', *Zoot Allures*, 1976.

[67]Ross Russell, *Bird Lives!*, 1972, p. 305.

'Find Her Finer' is a song of advice to the would-be male suitor. Zappa's elision of love object and audience makes this perhaps a bitter commentary on the poor commercial performance of *One Size Fits All* and its cosmic pretentions.

> Don't never let her know you are smart
> The universe is nowhere to start[68]

This sounds like a description of *Zoot Allures* itself, whose mainstream character can be surmised from the pared down song titles – 'Disco Boy' and 'Ms Pinky' (rather than the extravagance of 'Florentine Pogen' or 'Evelyn, a Modified Dog').

> Maybe you think this is crude
> And maybe you might think I am rude
> And maybe this approach I have spewed
> Is not the one for you
> But believe me, later on you'll find
> As you impress her with your mind
> You will just be left behind
> For a wiser fool[69]

'The Torture Never Stops' is in many ways a direct appeal to the glands. The line 'impress her with your mind' is a vivid absurdity, since the mind, a non-physical entity, cannot make a physical impression. 'Spew' is also a good image for 'The Torture Never Stops', which is offensive and reeks of inner fluids. Captain Beefheart – credited as 'Donnie Vliet' – completes this seductive slice of R&B with a bed of breathy mouth harp in the style used on *Bongo Fury*'s 'Cucamonga'.

'Find Her Finer' has a series of puns on mummies/wrapping/rapping/unwrapping.

> Find her finer, sneak up behind her
> Rap like a mummy till you finally unwind her
> Find her blinder, see who designed her
> Act like a dummy till you finally grind her[70]

'Ground mummy' was used as a spice in the nineteenth century (the bandages were impregnated in ancient Egypt and still kept their flavour). Unwinding a mummy means undressing it, making

[68]Frank Zappa, 'Find Her Finer', *Zoot Allures*, 1976.
[69]Ibid.
[70]Ibid.

it revolve: decoding the spiral, or playing a record. At the centre may be the invisible man, of course. This kind of concentrated poetry – evident in more abstract songs like 'Mr Green Genes' or 'Inca Roads' – tends to be overlooked in songs where the overt meaning is so blatant.

Roy Estrada, reunited with Zappa for the 1976 tour, plays bass on 'Black Napkins' and sings background vocals on other songs. His doowop expertise creates extraordinary connections. His falsetto over the teutonic militarism of 'Ms Pinky' sounds like an automated version of the girl's screams on 'The Torture Never Stops'; on 'Find Her Finer' his 'high weaslings' are virtuosic. *Zoot Allures* connects Roy Estrada's expert doowop falsetto with the extreme horror of concentration camps. It's a brilliant linkage, because doowop – as an expression of black and latino resistance to American mainstream culture – is also a cry of pain.

Zoot Allures, with its meditation on the libidinal aspect of concentration camps and its opening thrash about dead-end jobs, was a commentary on punks and their swastikas and dole-queue rock. It was also a commentary on disco. Giorgio Moroder had introduced deepthroat orgasm squeals over machine rhythms[71] and both 'Ms Pinky' and 'Disco Boy' parody robot beats. To turn Donna Summer's moans of ecstasy into screams of torture is a masterstroke. Each side ends with a song about masturbation: side one with 'Ms Pinky' and side two with 'Disco Boy'. Disco glamour is a front on loneliness and sexual frustration.

> They're closin' the bar,
> 'N she's leavin' with your friend!
> ... Disco boy, no one understands,
> But thank THE LORD
> That you still got hands
> To help you do the jerkin' that'll
> Blot out yer Disco Sorrow!
> It's Disco Love tonight
> Make sure you look all right[72]

Disco is the intrusion of the homogenized space of commodity exchange – the shopping centre – into the place of music. Just as Socrates denies death and sex, so the world of exchange cannot admit death or actual bodily sex or even defecation:

[71]Donna Summer, 'Love to Love You Baby', *Love to Love You Baby*, 1975, GTO Records GTLP008.
[72]Frank Zappa, 'Disco Boy', *Zoot Allures*, 1976; transcription from *Baby Snakes*, CD booklet, 1988.

'You never go doody!'
(That's what you think)[73]

The ideology of social democracy, that of responsible adults 'choosing' their governments, masks the real structures of power that shape our lives. By demonstrating our libidinal investment in images that revolt us, *Zoot Allures* is a desecration of the supposed consistency of the subject in bourgeois democracy, the integrity of the citizen who votes once every five years whilst ignoring third world wars, the concentration camps and butchery which prop up first world opulence.

> That voice was a lamentation. Calmer now. It's in the silence you feel you hear. Vibrations. Now silent air. Bloom ungyved his crisscrossed hands and with slack fingers plucked the slender catgut thong. He drew and plucked. It buzzed, it twanged . . . Thou lost one. All songs on that theme. Yet more Bloom stretched his string. Cruel it seems. Let people get fond of each other: lure them on. Then tear asunder. Death. Explos. Knock on the head. Outtohelloutofthat. Human life. Dignam.[74]

Bloom's thoughts as he wanders the streets of Dublin, a resumé of the cluster of symptoms played upon by *Zoot Allures*. Bloom is musing on Paddy Dignam's death, whose funeral he has just attended, and buzzing a cat-gut thong round a package in his pocket (it would be a rubber band if *Ulysses* had been set later than 1907). 'Ungyved' suggests Hamlet's dishevelment as reported by Ophelia: the account of string-plucking is charged with the same eroticism as in the discussion of the lyre in *Phaedo*. Bloom is thinking about the power of music to evoke, but how what it evokes is loss. The man is playing us an interior-monologue blues to a cat-gut guitar. Bloom plays on the cat-gut until it snaps, which is like the orgasm/death conclusion to 'The Torture Never Stops'.

Joyce is not quoted here to argue that Zappa is using *Ulysses* (though James Joyce is included in the list of names on *Freak Out!*), so much as to illustrate the accuracy of Zappa's imagery. In a society based on exchange, music speaks of the verities of mortality and desire. Joyce used a Jewish perspective to voice the exile of the self-enforced by commodity capitalism, just as Zappa uses the black perspective of the blues. Mortality, allure, twangs and cruelty: the Siren song as the voice of material truth.

---

[73]Ibid.
[74]James Joyce, *Ulysses*, 1922, p. 358.

CLOSE-UPS AND THE UNCONSCIOUS

Walter Benjamin has pointed out that the close-up in film is a means of revealing the unconscious: 'A touch of the finger is now sufficient to fix an event for an unlimited period of time. The camera gave the moment a posthumous shock, as it were.'[75] This is because the close-up reveals things to the viewer that were visible before *but not noticed*. An example of this is the attention paid to the wall below the radiator in David Lynch's *Eraserhead*. Close-miking achieves the same effect,[76] and *Zoot Allures* focuses attention on the plucking of strings with a new intensity. 'Friendly Little Finger' both as a title and via xenochrony focuses attention on the act of playing. 'Zoot Allures' begins with a glitteringly evocative feedback/whammy bar solo over chord progressions of unprecedented pungency. It compresses the whole atmosphere of 'The Torture Never Stops' into sound alone. Terry Bozzio is an extraordinary drummer, refining Elvin Jones's polyrhythms into an array of textures rather than metrical choices (in this he resembles jazz drummer Ronnie Burrage). The tune is strained and scraping, with little runs of notes that rise up like blood into a flushing face. Near the fade Zappa comes in with a stinging electric guitar solo that harks back to the clarity of T-Bone Walker. The contrast between this personal intensity and the adolescent glam-rock guitar that bursts in with 'Disco Boy' is quite absurd.

Zoot Allures also focuses on Zappa's voice in a manner still more intimate than the facetious adman voice of *Overnite Sensation* and *Apostrophe (')*, a close-miking that puts every tongue movement and saliva pop on record. Whereas *Uncle Meat* sounds like the chattering teeth of the flibbertigibbit, *Zoot Allures* ushered in a new preparedness to deploy the power of romanticism. This

---

[75]Walter Benjamin, *Charles Baudelaire: A Lyric Poet in the Era of High Capitalism*, 1938, p. 132.
[76]Here I part company with the otherwise admirable thesis of Linda Williams, *Hard Core*, 1990, who says, 'There is no such thing as a close-up of sound' (p. 124). True, sound recording cannot document male pleasure with the authority of the 'money shot' (though Zappa and the 1984 band claimed that '*spoo* is the little sound the white stuff makes when it comes out', Michael Brenna, 'The Spoo Show', *Society Pages*, No. 22, p. 21), but anyone who has responded to the electric guitar or heard free improvisers use contact-mikes must be aware of the special eroticism of close-miking. Sound may not be easily framed; it 'envelops' (p. 125) the spectator: but once the object under consideration – finger on guitar, lips in front of the microphone – is chosen, closer miking *can* reveal sounds that were previously repressed, directly comparable to 'close-up' photography. This may be because, unlike the collusive games of hard-core pornography, Benjamin and Zappa are not so much concerned with the 'revelation' of sights and sounds conventionally kept veiled, as in drawing attention to what is already there, but only unconsciously perceived.

close-miking of the mouth relates to a new romanticism in Zappa's music, of which the instrumentals in *Zoot Allures* were the first fruits. The physicality of the music blossomed into guitar exploits that are unprecedented in the history of the relationship of the body to electric music. In projecting minute digital manipulations into the public domain the electric guitar has a unique place in the interface between the private and public: *Zoot Allures* signalled a new level in the intensity of that dialectic.

CHAPTER 7
LÄTHER

Every article lathering leaving several rinsengs so as each rinse results
with a dapperent rolle, cuffs for meek and chokers for sheek and a
kink in the pacts for namby.
James Joyce[1]

A BUNCH OF LEGAL CRUD

At the end of 1977 Frank Zappa delivered four albums to Warner
Brothers: *Zappa Live in New York, Hot Rats III, Studio Tan* and
Zappa Orchestral Favorites. According to Zappa they refused to
pay the $240,000 due in the contract. He then re-edited the music
into the *Läther* four-record box set, the most ambitious of his
frequent not-to-be projects and the most highly rated of his countless 'bootlegs'.[2] He offered it to EMI and Mercury-Phonogram,
with the latter reaching the test-pressing stage. Zappa accuses
Warner Brothers of pulling strings to stop the deal. Incensed at this
corporate censorship, he broadcast all eight sides from Burbank-
Pasadena KROQ radio station, inviting listeners to tape the music
off the air. He sounded a little drunk, another unique feature
of this extraordinary broadcast. Although unwilling to bore the
listeners with a 'a bunch of legal crud', he explained the basic
situation, outlining a scenario in which he would not be able to
release any music for the next five years.

> FZ: (Semi-inaudible) I always did like songs that ended in 'ooh-la-la-la'.
> DJ: Wait a minute. In keeping with our situation here, use this one.
> FZ: All right. Ladies and gentlemen, this is Frank Zappa. I finally

---

[1]James Joyce, *Finnegans Wake*, 1946, p. 614, 4–7.
[2]Readers poll, *T'Mershi Duween*, No. 7, June 1989, p. 14.

managed to find this radio station lurking out in the fringes of Pasadena, yes this is quite an experience here, sitting trying to open a bottle of beer – it's one of those imported kind with tin-foil that's covering the top – and the guy here is asking me how I liked that record and since the microphone wasn't on you probably missed the fact that I'm deeply impressed with any song that fades out with the words 'ooh-la-la-la' and I'm sure you are too, otherwise you wouldn't be listening to this radio station. And so . . .

DJ: Have you faded out a couple of songs with 'ooh-la-la-la'?

FZ: Everything has to fade out with 'ooh-la-la-la'. If you're going to fade out, you have to fade out with those words, because those are the magic words. There are three or four really important words that happen in rock 'n' roll and other types of music that normal people like to listen to. 'Ooh-la-la-la', considered as one hyphenated word, would be one of the important words and the other thing that you definitely gotta watch out for are the three other important magic words that make radio stations go off the air, but we won't discuss them right now. Those are the most powerful words [*Strikes DJ's bell*] in America today, that's why we have such a wonderful place to live in. Now I'm here to play an album for you and I'm rapping a little – rapping is one of the words you say when you go on rock 'n' roll radio stations – I am rapping a little bit at this point to prepare each and every one of you for the grand and glorious experience of getting your little cassette machines out because I would like to have you tape record this album off the air because this album is not going to be available in the stores because Warner Brothers is trying to ruin my darn career. But we're going to play . . .

DJ: Boo!

FZ: Yeah, boo, hiss. Now I want you to . . . are you ready? Put your finger on the little red button, you have to push the red button and the one that says play at the same time and here comes the *Läther* album . . .

What followed was three and a half hours of music that ran the gamut of Zappa's art from *musique concrète* to orchestral composition, arena rock to chamber jazz, guitar extrapolations to cartoon soundtracks. Abandoning the sequencing of the original albums, which divided the music by genre, *Läther* revealed the hidden continuity of Zappa's ideas.

THE TRACKS

The full track-listing of *Läther* (and their subsequent appearance) was as follows. Changed song titles are indicated after album names.

312

1
Regyptian Strut – *Sleep Dirt*
Naval Aviation in Art – *Orchestral Favorites*
Little Green Rosetta – *Joe's Garage Acts II & III*
Duck Duck Goose – *Shut Up 'N Play Yer Guitar* 'Ship Ahoy'
Down in the Dew – Unreleased
For the Young Sophisticate – *Tinsel Town Rebellion*
2
Tryin' to Grow a Chin – *Sheik Yerbouti*
Broken Hearts are for Assholes – *Sheik Yerbouti*
The Legend of the Illinois Enema Bandit – *Zappa in New York*
3
Let Me Take You to the Beach – *Studio Tan*
Revised Music for Guitar and Low Budget Orchestra – *Studio Tan*
Redunzl – *Studio Tan*
4
Honey, Don't You Want a Man Like Me? – *Zappa in New York*
We've Got to Get into Something Real – *Sheik Yerbouti*
Black Page 2 – *Zappa in New York*
Big Leg Emma – *Zappa in New York*
Punky's Whips – *Zappa in New York*
5
Flambay – *Sleep Dirt*
The Purple Lagoon – *Zappa in New York*
6
Pedro's Dowry – *Orchestral Favorites*
Läther – *Zappa in New York* 'I Promise Not to Come in Your Mouth'
Spider of Destiny – *Sleep Dirt*
Duke of Orchestral Prunes – *Orchestral Favorites*
7
Filthy Habits – *Sleep Dirt*
What Ever Happened to All the Fun in the World – *Sheik Yerbouti*
Titties & Beer – *Zappa in New York*
The Ocean is the Ultimate Solution – *Sleep Dirt*
8
The Adventures Of Greggery Peccary – *Studio Tan*

The versions on *Sheik Yerbouti* and *Tinsel Town Rebellion* are different performances. By the time 'Little Green Rosetta' reached *Joe's Garage* it had become something altogether different. 'Flambay' was without the vocals dubbed on to the CD release of *Sleep Dirt*.

LÄTHER AND SAILORS

During a 1975 radio interview, Zappa found a recent record by Elliott Carter in the station library and insisted on playing it. He claims that *Double Concerto for Harpsichord and Piano*[3] got such a good response from the phone-lines that he played it twice, as well as the *Duo for Violin and Piano* on the other side. Researched to amplify the timbral qualities of the two instruments, Carter's *Double Concerto* seems to have influenced the flavour of the pieces of *musique concrète* that intersperse the tracks of *Läther* in the manner of *We're Only in It for the Money*. Elliott Carter has the usual reputation for formidable intellectualism thrust upon pre-minimal academic composers, but Zappa's use of his material shows a different side (in fact, Carter used to listen to jazz with his friend Conlon Nancarrow, and one can discern a rhythmic spark and soloist velocity in his *Oboe Concerto*[4] that is distinctly unclassical). Whereas the *musique concrète* of *Money* emphasized a vulgar physicality and blatancy in the urgency of its electric effects (a feature which can be found in John Cage's *Fontana Mix* and in Conrad Boehmer), the *Läther* segments use Carter's sense of spatial vastness: Zappa brings out the slithering delirium of Carter's music, the anxious beauties in its silvery sparkle. Set against Zappa's snatches of conversation, which centre on teen confusions over sexual identity, the serial harpsichord progressions and rattling percussion become psycho-drama of the most immediate kind.[5]

Läther begins with a choking sound of the kind rarely heard outside sex or weeping (or some such dishevelled state). Then a young male voice says:

> M1: Father, I'm glad you're here, I want you to hear this, I have a confession to make.
> M2: Well, spit it out, son.
> M1: L-l-l-leather!
> M2: Well, don't be ashamed.[6]

This exchange also served as an introductory PA tape on the 1979 tour. The idea of lather concentrates many ideas simultaneously.

[3]Elliott Carter, *Double Concerto for Harpsichord and Piano with Two Chamber Orchestras/Duo for Violin and Piano*, 1975, Nonesuch H71314.
[4]Elliott Carter, *Boulez Conducts Carter*, Erato, 1989, 2292–45364.
[5]Two of these links were used on side two of *Sheik Yerbouti*, 1979: 'What Ever Happened to All the Fun in the World' and 'We've Got to Get into Something Real'.
[6]Frank Zappa, link preceding 'Regyptian Strut', *Läther*, 1977.

One is of soapsuds in the washing machine, like the question on *Lumpy Gravy*: 'How do you get your water so dark?'. 'Washing linen in public' is a phrase that describes the public/private interface Zappa rejoices in, a metaphor also used in the Anna Livia Plurabelle section of *Finnegans Wake*: 'Panty Rap'[7] is an extrusion of that idea. Another aspect of lather is the onset of puberty: when the male adolescent starts to shave. Zappa's father

> used to work in his Dad's barbershop on the Maryland waterfront. For a penny a day (or a penny a week – I can't remember), he would stand on a box and lather the sailors' faces so his dad could shave them. *Nice job.*[8]

Sailors have always been used to portray comicbook notions of sexual frustration, as well male homosexuality. In 1968 Zappa played Ewan McColl singing 'The Handsome Cabin Boy' on the radio, chuckling over its ambiguities. It tells the tale of a beautiful woman who escapes to sea disguised as a cabin boy – evidently an excuse for homo-eroticism. 'Broken Hearts are for Assholes' mentions sailors.

> But you kissed the little sailor
> Who had just blew in from Spain
> *A few of these lovely little sailors to roll the stage back*
> And pull the chain attached to the
> Permanently erected nipples of Jimmy, *Nice*
> In a bold salute to pain[9]

The all-male situation of touring rock musicians in a way resembles that of sailors, and *Läther* continually speculates about homosexual activity. 'Assholes' is preceded by the following exchange:

> M1: What you say we go down the street for a few minutes?
> M2: No go on that . . . I er . . .
> M3: I don't like fag bars.
> M2: No.
> M1: Well . . . try 'em![10]

And, like rock musicians, sailors disseminate world culture, a point made by Zappa when discussing folk music with Paddy Moloney

---

[7]Frank Zappa, 'Panty Rap', *Tinsel Town Rebellion*, 1981.
[8]Frank Zappa, with Peter Occhiogrosso, *The Real Frank Zappa Book*, 1989, pp. 15–16.
[9]Frank Zappa, 'Broken Hearts are for Assholes', *Läther*, 1977.
[10]Frank Zappa, link preceding 'Broken Hearts are for Assholes', *Läther*, 1977.

of the Chieftains and Brian Hayes, interviewer of Radio 4's *Midweek*.[11]

> PM: I know one particular tune from India where the first eight bars are almost identical to an old style song from the west of Ireland. You can come across various little pieces and you hear it, and you think, 'My God, that's a jig, I know that' – a couple of little bars and you can match them. We have put together things like that.
>
> BH: How can you explain that, tunes cropping up on opposite sides of the world, where there couldn't have been any cultural exchange?
>
> FZ: [*Whispers*] Sailors! [*Much laughter*][12]

'The Legend of the Illinois Enema Bandit' celebrates anal sadism towards women, while 'Punky's Whips' examines the latent homo-eroticism exploited by publicity shots of heavy-metal bands. 'Assholes' switches from documentation of male gay S&M culture to heterosexual anality.

> Don't fool yerself, girl
> It's goin' right up yer poop chute[13]

As in *Story of O*, where Sir Stephen 'invariably used O as if she were a boy',[14] Zappa's interest in sadism drifts towards anality and sodomy. Zappa progressed from the heterosexual perversion of 'Penguin in Bondage' to male sadomasochism and leather sex in *Sheik Yerbouti, Joe's Garage* and *Thing-Fish*. Although his explicit position is 'not anti-gay',[15] Zappa's musical treatment of gays remains ambivalent, more concerned with the presentation of sociological material than expressions of a political solidarity. The development of his interests parallels something noticed by Linda Williams in hardcore film pornography: the role of sadomasochism in unlinking sexual activity from gender.

> This male-to-male fellatio is quite exceptional in feature-length hetero-sexual pornography. In fact, it is the only film of this period that I have seen that breaks the taboo against males touching males. Why does it occur here? Possibly the greater bisexuality and role-playing involved in sado-masochistic scenarios permits the admission of such a scene.[16]

---

[11]A relationship that flowered in a *soirée* at Zappa's house that included the Chieftains, Tuvan throat-singers, L. Shankar and Johnny 'Guitar' Watson – shown on Nigel Leigh's documentary for the *Late Show*, BBC2, 11 March 1993.
[12]Radio 4, 3 July 1991, transcription in *T'Mershi Duween*, No. 20, July 1991, p. 17.
[13]Frank Zappa, 'Broken Hearts are for Assholes', *Läther*, 1977.
[14]Pauline Réage, *Story of O*, 1954, p. 133.
[15]David Sheff, 'Frank Zappa Interview', *Playboy*, February 1993, p. 59; his sons Dweezil and Ahmet aren't homophobic either, because I asked them in an interview at Music for Nations, 30 September 1992, written up in *T'Mershi Duween*, No. 29, February 1993, pp. 20–23.
[16]Linda Williams, *Hard Core*, 1990, p. 220.

Male homosexual anal eroticism also combines with the scatological symbolism that runs beneath all Zappa's work. The sexual quandaries of the male adolescent – the primary target of rock marketing in the States – are used to unpick the certainties of sexual identity. In the collage interludes, the voices of Terry Bozzio, Patrick O'Hearn and engineer Davey Moire are placed next to effects derived from Elliott Carter, who dissolves the time-space certainties of classical music with purely formal procedures. Zappa fuses rock and classical music by making each fall apart.

The opening words could be those of a sinner to his priest. When the Church forces the individual to confess, it drags out personal secrets that social convention keeps hidden. By so doing it exerts powerful social control. Like William Burroughs, Zappa seeks to create an art that, by making public the private impulses exploited by morality and religion, will encourage resistance to that control. This private/public dialectic is articulated by shocking changes of register, as intimate conversations cut suddenly into rock arena hysteria or feedback-drenched guitar solos. Another meaning of lather is frenzy, as in 'to get into a lather' (describing the foamy saliva horses expel when they are excited). By spelling the title using the German convention of two dots to replace an 'e', it is pronounced 'leather', a fetish associated with S&M. The continuity behind the albums that Warner Brothers finally released in their original, genre-specific form (which Zappa followed in his CD release) – *Zappa in New York*, *Studio Tan*, *Orchestral Favorites* and *Sleep Dirt* – was revealed in *Läther* as the frenzy of forbidden practices, and the grotesque shock of revealing private matters on the public stage.

Dubious splendour

The opening confession segues into 'Regyptian Strut', a piece called 'Variant Processional March' when performed on the Grand Wazoo tour. Bruce Fowler's overdubbed brass fanfares and Ruth Underwood's martial tuned percussion recall Emperor Cletus in all his creaky splendour. It is an apt title, combining the idea of ancient Egypt with that of repetition and inauthenticity. Its fraudulent pomp introduces us to the hopes and dreams of adolescence.

It leads into 'Naval Aviation in Art?', which again has a sailor connection. When it was played by the Ensemble InterContemporain, Zappa added a sleeve-note, saying the music 'shows a sailor-artist, standing before his easel, squinting through a porthole for inspiration, while wiser men sleep in hammocks all around him'.[17]

This notion of evaporation of stability in naval-gazing is a good analogue to the way the the music of *Läther* has no secure stylistic base. As it finishes, a voice says, 'God that was really beautiful', just like Eric Clapton responding to 'Nasal Retentive Calliope Music' on *Money*, and we are plunged into 'Little Green Rosetta', evidently an out-take from the preamble to *Bongo Fury*'s 'Muffin Man'. It denigrates culture as the icing on the cake:[18] the careful accomplishments of art satirized as tacky ornament pooted forth on mass-produced commodities.

'Duck Duck Goose', subsequently released as 'Ship Ahoy',[19] is quite extraordinary. It sounds like overdubbed synthesizers, but is actually the coda to 'Zoot Allures' recorded at the same concert as 'Black Napkins' on the *Zoot Allures* album:[20] real-time guitar playing. It reveals a hair-trigger tension which is positively erogenous. Spoken words interrupt (a technique adopted in *Shut Up 'N Play Yer Guitar*), indicating a changed direction. 'Down in the Dew' (not yet officially released) starts with a pile-driver riff and screaming guitar, then abruptly cuts to laughter and falsetto operatics like something on *Weasels*.

> Won't ya take it down to C sharp, Ronnie?
> Whatcha gonna do when the well runs dry?[21]

The last phrase echoes Wynona Carr's hit 'Never Miss Your Water Till the Well Runs Dry',[22] a question Zappa answers with an extravagant piece of *musique concrète* and a bubbling guitar solo that ends in a classic Zappa melody.

'For the Young Sophisticate' is about paranoia over physical attributes. In an attempt at sympathy, the narrator assures the girl that the story she read in a magazine of a 'young sophisticator', who rejects a feminist 'agitator' for not shaving under her arms, is no cause for tears.

---

[17]Frank Zappa, *The Perfect Stranger*, 1984, Angel/EMI DS38170.
[18]'Flakes' takes a dim view of icing too: 'I am a moron and this is my wife / she's frosting a cake with a paper knife', *Sheik Yerbouti*, 1979.
[19]Frank Zappa, *Shut Up 'N Play Yer Guitar*, 1981.
[20]Frank Zappa, Osaka, 3 February 1976; 'Black Napkins', *Zoot Allures*, 1976.
[21]Frank Zappa, 'Down in the Dew', *Läther*, 1977.
[22]Wynona Carr, *Hit that Jive, Jack!*, 1985, Ace CH130.

> Forget that book I told her then
> Don't wanna hear about the book again[23]

This sounds as if Zappa is changing his mind about wanting the positions portrayed in the porn magazine in her father's bureau ('I don't believe you've never seen his book before'[24]). When asked if he would still love her if her hair grew 'all down the side of her kimono', he says yes – if it did not cause her to trip, 'or radiate a bad aroma'. 'Sick' is the final conclusion, the same comment that was passed on Fido's attempts to bring the slippers on 'Stink-Foot'. Hair growing down a 'kimono' is as absurd as clipping the poodle's 'managua'[25] – though in this context it has the intimidating ring of medical-textbook terminology. Anxiety about hair growth is a symbol for the confrontation of the natural body with social norms.

Zappa, though, refuses to recommend any particular course. Where the radio plays 'groups that are relevant to your lifestyle. Things that reinforce your ideas of self-worth and propulsion towards the future',[26] Zappa does not.

> FZ: If you're into heavy metal, you go for that kind of audio wallpaper and all it does is reinforce your idea of who you think you are.
> JOHN STIX: Rather than creating a mood, your music seems to demand that people listen and react.
> FZ: It's participatory. The music should interact with the person that's listening to it. What I do isn't designed to reinforce your lifestyle. It's coming from a different place; it's not product. Ultimately everything that gets released by a record company turns into product, but the intent of what I do is not product-oriented.[27]

Zappa is claiming that his is a critical, anti-ideological art, the very thing Adorno said was impossible to achieve in the mass market (and which postmodernism claims cannot be achieved anywhere at all). It is the contention of the negative dialectics of poodle play that Zappa is right on this point. It is not that his politics is always progressive or that his every opinion is full of uncontradictory wisdom, but that the records create problems with passive consumption. For a start, they refuse use as background music – a

[23]Frank Zappa, 'For the Young Sophisticate', *Tinsel Town Rebellion*, 1981.
[24]Frank Zappa, 'Dirty Love', *Overnite Sensation*, 1973.
[25]'Poodle Genesis', Osaka, 3 February 1976. Managua is actually the capital of Nicaragua, where the addressee of 'Yo Mama' is told to go.
[26]Frank Zappa, quoted by J. C. Costa, 'A Mother in the Studio', *Recording World*, 1976.
[27]John Stix, 'On the Record: Frank Zappa', *Guitar World*, September 1980, pp. 8–10.

commonplace criticism of Zappa's music that points to its critical status.

Although talking about 'Zappa' is convenient shorthand for the singer's position, it is important to grasp that these are *not* the same: the words of 'For the Young Sophisticate' should not be taken literally. Calling the situation 'sick' is not gauging things against an idea of natural health: it is more like Ghoulardi's catchphrase 'Stay sick!' that the Cramps used for an album title in 1990.[28]

The lather motif continues with 'Tryin' to Grow a Chin', a more organically 'rock' version than the layered synth-parodics it received on its legitimate release.[29] It is based on the circular folkrhyme 'Michael Finnegan', which gave *Finnegans Wake* its title and circular structure.

> There was an old man called Michael Finnegan
> He grew whiskers on his chin-a-gen
> The wind came up and blew them in again
> Poor old Michael Finnegan (begin again)[30]

Like America being unable to grow a beard ('200 Years'), 'Tryin' to Grow a Chin' is a song of immaturity. As Thing-Fish tells Harry and Rhonda: 'Y'all's takin' too goddam long to GROW UP IN ERMERICA!'[31] Featuring the 'archetypal' punk riff that Lowell George used on the Factory's 'Lightnin' Rod Man' in 1965, this was a showcase for Bozzio, whose explosive abilities became an important part of the stage act. The repetitions of the original rhyme hang over the tune as a criticism of youth-culture autism, a motif made more explicit in 'Teen-age Wind'.[32] Like *Money* predicting the Kent State University murders, the projection of the psychopathology of punk is chilling. Delivered to Warners at the end of 1977, Zappa carefully marked the date on a copyright declaration when the song appeared on *Sheik Yerbouti* in 1979. The deaths of Nancy Spungen and Sid Vicious in September 1978 made the words seem almost trite.

> I'm lonely 'n' green;
> Too small for my shirt

---

[28]The Cramps, *Stay Sick*, 1990, Enigma ENV1001.
[29]*Sheik Yerbouti*, 1979.
[30]From memory – Miss Sladdin's class in 3a.
[31]Frank Zappa, 'The Massive Improve' lence', *Thing-Fish*, 1984.
[32]Frank Zappa, 'Teen-age Wind', *You Are What You Is*, 1981.

If Simmons was here
I could feature my hurt . . .

I wanna be dead
In bed
Please kill me
'Cause that would thrill me
I wanna be dead
In bed
Please kill me
'Cause that would thrill me[33]

'Featuring one's hurt' is a phrase Zappa was using in interviews to castigate individualistic expression. 'Tryin' to Grow a Chin' showed where confusion between real life and artistic poses could lead.

ENEMA BANDITRY AND MALE CHAUVINISM

The psychoanalytic underpinning of 'The Legend of the Illinois Bandit' is dramatized on *Läther* by appearing directly after 'Broken Hearts are for Assholes', with its closing anal penetration and the phrase 'I knew you'd be surprised'. As someone who bought *Zappa in New York* in Cambridge at a time when the rapist was at large – he wore a ski-mask with 'Cambridge Rapist' emblazoned on it – this celebration of assault was particularly upsetting and difficult to justify (not helped by Malcolm McLaren's Cambridge Rapist T-shirts, showing that male chauvinism crosses all stylistic barriers in rock). *Down Beat* called it raising 'the doody joke to Wagnerian proportions'.[34] Jazz saxophonist Henry Threadgill managed to salute the bandit[35] without recourse to sexism at all. He explained his interest to Nat Hentoff.

A man was captured in Ohio around 1979. He started out in St Louis and worked his way up to Detroit and then moved across the midwest. He would tie people up. But he wouldn't rob them or hurt them. He would give them enemas. It wrecked the rooms in which it happened, but that's all he did. Richard Nixon was on his list, by the way, but he got caught before he got to Nixon. Why did he do it? He said he did it because people were full of shit. They didn't make him serve much time in prison. He had to do community work, and he had to see a

[33]Frank Zappa, 'Tryin' to Grow a Chin', *Sheik Yerbouti*, 1979.
[34]Chip Stern, '*Zappa in New York*', *Down Beat*, 1977.
[35]New Air featuring Cassandra Wilson, 'Salute to the Enema Bandit', *Air Show No. 1*, 1986, Black Saint BSR0099.

psychiatrist. Why did I write a piece about him? I thought he had something important to say. He was making a statement at that time, in the 1970s. When America was going backwards after the increase in freedom and honesty in the 1960s.[36]

Zappa turns the story into vengeance on 'college-educated women' and bourgeois anal retention in general. He does point out in the notes that the court scene where the women shout 'let the fiend go free' is a parody of blues mythology and that he himself wrote the final 'philosophical conclusion', where the bandit defends himself by saying, 'It must be just what they all needs.' This shows a scrupulous distinction between fact and his own embellishments.

There is already an undercurrent to *Freak Out!* which implies that the whole process 'which can't happen here' is sexual in nature. The strong heterosexual orientation in Zappa (something *Läther* starts to break down) makes the sexual person-to-be-'liberated' inevitably female. The distance between 'liberation' and 'harassment' was something that the 60s were not very clear about. If it is only men making the distinction the two become impossible to separate. Certainly the GTO's do not sound like victims, and *Permanent Damage* and Pamela Des Barres's *I'm with the Band* are important documents to consult when considering the argument that 60s counter-culture was an absolute disaster for women. Zappa correctly senses an obsequious hypocrisy in men posing as non-sexist, though his refusal to countenance any discussion has a reactionary aspect. His stock response 'I satirize stupid women, but I satirize stupid men too' is repeated by sidemen like drummer Chad Wackerman[37] and is really no answer at all. Zappa has no qualms about indulging the full-blown sexism encouraged by being part of a group of male rock musicians on tour, and such incomprehension of the woman's point of view is amply demonstrated by 'The Legend of the Illinois Enema Bandit'. If Zappa was likely to be raped himself, it would not be a song he would sing. On the other hand, when he claims that he is only making social documentary, the accuracy of his observations and the fact that he presents an absent moral centre come to his defence.

Some people note Zappa's lack of sympathy for the woman's point of view, condemn such sexism and refuse to listen to his music. Obviously, we are not going to do that – or you and I

---

[36]Henry Threadgill, quoted by Nat Hentoff, sleeve note, New Air, *Air Show No. 1*, 1986, Black Saint BSR0099.
[37]*T'Mershi Duween*, No. 25, June 1992, p. 15.

would not be so far into this book. It is precisely because Zappa refuses to 'put himself into other people's shoes', to bow to some predigested liberal consensus, that his art is so strong and raw and original. It also depends on how you view rape and its place in the oppression of women.

Some feminists call rape an 'assertion of male power', the act that keeps women in their place and legitimizes patriarchy, militarism and war. Such projection of rape to a global explanation is emotive but mythological. Rape is more akin to theft, murder and suicide: the self-destructive actions of the oppressed and exploitated on members of their own class. Interviews with rapists[38] reveal ignorance about sex rather than rational pursuit of 'male power'. Evidently, rape is used in war to subdue civilian populations, but this is part of the suppression of whole communities in the interest of ruling classes that control armed bodies of men, not 'sex war'. No doubt gangsters and pimps use rape to terrify and humiliate their prostitutes, but to generalize from this to male human nature works like Christian doctrines of original sin, with just such pessimistic and reactionary conclusions.

Although feminist ideas are currently weak in terms of active politics, they are strong in cultural criticism and censorship legislation, where they flow straight into the binary moralism of bourgeois ideology. This alliance reached an institutional expression in the 1986 Attorney General's Commission on Pornography, in which Andrea Dworkin begged the forces of the State to 'cut that woman down and untie her hands and take the gag out of her mouth and to do something for freedom'.[39] Commissioner Park Elliott Dietz wept in sympathy, and resolved to legislate against such images. The confusion between actuality and representation was complete: a right-wing government pursuing welfare cuts and anti-abortion legislation that actually harm millions of women's lives is suddenly in the vanguard of the fight for female liberation.

In this post-feminist morality, cultural products are lined up as good (female, sensitive, educated) versus bad (male, rude, low-class), ignoring the dynamics of the situation they operate in, and ignoring whether they are true to a material sexual substructure, or merely represent the consolation of pious wishes. In choosing to celebrate the Illinois Enema Bandit Zappa may offend liberal values, but he is also positing an absurdity, splattering shit over

[38]For example, *Why Men Rape*, ed. Sylvia Levine and Joseph Koenig, 1980.
[39]Quoted by Linda Williams, *Hard Core*, 1990, p. 21.

the audience as 'entertainment' (as the Mammy Nuns piss on Rhonda's fox-fur in *Thing-Fish*). At the end of the piece you can hear him say 'sit right down and make yourselves comfortable'. This, like the 'they're just not going to stand for it' before 'Titties & Beer' puts the tunes in an antagonistic relation to the audience.

Zappa's position may not translate well into politics, but it's a necessary for the pursuit of an art that can stir up forces worth playing with. *Thing-Fish* develops an absurd version of Southern nigger-speak that the NAACP condemned when used by Tim Moore on the *Amos & Andy* TV show. Their protests caused him to be fired. Zappa commented:

> It is in the tradition in America to reward artistry with contempt and ignorance with outrageous praise. Americans live in terror of excellence and will do ANYTHING to avoid contact with it . . . The entire Bible will be recited aloud by people who cannot read. Everyone will have a real estate license. They will all be Republicans.[40]

Zappa here gets close to the right-wing libertarian politics that made waves in California in the early 80s. He was actually invited by one libertarian delegate to run for president on that party's ticket; according to Meg Cox of the *Wall Street Journal*, Zappa's family were keen on the idea, but he decided their platform 'made no sense'.[41]

Cultural politics in America, where the progressive unity of the civil rights movement has decayed into squabbling 'minority rights' campaigns, is confused and in crisis. There is definitely something wrong when the left merely tail-ends the initiatives of different 'oppressed groups', as self-serving petit-bourgeois politicians build careers out of protest campaigns. Unlike socialist demands, which target objectives that cannot finally be achieved in the capitalist social order, such demands can be only too readily conceded to by conformist media programming. Initially progressive agitators end up operating protests hand-in-hand with right-wing fundamentalist censorship lobbies. Where it does not simply fail. The débâcle over the film *Basic Instinct* in 1992 is a perfect example. Vociferously condemned by gay groups, one expected to see a film of horrendous reaction: actually, lesbianism is used to *increase* the glamour and sexiness of the heroine. Turning

---

[40]Frank Zappa, *Them Or Us (The Book)*, p. 262.
[41]Meg Cox, 'Frank Zappa: Rocker and Businessman', *Wall Street Journal*, 10 February 1988.

upside-down the cliché of the blonde victim, making her into a psychotic killer, may not result in a film advertising equal rights for women, but it begs the question of why we go to films – to be morally uplifted or to realize our worst fears? There is a danger that any film that stretches the clichés to gain more impact will be the first to be proscribed. The Anti-Nazi League repeated such mistakes in England by picketing the Australian film *Romper Stomper* in 1993. In this sense the 'shock' of 'The Legend of the Illinois Enema Bandit' is to be defended.

Campaigns against media 'outrages' can carry the reactionary implication that the normal course of things is okay, that it is merely exceptional transgressions that are to blame for the state of the world. Radical art, in seeking to show the social processes involved in picturing the world, frequently challenges the limits of allowed representability: it will be the first to offend. The idea that the mass media is a riot of excitement that requires 'controlling' merely adds to its prestige. Mary Whitehouse and the pornographers are two sides of the same coin. Jeremy Prynne made an important point about 'snuff films' (the 'death-on-celluloid' movies that take the actuality of pornography to its most obvious extreme): obsession with such examples of modern urban folk devilry – whose very existence is questioned by informed sources[42] – seems hypocritical on the part of a legislature which is currently organizing its own snuff culture, which is the death penalty. Probably the nearest to actual 'snuff' are the films used to train interrogation personnel in various military dictatorships propped up by the USA.

Like the campaign against drugs, the campaign against pornography attacks a symptom: one delivering more electoral dividends (in a right-wing climate) than opposing, say, the Gulf War or welfare cuts. Despite Zappa's professed 'practical conservatism', which demands 'a less intrusive government and lower taxes',[43] and his hostility to the American public-school system, Zappa turns round the argument that rock corrupts the young into a criticism of the small amount of money the government spends on musical education.

> How can a child be blamed for consuming only that which is presented to him? Most kids have never come into contact with anything other than this highly merchandised stuff.

[42]Linda Williams, *Hard Core*, 1990, pp. 189–95.
[43]Frank Zappa, with Peter Occhiogrosso, *The Real Frank Zappa Book*, 1989, p. 315.

When I testified in front of the Senate, I pointed out that if they don't like the idea of young people buying certain kinds of music, why don't they stick a few dollars back into the school system to have music appreciation? There are kids today who have never heard a string quartet; they have never heard a symphony orchestra. I argued that the money for music appreciation courses, in terms of social good and other benefits such as improved behavior or uplifting the spirit, is far less than the cost of another set of uniforms for the football team. But I frankly don't see people waving banners in the streets saying more music appreciation classes . . . Once we're out of school, the time we can spend doing that type of research is limited because most of us are out looking for a job flipping hamburgers in the great tradition of the Reagan economic miracle. When all is said and done, that's the real source of America's barren and arid lives.[44]

Here Zappa's materialism leads him towards a left critique of Reaganomics, exposing the concern about 'porn rock' as a diversion. Bourgeois politics has an inevitable tendency to move from actual suffering and misery to *representation*. There is nothing the spectacle likes to do so much as talk about itself: a process which cannot possibly lead to any improvements, as – like commerce – the media operates as 'free' competition that obeys only one rule, which is to reach the greatest audience, a rule which obliterates any qualitative criticism. The campaign against *Basic Instinct* was an attempt to outflank that process, but ended in trying to enforce a cockeyed moralism that did not understand the art it criticized. Instead of seeking to prune and perfect the media, the most effective activities – strikes, riots, punk – give the lie to the entire edifice. Zappa's art works like the latter.

Excluded from the mainstream of American commercial culture for both his politics and his obscenities, Zappa is a pointer to the grey conformity and eventless boredom of the established media. His work acts like its unconscious: it shows its narrow limits by saying all the things they *don't* say. His political analysis may be flawed and naïve (he does not see the *connections*: between business and imperialism, the family and sexism, sexual repression and homophobia). On the other hand, it is precisely this refusal of abstract thought that makes his art so vivacious and pungent. Like William Burroughs – whose satirical vision is psychotically anti-women rather than merely rockist – Zappa has made it all up for himself. In art this is always a plus: in politics, less so.

[44]Frank Zappa, 'On Junk Food for the Soul', *New Perspectives Quarterly*, reprinted in *Society Pages*, No. 43, December 1988, p. 15.

The fact that Zappa's sexism alienates feminist listeners is both his loss and theirs, but it does not prevent his art acting as a flaw in the spectacle. Liberalism assumes that there is only one level on which to think, that to find Zappa's art important is to underwrite his every opinion; poodle play works otherwise. Zappa's very triviality degrades his 'point of view', which can only really be extrapolated from interviews and *The Real Frank Zappa Book*: the songs relentlessly construe a persona who is an absent centre. Offensive and annoying, Zappa's music is not what most sensitive, well-meaning people (including the author) would want to listen to. At the same time, it is radical precisely where the famous names who sit on the Amnesty and rain-forest panels are not, because it begs questions about the spectacle. The consciencemongers mouth liberal shibboleths, but in doing so they confirm the commercial structures that give superstars their privileged platform. Zappa thinks it stinks, and you can smell it in songs like 'The Legend of the Illinois Enema Bandit'.

Musically, the 'Illinois Enema Bandit' is bionic funk in the vein of Johnny 'Guitar' Watson's update on the blues, with Ray White's hard, gospel voice soaring into the stratosphere while Zappa's solo gutters with some of his most anal licks. Freud associated anal sadism with curiosity, and over the next decade Zappa's guitar frequently sounds as if it is excavating what Joyce – in a pun that links scatology to curiosity about origins and the mother – called 'amal matter'.[45] 'The Illinois Enema Bandit' perfectly frames the psychological processes involved in such blasphemies.

LÄTHER AND IRONY

Side three is a sequence that appears on *Studio Tan* (reordered on the CD release). Unusually for the *New Musical Express* of 1978, then in regular spats with Zappa over the relative value of punk, Ian Penman made some acute observations.

> The bouncy two minute disco-cert 'Let Me Take You to the Beach' is concerned with the state of stasis in American (and by implication British) culture: this is emphasized through the use of some 'neat' former vocabulary and textures (nostalgic parody of parodied nostalgia).[46]

---

[45]James Joyce, *Finnegans Wake*, 1946, p. 294n5.
[46]Ian Penman, 'Aunt Meat?', *New Musical Express*, 30 September 1978.

Some critics thought they heard Flo & Eddie on vocals, but Zappa had vowed never to work with them after the wheelchair episode: it is engineer Davey Moire's hysterical falsetto that graces this plastic Beach Boys 'perfect pop' masterpiece. Unaware that it was recorded between 1974 and 1976 (and probably throughout that timespan: it uses the Max Bennett/Paul Humphrey rhythm section from *Hot Rats*, Eddie Jobson on keyboards and Grand Funk Railroad's Don Brewer on bongos), Penman is thinking in terms of the discofied nonsense *Grease* made of the 50s in 1978. Of course the problem of nostalgia and repetition had been part of Zappa's project/object since at least *Ruben & the Jets*. Penman's comments do show how amenable Zappa's work is to anyone with a sense of irony. He's quite right: the airbrushed sleekness of 'Let Me Take You to the Beach' mocks contemporary pop by showing how close it is to pre-rock inanity. As usual with Zappa, the satire actually predates its target. Penman also noticed how glossy the succeeding 'abstract' music was ('Music for Low Budget Orchestra'), calling it Anthony Braxton produced by Robert Stigwood (*Grease*'s producer). Concerned to keep alive bebop's obstacle-course-for-improvisers integrity, Braxton's lines push at conventional rhythmic parameters and frequently resemble Zappa's. Though Braxton has taken the art-tack, thus limiting the field of sounds and ideas he can work with, the monstrous ambition of *his* project/object has much in common with Zappa's.[47]

'Revised Music for Guitar and Low Budget Orchestra' is a recast of the music Zappa wrote for Jean-Luc Ponty on *King Kong* (edited out from the official release on *Studio Tan* is a delightful burst of introductory effects that shows how closely Zappa's *musique concrète* can echo his 'real' composing). At first the sound of guitar and piano are so glossy they are Dali-esque – surrealist twists coated in epoxy-resin. Stravinsky-like 'marching' music resonates like an incursion by real instruments (strings and woodwinds uncredited on the CD notes, which only mention Duke, the Fowler brothers and Chester Thompson). The 'Duke of Prunes' theme used in the *King Kong* original is absent, but the lopsided ostinato of 'The Legend of the Golden Arches' is again

[47]Despite being marginalized by the culture industry, Braxton has been the subject of two important books: Graham Lock, *Forces in Motion: Anthony Braxton and the Meta-Reality of Creative Music*, 1988, gives a vivid account of the trials of the contemporary artist; less flawed by idealism – and astrological speculation poodle play blows its nose on – is Ronald M. Radano, *New Musical Figurations: Anthony Braxton's Cultural Critique*, 1993, a convincing illustration of the fact that negative dialectics may proceed without a poodle in sight.

used for the guitar solo, where an overdubbed horn-section doubles the improvisation (a technique used on 'Big Swifty'), giving a rhetorical flourish to the playing. 'Redunzl''s opening winds up the listener in the manner of a Nancarrow player-piano piece. Like the Escher print of gnomes climbing a staircase, it is as if the rising motif will never cease. However, it ultimately flows into the theme's soupy luxuriance, Zappa exploiting George Duke's widescreen harmonic imagination and the bright, hard edges of his soul-jazz Cuban rhythms. The guitar solo, soaring across Duke's mock pomp with verve and fire, has a tight rhythmic integration lacking in the loose Zappa/Duke jam of 'Po-jama People'. Chester Thompson's drumming here is just what Zappa needs: excitable explosions of fills over a rock solid tempo, funk-style rather than jazz. A section of parodic 'suspense' music ushers in a steaming Duke solo, replete with the sunrise romanticism that characterized 'Uncle Remus' on *Apostrophe (')*. The final coda shows Zappa's ability to score for real-time musicians the events of a piece like 'The Chrome Plated Megaphone of Destiny'. After the athletic eccentricities we have been through, the gross cliché of the 'pah-Damm' ending sounds absolutely magnificent (just the kind of effect Braxton's art-commitment disallows).

Side four of *Läther* begins with a little dialogue:

M1: It's gone.
M2: What, your talent for sucking?
M1: I never.[48]

'Honey, Don't You Want a Man Like Me' makes the kind of social observations that neither moral tetchiness nor simple chauvinism could achieve. It even received Chip Stern's grudging admiration in a *Down Beat* review that condemned Zappa's crowd-pleasing gross-outs: 'a reasoned, witty appraisal of the bar scene'.[49] It is immensely cruel to both sides of the 'romance', a callousness so off-the-leash it is positively exhilarating. In the *Läther* mix, just after Bozzio has done his imitation of her 'petulant frenzy', you can hear someone heckle from the back of the hall: 'fuck you, Zappa'. He responds 'and fuck you too, Buddy, fuck you very much' without dropping a beat. The exchange heightens the hysterical violence that characterizes the song, a cameo of frustration and inept manoeuvres.

---

[48]Frank Zappa, link preceding 'Honey, Don't You Want a Man Like Me', *Läther*, 1977.
[49]Chip Stern, '*Zappa in New York*', *Down Beat*, 1977.

PUCK

A much-quoted sentence in Frank Zappa's imaginary self-interview in a Warner/Reprise circular runs: 'Somebody out there in that audience knows what we are doing, and that person is getting off on it beyond his/her wildest comprehensions.'[50] It also said: 'We make a special art in an environment hostile to dreamers.'

The very 'accessibility' of late Zappa means that very few listeners give it the detailed attention that hermetic discourse demands. Where artists are evidently obscure – Mallarmé, *Finnegans Wake*, the Zappa of *Lumpy Gravy* and *Uncle Meat* – the need for interpretation is taken for granted. The vulgarity of 'Honey, Don't You Want a Man Like Me?' tends to block such an approach, even though there is just as much deployment of dream devices: displacement, word play and referral to arcane knowledge. What follows documents the train of ideas examination of any detail in the output macrostructure might provoke – provided the listener is prepared to follow the connective webs of meaning that figure the unconscious.

'Puck' is a key term in the lyric of 'Honey, Don't You Want a Man Like Me?'. The word was printed in capitals in the transcription on *Zappa in New York*.

> She was a lonely sort, just a little too short
> Her jokes were dumb and her fav'rite sport
> Was hockey (in the winter)
>
> He was duly impressed and was quick to suggest
> Any sport with a PUCK had to be 'bout the best
> As he jabbed his elbow in her (get it honey?)

The derivation of the word puck, as it used here, is probably from the verb 'to puck' which means 'to strike or hit', hence its application to the flat indiarubber disk used for a ball in bandy or hockey on the ice in Canada. The verb 'puck' is probably a variant of 'poke', which explains its association with male aggression here. His elbow jab is a perfect example of the sadistic quotient Freud detected in jokes of an obscene nature.

Quite apart from its links with violent words like 'poke' and 'fuck' (the latter's derivation from the Old German '*flecken*', meaning 'to hit', may be the etymological basis for its colloquial association with aggression), a 'puck' is also a mischievous male demon.

---

[50]*International Times*, No. 115, 1971.

In medieval England Puck was associated with the Devil himself. 'Titties & Beer', the track which ends side seven of *Läther*, sees Zappa outwitting the Devil by agreeing to everything he asks for. On the innerfold of *Zappa in New York*, where 'Honey' and 'Titties' finally appeared, Ruth Underwood is shown biting an apple (cropped in the CD release): as well as its use as a symbol for New York, the apple represents the fruit of the tree of knowledge of good and evil. 'The Torture Never Stops' (a version of which appeared on the CD release of *Zappa in New York*) includes the words:

> But a dungeon like a sin
> Requires naught but lockin' in
> Of everything that's ever been
> Look at her
> Look at him
> Yeah you!
> That's what's the deal we're dealin' in[51]

Fear of sin is fear of knowledge ('everything that's ever been'), which explains Zappa's relentless emphasis on the structures that channel desire.

Puck is also the name given to a bird more commonly known as a nightjar or goatsucker. In the United States the puck is known popularly as the 'whip-poor-will', which is echoic, after the bird's cry. Nightjar is also the name given to a disease in cattle (including goats) falsely attributed to the bird, which is meant to infest animals by sucking at their udders (this myth is built into the name of the bird's genus – *Caprimulgus*). This obsession with the mammaries of course recurs in 'Titties & Beer'; the fact that it is practised by stealth, at night, returns puck to its demonic root: a vampire or *incubus*, like the zomby woof. The nightjar derives its name from the peculiar whirring noise which the male makes during the period of incubation, which again points to an incubus.

The nightjar also appears in *Uncle Meat*.

> It's the middle of the night
> And your mommy & your daddy are sleeping
> It's the middle of the night
> And your mommy & your daddy are sleeping
> SLEEPING

---

[51]Frank Zappa, 'The Torture Never Stops', *Zappa in New York*, 1977.

> MOM & DAD ARE SLEEPING
> SLEEPING IN A JAR ... (the jar is under the bed)[52]

This repeated reassurance implies its opposite – which is that mom and dad are not asleep, but fucking. The primal scene, when the infant observes the parents copulating, is classically witnessed through a door which is ajar. The song segues into 'Our Bizarre Relationship', where Suzy Creamcheese's description of Zappa's sexual antics arouses in the listener a prurient, primal-scene-type curiosity. In *Läther* the wish-fulfilment reverie of 'A Little Green Rosetta' is abruptly terminated by Zappa exclaiming

> Whereupon the door closes violently!

which might interrupt observation of parental sexual activity, an exclusion which is paradoxically still more terrifying. The phrase works exactly like the irruption of horror in a dream, the sudden revelation of wish-fulfilments the child's ego refuses to acknowledge. The puck or nightjar: the moment of shock when the mind faces its unconscious impulses.

ACADEMIA

Whip-poor-wills in American lyric poetry, Puck in Shakespeare's *A Midsummer Night's Dream*: if Zappa were not in rock music, his poetic clusters would be generating Cultural Studies theses at the rate of *Finnegans Wake*.[53] The failure of American academia to interest itself in Zappa requires a sociological explanation.

> I'm talking 'university trained', trying to explain the average nerd who goes off, he's reasonably bright, he'll study in high school and then he'll go to college and get all fascinated and become a professor or something and he's a very good thinker within the assumptions of society. He's very learned and educated, he knows everything about everything. He's a pink, what we call a pink: he's programmed. He writes articles about creativity and writes about creative people but he's not creative in a truly new way; he doesn't have that vitality[54] like a Zappa has but he's creative enough to write stupid articles every week in the *Toronto Star* book review section or in journals, what's called academic but it's *not*

---

[52]Frank Zappa, 'Sleeping in a Jar', *Uncle Meat*, 1969.
[53]Which also mentions the nightjar. See James Joyce, *Finnegans Wake*, 1946, p. 449, 29–32, and Stuart Gilbert, 'Prolegomena to *Work in Progress*', Samuel Beckett *et al., Our Exagmination*, 1929, p. 70.
[54]Curiously enough, this was the word that Pierre Boulez used about Zappa when I interviewed him: *The Wire*, No. 84, February 1991, p. 28.

academic. There're all these journals popping up with educated people, who don't write in the official academic zone, who write for the popular culture journals like, well, *The Idler's* one, *The Journal of Wild Culture* is a new one; they're hundreds of those kind of nonacademic-but-not-lowbrow-musician-magazines. Those are educated, sophisticated people and they're creative within that world of their little cynicism or whatever they're writing about but the raw vitality of a Zappa as a monster fuckin' artist; they don't wanta deal with it. My generation lost interest in Frank and doesn't know what he did and the only reason they know about him now is because of the PMRC; kind of a puny topic for the average sophisticate: who gives a fuck about rock censorship? They're too busy worrying about what Barthes said about McLuhan or something. That's what I meant by saying that he fails to communicate to the university-trained. Not his fault but not the guy's fault either.[55]

Throughout the 70s and 80s Zappa remarked on how his audience got younger each year. His music remains part of the rock and drugs phase that ushers teen Americans into adulthood, refusing the tedium of either AOR (Adult Oriented Rock) or classical respectability. Although he later regarded the *One Size Fits All* band as a classic edition of the Mothers, and dedicated *Stage Vol. 2* to it, he also revealed that 'Po-jama People' was written about those musicians. As the cover of *Zoot Allures* showed, Zappa preferred being in the company of young persons, with their edgy creativity and insecurity.

> I think the overall impact of *that* group would be that it was between pseudo-jazzette and cranial. And the people who were in the band at the time – with a couple of exceptions – were genuinely boring people. I mean, I don't appreciate a band that likes to play chess in their off-stage hours. If you have to spend a lot of time with people who are interested in their chess boards and little card games and shite like that, it can drive you *nuts*.[56]

> I have had bands where everyone has been a reader. The most boring band I had was like that and ultimately led to the song 'Po-jama People'... engaging in intellectual, juiceless pursuits. I like to have guys on the bus who want to go out there and get laid.[57]

Läther was the opus that dealt with that in all aspects: both the anxieties of adolescence and the paradoxes of time and ageing. It presaged Zappa's rock period of the 80s.

[55]Bob Dean, quoted by jwcurry, 'Interview, 17 September 1990', *Cleaning up the Correlatives*, October 1990, p. 1, a stencilled newsheet available from Room 302, Books, 1357 Lansdowne Avenue, Toronto M6H 3Z9, Canada.
[56]Quoted by Cherry Ripe, 'Frank Zappa Has No Underwear', *New Musical Express*, 17 April 1976.
[57]Quoted by Paul Colbert, 'Frank Zappa', *Musicians Only*, 28 January 1980, p. 18.

'Honey, Don't You Want a Man Like Me' is followed by some *musique concrète* that was released on *Sheik Yerbouti* as 'We've Got to Get into Something Real' (retitled 'Wait a Minute' on the CD release). This is backstage chat: Zappa's in there spending thousands of dollars and the leather thing is two tours old. It is credited to Zappa, which revives the paranoia about authorship and control that threads its way through *200 Motels*. Like the anxiety about the well running dry, it segues into a bravura display of originality, this time with 'The Black Page', one of Zappa's most complex charts. The sight of a black page – a dense score with many notes to play – is known to drive young musicians into a frenzy.

> I've heard that people who select educational music take care to select pieces that are largely in crotchets and quavers, rather than semiquavers and demisemiquavers, in order to avoid the hysteria produced in young learners by a 'black page'.[58]

In a rebuff to Cardew's Maoist moralism, which declared that only simple music forms could 'serve the people', Zappa turned Terry Bozzio's hysteria in facing a black page into a pop concert event (he was also goaded into dialogue in 'Titties & Beer' and exposed in 'Punky's Whips'). According to Zappa, the tune is the missing link between 'Uncle Meat' and 'The Be-Bop Tango'. Like them, it has a weirdly static quality despite its torrent of small notes, a nagging insistence. The amount of musical material jammed into a few minutes is astonishing. Although the metrics strain at the limits of the players' imagination, there is a logic to the tune that recalls the semblance of unmediated mental reflection produced by the best jazz pianists. Along with Bozzio, marimba and vibes were necessary to lay out the 'statistical density' of the composition. In *Zappa in New York* there was a second version that added a disco vamp, at the end of which you can hear Zappa ask 'did anybody dance?' A feature of the 1978 tour was inviting up couples to dance to 'The Black Page'. Lured up by a regular beat, dancers were entertainingly flummoxed. At the Hammersmith Odeon on 26 January 1978

> Zappa invited two members of the audience who couldn't dance a step

---

[58]Cornelius Cardew, 'Wiggly Lines and Wobbly Music', *Studio International*, November–December 1976, reprinted in *Breaking the Sound Barrier*, ed. Gregory Battcock, 1981, p. 244.

to dance to the next number. 'Yes, for two minutes, the stage is yours.'
He ended up with two wonderful loonies, one who announced himself
as Eric Dolphy and had the slogan 'Out To Lunch' painted on the back
of his flasher's mac. They proceeded to jerk, frug, stomp and bomp to
an intricate jazz type number. They were great and rapturous applause
followed as they left the stage.[59]

Sounds missed the altercation that led to Out To Lunch getting
on to the stage (I know, because I was that loony). Zappa already
had a boy (named Rob Lipfriend) and his concept demanded a
girl.

FZ: Rob, you're just the kind of person we need up here. Now, one
matching female oaf.

OUT TO LUNCH: Me!

FZ: You're not a female oaf.

OTL: How do you know?

FZ: How do I know? Okay. With an answer like that, come up . . . [*OTL
climbs on stage*] . . . What's your name?

OTL: Eric Dolphy.

FZ: All right, Eric. He sure would turn in his grave over that one. Let's
pretend we've already achieved our objective – you people decide
which one is going to be the girl oaf. And now the reason we are not
going to go hog wild as they say in the trade, I mean the first night
we had too many people up here, it was so messy, here's the rules
and regulations of our dance contest. I hope you boys are paying
attention to this. This song is approximately two minutes long. At
the end of the song your time is up, voluntarily remove yourselves
from the stage. During those two minutes you are free to express
yourselves in any manner that you desire so long as you don't injure
each other, any member of the audience or harm any of our equipment
or any members of the rocking teenage combo, is that clear? Okay –
for a couple of minutes it's all yours, guys – and gals. The name of
this song is 'The Black Page Number Two', okay? 1–2–3–4![60]

The sound given the band in the monitors was crystalline in
comparison to that for the audience in the front row, so bright
and glowing it was quite unnerving. Although Lipfriend wanted
to waltz, I am capable only of an extended Charleston and found
myself doing tiny shoe-shuffles to the microscopic beats. I was
pleased to notice that Zappa made some similar steps.

On *Läther* 'Black Page #1' segues into 'Big Leg Emma',

[59]Edwin Pouncey, 'Zappa's Fun-filled Spectacular', *Sounds*, 4 February 1978.

[60]Frank Zappa, preamble to 'Black Page #2', London, 26 January 1978. By a strange coincidence
'1–2–3–4' is the name of OTL's first book (an edition of 200, printed on the Leeds SWP Roneo
in 1980).

originally released by the Mothers of Invention in April 1967,[61] abruptly descending from abstraction into pop. The massive forces at Zappa's disposal (a full horn section was hired for these 1976 New York shows) sound curiously cumbersome delivering such banalities. After a muttered 'that happened to me the same way', 'Punky's Whips' appears, an elaborately staged drama that applied Zappa's use of *musique concrète* splicing of words and sounds to real-time orchestration. Like Jasper Johns's beer-can 'sculptures' or Hitchcock making *The Rope* in seamless one-reel shots (a practice he later described as ridiculous, since his whole philosophy of film is about effective cuts) or John Zorn's scored hardcore, this kind of unnecessary bravura has a marked tendency to surface in technically advanced art. Lumpen art theory cannot see why 'real' splices (or beer cans or cuts or hardcore) are not 'sufficient', but to the acute observer (and art deserves nothing less) there is always an actual difference that makes the emulation worthwhile. In 'Punky's Whips' real-time orchestration gives the splices a romanticism, a velvet fog, entirely suited to the subject matter.

For Zappa the lips are a symbol of romance: in 'The Oracle Has It All Psyched Out', for example, he noted the 'kissable' publicity photographs supplied to fans by the Beatles.[62] The back cover of *Waka/Jawaka* (missing in the CD release) showed a pot plant in a dented, rusting bucket labelled 'ARALIA ELEGAT-ISSMA'. The pot plant reappeared in Schenkel's drawing of Uncle Meat's studio in *The Grand Wazoo*, this time labelled 'ECU DAMP PUCKERED RICTUS'. 'ECU' is a film-treatment acronym for 'Extreme Close Up'. Rictus is a term for the mouth that reappeared in 'Punky's Whips'. 'Punky's Whips' updated Zappa's earlier observations about the Beatles' commercial manipulation of adolescent fantasies by commenting on the glam look adopted by late 70s heavy-metal bands in the wake of the New York Dolls. Glamour is such a constructed thing that it is quite possible for make-up artists and hairdressers to make men look like female models, which the members of Angel certainly did. Written to commemorate Terry Bozzio 'jacking off to pictures of Punky Meadows',[63] the song dramatized teen sexual confusion in a

---

[61]Mothers of Invention, 'Big Leg Emma', 1967, Verve VS557.
[62]'The Oracle Has It All Psyched Out', reprinted in Dominique Chevalier, *Viva! Zappa*, 1985, p. 93. See, '*Uncle Meat*' in Chapter Two: Freakdom and the Hippies, '*The Grand Wazoo*' in Chapter Four: Music Music.
[63]Frank Zappa, 'Titties & Beer', *Zappa in New York*, 1977.

close-focus on *Läther*'s theme. It was introduced by the TV presenter Don Pardo, referring to 'the pooched-out succulence of his insolent, pouting rictus', and Bozzio sings

> Punky, Punky, give me your lips
> To die on . . . I promise not to come in your mouth

'Isn't it romantic, Punky?' asks Bozzio after a peal of bells that recalls *Symphonie Fantastique* by Hector Berlioz.[64] Various vocal contributions are recorded in different registers which gives them a hallucinatory spin, an effect magnified by a highly original mixture of electric guitars and saxophones. Such magical conjuring of emotional states makes most current classical opera look pallid. The concluding guitar solo, spurred by churning horns and magnificent strict tempo thrashing from Bozzio, is irresistibly propulsive.

Side five of *Läther* begins with 'Flambay', the love song of Drakma, the Queen of Cosmic Greed, to Hunchentoot the Giant Spider, though here without the vocals that were overdubbed for the CD release. Vocals actually serve to obscure the strange eloquence of its melody line: only Sun Ra could equal the queasy ambivalence of this cocktail jazz. The swelling theme is played by George Duke, Patrick O'Hearn's sumptuous upright bass just enough out of time to keep everything cockeyed. Voices talk about something 'breathtaking' that cost 'a small fortune': it could be a car or a tattoo or the next piece of music, 'The Purple Lagoon', which featured the high-price fusion session men Michael and Randy Brecker. 'Shit, I'm in hock up to my goddamn eyeballs' is pronounced with vowel sounds that seem to carry on into Patrick O'Hearn's gurgling bass guitar intro. 'Approximate', the old Wazoo and Sensation band piece that specifies rhythms but not pitches, is played against the portentous funk of 'The Purple Lagoon'. Ever ready with a phallic quip, Zappa's overdubbed guitar solo is referred to as 'a case of inevitable insertionism': his virtual-reality rock arena sound is fantastic, sitting strangely with the expertly shaped pattern of the solo. Randy Brecker's trumpet was run through a harmonizer three times, resulting in four-part harmony, making it sound like the Schälmei (a multi-headed German trumpet) played by Ronald Shannon Jackson. As with 'The Gumbo Variations' it repays a listen-through that focuses

---

[64] 'Isn't It Romantic' is the name of a song in Woody Allen's *Hannah and Her Sisters*, a fact Andrew Greenaway finds significant, *T'Mershi Duween*, No. 26, September 1992, p. 25.

attention on the drums alone; Bozzio is prodigious. The tricky metrics and unusual harmonies keep the soloists on their toes in a way that makes the academic complexities of regular fusion absolutely redundant. It seems that ignorance of Zappa's music must be the precondition for being impressed with jazz-rock.

PEDRO'S DOWRY

Side six reduces the introductory *musique concrète* to laughter at the start and 'Say, er, d'you still ball him?' at the close. 'Pedro's Dowry' was recorded at an orchestral concert at UCLA's Royce Hall on 18 September 1975. There is a story behind the music – a ballet – which Zappa related to the delight of the boisterous crowd.

> A woman with ocean-front property waits for someone named Pedro. She will launder his burlap shirt in a splendid sunset. He will play an inexpensive guitar. She will make him a stimulating drink. While he drinks it, she will put on some more lipstick. Later, they'll have a cheap little fuck and accidently knock over an ashtray. In the confusion she might have misplaced her necklace. Within moments Earl has cleaned her up.[65]

Although composed with the sounds of clichés – *Twilight Zone* effects, maundering suspense strings, dramatic thunder of drums – the example of Varèse leads Zappa to combine with an ear for new contrasts of timbre. Although completely orchestral, this is very physical music, with tensions and dispersals that correspond to bodily processes. It ends with a flurry and a ding-dong doorbell effect: as usual Zappa denies any transcendent meaning by a scrupulous reminder of petit-bourgeois banality. The title track of *Läther* follows, which the sleeve notes for *Zappa in New York* described as 'a sensitive instrumental ballad for late-nite easy listening' (there it was renamed with Bozzio's memorable line from 'Punky's Whips', 'I Promise Not to Come in Your Mouth'). It features a swooning, tingling Moog solo by Eddie Jobson that expertly duplicates the sensations of oral sex, a stunt that was repeated by Peter Wolf on 'Sy Borg'.[66] In answer to those people who maintain that electric instruments are cold and inhuman, Zappa makes them more intimate than you can really credit.

'Spider of Destiny' (again lacking the subsequent vocals) is a

---

[65]Frank Zappa, preamble to 'Pedro's Dowry', UCLA's Royce Hall, 18 September 1975.
[66]Frank Zappa, 'Sy Borg', *Joe's Garage Acts II & III*, 1979.

deftly original combination of acoustic (piano, marimba) and electric (wild guitar). Given the technical capabilities of the modern recording studio, it is quite extraordinary how bound by literal-minded realism is most recording of instrumental music, an indication of how often so-called 'listening' music merely serves to provide people with what they know – orchestral or jazz-band ambience. Here, studio wizardry folds two of *Läther's* sound-worlds – rock-arena frenzy and acoustic intimacy – into a single piece of music. 'Duke of Orchestral Prunes' is the Royce Hall version of the tune from *Absolutely Free*, though Tommy Morgan's harmonica solo has been replaced by whining feedback guitar played in the manner of 'Zoot Allures'.

FILTHY HABITS

'Filthy Habits', which begins side seven, lives up to its name, being one of the dirtiest guitar showcases Zappa has performed. Recorded with the same Parlato/Bozzio rhythm section as the title track of *Zoot Allures*, it evokes the images of 'The Torture Never Stops', full of the borrowings Bartók and Stravinsky made from Transylvanian and Slavic peasant music. At the end of the solo Zappa plays a keyboard lick that is unadulterated gypsy music. The tune's powerful riff underlies every overtracked slither, twanging like a monstrous heartbeat, a libidinal surge ready to swell at any instant. The fade quotes from Ray Manzarek's rippling keyboards on 'Riders on the Storm', a generic musical moment used to signify 'barbarian hordes' in Hollywood films. Susan McClary has pointed out how such non-tempered harmony has always meant 'otherness' in Western music, but her condemnation of European chauvinism does not stretch to seeing how such 'otherness' might be summoned from an oppositional ideological perspective – as, for example, the militant reggae band Dambala did in the classic 'Visions of War'.[67]

'Filthy Habits' segues into 'Whatever Happened to All the Fun in the World?' and 'Titties & Beer'. Zappa sets the scene, which is like something from a Meatloaf cover: the biker and his

---

[67]B-side of Dambala, 'Zimbabwe', 1978, Music Hive MHDisco001. This memorable keyboard threat was first introduced into pop by the Chantays with 'Pipeline', 1963, Dot, and shows up in the Mad Professor, 'Stepping Razor', *Who Knows the Secret of the Master Tape? Dub Me Crazy Part 5*, 1985, Ariwa ARILP021, and Man Parrish, 'Water Sports', on 'Brown Sugar', 1988, Bolts Records BOLTS8/12.

girlfriend Chrissy on a blasted heath with some ugly trees. The Devil pops up (played by Bozzio) and eats the biker's beer and his girlfriend. The biker wants them back but he will have to sell him his soul. Some lines of written dialogue, which had Zappa describing the soul the Devil is so keen to have, were dropped by the time the song was recorded (they surfaced on *Baby Snakes*):

> It's a mean little sucker about a thousand years old
> And once you've got it, you can't give it back
> You gotta keep it forever and that's a natural fact

The Devil is mortified at Zappa's immediate acquiescence and begins to back out. This then goes into improvised dialogue with Zappa goading Bozzio with whatever was going on at the time, jokes about pickles or Punky Meadows. On the *Läther* version he tells the Devil he is only interested in two things and asks him to guess what they are. Bozzio replies:

> Er, maybe Stravinsky and er . . .[68]

which is a perceptive remark, because the whole routine is a rewrite of the conflict between Devil and fiddle player in *A Soldier's Tale*. Zappa had actually played the part of the Devil in a performance at the Hollywood Bowl in 1972, conducted by Lukas Foss.[69] The loping funk riff of 'Titties & Beer' works like the 'marching music' that starts the Stravinsky. In the latter the Devil wins because the soldier attempts to return the past. When Mårten Sund, editor of *Society Pages* (the Zappa fanzine that subsequently relocated to the States), asked Zappa at the *Baby Snakes* conference in Oslo in 1980 if 'Titties & Beer' had a relationship with *A Soldier's Tale*, he laughed and said: 'That's funny. Sure, there's a relationship there. That's the most abstract question I've answered in about a year!'[70]

'Titties & Beer' pursues the idea of the 'world's greatest sinner', the idea that unhypocritical pursuit of desire transcends petty moralism, the Blakean road of excess leading to the palace of wisdom. At the end Chrissy explodes with indignation:

> I got me three beers and a fist fulla downs,
> An' I'm gonna get wrecked, so fuck you clowns!

The Devil farts and she's blown over a cliff. When the biker

[68]Frank Zappa, 'Titties & Beer', *Zappa in New York*, 1977.
[69]Frank Zappa, with Peter Occhiogrosso. *The Real Frank Zappa Book*, 1989, p. 116.
[70]13 January 1980.

returns to his pad his girlfriend is back: the whole episode has been a dream.

The last track on side seven is 'The Ocean is the Ultimate Solution', a title that performs the usual Zappa trick of finding poetry in material facts. Like 'Spider of Destiny' it pioneers a new instrumental balance, with upfront, glittering guitar, Patrick O'Hearn's acoustic jazz bass and Bozzio's boiling drums. When Zappa's electric solo arrives, dubbed over his acoustic chords, it is like a voice from another dimension: horizontal, streaked-sky notes that put the bubbling rhythm instruments into a totally different light. He uses his characteristic device of nagging repetition two thirds into the solo, his acoustic rhythm chords hammering on the electric guitar's siren wail. At the end, the tension uncoils in a strange opening out that recalls the final paragraph of *Finnegans Wake*, where the River Liffey flows out into the sea.

GREGGERY PECCARY

Side eight of *Läther* consists of 'The Adventures of Greggery Peccary', a virtuosic display of orchestration and studio editing that tells the story of a little pig who invents the calendar: 'Billy the Mountain' told in the style of *Apostrophe (')*. One of the problems of *A Soldier's Tale* is that, despite the attempt to popularize with narration, the high cultural level assigned to classical music means that the voices used will be RADA-trained – Sir John Gielgud[71] when Ken Dodd might be more appropriate. *Greggery Peccary* is definitely not in that class: because it uses every sonic trick in the book, it blocks high-art applause. Alongside the speeded up cartoon voices there is a jam-packed musical wit that is second to none. It is confusing to notions of cultural hierarchy to realize how close the music of *Greggery Peccary* is to the 'electronic chamber music' of *The Grand Wazoo*: the Wazoo road band played the march and the closing 'New Brown Clouds' section as instrumentals. The quick-fire succession of musical ideas on *Waka/Jawaka*, which makes most fusion look creatively poverty-stricken, uses similar devices to *Greggery Peccary*.

Belonging to a different generation (and coast), John Zorn

---

[71]Igor Stravinsky, *L'Histoire du soldat*, 1975, Deutsche Grammophon 2530609.

achieves similar concatenations of effects. He has been partly responsible for the aesthetic rehabilitation of Tex Avery and Carl Stalling in the late 80s. Zorn's approach stems from the wide variety of music available on record, a logical response to an increasingly universal condition for music listeners. Zorn does not degrade his sources with Zappa's besmirching leer, it is more a postmodern combination of elements, though a need for intensity (Zorn's hardcore affiliations) pushes it beyond the usual PoMo smugness. Zappa's eclecticism stems from a different source, which is the Varèsean discovery that any sound can be weighed for its external aspects, balanced regardless of considerations of genre. There is also Zappa's understanding of sound in terms of the body, a 60s-style belief in the blues that post-punk culture cannot credit, having witnessed both its commercialization as heavy metal and its ideological critique by feminism.

Greggery Peccary is also part of Zappa's ongoing philosophical speculation about time. In *Them Or Us (The Book)* Zappa proposed the Einsteinian thesis that time is an illusion in order to justify his free-associationist plot. Here, Greggery, sitting in his office at Big Swifty & Associates, Trendmongers, invents the calendar as a new trend.

> Greggery issued a memo on it
> Whereupon the entire contents of the Steno pool
> Identified with it strenuously
> And worshipped it
> And took their little pills by it
> And paid their rent by it
> And went back and forth from work by it[72]

Greggery is mobbed by a gang who object to the fact that the invention of the calendar means that they are now aware of the process of ageing. He escapes their clutches, narrowly escapes being eaten by Billy the Mountain and, puzzled by the 'brown clouds' of dust coughed up, decides he needs a 'philostopher' to assist him. Quentin Robert De Nameland (who later appears as the illegitimate crab-grass baby's father in *Thing-Fish*) gives a public lecture. He reveals that 'time is an affliction'. In the final mix, most of his lecture is replaced by an excellent Bruce Fowler trombone solo. *Hot Raz Times* printed an early version in 1973.

---

[72]Frank Zappa, 'The Adventures of Greggery Peccary', *Studio Tan*, 1979.

Well, folks
As you can see for yourself
The way this CLOCK over here is BEHAVING
TIME IS AN AFFLICTION . . .
This may be cause for alarm
Among a portion of you, as
From a certain experience
I tend to proclaim . . .
THE EONS ARE CLOSING!
(*Concerned mutterings from all in attendance*)
Now, what does this mean, precisely
To the layman?
Simply this: MOMENTARILY, THE NEED FOR
THE CONSTRUCTION OF NEW LIGHT
WILL NO LONGER EXIST!
Of course, some of you will say:
'Who is HE to tell me from this LIGHT?'
But, in all seriousness, ladies and gentlemen
A quick glance at the erratic behavior
Of the large, precision-built
TIME-DELINEATING APPARATUS beside me
Will show that it is perhaps
Only a few moments now!
Just look how funny it's
Going around there!
Personally,
I find mechanical behavior of this nature
To be highly SUSPICIOUS
When such a device
Doesn't go NORMAL
The implication of such a behavior
BODES NOT WELL!
And, quite naturally, ladies and gentlemen
When the mechanism in question
Is entrusted with the task of
The delineation of
TIME ITSELF . . .
And
If such a mechanism goes
ON THE BUM . . .
OR THE FRITZ . . .
Well
It spells TROUBLE![73]

After the lecture (to return to the version that appeared on *Läther*

---

[73]Frank Zappa, 'The Adventures of Greggery Peccary', *Hot Raz Times*, Vol. 1, No. 1, 1973, ed. Urban Gwerder, p. 13.

and *Studio Tan*) accomplices leap up to say to whom cheques are payable and the concluding chorus runs:

> Who is making those new brown clouds?
> If you ask a philostopher
> He'll see that you pays[74]

'Billy the Mountain' entertained anti-draft audiences in 1971 by stomping over airforce bases and toppling the government's representative Studebacher Hoch 200 feet to his death. The back cover of *One Size Fits All* used earth fissures as a figure for social upheaval. However, De Nameland does not refer to Billy the Mountain or talk about social collapse; instead he just talks about mechanical failure in clocks, the theme of decaying hardware that so upset Philip K. Dick.[75] It also comes up in 'Flakes',[76] the notes on 'He Used to Cut the Grass'[77] and 'Planet of My Dreams'.[78] More than any other prospect, it is American cultural stasis that feeds Zappa's satirical vision.

The transcript printed in *Hot Raz Times* concludes:

> Greggery takes leave of the *Therapeutic Assembly*, only to discover the mysterious dust storm is still in progress . . .
> GREGGERY: [*Miffed*] *That geek has ripped me off!*
> NARRATOR: [*Confidentially to Greggery*] *Perhaps it's a trend . . .*

A conclusion very like that of 'Cosmik Debris'.[79] The notion that time was an affliction is a tenet of the Situationists, who refused to wear wrist-watches, calling them the death's-head insignia of the bourgeoisie. When Greggery invents the calendar he rolls his eyes heavenward and angelic voices sing, 'Sunday, Saturday, Tuesday through Monday, Monday', with some of the sinister arbitrariness of the sequence in 'Billy the Mountain' that appeared round the star map on the back of *One Size Fits All*. The idea of the calendar appearing from heaven is appropriate since we live by the Christian calendar initiated by the birth of Christ. Enforced by wage labour and consecrated by religion, the calendar is a highly ideological construct that poses as natural: the idea of it being invented, however absurd, has a radical edge (one of the tracks on *Sleep Dirt* is called 'Time is Money'). It also returns to

---

[74]Ibid.
[75]For example, Philip K. Dick, *Ubik*, 1969.
[76]Frank Zappa, 'Flakes', *Sheik Yerbouti*, 1979.
[77]Frank Zappa, 'He Used to Cut the Grass', *Joe's Garage Acts II & III*, 1979.
[78]Frank Zappa, 'Planet of My Dreams', *Them Or Us*, 1984.
[79]Frank Zappa, 'Cosmik Debris', *Apostrophe (')*, 1974.

the theme of *Läther*, which is teen confusion about sexuality and its exploitation by such trend-mongers as Angel: ageing as a problem. Behind all the contempt and satire and degradation in Zappa is a vision of infantile joy, polymorphously perverse and as timeless as the unconscious.

ZAPPA IN NEW YORK

In 1977 Zappa hoped for an October release of *Läther*.[80] Journalists who were played its three and a half hours on headphones emerged stunned.

> *Läther* is nothing so much as a definitive overview of every mode the man has ever tampered with, utilizing new recordings and with few exceptions – notably a scorching 'Duke of Prunes' – all new material. If your interest in Zappa goes beyond mere frivolous acquaintance, it's essential.[81]

However, it was not to be. Despite Zappa's protests, Warner Brothers released *Zappa in New York*. Unlike the next three albums Zappa had provided them with artwork and extensive sleeve notes. The release was further vitiated by a threat of a lawsuit from Angel's record company. Punky Meadows had apparently okayed 'Punky's Whips' – being satirized by Zappa must seem to any young metal star the sign of having arrived – but Warners pulled the track, making sides one and two exceptionally short. Aggrieved customers even found copies that listed 'Punky's Whips' but omitted it (some copies with 'Punky's Whips', though, did appear in the shops).

Zappa in New York collected together all the live tracks from *Läther*, together with a special 'New York' version of 'Black Page #1', which added a disco vamp, spoken commentary and an introductory drum solo. There were also two new instrumentals: an arrangement of 'Sofa' and a crazy instrumental called 'Manx Needs Women'. Recorded at Halloween and between Christmas and New Year's Eve, you can make out tinsel stretched over Zappa's guitar monitor. The cover was a picture by Dweezil Zappa taken from a New York skyscraper, parked cars looking remarkably like a printed circuit. This impression is emphasized by lettering done

---

[80]*New Musical Express*, 1 October 1977.
[81]Paul Rambali, 'Stern Words in Knightsbridge', *New Musical Express*, 28 January 1978, p. 25.

in typical NYC neon tubes: it is as if Zappa has figured the city in the electronic circuits of his hardware.

Sleevenotes are friendly and direct, appreciative of New York's large and enthusiastic audiences. Programmed as the fourth side of a double, 'The Purple Lagoon' invites comparisons to 'Return of the Son of Monster Magnet' and, with its string of solos, 'King Kong'. With his recording career purportedly in limbo, Zappa continued to tour. Roy Estrada was replaced by Patrick O'Hearn, a friend of Bozzio's from San Francisco; he called round to see Bozzio at Zappa's studio carrying his upright bass and Zappa asked him if he 'could play that dog kennel'. It was O'Hearn's acoustic capability that enabled him to supply bass for the weirded-out jazz of 'Flambay' and 'Time is Money'. His electric playing has the bubbling flexibility of Jaco Pastorius. Like many musicians, working with Zappa was his chance to learn about the latest technology. He has since produced new-age synthesizer music.

In October 1976 Zappa toured with vocalists Ray White and Bianca Odin (another strongly gospel-inflected singer), Eddie Jobson (freed from Roxy Music as Bryan Ferry split for a solo career) on violin and keyboards and the O'Hearn/Bozzio rhythm section. With so few participants, there was less need for the elaborate arrangements used for larger forces, and the music was exceptionally fluid – the sound wet and live. There was room for a great deal of spontaneity. In Troy, New York, the road manager was shaved by Smothers on stage;[82] at the Cobo Hall in Detroit on 19 November guests included Don Brewer, the drummer from Grand Funk Railroad, Ralphe Armstrong and Flo & Eddie (despite Zappa's pronouncements in 1972), who performed 'Rudy Wants to Buy Yez a Drink', 'Would You Go All the Way' and 'Daddy, Daddy, Daddy'. After reading an article in the *Herald Tribune* about a friend of Memphis Slim's who was busking harmonica at Odeon Station in Paris, Zappa went and found him and got him to play at the Pavillon de Paris in front of 10,000 people. Sugar Blue later played harmonica on 'Miss You' by the Rolling Stones (though being a blues purist he hated the disco mix[83]). Long workouts on 'Pound for a Brown' had Zappa unfurling guitar solos of exceptional lyricism: the great guitar albums

---

[82]See 'Poodles and philosophy', Chapter 5: Bizarre to DiscReet.
[83]Phillipe Manoeuvre, 'Stones Harpist Located Down Paris Subway', *New Musical Express*, 23 September 1978.

the 80s came about through night after night of playing in such performance conditions. Presumably for reasons of audio quality, the tapes Zappa preferred to release are generally later concerts with Chad Wackerman rather than Terry Bozzio.

On the CD release of *Zappa in New York* four tracks were added (not counting the reinclusion of 'Punky's Whips'): 'Cruisin' for Burgers', 'I'm the Slime' – a riotously driving version with a near-hysterical Don Pardo – 'Pound for a Brown' and 'The Torture Never Stops'; all regular titles in the repertoire of the 1977 band, but here expanded by the four extra horns and the percussion of David Samuels and Ruth Underwood.

THE PANTER ALBUMS

Warner Brothers went on to release the original *Studio Tan*, supplying their own artwork by Gary Panter of *Raw* comic fame. They were bright and striking, but did not fit Zappa's current taste for low-key formality and photographs with suggestive details. The image for *Studio Tan* – a man sweating in a deckchair – was distinctive enough to turn up on a Vienna Art Orchestra album cover.[84] As Zappa toured with a band promoting *Zoot Allures* and material that was to arrive with *Sheik Yerbouti* – all heavily rock-based – Warner Brothers were releasing utterly contrasting music. *Studio Tan* did not have anything that was not on *Läther*. *Sleep Dirt* included two more tracks: 'Time is Money' and 'Sleep Dirt' itself. Without the agenda of the lyrics later revealed on the CD release, which start

> Time is money
> But space is a long long time[85]

the piece comes over as a sequence of portentous chords interleaved with strange lost moments and Zappa's characteristic urgent tumble of asymmetric rhythmic groupings. The words fit so closely that they must have preceded the tortuous complexity of the music. This spoken element, an application to thematic writing of vocalized R&B guitar (Guitar Slim, Johnny 'Guitar' Watson), explains both the intensity and the originality of Zappa's rhythms.

---

[84]Cover by Herbert Pirchner and Roland Wernbacher for Vienna Art Orchestra, *Tango from Ubango*, 1979, Art Records 1002.
[85]Frank Zappa, 'Time is Money', *Sleep Dirt*, CD only, 1991.

It is not just a matter of transcription (although the later experiments with 'meltdown' on *Man from Utopia* use such techniques). Like Sal Marquez transcribing a guitar solo for brass on 'Waka/Jawaka', such musical objectivization is taken into the compositional order itself. It is in a different league from the parochial academic smarts of a fusion band playing a Jelly Roll Morton tune in 5/8. As Zappa said to *Guitar* magazine, 'We can play in 4/4 and play some awful weird shit in 4/4. By the same token you can play in 9/16 and play some really boring stuff too, as evidenced by a lot of jazz-rock groups.'[86] The twists and turns of 'Time is Money' have a purpose; they abut the undocumented rhythms of verbal rhetoric to stringent musical form. It is the secret promise of *Pierrot Lunaire*: creating a two-way traffic between art and life.

The cosmic view of Drakma as she surveys a fucked-up earth is an absurd conjunction between pantomime sci-fi and the objectivity of critical politics. The guttering unease of the music – an electric guitar that darts and blusters, the hieratic tuned percussion, the scurrying drumset – erupts in fury like sunspots (or acne). Introducing money into Einstein's equation is a theoretical version of Zappa's insistence that the hierarchical separation of mind and body is an illusion, an ideology. 'Sleep Dirt', an acoustic guitar duet with James Youman, pursues the close-up intimacy of *Zoot Allures*, featuring an insistent motif that showcases Zappa's new ease with conventional evocation. His glistening tone and sliding left-hand give it a special flavour. Named after the secretion that accumulates in the corner of the eye during sleep, it has some of the dreamy intensity of half-conscious perception. Youman falters; Zappa asks 'You getting tired?'; 'No, my fingers got stuck.' This little exchange occurs before the eruption of 'Spider of Destiny', a strong example of Zappa's usual habit of upsetting the naturalistic ambience most recording is at pains to preserve.

Orchestral Favorites, the last of the Panter albums, collected together the orchestral works from *Läther* recorded at Royce Hall in September 1975, adding 'Bogus Pomp', a setting of the 'This Town is a Sealed Tuna Sandwich' theme from *200 Motels*.

---

[86]John Dalton, 'Shut Up and Play Your Guitar', *Guitar*, May 1979, p. 22.

CHAPTER 8
CBS AND CORPORATE ROCK

ZAPPA'S AUDIENCE, ZAPPA'S ATTITUDE

The lawsuit with Warner Brothers threatened to wipe Frank Zappa off the corporate map. Zappa's conceptual continuity requires a foot in the marketplace: his interest in high technology could not survive relegation to the avant-garde ghetto. In 1978 things looked bleak. His decision was to pursue the arena-rock aspect of *Läther*. Orchestral music could be financed from the proceeds and guitar solos would give a space for improvisation, but the groundbase of live work would need to be guitars and working within the touring infrastructure that had grown up around the rock music of the 1960s. Though Zappa remained independent of the corporate record industry by forming his own label, he played the same large venues as the big rock bands and relied on the majors for distribution. His project had ambitions – in terms of audience size, recording quality, key personnel – that only rock could deliver.

This explains his incomprehension of punk, which subverted the whole rigmarole, reasserting the potential of cheap production and audience interaction in small venues. *Sheik Yerbouti* made comments on punk ('Tryin' to Grow a Chin', 'I'm So Cute'), but the glorious polish of its production was the sound of money. The cover showed Zappa in Arab headgear, pushing his non-Aryan physiognomy to the fore (also showing the first white hairs in his moustache), printed with deluxe largesse on fine cardboard. Zappa insists that it was the cover that sold the album.[1] Stuffed with inventive music and subversive ideas, *Sheik Yerbouti* had the patina of professional product. If *Läther* had raised the ghosts of *Lumpy Gravy*, *Sheik Yerbouti* was music for the 1980s: slick, cynical, grandiose, entertaining. The strategy worked. Talking to Neil

---

[1] Dan Forte, 'Frank Zappa', reprinted in *Society Pages*, No. 10, May 1982, p. 19.

Slaven, Zappa explained: 'Before *Sheik Yerbouti* we were doing 50,000 to 70,000 units worldwide. *Sheik Yerbouti* sold 1.6 million units worldwide. I don't know the figure for *Hot Rats* but it's nowhere near *Yerbouti* – maybe 400,000.'[2]

However, this high gloss did not mean surrendering the anti-ideological aspects of Zappa's music. As anybody who has been involved with music promotion or sales is aware, 'going commercial' or 'selling out' is by no means the simple act rebel rock ideology makes of it. By pushing against prevailing ideas of the saleable a band can make a name; by tempering that originality, or merely working within new conditions they have helped to create, bands can hope to sell more, but they risk losing their initial support, entering into competition with bands who are playing the game more single-mindedly. The stranglehold of the record-pluggers on American FM radio introduces many other factors besides appeal to the taste of the average listener. Zappa has never had the budgets available to buy into the playlists of mainstream radio and has talked openly about corporate corruption. Gail Zappa explained the situation. For her, Fredric Dannen's exposé (he has talked to the Zappas about the problem) is more than a 'thesis'.[3]

> Whether it's the mafia or not, it's not like they don't have a lot of help. Whoever is finally benefiting in a huge way has the help of every single person in the industry because no one goes up against it. Consequently, the industry currently pretty much reflects itself, there's no real music, there's no real alternative music happening – forget about Seattle! I'm not denigrating anyone's talent, but in terms of introducing important musical ideas and having access to any kind of music you would ever want to hear or be able to hear, or even want to know about, it's impossible in this country. There is no airplay for anyone. I'm not just saying this as sour grapes, it's true. Everything sounds the same that's on the radio, everything is the same, it sounds formulaic, it sounds totally corporate.[4]

Down in the Zappas' office, a sticker produced by SST, the punk label set up by Black Flag, is prominently displayed: 'Corporate rock sucks!' Zappa's refusal to be involved in drugs also constitutes a denial of a stock-in-trade of the corporate-mafia-DJ interface. According to him, Warner Brothers representatives would come

---

[2]Quoted by Neil Slaven, 'Zappa Gets Frank', *Record Hunter*, supplement to *Vox*, July 1992, p. 6.
[3]For evidence that American radio payola is mafia-controlled, see Fredric Dannen, *Hit Men*, 1990.
[4]Gail Zappa, interview with the author, 27 October 1993.

backstage with suitcases of drugs. Apart from these social 'mal-practices' – as far as 70s corporate rock was concerned – turning to a rock sound does not immediately guarantee commercial success. Album sales are mediated by the industry's infrastructure, by marketing. Decisions made by executives about what to promote have a disproportionate effect on what constitutes the choices available.

> Now, how did they earn the *right* to be the gods of the record industry? These fuckers came from the shoe business, a lot of them. And they are the ones who finally make the decision of who gets the zillion-dollar push, the big endorsements, the big hosejob on MTV. These esteemed gentlemen, based on advice received from hip magazines that tell you what's hot, will then reshape the size and texture of American musical culture in their own pinhead image.[5]

If they are convinced that the music is 'commercial' they will push it, even if no one wants to hear – which is precisely what happened in the great disco slump of 1980. *Sheik Yerbouti* sounded more like viable product than, say, the non-vocal *Sleep Dirt*: Mercury-Phonogram (distributing Zappa's label in the States) and CBS (the label overseas) took the album seriously, tried to shift the units. Because it is mediated by what company personnel feel about the market, 'commercial' is never a stable term, a known quantity. When asked if he thought *Zoot Allures* was 'more commercial' than records made by the original Mothers of Invention, Zappa stared into his whisky and said: 'Every record I ever made I always thought was a hit. (*Pause*) ... That's how crazy *I* am. I thought *Freak Out!* was a hit.'[6]

Sheik Yerbouti was a guitar-based, song-oriented collection and this undoubtedly encouraged CBS to take it seriously: but what made it take off in Europe was 'Bobby Brown', a song with explicit lyrics that English-speaking radio would never pro-gramme. Speaking in 1992 of the success of *Sheik Yerbouti* in Europe, Zappa said:

> The reason was 'Bobby Brown'. Somebody in Norway decided that they liked the song very much and kept playing it in discos, and it became a hit in Scandinavia, then it was a hit in Germany. It was a Top Ten record again in Germany just last year. I don't know why.[7]

---

[5]Quoted by Matt Resnicoff, 'Poetic Justice: Frank Zappa Puts Us in Our Place', *Musician*, November 1991, p. 74.
[6]Quoted by Chris Salewicz, 'OK Frank Let It Roll ... The Frank Zzzzzzappa Snore-In', *New Musical Express*, 5 March 1977.
[7]Quoted by Neil Slaven, 'Zappa Gets Frank', *Record Hunter*, supplement to *Vox*, July 1992, p. 6.

Like the stock exchange, the charts, far from being the distillation of the finest in capitalist pop culture, are a lottery.

Newcomers to the band on *Sheik Yerbouti* were guitarist Adrian Belew and keyboardist Tommy Mars. John Swenson asked Zappa how he found Belew.

> I was in Nashville and he was working with this bar band and he was playing good Stratocaster and singing like – who was the guy that did 'Leah'? – Roy Orbison. He was doing Roy Orbison imitations. I said, Mmm, here's an interesting guy. I got his phone number, brought him to audition, he passed the audition and got the job . . . a lot of groups don't go out and hang around with normal people and go into little dip-shit bars and stuff and I do. And that's where musicians are at, out there workin', scufflin' along. Then the next thing that happens is when they come into my band they get a chance to work with better equipment, they get some discipline, they get a chance to be seen by hundreds of thousands of people for a period of time, they get mentioned in interviews and stuff – presto chango, they're fantastic musicians. But I don't think that some of the people who've been supposedly discovered by me would eventually have been discovered by any of the people they eventually went to work for, because those people don't know where to look.[8]

Adrian Belew subsequently left Zappa to work with David Bowie and King Crimson.

Tommy Mars had been playing piano in a cocktail bar, an experience he enjoyed about as much as Zappa enjoyed his tenure with Joe Perrino and the Mellotones.

> Well, the deal is that at the end of my 'piano bar' career I was getting incredibly distressed playing for men and women who would come in as perfect ladies and gentlemen and leave as animals. They would be sitting as close to me as we are sitting now and I could not resist the temptation to start singing to you and to you and telling to you how fucked-up you are, and what the hell are you doing to her? I was putting on the wrong mask for that gig, and it was just perfect that Frank needed somebody at the time to put on that mask for him, a perfect modulation. You don't keep that kind of a gig with that kind of an attitude long. Someone would say, can you play *Rhapsody in Blue* – I wouldn't just play the end part, I'd play the whole of *Rhapsody in Blue* for him. I was right at the end of my rope, I didn't know what to do, at my wit's end to try and keep some sanity as well as some artistry in that forum. I was never really meant to do that kind of performance. Personally speaking, I considered it great therapy every night to be able to look at you and point my finger at you and say, 'You're an asshole too! and you're an asshole!' or, 'Fuck me, you ugly son of a bitch!' –

[8]Dan Forte, 'Frank Zappa', reprinted in *Society Pages*, No. 10, May 1982, p. 19.

things that you get arrested for, for Christ's sake, you could do with him.[9]

Mars got to a Zappa audition via Ed Mann; the pair played in a band that did 'everything from Hindemith to Charles Ives, jazz and rock interpretations of these pieces as well as some of our own stuff and some bebop'.

On *Sheik Yerbouti* Zappa showed he knew what cultural level he was operating on with the opening track: 'I Have Been in You'. This was a reply to Peter Frampton's album *I'm in You*. On stage, Zappa would precede the song with a rap about the teenage girl/fan who had lured the English pop star back to her bedroom. At the Hammersmith Odeon in 1979 he had him remove safety pins from his face as he prepared for bed, which distressed the scattering of punk-sympathizers in the audience, since for them punk signalled an end to the arena-rock-divinity-groupie syndrome (besides which, safety pins were by then merely a tabloid concept of punk). At the climax of their fuck the pop star whispers into the girl's ear, using Zappa's stupidest cartoon voice, 'I'm in you!' On the record the song becomes doowop, the lushness of the production – the extraordinary space between the falsetto backup vocals and Zappa's leering, close-miked vocal – creating something quite unprecedented. The backing vocals have a desperation that recalls *Zoot Allures* and its progression from screams of torture to the howls behind 'Ms Pinky' and Roy Estrada's hysterical falsetto on 'Find Her Finer' (the original torture cries can be heard on *Sheik Yerbouti* behind the guitar solo on 'Rat Tomago'). As Zappa sings 'I'm going in you again', the song becomes an allegory of market penetration, of stepping into the emotional space of the listener: as so often, Zappa's own activities blend with those of the target.

> And while
> I was inside
> I mighta been
> Undignified
> And that is maybe
> Why you cried
> I don't know[10]

This encapsulates Zappa's use of sex, focusing on the moment when dignity slips, where the ego's armature becomes unravelled.

---

[9]Tommy Mars, interview with the author, 30 October 1993.
[10]Frank Zappa, 'I Have Been in You', *Sheik Yerbouti*, 1979.

Zappa's not-love songs have always symbolized an antagonistic attitude towards his audience; 'I Have Been in You' presaged a new twist, a delight in rubbing the audiences with their own base cravings. 'Dinah-Moe Humm' became the inevitable encore of late 70s concerts, frequently introduced as a 'stupid song'. Unlike most rock acts, Zappa's tight organization meant that he could make money from tours: he talked about having to sing 'Dinah-Moe Humm' a few thousand times in order to afford his orchestral projects.[11] It was played, Ramones-style, increasingly fast, as if to have done with it as soon as possible.

Zappa's post-*Läther* attitude was characterized in the English rock press as 'cynicism', as unhelpful a concept as the idea that instrumental music not geared towards the hit parade is 'self-indulgent'. His own pronouncements were highly contradictory. On *Zappa in New York* he had explained how the music had been played to 'a cosy group of 27,500 deranged fanatics . . . some of the nicest people we have had the experience of playing for (who we also hereby thank). New York last Christmas is what made this album possible.' Like any artist receiving critical flak, he liked to stress the pleasures of the audience versus the objections of those whose opinions got into print. On the other hand, he also developed the concept of stupidity: 'I just think the norm of the universe is stupidity. Stupidity is like hydrogen; it's everywhere, it's the basic building block of the universe.'[12] He said of 'Tryin' to Grow a Chin': 'The song was constructed using every kind of cliché that folk-rock brought to the world – all those stupid bass lines.'[13]

Concerts started to include 'stupid' events, like getting everyone to jump in the air or recite poetry. This argument is reminiscent of Devo, who derive expressive power from conscious reduplication of pop's streamlined alienation. When Zappa performed 'Broken Hearts are for Assholes', he would walk across the stage pointing at members of the audience, singing 'Because you're an asshole and you're an asshole'. Waiting for an autograph backstage at the Hammersmith Odeon, Out Of Gas (Gas Price) encountered members of the audience who wanted to beat up Zappa for 'having insulted them'.

---

[11]Frank Zappa, with Peter Occhiogrosso, *The Real Frank Zappa Book*, 1989, p. 146.
[12]Quoted by Michael Bloom, *Trouser Press*, February 1980.
[13]Quoted by Cherry Ripe, 'Frank Zappa Has No Underwear', *New Musical Express*, 17 April 1976.

FZ: If I feel like playing the guitar I'll play guitar.

JOHN DALTON: *Does this vary much from show to show?*

FZ: Well a lot depends on what kind of circumstance you're working in, what kind of venue and audience it is, whether they want to hear a lot of guitar or just be entertained. I can go both ways, I'm happy to play as much as people want to, but usually people would rather hear songs off a record, hear some words and see some funny stuff. That's what they bought the ticket for, they didn't come to hear a guitar extravaganza. They came to see a guy be a jerk. So great. Give 'em what they want.[14]

This offends the notions of sincerity and self-expression that underlies most post-60s rock and its critical afflatus. Freed from ethical moorings, Zappa's artwork floats in a queasy sea where the illumination it can cast on troubled waters is its sole reward. Instead of underlining ideology, the music promotes consciousness.

People like funny songs, I like funny songs. Why should you have serious songs all the time? That's what's wrong with the whole rock 'n' roll business. Everybody wants to be taken seriously – my art, my craft, my whatever it is. Who gives a fuck? Let's have a good time. But you can have a good time on a lot of different levels. You can laugh, you can listen to something, you can think about it, you can tap your feet, you can scratch your head, you can wonder what the fuck is going on. And then you can form opinions. That's a little bit more like real life.[15]

Bertolt Brecht called it *Verfremdungtechnik*; Zappa calls it funny songs. They both want the audience to observe their art with a certain detachment, an object of thought rather than social confirmation.

SHEIK YERBOUTI

The message of 'Flakes' collapses in on itself because it deftly removes the moral core required for the 'protest' singer. It starts out protesting at the poor quality of service delivered by West Coast businesses, but when the song is turned over to Adrian Belew as Bob Dylan impersonator, the absurdity of a 60s legend like Bob Dylan (or Frank Zappa) *protesting at lack of customer satisfaction* becomes so towering that it blots out the original idea. The degradation of 60s ideals into commercial transactions

---

[14]Quoted by John Dalton, 'Frank Zappa: Shut Up and Play Your Guitar', *Guitar*, May 1979, p. 21.
[15]Quoted by John Dalton, 'Frank Zappa: Part II', *Guitar*, June 1979, p. 26.

becomes a symbol of corporate rock. There is little sympathy for the victims either.

> I'm a moron, 'n' this is my wife
> She's frosting a cake
> With a paper knife
> Everything we got here's
> American made
> It's a little bit cheesey
> But it's nicely displayed[16]

This reflects the theme of useless ornament developed in 'A Little Green Rosetta'. The whole thing ends in a shower of shit.

> Well, the toilet went crazy
> Yesterday afternoon
> The plumber he says,
> *'Never flush a tampoon!'*
> This great information
> Cost me half a week's pay
> And the toilet blew up
> Later on the next day-ay-eee-ay[17]

Zappa is also voicing the kind of indignation you would expect from a well-off Californian. According to him, the flakes are 'protected by unions' and you are so 'greedy' you will probably join them. These are objectively reactionary ideas – the problems of our times caused by 'greedy unions' – but Zappa's delight in satire spares no one, and his own 'protest' is revealed as absurd as the protests of a millionaire like Dylan. 'Flakes' is a vision of the inefficiency of work in the commercial world, where exchange value supersedes use value. Like any good petit-bourgeois, Zappa may believe that personal integrity can make an unworkable system work, but his sharp observations of the current confusion are not hampered by such moralizing.

Patrick O'Hearn's enumeration of S&M tropes on 'Broken Hearts are for Assholes' varies from its previous version. The presence of two keyboard players in the *Sheik Yerbouti* band militates against the organic feel such tunes had on *Läther*: the carefully layered parodic-rock mix of *Sheik Yerbouti* is one of its delights. There is something daft about all this rock fury – and Terry Bozzio is dazzlingly angry on this record – being

---

[16]Frank Zappa, 'Flakes', *Sheik Yerbouti*, 1979.
[17]Ibid.

cross-woven with such rhythmically precise and silly-sounding synthesizers.

'I'm So Cute' is Bozzio's 'punk' showcase, pursuing the cute angel/ugly demon dichotomy used on the cover of *Zoot Allures*. As Zappa used to say from the stage (preserved on *Tinsel Town Rebellion*): 'Well, maybe you're sitting there and you're cute, maybe you're even beautiful, but there's more of us ugly mother-fuckers than you are.'[18]

Side two of *Sheik Yerbouti* is a masterpiece of programming. 'Jones Crusher' is a frenetic combination of rock 'n' roll velocity and castration-complex imagery. *Musique concrète* from *Läther* links into 'Rat Tomago' (tamago is the Japanese for egg; Zappa apparently liked the idea of a rat omelette). This brittle piece of in-yer-face guitar is in a different world from the solos on Mothers of Invention records. On Radio 1 John Peel had the temerity to follow it with some Duane Eddy to show how the guitar 'should' be played, airing punk prejudice against state-of-the-art recorded sound. The guitar sculpts the music and the other instruments coalesce round it. 'We've Got to Get into Something Real' was taken as evidence of creative flagging by some rather literal-minded reviewers[19] as the band talk about needing to come up with 'some new shit', but then Zappa sails in with the gorgeous melody of 'Bobby Brown' as if to demonstrate his limitless inventiveness.

'Bobby Brown' is part of Zappa's politically dubious specu-lation that women's liberation has turned men gay as they find career women 'would be like fucking a slightly more voluptuous version of somebody's father', as Harry-as-a-Boy puts it in *Thing-Fish*.[20] The historical actuality is that the rise of feminism has given the opportunity for all kinds of repressed sexual minorities to voice their identities. However, all considerations of fairness are swept aside in an outpouring of scandalous couplets over a lush, vibrant melody. It does not matter what Zappa actually believes – in *The Real Frank Zappa Book* he talks some half-baked nonsense about the duty of American citizens to breed the next generation – because of his ability to foment all the taboo areas in a single song.

> When I fucked this dyke by the name of Freddie
> She made a little speech then

---

[18]Frank Zappa, 'Dance Contest', *Tinsel Town Rebellion*, 1981.
[19]Brian Case, 'Frank Zappa: *Sheik Yerbouti*', *Melody Maker*, 3 March 1979.
[20]Frank Zappa, 'Harry-as-a-Boy', *Thing-Fish*, 1984.

Aw, she tried to make me say *when*
She had my balls in a vice, but she left the dick
I guess it's still hooked on, but now it shoots too quick[21]

Bobby Brown 'jingles his change' (a witty rephrasing of the album's title) but is 'still kinda cute'. Zappa's declared 'position' on gays and women is ambivalent because he reckons that freak individualism transcends the need for social pressure groups.

> It's as much of a hype as punk rock as far as I'm concerned. Some of the things they wish to achieve are quite noble, but I resent the manner in which they are being advertised. It's not the ideals, it's the packaging. I find it repulsive and think it's an insult to men and demeaning to women.[22]

This is an *aesthetic* repudiation of feminism, suspicious of its use of bourgeois moral categories, and its concomitant reinvention of guilt and sin. 'Bobby Brown' came up as a success in discos, where gay culture is at its strongest: its specific politics were ignored because of the joy of finding a pop record that actually mentions all these things. It does not matter what the explicit message is, the song mentions us therefore we exist – to paraphrase Zappa on teenagers and *The Blackboard Jungle*.[23] Only an idealist politics, one that seeks a sterile enumeration of right-on tenets, a purism more connected with religious ideas of personal morality than politics, could condemn 'Bobby Brown'. As it actually worked in the clubs it was a blow for liberation.

'Bobby Brown' puts the succeeding instrumental in the most lurid light. In the sleeve note Zappa described xenochrony for the first time (though here he calls it 'experimental resynchronization'): he placed a bass solo by Patrick O'Hearn alongside a Terry Bozzio drum part on the multi-track, creating 'interplay' that 'never actually happened'. This is a high-tech version of the kind of experimentation Charles Ives established as an American tradition: while a boy he would sing one hymn while his father played the accompaniment to a different one. In 'Rubber Shirt', the deliberate mismatch produces an extraordinary piece of music. Given the slippery sensuality of O'Hearn's playing, its title seems exceptionally appropriate. Bass notes have always been

---

[21]Frank Zappa, 'Bobby Brown', *Sheik Yerbouti*, 1979.
[22]Quoted by Paul Rambali, 'Stern Words in Knightsbridge', *New Musical Express*, 28 January 1978, p. 25.
[23]Frank Zappa, 'The Oracle Has It All Psyched Out', *Life Magazine*, 1968, reprinted in Dominique Chevalier, *Viva! Zappa*, 1985, p. 94.

associated with the lower parts of the body and the bowels: 'Rubber Shirt' seems to use them with the exploratory pleasure of fistfucking rather than the anal-sadism of Zappa's guitar.

Side two ended with 'The Sheik Yerbouti Tango'. Gay culture has always stressed the flamboyant and exaggerated. Hi-Energy disco frequently uses lopsided gypsy rhythms and tangos. It is no accident that Eartha Kitt – doyen of New Orleans exoticism – had a new lease of life camping it up on disco numbers. Like Zappa with the bouzouki and Bulgarian folk-music (and Coleridge with the *chinoiserie* of 'Kubla Khan'), gays use kitsch and camp to undermine oppressive notions of authenticity. Although Zappa does not adopt gay politics, his 'satirical' interest in gay culture reveals strong affinities.

Side three of *Sheik Yerbouti* presented five rock tracks, only one of which – 'Tryin' to Grow a Chin' – had appeared on *Läther*. 'City of Tiny Lites', previously a vehicle for Ray White's gospel voice, was now adopted by Adrian Belew.

> City of tiny lites
> Don't you wanna go . . .
> Tiny blankets
> Keep you warm
> Tiny pillows
> Tiny sheets
> Talkin' 'bout those tiny cookies
> That the people eats . . .
> Every cloud is silver line-y
> The great escape for all of you[24]

This is satire of private wish-fulfilment worlds – whether induced by drugs or holy communion or even records – similar to that of Philip K. Dick's 'The Days of Perky Pat',[25] in which miserable Martian colonists housed in spartan domes called 'hovels' chew a drug named 'Can-D' and inhabit the 'Perky Pat' doll in her doll house. The cover of *Zappa in New York*, by reducing parked cars in the city to electronic circuits, conveyed a similar idea of miniaturization.

> Maybe you should know
> That it's over there
> In the tiny dirt somewhere[26]

---

[24] Frank Zappa, 'City of Tiny Lites', *Sheik Yerbouti*, 1979.
[25] Philip K. Dick, 'The Days of Perky Pat', 1963, *The Days of Perky Pat Collected Stories Vol. 4*, 1987, a story later incorporated into *The Three Stigmata of Palmer Eldritch*, 1964.
[26] Frank Zappa, 'City of Tiny Lites', *Sheik Yerbouti*, 1979.

This implies that it is in the parts of the environment considered to be *without* value that the truth is to be found: the suppressed realities of the body that Zappa – along with Freud – always returns to.[27]

'Dancin' Fool' mocked the disco syndrome, while 'Jewish Princess' was a leering song of lust that focused on non-Aryan body traits. The Anti-Defamation League of the B'nai B'rith demanded an apology.

> They asked me to apologize and I refused. I still have their letter nailed to the wall. They got a lot of mileage out of it, but it was a tempest in a teapot. They just wanted to give the impression that here, in the world of rock, was this rabid anti-Semite who was besmirching the reputation of everybody in the Jewish faith. Well, I didn't make up the idea of a Jewish princess. They exist, so I wrote a song about them. If they don't like it, so what? Italians have princesses, too.[28]

Critical opinion was divided on the song. Brian Case said: 'Maybe I'm missing some subtle indictment of racialism and sexism, but "Jewish Princess" seemed to me to fall midway between Julius Streicher and the Mailer of *The Time of Her Time*.'[29] In the *New Musical Express* Nick Kent said it would be anti-Semitic 'if it weren't so damn feckless'.[30] Hugh Fielder in *Sounds* called it 'another lascivious ballad in praise of Frank's ideal woman'.[31] The instrumentation seems to be massed kazoos – or comb-and-paper: the whole thing sounds like a rude mouth noise.

Awright, back to the top ... everybody twist![32]

Zappa's response to the flak was to write a song about Catholic girls 'with a tiny little moustache' commemorating his own racial type, a typically obtuse response to liberal condemnation. Abstractly, 'Jewish Princess' is an extension of the theme of Near Eastern exoticism that imbues both the music and the cover. 'With

[27]This recalls variously: 'secret smut & lost metal money', 'Sofa No. 2', *One Size Fits All*, 1975; 'And so slowness is / interesting and the dust, in cracks between / boards . . . Fluff, grit, various / discarded bits & pieces: these are the / genetic patrons of our so-called condition', Jeremy Prynne, 'A Gold Ring Called Reluctance', *Kitchen Poems*, 1968, *Poems*, 1982, p. 22; and Paul Hession's notorious statement, 'I'm attracted to dirt', sleeve note to Hession/Wilkinson/Fell, *foom! foom!*, 1992, Bruce's Fingers BF5, which caused him to be compared to the sewage-cleaning robot Ro-Jaws from the *2000AD* strip 'ABC Warriors'.
[28]Quoted by David Sheff, 'Frank Zappa Interview', *Playboy*, February 1993, p. 59. Much the same point is made in Frank Zappa, with Peter Occhiogrosso, *The Real Frank Zappa Book*, 1989, pp. 225–6.
[29]Brian Case, 'Frank Zappa: *Sheik Yerbouti*', *Melody Maker*, 3 March 1979.
[30]Nick Kent, 'Overly Sub-Standard', *New Musical Express*, 3 March 1979.
[31]Hugh Fielder, 'Up Yours', *Sounds*, 10 March 1979, p. 36.
[32]Frank Zappa, 'Jewish Princess', *Sheik Yerbouti*, 1979.

a garlic aroma that could level Tacoma' is replicated in the extraordinarily cheesy instrumentation: as with the S&M images that precede 'Rubber Shirt', 'Jewish Princess' supplies the imagery for 'Rat Tomago' and 'The Sheik Yerbouti Tango'. According to Zappa, Vinnie Colaiuta has an expression, 'It has no *garlic* in it',[33] for bland, academically correct music; Zappa's music is garlic all the way.

> To specifically happen with a pee-pee that's snappin' . . .
> With Roumanian thighs, who weasels 'n' lies
> For two or three nights
> Won't someone send me a princess who bites[34]

The fade-out connects the Jewish Princess to the poodle who bites and snaps on the fade-out to 'Dirty Love'. The poodle represents the site of punished nature: 'Jewish Princess' extends that to ideas of race and sex. Adorno was convinced that anti-Semitism found in Jews a scapegoat, a container for all their repressions. Psychoanalysis of racist rhetoric bears that out.

In *Enemy of the Stars*, Wyndham Lewis has the Aryan hero Arghol say to his sidekick, the 'jewbeaked' Hanp: 'I found I wanted to make a naif yapping poodle-parasite of you.'[35] Zappa is tracing similar patterns. In Zappa's unconscious schema the poodle/princess *bites*: the zero becomes a mouth, sprouts teeth and threatens the oppressor with *vagina dentata*. As it went in 'Jones Crusher':

> Deadly jaws, better get the gauze[36]

Or the vice Freddie the dyke applied to Bobby Brown's balls. The panic and urgency of *Sheik Yerbouti* derives from these anxieties.

It is not pleasant to deal with texts that the Anti-Defamation League is calling anti-Semitic. However, 'Jewish Princess' extends the scope of *Sheik Yerbouti* so that it covers issues of desire and bodily difference and exoticism. Zappa refuses to adopt a conscious, abstract politics that would prevent his intuitive research. It is not a matter of 'justifying' his excesses. As Theodor Adorno wrote:

> The central concern is not social justification, but the establishment of

---

[33]Frank Zappa, 'Absolutely Frank: Putting Some Garlic in Your Playing', *Guitar Player*, December 1982.
[34]Frank Zappa, 'Jewish Princess', *Sheik Yerbouti*, 1979.
[35]Wyndham Lewis, *Enemy of the Stars*, 1932, p. 9.
[36]Frank Zappa, 'Jones Crusher', *Sheik Yerbouti*, 1979.

social theory by virtue of explication of aesthetic right or wrong lying at the very heart of the objects which are property.[37]

It would weaken Zappa's exploration of the social aspect of the music he uses – the pull of the non-Western, the working of lust – to remove this inclusion of the Jewish question.

Side four consists of two tunes: 'Wild Love' and 'Yo' Mama'. 'Wild Love' is a reflection on changed sexual customs, delivered with documentary objectivity. When Zappa said why he liked 'funny songs' that let the audience form their own opinions, he explained that this was in preference to 'have somebody dump their emotional freight on your doorstep and tell you about their broken heart or how they feel about wind blowing and leaves falling off trees. That's crap.'[38]

'Wild Love' takes words straight out of that comment.

> Many well-dressed people
> In several locations
> Are kissing quite a bit
> Later in the evening
> Leaves will fall
> Tears will flow
> Wind will blow
> Some rain, some snow[39]

Carefully orchestrated with hip chord changes and a slick, upbeat swing reminiscent of Steely Dan, the song contrasts the 'days of long ago' when couples would not go all the way and now, when

> Now'days you get dressed up
> 'N' later you get messed up
> But still you're pretty hip[40]

concluding 'But who's to say/Where it will go'. It is as if the removal of sexual taboos has taken the meaning from sex.

'Yo' Mama', a song dedicated to a road manager who did not make the grade, tells him to retreat to maternal shelter. Like 'Wild Love' the song asserts an objective viewpoint. Zappa delivers some of his most extreme guitar (according to the notes, it was taken from a performance at Nürnberg and applied xenochronously over a different rhythm – Mars recalls welding together three separate solos). The accompaniment seems entirely conjured up by his

[37]Theodor Adorno, *The Philosophy of Modern Music*, 1948, p. 26.
[38]Quoted by John Dalton, 'Frank Zappa: Part II', *Guitar*, June 1979, p. 26.
[39]Frank Zappa, 'Wild Love', *Sheik Yerbouti*, 1979.
[40]Ibid.

playing, but it was actually down to a lot of hard work on the part of Tommy Mars.

> That piece fuelled me for years. When people say, What's the heaviest thing you've ever done musically? and you're talking to a guy that's played all the war-horses of classical music, I've played *concerti* with different orchestras . . . I couldn't believe that I was a compositional part of this! It's like when you put a freeway together, you have to chop down this section of woods, you have to drill through that granite, you have to cross this water to get where you're going. He just had this idea of these three guitar solos and it was just like that. One of the most difficult parts on that was where it came back to the tune, the notes that Patrick played in that part of the show, there's a lot of poetic license there, nearly impossible, the number of takes I had to do on the mini-moog to fit what he was doing and then reorchestrate chords over that which would fit![41]

Some of the most exciting moments in modern classical music – Varèse, Boulez, Stockhausen – develop an extraordinary objectivity, a hugeness of event like quasars exploding in space. Zappa's solo is like that. Because Zappa is so astute at selecting the icons that stimulate and upset, there is a tendency to read off his music as expressionist. The solo on 'Yo' Mama' serves as a reminder of the objectness of art. Zappa is an artist who arranges material, leaving us to draw our own conclusions.

NEW MUSICIANS: CUCURULLO, SHANKAR, WILLIS

The revelation of the first 1979 tour was Warren Cucurullo from Brooklyn (whom Zappa introduced at Hammersmith, confusingly, as 'Sophia Warren'). He originally approached Zappa as a dedicated fan; he actually knew how to play more of Zappa's back-catalogue than most of Zappa's musicians and had learned to play all of Zappa's solos.[42] His cassettes impressed Zappa, but he was so young Zappa told him to come back in a few years. His technique is absolutely astonishing. A faster player than Zappa, he plays as rhythmically out, but picks each note cleanly, giving a hard-edge new-wave feel to his solos. Their contrasting approach meant that they could play together successfully: their duet on 18

---

[41]Tommy Mars, interview with the author, 30 October 1993.
[42]Tom Mulhern, 'I'm Different', *Guitar Player*, reprinted in *Society Pages*, No. 14, February 1983, p. 10.

February (second show) at the Hammersmith Odeon ('Pound for a Brown') was devastating.

In 1980 Bozzio, O'Hearn and Cucurullo formed Missing Persons – new wave as conceived by West Coast musos. The lead singer, Dale, was Bozzio's wife, and appeared on *Joe's Garage*, Zappa's next recording project. Zappa cited Bozzio's tenure as the fourth stage in a recording career he divided into five.

> The earliest five albums definitely owe their sound and their attitude to the personalities of the people who played on them. Not only their physical performances, but their aura. Included on those sessions were Roy Estrada and Ray Collins. The next incarnation was with Mark Volman and Howard Kaylan, then George Duke and Ruth Underwood, a series of bands featuring Terry Bozzio on drums and the latest line-up is with Vinnie Colaiuta in the seat and Warren Cucurullo on rhythm guitar.[43]

As it became obvious that Zappa's band changed year by year, other figures appeared. Born in Madras on 26 April 1950, Lakshminarayana Shankar was singing ragas at the age of two and started lessons with his father on violin at age five (his father is V. Lakshminarayana, the violinist, not Ravi Shankar, the sitar player, as widely reported). In 1969 he moved to the States and took a degree in ethnomusicology at the Wesleyan University and played with Ornette Coleman and Jimmy Garrison, Coltrane's bass player. In 1973 he began working with the English guitarist John McLaughlin, then in *Love, Devotion & Surrender* phase, under the tutelage of Guru Sri Chinmoy. In 1975 they formed Shakti in order to play an acoustic jazz-Indian classical fusion. Shakti broke up in 1978. That year Shankar played duets with Zappa in New York at the Palladium on Halloween.[44]

Zappa likes to solo within a static harmonic environment – he has expressed a distaste for the busy chord progressions of bop – and his interest in extended rhythmic patterns has an affinity for Indian music. L. Shankar and Zappa played scorching music together. Zappa produced a record for Shankar called *Touch Me There*. It used respected British rock session musicians, but apart from Shankar's slurring, sly violin sound (and the incongruity of an ex-McLaughlin musician collaborating with the author of 'Cosmik Debris', which attacked Sri Chinmoy), it had little to

---

[43]Quoted by Paul Colbert, 'Frank Zappa', *Musicians Only*, 26 January 1980, p. 15.
[44]His playing on 'Thirteen' and 'Take Your Clothes Off When You Dance' appears on *You Can't Do That on Stage Anymore Vol. 6*, 1992.

recommend it. The musicians do not seem to seem to pick up on his playing beyond an ability to get faster and louder on the solos.

Zappa contributed 'Dead Girls of London', a typical bit of deadpan social critique. Van Morrison had telephoned Zappa, asking if he would like to use his voice, and was duly recorded on it. When his manager got difficult, he was offered half the publishing, but permission was still not forthcoming. During the lawsuit Zappa had toured with a 'Warners sucks' banner and had not maintained industry protocol to interviewers: according to Zappa, Mo Ostin of Warner Brothers personally scuppered the deal.[45] Morrison's singing was actually not quite right for the song:[46] his soulman's bark sounded too upset, as if the song was tragedy rather than a tease. In the end Zappa and Ike Willis did better (under the name Stucco Homes), full of leering, distended vowel sounds and 'foo-ee', Willis's currently favoured exclamation. Ike Willis was a crucial discovery.

> I met Ike at an outdoor college concert we did in St Louis. He was one of the student roadies. He had a summer job on a garbage truck and played on the football team. He said he played guitar and sang, and the guy was great! He just sings his ass off, it's fantastic. I told him at that time that when we were having auditions, I'd bring him out.[47]

On Willis's English début at Knebworth on 9 September 1978, one missed the leather-tonsil gospel power of Ray White's voice for a song like 'Bamboozled by Love', but on *Joe's Garage* his subtlety and adaptability were virtuosic.

JOE'S GARAGE

The session for *Joe's Garage* started out with the intention of recording a single ('Joe's Garage' c/w 'Catholic Girls') and ended up with seventeen songs and a triple concept album. By improvising (in the space of a single weekend[48]) a story loosely based on the life-story of a musician, Zappa constructed a parable of music in hard times that was both touching and ridiculous. As usual with a Zappa release, the sound of the record was radically

[45]Christopher Kathman, 'Who Else But Zappa Still Plays for the Ugly People', *Sounds*, 16 September 1979, p. 3.
[46]It appeared on the bootleg *Leatherette*.
[47]Christopher Kathman, 'Who Else But Zappa Still Plays for the Ugly People', *Sounds*, 16 September 1979, p. 3.
[48]Paul Colbert, 'Frank Zappa', *Musicians Only*, 26 January 1980, p. 15.

different from its predecessor. Instead of the elaborate rock frenzy of *Sheik Yerbouti*, drums were recorded with the spacious resonance of contemporary soul records. *Sheik Yerbouti* used live recordings as basic tracks; *Joe's Garage* tracks were built up in the studio using 'just Wurlitzer, bass and rhythm guitar'.[49] Instead of the edgy discipline of live rock and its coherent blasts of power, riffs begin during the interminable whisperings of the Central Scrutinizer, fade out into theatrical cameos. The slithering freedom of elements used in 'I Have Been in You' has become the entire sonic universe.

The guitar solos on *Joe's Garage* were live playing Zappa isolated on tape and then applied over the studio rhythm tracks (the engineer called it 'the Nagra guitar' because all Zappa would do was turn the switch on the tape machine).

> I came back with a stereo Nagra tape of just guitar solos and thought of songs where they could go. You try to find something that's in the same key but the time signature could be different. In 'Packard Goose' the backing is in 4/4 and the solo was played in 15/16 in a totally different tempo. It was from the last show in Zurich during a song called 'Easy Meat'. The solo in 'Keep It Greasey' – the rhythm background I think is in 21/16 and the guitar is in 11/4. The beats come together about once a month.[50]

This use of chance resembles the procedures of John Cage and the fold-in of William Burroughs: although it provocatively challenges notions of intention, it does so in such circumstances that there is no doubt as to the character of the composer. Every element is so original, so patently Zappa-esque, that random recombination merely sparks further possibilities: the xenochronous guitar solo 'Toad-O Line'[51] is one of Zappa's greatest pieces of music.

On the infectious sleaze of 'Crew Slut' (an update of 'Motherly Love'), Dale Bozzio's voice has the strangely affecting, undefended quality that characterized Zappa's snatches of dialogue from Suzy Creamcheese and the GTOs. The difference is that we know she's acting: the whole of *Joe's Garage* is marked by an aspect of charade ('It's sort of like a really cheap kind of high-school play . . .' runs the liner note), emphasized by Zappa's appearance on the cover in black-face and holding a mop. Professionally involved with the cycle of tours and recordings, Zappa finds it harder to achieve

---

[49]Ibid.
[50]Ibid.
[51]Renamed 'On the Bus' on the CD, 1989.

the documentary realism of the early days. The free-floating nature of the music seems to be the perfect corollary of this postmodern dilemma.

'Wet T-Shirt Nite'[52] is satire of American night-life inanity that makes 'America Drinks and Goes Home' sound like a demo. As Buddy Jones, Zappa uses the front of the gross MC to stir all kinds of ghosts. Mary wants the fifty bucks so she can get home: 'Yeh, I know, your father is waiting for you in the tool shed,' recalls Magdalena and the sexual abuse she received from her father. 'Ain't this what living is really all about?' pokes out of the shambles like the question, 'Is this waste of time what makes a life for you?' on *Greggery Peccary*. 'Sounds like you just got an ice pick in the forehead' refers to Zappa's description of the sound of the R&B guitarists he admires: the 'ice-pick in the forehead tone' of Guitar Slim and Johnny 'Guitar' Watson. Absurd to mention Leon Trotsky's demise in this context, but it is there for those who see a connection between the silenced opponent of both Stalin and capitalism and the issues of censorship and suppression in *Joe's Garage*.

Gazing out into his increasingly young audience, Zappa seems to have had a pretty dim view of his function as an entertainer. The position had not really changed much since 'You're Probably Wondering Why I'm Here' on *Freak Out!*. Tim Schneckloth of *Down Beat* said to him in 1978 that he must have kept his original audience, 'people who are around thirty now'.

> Some of them still come to our concerts. But usually they don't, because now that they have wives, kids, mortgages, day jobs and all the rest of that stuff, they don't want to stand around in a hockey rink and be puked on by some sixteen-year-old who's full of reds. So consequently, our audience gets younger and younger. We've picked up a larger number of female audience participants and there's an increase in black attendance.[53]

A note for 'Wet T-Shirt Nite' describes Zappa's rap as MC.

> BUDDY JONES, like a true WET T-SHIRT EMCEE type person, proceeds to say various stupid things to waste time, making the contest itself take longer, thereby giving the mongoloids squatting on the dance floor an opportunity to buy more exciting beverages . . . liquid products

---

[52]Renamed 'Fembot in a Wet T-Shirt' on the CD, 1989.
[53]Quoted by Tim Schneckloth, 'Garni Du Jour, Lizard King Poetry and Slime', *Down Beat*, 18 May 1978, p. 16.

that will expand their consciousness to the point whereby they might more fully enjoy the ambiance of *Miami by Night* . . .[54]

Buddy Jones's 'stupid' act corresponds almost precisely to Zappa's onstage demeanour at the time. Whereas *Freak Out!* had celebrated the 'hungry freaks', 'Wet T-Shirt Nite' characterized the audience as *craving*, with its (etymologically unsubstantiated) resonance of *craven* (defeated, subservient, crawling).

> 'Cause the sign outside says it's WET T-SHIRT NIGHT
> 'N' they all crave some pink delight . . .
> 'N' all of the fellas, they wish they could bite
> On the cute little nuggets
> The local girls are showin' off tonite
> You know I think it serves them right[55]

Contrasting studio and live work, Zappa said: 'On stage you get one shot at it and also you have the audience and their craving and need to be entertained at all costs.'[56]

At concerts the presence of other guitarists – Ike Willis, Warren Cucurullo, Denny Walley – meant that Zappa only needed to play on his solos. He would sit on a stool to the side, drink coffee, light up a Winston. Some people thought he looked bored and disengaged, though he said he was actually listening to the music his band was playing. He would also pick up a microphone and talk to the audience, a practice he described as 'walking around with a microphone being a buffoon'.[57] This ambivalence towards the *value* of his art offended rock critics. It transgresses an unwritten law of all those involved in the industry, which is to guarantee the status of the commodities they are pushing. Unlike rice and soap, the use value of art is conceptual: the music industry is built around guaranteeing that product has meaning, when precisely being made product devalues it.

Attentive listening to 'Wet T-Shirt Nite' reveals a quite astonishing passage of scored music ('They all crave some pink delight'). It flashes by with the illusionistic grace of Nancarrow or Braxton: really taxing work for Ed Mann, whose skill here is incredible. Naturally, such moments were forgotten in the general indignation about the subject matter. Although Zappa has no time

---

[54]Sleeve-note to Frank Zappa, 'Wet T-Shirt Nite', *Joe's Garage Act I*, 1979.
[55]Frank Zappa, 'Wet T-Shirt Nite', *Joe's Garage Act I*, 1979.
[56]Quoted by Paul Colbert, 'Frank Zappa', *Musicians Only*, 26 January 1980, p. 15.
[57]Quoted by John Dalton, 'Frank Zappa: Shut Up and Play Your Guitar', *Guitar*, May 1979, p. 21.

for the limitations of good taste, he is not unconcerned with sexism.

> Our big prize tonight is fifty American Dollars to the girl with the most exciting *mammalian protuberances* as viewed through a thoroughly soaked, stupid looking white sort of male person's conservative kind of middle-of-the-road COTTON UNDER-GARMENT! Whoopee![58]

The description shows literally how the female is viewed in the wet T-shirt contest, but also, by metaphorical extension, sociologically: through drunk, stupid, white, male, conservative, middle-of-the-road eyes. Zappa uses the wet T-shirt contest in a 'philistine' manner in order to denigrate idealism (though it should be noted that, despite his impatience with feminist prescriptions, Zappa has never used visual images of women to sell records). But he *also* uses the wet T-shirt contest to criticize his audience. It cuts both ways: the listener cannot help being tempted by the idea of looking at Dale Bozzio's breasts. Like 'The Torture Never Stops', Zappa is concerned to implicate the listener in the stupidities he condemns. There is no moral way out – but that is the point.

Like *Läther*, it is the interface between private and public that hinges the whole project. Speaking through a cheap plastic megaphone which is only abandoned on side four, Zappa is 'The Central Scrutinizer' who explains:

> It is my responsibility to enforce all the laws that haven't been passed yet. It is also my responsibility to alert each and every one of you to the potential causes of various ordinary everyday activities you might be performing which could eventually lead to *The Death Penalty* (or affect your parents' credit rating).[59]

Zappa was involved in real-life controversy over such issues when he appeared versus Judith Toth at the State Senate proceedings in 1987 (dialogue included in *Video from Hell*): 'This is talking about human masturbation as an *"illicit sexual act"* [*Laughter*].'[60] Zappa is addressing the issue of morality and its use by the right as justification for repressive legislation. 'The Central Scrutinizer' is a parody of the super-ego or conscience, the voice of social authority in the individual: 'Sometimes when you're not looking he just sneaks up on you.'[61]

This is like the force that Howard Kaylan denounces during

---

[58] Frank Zappa, 'Wet T-Shirt Nite', *Joe's Garage Act I*, 1979.
[59] Frank Zappa, 'The Central Scrutinizer', *Joe's Garage Act I*, 1979.
[60] Frank Zappa, with Peter Occhiogrosso, *The Real Frank Zappa Book*, 1989, p. 285.
[61] Frank Zappa, sleeve note to 'The Central Scrutinizer', *Joe's Garage Act I*, 1979.

'Strictly Genteel' on *200 Motels*: Zappa himself. As Jonathan Jones explains it:

> Zappa positions himself as the organizing Intelligence, overseeing and mastering his monstrous creations. He orchestrates a travesty of power, like that other humbug controller, the Wizard of Oz, who also hid behind voices.[62]

'Why Does It Hurt When I Pee?' was inspired by a road manager's howl of pain in the toilet of the tour bus. On 'Lucille Has Messed My Mind Up' Ike Willis adopts his best modern-soulman tones, exploring some of the unusual parts of the throat brought to public attention by Will Downing in the early 80s.

In the sleeve note to *Joe's Garage Act I* (issued as a 'taster' for the double album *Acts II & III*), Zappa refers to developments in Iran, then in the grip of Khomeini's counter-revolution.

> If the plot of the story seems just a little bit preposterous, and if the idea of *The Central Scrutinizer* enforcing laws that haven't been passed yet makes you giggle, just be glad that you don't live in one of the cheerful little countries where, at this very moment, music is severely restricted . . . or, as it is in Iran, totally illegal.[63]

The popular upsurge that toppled the Shah shook world imperialism, but due to the pusillanimity of the Moscow-controlled Communist Party, which failed to argue for any independent, socialist, working-class politics, leadership of the revolution fell into the hands of the mullahs and fundamentalists. Ayatollah Khomeini arrived from exile and proceeded to impose bourgeois 'order', reviving the secret police and many of the worst aspects of the Shah's regime. He cultivated popular opinion by condemning all aspects of 'Western decadence', which included cabaret pop, the Turkish-inflected Euro-disco played in over 500 nightclubs in pre-revolutionary Tehran.

In the early 80s Ronald Reagan used fear of Islamic fundamentalism as a replacement for an increasingly less credible communist threat. Elsewhere, by connecting Islamic fundamentalism to the Christian variety Zappa recovered a critical, anti-nationalist stance.[64] Certainly Khomeini's suppression of music – not just Yankee disco, but also Persian classical music according to Shu Sha, an Iranian musician who was interviewed by the *New Musical*

---

[62]Jonathan Jones, 'A World of Secret Hungers', *Eonta*, Vol. 2, No. 2, July/August, 1993.
[63]Sleeve note to Frank Zappa, *Joe's Garage Act I*, 1979.
[64]Frank Zappa, 'Dumb All Over', *You Are What You Is*, 1981.

Express in 1980[65] – showed how suspiciously music is viewed by authoritarian regimes. *Joe's Garage*, inspired by Zappa's experiences with Warner Brothers, showed how the dictates of commercialism have a tendency to operate in the same way.

> A guy from a company we can't name
> Said we oughta take his pen
> 'N' sign on the line for a real good time
> But he didn't tell us when
> These 'good times' would be somethin'
> That was really happenin'
> So the band broke up
> An' it looks like we will never play again...[66]

This is the experience of countless bands who want to play, but whose music does not suit the record company strategies for maximizing profits. Despite Zappa's paranoid view that punk was a creation of the music industry working in tandem with journalists and bands (instead of the conflict it actually was), Zappa indicts the same conditions punk protested.

Joe's Garage Acts II & III arrived as a double-album package. Artwork throughout was by John Williams, who had done interior layout for both *Hot Rats* and *Burnt Weeny Sandwich*. In *Act I* he took up the liner-note theme of music's reliance on the oil industry (Zappa was suggesting that the US government might use the oil shortage to justify the abolition of music, pointing out that records are made of oil) with diagrams that connected fossils, oilwells, tankers, records, stylus technology and the listening ear. 'You are here' read a note, pointing at a house without windows.

Opposite this diagram was a collage that assembled icons of art and science from ancient Egypt to submarines and (wrong way up) Japanese characters. It included a nineteenth-century *odalisque*, a flying boat, a diagram of a tooth, medieval lute tablature, Zappa's face in various degrees of close-up (in one his mouth is surrounded by anemone tendrils) and a sequence from Eadweard Muybridge's famous nineteenth-century photographic study of movement. As Linda Williams has pointed out,[67] Muybridge's scientific use of photography to find out about the body begs the question of pornography. Curiosity and the thirst for knowledge immediately foment criticism of social restraints. These images

[65]Andrew Tyler, 'Working for the Clampdown', *New Musical Express*, 22 March 1980.
[66]Frank Zappa, 'Joe's Garage', *Joe's Garage Act I*, 1979.
[67]Linda Williams, *Hard Core*, 1992, p. 36.

imply that *Joe's Garage* puts at stake nothing less than the whole of the accumulated knowledge of civilization.

The lyric sheet included thematic illustrations: guitar and saxophone, a Central Scrutinizer made of collaged nineteenth-century engravings, a Dodge, a Fender Champ amplifier. The full-page spread showed men in gas masks and overalls from the 1930s, a map of America with a mysterious footprint and, like the back cover of *Overnite Sensation*, a floating doughnut (the one given to Joe by his counsellors after his brush with the law). On the back of the lyric sheet John Williams uses his characteristic thought-bubble technique to show a doctor thinking of world domination as he surveys a patient on an examination table (presumably Joe with his 'unpronounceable disease').

The photograph (by Norm Seeff) selected for the cover of *Acts II & III* is especially inspired, showing a woman removing the black-face paint from Zappa's eyes. On the left her red fingernails recall the dummy's hand on the cover of *Burnt Weeny Sandwich* in Cal Schenkel's collage, and which pokes up below the M of 'Mothers' in the *Money* tableau. Zappa has always had images of hands entering his visuals, indicating the manipulated nature of his art. This is like a photo-realist version of the threat of *Uncle Meat*, as we fear Zappa will receive a poke in the eye. This interference with body space, a tension about inside and outside, runs throughout *Joe's Garage*, but in a manner so different from the chattering bare bones of *Uncle Meat* the similarity is easy to miss.

Inside, John Williams again uses the idea of the product flow-chart. A man in industrial protective goggles (presumably L. Ron Hoover) disseminates power via robots, a propagandist indoctrinating via the school room and television, finally reaching an array of lower life-forms: beetles, flies and an anenome. Facing it is a head taken from a medical picture where the face tissue has become transparent: we can see the sinus cavities and teeth beneath nose and lips, a return to the horrors of Zappa's childhood radium 'treatment'. He is surrounded by torn scraps of *Act I*'s collage, iced muffins and a green rosetta. This is a pictorial equivalent to the closing track, 'A Little Green Rosetta', where Zappa throws up all the elements of his music in an improvised live event.

The lyric sheet pursued the thought bubble method to link its images. A brilliant sequence shows a doctor using a catheter to examine a man's penis while thinking of spraying DDT; meanwhile a man disinfecting a toilet thinks of a salami. John Williams's connections are as tenuous as the Central Scrutinizer's narrative links between songs, but similarly revolve around the ideas of work, daydreams, domestic chores, physical abuse vented on the body – the strange connections between things in the unconscious mind.

Side one of *Acts II and III* starts with 'A Token of My Extreme', a song Beefheart sang with the Mothers in 1975. Here it is sung by Frank Zappa as L. Ron Hoover of the First Church of Appliantology. This is in the line of Zappa's great onslaughts on mysticism, from 'Absolutely Free'[68] to 'Oh No'[69] and 'Cosmik Debris'.[70] Fusion players, looking to extend Coltrane's ideas as well as his music, frequently found in Scientology a religious package that corresponded to their own commodification of Trane's musical quest. Here Zappa poses as an alternative Hubbard.

> Don't you be Tarot-fied
> It's just a token of my extreme
> Don't you ever try to look behind my eyes
> You don't wanna know what they have seen[71]

Throwing a 'mean Tarot' was one of Camarillo Brillo's accomplishments, part of her panoply of hippie junk. Zappa advises us to be neither terrified nor mystified by his art. The lines about his eyes recall the final scene of *200 Motels*, which repeatedly cut to Zappa's staring eye: the idea of some enormity that lies behind the everyday surface. L. Ron Hoover persuades Joe to give him fifty bucks in order to go to the Closet and find a sex appliance. He will need to learn German (a reference to German high-tech manufacturers who fail to provide manuals in English). L. Ron Hoover concludes:

> If you been *Mod-O-fied*,
> It's an illusion, an' yer in between
> Don't you be *Tarot-fied*,
> It's just a lot of nothin', so what can it mean?[72]

Zappa is talking of his art again, something that is meant to provoke questions and then self-destruct.

'Stick It Out' was originally part of the sofa routine performed

[68]Frank Zappa, 'Absolutely Free', *We're Only in It for the Money*, 1968.
[69]Frank Zappa, 'Oh No', *Weasels Ripped My Flesh*, 1969.
[70]Frank Zappa, 'Cosmik Debris', *Apostrophe (')*, 1974.
[71]Frank Zappa, 'A Token of My Extreme', *Joe's Garage Acts II & III*, 1979.
[72]Ibid.

by Flo & Eddie in 1971, the song God's girlfriend sings to Squat the Magical Pig. It also includes some lines from 'Latex Solar Beef':

Feel the steam
Touch the steam
Hear the steam
Feel the steaming hot black screaming
Iridescent naugahyde python gleaming
Steam roller[73]

'Steam' becomes 'chrome', as Joe is now singing the song to 'a cross between an industrial vacuum cleaner and a chrome piggy bank with marital aids stuck all over its body'. The tune develops a pounding disco beat of quite awesome brutality. Zappa is parodying Giorgio Moroder's self-consciously mechanized disco music (at the time running high in the charts), but he is also referring to the allure of the inorganic, the confusion between object and person incumbent in a commodity system. Just to make sure non-disco listeners are not left off the hook, it also lays bare our relationship to the record player: when we emote to recorded music we are responding emotionally to a mechanical device. It is like Pierre Boulez pointing out that people who listen to a record of Tchaikovsky are in fact listening to electronic music. Zappa is bringing to consciousness aspects of modern music-listening that are suppressed by those who wish to treat the medium as transparent, value-free, natural.

'Sy Borg' has the appliance give Joe a blow-job, Peter Wolf's keyboard solo reaching the same tingling extremity as 'I Promise Not to Come in Your Mouth'.[74] The general critical opinion was that the surrounding words ruined an otherwise 'beautiful' piece of music; actually, the idea of oral sex performed by a machine corresponds very precisely to being ravished by the beauty of a synthesizer solo etched into a piece of black plastic.

'Dong Work for Yuda' was about Zappa's bodyguard John Smothers and his habitual mispronunciations: a delight in non-communication, the substance of language rather than its ideational content, which resurfaced in the language of *Thing-Fish*. The critical consensus was that this delight is childish, and indeed it is, and so is *Finnegans Wake*. In adopting the communicative networks

---

[73]Frank Zappa, 'Latex Solar Beef', *Fillmore East June 1971*, 1971, as transcribed (Corrected by Zappa) in *Frank Zappa Plastic People Songbuch (Corrected Copy)*, 1977.
[74]Frank Zappa, 'I Promise Not to Come in Your Mouth', *Zappa in New York*, 1977.

of the adult world people sacrifice infantile, immediate pleasures for social power: precisely what so much modern art reneges on. Where the real world deals in tokens, an ever-delayed postponement of fulfilment that in capitalism assures profits for the few, modern art wants its pleasure now. Conventional rock criticism (postmodern or merely dim) has not looked favourably on such insistence on the material of speech and sound, but from a materialist point of view, it is a sign of the integrity of the art object.

After plooking the sex appliance to death and finding he cannot pay for it, Joe is sent to prison, where he is gang-banged by record executives: 'Keep It Greasey' (this song that does not quite fit the continuity, as it is in the vein of 'The Legend of the Illinois Enema Bandit', an advertisement for heterosexual anality). He emerges from the fray with 'Outside Now'. Its words were extraordinarily resonant when the song was performed out of its narrative context, as it was in both the 1980 and 1988 tours.

> These executives have plooked the fuck out of me
> And there's still a long time to go
> Before I've paid my debt to society . . .
> I'll dwindle off into the twilight realm
> Of my own secret thoughts
> I'll lay on my back here 'til dawn
> In a semi-catatonic state
> And dream of guitar notes
> That would irritate an executive kinda guy[75]

Zappa then played some scabrously low notes. In *200 Motels* Jeff Simmons (played by Martin Lickert) says the secret of commercial success is to sing high (advice proved accurate by the Bee Gees' subsequent success); here a sleeve note mentions that only high squealy guitar notes get to be hits (unless it is Duane Eddy). This dichotomy between high and low repeats the contrast between beautiful and ugly in Zappa's reverse-psychology commercialism.

As Joe sings repeatedly:

> I can't wait to see what it's like
> On the outside now . . . [76]

The meaning of 'outside now' drifts from 'outside the prison' to 'outside now' in terms of time: outside the present. The phrase sums up the net impact of the xenochronous guitar solos, which

[75]Frank Zappa, 'Outside Now', *Joe's Garage Acts II & III*, 1979.
[76]Ibid.

phrase according to a different time zone than the 'now' of the backing. In 'Canarsie' on *Shut Up 'N Play Yer Guitar* Zappa was asked to 'identify your last port of entry, space wanderer'. Zappa speculated to John Swenson that only ESP could explain how the band could come together after such lengthy detours when playing live.[77] On 'Outside Now' it is even harder to explain, because he is 'actually' soloing to a different backing. Xenochrony is technological recognition of the expanded potential of comprehension in the modern listener, a simultaneity already promised by the overlayered tempos of Eric Dolphy's *Out to Lunch* and Ornette Coleman's free jazz. In the fanzine *T'Mershi Duween* Matt Galaher's column, 'Statistical Density,' regularly transcribes xenochronic 'coincidences' that are astonishing.

In the jazz tradition playing 'outside' means playing outside the chord changes and fixed tempo; 'inside' means playing according to the rules. During the bop era the modernists were referred to as 'out-cats'. These also correspond to notions of social acceptability. 'Outside Now' recognizes the utopian aspect of music, but also its lack of social impact: the guitar solo is 'imaginary'.

When Zappa did the interviews for *Joe's Garage* he had to weather the scorn of journalists who reckoned he had abandoned the responsible social critique of the story for sex-play, but it was precisely by making *Joe's Garage* a controversial record that he could test the limits of rock representability. The artwork interacts with society rather than representing it. In 'A Token of My Extreme' Joe thinks to himself:

> Some people think that if they go too far
> They'll never get back to where the rest of them are
> I might be crazy, but there's one thing I know
> You might be surprised at what you find when ya go![78]

When Zappa talked of preferring sex to drugs, he mentioned that sex is 'closer to the way things are really constructed'.[79] The most interesting aspect of far-out behaviour is the light it can cast on the norm.

'He Used to Cut the Grass' has Joe out of prison in a world where music is illegal, stumbling over 'mounds of consumer goods formed into abstract statues dedicated to the Quality of American

[77]John Swenson, 'Frank Zappa: The Interview', *Guitar World*, March 1982.
[78]Frank Zappa, 'A Token of My Extreme', *Joe's Garage Acts II & III*, 1979.
[79]Radio interview with Jim Ladd, 'Zappa on Air', *Nuggets*, No. 7, April/May 1977, p. 18.

Craftsmanship', imagining yet more extraordinary guitar, finally even imagining enraged neighbours, damning reviews in the music press and 'Packard Goose', a heavily scatological attack on critics.

> Maybe you thought I was the Packard Goose
> Or the Ronald MacDonald of the nouveau-abstruse[80]

Almost deliberately packing these lines with American references British punk journalists would not have the background to interpret (Vance Packard wrote the 1950s bestseller[81] that lifted the lid on advertising's manipulation of the American people; Ronald MacDonald is a US media clown for kids), Zappa is denying that his music is either commercial or avant-garde. The song disintegrates into a vision of Mary, who says:

> Information is not knowledge
> Knowledge is not wisdom
> Wisdom is not truth
> Truth is not beauty
> Beauty is not love
> Love is not music
> Music is THE BEST[82]

which sets up a kind of self-cancelling hierarchy, until word play and free-association trashes the whole speech

> Wisdom is the domain of the Wis (which is extinct)
> Beauty is a French phonetic corruption
> Of a short cloth neck ornament
> Currently in resurgence[83]

and she is obscured by a flock of bow-ties. Any attempt at transcendence is immediately rubbished in a welter of trivial Americana.

Joe's Garage nears its end with a guitar showcase called 'Watermelon in Easter Hay', a phrase used by the musicians to describe how difficult it was to solo in this band of virtuosi: as difficult as 'growing a watermelon in Easter hay'.[84] The contrast between wet and dry in the phrase works like the contrast between the guitar's romanticism and the precision of the backing. The yellow hair of the make-up artist on the cover of *Joe's Garage Acts II & III* (who also appears on the cover of *Baby Snakes*, extending her tongue) looks like a bale of hay. Watermelons are a Southern black

[80]Frank Zappa, 'Packard Goose', *Joe's Garage Acts II & III*, 1979.
[81]Vance Packard, *The Hidden Persuaders*, 1957.
[82]Frank Zappa, 'Packard Goose', *Joe's Garage Acts II & III*, 1979.
[83]Ibid.
[84]Quoted by John Swenson, 'Frank Zappa: The Interview', *Guitar World*, March 1982.

icon to go with Zappa's black-face; cut open they are red like a vaginal invitation: sexual poetry again, just like 'Ritual Invocation and Dance of a Young Pumpkin'. The tune seems to have been written to make maximum use of the extraordinary space of the mix (it is the record's one non-xenochronous solo). Once you have got over the idea of Zappa playing a soaringly beautiful tune (the *Down Beat* reviewer did not – he hated it, and said so) its power imprints itself on the memory.

'Little Green Rosetta' is like a 'Return of the Son of Monster Magnet' thirteen years later: this time the massed extras don't freak out, they sing along like a muppet chorus. Zappa discards his plastic microphone and leads them in a series of wisecracks and free-association gibberish, deliberately degrading any idea of meaning. Compared to this, Black Mountain School happenings were rituals of consummate bourgeois elegance. It may well be a load of rubbish, but there is nothing quite like it in Western art. Zappa refers to the third world ('the kerosene record player is not a very efficient device'), mocking the desperate attempts to copy American consumerism which merely result in trash anyway.

> And if all else fails, throw the record away . . . build your own green rosetta . . . try this recipe: We'll start with a lump of grass . . . the grass bone connected to the ankle bone . . . the the knee bone connected to the wishbone . . . and then everybody moves to New York and goes to a party with Warren. Hey![85]

Zappa went to Thanksgiving at Warren Cucurullo's home – he was so impressed with his parents' Italian-family largesse ('so New Wave') that he took a camera crew along with him the next year. The word 'wish' triggers the reference to Warren as he goes straight to his own idea of fun: it short-circuits everything on *Joe's Garage* and yet also completes it, because the whole theme has been about wish-fulfilment anyway. He also manages to make one of his most succinct statements of his predilection for 'stupidity':

> They're pretty good musicians
> But it don't make no difference
> If they're good musicians
> Because anybody who would buy this record
> Doesn't give a fuck if there's good musicians on it
> Because this is a stupid song
> AND THAT'S THE WAY I LIKE IT[86]

[85]Frank Zappa, 'A Little Green Rosetta', *Joe's Garage Acts II & III*, 1979.
[86]Ibid.

'Pretty good musicians' was a phrase used by one of the contemporary band defending himself against criticism from an ex-Zappa sideman. It became a running joke. Players like Ed Mann and Vinnie Colaiuta and Warren Cucurullo are absolute virtuosi. On the other hand, fetishism of musical skill has had amazingly poor musical results in both heavy metal and jazz-rock (a point made by Zappa when he says he prefers the sound of the old blues guitarists to the 'freeze-dried' technique of the metal superstars). Zappa's 'stupid songs' betray an attitude that is stronger than technique. It is the way it rubs against his musicians' skills that produces great music, just as the way his jokes and obscenities rub the listener the wrong way and generate sociological perceptions.

I Don't Wanna Get Drafted

In 1980, in answer to the new cold war instituted by Ronald Reagan, Zappa released a single: 'I Don't Wanna Get Drafted'. At concerts he sold a badge with the same slogan, the phrase scribbled in his hand in orange on US Army olive-green. Tommy Mariano (later known as Tommy Mars) replaced Peter Wolf on keyboards and Arthur Barrow replaced Patrick O'Hearn on bass. Ray White was back, resplendent in a flowery silk shirt.

Recorded in the home studio with his kids Moon and Ahmet on vocals, the words reflected Zappa's current absurdism.

> Rollerskates and disco is a lot of fun
> I'm much too young and stupid to operate a gun[87]

The Mothers had never adopted a militant condemnation of the war in Vietnam; opposition to the war went without saying. Zappa's interest in the connections between violence, horror and mutiny went beyond singing along with Mungo Jerry, as the incident with the Marines at the Garrick Theater showed. *Absolutely Free* had attacked the hypocrisy of selling war-toys at Christmas ('Uncle Bernie's Farm'), giving the reference to toys in 'I Don't Wanna Get Drafted' a conceptual link. The cover showed the band lined up behind Zappa, giggling like a bunch of schoolboys: only Zappa looks dour. The back cover was a Cal Schenkel montage showing toppling buildings and Uncle Sam in conflict with the Russian bear: 'IS THIS TRIP REALLY NECESSARY?' it asked

---

[87]Frank Zappa, 'I Don't Wanna Get Drafted', 1980, Zappa WS7-73000.

in mock-Cyrillic. The graphic was also used for the back of the 1980 tour programme.

It is not necessary to construct a 'militant' image in order to make a political point. The distributors in the States (Mercury-Phonogram) realized this: as if confirming the paranoia *Joe's Garage* joked about, they refused to handle the record as it was 'unpatriotic'. Ten years later Zappa's mail-order cottage industry was still selling the unsold backlog at $1 a throw. The flip side was a guitar solo recorded live at the New York Palladium at Halloween in 1978 titled 'Ancient Armaments', majestically slow and melancholy.

TINSEL TOWN REBELLION

Zappa was accused of commercialism for the albums *Tinsel Town Rebellion* and *You Are What You Is*. They included few instrumentals. The critics were not to know that Zappa was busily working on orchestra scores all the while, or had built up a repertoire of staggering rock instrumentals for live performance. In 1981 he told John Swenson that his current band had enough instrumental numbers in the repertoire to do a two-and-a-half hour show with no vocals whatsoever.[88] Actually, the *Shut Up 'N Play Yer Guitar* series outsold both vocal albums;[89] the decision to use vocals was apparently political rather than commercial: 'I've got some lyrics that are worth hearing. It's a bit difficult to make a pointed statement about the Moral Majority with an instrumental.'[90] A curious argument. *You Are What You Is* contained four songs dealing with the new right (out of twenty), while the nearest *Tinsel Town Rebellion* got to a comment on the moral majority was a cover of 'Brown Shoes Don't Make It'.

Cal Schenkel's *Tinsel Town Rebellion* cover collage showed a scene of early-century decadence. Austro-Hungarian army officers in full-dress uniform carouse with champagne as the building topples about their ears. Zappa presides over this chaos in the role of bemused entertainer. 'Fine Girl', the opener, was described in the sleeve notes as 'a studio cut, included so that conservative radio stations can play something on the air, alerting people to the

[88]Dan Forte, 'Frank Zappa', *Musician*, 1981, reprinted in *Society Pages*, No. 10, May 1982, p. 18.
[89]John Swenson, 'Frank Zappa: The Interview', *Guitar World*, March 1982.
[90]Dan Forte, 'Frank Zappa', *Musician*, 1981, reprinted in *Society Pages*, No. 10, May 1982, p. 18.

fact that this album exists', an innocuous description for a systematic collation of symbols of women's oppression. Multi-part singing, overemphasized black accents ('de' for 'the') and a reggae beat all serve to make its plea for subservient females iconic and unreal.

> She do your laundry
> She change a tyre
> Chop a little wood for de fire . . .
> She do the dishes
> If you wishes
> Silverware too
> Make it look brand new . . .
> With a bucket on her head
> Fulla water from de well
> She could run a mile . . .
> She didn't need no school
> She was built like a mule
> With a thong sandal
> Well, wasn't no kinda job she could not handle[91]

This evokes the slave girls of John Norman's *Gor* series, the fantasy planet where women are reduced to their 'natural' state of sexual slavery: titillating S&M scenarios in endless permutation. In one passage Norman actually argues that wearing a sandal with an ankle strap 'proves' that a woman is really a slave destined for a collar and bondage. The explicit argument (there are many passages where the narrator – master or slave – expounds the philosophy of Gor) is for a return from the hypocritical 'equality' of liberalism to the 'natural' state of female subservience. The regression of sex is used as an argument for social regression. Norman's polemics are argued very like those of Ayn Rand, the McCarthyite sci-fi writer of the 50s, though his twist is male chauvinist rather than anti-communist. Rand pressed readers to join her own right-wing organization, pioneering the direct-mail politics that contributed so devastatingly to Reagan's victories in the 80s. Fantasies about a natural, purer, simpler state were likewise what attracted Ezra Pound to Vivaldi in music and to Mussolini in politics.

It is a shibboleth of structuralist and postmodernist criticism that the 'natural' is a locus of ideology. Though this is invariably correct, it can lead to a knee-jerk response that means that vast tracts of popular culture – and the yearnings they service – are simply disregarded: snobbery with a political gloss. Linda Williams has achieved a great deal in removing this block as far as film

---

[91]Frank Zappa, 'Fine Girl', *Tinsel Town Rebellion*, 1981.

pornography is concerned.[92] The Gor books rehearse a desire for regression to the animal which is as widespread as civilization itself, though Norman's sexist slant makes the female the sole site of this regression. He rarely – and unconvincingly at that – explores male masochism, actually (despite feminist paranoia) a much commoner tendency than sadism.[93] Both Norman and Rand have problems relating their fantasies to their politics. In using individual desire as a criticism of liberal hypocrisy they bypass the reality of the family, which is how sexual oppression is actually mediated. Nevertheless, Norman and Rand reach large audiences by immersing their reactionary theories in fantasies that genuinely address the impoverishment of personal experience under capitalism.

Where liberalism merely seeks to avoid contact with such unsavoury manifestations of sexual protest, radical culture seeks to harness these energies to a libertarian programme. In actually practising sadomasochism, and suggesting that we do too, writers like Larry Townshend[94] and Pat Califia[95] convert such impulses into a critique of the family and sexual oppression. They declare they are bringing to consciousness patterns that condition arousal and thereby challenging the idea that sex is solely a matter of forming stable partnerships and raising the next generation. Zappa's attitude towards such politico-sexual deviation from norms is ambivalent and confused (see *Thing-Fish*). 'Fine Girl' is a typical example of his procedure, which is to present material rather than give opinions. By accurately enumerating the demeaning aspects of 'primitive sexuality', 'Fine Girl' questions return-to-nature ideology. It raises spectres for fans of world music and their assumption that non-Western music necessarily constitutes a soundtrack for a more enlightened lifestyle – but it also questions Zappa's own enthusiasm for the blues. Satire which leaves no one comfortable.

'Fine Girl' segues into 'Easy Meat'. Judging solely by the words, the song should indeed be the 'sleazy juvenilia' denounced by the critics,[96] but the joke is the concerto in the middle, which performs sexual-materialist reductionism on Michael Nyman's

---

[92]Linda Williams, *Hard Core*, 1990. Thanks due to Matthew Caygill for recommending this book.
[93]'A one-to-three ratio, in favour of the M', Larry Townshend, *The Leatherman's Handbook*, 1972, p. 29.
[94]Larry Townshend, *The Leatherman's Handbook*, 1972.
[95]Pat Califia, *Macho Sluts*, 1988.
[96]Jonathan Romney, 'Fast Licks', *The Wire*, No. 102, August 1992, p. 70.

revival of the baroque. Portentous keyboard pontifications over-dubbed by Tommy Mars (Zappa termed this pounding pomp 'the classical section' in the sleeve notes) function like the rush of blood to an erection, culminating in a splashdown with a blatantly sexual resonance. As Susan McClary says:

> The standard explanation would be that while popular music admittedly addresses issues such as sexuality, classical music (the standard concert repertory of the eighteenth and nineteenth centuries) is concerned exclusively with loftier matters. Indeed, it is precisely this difference that many devotees of classical music would point to as proof that their preferences are morally superior to those of the pop music fan: their music is not contaminated by the libidinal – or even the social. I will be arguing . . . that classical music – no less than pop – is bound up with issues of gender construction and the channeling of desire.[97]

Zappa's status as 'sleazy juvenilia' in critical circles means that it is unlikely that McClary will ever hear this hilarious confirmation of her thesis. 'Easy Meat' evokes 'classical' excitement and then slides it into orgasmo-penetrative pornotopia with an ease that begs questions less about Zappa's proclivities than the 'abstractness' of velocity in classical music. After the splashdown/penetration, there is free-form saxophone, croaking that sounds like underwater marine life (perhaps a segment of the introduction to 'Manx Needs Women' on *Zappa in New York*), a clavinet chord and a voice saying:

> They're just not gonna stand for it!

which is the line that introduced 'Titties & Beer' on *Läther*.[98] Then, with a vertiginous opening out of the recording space, we are tipped into an outstanding guitar solo, as if the guitar is exploring the infinite recesses of sexual intercourse.

Before the keyboard section she offers to take him to her house and beat him off with a copy of *Rolling Stone*; after the solo he explains:

> I told her I was late
> I had another date
> I can't get off on the *Rolling Stone*
> But the robots think it's great[99]

[97]Susan McClary, *Feminine Endings*, 1991, p. 54.
[98]'What Ever Happened To All The Fun In The World', *Sheik Yerbouti*, 1979, is the same link, with this final line omitted.
[99]Frank Zappa, 'Easy Meat', *Tinsel Town Rebellion*, 1981.

But by the end:

> Saw her tiny titties
> Through her see-through blouse
> I just had to take the girl to my house[100]

This expresses Zappa's refusal to believe in transcendent cultural values that set you apart from the mass, acknowledgement of the ineluctable allure of what McClary calls 'popular culture' (and Zappa calls 'Cheepnis'). As Zappa collected articles of 'feminine underclothing' at Berkeley Community Theater for artist Emily James's quilt, he said:

> No, we are not going to play 'Cheepnis' – that's right – but we are collecting underpants . . . So far, ladies and gentlemen, the response from this particular community has not been especially gratifying. Perhaps you're a little bit too intellectual here . . .[101]

Critics were amazed that Zappa should not only collect underwear, but have every word of the ensuing dialogue transcribed on the sleeve. It is only when you put these seemingly random moments against the big picture – Zappa's refusal to underwrite the hierarchies of mind and body, of social class – that the details gleam with significance.

Zappologist Jonathan Jones took the quilt as emblematic of Zappa's entire work.

> Whether or not the quilt was actually made, the very idea of it captures the essentials of Zappa's work. Looking back over twenty years, what has it been but a public display of America's dirty linen? But it is also worth considering the nature of a quilt, a fabric which is stitched together out of leftovers, discarded bits and pieces, remnants and scraps. Zappa's music is just such a heterogenous assembly.[102]

'Easy Meat', with its combination of sleaze and pomp, *Rolling Stone* and baroque, Philadelphia (the main song) and Santa Monica (guitar solo), along with overdubbed keyboards and snatches of *Läther, Sheik Yerbouti* and *Zappa in New York*, is a perfect illustration of such 'heterogeneous assembly'.

'For the Young Sophisticate' is the *Läther* song re-recorded in the queasy, marimba-heavy style of 'Little Green Rosetta' on *Joe's Garage*. Zappa turns it around by goading the drummer Vinnie

---

[100]Ibid.
[101]Frank Zappa, 'Panty Rap', *Tinsel Town Rebellion*, 1981.
[102]Jonathan Jones, 'A World of Secret Hungers', *Eonta*, Vol. 2, No. 2, July/August 1993. Respect due to Jones for his ability to see through the nearly opaque effrontery of this particular moment to the aptness of its metaphor.

Colaiuta throughout, part of the dissolution of song lyrics into band in-jokes that characterized the 80s. Using a mismatch of elements draws attention to the material used to make representations – songs reduced to the banter of musicians on the road.

On side two 'Panty Rap' appears in the midst of revived oldies. The utterly different tone of voice the old numbers are sung in, let alone the bionic precision of the playing, indicated changed times. Dismissing the efforts of Don Preston and Jimmy Carl Black, who were touring as the Grandmothers, Zappa commented on attempts to 'revive an era'.

> First of all, they can't do it. The era itself is gone. The reason the Mothers were what they were was a combination of these ingredients: the time in which they appeared and the personalities of the individual members in that particular year of their growth as people. People change. Motorhead of 1967 is not Motorhead of today, nor is the Don Preston of 1967 the Don Preston of today. The Don Preston of today has been on the road with – what's that guy's name? – Leo Sayer, right? He was with Leo Sayer a number of years. It changes a guy, you know.[103]

The reference to Leo Sayer (really a blow below the belt!) shows how bitter the conflict with his old sidemen had become.

'Tinsel Town Rebellion', Zappa's putdown of LA punk, merely confirmed what punk ears could conclude from the sound of his albums: here was someone committed to the piece of the action granted him by his place in the 60s rock revolution. The guitar solo at the end of side two, 'Now You See It – Now You Don't', taken from a performance of 'King Kong', is an astonishing piece of twirling invention over a reggae pulse. The skill of his accompanists allow him a freedom very different from the linear squirming of his solos with the Mothers. He remarked to *Guitar World* in 1982:

> Improvisation is a communal effort... Prior to today I have not had an ensemble that was capable of that type of aesthetic realization. The early Mothers weren't that musically skilled. I mean they had their own qualities, but to be able to support me in doing the kind of thing I'm doing now, they couldn't do it. And my technique has improved, and my equipment has improved, so now aside from playing the notes that I want to play it's easier for me to make the sounds that I want to make.[104]

---

[103]Quoted by Dan Forte, 'Frank Zappa', *Musician*, 1981, reprinted in *Society Pages*, No. 10, May 1982, p. 21.
[104]Quoted by John Swenson, 'Frank Zappa: The Interview', *Guitar World*, March 1982.

In the jaundiced view of the album's title track, punk was merely about securing record deals: an easy slur from someone who already ran a record company. What excited Zappa about younger musicians was chops and a commitment to his own music. When bored Berklee student Steve Vai sent him a transcription of 'Black Page' with a cassette of his band Morning Thunder, it proved that Cucurullo was not a one-shot deal. Zappa's 'Tinsel Town Rebellion' vision of musicians learning 'dumb' riffs in order to relate to the new wave was closer to his own ex-sidemen in Missing Persons than the actuality of LA punk: Black Flag, Saccharine Trust, Universal Congress Of, Tupelo Chain Sex were playing something real. Zappa was attempting to get his current musicians into the Turbans and Young Jessie: 'I'm trying to get these guys interested in that form of music. I love that stuff. And they're coming along, they're starting to get more enthusiastic about it.'[105]

Tupelo Chain Sex could relate better to genuine R&B than Zappa's Berklee-educated musos: they proved as much by recording some scorching harmolodic ska featuring Sugarcane Harris.[106] Like any new artistic generation, punk showed up the limitations of their predecessors, including Zappa. He accused the punks of doing cocaine, when it was actually – due to its expense – the scene's uncoolest drug. Making a virtue out of poverty, the Straight Edge movement was denying drugs and drink altogether. Zappa's accusations are like Frank Sinatra declaring that rock 'n' roll singers were only doing it for the money – stupid.

On the other hand, 'Tinsel Town Rebellion' included lines of inimitable abuse for

> ... all those record company pricks
> Who come to skim the cream
> From the cesspools of excitement
> Where Jim Morrison once stood[107]

Zappa's indignation sticks out like a spring from a broken-down sofa. As with 'Flakes' the message twists and becomes absurd, a fountain of vitriol that exceeds the subject: Zappa is singing about capitalism rather than punk rock. Even when seeming to deliver a 'straightforward' song, there is always a moment where the thing

---

[105]Dan Forte, 'Frank Zappa', *Musician*, 1981, reprinted in *Society Pages*, No. 10, May 1982, p. 21.
[106]Tupelo Chain Sex, *What is It*, 1982; *Ja-Jazz* 1983; *Spot the Difference*, 1984. Thank you to producer Jason Mayall for sending me a tape; if Dave Dahlson is still about, I wish he'd get in touch.
[107]Frank Zappa, 'Tinsel Town Rebellion', *Tinsel Town Rebellion*, 1981.

seems to break down. Zappa was asked about the way he seems to sabotage what might otherwise be 'straight-ahead, accessible compositions'.

> That misunderstanding derives from this fact. People who deal in rock 'n' roll criticism are all part of the machinery that thrives on the idea that the largest number of units sold equals the best music. And if somebody does something without wanting to sell billions of platinum units, then this is incomprehensible to the average rock 'n' roll critic, because they believe that anybody who doesn't play the same game is crazy or dangerous or both. So they can't compute the idea that maybe the concept of the song that they perceive as a perfectly acceptable, viable, nice little rock 'n' roll ditty that they think was sabotaged – maybe the *sabotage* is the actual information in the song, and the rest of the stuff surrounding it is something that will attract the attention of the people who need to hear that other information. It's the carrot on the end of the stick to make you experience that other information. The part in the song that turns out to be weird to those particular critics is the part that's important, and the other stuff is just something to set you up for the little twist that's in there. Without the setup, the twist doesn't work, and oftentimes the compositions are designed to lead you right down the primrose path until you hit the brick wall.[108]

Zappa's professed favourite track on *Tinsel Town Rebellion* was 'The Blue Light', which consists of nearly unadulterated sabotage. It introduced his new kind of *sprechstimme*, which the band called 'meltdown', a further extension of Zappa's leering silly-voice taunting that included improvised words and notes. The song revisits the hopeless, drug-addled stupor of the 60s generation touched on in 'Pygmy Twylyte' and 'City of Tiny Lites'. The hippie imagery of Donovan and Todd Rundgren turns into a vision of the polluted Atlantic ('The seepage, the sewage, the rubbers, the napkins . . .'). Ideological disintegration has invaded the song structure itself.

'Pick Me I'm Clean', a recital of phrases spoken by groupies, orchestrates the band members' underlying hostility in a way that seems callous and jaded compared to Flo & Eddie's hysterical enthusiasm. Bookended by the tight, repetitious lyric, Arthur Barrow's wonderfully judged bass – close to the jazzy fluidity of 'Inca Roads' – provides expansive backing for a beautiful guitar solo. Whatever the surrounding unpleasantness, sex and music are always sites of utopian freedom in Zappa.

'Bamboozled by Love' is a terrifying song of stomping jealousy

---

[108]Dan Forte, 'Frank Zappa', *Musician*, 1981, reprinted in *Society Pages*, No. 10, May 1982, p. 20.

in which the male protagonist finally kills the object of his puzzle-ment, a rock *Carmen* that churns up excitement without allowing resolution in tragedy as an aesthetic experience. The album con-cludes with two covers, 'Brown Shoes Don't Make It' and 'Peaches en Regalia' (here renamed 'Peaches III' since it appeared on both *Hot Rats* and *Fillmore East June 1971*), bravura displays of the band's onstage discipline. Played live, it is clearer how 'Brown Shoes' uses rock riffs to involve the listener's libido in unwhole-some urges. In the new arrangement 'Peaches' becomes something of smoke and mirrors, its original dialogue between comic fanfares and rock strut turned into a series of illusionist façades. Towards the end the rhythm is revealed as the labour of cartoon robots. Zappa's sign-off has Warren Cucurullo play tributes to various great Italians, including Conlon Nancarrow (to whose 'bionic ragtime' sensibility Cucurullo's zigzag playing style has many affinities).

YOU ARE WHAT YOU IS

You Are What You Is was conceived as a political onslaught, an intervention in the increasingly restricted world of mainstream rock. It stiffed. The video for the title track was banned from MTV because it showed a Ronald Reagan look-alike being strapped into an electric chair. It included as 'decorative filler material' an article *Newsweek* commissioned from Zappa and then rejected as 'too idiosyncratic'. It blamed the state of America on stupidity, the media, committees, unions, accountants – using the image of cheese (a symbol of cultural collapse in the pizza of 'The Blue Light' on *Tinsel Town*). Using the colour-printing available on a record sleeve, the word 'cheese' was picked out in yellow. Like his overuse of emphases in *The Real Frank Zappa Book*, this device is typi-cal of Zappa's refusal to accept the usual parameters of literary production (the same synaesthetic 'idiosyncrasy' also characterizes the work of William Blake, the difference being that Blake managed to release his books only in editions of nine or so). Picked out in red was a return to poodle imagery: a sneer at the sacred *Prime Rate Poodle*, the 'bottom line' of profit. As Adorno never tired of pointing out, the argument of commercial viability is in the end as repressive and restrictive as fascism. Never mind that a genuine political critique requires a full-blooded denunciation of capitalism (a denunciation Zappa's own small-business interests cannot permit), Zappa was responding to the Reagan–Thatcher orthodoxies that were sweeping the world and defending his own patch with clear-sighted integrity. Having served as a figure for every inexpressible concept, the poodle now served to symbolize the most ruinous fetish of all: the profit motive.

> The *Quality of Our Lives* (if we think of this matter in terms of '*How much* of what we *individually* consider to be *Beautiful* are we *able* to *experience* every day?') seems an irrelevant matter, now that all decisions regarding the creation and distribution of *Works of Art* must first pass *under the limbo bar* (a/k/a 'The Bottom Line'), along with things like *Taste* and *The Public Interest*, all tied like a tin can to the wagging tail of the sacred **Prime Rate Poodle**. The aforementioned festering *poot* is coming your way at a theater or drive-in near you. It wakes you up every morning as it droozles out of your digital alarm clock. An ARTS COUNCIL somewhere is getting a special batch ready with little tuxedos on it so you can think it's precious.[109]

The remark about tuxedos shows how little Zappa's subsequent work with classical orchestras had to do with aspirations to highbrow status. Zappa hits the nail on the head: making aesthetic distinctions in an arts-funding environment is like mentioning the concept of class in bourgeois politics. It puts the ball right out of the court.

By the 80s, rock music had become integral to the conditioning of white America, a stage associated with adolescence and abandoned with the onset of maturity. *You Are What You Is* knew its constituency and addressed it with its opening number, 'Teen-age Wind'. This uses repetition in a highly symbolic manner: reiteration of words about freedom become the very opposite of what they are saying. Transcription in capitals reinforced the sensation of stuck-record stasis.

> FREE IS WHEN YOU DON'T HAVE TO PAY FOR NOTHING
> OR DO NOTHING
> WE WANT TO BE FREE
> FREE AS THE WIND[110]

Grateful Dead concerts, tightening the headband during a solo, midnight showings of *200 Motels*: Zappa is as scathing about his audience as he was on 'Flower Punk' in 1967. The accurate

---

[109]Frank Zappa, 'Say Cheese . . .', sleeve note, *You Are What You Is*, 1981.
[110]Frank Zappa, 'Teen-age Wind', *You Are What You Is*, 1981.

tracking of the words by the drums and their unreal clarity give the song an hallucinatory quality. Jimmy Carl Black quotes some of his lines from *200 Motels* on 'Teen-age Wind' before reviving his redneck persona for 'Harder Than Your Husband', a superbly callous C&W rejection song with slide guitar by Denny Walley. 'Doreen' is a work-out for Ray White's muscular voice, an extravagant widescreen symphony of multi-tracked singing and guitars, in complete contrast to 'Goblin Girl', which works the cheesy smut of 'Jewish Princess'. Then Zappa overlays 'Doreen' over 'Goblin Girl', creating an Ivesian complexity out of two simple songs. It finishes with a chorus about how Coy Featherstone's green light makes the black guys in the band look like 'they've got scales all over their body'. As in *Tinsel Town*, the listener is continually reminded of the musicians behind these songs.

Side one's suite of pop songs concludes with the ominous 'Theme from the 3rd Movement of Sinister Footwear'. The guitar sounds huge; it thrashes around like a dragon, guitar and percussion and bass clarinet flailing off like sparks. No one else would even think of putting this massive rock timbre up against such rhythmically refined accompaniment. This piece of music could not have been achieved without the services of Steve Vai, who wrote a transcription at Zappa's request.[111] Zappa then asked him to learn to play it on guitar; in three days he had learned it. Steve Vai told *Society Pages*:

> But it wasn't for a while that I got to record it, so I kept practising it harder and harder. If you listen very carefully to the *You Are What You Is* album, I'm doubling the melody in one speaker and Frank's original guitar track is coming out of the other. Ed Mann, the percussionist, learned the melody on the different percussion instruments, and he recorded it. David Ocker learned the part on bass clarinet and doubled it.[112]

Society Pages had printed an early transcription (not what finally appeared in *The Frank Zappa Guitar Book*[113]). Vai commented:

> This originally started out as the opening of a show, I think it was Halloween in New York. The rhythms that appear in this transcription are transcribed rhythms from the original version which was called

---

[111]Vai was first taken on as a transcriber rather than a guitarist; he finished the massive *Frank Zappa Guitar Book* just in time to go on the 1982 tour.
[112]Quoted by Michael Brenna and Rune Karlsen, 'Stevie's Spanking', *Society Pages*, No. 12, September 1982, p. 9.
[113]*The Frank Zappa Guitar Book*, 1982, Munchkin Music; distributed Music Sales Ltd (UK and Eire), Music Sales Pty Ltd (Australia), Hal Leonard Publishing Corporation (USA and Canada).

'Persona Non Grata'. If you try to read this piece of music right here in your magazine along with the record, you'll find it inaccurate, because Frank took his guitar part, and the percussion plus guitar plus clarinet overdubs and played them on a totally different rhythm track, I think the actual rhythm track from a solo from 'Easy Meat', because it's the same type of vamp, it's 3/4 E. Lydian. All this is why David Logeman was on it. He didn't play it when the actual thing was being recorded live, that was Vince [Colaiuta]. The rhythm track on the album consisted of Arthur Barrow playing bass, and I think it was Tommy Mars playing Rhodes and David Logeman playing drums. So the actual sense of time on the 'Sinister Footwear' that appears on the record is slightly different than what is transcribed here. A musician who can understand this would have a hard time to follow it. I don't know how you got hold of this, it *is* my transcription, which is yet unpublished. I can recognize the copying of Richard Emmet, who did it, and I don't know if it would be a good idea to let Frank see it, not at all.[114]

Steve Vai's diagnosis of xenochrony has since been challenged.[115] Either way, Zappa is dealing with a cross-fertilization of rock and classical that is absolutely unique. He has pointed out many times that the kind of improvisations he achieves on stage would be impossible in a studio. To take these and make them into scores, double up the instrumentation with the precision of new-complexity chamber music *and* to spread it across an alien rhythm track is truly alchemical. 'Sinister Footwear' concludes with a clacking piece of percussion that recalls the noises of 'Chrome Plated Megaphone of Destiny'. Just when you think that it had finished it rattles again, a sinister ratchet reminder. Transcription gives Zappa's temporal excursions the externality of spatial objects. The music seems to result from twanging on some pre-existent structure (as indeed, someone playing from a score would be), which is why the resonant piano space of the *Lumpy Gravy* dialogues (or the plucked piano wires of 'Megaphone of Destiny' or the harp of 'Zoot Allures') seem such appropriate poetic extensions of his music. Improvisation is the quickest way to achieving personal expression; scores posit music as an external object. Zappa moves between these in a practical dialectic that uses the skills of key personnel: recording engineers, musicologists, musicians.

'Society Pages', 'I'm a Beautiful Guy', 'Beauty Knows No Pain', 'Charlie's Enormous Mouth' and 'Any Downers?' were performed as a suite on the 1980 world tour, and appear in the same

[114]Quoted by Michael Brenna and Rune Karlsen, 'Stevie's Spanking', Society Pages, No. 12, September 1982, pp. 9–10.
[115]By Marc Ziegenhagen, 'Didja Know ...?' Society Pages USA, No. 2, undated, p. 53.

order on the record. Schenkel's graphics for the tour programme reinforced political aspects of the lyrics. 'Society Pages' was illustrated by a photograph of dignitaries in evening dress under the Stars and Stripes. In the corner a clipping from a 50s comic strip has members of the ruling class at dinner.

> SENIOR GENT: Our winter home is in Washington. I hope you'll call on us.
> JUNIOR GENT: I'm honored, sir. I certainly shall.
> YOUNG LADY: [*Thinks*] He's my idea of a handsome man.[116]

'Charlie's Enormous Mouth' was illustrated with the skull from *Uncle Meat* branded with the year of the Black Death, 'Easy Meat' with hardcore erotica blown up out of recognition. Schenkel provides another *Tinsel Town*-style vision: here the band is bannered 'Fab Poodles' and in the distance there is a Busby Berkeley-style arrangement of dancers in devil costumes against pit-of-hell scenery. The dog-eared man from *Lumpy Gravy* makes another appearance and at the top right corner there is the photo of old-fashioned dancers used for the innerfold of *Lumpy Gravy*.

'I'm a Beautiful Guy' detected the élitism and racism at the heart of the yuppie health fad.

> They're playing tennis
> Their butts are tighter
> What could be *whiter*?[117]

'Beauty Knows No Pain' registered the impact of commodification on the body (continuing the critique of 'Plastic People' and 'Mom & Dad').

> Beauty is a bikini wax 'n waitin' for yer nails to dry
> Beauty is a colored pencil, scribbled all around yer eye
> Beauty is a pair of shoes that makes you want to die
> Beauty is a
> Beauty is a
> Beauty is a
> Lie[118]

These songs demonstrated what Zappa could achieve with a team of crack musicians, the music swerving and accelerating like a well-built sports car, words seamlessly welded to the melodies.

The title track parodied the pretensions of those who are not

---

[116]Cal Schenkel, *Zappa 1980 World Tour* brochure, p. 6.
[117]Frank Zappa, 'I'm a Beautiful Guy', *You Are What You Is*, 1981.
[118]Frank Zappa, 'Beauty Knows No Pain', *You Are What You Is*, 1981.

prepared to accept what race they are. Like Zappa's contempt for cosmetics, his hatred for illusions could be construed as intransigence to people's development and potential, laying him open to charges of sexism and racism. Rather than inveigh in the abstract against 'bad thoughts', he documents the distortions and disasters brought about by oppression and exploitation. By keeping to specific instances Zappa saves himself from the utterance of empty pieties; it explains the shocking intensity of his words and stories. The way he cuts in his own voice to say the word 'nigger' in the line 'Now he says to himself, I ain't no nigger no more' shows precisely Zappa's willingness to accumulate on himself all the nastiness of modern America. Nevertheless, as the Devil said in 'Titties & Beer':

> You can't fool me, man, you ain't that bad
> I mean you shoulda seen some of the souls I had
> Why there was Milhous Nixon 'n Agnew too
> 'N both of those suckers was worse 'n you[119]

The out-chorus of 'You Are What You Is' has Ike Willis and Ray White sing key phrases from 'Wino Man', 'Harder Than Your Husband' and 'Jumbo, Go Away'. The song also meshes with a preview of 'The Mudd Club'. Like both Cal Schenkel's cover for *Tinsel Town* and his vision of hell in the 1980 tour programme, the music threatens to mash everything together in one horrible torrent.

'Mudd Club' was the result of Zappa's 'sociological investigation' of discos in New York (Schenkel included the 'man with the blue mohawk' in both montages). Zappa's documentation of S&M asks questions about the place of pain and punishment in a secular society, a brief that then expands to deal with religion and militarism. 'The Meek Shall Inherit Nothing' cackles with de Sade's anti-religious laughter. Zappa's strength has always been his sensitivity to the political resonance of form: his abstract political views, pushed into song form in 'Dumb All Over', read like doggerel.

> You can't run a country
> By a book of religion
> Not by a heap
> Or a lump or a smidgeon
> Of foolish rules
> Of ancient date

---

[119]Frank Zappa, 'Titties & Beer', *Zappa in New York*, 1977.

> Designed to make
> You all feel great[120]

However, hearing these lines whispered in guttural cyberspeak and phased in stereo over a relentless machine rhythm makes them spooky rather than daft: the mad mutterings of some prophetic loon everyone ignores, like John the Baptist's voice-from-the-well in Richard Strauss's *Salomé*. With its lines about the stupidity of revenging the crusades, 'Dumb All Over' was particularly timely for a record released during the Iranian hostage crisis.

'Heavenly Bank Account', a song about money-making evangelism, is sung like a church service, the luxuriance and smugness of the melody perfect for its subject matter. After the words

> They won't get him
> They will never get him
> For the naughty stuff
> That he did[121]

there is a peal of munchkin laughter out of 'Goblin Girl'. One of Zappa's strategies is to trivialize the heinous crimes that can topple hypocritical leaders – he is laughing about blow-jobs, Jimmy Swaggart is not.

Despite the epic political scope of such songs, *You Are What You Is* returns (like side two of *We're Only in It for the Money*) to songs about specific people. 'Suicide Chump' pursues Zappa's unsentimental rationalism, appropriately set to a brisk blues. Like the Sex Pistols' 'Problems', it removes sympathy in a radical gesture of defiance to conventional morals. 'Jumbo, Go Away', one of Zappa's nastiest songs, is the tale of a dependent groupie who tried to give a band member an unwanted blow-job in a restaurant.

> You got to realize
> Our little romance deal
> Will not materialize
> Into a thing that you'd call REAL . . .[122]

This is sung by Bob Harris in a falsetto, the soaring line surpassing every hysterical cliché of post-Beatles pop. The tune takes off into a dazzling section of rhythmic complexity over which Jumbo says, 'I think I have worms.' It is hard to listen to the next words without wincing.

---

[120]Frank Zappa, 'Dumb All Over', *You Are What You Is*, 1981.
[121]Frank Zappa, 'Heavenly Bank Account', *You Are What You Is*, 1981.
[122]Frank Zappa, 'Jumbo, Go Away', *You Are What You Is*, 1981.

394

Jumbo better get back
Or your eye will get black
When I give you a smack
(*No Denny don't hit me*)[123]

and the chorus sings 'wash up your pie' as Zappa deals Jumbo an old sexist routine.

FZ: There are three things that smell like fish.
J: Really? What are they?
FZ: One of them is fish.
J: Oh.
FZ: The other two . . .
J: What do you mean, the other two?
FZ: . . . are growing on you!

It is likely that many male bands behave like bastards on the road; it is Zappa's need to stick it right under the listener's nose which is unusual. The assumption that Zappa is therefore a bastard is precisely the reflex his music is designed to question, of course, but it has to be admitted that he gets his effects by sailing pretty close to the wind.[124]

'Jumbo, Go Away' segues into 'If Only She Woulda', a tune that uses the same Cuban riff the Doors used to solo on. It inevitably recalls the 60s and Vietnam (a connection cemented by the *Apocalypse Now* soundtrack) and prepares the way for a version of 'I Don't Wanna to Get Drafted', now named 'Drafted Again', with Ahmet Zappa delivering the lines about being too young and stupid to operate a gun. The closing line

Leave my nose alone, please[125]

relates to Zappa's childhood experience of radium treatment:[126] radiation can damage your children's health. Zappa later speculated that there was simply too much being said in *You Are What You Is* for DJs to pick up on it: radio-play was dismal and sales poor. It remains one of the most ambitious public stands against Reaganism in the 80s.

---

[123]Ibid.
[124]See 'Epilogue', where I ask him about this song.
[125]Frank Zappa, 'Drafted Again', *You Are What You Is*, 1981.
[126]Acknowledgements for this insight to Jonathan Jones, 'A World of Secret Hungers', *Eonta*, Vol. 2, No. 2, July/August 1993.

SHIP ARRIVING TOO LATE TO SAVE A DROWNING WITCH

The lottery of the charts was nowhere so well illustrated as in June 1982 with the chart success of 'Valley Girl'. It was caused by fourteen-year-old Moon Zappa's contribution.

> It's not my fault – they didn't buy that record because it had my name on it. They bought it because they liked Moon's voice. It's got nothing to do with the song or the performance. It has *everything* to do with the American public wanting to have some new syndrome to identify with. And they got it. There it is. That's what made it a hit.[127]

The CD release includes a sweet handwritten note from Moon asking for a chance to 'work' on a recording; Zappa actually woke her up in the middle of the night to perform on 'Valley Girl'. Selecting phrases from a routine in which she mocked the mannerisms of San Fernando Valley little rich girls, Zappa framed her with the alertness to ambience and the specific poignancy of the unguarded voice he had used for Suzy Creamcheese and the GTO's. According to Moon: 'Bar mitzvahs is where it started. I would go to bar mitzvahs and come back speaking Valley lingo that everyone at the bar mitzvah was speaking and the song came out of that.'[128] Zappa encouraged Moon to embroider what she heard. The expression 'bag your face' was extended to 'bag those toenails'. 'And I was saying Mr Bu Fu, and he said, wait, try Lord God King Bu Fu, and I just threw that one in.'[129]

Zappa looked on in bemusement at all the trappings of having a hit in the 80s. Moon was interviewed by *Time-Life* and *Playboy*, there was franchising of Valley Girl T-shirts, lunch-boxes, cosmetics, offers for a TV series and a feature film (which was eventually made, though without Zappa's involvement). Both Moon and Frank were adamant that she was not actually a Valley Girl: as usual Zappa's ironies bypassed the media circus. According to Moon, the song was 'by no means offensive, it isn't – it's funny, it's comedy',[130] but Zappa made dark hints that 'Valley Girl' was not simply a celebration.

---

[127]Quoted by Tom Mulhern, 'Frank Zappa: I'm Different', reprinted in *Society Pages*, No. 14, February 1983, p. 12.
[128]Moon Zappa, quoted by Michael Goldberg, 'Frank & Moon', *Creem*, Vol. 14, No. 6, November 1982.
[129]Quoted in *High Times*, No. 87, November 1982.
[130]Quoted by Michael Goldberg, 'Frank & Moon', *Creem*, Vol. 14, No. 6, November 1982.

Well you have to understand that I'm not too thrilled about the Valley as an aesthetic concept. You know, I mean the San Fernando Valley, to me, represents a number of evil things. I probably shouldn't be saying that because a lot of people think this is a nice, cute, harmless song. But I don't like the valley. I shouldn't say anything more than that.
MICHAEL GOLDBERG: *Why?*
No, I'm not gonna. I don't want to spoil anybody's fun. It's better that they should think it's a nice little song.[131]

'Valley Girl' appeared on *Ship Arriving Too Late to Save a Drowning Witch*. The album contained another song about life in Hollywood which the media chose to ignore. It was called 'Teen-age Prostitute'. On the English single release it was the B-side:[132] quite literally the other side of 'Valley Girl'.

> She ran away from home
> Her mom was destitute
> Her daddy doesn't care
> She's a teen-age prostitute
> '*I have got a pimp*
> *He treats me like a dog . . .*'
> (All the stuff she's shooting
> Keeps her in a fog)[133]

The last song on the album, it mashes together thunderous marimba playing, a frenetic 'Peter Gunn' riff, blaring synthesized horns and the glass-endangering top notes of the opera singer Lisa Popeil: a panic-inducing onslaught of considerable power. It is like an explosion of the frenzy that has been building throughout the record.

Ship Arriving Too Late is one of the most succinctly *paced* Zappa records. The opener, 'No Not Now', has Roy Estrada's falsetto in three-part harmony with itself. Zappa described it as 'country and western on PCP'. The orchestration of different voices – Estrada's nasal falsetto, Ike Willis's choked sincerity, Ray White's iron tonsils, Zappa's sneer – is complex, pursuing the widescreen scope of the out-chorus of 'Doreen'. It is all anchored in guitar sounds that are positively sinoidal in their vocal intensity. The pounding, dumb backbeat reflects the relentless roll of the truck the subject is driving. He is driving string beans to Utah, home of the Osmonds.

---

[131]Ibid.
[132]The Barking Pumpkin single – WS9 02972 – had 'You Are What You Is' on the B-side; the CBS UK release – CBS A2412 – had 'Teen-age Prostitute'.
[133]Frank Zappa, 'Teen-age Prostitute', *Ship Arriving Too Late to Save a Drowning Witch*, 1982.

Donny 'n Marie
Can both take a bite
(*Bite it Marie*)
Hawaiian – Hawaiian – Hawaiian
Lunch[134]

The driver's thoughts consist of the random images that pass through the mind during boring work. 'Valley Girl' has a chorus in a similar style and a bouncing, mongoloid bass line. Moon's rap provides textural relief, something without velocity, poignant moments.

'I Come from Nowhere' has Bob Harris revive Ricky Lancelotti's zomby vocalese. His own lips seem to be stuck in the strange contortions of the insincere people the song attacks. The singing drifts out of tune in the manner of Zappa's 'meltdown'; Iggy Pop started singing out of tune the same year,[135] as if the horror of the new decade had now sunk in, requiring something desperately out-of-kilter from the old hands. Harris's singing is so strained that the guitar solo comes as a relief, Zappa indulging some of his densest distortions. Patrick O'Hearn's bass here is wonderfully free: through Chad Wackerman's drum blizzard bass and guitar twist and turn and argue like living things. This section is *out* like the Hendrix Experience or Cream during a live excursion, a complete aberration for a hit record in 1982. The *Los Angeles Times* reported on 20 June:

> The album moved up an incredible 101 places on the Billboard chart last week, from 172 to 71. A jump of that magnitude rarely happens, a Billboard spokesman said.
> More than 125,000 albums have been sold nationwide since release three weeks ago. It is selling better than any previous album according to a spokesman for Barking Pumpkin Record Co., the label on which Zappa records.[136]

Side two of this pop record went to even further extremes, showing anyone who felt that *Tinsel Town* and *What You Is* neglected instrumental music that Zappa was still pioneering monster compositions.

The title of the album came from a book of puzzle pictures by Roger Price called *Droodles*, which was published in 1953. A diagram that could be read as 'ZA' was titled: 'Ship arriving too

[134]Frank Zappa, 'No Not Now', *Ship Arriving Too Late to Save a Drowning Witch*, 1982.
[135]Iggy Pop, *Zombie Birdhouse*, 1982, Animal CHR1399.
[136]David Frenznick, 'Is "Valley Girl", "Fer Real"?', *Los Angeles Times*. Thanks to Wee John and Mary-Lou for this cutting.

late to save a drowning witch' (this was emphasized in John Vince's design, which reproduced Price's graphic with 'Zappa' written above using triangles for 'A's). The psychoanalyst Jacques Lacan talked of the 'name of the father', finding in it the principle of order which founds patriarchy. Prompted by Roger Price's caption, Zappa gazes into the literal aspect of his father's name and came up with a monster movie vignette, told in the key-free manner of 'meltdown'. Like 'The Blue Light', it is a vision of pollution.

> Not even a witch ought to be caught
> On the bottom of America's spew-infested
> Waterways, *hey-hey*[137]

Mutating due to radiation, with 'Sardines in her eyebrows... Lobsters up 'n down her forehead', she goes ashore and causes monster-movie-type chaos.

> Maybe a submarine could save her,
> And bring her home to the Navy...
> For some kind of *ritual sacrifice*...[138]

According to Susan McClary, this is the schema that underlies tonal classical music, where challenges to the fundamental key are played with, but finally eliminated: just as the 'threat' of the feminine is disposed of in classical narrative. Circulating a heterogeneous motley of cultural junk, Zappa's story degrades these elements, asking us to observe these motifs with the same degree of levity we might bring to a 50s monster movie.

Before he sings 'ritual sacrifice', Zappa goes 'ooh-ooh-ooh-aah-aah, aah-ooh-ooh-ooooh-ooh-ooh-aah-ah-hah-wah', gibberish just sufficiently organized to tempt the transcriber, but which then turns into vocal expression, making accurate transcription as an abstract sequence of countable oohs and aahs nearly impossible. It sums up the problems facing Steve Vai when transcribing guitar solos. In Zappa the classical dialectic of tonality and chromaticism is replaced by a dialectic between free improvisation and scored order. Despite the male chauvinism of its lyrical trappings, and its dramatic use of the symbols of the castration complex, this sadomasochistic dialectic – between flesh and bond, impulse and restraint – finally transcends gender. Though feminism, reacting to the commercial exploitation of sadomasochism in a sexist

---

[137]Frank Zappa, 'Drowning Witch', *Ship Arriving Too Late to Save a Drowning Witch*, 1982.
[138]Ibid.

society, sees it all as a male plot, developments in radical gay culture are starting to show how, because it is based in regressive *play*, sadomasochism holds the promise of a sexuality beyond sexual difference.[139]

Against the cartoon croaking of the witch's laughter, Zappa's musicians take off into one of his most involved compositions, the classic Scott Thunes/Chad Wackerman rhythm section providing firm scaffolding for an utterly excruciated guitar solo. The composed section is followed by a more open patch of playing. As Thunes begins to vary his line in response to Zappa the music moves like some exotic beast. Tommy Mars unzips flourishes across the keyboard that luxuriate in Zappa's strange harmonies. Whereas during Mothers of Invention improvisations there would generally be one musical event to watch, here everything moves at once. The clarity of the sections resembles 'Andy', though improvement in both playing (most of the guitar-lines are Vai playing notes specified by Zappa) and recording technology (all the feedback documents live situations) have given the guitar sound a new succulence. Following Vai's transcription, Ed Mann's marimbas can echo the guitar notes because the solos are in fact orchestrally conceived: a characteristic feature of Zappa's writing for the Thunes/Wackerman bands is an ability to make static, floating areas suddenly develop the closed quality of written composition. The final mix used edits from fifteen live performances, some of them two bars long. The band's ability to maintain a strict tempo was crucial. Asked if he met mismatches working this way, Zappa replied:

> You start off with a band that is highly rehearsed, that maintains their tempo. They learn it at a certain tempo, then they'll play it the same way night after night... Everybody tunes to the vibes, because their tuning doesn't drift. We calibrate all our Peterson Strobe Tuners to them. That gives you consistency.[140]

Ship Arriving Too Late is an album that draws the listener in gently: once the sound of the instruments is established they are taken and twisted into ever more perverse and anguished shapes. 'Envelopes', rather like 'Redunzl', is a compressed set of illusions, a geometry of up and down that seems to blow all logic apart yet

---

[139]See Linda Williams, *Hard Core*, 1990, p. 220. David Osmond-Smith's treatment of sado-masochism in Mozart is awaited with impatience.
[140]Quoted by Tom Mulhern, 'Frank Zappa: I'm Different', reprinted in *Society Pages*, No. 14, February 1983, p. 12.

fits together like a gleaming machine. What sound like speeded-up keyboards dart in with Nancarrow-like urgency, building up to a crazed peak (surmounted by witch laughter), until the theme comes back as a kind of relief. Then the unbearable panic of 'Teen-age Prostitute' blows all before it.

MAN FROM UTOPIA

When Zappa performed in Palermo in 1982 the concert ended in a riot, with police using teargas to quell the crowd. Zappa's Italian was restricted to *'Seduti, per favore.'* Using Italian, promoter Massimo Basoli asked everyone to calm down. The event was comme-morated by a cover commissioned from Gaetano ('Tanino') Liberatore, a celebrated Italian comic artist whose work was appearing in European anti-establishment magazines in the early 80s (the Italian *Frigidaire* and the French *L'Echo des Savanes*). As an art student Liberatore copied the work of Michelangelo a great deal, which shows in the massive muscles he gives Zappa, who is cast as his robot creation Rank Xerox (originally with green skin too, but Zappa asked for flesh tone[141]). A Milan concert on the same tour, in a 'park' by a mosquito-infested lake in an industrial zone, also supplied some imagery, with Zappa wielding a fly-swatter.[142] On the reverse you can see the audience choking in the teargas, police with riot shields, a bare-breasted woman waving a copy of *Frigidaire*, the Pope with Swiss Guards, two men snorting cocaine. 'Cocaine Decisions' opened the album and may be heard live, interrupted by the 'crack' of a teargas grenade being launched, on *You Can't Do That on Stage Anymore Vol. 3*.[143] A banner '3–1 Vaffanculo' refers to Italy's 1982 victory over Germany in the World Cup, something that happened just prior to the perform-ance at Genoa.[144] The bottom left corner shows John Smothers, the bodyguard celebrated in 'Dong Work for Yuda' (*Joe's Garage Acts II & III*), crushing a photographer's head.

Man from Utopia moved on from the teen-heavy-metal sound and political sweep of *You Are What You Is* to more self-con-tained and compact songs. A crisp, incisive recording quality

[141]*Society Pages*, 30 September 1991, p. 53.
[142]Songs from this gig – 'Fine Girl' and 'Zomby Woof', 1982 – may be heard on *You Can't Do That on Stage Anymore Vol. 1*, 1988.
[143]Frank Zappa, 'Cocaine Decisions', 1982, *You Can't Do That on Stage Anymore Vol. 3*, 1989.
[144]Frank Zappa, 'Sofa 2', 1982, *You Can't Do That on Stage Anymore Vol. 1*, 1988.

characterized all three styles of the record: 'message' pop songs, driving instrumentals and wacked-out experimentation. 'Cocaine Decisions' featured the harmonica of Craig 'Twister' Steward, as Zappa ticked off cocaine users for unprofessional behaviour while under the influence. Despite the disclaimer

> You are a person who is high class
> You are a person not in my class[145]

it is a song of righteous indignation written by a fellow professional. The arrangement is incredibly tight, its crystal clarity both echoing cocaine-induced insight and mocking the chaos drug-use brings in its wake. The way the melody swoops down (for the lines about 'flying to Acapulco') shows a contempt for the Californian lifestyle that is refreshing in its vitriol. As usual, Zappa's own complicity in what he attacks – this is miles away from an LA punk diatribe or a song by Victor Jara denouncing Yankee imperialism – gives the song an acrid twist that doubles the hurt.

'The Dangerous Kitchen' introduced transcribed vocalese with overdubbed accompaniment. Steve Vai transcribed Zappa's pitches – sung in the toneless *sprechstimme* of meltdown – and learned the part on the guitar. He then played the line on acoustic over Zappa's original concert recording. The result is a monstrous fusion of inspired free-form foolishness and meticulous virtuosity: like Jasper Johns' 'sculpture' of a beer can, it begs all sorts of questions about value. In the airbrushed, homogenized world of chart music any old rubbish suddenly looks like the most intricate, faceted art on display.

'Tink Walks Amok' was written for bassist Art Barrow ('Tink' is his nickname), a pattering set of figures for drums and bass that borrows from the irrational metrics of a Beefheart song like 'Pachuco Cadaver', but converts them into something low-key and streamlined. Its complete control (not 'amok' at all) sets off the vagaries either side. 'The Radio is Broken', a celebration of sci-fi stupidities, combines leering, atonal vocals from Zappa and Bob Harris with sections of 'Tink Walks Amok' style tightness. The provocative 'self-indulgence' of its humour serves to block such appreciation, but on a formal level the contrast between the aural fuzz of the distorted singing and the snap of the instrumental sections is reminiscent of the contrasts between 'smooth' and

[145]Frank Zappa, 'Cocaine Decisions', *Man from Utopia*, 1983.

'striated' time in Boulez. The repeated refrain, 'The radio is broken
– it don't work no more', turns into a general comment on the
disintegration of America's ability to communicate with itself, as
the song crumbles into the social reality of 50s monster movies –
sex in the back seats.

> You spilled your coke
> You're stepping on the popcorn
> *JOHN AGAR!*
> Uh-oh...
> (*Dwarf Nebula*)[146]

'Stepping on the pop corn' works as a definition of Zappa's music;
the final 'dwarf nebula' recalls both the 'Processional March' from
Weasels and what God's girlfriend wants to see when she fucks
Squat the Magic Pig.

'Möggio' begins and ends in magnificent snorks, the like of
which had not appeared on a Zappa record since *Uncle Meat*.
Through-composed, 'Möggio' reveals the pressurized inventiveness that flowered in the Synclavier compositions, Nancarrow's
zipping glissandi and dadaist superlogic exfoliating a characteristic
dawn-dew parody romanticism. The bionic musicianship capable
of delivering this kind of modernism has left the emotional
weight of R&B far behind, as illustrated by the medley of 'The
Man from Utopia' and 'Mary Lou'. The rubbishing of sincerity
and expressionism in 'The Radio is Broken' produces extraordinary formal innovations, but comparison with the emotional
force of the R&B originals produces impatience with Zappa's
mocking disengagement.

'Stick Together' is Zappa's anti-union song. People who are
aware of Zappa's radical opinions on other subjects are frequently
surprised with his hostility to unions, in England at least a sign
of Thatcherism – precisely the right-wing ideology *You Are What
You Is* was protesting about. Sung over a reggae beat – cleverly
guying a music which is all about solidarity and a collective
response to capitalist oppression – Zappa admits that 'once upon
a time the idea was good'. His observation that the American
labour movement has 'the Mafia' curse is not ill-founded. Mike
Davis, who has written the best accounts of recent American
history, put it this way:

At the height of the anti-war and Black-power movements in 1968–70,

---

[146]Frank Zappa, 'The Radio is Broken', *Man from Utopia*, 1983.

the old-line craft unions, along with their allies in the Mafia-controlled teamsters and maritime unions, wrecked any hope of a New Deal-type social alliance by viciously attacking anti-war protests, opposing schemes for Black control of local institutions (like the police or schools), rejecting demands for affirmative action in apprenticeship programs, and, in a majority of cases, aligning with the urban-Democratic *anciens régimes* against ghetto and campus demands, even frequently against newly unionized public-sector workers.[147]

Zappa was recording much the same instance of working-class conservatism when he described the anti-hippie, communist-stomping redneck Lonesome Cowboy Burt in 1971.

> He's a unionized roofin' old
> Son-of-a-gun.[148]

However, by 1983, Zappa's condemnation of unions is sounding distinctly right-wing. Mike Davis argues that it was the unions' defensive, collaborative attitude that led to the movement of industry southward to the un-unionized Sunbelt in the 70s and 80s. If the established unions had tried to organize in the south – rather than trade for privileges – the American working class would not have suffered its first decline in real wages since the war. Davis draws socialist conclusions from union corruption, whereas Zappa rubbishes the whole idea of solidarity. After hearing Zappa complain about a Chicago stagehands' union demanding a $3,000 fee for the right to record a concert, TV interviewer Sandi Freeman asked if Zappa wanted a return to nineteenth-century conditions. Zappa baulked at espousing total anti-unionism, but could only reply with the stalest of shopkeeper's adages: 'I'm not saying that at all. I'm saying honesty is the best policy ... no one wants to be honest any more because if you're honest you finish last.'[149]

Zappa's indignation is classically petit bourgeois – the cry of the small businessman squeezed between capital and labour. Though Zappa's art has no place for élitism, his sympathy for the 'man in the street' does not extend to understanding the structural position of the worker in capitalist society. The words of advice ring hollow.

> Common sense is your only hope

[147]Mike Davis, *Prisoners of the American Dream*, 1986, p. 211.
[148]Frank Zappa, 'Lonesome Cowboy Burt', *200 Motels*, 1971.
[149]Frank Zappa to Sandi Freeman, 'The World isn't Ready for Me', *TV Special*, 1984.

When the union tells you it's time to strike
Tell the motherfucker to go take a hike[150]

Reagan's defeat of the air-traffic controllers in 1981 was one of the key battles that established the hegemony of the right in the States in the 80s. The working-class activist's repeated experience (one admittedly only generalized to those involved in socialist politics) is of attempted fightbacks continually *defused* by the trade-union bureaucracy. The idea that it is trade unions that manipulate workers into strikes is a petit-bourgeois fantasy – fed by precisely the media misinformation Zappa claims to disbelieve.

'Stick Together' produces a crack in the edifice a misguided left-wing aesthetic – an insufficiently negative dialectic, or one without poodle play – might try and build on Zappa's work. After the rhetoric of *You Are What You Is* one might expect Zappa to have some realistic political programme (much in the way that the LSE and Berlin students expected to hear him make anti-capitalist statements in the late 60s). However, it is not what Zappa *represents* that makes him politically interesting, but what he does to representation. By stressing the material factors of production – the band's backstage chat, studio tomfoolery, mixing-desk techniques, tape-splices and jumps – he gives the smooth inevitability of the spectacle the lie. His political 'message' cannot be consumed; it requires *work*.

It is worth contrasting Zappa with a band like the Clash. Their explicitly left-wing politics contributed an important strain to punk at a time when the rise of the National Front (and McLaren's 'subversive' use of the swastika) meant many were giving it a right-wing interpretation. One of their songs was 'I'm So Bored with the USA', which went along with punk's discovery that you could sing in an English accent (even if Joe Strummer's cockney was a put-on). However, being bored with the USA also harked back to a time when the English ruled pop music with the Beatles and the Stones (Paul Simonon's Union Jack in the photo on the cover of their first album was evidence of such patriotic populism). In their film *Rude Boy* they showed a liking for élitist 'red terror' politics that is way over the head of a racist fan, who is not argued with but quietly dropped – Strummer showing the disdain for working-class 'backwardness' characteristic of highbrow liberalism. On their second album the Clash brought in Sandy

---

[150]Frank Zappa, 'Stick Together', *Man from Utopia*, 1983.

Robertson, producer of Blue Öyster Cult, in order to obtain the currently saleable heavy-metal guitar sound. The idea was to break big in America. Their intentions were revealed as susceptible to commercial ploys, which compromised their politics as much as Labour Party politicians (or trade-union bureaucrats) who promise to fight for socialism and then sell out. The explicit political statement is no guarantee of integrity in art.

Zappa's aesthetic integrity works via a grasp of the concrete situation he operates in. He wishes to dramatize the material situation in which he is in rather than produce grand statements. His hostility towards unions arises from his economic position within music. 'Rudy Wants to Buy Yez a Drink' (*Chunga's Revenge*, 1970) had already exposed how useless the musician's union – designed for classical and jazz musicians – was in relating to rock. It was, though, Zappa's experiences in the classical field that gave him an undying hatred of what he saw as 'union mentality': 'Why should I pay these guys who don't care about what I'm doing?'[151]

Zappa has on tape an orchestral shop steward shouting 'time!' in order to ruin a take an extra ten seconds would have completed. In spending the cash raised through singing 'Dinah-Moe Humm' Zappa encountered the intransigence of unions in protecting the interests of an alienated workforce. It is naïve of him to expect bought craftspeople to exhibit the same commitment as his band members, but in the absence of any politics connected to working-class struggle it is easy to see why such a typical petit-bourgeois attitude towards unions should fit. Talking of his Synclavier, John Diliberto of *Music Technology* magazine asked Zappa why he needed all this investment in hardware when previous composers did not.

> FZ: Because back then they didn't have a musicians' union. Maybe they had more rehearsal time and they could write things that would get played.
>
> JD: So you think that the musician's union is holding back you and other artists?
>
> FZ: No! I think all unions are. I don't mind saying I am anti-union. The union mentality has affected the arts drastically in the United States. The worst example would be the stagehands' union, which in many instances earns more than the musicians who are playing.[152]

---

[151]Frank Zappa to Sandi Freeman, 'The World isn't Ready for Me', *TV Special*, 1984.
[152]Quoted by John Diliberto, 'Frank Zappa and His Digital Orchestra', *Electronic Musician*, September 1986, p. 54.

In using capitalist means to realize his music Zappa inevitably starts thinking like a capitalist.

'Sex' manages to be utterly offensive in a way only Zappa knows how. Ostensibly decrying the stress on slimness that marks American commercial imagery, it does so in a manner that talks about the woman as a fuckbag.

THE BIGGER THE CUSHION, THE BETTER THE PUSHIN'[153]

On the other hand, the remark about 'riding on an ironin' board' is so deftly accurate – in a shamefully undocumented area – that the (male) listener has to laugh.

> Some girls try it 'n they don't like it
> They complain 'cause it don't last[154]

Zappa's lyric operates in this sensitive area like a bull in a china shop, exposing such widespread social ignorance of sexual matters that its caustic stringency is finally redemptive. Or not. You decide.

'The Jazz Discharge Party Hats' further documents the band's knicker fetish with more overdubbed meltdown. If the 'bizarreness' of the band's behaviour seems lame in comparison with the original Mothers, this merely indicates changes in the relationship of personal life to public morals in the intervening years. As usual Zappa presents us with material. Frequently it is the most barren stretches of his music that in later years comes to sparkle with suggestive social comment as conceptual continuity works its charm (Zappa actually cites it as one of his most innovative recordings). As yet, the negative dialectics of poodle play finds this track inert, a sure sign of some repressed excitement someday to erupt. Although this may sound like the worst case of 'special pleading', the experience of rubbish-transmutation in Zappa is so regular that it has become impractical to condemn anything – even a track like this.

The closing 'We are Not Alone' makes use of Marty Krystall, the West Coast tenor saxophonist. Krystall's credits include Charlie Haden, Jaco Pastorius, Aretha Franklin and impressive work with Buell Neidlinger.[155] 'We are Not Alone' combines

---

[153]Frank Zappa, 'Sex', *Man from Utopia*, 1983.
[154]Ibid.
[155]Marty Krystall can be heard to advantage with Buell Neidlinger's String Jazz on *Swingrass '83*, 1982, Antilles AN1014, and *Locomotive*, 1988, Soul Note 121161, a brilliant band: Western Swing meets Duke and Monk. Krystall and Neidlinger also played with Don Preston on *Aurora*, 1988, Denon CY73148.

R&B simplicity with shimmering irregularity in a concise squib. The relationship between the drum's heavy pattern and the keyboards is subtly displaced, creating a strange multiplicity. *Man from Utopia* reached number 153 in the *Billboard* charts in April 1983.

BABY SNAKES

Billed as 'a movie about people who do stuff that is not normal', the film *Baby Snakes* was premièred on 21 December 1979 at the Victoria Theater, New York. It featured the 1977/8 band with Adrian Belew and Terry Bozzio both on- and offstage, Roy Estrada and the amazing clay animations of Bruce Bickford. Zappa found that Bickford's grotesque transformations were so suggestive that they frequently suited music they were not designed for. Although it received the Premier Grand Prix for a musical film in Paris in 1981, it was not a success and very rarely shown. In 1982 Barking Pumpkin released a picture disk with some live tracks from the film.[156] It featured another Norman Seeff photograph: as Zappa stares out with a look of sinister sleaze, stray hair curling over his face, the make-up woman from *Joe's Garage* proffers her tongue. Side one was a stonking live suite; side two featured a 'Dinah-Moe Humm' encore and an eleven-minute 'Punky's Whips'. During the 'Titties & Beer' dialogue with Bozzio, Zappa explains that he has already *been* to hell – he was signed to Warner Brothers 'for nine fucking years'. To hear a multinational entertainment conglomerate abused in front of a large, excited rock audience is exhilarating. It was an imposing document of an unstoppable band, a rock release in the midst of a turn to classicism.

---

[156]Frank Zappa, *Baby Snakes*, 1982.

CHAPTER 9
MORE GUITARS

The mouth of the puppy should be cleared of mucus by rubbing round it and inside with a white handkerchief or a piece of gauze. If the after-birth has been expelled, the cord joining this to the puppy must be severed. The cord should be tied tightly with cotton about an inch from the puppy's abdomen and then the rest of the cord and the placenta cut off with a pair of sterilized scissors.

Margaret Rothery Sheldon and Barbara Lockwood, *Breeding from Your Poodle*[1]

SHUT UP 'N PLAY YER GUITAR[2]

Tommy Mars read out the words of this chapter's epigraph during 'Pound for a Brown' when Frank Zappa played the Hammersmith Odeon in London on 17 February 1979.

> Just when they wind up the Nanook section ('Don't Eat the Yellow Snow' and 'St Alphonso's Pancake Breakfast') and the act seems under control, Zappa starts leafing through a book that someone's handed him from the front row. He looks *delighted*. It's passed around the whole band, who all crack up in hysterics. We're treated to an extract – a clinical aid to the canine birth process, advising the use of sterilized scissors.[3]

The poodle text provides a perfect description of Zappa's guitar-playing: living gristle sliced at by a musical wit both clinical and razor-sharp. In being severed from the mother the puppie suffers irreparable loss, a trauma relived by the castration complex – you can also hear this in Zappa's playing. Since Hendrix's untimely death all guitar-playing has been disappointed, his stance thieved

[1] Margaret Rothery Sheldon and Barbara Lockwood, *Breeding from Your Poodle*, 1963, p. 53.
[2] Thanks to Mårten Sund for running an early version of this chapter, *Society Pages*, No. 9, March 1982, pp. 9–13.
[3] Mark Ellen, 'A Tasty Change from So-so Soup', *New Musical Express*, 24 February 1979.

by innumerable charlatans. This is why, however assertive or grand or filthy they are, a melancholy always invades Zappa's solos, the claustrophobia that has haunted his lyrics from 'Stuff up the cracks, turn on the gas, I'm gonna take my life'[4] to 'confinement loaf', the bread designed to keep convicts docile.[5] Despite all the freedoms taken there is a recognition of limits which is very moving.

Breeding from Your Poodle entered Zappa's universe by its presence in remaindered bookshops in Britain in the late 70s. It was passed to Frank Zappa by photographer John McQueenie, who was sitting in the front row. Zappa's music is like some hungry amoeba – a fast 'n bulbous jelly – in the way it can absorb extraneous materials and use them to extrude itself into new areas.[6]

In the post-*Roxy* bands Zappa's guitar became the pre-eminent focus for improvisation.

> I enjoy going on stage and improvising a guitar solo. You know, you can't do that at home. You can sit around and noodle on your guitar, but it's the instant challenge of going against the laws of physics and the laws of gravity and playing something nobody ever heard before. And no one would dare to play. That's what I like to do. That's ... I mean, that's sex. It's better than sex. That takes you into the realm of science.[7]

Shut Up 'N Play Yer Guitar was originally designed for specialist, guitar-oriented listeners and therefore made available through mail order only. It was successful, and subsequently appeared in the shops as a three-record box set, distributed in America by Phonogram and worldwide by CBS. It is mainly full-flight electric guitar using feedback and no-holds-barred rhetoric, relieved by only three acoustic tracks and two where Zappa's use of his Strat with Di Marzio pick-ups (rather than the handmade Gibson copy sold to Zappa by its maker backstage, with its extra fret[8]) results in a radically different tone. The massiveness of the rock sound has led to criticism of the album as monotonous, but actually the close focus gives room for highly evolved permutations. If listeners

---

[4] Frank Zappa, 'Stuff up the Cracks', *Ruben & the Jets*, 1969.
[5] Frank Zappa, 'Any Kind of Pain', *Broadway the Hard Way*, 1988.
[6] Danny Houston and I became credible to each other when it was discovered that we each had not only a copy but *several* copies of *Breeding from Your Poodle*. Credit must go to him for organizing the book's presentation at Hammersmith Odeon. A copy was subsequently sent to Mårten Sund, who photographed Zappa with the book in Oslo (see frontispiece).
[7] Quoted by John Swenson, 'Frank Zappa: The Interview', *Guitar World*, March 1982.
[8] Steve Rosen, 'Frank Zappa', *Rock Guitarist*, 1977, reprinted in *Society Pages*, No. 26, July 1985, p. 21, and *Music UK*, No. 30, June 1984, p. 28.

are prepared to immerse themselves in the music, it is about as monotonous as late Trane or Last Exit – or, as Zappa told *Guitar*, Jimmy Reed, the Chicago bluesman.

> Some people listen to one Jimmy Reed record and say, Hey, it all sounds the same. To the uninitiated ear it does, because it's almost exactly the same record after record, but if you like that sort of stuff and can appreciate the subtleties that are involved in the way the boogies are played and so forth, then it opens up a whole new world for you and you don't get bored with it.[9]

As if to showcase his fertility of ideas Zappa presents no less than *four* solos from the same song. 'Inca Roads' is the occasion for 'Shut Up 'N Play Yer Guitar' from the Hammersmith Odeon matinée on 18 February 1979; 'Shut Up 'N Play Yer Guitar Some More' from Hammersmith on 17 February; 'Return of the Son of Shut Up 'N Play Yer Guitar' from Hammersmith on 19 February; and 'Gee, I Like Your Pants' from the Hammersmith evening performance on 18 February. All recorded within three days and hardly a lick repeated.

The blurb on the back of the box made out it was Zappa's bid for cultural credibility, the musical muscle the critics were deaf to in their rush to condemn his naughty words – the CD release included a review from *Guitar Player*. The box the records appeared in was super-glossy, the inner sleeves stylish and smart, the text set with a right-justified margin so that the interested party always looks at it upside down first. On the cover Zappa sat at his grand piano holding his customized Les Paul and wearing a Panama hat, looking out of these trappings of success with teeth-gritted determination: a deluxe chocolate box of live nuggets wrapped in imitation gold leaf.

It kicked off with 'five five FIVE', wrongly credited to Hammersmith, 17 February,[10] a fury that combines rock onslaught with East European peasant swirl, until Zappa suddenly slows down and plays a series of notes *against the backing*, making the music suddenly alien and unplaceable, no longer 'rock' but some weird rumble. The title refers to its metric scheme. Zappa explained it thus: 'It's in 5/8, 5/8, 5/4. You count it like this: One two one two three, one two one two three, one-and two-and three-and four-and five-and.'[11] The rhythmic precision of his

---

[9] Quoted by John Dalton, 'Frank Zappa Part II', *Guitar*, June 1979, p. 26.
[10] Actually it is the coda to 'Conehead', performed at the start of the set on 19 February 1979.
[11] Frank Zappa, 'Absolutely Frank: First Steps in Odd Metres', *Guitar Player*, November 1982.

411

accompanists, particularly Vinnie Colaiuta's flexi-directional multiplicity, gives Zappa freedom to invent on the spot. Zappa called him:

> the best guy I've ever had a chance to work with in terms of following what I play. He is really astute and he can subdivide a bar like nobody's business and still come out on the beat. He's really good.[12]

A tiny segment of vocal surprise leads into 'Hog Heaven', extracted from a performance of 'The Illinois Enema Bandit'. It opens with what sounds like slowed-down guitar and gradually winds up to regular pitch and then sticks on a repeated figure. It is as if Zappa is playing in real-time the temporal dislocations of his tape-splice collage. The voice from *Läther* says, 'God that was really beautiful', and the listener is plunged into the majestic harmonies of 'Inca Roads'. On *Läther* the phrase mocked the high seriousness of 'Naval Aviation in Art', here it hinges a transition between ugly rock violence and a confidently surging piece of jazz, Arthur Barrow's bass moving with a fluency uncharacteristic of rock. Whatever his unarguable talents, Zappa's real claim to fame lies in the moments where there is no calibrated assurance that what he is doing is well achieved or brilliant. The way his material can be split apart and recombined almost at random, and still come out with suggestive moments, a ricochet of meanings, is quite unique.

Side one ends with 'While You Were Out', named after the heading printed on Post-its, the removable yellow notelets that invaded offices in the 1980s (Zappa as usual conjuring poetry from the everyday). Recorded in the studio with minimal percussion accompaniment, it was played on an acoustic Black Widow plugged directly into the recording console. It is in the reflective, consolatory vein of *Uncle Meat*'s 'Nine Types of Industrial Pollution' – the music of incipient sleep, where gaps keep shutting down across the continuities of conscious thought.

Side two begins with 'Treacherous Cretins'. Like 'Deathless Horsie' on side four, it is the tune Zappa used to open with in 1979, an insinuating, hypnotic riff carried by Warren Cucurullo's electric sitar on the first and Ed Mann's vibes on the second. Zappa used a radio mike and would start playing while offstage, making the music sound still more etherial and detached. Like 'Hog Heaven', 'Soup and Old Clothes' is an 'Enema Bandit' out-take.

---

[12]Quoted by John Dalton, 'Frank Zappa: Shut Up and Play Your Guitar', *Guitar*, May 1979 p. 22.

The stomping rhythm develops a tilted tango propensity. Zappa's dips and wriggles pursue arguments to rival the prose of late Henry James in their baroque, focused intelligence and sinister power. The contrast between the repeated synthesized horn riff and the guitar's squirmiferous oozing is abetted by Colaiuta's camp drum-rolls.

'Variations on the Carlos Santana Secret Chord Progression' sounds like it has been lifted from 'If Only She Woulda', its Doors-like rhythm providing a solid frame for Zappa's hard shapes. 'Gee, I Like Your Pants' features a burst of the star-spangled notes used sparingly in the classic 'Inca Roads' solo on *One Size Fits All*. The title is a phrase from 'Dead Girls of London', reviling the English obsession with clothes (though what English person swears 'Gee'?). The New York Dolls noticed the same thing (but with approval), giving credibility to Zappa's claim to be documenting cultural folklore.

> Johnny got a drape in blue with a black velvet collar. We loved to dress up. Here in America, nobody gives a shit about clothing, but in Europe, somebody will go 'What the fuck are you doing with those crazy pants'. That might get you to be cool.[13]

Down Beat's champion of jazz's post-harmolodic rediscovery of the electric guitar, Bill Milkowski, proves (naturally) to be an informed Zappa fan. He asked Zappa about the 'Bulgarian bagpipe technique'.

> With your left hand you're fretting the notes and with your right hand you're also fretting the notes with a pick. Instead of plucking the string you're fretting the string, you hit the string and then that presses it against the fret so it actuates the string and also determines the pitch, and you can move back and forth real fast that way . . . just aiming it straight down the string. On the guitar album you can hear it on 'Gee, I Like Your Pants' and 'Variations on the Carlos Santana Secret Chord Progression'. Actually, I learned it from Jim Gordon, who is a drummer, and he picked it up from some other guitar player. He showed it to me in 1972.[14]

'Canarsie' begins with a band member saying 'Identify your last port of entry, space wanderer' and 'Canarsie, where everyone looks the same' (Canarsie is where Warren Cucurullo's parents

[13]Sylvain Sylvain, quoted by Jon Savage, *England's Dreaming: Sex Pistols and Punk Rock*, 1991, p. 59.
[14]Quoted by Bill Milkowski, 'Frank Zappa: Guitar Player', *Down Beat*, February 1983.

live; he is playing electric sitar here). Patrick O'Hearn's jaggedly alien bass riff provokes some of Zappa's most abstract playing.

'Ship Ahoy' ('Duck Duck Goose' on *Läther*) has Bozzio's drums and Estrada's bass rattle in sympathy as if they are part of the all-enveloping feedback; the notes sound as if they are swallowing themselves, a sensitivity that is positively erogenous. Sheer *sound* is shaping the direction of the music: appropriate that André Lewis – associate of Buddy Miles and the funk musicians Hendrix was gravitating towards before his death – is playing keyboards. The spoken phrase 'ship ahoy' preceding the track sounds as if someone engaged in gay-bar cruising has found the object of his desire (a version of 'hello, sailor'). This relates to *Läther*'s focus on sexual quandary, but the music sounds like the bubbling waters of a ship's wake: buoys and gulls and dissolution into the ocean.

'Pink Napkins' is 'Black Napkins' played on the Strat with Di Marzio pick-ups. The colour pink points to its sound-world: organic gurgles and plops, pink with the embarrassing tenderness of dolls' legs in rubber latex. 'Beat It with Your Fist' is short, hard and clear, with a jumble of voices that include some dialogue from *Lumpy Gravy*, indicating that Zappa had successfully wrested the masters from Herb Cohen. 'Pinocchio's Furniture', from a 1980 rendition of 'Chunga's Revenge', returns to gypsy-mutant-industrial-vacuum-cleaner guitar. Its title pursues Zappa's surrealist view of commodity society: the discomfort of the wooden doll staring at his wooden furniture. 'Why Johnny Can't Read' (the title refers to 'Johnny Can't Read' by the Eagles) has the alien feel of 'Canarsie': big sonic events triggered in space. Zappa is pioneering a new agenda for improvisation, where free soloing is abetted so closely by the accompanists that the music sounds completely organized.

Like most of Zappa's record sets, the last side presents the musical *tour de force*. 'Stucco Homes' derives its name from Zappa's own description of residences in Beverly Hills (as well as being his alias when singing 'Dead Girls of London' with Ike Willis on L. Shankar's *Touch Me There*) and features private acoustic reflections, possible melodies skittering off in all directions through Vinnie Colaiuta's spacious percussion. 'Canard du Jour' translates as 'Hoax of the Day': Zappa plays bouzouki to Jean-Luc Ponty's baritone violin. When Zappa first gave interviews he would say that the only instrument he thought sounded like his guitar was the bouzouki. When Ponty first started improvising he laid aside his prize-winning classical violin and took up saxophone.

laid aside his prize-winning classical violin and took up saxophone. The hoax could be Zappa imitating guitar on a bouzouki and Ponty imitating a horn on his violin (at times his bowing sounds astonishingly like breath). Zappa is acutely aware of the hypocrisies of pseudo-authenticity: when acting as a DJ in 1980 he found a sleeve note description of Brian Jones taking to the sitar 'like a native' utterly preposterous.[15] The hoax could be a reference to ethnological forgeries, as the music bounds off into folk melodies and jigs. After the stridency of the live rock tracks, it is a demonstration of what can be achieved with limited means by touching off memories of other cultures, other instruments. 'Canard du Jour', lacking as it does either rock timbre or a pounding beat, recalls the folk-delvings of Bartók and Stravinsky.

RHYTHM

When Zappa is asked what he considers special about his playing, he often mentions rhythm. *The Frank Zappa Guitar Book*[16] was produced in tandem with *Shut Up 'N Play Yer Guitar*, with a photograph of Zappa from the same session on the cover. It consisted of transcriptions by Steve Vai of Zappa's solos. It emphasized how unacademic Zappa's approach is. When frozen on the page, his music looks like something out of the new complexity.

> FZ: That's one of the things I'm doing that other people aren't. I think most of the people who are rated as really fantastic guitar players are dealing with rhythmic material that has been beaten to death, and there's nothing subtle about it at all, because what they do is either divided in triplets or straight up and down, really fast 32nd notes and stuff like that. Shit, anybody can do that if they sit down and practise their scales. But mine is based on something else.
>
> JOHN DALTON: You use groups of fives and sevens on beats.
>
> FZ: Yeah, and across bars and stuff like that. 'Sheik Yerbouti Tango' is kinda interesting. Here there are groups of septuplets but they're accented in five, culminating in this little chingus here which has ten in the space of a dotted quarter, with ornaments inside the ten.[17]

In a series in *Guitar Player* magazine called 'Absolutely Frank' in

[15]Frank Zappa, *Star Special*, BBC Radio 1, January 1980.
[16]Frank Zappa, *The Frank Zappa Guitar Book*, Music Sales Ltd, 1982.
[17]Quoted by John Dalton, 'Frank Zappa: Shut Up and Play Your Guitar', *Guitar*, May 1979, p. 22.

December 1982 (changed at his request in 1983 to 'Non-Foods'[18]), Zappa was asked about the note-groupings within 'Gee, I Like Your Pants'.

> It's only a mystery hemiola [rhythmic relationship of three against two], but the thing that's fascinating about it is that we end up right on the beat. One, two, three, four, one – then it comes back on the beat of the second beat of the bar. Anybody can do that if they want to. And then after you've done it, who do you impress with it? Do you play it for your girlfriend and say, 'Hey, 27 over 3!' She'll say, 'Big deal. *Why?*' When people hear it, they won't say it sounds like 27 over 3, but they will know that it sounds different.[19]

Zappa is aware of the deficiencies of Western classical music as regards rhythm. The transcriptions – made possible by Steve Vai's Berklee education and a long apprenticeship of Zappa obsession – were an attempt to bridge the gap. Minimalism claims to open out classical music to other cultures, yet never faces non-classical sound in its specific complexity. Zappa's scores makes such world-music pretensions look like the sorry excuses they are. They also explain Zappa's need for virtuosi, even if these young players lack the character of the original Mothers or the mature musicianship of the *Roxy* players.

> If you learn music in school, most of what they teach you is straight up and down. You know: One, two, three, four. It's all real square; it's all real boring. It's like this: in the realm of mathematics, there is something beyond adding and subtracting, it goes all the way out. And it's the same in music. The type of music that people are taught in schools, especially from the rhythmic standpoint, never gets beyond addition and multiplication. There's no algebra out there. There's certainly no physics, and there's no calculus or trigonometry. There's nothing interesting in musical rhythm that they teach you in school. Most academic situations tend to ignore this type of rhythmic approach – not just mine, but anybody's that's polyrhythmic. They ignore that approach because the great bulk of the repertoire that a graduate of a classical institution is going to play doesn't have to have any of that, so they concentrate on stuff that's going to be useful to them when they take jobs in orchestras and have to play Beethoven's Fifth for the rest of their lives.[20]

This shows a fascination for the moment at which abstractions

---

[18]Used in American supermarkets to indicate the hardware section of the store (only introduced to England in the mid-80s), this bizarre coinage combines both the biblical 'Man may not live by bread alone' and the negativity poodle play applauds in modern art.
[19]Frank Zappa, 'Non-Foods: Coming to Grips with Polyrhythms', *Guitar Player*, reprinted in *Society Pages*, No. 16, June 1983, p. 29.
[20]Ibid.

like rhythm or number begin to develop the capacity to figure the real world. It is a statement of dialectics – completely at odds with poststructuralist despair at thought ever encountering the real, or postmodernism's blithe satisfaction with the building blocks of discourse. Zappa takes the line that it is atonality that makes people object to avant-garde classical music. People can enjoy polyrhythm in, say, African drumming, even if they cannot count it.

> If you have a diatonic setting or even a bitonal setting with complicated rhythmic stuff on it, there's no reason why it shouldn't be appealing to a wide range of people. People *like* rhythm. And the thing that makes the rhythm work is whether people are playing it *right*. There is such a thing as a quintuplet played in a bad way so that you don't really hear five in the space of whatever amount of notes it is taking the place of. And it doesn't impress you when you hear your quintuplets played stupidly. But in a real good five over a real good four or a three sounds great. And when it lines up it makes another rhythm – it makes a rhythmic *difference* tone . . . There's another rhythm that is created when you do *anything over anything*. If one guy is playing exactly the 4/4 of the bar and another guy is playing nine beats against that you're going to get another rhythm . . . and that's the difference tone, the *mystery note*. You know that it's there: your foot is tapping even though the musician isn't playing the four beats, your foot is tapping in the basic time signature of the song. And there is a clock inside your body that's saying 'We're in 4/4.' And somebody plays nine across it, and inside your body you hear the difference, and that's part of the excitement of that kind of rhythm.[21]

This stress on what people *like* and the *physical* communication of music sets Zappa apart from the right-wing interpretation of Adorno, which ignores the dimension of social critique in order to emphasize mandarin purism. A technical analysis of Zappa's music – including the supposedly 'stupid' songs – reveals astonishing rhythmic complexities. Jazz-rock ideology consecrated complexity as a mark of superiority, just as minimalism consecrates simplicity: both ignore the fact that musical progress is achievable only by a dialectic between musicianship and the needs of the expressive body. It is possible to use a sliderule to 'demonstrate' Zappa's contribution to music, but it is his placement of complexity in context, as a problem for both players and the music industry, that makes his art so charged and urgent. Tommy Mars

---

[21]Ibid.

was certain that something extraordinary was happening in the pursuit of unusual rhythms.

> I feel it very spiritually when you have these relationships, even a simple 5 over 4, type of things that aren't really natural to the Western culture. For me personally I have to blank out, I feel it, it's not so much the actual literal arithmetic numerical equation of how those notes work together, it's a feeling and when I'm there I really feel like I'm floating, it's very very strange and I've only really been able to do that with Frank's music. When you're playing from a four-square concept you're used to that, but when this four-square thing leaves and you feel this strange phrase, it's a very surreal experience – and some nights are better than others, too. Some nights you can really nail it and you're dealing with a whole band here, it's not as if it's just one person who's doing it, there's a group business that takes over there – that's quite an experience too. We're all grateful as musicians that Frank wrote things like that. I know when Vinnie [Colaiuta] first got in the band, we'd call each other on the phone like we were little chipmunks working on the nuts, man, we would go over certain things we did at rehearsal, it was a real *esprit* in those days.[22]

MORE AND MORE GUITARS

The CD release of *Shut Up* included a reprint of John Swenson's appreciative review in *Guitar World*. Besides pointing out that Brian Eno's much publicized intellectualism is tiddlywinks compared to Zappa's experimental attitude, it pointed out that more guitar records could appear: 'Theoretically, Frank Zappa could release an infinite number of new records just working from the boxes and boxes of guitar solos stacked up in his basement recording studio. *Shut Up 'N Play* . . . is only the tip of the iceberg.'[23]

Titled simply *Guitar*, more of the iceberg was revealed on both vinyl and CD in 1988. The double album featured nineteen cuts and the double CD thirty-two. At this point Zappa started to exploit the full potential of the new format: along with the six *You Can't Do That on Stage Anymore* double sets, the five CDs derived from the 1988 tour and the two boxes of 'official' bootlegs, the sheer amount of material caused even devotees to flounder. Like the map in the Borges story that is so detailed that it dupli-

[22]Tommy Mars, interview with the author, LA, 30 October 1993.
[23]John Swenson, 'Frank Zappa: Shut Up 'N Play Yer Guitar', *Guitar World*, Vol. 2, No. 6, November 1981, reproduced in CD issue of *Shut Up 'N Play Yer Guitar*, 1990.

cates the terrain, Zappa's art appears to stretch off into a world of infinite variations.

Guitar is recorded with still greater fidelity than *Shut Up*, achieving a three-dimensional, sculptural massiveness that makes the previous record sound emaciated. The tracks are no longer bridged by vocal exclamations. Apart from three tracks which feature the 1979 band with the Arthur Barrow and Vinnie Colaiuta rhythm section, the band is always from one of the two 80s line-ups, which both featured the Scott Thunes and Chad Wackerman rhythm section. It opens with a blues vamp entitled 'Sexual Harassment in the Workplace', which sounds like an attempt to invade the regular world inhabited by the likes of Stevie Ray Vaughan, but Zappa soon veers off into his characteristic pungencies. Yet the rhythmic complexity is not contrived.

> The hardest thing for me to do is play straight up and down, absolutely the hardest to do. Stuff that everybody else does naturally just seems as impossible as shit to me. I don't think in little groups of twos and fours and stuff; they just don't come out that way. I can sit around and play fives and sevens all day long with no sweat. But the minute I've got to go *do*-do-do-do *do*-do-do-do it feels weird, it's like wearing tight shoes.[24]

The space and flexibility of his accompanists is staggering: Zappa has invented a new kind of music, the glistening precision of drums and bass and keyboard framing positively scabrous invention. The playing is less frenetic than *Shut Up*, but each solo carves its own shape. Zappa is looking for something on these solos, and communicates the excitement of his search. The 1984 band had no percussionist, but Tommy Mars uses his synthesizer in a percussive way.

'Chalk Pie' ends with some stirring low notes that sound like the 'skidmarks' Zappa notices in female underwear.[25] They were played on his 'Hendrix Strat', the guitar Hendrix burned at the Miami Pop Festival.

> It was given to me by the guy who used to be his roadie. I had it hanging on the wall in the basement for years until last year when I gave it to Rex Bogue and said, 'Put this sucker back together', because

---

[24]Steve Rosen, 'Frank Zappa', *Rock Guitarist*, 1977, reprinted in *Society Pages*, No. 26, July 1985, p. 23, and *Music UK*, No. 30, June 1984, p. 30.
[25]Frank Zappa, 'Panty Rap', *Tinsel Town Rebellion*, 1981.

it was all tore up. The neck was cracked off, the body was all fired, and the pickups were blistered and bubbled.[26]

At the end of 'When No One was No One' you can hear someone in the audience shout 'Who are the Brain Police?' at the top of their lungs, just before Zappa cuts into 'Once Again, without the Net'. 'Outside Now (Original Solo)' presents the solo in its original context, before its xenochronous presentation on *Joe's Garage*. 'For Duane', logically enough, is an excerpt from 'Whipping Post'. 'Systems of Edges' is yet another solo from 'Inca Roads', making use of Colaiuta's jazzy fluency; 'Do Not Try This at Home' uses Chad Wackerman's explosive accuracy, the guitar whining like a siren in a Varèsian future-scape. In live performance a hand-signal – twirling rasta braids – could enforce a 'reggae' beat (a two-four emphasis rather than one-three), which, while sounding nothing like reggae (one tune is called 'That's Not Really Reggae') due to the sound of the instruments, gives yet another tilt to the rhythmic matrix. For 'Watermelon in Easter Hay', the beautiful guitar show-case tune from *Joe's Garage*, Zappa develops a piping sound on his customized Strat reminiscent of the *Bongo Fury* solos.

The last track on the CD, 'It ain't Necessarily the St James Infirmary', combines two famous jazz tunes. This squint-eyed view of America's pre-rock musical heritage turned up again on *Make a Jazz Noise Here*. Given the moribund nature of rock music on the corporate level Zappa was working on, it is as if he needed to look to jazz to find his equivalents.

[26]Steve Rosen, 'Frank Zappa', *Rock Guitarist*, 1977, reprinted in *Society Pages*, No. 26, July 1985, p. 21.

CHAPTER 10
ORCHESTRAS AND BROADWAY

THE LONDON SYMPHONY ORCHESTRA

Zappa was only able to realize his orchestral ambitions by financing them himself. In *The Real Frank Zappa Book* he outlines two failed projects – 'orchestral stupidities'[1] – that explain why this should be so. *London Symphony Orchestra Vol. I* appeared in an austerely classical sleeve, with black lettering embossed on a matt-grey background. The LSO's emblem and the words 'Conducted by Kent Nagano' appear on the front, along with Nagano's career biography on the inner sleeve. The cover emphasizes its straightness to the point of being weird, actually looking more like the cool 'classicism' of next year's Chicago house compilations.[2] Zappa's back-cover shot by Steve Schapiro makes him look reasonable and friendly in the manner of classical-music promo shots. The LSO was spiced up with the addition of David Ocker (solo clarinet), Ed Mann (percussion) and Chad Wackerman (drums). Recorded at Twickenham Film Studios on twenty-four-track in January 1983, it eschewed the usual 'central mike' recording of orchestras for spot mikes and controlled mixing.

The music has a relaxed lushness that is very different from the orchestra parts of *200 Motels*, which, apart from the heroic cheesiness of the overture, tended towards the explosive sound-world of Boulez and the strained textures of Gyorgy Ligeti. The reviewer in *Society Pages* compared the music to a dinosaur: unlike Zappa's small group work, his musical nervous energy did not have the strength to animate all the parts. This image was actually coined by Zappa himself when trying to explain how hard it was to motivate orchestras: 'The head is real tiny and the body is real

---

[1] Frank Zappa, with Peter Occhiogrosso, *The Real Frank Zappa Book*, 1989, pp. 146–50. A text which originally appeared in *Musician*, No. 36, September 1981.
[2] For example, Steve 'Silk' Hurley, 'Jack Your Body', 1985, London LON117.

big and by the time the thought goes from there to here, the tail has already rotted off.'³

Richard Barrett, one of England's new complexity composers, has argued Zappa's music suffers from generic apartheid in the 80s. The separation of rock and orchestral music denies the miscegenation of elements that was previously so fascinating. Attending Zappa's Barbican showcase for the LSO scores, he appreciated Zappa's 'studio mixer's ear' in the arrangements, but sensed a lack of musical material.

Both the *Society Pages* reviewer and Richard Barrett are registering disappointment that the manic energy of Zappa's rock music has somehow not translated into the full orchestral version. It is as if the large forces have diluted his music. Whereas the Royce Hall performances for *Orchestral Favorites* were buoyed by electric guitar and bass as well as band members' drums and percussion, the music as played by the LSO seems somewhat grey and eventless. Zappa himself was not too taken with the results.

> Thanks to songs like '*Dinah-Moe Humm*', '*Titties 'n Beer*' and '*Don't Eat the Yellow Snow*', I managed to accumulate enough cash to bribe a group of drones to grind its way through pieces like '*Mo 'n Herb's Vacation*', '*Bob in Dacron*' and '*Bogus Pomp*' (eventually released on *London Symphony Orchestra, Volumes I and II*) – in performances which come off like high-class 'demos' of what actually resides in the scores.⁴

It is difficult to say whether the lack of energy results from accepting the splits of modern music – bribing unwilling 'drones' with the proceeds of rock music exploitation – or from bad performances: both seem to be aspects of the same problem.

Viewed from the perspective of Darmstadt and the new complexity, which is concerned with the new colours and intensities to be squeezed from classical orchestration – the work of Giacinto Scelsi, Michael Finnissy, James Dillon, Chris Dench and Barrett himself – Zappa's orchestral music is indeed 'preposterously non-modern' (a description used by Zappa in the sleeve-note to *The Perfect Stranger*). However, this mistakes his surrealist intent. Zappa fits better into a tradition that might comprise Kurt Weill,

---

³Quoted by Josef Woodard, 'Zappa: The Licence to be a Maniac', *Musician*, 1986, reprinted in *Society Pages*, No. 33, December 1986, p. 18.
⁴Frank Zappa, with Peter Occhiogrosso, *The Real Frank Zappa Book*, 1989, p. 146.

Friedrich Gulda and the Stravinsky of *Ebony Concerto*[5] than to an overtly modernist line of development.

'Sad Jane' is a lugubrious concoction of film-music clichés, the mournful melancholia that frequently sets the scene for psychic possession or poltergeist violence. It uses a simple chord sequence played on the harp, reminiscent of 'Watermelon in Easter Hay'. After the initial statement, bassoons and basses are used in a positively salacious manner to introduce one of those Varèsean moments which seems to squeeze a thin line of gold from the chords. There is a tinge of Webern to some of the sparser writing, but the swathes of strings are direct-from-Hollywood. The contrast between plaintive clarinets and growling brass is milked and there is a puffing flute line whose strenuousness recalls similar moments on *Lumpy Gravy*. In the middle Chad Wackerman introduces the main theme on drums. The tune works like a Zappa guitar solo, full of humorous 'Twilight Zone' riffs and wilful leaps. Although lacking the ice-pick-in-the-forehead virulence of most of Zappa's music, the attention to the timbral mix means that nothing is ever predictable. Every note has a sense of purpose.

'Pedro's Dowry' is presented in a different arrangement from *Orchestral Favorites*, where it used only forty pieces. There is a diminution of swagger, as if the string players are having difficulty in relating to its vulgar romanticism, but the brass and percussion are great. The regular beat offsets the dada fidgets (an orchestration of the pleasure of hearing Zappa's guitar stretch out against drummers like Colaiuta or Wackerman). By the end the strings appear to have gained interest and pile into their musical crevices like a swarm of wasps. The seasick lurching between onward velocity and stasis is a musical version of the seduction of the story. Before the 'disco section' featuring the 'enticingly Australian violin' of Ashley Arbuckle, the need to stuff in as many metrical ideas as possible causes great tension. The music winds itself into a passionate surge before concluding in the bathos of the 'ding-dong' doorbell.

'Envelopes' makes a fascinating contrast to the rock band version on *Drowning Witch*. Cheapo *film-noir* jazz vamps are distributed over the orchestra sections with a deep sense of silliness. Massed strings are used to give a flustered, astral texture to the

---

[5]As actually programmed by the American conductor Clark Rundell at the Royal Northern College of Music on 1 April 1992.

climax. The later stringless version[6] has a clearer sense of direction. As Zappa points out in *The Real Frank Zappa Book*,[7] string players tend to be the most buttoned-down members of the orchestra. They are, after all, playing instruments that go back to the craft era of musical production (emphasized on *LSO Vol. I* by listing the string players' instrument and vintage alongside their names). Brass instruments were a development of industrial technology and were mass-produced[8] – hence the working-class tradition of brass bands (and the lack of 'vintage' brass instruments). Orchestral lore therefore has brass-players cast as uncultured buffoons. String-players, by contrast, tend to be the inhibited, conservative wing of any orchestra, which is perhaps why the stringless 'Envelopes' works better.

'Mo 'n Herb's Vacation' is a twenty-seven-minute symphony in three movements. It begins by making prolific use of the clarinet's ability to pose intelligent, modernistic intervals, a showcase for David Ocker. The beauty of Zappa's orchestral music is a fresh, unacademic weighing of particular sounds: you can hear him think as he balances drum rolls and string scratching against the clarinet line. The second movement uses strained violins playing extended discords and scurrying basses and cellos. A heavier work-out of the ideas of 'Naval Aviation in Art', it uses some highly original effects (twinkling string scratches and metallic chimes) and consummate Varèsean percussion (woodblocks and drums). Again, the massed strings evoke a dreary landscape of classical fraudulence into which brass and percussion burst like shafts of sunlight and welcome thunder. When they break up into separate voices the music becomes complex and iridescent: the cellist is able to relate to Zappa's line even if, in these surroundings, its romanticism is distinctly parodic. The last movement welds Varèsean events into a murky kind of American pastorale.

Zappa is an extremely linear – or real-time – composer. His musical decisions result from the attention of the listening ear. Whereas Darmstadt composers frequently pursue a dialectic of schematic, mathematical invention versus playability and audibility, Zappa uses scores to direct musicians rather than to figure abstract shapes. This means that he very rarely attains the complex simultaneity that characterizes Boulez or early Stockhausen. In

[6]Same concert as the above.
[7]Frank Zappa, with Peter Occhiogrosso, *The Real Frank Zappa Book*, 1989, p. 142.
[8]A point made by Andrew Blake, *The Music Business*, 1992, p. 47.

writing for full orchestra, without the automatic simultaneity of playing with an improvising band of musicians, he does not exploit the specific potential of scores, which is to generate separate – but simultaneous – events. However, what he does contribute is a sense of freewheeling absurdity that academic composers find impossible to attempt without sounding tiresome. Zappa's materialism – an interest in sounds themselves, a complete lack of commitment to any particular social mode of realizing them – frees his orchestral music from repressive purism. As horns blurt and drums rumble at the end of the piece we know that here is music that is not a Platonic ideal whose existence as sound is merely temporary. It does not add up. This is its strength.

As Zappa explained in some spiky sleeve notes, *Vol. II* was delayed some years as he tried to find an editing method that could clean up the mistakes of an inebriated trumpet section.

> Rock journalists (especially the British ones) who have complained about the 'coldness', the 'attempts at perfection,' and missing 'human elements' in *Jazz from Hell* should find *LSO Vol. II* a real treat. It is infested with wrong notes and out-of-tune passages.[9]

Like the 'nine years of hell' with Warner Brothers Zappa denounced from the stage of the New York Palladium,[10] the attack on the musicians is a characteristic dramatization of the material conditions of musical production. 'Bogus Pomp' – extended from *Orchestral Favorites*' thirteen minutes to twenty-four and arranged by David Ocker – is professedly 'a parody of movie music clichés and mannerisms . . . supported by cheesey fanfares, drooling sentimental passages and predictable "scary music".'[11] After the viola player's solo there is a 'psychodrama' from the orchestra as they explode with indignation that such a 'lowly' instrument be granted the limelight. The strongly melodic nature of the material – principally themes from *200 Motels* like 'This Town is a Sealed Tuna Sandwich' and 'Would You Like a Snack' – were better realized on the more compact *Orchestral Favorites* version; this simply seems more dilute. 'Bob in Dacron' is a companion piece to 'Sad Jane': in the ballet conducted by Kent Nagano with the Berkeley Symphony Orchestra, depicting the opposite number in a singles-bar encounter. It is a densely woven piece, exploiting Zappa's ability to charge his musical figures with an organic sense of

---

[9]Frank Zappa, sleeve note, *LSO Vol. II*, 1987.
[10]Frank Zappa, 'Titties & Beer', *Baby Snakes*, 1982.
[11]Frank Zappa, sleeve note, *LSO Vol. II*, 1987.

independent life. Its lack of any dramatic shape, though, makes it somewhat monochrome. 'Strictly Genteel', a beautifully recorded rendition of the *200 Motels* chestnut, sounds as fabulous as it always does: the extra pieces of percussion are productively employed. One of Zappa's great assets is his ability to write suggestively inauthentic melodies, and this is one of his great ones.

This orchestral music is an essential adjunct to the project/object. Not only does it allow us to hear Zappa's music refracted through the traditional vehicle of bourgeois expression, it also demonstrates the economic vicissitudes and social contradictions involved in the area. Just as much as the *200 Motels* court case, Zappa uses the opportunity to make all kinds of fissures appear in the for-granted status of traditional practices. But it cannot be said that Zappa has left the field of classical composition behind as he has left fusion (or 'abstract music using rock sonorities'): a burnt-up field. If the postmoderns were correct, and the high-art avant-garde were utterly moribund, Zappa's work would stand out heroically against minimal piety and neo-religious obfuscation. However, new sounds are still being generated with the symphony orchestra, as the work of James Dillon demonstrates. In this context, Zappa's orchestral style sounds like an intriguing burlesque in a side alley.

On the other hand, maybe one should not be overhasty in making conclusions based on these 'drone' performances. When the Royal Northern College of Music students – in a stringless classical/jazz collaboration led by Clark Rundell – played 'Envelopes' and 'Dog Breath' in 1992, Zappa's music suddenly *did* sound like an emotive, attractive third stream that could import humour and noise without the usual creaking condescension.[12] It is possible that the RNCM student versions would offend Zappa's horror of 'mistakes' – the percussionist I spoke to admitted that some of the demands made of him were 'ridiculous' – but attitude and attack count for a lot. The increased rhythmic bite of pop music since rock 'n' roll has produced a generation of musicians with ears for Zappa's approach. There is something middle-aged about the LSO's attack that vitiates the music: the RNCM concert pointed exhilaratingly to a future for Zappa's scores in the classical world.

---

[12] Reviewed by a (Fr) edited-together multiple personality of myself, Otto Smart and Geoff Wills, *T'Mershi Duween*, No. 25, June 1992.

Zappa made contact with IRCAM, the centre for sonic exploration built beneath the Pompidou Centre in Paris and run by Pierre Boulez, when he visited to experiment with Giuseppe di Giugno's 4X digital signal processor. That Zappa's music should be conducted by Pierre Boulez with the Ensemble InterContemporain was generally greeted by incredulity. Anthony Braxton was indignant.

> To this day, IRCAM has never tried to help me do anything. I wanted to study electronic music there, but they wouldn't let me in. I think Boulez himself probably doesn't have any respect for me. He would later bring in people like – who's that rock performer? Frank Zappa? – and give him the opportunity to have a symphonic work performed which Boulez himself conducted; but they wouldn't even let me walk in the place. That's the nature of the political dynamics at IRCAM.
>
> It's not that I want to accuse any one individual of racism, it's just that when it comes to dealing with Africans and African-Americans it's *business as usual*. They can use black people in the Pigalle section where there's a lot of, you know, good fun and 'black exotica'; but because I have the same kind of visions as a Stockhausen, in terms of the projects I wanted to do, I was seen as an arrogant nigger.[13]

It is true that the European academic, institutional approach encodes racism in its denigration of improvisation and audience participation. However, in his insistence on new work Boulez is actually in an antagonistic position as regards the usual function of classical music. He can see that improvisers have greater scope for the realization of new music.

> I think in the matter of this jazz business generally that they are forced to be more inventive individually, because they don't have a repertoire – they have to make up their own repertoire as individuals, and also they do not have the burden of repertoire music to be performed, to be performed, to be performed, so the creativity goes completely away. That is the difference between a small group and a big orchestra group where the creativity is pushed down.[14]

Despite such statements, Boulez has not listened to jazz with the attention of Elliott Carter or Conlon Nancarrow. Although being in America means that jazz is culturally less avoidable, it is disappointing that someone like Boulez cannot see that Misha Mengelberg and Derek Bailey and Willem Breuker (and Adrian

---

[13]Quoted by Graham Lock, *Forces in Motion*, 1988, pp. 95–6.
[14]Pierre Boulez talking to the author at Maida Vale, BBC Studios, London, 18 November 1990.

Sherwood) are parallel forces. Like many artists who pursue their goals through to conclusion, there is a certain narrowness in his approach. He comes from a previous generation, from a period when Adorno's embattled attitude towards the culture industry seemed the whole picture, a set of music theorists who were not young enough to be touched by Hendrix or Coltrane. Disappointments about someone's limits often lead to unbalanced pronouncements. The fact that Boulez should take Zappa seriously is less an example of racism than welcome recognition of Zappa's place in the tradition of Debussy, Stravinsky and Varèse in which Boulez himself stands. Braxton's tendency to Stockhausen-type mysticism is also unlikely to appeal to Boulez's materialism, though in 1972 it is more likely that IRCAM's rejection was based on sheer ignorance of Braxton's work.

Boulez was also intrigued by Zappa's hardware. Keyboardist Tommy Mars, himself classically trained, recalled the encounter between two cultures.

> The night he was in Paris, I believe it was one of the first evenings that Frank and Pierre had finally gotten together, they had only corresponded before. Frank was extremely sick – he was coming down with walking pneumonia or something, he was really pale and he had a fever. We're all looking at Pierre Boulez, God this is an incredible experience. For some reason Frank had to postpone the major part of their meeting together and he said, Would you take Pierre up on stage and show him your set up. I said, What? He said, He'll really appreciate it, show him the Poly-box. So, I went on stage and there were people there – we were half an hour from playing and the hall was filling up. I didn't want to be anti-climactic and really blow and show what was going on, but I showed him this instrument that I had brought to Frank called the Poly-box, made by Electro Comp, it was a parallel chord follower, but it had a lot of life to it because you could just hit another chord and it would stay there, it would remember that chord so that you could continue during measures to keep changing chords, so it wasn't like a total parallel type of deal . . . and Boulez's eyes just lit up and he said, I've been writing stuff like this! I had a woodwind sound coupled with a piccolo and a couple of French horns at the bottom, and he was intrigued because that right there was what he was doing currently. Frank was really pleased. During the show, it was like taking him down the K-Mart for a blue-light special, he was having everyone in the band illustrate things with their new gear, it was so funny – I was saying to myself, This is Pierre Boulez! I was awed, truly awed.[15]

Boulez avoids terms like 'spirit' when talking about his music, in

---

[15]Tommy Mars, interview with the author, 30 October 1993.

marked contrast to the current fashion for new-age pieties in the classical arena. When asked about this, his answer was surprisingly like the demands for an energized, active listening that have distinguished Zappa's music since *Freak Out!*.

> Some people say that if you take away the occult, you take away god, you take away religion, everything is so dry. But you're saying it's not dry at all . . .
>
> PIERRE BOULEZ: It's richer because you have to have a metaphysics of yourself, something not imposed on you by education. For me it is more interesting for someone to invent his own situation than to accept his situation.[16]

By conducting Zappa's pieces, Boulez showed that these words were not just rhetoric. However, he would not let the collaboration be read as 'endorsement' of Zappa, and puzzled the press with his reticence in praising Zappa's scores. 'I reserve judgement about all the qualities of Zappa's music,' he told *Libération*.[17] Out of the press conferences, though, he replied to a question asking if he liked Zappa's music by saying, 'Certainly. I found a kind of vitality and it was very good for our musicians to do that: they were not accustomed at all to it, and that's good to work on it.'[18]

The pieces come across much more strongly than the *LSO* albums, though only three scores were finally played. Zappa was used to the absolute dedication of virtuosi like Cucurullo, Vai and Mann, who live for Zappa's music in the manner of Sun Ra's musicians. He was not happy about the performances at the première, and was mortified to have to take a bow.[19] The pieces were recorded the very next day.

The Perfect Stranger appeared on EMI's classical subsidiary Angel, showing that recording conglomerates use the same imagery for the otherworldliness of art as rock bands, and contributing nicely to conceptual continuity. The cover used a painting by Donald Roller Wilson. It showed Patricia, the dog, in a high chair, alongside beautifully caught bottles of Heinz tomato ketchup, Budweiser beer and baby's milk. The full title of the painting – written in the style that may have inspired 'Evelyn, a Modified Dog'[20] – is eighteen lines long.

---

[16]Pierre Boulez, London, 18 November 1990
[17]Quoted by Julian Colbeck, *Zappa: A Biography*, 1987, p. 181.
[18]Pierre Boulez, London, 18 November 1990.
[19]Frank Zappa, with Peter Occhiogrosso, *The Real Frank Zappa Book*, 1989, p. 196.
[20]Frank Zappa, *One Size Fits All*, 1975.

PATRICIA'S LATE-NIGHT COMPLEMENTARY SNACK AT MONTE'S
AND RICHARD YOAKUM'S BOULEVARD HOUSTON TOWNHOUSE
WHERE (THE NIGHT BEFORE) DON HAD GONE UP IN SMOKE

PATRICIA'S THICK GREEN LENSES FILTERED OUT THE SHADES
    OF RED
REFLECTED FROM THE HEINZ-SIGHT OF HER BOTTLE –
(THAT BRAND OF KETCHUP WE ALL LOVE SO WELL)

BUT MRS JENKINS' GLASSES LENSES WERE A ROSY RED
AND WHEN *SHE* SHOOK THE CONTENTS OF THAT BOTTLE –
(THAT KIND OF KETCHUP WE ALL LOVE SO WELL)

SHE DIDN'T THINK TO SHIELD HER EYES TO NULLIFY THE RED
AND THE HOT BRIGHT LIGHT HAD LEFT HER BLIND;
    BUDWEISER
(THAT TYPE OF BEER WE ALL LOVE SO WELL)

SO, WHILE PATRICIA WATCHED THAT NIGHT, HER FRIEND WENT
    UP IN SMOKE
LIKE DON HAD DONE; HER FLAMES LEAPED HIGHER AND
    HIGHER
(PAT FEARED THAT JENKINS SURELY WENT TO HELL)

BUT PATRICIA WAITED YEARS AND YEARS TO SEE IF SHE'D COME
    BACK
SHE WAITED BY THE TABLE WITH HER BOTTLE
(ENGAGED AND FAITHFUL IN HER SENTINEL)[21]

Without the overplayed allegories that mar Wilson's grander paintings, the piece falls midway between photo-realism and the post-metaphysical still-lifes of Giorgio Morandi. The associations of oil paint – luxuriance, expense, sensuality – fitted Zappa's mid-80s sense of quality product in both classical and rock fields.

Despite Zappa's misgivings, the Ensemble InterContemporain play firmly and with expansive fantasy. On the record sleeve Boulez is thanked for 'having the patience to demand accurate performance of the *killer triplets* on page eight',[22] Zappa wrote absurdist stories to go with each piece. The title track tells the tale of a door-to-door salesman selling a gypsy mutant industrial vacuum cleaner, representing the values of *'chrome, rubber, electricity'* and *'household tidiness'*, to a slovenly housewife, with whom he 'cavorts licentiously'. The 'demonstration' dirt he sprinkles on the carpet works as a metaphor for Zappa's art. The piece

---

[21]*The Paintings of Donald Roller Wilson*, Introduction by Peter Frank, 1988, p. 89.
[22]Frank Zappa, sleevenote, *The Perfect Stranger*, 1984.

has some of the burnished clarity of 'Music for Electric Guitar and Low Budget Orchestra',[23] though it lacks any regular bass-line. The concluding dada histrionics of the brass fanfares beg all sorts of questions about pomp and legitimacy.

'Naval Aviation in Art' is played in a more fulsome manner than on *Orchestral Favorites*, emphasizing the careful timbral stripes of its stacked-up chords rather than merely a silvery stretchedness. Side two concludes with the first of Zappa's Synclavier pieces, 'The Girl in the Magnesium Dress'. The influence of Conlon Nancarrow is immediately apparent. With the release of Nancarrow's player piano pieces[24] it is becoming clear that his use of steam technology is going to become an important example for those using computers to realize compositions. The Synclavier sounds are glittering and chime-like. As Zappa's experience with the Synclavier increased – and he spent more on memory – he began to achieve dirtier, more timbrally complex sounds. None the less, the genesis of the rhythms in 'Magnesium Dress' show Zappa's characteristic interest in breaking rules, in finding what the machinery *can* deliver rather than in simply making it work – a high-tech version of being interested in sex rather than sports.

> The piece was made from Synclavier digital dust. It's hard to explain, but when you look at the G page on the Synclavier, you'll see note names and numbers, but that's not all that lives on a track. There's subterranean information which can only be viewed when you go out of the user-friendly part of the machine and into the mysterious world of XPL programming. At that point, you can see these things that live on the track that are giving these secret instructions to the machine telling it what to do. One classification of these secret instructions is something called 'G numbers', which would be derived from plugging in a guitar. They have this guitar unit that you can plug in, and besides recording the note that you play, it records a bunch of data in the form of G numbers. So we found a way to convert bunches of G numbers into note blanks. And G numbers occupy points in time. They indicate that something happened on the guitar string at a certain point in time. It takes a little piece of eternity and slices it up, and if your finger moved, there's a G number that says what your finger did besides just playing the note. So we converted this dust into something that I could then edit for pitch, and the dust indicated a rhythm. So what I did was take the rhythm of the dust and impose pitch data on the dust and thereby

---

[23]Frank Zappa, *Studio Tan*, 1978.
[24]Conlon Nancarrow, *Studies for Player Piano Vols. I and II*, 1991, Wergo WER6168–2; *Vols. III and IV*, 1990, Wergo 60167–50; *Vol. V*, 1988, Wergo 60165–50.

move the inaudible G number into the world of audibility with a pitch name on it. That's how 'Magnesium Dress' was built.[25]

The final outcome was the rendition of this 'digital dust' by a real-time orchestra – the Ensemble Modern – in 1993.[26]

'Outside Now, Again' returns to the hypnotic motif from *Joe's Garage*. The Synclavier's gong-sound works with the pentatonic riff to provide a hypnotic, oriental flavour unusual for Zappa. This piece would sound good programmed between John Carisi's 'Moon Taj',[27] Jan Steele's 'All Day',[28] Claude Debussy's 'Masques'[29] and Malcolm McLaren's 'Obatala',[30] being what is known in the trade as a 'hypno-classic'. Although its oriental charm is echoed in countless minimal and new age atmospheric 'tricklers', the 'right-hand' variations (as with Nancarrow's player piano, the bionic implausibility of this kind of music is rooted in known practices) build a genuine musical argument. Highly purposeful harmonic choices give it a pungency lacking in the C-major blandness of most minimalism. However, noting its superficial similarities, Zappa added a caustic sleeve note in line with his view that minimalism is essentially part of Reaganite cost-cutting policies:[31]

> 'Outside Now, Again' shows the entire cast in an endless soup line. This pitiful sustenance (dished out by people dressed to look like grant-givers from the *National Endowment for the Arts*) is perfectly suited to minimalist choreography.[32]

This sudden return of the themes of *Joe's Garage* is a hilarious contextualization of the airy idealism of minimalism, as well as a premonition of the current economic crisis and welfare cuts.

'Love Story' depicts an elderly Republican couple attempting sex while break-dancing, a perfect way of describing its combination of American romanticism and jagged high-tech metrics. The sound of bed-springs bursting through the mattress: a Synclavier

---

[25]Frank Zappa, quoted by Don Menn, *Zappa!* (a supplement from the publishers of *Keyboard and Guitar Player*), ed. Don Menn, 1992, p. 60.
[26]Frank Zappa, 'The Girl in the Magnesium Dress', *The Yellow Shark*, 1993.
[27]The Gil Evans Orchestra, 'Moon Taj', *Into the Hot*, 1961, Impulse MCAD39104.
[28]Jan Steele, 'All Day', Jan Steele/John Cage, *Voices and Instruments*, 1976, Obscure No. 5.
[29]Claude Debussy, 'Masques', 1904.
[30]Malcolm McLaren, *Duck Rock*, 1983, Charisma MMLP1.
[31]'It used to be that they would fund only *boop-beep stuff* (serial and/or electronic composition). Now they're funding only *minimalism* (simplistic, repetitive composition, easy to rehearse and, therefore, *cost-effective*). So what gets taught in school? *Minimalism. Why?* Because it can be FUNDED. Net cultural result? **Monochromonotony**', Frank Zappa, with Peter Occhiogrosso, *The Real Frank Zappa Book*, 1989, p. 189.
[32]Sleeve note, Frank Zappa, *The Perfect Stranger*, 1984.

realization of some of the ideas of 'The Chrome Plated Megaphone of Destiny'.[33] 'Dupree's Paradise' is the third of the orchestral compositions. It was originally a vehicle for Napoleon Murphy Brock's flute, evoking night-time jazz bohemia, jam sessions and social degeneracy. The surging chintz of its theme structures the glancing musical events beautifully; the Ensemble InterContemporain sound well in charge.

'Jonestown' is named after the South American jungle city where hundreds of born-again Christians took arsenic in an act of community suicide. It is appropriately sick, strange and eerie. The chime sounds become differentiated enough to give an idea of collapse and disintegration: the music works like a gamelan transmuted in outer space, both sensually gratifying and threatening. Promising well for his investment in Synclavier technology, this is one of Zappa's most powerful pieces of music.

The Perfect Stranger, however fortuitously, works well by combining virtuosic classical musicianship and state-of-the-art computer manipulation. Like *Studio Tan* there is a threatening quality to the gloss, as though that album's Léger-like dazzle has been warped into something more nearly resembling Max Ernst, a decalcomania dripping with dangerous flowers, eyeballs growing from tree trunks alongside weirdly glistening patches of moss.

FRANCESCO ZAPPA

James Joyce became interested in a poet called James Stephens because his name combined his own with that of Stephen Dedalus, the hero of *Portrait of the Artist as a Young Man*. Frank Zappa discovered that *The New Grove Dictionary of Music and Musicians* listed a Francesco Zappa, who 'flourished' between 1763 and 1788. In collaboration with David Ocker, Zappa located his scores at the Bancroft Library at the University of California, Berkeley, and at the Library of Congress, Washington, DC. Realized on the Synclavier in early-days chiming mode, this digital version of by-numbers baroque sounds like a musical Christmas card.

David Ocker's provocative sleeve note suggests – horror of horrors – that in the 'golden age' of classical music that gave birth to Mozart, composers may have been more interested in flattering

---

[33]Frank Zappa, *We're Only in It for the Money*, 1968.

their noble customers than in achieving transcendent art. *Them Or Us (The Book)* makes great play of the upset in linear time created by imagining Zappa's attempts to make music in a different era. Francesco Zappa also appears as a character in *Thing-Fish*.

Francesco works like a *Cruising with Ruben & the Jets* fifteen years on, a release whose stiffness and banality offsets its companion releases. Its most intriguing aspect was the mechanized feel of the computer-generated sounds, reminding us that at the time 'Europe was ablaze with new inventions like the steam engine'.[34] Enough to make an authentic instrument enthusiast gag on a spoon, this reminder of the inert rationalism of baroque is welcome at a time when early music is so frequently sentimentalized as 'truly human' in comparison to twentieth-century developments. *Francesco*'s importance is conceptual rather than musical, though it deliberately makes such distinctions hard to draw. Just as you think you can dismiss it as supermarket tweeness, it generates a new perspective on the issues of musical objectivity, science and technological progress as expressed in musical genre. Certainly *Francesco* successfully jump-starts more ideas than the average classical release of 'dead composer' music.

THING-FISH

Thing-Fish was planned as a Broadway musical, but it became a triple-album box set instead. It is probably the most offensive – and least defended – of all Zappa's creations. In his biography Julian Colbeck dismissed it in a mere three lines: 'A boxed set of records for a musical comedy entitled *Thing-Fish*. Many of the basic tracks for the latter had been recorded back the previous year.'[35]

The use of previous backing tracks blunted *Thing-Fish*'s impact for Zappa connoisseurs (and who else was going to buy the thing?), who felt short-changed. This antagonistic relationship between product and the fans has been a continual feature of Zappa's œuvre, an aspect that has the intriguing effect of generating *work* on the part of the fan.

The highly suggestive nature of Zappa's art to those aware of the avant-garde – in the sense of technical innovations in the

---

[34]Sleeve note by David Ocker, Frank Zappa, *Francesco Zappa*, 1984.
[35]Julian Colbeck, *Zappa: A Biography*, 1987, p. 183.

material procedures of art – was well illustrated by an article on *Thing-Fish* by jwcurry, published in *Rampike*, the Canadian literary journal.[36] His thesis is that Zappa's lyric writing is a 'theory of excess' that results in 'verbal confrontations', with *Thing-Fish* cast as the most lyrically excessive album Zappa has yet released. It is dominated by Ike Willis's Thing-Fish, the name a corruption of Tim Moore's TV character Kingfish (whose language the white man 'from the middle-class family' imitates in 'You are What You is'). As Zappa put it in *Them Or Us (The Book)*, which reprints much of the *Thing-Fish* libretto, Thing-Fish's language

is a pseudo-negrocious dialect, originated by an actor named Tim Moore in the TV version of *Amos & Andy*. He was severely punished for it. The NAACP made him pay for his own 'one-way ticket to Fresno.'[37]

Far from being racist, *Thing-Fish* is a virulent trashing of the condescension and racism of Broadway's association of entertainment with happy all-singing all-dancing black folk: 'They told me it had c-c-colored folk in it, RHONDA, and that's ALWAYS a sure sign of GOOD, SOLID, MUSICAL ENTERTAINMENT!'[38]

It works like a great eruption of pus, akin to pricking an extremely unpleasant boil, which Broadway does indeed represent. However, as usual with Zappa, an assertion that his art is 'non-racist' or progressive in any manner can only be achieved by *work* on the part of the auditor: he manages to offend against practically every shibboleth liberal culture has ever formulated.

Thing-Fish tells the tale of a conventional yuppie couple who are drawn into all kinds of perversions by the magic of stagecraft. Instead of being stranded at Frank 'N Furter's castle *à la Rocky Horror Show*, they are attending a Broadway musical, but are soon intimately involved. They go further than merely dressing in stockings and suspenders: Harry ends up chained by rings through his nipples, lusting after a miniature rubber doll named Ob'dewella 'X'; Rhonda ends up fucking her briefcase and making Harry smell the fountain pen she has been using as an anal dildo (perhaps a parody of the wealthy husband–wife scene in *The Sound of Music* where a fountain pen is bandied about as a possible birthday

[36]jwcurry, 'Grammatical Sabotage: Conversing with Frank Zappa's *THING-FISH*', *Rampike*, Vol. 7, No. 2, 1992, pp. 72–77. *Rampike* is published from 95 Rivercrest Road, Toronto, Ontario M6S 4H7, Canada.
[37]Frank Zappa, *Them Or Us (The Book)*, 1984, p. 262.
[38]Frank Zappa, 'Harry & Rhonda', *Thing-Fish*, 1984, booklet, p. 4.

gift). A photographic depiction of these events – with a variant storyline – was reproduced in *Hustler*,[39] with prosthetic rubber masks by Jene Omens.

jwcurry quotes a Zappa monologue from the end of an onstage rendition of 'Packard Goose'[40] which has a lot of bearing on the shock tactics of *Thing-Fish*.

> I'd like each and every one of you to fantasize along with me this evening that, in some small way, the process of performing this show will rid you of your own personal demon, whatever it is that's bothering the shit out of you this year. Just ... Just ... you know what I mean? Because you guys in New York should know more than anybody else in the world that the only way that you're ever going to make it through life without going completely crazy is by finding some one or some thing to say 'Fuck You!' to. See? Now, in the past, in the past, many governments and religious leaders have paraphrased that expression in such a way as to make a certain religious or political or ethnic minority the victim of their cruel disregard. But today it's the time for the people who have been the victims of that disregard to turn around and disregard something else. So, have a good time ...'[41]

Zappa here summarizes the key ideologies – religion, politics, race – that have been used by the American ruling class to deflect the precipitation of a unified working-class consciousness in the States. However, instead of producing an ideal resolution of those conflicts by proposing a series of liberal taboos, Zappa proposes the use of all those taboos by the underdog, not just a return, but a *revenge* of the repressed. This was the aspect that appealed to Matt Groening, creator of *The Simpsons* and long-time Zappa fan.

> Dan Quayle talked about how he's wearing the 'scorn and ridicule' that he receives like a badge of honor. And I thought, 'Scorn and ridicule – yeah, that's what I got to keep remembering to get back to.' Something that Zappa does so well. Not to suffer but to *offer* your scorn and ridicule.[42]

Groening's last phrase works as a perfect description of the motivating force behind *Thing-Fish*'s assault on yuppie sensibilities.

The *Thing-Fish* chorus consists of 'Mammy Nuns'. Like the Thing-Fish himself they have potato heads, duck lips and stereotypical Aunt Jemimah clothes. With the Mammy Nuns Zappa was

---

[39] *Hustler*, No. 10, April 1984.
[40] From the bootleg *Show & Tell*, undated.
[41] Quoted by jwcurry, *Rampike*, Vol. 7, No. 2, 1992, p. 73.
[42] Matt Groening, *Zappa!* (from the publishers of *Keyboard and Guitar Player*), ed. Don Menn, 1992, p. 26.

reviving an idea of grotesques that started with the Grunt People, the film that was to star Captain Beefheart in 1965. He described the Grunt People to *ZigZag* magazine.

> They're these people on the moon, who wear these clothes which are like burlap bags with fish and garbage sewn on them. They are the villains of the story, but turn out to be the victims of a government agent. It's a little warped – just enough to retain clarity – like a mirror that makes your arm look a little larger.[43]

In the mid-70s Zappa had a habit of introducing himself onstage as 'Rondo Hatton'. Originally voted 'handsomest boy of his year' in high school, Hatton had a career as 'the ugliest man in pictures' after a traumatic gassing in the trenches which caused his face to swell and distort, combining, Zappa's pet themes of poison gas, war and inverted glamour.[44] 'San Ber'dino' introduced 'Potato Head Bobby'; by 'Advance Romance' he has grown several eyes in his potato head as he queues in the food-stamp line. He reappears in *Thing-Fish* as a Mammy Nun, as does Ob'dewella 'X', Zappa's pseudonym on George Duke's *Feel*[45] and Andy DeVine, the cowboy actor from *One Size Fits All* (as Sister Anne de DeVine). Thing-Fish and the Mammy Nuns represent the ugliness of poverty in the eyes of the respectable moneyed classes. Like the police preparing to assault the 'scum'[46] on the Trafalgar Square anti-poll tax march of 1991 (which provoked the riot that toppled Margaret Thatcher from power), the association of the poor with dirt and disease – now tragically cemented by Aids – has always underlain ruling-class contempt for the oppressed.

Thing-Fish is a parable based on Zappa's theory that Aids is the result of biological warfare waged against America's own population, exploited by the moral right as evidence of divine retribution. Thing-Fish puts it in his own inimitable way:

THING-FISH:
Dey booked in de heavy pseudo re-LIJ-mus talent to pronunciate de
doc-TRINE of BIBLICAL RETRIBUTIUM!

---

[43]Quoted by Pete Frame, *ZigZag*, No. 8, December 1969, p. 43.
[44]Pointed out by Andrew Greenaway, 'Frankie Goes to Hollywood', *T'Mershi Duween*, No. 26, September 1992, p. 25.
[45]'Love' and 'Old Slippers', *Feel*, 1974, MPS 2122312–4.
[46]Actually overheard by Audrey Farrell, whose statement, 'For the police the working class in struggle are scum, just as the unemployed are scum, as prostitutes are scum, as blacks are scum, as gays are scum – and will be as long as they are there to protect bourgeois property and the bourgeois family from what they have to see as an enemy class', at an SWP branch meeting helped to formulate this socialist reading of *Thing-Fish*. Her book on the police is highly recommended: Audrey Farrell, *Crime, Class and Corruption: The Politics of the Police*, 1992.

ENSEMBLE:
Moving the project forward!
THING-FISH:
Figgin' dat to be . . .
ENSEMBLE:
Da-da-dee-dahh!
A sho-fi' explumation, suitable fo' Domestical . . .
ENSEMBLE:
Assuagement![47]

It parallels Zappa's conviction that LSD was researched, synthe-sized and unleashed on the population by the CIA. This expla-nation of Aids is generally dismissed as conspiracy theory, though when Zappa quotes from a book on American weapons tech-nology that talks about the feasibility of 'ethnic chemical weapons' it does not seem quite so crazy. A 1969 Senate appropriations hearing was presented with 'testimony (speaker unidentified) regarding the development of a new class of biological weapons (note the plural) which would be 'refractory' to the human immu-nological system'.[48]

Whether or not the American government hatched the intro-virus, its neglect of the care of victims and the education of its target groups has been criminal. As Thing-Fish says

Now . . . how many you folks is CONVINCED de gubnint be totally 'UNCONCERNED' wit de proliferatium o' UNDESIRABLE TEN-ANTS in de CONDOMINIUM o' LIFE?[49]

Convincing as an explanation of Aids or not, *Thing-Fish* provides a scary metaphor for understanding the American ruling class's contempt for those whom sexual-orientation or poverty deflects from the monogamous heterosexual ideal – an ideal which is itself a hypocritical smokescreen, as attested by the continual emergence of scandals about members of the Kennedy family and top TV evangelists.

Harry and Rhonda's immersion in the world of Thing-Fish's Broadway is comedy of the highest order. Evidently thinking about 'The Torture Never Stops', Ian Penman made the point that *Zoot Allures* 'was a portrait of the "average man" listening to *Zoot Allures*';[50] likewise Harry and Rhonda provide a reflexive commen-

---

[47]Frank Zappa, 'Galoot Up-Date', *Thing-Fish*, 1984, booklet, p. 5.
[48]Frank Zappa, with Peter Occhiogrosso, *The Real Frank Zappa Book*, 1989, p. 352. The book referred to is Jeremy Paxman, *A Higher Form of Killing*, Hill and Wang, p. 41.
[49]Frank Zappa, 'Galoot Up-Date', *Thing-Fish*, 1984, booklet, p. 5.
[50]Ian Penman, 'Frank Zappa: *Studio Tan*', *New Musical Express*, 30 September 1978.

tary on one's own feelings while listening to *Thing-Fish*. Just as 'Wet T-Shirt Nite' had a 'pretend' soaking, so no one is very sure what it means to be pissed on by the Mammy Nuns.

The Ensemble lifts their skirts, revealing customised lawn-jockeys with the out-stretched lantern-bearing arm positioned between their legs. Instead of a lantern, the hand of each jockey clutches a shower-head plumbing fixture. On cue, what appears to be piss sprinkles onto HARRY, RHONDA and the other FIRST NIGHTERS.[51]

Racist garden statuettes of negro stableboys constituted one of the themes of 'Uncle Remus'.[52] Rhonda wants to leave, but Harry says they cannot afford to 'at these ticket prices', which is similar to the listener who has just invested in the triple-album box set. Harry tells Rhonda that the piss is 'only theater piss', which is a perfect symbol for the dubious ontological status of offence in Zappa's art. As Harry and Rhonda are chained, they argue about whether or not these are just 'theater chains'. Is the art really offensive, or is it all part of the artwork? 'D'ja get any on ya down dere?' asks Thing-Fish, a flashback to the title of the first track of *Weasels Ripped My Flesh*, which also played on the idea of art as abuse (the title track's two minutes of feedback).

The Mammy Nuns wreak revenge on the whole institution of Broadway. The new disease turns blacks and gays into Mammy Nuns, all sporting the 'napkin' which nigger minstrels would use to sop up their sweat (Louis Armstrong and his handkerchief caused a lot of anguish for his younger and more racially conscious jazz fans). This symbol of oppression is now no longer just costume: 'de nakkins we's wearin' atch'ly be GROWIN' outs our bodies'.[53] This is precisely what racism does to the body itself, perhaps explaining why superstars like Michael Jackson resort to plastic surgery. The key phrase is: 'We ugly as SIN!'[54] which relates to the message of 'The Torture Never Stops'. This song explained its association of punishment and libido by reference to the need for knowledge of 'everything that's ever been': a summary of sexual excitements in a society of domination.

> ... a dungeon like a sin
> Requires naught but lockin' in

[51]Frank Zappa, 'The Mammy Nuns', *Thing-Fish*, 1984, booklet, p. 3.
[52]Frank Zappa, 'Uncle Remus', *Apostrophe (')*, 1974. See above, 'Music, No Words, Orgasm vs. Anal Retention' in Chapter Five: Bizarre to DiscReet.
[53]Frank Zappa, 'Galoot Up-Date', *Thing-Fish*, 1984, booklet. p. 5.
[54]Frank Zappa, 'The Mammy Nuns', *Thing-Fish*, 1984, booklet, p. 4.

Of everything that's ever been
Look at her
Look at him
Yeah you!
That's what's the deal we're dealin' in[55]

In the version of 'The Torture Never Stops' on *Thing-Fish*, the musical is itself the dungeon that will accumulate all knowledge.

But, a MUSICAL, like we's in,
Require a WHOLE BUNCH O' EVERYTHIN'!
We talkin' EVERYTHIN' DAT EVER BEEN![56]

This restates the idea of Kafka's torture machine in *We're Only in It for the Money* and the confessional of *Läther* – the work of art that will bring repressed impulses to consciousness and highlight collusion with societal oppression.

The Evil Prince wishes to restore the old characters of Broadway – his zomby accomplices are from *Peter Pan*, *Hello Dolly*, *Oklahoma* and *Annie*. His disease targets blacks and gays.

Fairies and faggots and queers are
'CREATIVE'
All the best music on Broadway is
'NATIVE'[57]

'Ugly as sin', the Mammy Nuns bring up all the issues – racism, poverty, Aids – that the yuppie couple do not want to face. As they flinch from everything around them, they begin to suffer from the same symptoms, like the president intoning the dumb 'doot doot doot' of 'Louie Louie' on *Absolutely Free*.[58]

I want REAL BROADWAY ENTERTAINMENT! . . . And what do I get? A Potato-headed jigaboo with Catholic clothes on! Incomprehensible duck lips! Weak bladders draining through *abnorminably* large organs! Jesus, HARRY! What the FUCK is going on here?[59]

Rhonda's 'abnorminably' is part of the linguistic disintegration of *Thing-Fish*: even while she is complaining about his incomprehensibility her own language suffers infection. 'Galoot Up-Date' uses both instrumental and vocal tracks from 'The Blue Light' (*Tinsel Town Rebellion*), which had Zappa sneering at the quandaries of the white middle classes.

[55]Frank Zappa, 'The Torture Never Stops', transcription from *Zappa in New York*, CD, 1991.
[56]Frank Zappa, 'The Torchum Never Stops', *Thing-Fish*, 1984, booklet, p. 6.
[57]Ibid.
[58]Frank Zappa, 'Plastic People', *Absolutely Free*, 1967.
[59]Frank Zappa, 'Harry & Rhonda', *Thing-Fish*, 1984, booklet, p. 4

You go to *Straw Hat Pizza*,
To get all those ingredients
That never belonged on a pizza in the first place
(But the white people really like it . . .)[60]

Zappa is separating himself from the white race as an Italian, recalling Charles Mingus and his famous distinction (after he declared he had never played with whites, he was asked about Charlie Mariano – 'But he's Italian,' he replied). The song continues

Your ethos, your pathos,
Your flag pole, your port hole
Your language
You're frightened
Your future
You can't even speak your own fucking language.[61]

Flag pole/port hole is an extraordinary jump, going from salute-the-flag patriotism to alienation (the port holes of 'Excentrifugal Forz' and 'Naval Aviation in Art'). When Thing-Fish is faced with this accusation, part of the original backing track, he replies: 'What on urf do you mean: "MY LANGUAGE"? I got yo language hangin', boy.'[62] Thing-Fish is hanging the English language as vengeance for Ku Klux Klan lynchings. In the wordplay of *Thing-Fish* there is a desperate energy that comes from its close tracking of urgent social issues.

In *Them Or Us (The Book)*, Buddy Wilson, desperate to explain to his kids how Uncle Willie has managed to appear beyond the grave, establishes that time is an illusion:

Well, let's look at it ANOTHER way . . . TIME is not like what people THINK it is. It doesn't START OVER HERE and then GO OVER THERE . . . TIME is just one big LUMP OF STUFF . . . EVERY-THING IS HAPPENING *ALL THE TIME!*[63]

Zappa shows an acute grasp of the illusory nature of scientific 'certainty' in a society based on war ('Will it explode?') and the profit motive ('Will this effect real estate values?'). The whole passage reads like an expressionist account of Zappa's childhood anxiety about his father's work for the military.

[5] All unknown 'facts' pertaining to Universal Mechanics are sought in

[60]Frank Zappa, 'The Blue Light', *Tinsel Town Rebellion*, 1981.
[61]Ibid.
[62]Frank Zappa, 'Galoot Up-Date', *Thing-Fish*, 1984, booklet, p. 5.
[63]Frank Zappa, *Them Or Us (The Book)*, 1984, p. 62.

an order of priorities determined by what people think they WANT to know. (First: 'Will it explode?'; Second: 'How will this effect real estate values in our area?')

[6] Even without suggesting that all human knowledge be re-thought, we ought to at least *consider the possibility* that centuries of accumulated errors, misjudgements, inaccurate observations, erroneous evaluations of data, etc., could have emulsified into the Cretin's Porridge now being served up as THE HOLY SOFTWARE SNACK-PACK we refer to as 'OUR BODY OF KNOWLEDGE IN ALL MATTERS SCIENTIFIC'.[64]

Like David Ocker's sleeve note to *Francesco Zappa*, which questioned the idea of the transcendence of baroque musical value by pointing out that it was produced to accompany bewigged aristocrats while they dined, this kind of thinking is extremely subversive. Its materialism goes beyond bourgeois faith in science and seeks to understand its roots in the requirements of social forces. In its naïvety and power it recalls William Blake's critique of the oppressive authoritarianism of organized religion.

However, the theory of time in *Them Or Us (The Book)*, although using images drawn from Einstein's relativity (*The Real Frank Zappa Book* is dedicated to Stephen Hawking), is really about the psychical simultaneity of both memory and the forgotten (the unconscious), a point made by Freud in 1907, the same year as the setting of *Ulysses*, which also posited a non-narrative of simultaneous themes.[65] Zappa is talking about how he – and the listener who is familiar with his œuvre – can imaginatively entertain all his records at the same time, a feature which repro-duces the timelessness of the unconscious. In *Them Or Us (The Book)* this manifests itself in a hallucinogenic merging of narrative moments from records all over his career; in *Thing-Fish* by the appearance of a character called Harry-as-a-Boy.

Harry-as-a-Boy allows Harry and Rhonda to observe Harry's early life enacted on Stage. He explains turning gay according to the theory outlined in 'Bobby Brown':

HARRY-AS-A-BOY:
I lost all desire for intercourse with females when they started carrying those briefcases and wearing suits 'n ties.
RHONDA:
WHAT?

---

[64]Ibid., p. 61.
[65]Sigmund Freud, *Psychopathology of Everyday Life*, 1901 (added 1907), p. 339n1. See above 'Timelessness' in Preface.

442

Let's face it: that would be like fucking a slightly more voluptuous
version of somebody's father! I'm far too sensitive for such a traumatic experience!

Harry-as-a-Boy also rehearses the idea that gayness is a government plot to contain the population explosion, as well as being a
'selfish' refusal to devote one's time to bringing up kids. This
absurd homophobic fantasy – when it is precisely the right's moralistic stress on family values and sexuality as only permissible as
a means of reproduction that leads to oppression of gays – produces a moment of high comedy as Rhonda reacts by calling her
husband an 'overeducated cock-sucker'. The musical dissolves into
ever more ludicrous sexual scenarios and parodic politics. The
Mammy Nuns sing 'He's So Gay', an enumeration of leather-sex
clichés. To Rhonda's disgust and Thing-Fish's amazement, Harry
then decides he wants to have sexual relations with a Mammy
Nun. He tries to sing a love song, while Thing-Fish tells him that
his 'unrequited desirin's be mo'' suited to de ZOMBY-FOLK up
in de EVIL PRINCE's lab-mo-to-rium!':[66] Love interest is part of
the old Broadway that the Mammy Nuns have replaced. Harry-
as-a-Boy complains that the plot is in a mess.

HARRY-AS-A BOY:
I think this is going too far, Mr THING-FISH! I haven't even
had a chance to fall in love, or to grow to maturity yet! The
ARTIFICIAL RHONDA is pining away for my wholesome
companionship, just over there! This isn't right! You're letting
everything get all out of sequence!

Harry-as-a-Boy then asks Artificial Rhonda – who turns out to
be Ms Pinky, the lonely person sex device – to dance, using all
the phrases that from 'America Drinks and Goes Home' to
'Dancin' Fool' and 'Sy Borg' have been Zappa's icons of modern
America's grotesque inadequacy at sexual communication.

Harry-as-a-Boy and Artificial Rhonda then become participants in a nativity scene on Francesco's front lawn in New Jersey.
Harry-as-a-Boy is the cuckolded Joseph; Artificial Rhonda has
been 'knocked up', not by the Holy Spirit but by Quentin Robert
De Nameland, the fraudulent 'philostopher' of *Greggery Peccary*
and video preacher denounced in the *Thing-Fish* version of 'The
Meek Shall Inherit Nothing'. The infidelity occurs during 'Clowns

---

[66]Frank Zappa, 'The Massive Improve'lence', *Thing-Fish*, 1984, booklet, p. 10.

on Velvet', a track named after Zappa's jaundiced term for what most guitarists do when asked to decorate a stretch of time: the default idiocy. Here such convention is flummoxed by having a TV evangelist fuck an inflatable rubber woman while his wife gives the bellboy an enema.

Baby Jesus in the manger is played by the Crab-Grass Baby, whose voice is a computer-generated series of twisted gutturals. It is here that jwcurry's analysis, which stems from a background in concrete and visual poetry, seems particularly perceptive. Zappa overlays so many sabotaged discourses that one can view the results as abstract patternmaking. The computer voice recites Motorhead's speech from *Lumpy Gravy*. Harry-as-a-Boy is besotted.

CRAB-GRASS BABY:
I pooped my pants, pooped my pants, pooped my pants!
I went doody, faaather, sob-sob-sob-sob-sob.
HARRY-AS-A-BOY:
His vocabulary is astonishing![67]

Meanwhile, Artificial Rhonda attends a consciousness-raising group and contemplates a career of her own. Harry-as-a-Boy becomes the protagonist of 'No Not Now' from *Drowning Witch*, a trucker driving stringbeans to Utah. The former selves merge with their later manifestations. Harry is wearing S&M gear and is chained by the nipples. Rhonda wears a Santa Claus outfit over a rubber suit designed to look like Artificial Rhonda 'carried to its most alluring extreme'.[68] She unzips the Santa Claus costume, straps on a dildo and fucks her giant briefcase. Meanwhile, Brown Moses, sung by Johnny 'Guitar' Watson, arrives to denounce the couple for leaving the baby outside in the crab-grass while they have been indulging their sexual pursuits. We can hear an echo here of Zappa's moralistic words about familial duty in *The Real Frank Zappa Book*,[69] where he accuses yuppie single-child families of using their child as a status object. Brown Moses ends up begging for money, though, and offers the Crab-Grass Baby as collateral; he is not a centre of value either.

Meanwhile, the Evil Prince and his Broadway zombies have started sprouting 'nakkins' and talking like Thing-Fish, who decides they are not a 'prov'lem' any more. Sister Ob'dewlla 'X'

---

[67]Frank Zappa, 'The Crab-Grass Baby', *Thing-Fish*, 1984, booklet, p. 11.
[68]Sleeve note, Frank Zappa, 'Briefcase Boogie', *Thing-Fish*, 1984, booklet, p. 14.
[69]Frank Zappa, with Peter Occhiogrosso, *The Real Frank Zappa Book*, 1989, p. 258.

declares she wants to fuck the Crab-Grass Baby and Thing-Fish pumps the two dummies up and down, unleashing a sinister combination of computer mutterings and wild screams. Harry declares he will return to Long Island in his S&M gear feeling fulfilled. Rhonda reveals that she has schemed for years to overtake her husband.

> We learned how to hide SECRET STUFF, wrapped up in the middle of those severe little terminal BUNS we wear! Little TRANSMITTERS, HARRY! Oh... don't pretend to be surprised! We even had ROOM LEFT OVER in there for all of our most favorite little embroidered delicate secretly feminine child-like helpless pathetic sentimental totally useless PERSONAL 'GIRL-THINGS' that smell like the stuff they put in the toilet paper.[70]

Having used Thing-Fish's fountain pen as an anal dildo, she makes Harry sniff it, and he 'assumes the traditional pose of the RCA dog'. 'Won Ton On' ('No Not Now' backwards) closes the musical, as the Mammies corn-hole a grateful Evil Prince, Francesco gives Opal an enema and Quentin Robert De Nameland corn-holes Brown Moses. The Crab-Grass Baby is returned to Harry-as-a-Boy and Artificial Rhonda. This is a sexually revolutionized version of the pairing off of characters that usually concludes musicals. As in 'Strictly Genteel', the *200 Motels* finale, there is a festival atmosphere: the protagonists process through the audience in a conga-line. Thing-Fish says: 'Wave good-night to de white folks, 'DEWLLA!'[71]

As with transcribing the dialogue of *Lumpy Gravy*, this account of *Thing-Fish*, by tracing one narrative, severely limits its resonance and complexity. Although one can detect a certain amount of moralism and contempt for 'aberrant' sexual practices, there is a swirling flamboyance about the *offensiveness* of the words and actions that prevents a clear assessment of any argument. *Thing-Fish* is therapy, an immersion, not a lecture. As jwcurry concluded about it (inconclusively):

> Zappa is an observer, a funnel with a filter translating everything that passes through it into music... The density of information consumable from it prevents me from even *wanting* to come to any kind of conclusions about it as a whole... Rich on many levels of experience,

[70]Frank Zappa, 'Drop Dead', *Thing-Fish*, 1984, booklet, p. 16.
[71]Frank Zappa, 'Won Ton On', *Thing-Fish*, 1984, booklet, p. 16.

Thing-Fish, calculatedly easy to ignore, is not a work to be ignorant of: 'Stupidity has a certain charm – ignorance does not.'[72]

Musically, from the opening descending bass motif that starts with Ike Willis's 'Once upon a time . . .', *Thing-Fish* has a uniquely unstoppable flow. Basic tracks are sourced as follows:

1
Prologue
The Mammy Nuns
Harry & Rhonda
Galoot Up-Date – 'The Blue Light', *Tinsel Town Rebellion*

2
The 'Torchum' Never Stops – *Zoot Allures*
That Evil Prince
You Are What You Is – *You Are What You Is*

3
Mudd Club – *You are What You is*
The Meek Shall Inherit Nothing – *You Are What You Is*
Clowns on Velvet
Harry-as-a-Boy
He's So Gay

4
The Massive Improve'lence
Artificial Rhonda – 'Ms Pinky', *Zoot Allures*
The Crab-Grass Baby
The White Boy Troubles

5
No Not Now – *Drowning Witch*
Briefcase Boogie
Brown Moses

6
Wistful Wit A Fist-Full
Drop Dead
Won Ton On – reverse transcription of 'No Not Know', *Drowning Witch*

The backing on *Thing-Fish* is kept subservient to vocals and narrative, but is nevertheless sophisticated and richly mixed. Some original tracks brought in Chuck Wild for 'Broadway' piano and Jay Anderson on string bass. David Ocker and Steve De Furia helped with the Synclavier programming. Zappa's version of Broadway

---

[72]jwcurry, *Rampike*, Vol. 7, No. 2, p. 75. The quotation is from Frank Zappa, with Peter Occhiogrosso, *The Real Frank Zappa Book*, 1989, p. 241.

pomp, best showcased on the Mammy Nun choruses, warps all-singing all-dancing inanity into something polluted, industrial and threatening. The Nuns of *The Sound of Music* have become something entirely warped. The fast flow of verbal and sexual grotesques is so tantalizing that one can miss quite how good the new tunes are: it is therefore instructive to hear 'The Mammy Anthem' played by the 1982 band in Sicily[73] and 'Brown Moses' and 'The Evil Prince' played by the 1984 band in Hollywood and Hammersmith.[74] Ignored even by the cognoscenti, *Thing-Fish* repays more than the 'annual' listen some Zappologists[75] give it.

THEM OR US

1984 was a bamboozling year for Zappa consumers: *The Perfect Stranger, Francesco*, the triple-box *Thing-Fish* and then, as if that was not enough, a full-scale double rock album of new tunes, *Them Or Us*. The record tied in with the classical releases visually by sporting yet another Donald Roller Wilson painting. The ketchup and baby's milk bottles have been chosen from the clutter on the table of *The Perfect Stranger* and placed on wall brackets. The incompatibility of the two foods pack the same confrontational dialectic as the title, which was a statement of defiance: them (the religious right) or us (rock musicians), also making later references to Heinz[76] and ketchup[77] resonate. Roland Barthes pointed out that French political rhetoric contrasts milk to wine;[78]

---

[73]Frank Zappa, *You Can't Do That on Stage Anymore Vol. 1*, 1988.
[74]Frank Zappa, *You Can't Do That on Stage Anymore Vol. 4*, 1991.
[75]This was originally aimed at Chris Dean in Bradford, who was subsequently mortified that his annual *Thing-Fish* 'ritual' should be quoted to Zappa as an example of lack of enthusiasm for the work, when in fact it's precisely designed to address its awesome immensity. The dialogue after reading out this chapter to Zappa on 26 October 1993 went as follows:

> OTL: I've got a footnote to my friend who lives in Bradford, who says, That thing – I can only listen to it once a year! It's my little message to him . . .
> FZ: Uh-huh.
> OTL: . . . saying he should listen to it more. Not adequate, it's such a big thing, *Thing-Fish*, you can go on and on with it.
> FZ: I think you did a good job: it's a major challenge to describe it in any terms. I love 'Brown Moses', it's a great song to sing, it's a fun song to sing. Actually I'm a pretty decent composer of Negro spirituals.

The keyboardist on the date agreed: 'I remember when we were doing "Brown Moses", there was Ike, Ray, Napoleon and Johnny and Frank and I, and that was such a cool session, man, getting those harmonies, so cool', Tommy Mars talking to the author, 30 October 1993.
[76]'Heinz make food' so far unattributed.
[77]'Ketchup is a vegetable', Frank Zappa, 'When the Lie's So Big', *Broadway the Hard Way*, 1988.
[78]Roland Barthes, 'Wine and Milk', *Mythologies*, 1970, trs. Annette Lavers, 1973, pp. 65–8.

here ketchup figures stage blood, a symbol of the ritual violence behind performance, while milk figures the cosseting of the evangelical right in the person of the PMRC, the 'Mothers' of Prevention'[79]. Sound production was another step on from *Sheik Yerbouti*: the music has a glossy, oiled power full of menace.

The record begins with a cover of the Channels' hit 'The Closer You Are', which was credited in 1956 to lead singer Earl Lewis and Whirlin' Disc label owner Bobby Robinson,[80] the latter probably just taking a royalties cut. At the time of *Them Or Us* Robinson was riding a new wave of street creativity with such groups as the Treacherous Three and Fearless Four on the Enjoy! label. The Channels were recorded in New York, a regional hit restricted to the East Coast (unusual for a Zappa favourite). In 1980 Zappa played it on the radio between 'Straight Lines' by New Musik and 'Hyperprism' by Varèse. He segued the Channels into 'Hyperprism', he explained, because 'these are two of my very favourite records and I think they should be heard as a pair.'[81]

Although most tunes on *Them Or Us* are based on live tracks, the mixed personnel on 'The Closer You Are' does not reflect any particular road band. It uses bassist Art Barrow (who left in 1980) and Chad Wackerman (who replaced Vinnie Colaiuta on drums in 1981). Who overdubbed whom is practically impossible to verify as Zappa would frequently invite back veterans for studio work, dubbing over more 'recent' players or indeed themselves. The song is recorded in the style of 'I Have Been in You' which opened *Sheik Yerbouti*, with background vocals swooping ecstatically into the stratosphere and Zappa leering up front, the new production practically hallucinogenic in its sculptural presence.

'In France' is a scurrilous attack on the country of Pierre Boulez which shows that even if *The Perfect Stranger* required his 'killer triplets' Zappa was not in awe.

> The girls is all salty
> The boys is all sweet
> The food ain't too shabby
> An' they piss in the street[82]

The chorus echoes the old doowop number 'Down in Mexico' by

---

[79]Frank Zappa, 'Porn Wars', *Meets the Mothers of Prevention*, 1985.
[80]Inexplicably changed to Morgan Robinson in the CD release, 1990.
[81]Frank Zappa, *Star Special*, BBC Radio 1, 27 January 1980.
[82]Frank Zappa, 'In France', *Them Or Us*, 1984.

the Pelicans.[83] Johnny 'Guitar' Watson gets right inside the lyric, spitting out its obscenities with just the right degree of gleeful provocation – after all, it was from Johnny 'Guitar' that Zappa learned the *attitude* that all good guitar playing comes from in the first place. In singing about the mystery blow-job that would 'turn your peter green', Watson also wreaked revenge on Peter Green, who, as guitarist in the original Fleetwood Mac, spearheaded the white blues assault on the charts.

Like 'Won Ton On' on *Thing-Fish*, 'Ya Hozna' uses backwards recording. By reversing tapes of heavy-metal bands various Christian extremists – including influential TV evangelists – purported to hear instructions to worship Satan and commit suicide. They were calling for legislation to make what they termed 'backwards masking' illegal. In court, in answer to the 'expert' Wilson Bryan Keyes, who accused them of recording 'do it' backwards on *Stained Class*, Judas Priest used the tactic of playing their records backwards themselves and 'discovering' all kinds of ludicrous messages. Like finding faces in wallpaper, the brain can make 'sense' of practically anything. Finding calls to Satan in the blips and blats of reversed metal albums showed more about the obsessions of the accusers than anything in the music they were attacking.

Of course, to the religious, who fix on ritual as a practice that encodes special powers, the idea of *reversal* is an ever-present fear. This is the basis of the medieval Black Mass in which the Lord's Prayer is recited backwards while walking widdershins (anticlockwise) round a church. Backwards tapes of singing and speech are frequently used in horror films because their simultaneous familiarity and 'wrongness' is disorienting. To impressionable viewers of religious TV broadcasts Judas Priest sounded pretty scary when played backwards. Zappa called the fundamentalists' bluff by issuing a song in which the entire vocal runs backwards.

The title of 'Ya Hozna' is a transcription of how the opening words sound (i.e. the last words of the backwards vocals – 'I'm a sofa ya hi-hi'). The backwards vocal track is placed over a pounding rhythm track, the kind of propulsive fuzz rock-out only Zappa can engineer. One can pick out an insane guttural voice belonging to a *bon viveur* on speed; a blaring male chorus sounding like

---

[83]Recorded for Imperial in 1954 – check the wayward guitar solo!

449

Magma (Christian Vander's alchemical attempt to reincarnate John Coltrane in outer space); and a strenuous Scandinavian health leader exhorting a class to exercise. The words may be heard forwards by the simple expedient of taping the tune, unscrewing the cassette box, reversing the tape on the spool and reassembling the box. Just like the prohibition on masturbation, it is the way religious fanatics attempt to suppress the most obvious experiments (actions that are so simple to perform that prohibition is bound to be ineffective) which is so insulting. It will not come out very hi-fi, but you can make out the words.

I am the heaven
I am the water
Ich bin deine Gerrisse
Ich bin deine Gerrisse und Sprunggerrisse
I am the clouds
Ich bin der Chrome Dinette
Ich bin Eier aller Arten
Ich bin alle Tage und Nächte
Ich bin alle Tage und Nächte
I am embroidered
Ich bin der Dreck unter deinen Walzen
Oh no, whip it on me, honey
Ich bin hier
Ich bin der Autor aller Falten und Damastpaspeln
Ich bin der Chrome Dinette

You're a lonely little girl
But your mommy and your daddy don't care

Ich bin hier
Und du bist mein Sofa
You're a lonely little girl
Ich bin hier
Und du bist mein Sofa
Ya, hi-hi, you are my sofa ya hi-hi

And like REACH and like SQUAT and like CRAWL
Repeat . . . like CRAWL. Everybody like REST . . .
OK, like PULL like PUSH and like . . .
OK like BLOW and BLOW

Ich bin dein geheimes Schmutz und verlorenes
Metalgeld
Ich bin hier
Und du bist mein Sofa

You're never too old to like BLOW and like BLOW and like BLOW . . .
OK, like . . .

Ich bin hier
Und du bist mein Sofa
Ya, hi-hi, You are my sofa ya hi-hi

All right, faster, faster . . . Go, do it, do it!
Like YEAH! . . . I'm feelin' GOOD and I'm looking GREAT
Yeah, FER SURE . . . Like NO WAY!

Ich bin hier
Und du bist mein Sofa
Ya, hi-hi, You are my sofa ya hi-hi
Ich bin hier
Und du bist mein Sofa
Ya, hi-hi, You are my sofa ya hi-hi[84]

The 'three' voices turn out to be George Duke with his 'Ya hi-hi'; a chorus of George Duke, Napoleon Murphy Brock and Zappa; and Moon Zappa. Like the Crab-Grass Baby Jesus in *Thing-Fish*, the lyric combines lines from several songs: 'Sofa No. 2' from *One Size Fits All*; 'It's His Voice on the Radio', from *We're Only in It for the Money* (usually known as 'Lonely Little Girl'); and Moon's Valley Girl exercise routine that appeared on the *Thing-Fish* demo's 'I Don't Wanna Get Drafted' (Zappa talked at the time about releasing a Valley Girl exercise record with contortionist music, an idea that provided the title for 'Aerobics in Bondage'[85]). Frank Zappa from 1967, George Duke, Napoleon Murphy Brock and Frank Zappa from 1975 and Moon Zappa in 1982. It contains the heavy blasphemy of 'Sofa' but also the innocent good humour of Moon and the compassion of 1967, *all* sounding equally weird and 'evil' – or simply 'backwards', to take a literal viewpoint.

'Ya Hozna' is a typical example of Zappa's willingness to contradict reactionary mystification by practical experiment. It is interesting, in view of the way Zappa inverted the title of 'No Not Now' for *Thing-Fish* (and came up with the name of a Chinese soup), that Moon's 'blow!' actually sounds like 'wolb!' Whoever would have guessed that American vowel sounds are simply Scandinavian ones reversed? The fundamentalist 'backwards masking' scare was an extraordinary demonstration of how

---

[84]Ben Watson, 'Anzoh Ay', home tape, 1984, constructed from Frank Zappa, 'Ya Hozna', *Them Or Us*, 1984. Thanks to my mother, Katherine Watson, for helping me transcribe the German. For an English translation see Axel Wunsch, 'New Zappa LP', *Society Pages*, No. 22, November 1984, p. 8. This 'non-critical', fact-rich article by 'Axel Grease' proved very helpful in preparing this overview of *Them Or Us*.
[85]Frank Zappa, *Jazz from Hell*, 1986.

little people in the States understand the machinery they use at home, the confusion between strips of magnetic tape and nature itself: and by extension, of course, the representations of television, the words of the presidential address, the whole debilitating illusion of the spectacle. 'Ya Hozna' – ostensibly an 'incomprehensible song without a message' – is a perfect example of the subversive tendency of Zappa's materialism. Steve Vai added a (forwards) guitar solo of quite gobsmacking velocity.

'Ya Hozna' was followed by 'Sharleena', the classic love song from *Chunga's Revenge* (1970). Played with steely virtuosity, its proud, stilted hurt no longer has the old ache. Zappa's son Dweezil plays a solo that zips about a lot, evidently impressed by Vai's approach. The accumulation of new, young, *loud* guitarists seems to be an attempt to stack a lot of *Us* versus *Them*.

Side two starts with *Sinister Footwear II*, the second of three movements of a ballet which was given its world première by Kent Nagano with the Berkeley Symphony at the Zellerbach Auditorium on 16 June 1984 (the third appeared on *You Are What You Is* as 'Third Movement of Sinister Footwear'). As there and on 'Drowning Witch', the combination of electric guitar grossness and *pointilliste* musicianship is quite bizarre. Given the qualities of rock sonority and classical precision, it is an obvious fusion to make, but since only Zappa seizes this obviousness what emerges seems 'merely' quintessential Zappa. Bartók's *Bluebeard's Castle* invaded by the dragon of your dreams, it is a blistering piece of modern music that nevertheless frames its huge moments in dinky arpeggios. A new, ringing clarity in the production makes use of the moral space created by the songs on the other side of the vinyl: this abstract music really benefits from the sense of toppling restrictions created by the scurrilous disregard of side one.

Side two of *Them Or Us* (like side two of *Sheik Yerbouti*) is one of the great Zappa sequences. After eight minutes of brain-curdling data overload with 'Sinister Footwear' it breaks into a *country and western song*, the assumed locus of ultimate stupidity. The crude facts of 'Truck Driver Divorce' abut the tremulous, compacted densities of 'Sinister Footwear' in a metaphorical turn-about such as no other twentieth-century art has the scope to offer. It is hilarious and ghastly at once. After pissing – in characteristically venomous, petit-bourgeois, irresponsible, yet strangely accurate manner – all over the on-the-road romanticism of

452

The bold & intelligent
MASTERS OF THE ROAD
With their Secret Language
And their GIANT
OVER-SIZED
MECHANICAL
TRANS-CONTINENTAL
HOBBY-HORSE![86]

by pointing out the pitfalls of night-time employment

Sometimes when you get home,
Some ugly lookin' son-of-a-bitch
Is trying to pooch yer
HOME-TOWN SWEETHEART![87]

Zappa unleashes a guitar solo that completely turns round the listening space we have been inhabiting.[88] This is achieved by the xenochronous laying of the guitar solo from 'Zoot Allures', recorded in New York on 11 November 1981,[89] over a foreign backing. The solo goes beyond even that of *Sheik Yerbouti*'s 'Yo' Mama' in establishing the guitar as the pre-eminent force in carving out abstracted sonority. The grinding repetitions of 'No Not Now' suddenly fall into place as background to this scorificatious desecration of the tedium of paid labour.

'Stevie's Spanking' is not to be confused with *Cadillac Extravaganza*, the Austrian film-short from 1978, where a critic of Zappa's 'opulent' lifestyle was spanked by Smothers inside the Cadillac that 'symbolized the American way of life' (according to the spankee). 'Stevie's Spanking' documents Steve Vai's spanking by Laurel Fishman, whom Zappa consulted about the song and who signed an official release.[90] Again, Zappa lets loose the new metal heroes – Steve Vai and Dweezil – over a classic riff, though the band plays in such a characteristically tight way that it does not really sound like Van Halen at all. 'Baby, Take Your Teeth Out' was the single, a mocking song in the cheesy twist tradition of 'Jewish Princess', lasting a mere one minute twenty-four seconds. The 'reggae' of 'Fine Girl' has become an idiotic calypso, complete with steel pans. Presumably a request for gummy oral sex, it is

[86]Frank Zappa, 'Truck Driver Divorce', *Them Or Us*, 1984.
[87]Ibid.
[88]Thanks to Alan Wilkinson, sax-terrorist saviour of improvised music, for pointing out this particular felicity.
[89]Marc Ziegenhagen. 'Didja Know . . .?', *Society Pages USA*, No. 2, undated, p. 54. Another fact-rich article which was again very helpful.
[90]Frank Zappa, with Peter Occhiogrosso, *The Real Frank Zappa Book*, 1989, p. 214.

curiously weightless, as if the absurdism of the 'Jones Crusher' castration-complex tack is going to make the song evaporate. The middle section has Ike Willis sighing and grunting in a white mist of directionless vagary. Quite the oddest structure for a chart contender.

'Marque-Son's Chicken' (Marqueson is a nickname for monitor-board engineer Marque Coy), a live solo from 1982, accumulates repeated figures with a speed and eccentricity reminiscent of 'Tink Walks Amok', Ed Mann and Steve Vai pacing each other through fine-mesh intricacies. Then a highly original brand of heavy-rock swing pushes Zappa into his guitar solo, Scott Thunes's bass particularly rugged and raunchy. Zappa clambers about the harmonies like a child exploring a climbing-frame, a fresh enthusiasm that shows that, for all their nervous energy, Steve Vai and Dweezil do not challenge Zappa for curiosity about the interstices of musical structure. The dogged bass-line becomes more and more absurd against Zappa's liberties, which develop a chafed rawness before the theme crashes in again. 'The Planet of My Dreams', another excerpt from the *Hunchentoot* musical, concludes side three with a soaring soprano vocal from Bob 'Harry-as-a-Boy' Harris. It is also a proud boast of integrity from Zappa himself – though, like much of *Them Or Us*, he is not actually performing on the song. Thana Harris, who applied vocals to the *Hunchentoot* tunes ('Flambay', 'Spider of Destiny', 'Time is Money') on the CD release of *Sleep Dirt*, sings in the chorus. The presence of George Duke (who quit in 1975) on piano and Patrick O'Hearn (who quit in 1978) on bass plus current players suggests that the track had been worked on at the Utility Muffin Research Kitchen for nearly a decade.[91]

Side four begins with 'Be in My Video', a sequence of video clichés mainly derived from David Bowie's 'China Girl' and 'Dance the Blues'. As David Bowie told Kid Jensen in 1983, 'I'm not really a roots person in terms of home.'[92] When postmodernism

---

[91]A supposition supported by the existence of a 70s out-take of the track with only Bob Harris, George Duke and Patrick O'Hearn. Marc Ziegenhagen, ever vigilant about the facts, argues that Bob Harris's involvement elsewhere in *Them Or Us* throws this mid-1970s provenance into doubt ('Didja Know...?', *Society Pages USA*, No. 2, p. 54). With his busy schedule – Miles Davis, Nelson Mandela celebrations, his own tours – it is surely unlikely that George Duke would pop in for a session in the 80s. Bob Harris is a long-term accomplice – he was in the Mothers of *Fillmore East June 1971* – so a 70s track overdubbed in 1984 still seems most credible. The Duke/O'Hearn out-take must be part of the *Hunchentoot* songs of '*circa* 1974–6' that surfaced on *Läther* and the vinyl release of *Sleep Dirt*.
[92]BBC Radio 1, 25 March 1983.

was merely a twinkle in Fredric Jameson's political unconscious, Bowie was purveying commercial glamour as a fine-art pose: Zappa is truly his nemesis. To add insult to injury, it is recorded in straight-ahead 4/4 in the key of C major. The exuberance of the varieties of silly voice used here begs comparison to the Mothers on *Absolutely Free*. Zappa was not merely castigating Bowie's clichés; the song came from a considered view of the limited possibilities of video in an MTV-oriented rock industry.

> There's an exteme unfairness involved for the groups involved in making videos. The record company may advance the money for the production but before the group sees any record royalties the company gets all the money for the video back. Some group has to take a chance and invest in the video – so what do they do? They want to make sure that their video's gonna go on, so they insist on making sure it looks exactly the same as the other guy's video, so consequently you have a handful of directors who do all the videos because they can make them look all the same because they actually *made* the last one, y'know, so everything shrivels down to nothing. And meanwhile the audience that really just wants entertainment, they like music, they want to see pictures moving in time with the music, don't realise the grim aspects of what's really going on behind the scenes, and in some instances – I don't wanna use this ugly word – but there is [silly announcer's voice and holds his hands like a megaphone – as per 'enforced audience participation' on the 1979 tour] *payola* involved. So if you've made this video that looks like everybody else's video even that's not going to get it on the air unless you *pay off* to make them play your bland average video.[93]

The title-track 'Them Or Us' is recorded in the stand-out production style that makes *Guitar* the Zappologist's desert-island disc. It was originally performed in Bolzano, Italy, on 3 July 1982 as a solo on 'The Black Page'. The sonic events resemble nuclear Armaggedon presented on a wraparound screen by Steven Spielberg: it is as if every other guitar player (apart from Hendrix) has been playing in only two dimensions before. Towards the end the filth and crunch is simply outrageous, a reminder that sheer rock heaviness can still sound like an affront.

'Frogs with Dirty Little Lips' answers those critics who damn Zappa's lyrics as 'infantile' by setting lines made up by his son Ahmet. The basic rhythm track consists of humorously sinister frogs-and-crickets noises and the chorus, which includes Roy Estrada, sets a new benchmark for march-time pomp and stupid circumstance. The basic track was recorded at one of only three

---

[93]Frank Zappa, *Video22*, 1984.

live performances of the song.[94] 'Whipping Post' was prepared for the 1984 band after some heckling at a concert in Helsinki on 22 September in 1974.[95] It was an interesting moment because the request actually left Zappa nonplussed. The jazz-tinged *Roxy* band had got so far from regular rock that the idea of playing Allman Brothers' second-to-none guitar blow-out[96] seemed utterly incongruous (and hence, in Zappa's terms, *de rigueur*). His riposte – asking the heckler to sing it and, hearing nothing, saying it must be a John Cage composition – is characteristically sharp, but he is evidently rattled: he keeps referring to 'Whipping Post' during 'Montana'. He told *Guitar Player* magazine:

> He just yelled out 'Whipping Post' in broken English. I have it on tape. And I said, 'Excuse me?' I could just barely make it out. We didn't know it, and I felt kind of bad that we couldn't just play it and blow the guy's socks off. So when Bobby Martin joined the band and I found out that he knew how to sing that song, I said, We are definitely going to be prepared for the next time somebody wants 'Whipping Post', in fact we're going to play it before somebody even asks for it.[97]

It was the ideal song to conclude an album that set up rock as an oppositional culture to the Christian right (even if the precision of Zappa's musicians give it a strangely modulated feel). The backing was Zappa's patented pseudo-reggae beat, but it has sufficiently wilful mass and lyricism to recall Duane Allman in all his glory.

[94]Santa Monica, 11 December 1981, and San Diego, 12 December 1981 (two shows), the final nights of the tour.
[95]Frank Zappa, 'Montana (Whipping Floss)', *You Can't Do That on Stage Anymore Vol.* 2, 1988.
[96]The Allman Brothers Band, *At Fillmore East*, 1971, Capricorn SD2–802.
[97]Quoted by Axel Wunsch, 'New Zappa LP', *Society Pages*, No. 22, November 1984, p. 12.

CHAPTER 11
SYNCLAVIER AND TOTAL CONTROL

SYNCLAVIER AND COMPOSITION

Zappa has always been clear that his goal is to realize his compositions: play music that *he* wants to hear. Musicians are therefore a means to an end. Though he enjoys, and documents, band-member behaviour, he would just as soon write songs about amplifiers ('Electric Aunt Jemimah') or Hammond organs ('Florentine Pogen'). In *The Real Frank Zappa Book* he remarks that he cannot be friends with his musicians because he employs them.[1] Michael Gray notes Zappa's commodity relationship to his players: 'Zappa has come to see his musicians as purchasable units, like editing suites or amplifiers – part of the baggage a present-day composer needs.'[2]

In 1982 he was one of the first to buy a Synclavier, a computer for editing digital sound. He was not impressed with Synclavier's guitar interface (you had to play too slowly) and never bought it. Music is entered via piano-keyboard, terminal (VDU-presented score with qwertyuiop-keyboard or mouse) or Roland octapad ('this little set of plastic squares that you hit with a stick and it has a MIDI output on it'[3]). It was expensive, but, as he said to *Electronic Musician* in 1986, 'I could have bought two of these machines for what the *London Symphony Orchestra* album cost

---

[1]Frank Zappa, with Peter Occhiogross, *The Real Frank Zappa Book*, 1989, p. 251.
[2]Michael Gray, 'The Double Life of Frank Zappa', *Daily Telegraph*, 18 September 1992. Thanks to James Rushton at Chester Music for this cutting. The shock of seeing Charles Shaar Murray (*Oz, Frendz, NME*), Tony Parsons (*NME, Socialist Worker*) and Michael Gray (who had the leftist insight to mention how the Communist Party betrayed the 'oh-so-nearly a revolution' of May 1968 Paris in his book *Mother! is the Story of Frank Zappa*, 1985, p. 94) occupying the entire music page of the Tory *Daily Telegraph* is a salutary lesson on the limits of music-writing as a vehicle for social change.
[3]Quoted by John Diliberto, 'Frank Zappa and His Digital Orchestra', *Electronic Musician*, September 1986, p. 53.

me'.[4] Like any employer, Zappa dreams of replacing troublesome employees with machinery, relishing the chance to offend those who sentimentalize the 'human element' in art.

However, Zappa is too much a realist to imagine that this can really be the case. In *The Real Frank Zappa Book* he weighs the Synclavier pros (doesn't get bored, precision) versus the cons (expression requires a lot of input, no improvisation or spontaneity) and admits he is '*almost* tempted' by the 'human'.[5] It would be strange indeed if someone who has toured for the last quarter-century *really* did not enjoy working with musicians. Like Malcolm McLaren's reputation for 'manipulation', people seem all too willing to take Zappa's statements at their face value, rather than examine what he actually does. When Miles Davis used a Synclavier on *Tutu* he was not accused of misanthropy. In 1979, explaining why he preferred brass musicians playing a transcription of his solo on 'Revised Music for Guitar and Low Budget Orchestra'[6] to orchestral tracking by a machine, Zappa said:

> I actually think the overdubbing makes it sound better, because you have all the imperfections which make it sound more interesting. If you had something tracking it absolutely I think it would tend to be a little bit dull. I like the idea of several instruments all trying desperately to play the same line.[7]

Most established names merely play a few large venues to boost the sales of a new album. Zappa's touring schedule has been strenuous and persistent: decades of regular live gigs. Zappa has probably played with more musicians, and more often, than anyone else in rock.

Zappa is just as fascinated by technology, though, and it was with the Synclavier that he applied himself to electronically generated music (after a little dabbling with the Moog synthesizer on *Zoot Allures*). He was wildly enthusiastic.

> It's beyond the orchestra. Because what it enables me to do is the same thing a painter gets to do. You get to deal with the material in a real and instantaneous way. You go boop and it's there. You don't sit down and write it out painstakingly over a period of years and have the parts copied and hope that some orchestra will have enough time to devote to a rehearsal so they come within the vicinity of what your original idea is. There is no doubt about it that if you can play on this

---

[4]Ibid., p. 51.
[5]Frank Zappa, with Peter Occhiogrosso, *The Real Frank Zappa Book*, 1989, p. 173.
[6]*Studio Tan*, 1978.
[7]John Dalton, 'Frank Zappa Part II', *Guitar*, June 1979, p. 24.

thing and hear what you're playing, you have total control of your idea. Good, bad, or indifferent, you get to take the rap for it without having to share any blame with some malfeasance on the performance level when you write it out in the normal way.[8]

In February 1987 he posed on the cover of *Music Technology* magazine under the heading 'Shut Up and Play Your Synclavier', one of his scores glowing on the VDU, his finger poised over the terminal's keyboard. Interviewer Rick Davies expressed surprise that he could find inspiration without playing an instrument. 'No, I just go in there and go to work. Sit down and start typing. I like it.'[9] This recalls Zappa's original fascination with the score. On hearing how musical scores operated – long before he played an instrument, and before he had learned the real conventions – he immediately scribbled down some notes and began pestering musical 'craftspersons' to play his music.[10]

> It was fascinating to me that you could see the notes and somebody who knew what they were doing would look at them and the music would come out. I thought it was a miracle. I was always interested in graphics, and I spent most of my creative time in my early days in school drawing pictures. I got a Speedball pen and a jar of Higgins India Ink and some music paper and, shit, *I could draw those.*[11]

This is less an indication of an inability to relate to people than of a fascination with *transformation*, the alchemy by which spatially arranged signs become a piece of time: the idea of the score is the background to Zappa's interpretation of Einsteinian space-time unity in both *Them Or Us (The Book)*[12] and 'Time Is Money'.[13]

In February 1987, Zappa was in no doubt about the superiority of the machine to the human element. Asked which he preferred to work with, he answered:

> With a machine. No question. No contest. The problem with doing anything with live musicians is that they're entitled to earn a living, so you have to pay them. And it gets expensive. When a tour is over, the band is free to go out and do whatever other things they can get in their spare time. I don't keep them on salary all the time – I can't afford them. So the best way to do music is by typing it in, pushing the button and listening to it play back correctly.[14]

---

[8] Ibid., p. 52.
[9] Quoted by Rick Davies, *Music Technology*, February 1987, p. 45.
[10] Frank Zappa, with Peter Occhiogrosso, *The Real Frank Zappa Book*, 1989, p. 142.
[11] Quoted by David Sheff, 'Frank Zappa Interview', *Playboy*, February 1993, p. 62.
[12] Frank Zappa, *Them Or Us (The Book)*, 1984, p. 63.
[13] Frank Zappa, 'Time is Money', *Sleep Dirt*, lyrics on CD only, 1991.
[14] Quoted by Rick Davies, *Music Technology*, February 1987, p. 48.

Zappa said he was working on between 250 and 300 compositions. Every time he upgrades software and RAM (random access memory) he revises them all: everything is in a state of flux. Between *The Perfect Stranger* (1984) and *Meets the Mothers of Prevention* (1985) you can hear advances in timbral complexity: the chiming purity of the former is overtaken by Zappa's patent visceral intensity as he adds more complex harmonics and carves more interesting timbres. At this point few of the pieces existed in hardcopy: even with the Synclavier's score-print option, printing on a graphics printer (Zappa had not yet bought a laser printer) was too slow.

Zappa does not see the Synclavier simply as a gadget to realize scores: he also uses it to achieve the effects of *musique concrète*, either by associating samples with particular keys (a process called 'patching') or using a razor blade, like in the old days.

> I still do razor blade edits. Sure! If you've got 16 tracks and you have complicated orchestration in there and you suddenly want to make a drastic change from one section to another, the only way to do it is to, unless you have more channels or more RAM, is to print the two sections onto the tape and cut them together.[15]

When questioned by Den Simms as to what constitutes 'true' xenochrony – shocked that Zappa would describe as 'xenochronous' alien drums and guitar with a bass player 'splitting the difference' between the two time signatures – Zappa revealed a similar kind of pragmatism.

> I mean, basically, what you're looking for is a musical result that works, y'know, so . . . there's nothin' 'pure' about me, and the tools that I use. I mean, I'm the guy that sticks 'Louie Louie' in every fifteen minutes.[16]

While Zappa's music ceaselessly reminds us of its means of production, rubbing our noses in its provenance, it is not *experimental* in the manner of Stockhausen's late 60s music, which demotes aesthetic choice in favour of hearing the results of certain procedures. There is no ideological commitment involved in using digital edits, tape splices or live snorks: composition is finally a matter of the decisions of the listening ear. Thus Zappa bypasses one of the great conceptual cul-de-sacs of twentieth-century art music.

---

[15]Quoted by John Diliberto, 'Frank Zappa and His Digital Orchestra', *Electronic Musician*, September 1986, p. 52.
[16]Quoted by Den Simms, 'He's a Human Being, He Has Emotions Just Like Us Part 2', 12 January 1991, *Society Pages*, No. 7, September 1991, pp. 19–20. Sure enough, in the midst of the classical concert *The Yellow Shark*, 1993, 'Louie Louie' arrives: 'Welcome'.

Meets the Mothers of Prevention in 1985 was the first 'rock' use of the Synclavier (it had previously been used only on the 'classical' records *The Perfect Stranger* and *Francesco Zappa*, both from 1984). Though such generic distinctions become blurred in the world of digital editing, *Mothers of Prevention* established its rock orientation with side one, which was played by the touring band: Willis, Vai and White on guitars, Mars and Martin on keyboards and the Thunes/Wackerman rhythm section.

'We're Turning Again' also addressed issues germane to rock by rubbishing the American media's fixation on the 60s. The old irritant of flower power had been made worse by the assumption made by younger rock writers that Zappa was a product of that era.

> They walkin' around
> With stupid flowers in their hair
> And everywhere they go they try and
> Stuff 'em up the guns
> And the servants of the law
> Who had to push 'em around
> And later mowed them down
> But they were full of all that shit
> That they believed in
> So what the fuck?[17]

In 'Mom & Dad' on *We're Only in It for the Money* in 1968 Zappa had written an elegy for anti-war protesters killed by the authorities, three years before the Kent State University killings when the National Guard fired on demonstrators. In retrospect he desecrates their memory, just as he offends rock listeners by enumerating the deaths of Hendrix, Joplin, Morrison and Keith Moon, complete with silly sound-effects, Ike Willis using his Thing-Fish 'negrocious' dialect. It is the one song of Zappa's that Steve Vai felt unhappy about.[18]

> Everybody come back!
> No one can do it like you used to
> If you listen to the radio
> And what they play today

---

[17]Frank Zappa, 'We're Turning Again', *Meets the Mothers of Prevention*, 1985.
[18]Steve Vai, 'Zappa Now and Then', *Guitar*, May 1986.

You can tell right away
Those assholes really need you[19]

Zappa's lines offend notions of correct prosody, the shoddiness of the language expressing his contempt for his targets. 'The Blue Light'[20] had also referred to Donovan – 'the guy in the brocade coat' – as an icon of the hopeless nostalgia indulged in by the middle-aged. Zappa's indignation and offence rend the piety with which the 60s are regarded by institutions like *Rolling Stone* with a venom that puts everything into play. Musically, the piling up of marimba, weirdly timed drums and effects presents a data-overload that gets overlooked because of the pungency of Zappa's words.

The contempt of 'We're Turning Again' has a curious effect on the following track, 'Alien Orifice', where the technically astonishing runs by Ed Mann are made to sound mocking and vacuous. Based on a motif that seems to find ever more incongruous reasons to return to the same note, it presents indecision as a patterning device. Scott Thunes's bass part can be listened to as a composition in itself. An extension of 'The Black Page', the closely written section breaks into a ridiculously ecstatic cadenza on cheesy Wurlitzer samples before a devastating piece of Zappa guitar that recalls the poise of his solo on 'Redunzl'.[21] Before the theme is reprised, Ed Mann is unleashed on a quite absurd progression. 'Alien Orifice' jampacks so many musical ideas that it fully justifies Zappa's use of such technically advanced players; the unerring logic of its convolutions – simultaneously a challenge to musicians and a joy to listeners – is reminiscent of jazz compositions by Andrew Hill and Thelonious Monk.

'Yo Cats' attacks the session musician mafia in appropriately seasick jazz tones: 'I play shit but I love that loot', despising 'those schmucks with electric guitars'. In one sense Zappa is still fighting the rock 'n' roll wars, in another he is celebrating the liberating effect of technology for the composer. With his Synclavier he can do without musicians altogether. Ike Willis delivers one of his best performances, all smarm and greasy charm as he works his way through Zappa's scabrous innuendo.

---

[19]Frank Zappa, 'We're Turning Again', *Meets the Mothers of Prevention*, 1985.
[20]Frank Zappa, *Tinsel Town Rebellion*, 1981.
[21]Frank Zappa, *Studio Tan*, 1978.

Watch your watch, play a little flat
Make the session go overtime, that's where it's at[22]

Tommy Mars's expert use of Hammond organ samples reinforce the sense of night-club sleaze.

'What's New in Baltimore' had words in public performance and the words of the title precisely fit the melody that arrives half-way through. It begins with variations that churn up to a peak of differentiated rhythm before exploding with the arching glory of the theme itself. Like 'Black Napkins' and 'Watermelon in Easter Hay', it is an unashamed vehicle of guitar romanticism that both parodies and exults in its preposterous arousal. Distinguishing it from 70s cosmic guitar is the firmness of Zappa's harmonic development and Chad Wackerman's extraordinary rhythmic interaction, his dropouts and comments. Towards the fade-out Zappa plays some growling figures, a heavy version of the way Johnny 'Guitar' Watson rocks against his backing rhythm.

Side two was realized on the Synclavier. 'Little Beige Sambo' – the title reflects Zappa's critique of the new black middle class – is a dazzling piece. Zappa establishes his samples in naturalistic ways and then stretches them beyond possibility. Zappa entered most of the music via the keyboard, and there is a decidedly pianistic feel to it. Thus a skittering top line sounds like Ed Mann on xylophone, but revs up beyond even his lightning touch. A busy, gruff bass figure anchors the torrent of sprinkled notes which add up to a piece of typical sunrise pastoral. Like a Nancarrow player-piano piece, it climaxes in utterly 'impossible' glissandi.

'Porn Wars' was the fruit of Zappa's stand against the Parents Music Resource Center, an organization formed to force the record industry to 'rate' albums in the manner of films. They favoured such designations as 'D/A' (drugs/alcohol), 'X' (sex), 'V' (violence) and 'O' (occult). This last revealed their ideological roots in the evangelical right, as well as infringing First Amendment prohibitions of legislation pertaining to religious freedom. Zappa was convinced that rated albums would effectively be dropped from the stores; commercial interest would lead towards self-censorship by the industry. Using actual soundbytes from the Senate house hearing gives a stark taste of the authoritarian pomposity Zappa was up against. In a courageous act of solidarity, Zappa did precisely what the rap group 2 Live Crew had done to their pros-

---

[22]Frank Zappa, 'Yo Cats,' *Meets the Mothers of Prevention*, 1985.

ecutor Jack Thompson – released a record using their enemy's voices – and been sued and banned for. As Zappa pointed out, the PMRC assumed that attacking a group of young, poorly resourced rappers would be a pushover; taking on Zappa – wealthy, independent of the record industry yet well known as articulate and newsworthy – was another matter.

'Porn Wars' opens with quotes showing how contradictory the right's position was – one senator claims that the hearing is not about framing legislation while Senator Ernest Hollings talks of finding 'any constitutional means' of stopping this 'outrageous filth'. In defence of the idea of rating rock albums, the manner in which toys are sometimes labelled with 'age ranges' was brought up.

> SENATOR PAULA HAWKINS: I'd be interested to see what toys your kids ever had.
> FZ: Why would you be interested?
> SPH: It would be a point of interest in this, uh . . .
> FZ: Well come over to the house, I'll show them to you [*Laughter*] . . . really.
> SPH: I might do that.[23]

The attempt to make out Zappa as some kind of freak is deflated by the invitation, neatly exposing the paranoia that fuels right-wing moralism. When Ike Willis – in his Thing-Fish persona – interrupts to ask for a vote (a section borrowed from *Thing-Fish*) – he refers to Zappa with words that originally applied to Harry: 'We'll get back to the wimp and his low-budget conceptium of personal freedom in just a moment.'[24]

It is precisely the 'low-budget', unrhetorical side of Zappa's argument that makes it so effective. Dialogue left over from *Lumpy Gravy* – the freaks discussing the 'pigs and ponies' and their rhinestone collars and gold-lamé hoof covers – reruns the 'them or us' theme. The humour and intimacy of Zappa's poetic world grates against the pompous formality and disdain of the senators.

> SENATOR ALBERT GORE: I think that your suggestion is a good one, to print the words, that would go a long way to satisfy everyone's objections.
> FZ: All we'll have to do is find out how it's going to be paid for.

---

[23]Frank Zappa, 'Porn Wars', *Meets the Mothers of Prevention*, 1985.
[24]Ibid.

Zappa's 'low-budget' conception also entails a stringent view of economic necessity. The piece ends as the next witness is called – singer-songwriter John Denver.

Of course, in something he himself constructs, Zappa is bound to have the last word. However, the piece works by presenting a stack of material rather than by shaping a polemical argument. Speeded-up and distorted quotes are repeated in a quilt of words. 'Bend up and smell my anal vapour'; 'fire and chains and'; 'maybe I could make a good rock star, I don't know'; 'porn rock'; 'sex'; 'listen you little slut, do as you're told'; 'outrageous filth'; 'tools of gratification in some twisted minds'; 'the effects of such lyrics on the well-adjusted child'; 'pyromania'; 'burn burn burn'; 'come with Daddy'; 'drive my love inside you'.

The effect of this verbal pot-pourri is to dramatize how people draw their own meanings from words and phrases. Senator Ernest Hollings from Texas found difficulty in assessing any 'redeeming social value' in the music in question because the words were 'inaudible'; he also commented that his accent was frequently misunderstood in different parts of America (which is where the phrase 'maybe I could make a good rock star, I don't know' derives from). Zappa has pointed out that the Bible's Song of Solomon contains an account of fist-fucking[25] and that *Carmina Burana* is based on a pornographic Latin text (when told this on TV, Kandy Stround, the PMRC's solicitor, looked pained and said, 'Actually it's one of my favourite pieces').

Although structuralist literary criticism has celebrated the way James Joyce and Jean-Luc Godard[26] force the audience to become aware of how meaning is created, Frank Zappa has managed to take such processes out of the art world into pop politics. Unlike Sting and U2, who ask us to admire their actions on our behalf, Zappa sets up a series of questions about meaning and its social control that encourage our own speculation, preserving the utopian message of the hermetic world of *Lumpy Gravy*. Some of the

---

[25]Song of Solomon, 5: 4.
[26]Particularly Colin MacCabe, *James Joyce: The Revolution of the Word*, 1978: *Godard: Images, Sounds, Politics*, 1980. The book on Jean-Luc Godard is much inferior, as MacCabe has to defend Godard's shabby Maoist politics. Unlike Vaneigem's attack on Zappa, the SI's condemnation of Godard – who came from the same milieu, merely recycling ideas Guy Debord had pioneered with his films in the 1950s – was conclusive: 'The Role of Godard', *International Situationniste*, #10, March 1966, reprinted in *Situationist International Anthology*, ed. Ken Knabb, 1981, pp. 175–6.

most 'diabolic' noises – also used as samples on the 1988 tour[27] – are just a kid burping:

> That's my nephew, Jade. He has the ability to burp very loud and very long, and he can also burp words. So when he was here visiting in '87, we had a sampling session with Jade. In fact, he got the same as any other musician that comes in here to do samples. I stood him in front of a microphone and let him do an assortment of burps, and then gave him a list of words and phrases to burp, and some of those things were put into the Synclavier, and that's what you heard.[28]

'Porn Wars' shows that 'obscenity' and 'evil' are not fixed terms, but taints applied in the course of exacting social power: a vindication of the effectiveness of modernism as a political instrument.

After 'Porn Wars' the 'pure' music of 'Aerobics in Bondage' sounds deeply satirical, as if Zappa has frozen the social conflicts of the Senate hearing into art-mannequin cameos. This is the old idea of inverting the relationship of art to reality that came with the *200 Motels* press kit, conceptual continuity as the landscape we are living in ('Imagine that *you* could be living there and working there and not even know it. Whether you can imagine it or not, that's what the deal is.'[29]) The beauty of the music's construction, its symmetries and logic, are placed in distinction to the accusations of boorishness and insensitivity in 'Porn Wars'. Like the music of *Lumpy Gravy*, it seems to pursue the verbal arguments that proceed beyond the threshold of consciousness. It finishes with a fluttering luxuriance that is highly virtuosic.

Zappa decided that 'Porn Wars' was of mainly American interest and replaced it with three new tracks in a 'European Version' (an indication of this replaced the anti-rating 'Warning Sticker' on the American issue). The phrase itself actually goes back to *200 Motels*.[30] Johnny 'Guitar' Watson was brought in to sing and play guitar on 'I Don't Even Care', backed by Ray White. It's a turgid, knotted song, with boiling rhythm guitar, taking up where Watson's 'protest' hits ('Ain't That a Bitch', 'A Real Mother for Ya') left off.

> I don't even care
> So let me tell you why this evening

[27] See Frank Zappa, 'A Few Moments with Brother A. West', *The Best Band You Never Heard in Your Life*, 1991.
[28] Frank Zappa, quoted by Den Simms, 'The Obsessive Analyst', *Society Pages*, No. 7, 30 September 1991, p. 2.
[29] *International Times*, No. 115, 1971.
[30] Frank Zappa, 'The Girl Wants to Fix Him Some Broth', *200 Motels*, 1971.

Listen!
Now enough has been said
About the white the blue and the red
Everybody just running along scared
Ow!
Talkin' about me y'all
I don't even care
No I don't, no I don't
Standing in the bread line
Everybody line to line[31]

Zappa gives Watson space for his inimitable asides, which include some of Zappa's running jokes ('Listen! Ain't that some spoo!') and the utterly characteristic twang of his guitar: *the* voice of West Coast R&B rides again.

'One Man – One Vote' is a Synclavier track in the perverted-fusion style of *Jazz from Hell*. A slippery bass figure kick-starts absurdly jolly melody-rapture, until a sinister modulation finds a darker tone. When the theme returns it bursts up through splinters of sound like a sea-monster breaking through the waves. 'HR 2911' anthologizes some of the music from 'Porn Wars', Webern string-sounds gracefully unfurling through snorks and grunts and ratchet percussion. After learning to recognize the haunting tune, its appearance on 'Porn Wars' becomes still more poignant. The title referred to House Resolution 2911, the clause which explained why the record industry was ready to concede album-rating: it was also petitioning for a tax on blank tapes. By giving in to the PMRC on 'voluntary' labelling of rock records, the industry hoped to ease HR 2911 through Congress (helped by the fact that the PMRC was founded by senators' wives). Gail Zappa described the situation.

In fact, the whole thrust of those hearings was to guarantee the sales tax on blank audio tapes. If you look at the names of the ladies who signed the original letters before the PMRC was formed, and you look at the names of the senators who were involved . . . this is what we put in the Z Pack, which the news never wanted to touch. The blank-tape tax is collected by the US government for the benefit of the record companies that distribute product – the big six or five or three or whatever. The major distributors in this country are the beneficiaries of this tax, which tax payers are paying the government to collect for them, which they then divide up. I'd like to see *those* audits! RIAA and everybody else in the industry was bending over – in the same way that

---

[31]Frank Zappa, 'I Don't Even Care', *Meets the Mothers of Prevention*, 1985.

gazelles *pronk*, y'know – to accommodate these people, because they knew they were going to make a fortune off of those tax monies.[32]

Despite Zappa's proprietary attitude towards his art (resulting in campaigns against bootlegs, the use of samples of his music, even writers daring to quote his lyrics), he militantly opposed this acceptance of censorship in exchange for monetary gain. He was also clear how little of the blank-tape tax would actually accrue to the artists whose work is allegedly filched by home-taping: 10 per cent.[33] The CD release of *Meets the Mothers of Prevention* collected together both track runnings.

JAZZ FROM HELL

Apart from one guitar showcase, *Jazz from Hell* is a pure Synclavier album, and an instrumental one at that: vocals are restricted to fleeting samples of phrases and 'mouth noises'. Now that *Sleep Dirt* has been overdubbed with vocals, *Jazz from Hell* joins the classical and guitar albums as the only 'music music' in Zappa's catalogue.

Zappa quite rightly dismisses the sentimentality of critics who view the Synclavier as 'inhuman' (in distinction to the supposed 'humanity' of a domestic appliance reproducing the polyvinyl wiggles of, say, John Denver). Although Zappa lost no opportunity to declare that at last he was free of the troublesome necessity of employing musicians, he was aware that the presentation of electronic music in performance raised problems. Who wants to go out and see someone push a 'start' button?[34] In 1988, when Zappa went on the road again, he took eleven musicians with him. Despite his rhetoric, there *are* still aspects of music a machine cannot deliver.

The Synclavier can theoretically synthesize any music under the sun, but *Jazz from Hell* nevertheless sticks in the main to models created by drum-bass-melody-instrumental formats. The basic form is closer to fusion than it is to the electronic blow-outs perpetrated by Karlheinz Stockhausen and his accomplices at the

---

[32]Gail Zappa, interview with the author, 27 October 1993.
[33]Frank Zappa to J.B. Peterson, Pacifica Radio KPFK, 21 June 1990, transcribed in 'Zappa on Censorship', *Society Pages USA*, No. 3, undated, p. 29.
[34]He did not reply to the northern English promoters Leeds Jazz, who invited him to come and present his Synclavier compositions as background to him playing his electric guitar.

Cologne Electronic Studio in the late 50s. Like Conlon Nancarrow, whose player-piano pieces are based on two-hands piano-playing, Zappa likes to establish an illusion of reality and then push the technical limits beyond belief.

Although widely denounced as abstract and unlistenable by those who regard Zappa as a comedy act, *Jazz from Hell* is actually a wonderful demonstration of Zappa's continuing ability to compose tunes. In modern classical music, tunes are invariably a sign of flatulence and inertia, as historical imperatives are abandoned for whimsy and pastiche. However, Zappa's surrealist ear for sonority makes a tune less a matter of a series of dots on score-paper than a way of realizing social-satiric energies bound up in what he calls the 'aroma' of different instruments. Though he has abandoned musicians, the Synclavier is not an excuse to forget the social resonance of musical sound. This is of course why lyrical barbs and musical invention are so closely related in his music: they both reveal a perverse impulse to upset the applecart. Zappa's music has always been about the issues of freedom and necessity: *Jazz from Hell* gives close focus to the musical ramifications of that polarity.

'Night School' starts with a conventional 80s booming drum sound snickered up with rasping castanets and automatic hand-claps, and then introduces a portentous organ figure. The piece is organized around a keyboard 'solo' that chooses a bizarre route through the harmonies, a dazzling dada performance that is saved from mere wackiness by its dialectical relationship to the 'backing'. Things happen, chords are discovered, harmony transforms itself. The title relates to a proposal for a TV series on current affairs that Zappa prepared in the late 80s[35] in which 'tits on TV' were to be used to gain viewing figures for anti-establishment politics – a Hollywood version of Cicciolina, the Italian porn star who campaigns against nuclear energy and the death penalty and who shot to fame outside Italy in association with artist Jeff Koons.[36] Zappa's melodic lines frequently resemble TV quiz-show themes, which equate odd intervals with wit and speed of thought, but the difference is that he takes risks. He avoids TV triteness by dissolving the security of a 'home' key. In 'Night School' the entire accompanying 'orchestra' keeps having to modulate in order to keep up with the solo's perverse twists.

[35]Frank Zappa, with Peter Occhiogrosso, *The Real Frank Zappa Book*, 1989, pp. 40–43.
[36]Ilona Staller, *Cicciolina*, 1992.

Zappa uses 'the beltway' as an expression for the unseen processes of establishment politics:[37] like 'Treacherous Cretins',[38] the
title 'The Beltway Bandits' refers to his political enemies. The
Synclavier can hold only an eight-character name for a composition: with over 200 pieces on disk, Zappa had to resort to cryptic
codes which he admitted gave him little clue as to the music inside.
The names of the compositions are therefore less integral to the
compositions than tunes with lyrics developed on the road with a
group of musicians. Nevertheless you can make out a regular
squeaking sound that sounds like a strop on a wheel. Again there
is a questioning solo, this time a whining approximation to a sax
or violin, a kind of articulate siren (Zappa was particularly excited
with mutating samples into each other, so a line could gradually
change from one instrument to another). The backing includes
mouth noises and body sounds. The idea of repetition and circu-
larity in the title – conveyor belts, rubber bands – is neatly wound
into the solo, which fixes itself into a four-note loop that only
breaks once it has drawn attention to itself as repetition rather
than expression. André Lewis used a similar device in his solo on
'Dirty Love' on *Mandré*[39] the pioneering all-synthetic soul album
he made in 1977. The studied arbitrariness of post-Ornette improvisation, the attempt to allow undirected, unconscious choice
leeway, here generates a repetition that only a conscious and flamboyant flourish (which comes as a distinct relief) can dissipate.
Computer programmers are familiar with what are termed 'loops'
in procedural code, and this 'stuck' motif amusingly illustrates a
common bug: the 'eternal loop'. It is like watching a rat run round
and round a maze.

'While You Were Art II' started life as a guitar solo, one of
the chamber improvisations that provided respite from feedback
mania on *Shut Up 'N Play Yer Guitar*.[40] The score was transcribed
by Steve Vai[41] and arranged for Synclavier by Zappa (the inability
to track complex rhythms – precisely the point of Vai's transcriptions – is the main reason Zappa does not use the Synclavier guitar
interface). The original improvisation is open and reflective in the

[37]'The think tanks that exist inside the beltway, all these organizations who develop position
papers and slide 'em under the White House door, they are still exerting influence through these
study groups and think tanks', Frank Zappa on 'The Bob Lesh Show', Radio KTKK, Salt Lake
City, 22 June 1991, reprinted in 'Frank Observations', *Society Pages*, No. 10, 24 August 1992, p. 45.
[38]Frank Zappa, 'Treacherous Cretins', *Shut Up 'N Play Yer Guitar*, 1984.
[39]Mandré, *Mandré*, 1977, Motown M6–886S1.
[40]Frank Zappa, 'While You Were Out', *Shut Up 'N Play Yer Guitar*, 1981.
[41]*The Frank Zappa Guitar Book*, 1982, p. 44.

extreme. Here Zappa uses the Synclavier's sampling capacity to the full, painting in the notes from a wide palette. The expressive line of the original guitar solo becomes an absent centre, resulting in a delicate, sparse world of glancing notes that are reminiscent of Webern (a nod to a high-art context is made in the altered title). However, the rhythmic drive of these dislocated fragments is in a different world from Webern.

'Jazz from Hell', the title-track, mixes the fragmented world of 'While You Were Art II' with purring bass and snuffling saxophone samples reminiscent of the tweaked fusion of 'Night School'. When asked if the title was meant to upset the PMRC, Zappa said he was using it in the sense that a diabolically bad lounge-crooner might be called 'an entertainer from hell'. If this music is jazz, it is jazz from hell. 'G Spot Tornado', in reference to the mid-80s discovery of a 'new' site of sexual excitation, arrives appropriately flushed and dishevelled, with female throat samples that might come from either 'Dinah-Moe Humm' or 'The Torture Never Stops'. The *Bluebeard's Castle* tonality of the latter is revved up to sound like a Cossack dance on poppers. The hard speed of the bass line is reminiscent of 'Möggio'.[42] At the end, the sound of the drum beats decaying is a tribute to the vast amount of RAM (random access memory) Zappa bought in to give his samples a real-time feel.

'Damp Ankles' is named for a friend of Zappa's who works in a psychiatric institution. Apparently the patients would show their appreciation of his efforts on their behalf by licking his ankles. As with 'The Beltway Bandits', a 'complex' rhythm is disguised as what sounds like squeaking machinery. The compressed musical thought in these works can leave the ear stunned, unable to cram in any more ideas. Notes hover and dart like dragonflies. The piece is sandwiched between environmental sounds of insects, animals and running water.

'St Etienne' is a guitar showcase played with real musicians. Considering the number involved (the full 1982 touring band: seven pieces excluding Zappa) it is extraordinarily spacious. They seem to be deliberately reproducing the floating feel of the guitar solos on *Joe's Garage*. The solo ends with a lovely example of Zappa's famous 'bagpipe' technique. 'Massaggio Galore' is heavy on vocal samples: you can hear Ike Willis gibber and moan and

---

[42]Frank Zappa, 'Möggio', *The Man from Utopia*, 1983.

471

make his 'Hi-ho Silver!' running joke (very speeded-up). It dramatically exaggerates a common feature of the pieces on *Jazz from Hell*: the musical levels operate in different time zones. The bass and drums are agitated and urgent but the melody floats about somewhere else. Xenochrony has penetrated to the heart of Zappa's compositional method: he is now deliberately scoring these stretches of non-synchronicity with their long-delayed resolutions.

Zappa was amused to note that the PMRC wanted *Jazz from Hell* to carry a warning sticker. As there were no rude words at all on the album, it proved his point that they were really out to X-rate certain artists, not particular records. It was awarded a Grammy for 'best instrumental rock record'. Zappa declared that this was preposterous and that he doubted that any of the jury had even listened to it. Many speculated that it was a sop from the industry to try and keep him quiet. Needless to say, it did not work.

CHAPTER 12
STAGEISM, OR, ISSUING THE ŒUVRE

STAGEISM

The CD medium gave Zappa the means to release the collected history of live Mothers music he had been promising since 1969. The records came in six volumes of double CDs, over thirteen hours of music chosen from a formidable archive of material, ranging from early four-track through to the forty-eight-track digital recordings made on the 1988 tour. With the release of two boxes of 'Beat the Boots', a selection of Zappa's vast bootleg legacy issued by Rhino Records with Zappa's blessing (but not his involvement), the *Stage* series swamps the listener with material, giving a similar sense of vertigo as that induced by contemplating the discography of Duke Ellington or Sun Ra. As Zappa has pointed out, the *Stage* series is primarily of interest to 'hardcore' fans already familiar with the canon: one of its delights is to register differences between live and studio versions of familiar tunes. Next to no visual aids – the same 'Hollywood epic' lettering on every cover, distinguished only by colour (*Vol. 1* red/yellow; *Vol. 2* yellow/blue; *Vol. 3* pink/green; *Vol. 4* orange/blue; *Vol. 5* pink/red; *Vol. 6* pink/orange) – and no overdubs[1] mean that the music is reduced to the actions of musicians recorded in real-time, a continuous flow of some of the most detailed compositions ever committed to musical memory (the only Zappa band to make substantial use of charts onstage was The Grand Wazoo orchestra, sadly absent from the *Stage* series).

The *Stage* series was met by rumblings of discontent from hardcore Zappaphiles. The existence of a global network of Zappa fans who swap live-performance tapes – an inevitable result of Sony's high-quality tape-recorder miniaturization with the

---

[1] Except 'Lisa's Life Story' on *Vol. 6*, fact fans, which has overdubbed drums (twelve hours fifty-seven minutes out of thirteen hours is not bad).

Walkman of the early 80s – meant that fans could collect their own versions of Zappa's live archive. Their corrections – printed in the booklet for *Stage Vol. 2* and in the fanzine *Society Pages* – showed that these hardcores were more meticulous about dates than Zappa himself. Obviously such collectors have their own ideas about favourite performances; one of the hazards of tape-collecting – impatience with much-performed songs – was illustrated by Out To Lunch's heckling of the 'Dinah-Moe Humm' encore in 1978.[2] Of the two fanzines in English, *T'Mershi Duween*, based in Sheffield, England, and hence less of a mouthpiece for Zappa's own views, was the most critical of *Stage* choices. The relocation of *Society Pages* to America and close contact between its editors and Zappa made it more liable to applaud every move (they went so far as to repudiate a useful book by one of their own contributors – Dominique Chevalier[3] – at Zappa's request). However, though *Society Pages* (quite rightly) dismisses vinyl and CD bootlegs as exploitation of record-buyers without access to the tape pool, it does not discourage equitable swapping of live tapes. Fans can build up their own live archive with Zappa's blessing: *Stage* is Zappa's own selection. As usual with Zappa's productions, they have a tendency to reveal their felicities after initial frustrations (a process which can take years). Certainly no tape collection can emulate their audio quality, which is sterling.

STAGE ONE

As a figure for recorded sound – the lifeless residue of human activity – the Muffin Man's phrase 'dried muffin remnants'[4] is a charming image in comparison to that which opens the *Stage* series.

MV: Can I just ask everybody here, did anybody see me puke on stage?
HK: Didja?
MV: I puked on stage.
HK: You puked on stage?
MV: It was right in the middle of us singing 'Easy Meat' or something and all of a sudden I started puking out of my mouth and I just put my hand over my mouth . . .
HK: Ohh. Outasite!

[2] See 'John Ruskin and Dinah-the-dog', Chapter 5: Bizarre to DiscReet.
[3] Dominique Chevalier, *Viva! Zappa*, 1985.
[4] Frank Zappa, preamble to 'Muffin Man', *Bongo Fury*, 1976.

MV: I thought you guys caught that, man. I got really sick, jumping around 'n stuff, all that Scotch and wine. It was weird, I only did it for a about a second, it was just like a little spew, I kind of shoved it back down my throat and went on singing.
HK: Yeah, that is strange, man, *razzo rizzo*.
FZ: He saved it because he might be hungry later.
MV: Eeee-errrgh – get the big pieces![5]

Occluded in the usual entertaining grossness of Zappa on-the-road documentation are some highly charged themes. There is an oblique reference to the notorious eating-a-shit-on-stage myth (does Mark Volman eating puke on stage suffice?), as well as a reminder of conceptual simultaneity, as the song 'Easy Meat' appeared on vinyl only with *Tinsel Town Rebellion* in 1981, eleven years after this exchange.

'He saved it because he might be hungry later' as usual gives Zappa the last word. It is an old joke, but it also echoes the biblical adage 'As a dog returneth to his vomit, so a fool returneth to his folly.'[6]

These live moments are preserved by Zappa because they are unrepeatable, something indicated by the title of the series: *You Can't Do That on Stage Anymore*. The cover of the concurrent *Make a Jazz Noise Here* made the point that the record industry was busily eradicating live music as a viable part of American mass entertainment. However, in his characteristic manner, Zappa tempers such claims with a reminder that these discs may only be the sounds of a fool returning to his folly.

Volman's 'get the big pieces!' segues to Zappa's most large-scale concept, the epic blasphemy of 'Sofa'. It is put in context by preceding it with the routine in which Mark Volman poses as God's fat floating maroon sofa, which 'stretches in all the right places' (just like the universe).[7] The entire *Stage* series is book-ended by 'Sofa' and 'Strictly Genteel' (which finishes the second disc of *Vol. 6*), a movement from denunciation of religious fraud to the benign secularism that underlines Zappa's materialist philosophy. 'Sofa' comes from the concert at the Rainbow, where Zappa was pushed offstage by an irate fan; there was speculation that the fire at Montreux a week before and this incident were divine

---

[5]Mark Volman, Howard Kaylan, Frank Zappa, 'The Florida Airport Tape', April 1970 (unconvincing *Stage Vol. 2* correction), *You Can't Do That on Stage Anymore Vol. 1*, 1988.
[6]The Bible, Proverbs: 26; 11.
[7]Frank Zappa, 'Once Upon a Time', 1971, *You Can't Do That on Stage Anymore Vol. 1*, 1988. See 'Sofa', Chapter 5: Bizarre to Discreet.

retribution for its blasphemies. If so, by beginning the *Stage* series with 'Sofa', Zappa is once again challenging the Godhead to do His worst.

'The Mammy Anthem', recorded in 1982 at Palermo, has a surpassing grandiloquence equal to 'Sofa' (a feature unnoticed by those who dismissed *Thing-Fish* as a bunch of dubious racial and sexual slurs overdubbed on old backing tracks). Played live and without vocals, it is clear how much it relies upon the glorious sleaze of Zappa's feedback guitar. Like the tracks 'Zoot Allures' and 'Them Or Us', it celebrates the power of the electric guitar to blaspheme, helped by recalling the words 'we as ugly as *sin*' from its original version.[8] When the band returns to the theme (at 4.38), there is an odd moment of digital interference, reminiscent of the artificial dialogue of the Crab-Grass Baby. Although the *Stage* series insists on its integrity as a document of real-time performance, as much as the super-discipline of his bands' musicianship, Zappa's use of high-technology fractures the notion of directly-from-the-heart guitar expression. This weird beep is a reminder of the exactions of factory work and silicon-chip automatism.

In jump-cutting between bands of different eras one remarks an extraordinary tightness and velocity in the bands of the 80s: Scott Thunes and Chad Wackerman providing a nimble rhythm track that is quite astonishing. 'You Didn't Try to Call Me' from 1980 has a bionic bounce that freeze-frames the original version on *Freak Out!*. 'Diseases of the Band', recorded at Hammersmith in 1979, lists some of the hazards of going on tour, then shuffles in recordings from 1969, 1971, 1974 and 1973 in quick succession, before showing what the diseased band was capable of. Originally written to showcase Terry Bozzio's explosive temper, 'Tryin' to Grow a Chin' is sung by Denny Walley, showing that however central Bozzio had become in 1977, he was still replaceable, some-thing he ruefully acknowledged in later interviews. Zappa also sings words to Sam the Sham's 'Wooly Bully' over the iconic dumbness of the tune's riff. This, and Napoleon Murphy Brock's rewrite of 'Louie Louie' as 'Ruthie-Ruthie', serve to introduce archetypal rock stupidity, a thematic link throughout the *Stage* series. Like the version of 'The Mammy Anthem', a wordless medley of three songs played by the Mothers of Invention indi-

---

[8]Frank Zappa, 'The Mammy Anthem', *Thing-Fish*, 1984.

cates how words – in this case the unprotected ejaculation of 'Harry, You're a Beast' – can serve to distract from the musical logic of Zappa's compositions.

Flo & Eddie's 'The Groupie Routine' shows how much improvisation Volman and Kaylan put into the *Fillmore East June 1971* dialogues. According to Volman, Zappa encouraged them to talk to fans each night in order to establish elements of local folklore. Aware of the tension in mass-marketed art between the homogeneity of product and the local colour of its consumers, Zappa uses Flo & Eddie's guileless genius for spontaneity to bring some of the energized clutter of particular circumstance into his operatic superstructure.

Like any art worth its salt, Zappa keeps saying the same thing in different ways: microstructural icons of his whole approach stack up into the texture of the art much as DNA is replicated in every cell of the organism. In a spoken introduction to 'Ruthie-Ruthie' Zappa drew a parallel between audience cravenness and his penguin- and poodle-baiting routines.

> I can't see you but I know that you're out there. It's that little voice, that same little voice at all of the concerts, of the guy in the back of the room who's going *'wenn-hinn, wenn-hinn-in-hinn-in-hinn, wenn-hinn-in-henn-in-henn'*. Couple of years ago, there was a guy who used to come to all the concerts on the East coast, I swore I heard him every night for a month, that he was somewhere in the audience, there was the little voice and he would say, *'Freak-me-out, Frank, freak-me-out! Freak-me-out, Frank!'* Okay, here we go. *Arf arf! Renn-hinn! Arf!*[9]

The way Zappa imitates the sound of the heckler is similar to the complex cry-of-the-bondee in 'Penguin in Bondage'. 'Arf!' is Fido's bark in *Apostrophe (')*. For musicians onstage, surrounded by the hardware of amplification, the audience is reduced to a subjugated, nagging, one-dimensional cartoon of anguish. In playing with his poodle thematics and cartoon voices Zappa hits on moments that lay bare the relationship of producer to consumer in commercial art, a satirical exposition of the audience's reduction to zero which revolves a panoply of the marks of the oppressed.

In linking 'Louie Louie' to 'Babette', a doowop song for Marty Perellis and his 'fondness for the canine species and the orifices attendant thereto', Zappa indulges the speculation about periodization that characterized his preamble to 'The Bebop

---

[9]Frank Zappa, introduction to 'Ruthie-Ruthie', 1974, *You Can't Do That on Stage Anymore Vol. 1*, 1988.

Tango'.[10] George Duke's atonal electric piano and Ruth Underwood's tinkling percussion evoke the cosmic uncertainties that were nailed into 'Inca Roads' as Zappa explores the different aromas of the years of the 50s. A delightfully ragged 'I'm the Slime' and a devastating 'Big Swifty' from 1973 bring this disc to a musical peak.

The diseased 1979 band returns with a bravura version of 'Don't Eat the Yellow Snow', which combines highly scripted reproduction of *Apostrophe(')*'s complex edits with improvised fluency. Zappa played two shows on that day and his interest in spontaneous poetry recitals from audience members seemed in keeping with the matinée flavour of the first concert. The way the band negotiate audience recitals and other tomfoolery without losing their poise is impressive.

Warren Cucurullo's description of watching girls on the bus in Leftrook City has been cut. Zappa's contribution is in fact from Dylan Thomas's *Under Milk Wood.*

> Alone in the hissing laboratory of his wishes, Mr Pugh minces among bad vats and jeroboams, tiptoes through spinneys of murdering herbs, agony dancing in his crucibles, and mixes especially for Mrs Pugh a venomous porridge unknown to toxicologists which will scald and viper through her until her ears fall off like figs, her toes grow big and black as balloons, and steam comes screaming out of her navel.[11]

It is a good example of Zappa's powers of near total recall (he misses out 'tiptoes through' and 'agony dancing in his crucibles' and substitutes 'prepares to compound' for 'mixes especially'). He makes the misogynistic secret laboratory seem entirely his own: Zappologists unaware of *Under Milk Wood* would conclude that this was merely another episode in the story of Uncle Meat (or *Thing-Fish*'s Evil Prince). Interestingly enough 'unknown to toxicologists' becomes 'hitherto unknown to toxicologists', modelled after 'a vigorous circular motion, hitherto unknown to the citizens of Canarsie, but destined to take the place of the mud shark in your mythology' that Zappa sang earlier in the song. It also connects with 'scientists know this exquisite little inconvenience as bromidrosis' from 'Stink-Foot': Thomas's poetry has become so embroiled in conceptual continuity that Zappa's evident amusement appears to be at words of his own devising.

Disc two of *Vol. 1* proceeds in a similar way to disc one,

[10]Frank Zappa, 'The Bebop Tango (of the Old Jazzmen's Church)', *Roxy & Elsewhere*, 1974.
[11]Dylan Thomas, *Under Milk Wood*, 1954, p. 63.

jumping from different bands and year to year in a convincing demonstration of the way Zappa's music can be entertained as a simultaneous artwork. It opens on 13 February 1969: the smaller venue played by the Mothers of Invention at that date is instantly detectable as Zappa makes announcements about hamburgers and illegally parked cars. 'Plastic People' is the second use of Richard Berry's 'Louie Louie' in *Vol. 1*, the simple version before the interpolations used on *Absolutely Free*. The closing lines, 'I'm sure that love will never be / A product of plasticity', segue into 'The Torture Never Stops' from 1977, the ideal introduction to this Gothic vengeance on romantic aspiration.

'The Torture Never Stops' includes the quote from 'The Chatanooga Choo Choo'[12] that 1977 renditions favoured. Terry Bozzio's sumptuous, cymbal-rich drumming sounds like its textures were made for the song. Before 'Be in My Video' Zappa drops in a charming bit of backstage chat from 1970 which has an English sounding band-member (Aynsley Dunbar?) negotiating blow-jobs for all the band from a groupie who wants to fly to Orlando with them. The weird thing is that he appears to say 'wolb-job', the same backwards version of 'blow' that appeared on Moon's exercise instructions on 'Ya Hozna'.[13] 'Be in My Video' substitutes 'and then we'll mine the harbour' for 'and then we'll dance the blues', referring to Ronald Reagan's controversial attempt to exclude Nicaragua from multinational trade, such arrogant imperialism providing a parallel to David Bowie's appropriation of the blues.

The politics become more overt in three songs from *You Are What You Is* that Zappa proudly mentions were part of an MTV broadcast, adding darkly, 'It is unlikely that they'll ever let us get away with that again.' It is surprising that Ray White, whose gospel intensity Zappa was essentially poaching from the other side (his lay-offs in 1978 and 1979 have been attributed to religious scruples about Zappa's lyrics), can sing the introduction to 'Heavenly Bank Account' with quite such urgency and conviction. Zappa uses the MTV platform to deliver his political message: 'Tax the churches! Tax the businesses belonging to the churches!' The 'Suicide Chump' blues features some lovely swapping of fours among the band. Ray White's big blocky guitar sound has a closeness to the sound of his singing voice that is reminiscent of

---

[12]Thanks to Caroline Arscott for pointing this out.
[13]Frank Zappa, 'Ya Hozna', *Them Or Us*, 1984.

Guitar Slim. Bobby Martin uses some great Hammond samples in his keyboard solo and Tommy Mars simply bubbles with invention.

You Can't Do That on Stage Anymore Vol. 1 finishes with another version of 'Sofa', illustrating what a wide range of sonorities the 1982 band could deliver. Arriving after the frenetic velocity of 'Tell Me You Love Me', it piles up rich, impacted layers of pomp and percussion and ghostly synths. Some writers who theorize avant-garde music argue that to advertise 'no overdubs' is simply Luddite refusal of technology.[14] However, those who think of music as something other than the consumption of prerecorded artefacts recognize the rhythmic punch that arrives in real-time playing. The infinite choices of overdubbing have a tendency to pad out the musical trajectory: Zappa's 80s bands were quite unique in the timbral complexity they could stack into streamlined urgency. It is not a matter of stunts or sentimentality about 'real' playing – this music simply could not be realized in the studio. Records like *Jazz from Hell* indicate how ready Zappa is to use the studio to create gargantuan music; the *Stage* series documents a completely different approach, one with its own specific rewards.

STAGE TWO

The second volume in the *You Can't Do That on Stage Anymore* series is devoted to a single concert by what is basically the band that recorded *Roxy & Elsewhere*, though Bruce Fowler (trombone) had left and Chester Thompson had learned to handle Zappa's complex metres unaided by Ralph Humphrey. The repertoire is also much the same as *Roxy*, though Zappa points out that 'the fast tempos on the more difficult tunes demonstrate what happens when a band has played the material for a year'.

Disc one opens with an instrumental version of 'A Token of My Extreme', the portentous song that is put in the mouth of L. Ron Hoover of the First Church of Appliantology at the start of *Joe's Garage Acts II & III*. Over this swelling theme Napoleon

---

[14]For example, David Toop's review of Scott/Casswell's *The Magificence of Stereo* in *The Wire*, No. 105, November 1992, p. 63, or Robert Sandall's dismissal of Fred Frith and Tim Hodgkinson on Radio 3's *Mixing It*, 19 October 1992. Obviously those who fetishize specific musical methods are in danger of subsuming actual music into abstract moralism, but there is no denying that real-time interaction still produces unique sonic continuities – however offensive this may be to technophiles.

Murphy Brook and George Duke engage in the irreverent, good-natured jive that also characterizes the musical alchemy of this edition of the Mothers. With George Duke's rocking accompaniment, 'Stink-Foot' sounds particularly attractive and 'Inca Roads', though it lacks the lustrous mix of *One Size Fits All*, sounds gorgeous. If the guitar solo sounds familiar, that is because parts of it were dropped into the vinyl version. In a live context it becomes still clearer what a put-on the song is.

The song's title puns to the words 'ink erodes'. As befits one of Zappa's most pungent concentrations of poetic images, it connects to the hermetic tradition of verbal play by which poets use the pen to erode the certainties of rational thought. The epigraph to the preface of this book has Hart Crane speak of 'incandescent wax',[15] which connects this Incan descent to Icarus and his fall and watery demise. Hart Crane himself committed suicide by leaping to his death from a liner somewhere in the Caribbean archipelago. As the doubling of Napoleon's flute and Ruth's marimba describe the descent of the flying saucer towards the positions marked by the ancient Incas, Zappa lights up an iridescent thread in literary history. The apparatus of *One Size Fits All* and its absurdist alchemical trappings like those of Sun Ra, connect to the truly magical, which is the spontaneous interaction of the human body in music and sex. The majestic melancholy of Zappa's guitar solo seems to mourn that this joy is currently not the substance of everyday life. The cosmic questioning of George Duke's lines are answered in the childish horseplay of the band; sexual reductionism as a solution to mystical blandishment.

'Village of the Sun' is taken at a faster lick than on *Roxy*, but still retains its evocative charm: the versions of 'Echidna's Arf' and 'Don't You Ever Wash That Thing' are astonishing, as heavy blues changes – similar modes to those used by contemporary blues artists like Johnny 'Guitar' Watson and Etta James – are mixed with lightning percussion rhythms and playful, dadaistic changes of direction. 'Room Service' reports the adventures of the band were currently having in Finnish hotels. Napoleon's elastic voice – similar in its suggestive microtonality to Jean-Luc Ponty's violin – is admirably suited to 'Idiot Bastard Son'. 'Cheepnis' has Chester Thompson drumming up a panic storm on cymbals. Although the culture industry continually recuperates such strategies to its own

---

[15]Hart Crane, 'The Marriage of Faustus and Helen', 1926, *The Complete Poems and Selected Letters*, ed. Brom Weber, 1966, p. 31.

use – smug TV series that present us with 'highlights' of 'bad' movies – 'Cheepnis' is just as much a manifesto for critical survival in consumer society as Walter Benjamin's 'The Work of Art in an Age of Mechanical Reproduction'.[16]

'Approximate', which also appears in *Stage Vol. 4* performed by the 1982 band, specifies rhythms but not pitches, and can therefore be performed on instruments or voices or stamping. All three methods feature here. 'Dupree's Paradise', prefaced at performances attended by English speakers by a long description of a typical after-hours jazz-dive, is introduced by George Duke's ongoing story of backstage antics. Unusually for Zappa, the improvisations precede the head, giving Napoleon and George ample opportunity to indulge their funky genius. The theme itself, later arranged for the Ensemble InterContemporain,[17] is a slippery progression closer to something by Olivier Messiaen than anything in jazz. The Finnish composer Unto Mononen's popular tune 'Satumaa' is then thrown in as a crowd-pleaser, a *Third Man*-type piece of zither music which the musicians read from sheet music. Napoleon's imitation Finnish is suitably absurd and Zappa interjects the James Brown quote 'Ain't it funky now!', a phrase he maintains is ridiculous for any white person to use. Duke funks it up beautifully and Zappa's guitar seems to explode (throughout the concert, beginning with 'Stink-Foot', Zappa's guitar breaks are characterized by a marvellously accentuated sound). 'T'Mershi Duween' follows, an obscure ninety-second miniature consisting of tight rhythmic runs (which, in an appropriately perverse manner, christened the English Frank Zappa fanzine). Two tunes from *Uncle Meat* are lifted out of their original quirkiness by the band's musicianship, sounding gloriously rich and strange.

'Building a Girl' is a unique document of Zappa's 'conduction', where band members follow his gestures with musical effects: Napoleon's flute and Duke's synths bounce off each other – one minute of extraordinary experimental music (at the Hammersmith Odeon in 1978 Zappa 'built' both a man and a woman, had them copulate furiously, bundled them into a ball and tossed them aside). 'Montana' is subtitled 'Whipping Floss' because of the request for the Allman Brothers' 'Whipping Post' – fulfilled a decade later by

---

[16]Walter Benjamin, 'The Work of Art in the Age of Mechanical Reproduction', 1936, *Illuminations*, trs. Harry Zohn, 1968.
[17]Frank Zappa, 'Dupree's Paradise', *The Perfect Stranger*, 1984.

its appearance on *Them Or Us*. Zappa's guitar solo climbs up and down with a clipped attention to harmonic steps that is in marked contrast to the bluesy outbursts of 'Stink-Foot' and 'Cheepnis'. In many ways it predicts the hard-edged modernism Warren Cucurullo's playing brought into the band at the end of the 70s. 'Big Swifty' serves merely as a coda to 'Montana', reduced to the dithering head and the opulent careering of Sal Marquez's guitar-solo transcription. Topped and tailed by Zappa's careful name-checks, the concert fits beautifully onto two CD discs (it was also released as a box set of records, perhaps so that Finnish fans – behind in hi-fi technology – would have a chance to hear it). *Stage Vol. 2* is a fantastic document of a band whose ease and fire and swing Zappa never bettered.

STAGE THREE

For those who feel that Zappa's 80s bands never had quite the personality of his preceding aggregations, *Stage Vol. 3* is probably the least attractive of the series. Disc one features the 1984 band, while disc two includes a suite of songs from *You Are What You Is*. Disc one opens with Dweezil Zappa's first performance with his father – a version of 'Sharleena' from *Chunga's Revenge*. Zappa introduces it as a song from the *Them Or Us* album, indicating how little his audience coasts on 60s nostalgia. A brittle reggae beat freezes the tune into its separate moments. Dweezil shows that he is adept at what his father calls Van Halen's 'freeze-dried' guitar figures, volleys of notes emerging like boinging bedsprings. Zappa *père* joins him for a stirring duet: Dweezil's clarity and relative orthodoxy offset Frank's visceral slithers.

The 1984 band's 'Bamboozled by Love' illustrates the manner in which their bionic musicianship gives a sense of unreality to the music they play. The riff is played at a tidy clip far removed from the heavy rock that characterized the song's initial perform-ances by the 1978 touring band. Synthesized handclaps and syn-thetic whistling (similar to the digital blemish that surfaces in the guitar solo to 'The Mammy Anthem') reinforce the sensation of cybernetic efficiency. During the guitar solo the band drop into the riff from 'Owner of a Lonely Heart' by Yes, a band whose other-worldliness pretended to fly by the sweaty sexism of 'Bam-

other-worldliness pretended to fly by the sweaty sexism of 'Bamboozled by Love'. Zappa highlights the problems of skilled musicians basing their music on such a crude form as rock.

A version of 'Advance Romance', the loose blues vehicle from 'Bongo Fury', provides a perfect example of the precision and unbending ferocity of the 1984 band. Blues ease has become hard-angled power, though there are still plenty of in-joke asides. Two songs from Seattle ('Bobby Brown' and 'Keep It Greasey') show the disintegrating effect repetition has on meaning as Ike Willis's references to the Lone Ranger cause Zappa to ad-lib changes. By the end of 'Bobby Brown' Ray White can hardly sing for mirth. It is like watching a painting flake off before the eyes as the song's anal-sadistic affront disappears into giggles which have nothing to do with the subject of the song. Whether one characterizes this erasure of significance as 'creative improvisation' (Zappa comments that the Synclavier will not suddenly crack him up by inserting 'Hi-ho Silver' at some unlikely moment) or simply boredom with oft-repeated songs, the effect is subtly terrifying. Though 'hardcore' Zappa fans applaud these jokes – holding up banners saying 'What's the secret word tonight?' at gigs – the way these highly offensive songs crumble away into uncontrolled laughter says as much about the semiotic erasure wrought by repetition and work-discipline as do deliberately constructed ironies like 'Dinah-Moe Humm'.

'Honey, Don't You Want a Man Like Me?' re-establishes some kind of dialogue with the audience by instructing them to replace Helen Reddy with Twisted Sister as 'her favourite group'; the scabrous lyrics of 'In France' inject some urgency. 'Drowning Witch' includes the disc's only non-84 segments, necessitated by that band's apparent failure to play the difficult instrumental section properly. Zappa's meltdown is particularly effective as scraps of Broadway rhapsody pan through improvised gibber. The instrumental section, working Zappa's guitar into the interstices of a highly detailed arrangement, shows the necessity of all the annoying aspects of the 'secret word' in-jokes that have preceded it. Just as the lyrics freeze verbal free association into a poetic vision, so the composition is built out of arbitrary and perverse moments, but welds them into something undeniably solid.

Zappa designs his music so that its musicality rears up when you least expect it. 'Ride My Face to Chicago' is based on graffiti in the toilet in the Whisky-a-Go-Go in 1965, some fast rock 'n'

blossoms into a catapulted Zappa solo over synthetic handclaps and reggae bass and drums that have more separate and independent rhythms going on than anything since Eric Dolphy's *Out To Lunch*. Thunes and Wackerman outdo themselves: the suspended rhythmic thinking here is heart-stopping. Zappa has never played better. Appropriately enough, it was recorded in Chicago.

'Carol, You Fool' is doowop reggae sung by a male quartet, with synthetic steel drums in the manner of 'Fine Girl'. Ray White soars beautifully and there is a great electric piano blues break. According to Zappa, any resemblance between 'Chana in De Bushwop' and Lee Dorsey's 'Working in a Coalmine' is coincidental; like 'Dong Work for Yuda' it is in the generic style of a Southern work song. Another incident dramatizes the hazards of live performance: Zappa pushes Alan Zavod aside in order to parody his usual crowd-pleasing 'volcano solo'. 'Joe's Garage' again sees the song's original meaning disappear into a welter of band jokes. Some things never seem to change, and the band found 'Why Does It Hurt When I Pee?' completely relevant to the current tour, enabling Zappa to dedicate it 'to the two guys in the crew who went to see the doctor this afternoon'. Zappa's parodic 'Layla' riff sounds particularly raw and immediate on the closing measure.

Disc two presents a relief from the stadium ambience of the 1984 tour: a recording at the Roxy from 1973 which has road manager Marty Perellis asking the audience to pass their glasses along to the waitresses. Despite a fuzzy bass quality obscuring Bruce Fowler's trombone, Napoleon Murphy Brock's humour is infectious and the blues feel warm and embracing. As Jonathan Jones[18] has pointed out, the comments about phone-tapping and tape-recorders relate to the speculations in *We're Only in It for the Money* and *Joe's Garage* about power and recorded sound. Zappa's guitar lacks the keen bite and rhythmic extrapolation of his 80s playing, but buoyed by George Duke's comping it has a rich bluesy exoticism: the humour and spontaneity of the blues pitched against the evil machinations of Watergate – a similar attitude to that which pervaded George Duke's *I Love the Blues, She Heard My Cry* and Johnny 'Guitar' Watson's mid-'70s 'protest' funk.

---

[18]Jonathan Jones, 'A World of Secret Hungers', *Eonta*, Vol. 2, No. 2, July/August, 1993.

'Hands with a Hammer' has Terry Bozzio bewailing the state of his hands after 'beating the shit out of the drums two shows two nights in a row', backstage dialogue similar to that used on the linking *musique concrète* of *Läther*. As Bozzio explains that 'I work for this man, I love this man', it echoes the controversy that surrounded Big John Mitchell and his loyalty to Richard Nixon over his own wife. As *Läther* emphasized, homosexuality lurks in the structures of male bonding: here it is connected to the power structures of work discipline. As Zappa directs his listeners to the benefits of hearing 'real drums' – where 'artificial' drums are associated with the 'phoney' (gay) music of Boy George, Hi-Energy disco and House – Bozzio's explosive and passionate outburst points elsewhere.

The start of 'Zoot Allures' is a tantalizing taste of the feedback chamber-music played by the 1975/6 small band of Brock, Lewis, Estrada and Bozzio before it cuts into the familiar reggae of 1982 for Zappa's solo. A sequence of songs from *You Are What You Is* is a technical marvel, since the songs being replicated had 'layer upon layer of overdubs and many bizarre edits'.[19] The live aspect gives the tunes an attractive thrust (three other songs from this New York Palladium concert for MTV appeared on *Stage Vol. 1*, presumably because of Zappa's eighth theoretical criterion for inclusion in the *Stage* series: 'Is there film or video tape of the performance?'). As usual, Scott Thunes's bass-playing is impressive, and the tightness of the 'chaos effects' are bravura as Zappa numbers the defects of drug-ridden yuppie America. The lack of 'secret word' tomfoolery reflects both the discipline needed to reproduce the record and the perceived political urgency of the situation after Reagan's electoral victory at the start of the 80s (though Zappa manages a conceptual 'arf!' during 'Beauty Knows No Pain'). The second part of 'Cocaine Decisions' and 'Nig Biz' were recorded during the teargassing of the crowd at Palermo in 1984. Both have the usual uncompromising realism of Zappa's social reportage; the previously unreleased 'Nig Biz' is a particularly telling account of how record companies exploited black R&B singers in the 50s. As we hear the crowd scream and the 'crack' of teargas canisters being launched, Zappa's 'please sit down and be calm so we can play music' rehearses the impotence of all art in social conflict. Ray White's 'it was all just a game' seems

---

[19]Sleeve-note, Frank Zappa, 'Charlie's Enormous Mouth', 1981, *You Can't Do That on Stage Anymore Vol. 3*, 1989.

and be calm so we can play music' rehearses the impotence of all art in social conflict. Ray White's 'it was all just a game' seems particularly apt as Zappa says 'now's the time to play the blues' and White launches into the first of his two gritty solos. The different keyboard sounds (Mars and Martin) work particularly well together here, but it is Ray White's mighty vocal that steals the show.

The twenty-four-minute 'King Kong' merges performances from 1982 in Metz and Dijon in France and Hammersmith in England together with the ill-fated Rainbow Theatre performance of 1971. Ed Mann's vibes whip out the theme around the reggae beat with graceful ease: by contrast, the original Mothers played the tune with such studied concentration! After the action-packed tightness of the *You Are What You Is* suite, the open improvisation, with the band's shouts of 'blow-job' echoing around the auditorium, is particularly welcome. By contrast the 1971 band sounds small-scale, concertinaed both by audio-quality and musicianship, though Ian Underwood's wah-wah pedal alto sax solo has the rawness that makes his contribution to *Hot Rats* so crucial. Struggling with a 'mini-guitar' that 'absolutely refused to stay in tune' Zappa (1982 in Dijon) produces a reflective, non-feedback solo full of delightful twists. Tommy Mars contributes inventive electric piano with Scott Thunes in brilliant counterpart, as Zappa (1982 in Hammersmith) starts up an 'I want a garden' meltdown to which Bobby Martin responds 'I want a nun', imitating Harry's serenade to Sister Ob'dewella 'X' in *Thing-Fish*. The unstoppable conviction of these spontaneous improvisations is the definitive answer to 'those who still believe the only "good" material was performed by the earliest groups'.[20]

Stage Vol. 3 ends with a version of 'Cosmik Debris' from 1984, with Ike Willis extending the Lone Ranger motif with references to a Lenny Bruce routine. Willis and Zappa chuckle as they weave 'Hi-ho Silver' references into the song. As usual, Zappa ends the disc with a concert finale and as the crowd roars its approval one can only marvel that such private repartee can provide a spectacle for the packed denizens of the Paramount Theater in Seattle.

---

[20]Frank Zappa, General Information note in every booklet to *You Can't Do That on Stage Anymore Vols. 1–6*, 1988–92.

Much to the fans' disappointment, the booklet for *Stage Vol. 4* dispensed with Zappa's annotations, indicating perhaps a degree of exhaustion with the project. Disc one begins in 1979 with Denny Walley and Zappa joking about pneumatic sex toys ('Little Rubber Girl'). 'Three holes, no waiting,' Zappa comments as it segues into 'Stick Together' from 1984. Offensive sexism, anti-union songs – sometimes even the most ardent Zappologist baulks at the material. However, this would be a shame as this disc unfurls into one of the best in the series. 'Little Rubber Girl' actually starts out as 'Go Cry on Somebody Else's Shoulder', but evolves into an improvisation in praise of the inanimate sex object. As with 'Bamboozled By Love', Zappa's ambivalence redounds to no one's advantage: the stoic individualism of the *Freak Out!* song is reduced to masturbatory autism. 'Stick Together' is quickly curtailed as if the generational warfare of the next cut – 'My Guitar Wants to Kill Your Mama' – holds more interest. Even on *Weasels* this song had been a tribute to punk antagonism rather than direct expression: here it becomes still more of a formality, though Thunes's funk bass riff is enticing.

The closing chords of 'Willie the Pimp' are shot through with the opening guitar figure of 'Montana', but instead of proceeding with the song as performed at Hollywood's Universal Amphitheater in 1984, Zappa drops in a performance from the Roxy in 1973, reverting to 1984 towards the end with the words, 'I don't care if you think it is silly, folks.' The warm acoustic of the Roxy band – with Bruce Fowler's virtuosic trombone doubling the tricky melodies – contrasts with the shining clarity of 1984, but otherwise the song is still as inspirationally ridiculous as ever. 'Brown Moses' lacks Johnny 'Guitar' Watson's wonderful vocal on *Thing-Fish* (Watson nearly went on tour with Zappa in 1984 but asked for too much money – he has always been reluctant to venture away from home), but this and 'The Evil Prince' are welcome glimpses of the huge, knotted, complex scenario of the musical. Ray White replaces Bob Harris as the voice of the Evil Prince. The guitar solo is played over a fantastic fabric of percussion, samples and rippling keyboards, contrasting metres used to allow different sonic textures to poke up and shine.

From here on, disc one turns to instrumental music, with light relief supplied in the form of 'Love of My Life' performed at New York's Mudd Club in 1980 with the short-lived sextet of Willis, White, Mars, Barrow and Logeman. 'Approximate' manages to press the random joke vocals of the 1982 band into its strict metrical patterns, Zappa's 'there's a '39 Buick blocking the drive' serving as a reminder of the car announcements that began disc two of *Stage Vol. 1.* Tommy Mars sounds especially good on these moments of untrammelled freakdom, as he does later on his 'Pound for a Brown' solo.

'Let's Move to Cleveland – Solos (1984)' has a surprise appearance by Archie Shepp, the original angry young man of '60s free jazz. Without Shepp's projection of honking R&B into artspace it is difficult to imagine how the original Mothers would have managed the saxophonics of *Weasels Ripped My Flesh*. His 'On This Night'[21] – a setting of a revolutionary text by W. E. B. Dubois full of utopian Marxist optimism – provides a parallel fusion of classical grace and improvised power to many of Zappa's best moments. Here, his mournful, tortured tenor receives quite uncanny support from Zappa's sidemen. Like the Brecker Brothers' performances with Zappa[22] it is an indication of how much jazz would benefit from attention to Zappa's use of rock rhythm and sonority. The Shepp piece aptly segues into some far-out improvisation from the Mothers in 1969 which begs comparison to contemporary experiments by Stockhausen or AMM or records released on the Parisian BYG label. Characteristically, you can also hear the sound of an audience being thoroughly entertained by all this 'difficult' modern music, as they also were by the 1984 band playing 'The Black Page' in Vancouver.

'Take Me out to the Ball Game', recorded live in Bilbao, Spain in 1988, connects to the critique of sport and TV started in 'Trouble Every Day'. It turns the waffling stupidity of TV baseball and its march-band accompaniment into a spontaneous verbal improvisation between Ike Willis and Walt Fowler. When the latter plays his excruciatingly beautiful trumpet solo, the contradiction between his lyricism and the idiocy all around has a true poignancy: music as transfigured daily life. Ike Willis begins to sing like a jazz balladeer in answer to Fowler's trumpet.

'Filthy Habits' is again from the 1988 tour, benefiting from

---

[21]Archie Shepp, *On This Night*, 1966, Impulse/GRP GRD125.
[22]Frank Zappa, 'The Purple Lagoon', *Zappa in New York*, 1977, and 'Black Napkins', 1976, *You Can't Do That on Stage Anymore Vol. 6*, 1992.

the plushness of a full horn section: it crashes into the plaintive raggedness of the preceding track, its barbarian-horde purple completely at odds with ball-game inanity. 'The Torture Never Stops' is from the Armadillo, Austin, Texas, in 1975, where much of *Bongo Fury* was recorded. Sung by Captain Beefheart (for whom it was originally written), it uses a storming 'Smokestack Lightnin'" riff Howlin' Wolf's guitarist Hubert Sumlin would have been proud of. Beefheart's delivery is devoid of Zappa's leering relish; without the ambivalent orgasm/torture cries added on *Zoot Allures*, the evocation of the dungeon sounds like a protest rather than a proposition. Denny Walley's slide guitar sounds particularly succulent next to Beefheart's harmonica. Bruce Fowler's trombone – also prominent in the sordid splendour of the preceding 'Filthy Habits' – adds a golden tinge to the chorus.

Disc two begins with an anti-Church rap that manages to combine the sexual antics of Steve Vai and Laurel Fishman with a critique of the concept of sin and Zappa's low opinion of France. He was recycling a joke he used in 'Titties & Beer'[23] when he told the Devil that he is not frightened of hell because he has already been there, having been signed to Warner Brothers for nine years. This time he explains that Steve Vai need not fear he might go to hell for having fucked a girl with his organ, a zucchini, a vibrato bar, etc., because, 'ladies and gentlemen, there is no hell, there is only . . . France!' This segues into 'Stevie's Spanking', recorded in Rome. This track has received a lot of flak from even devoted fans for its 'dumb' heavy-metal chords. Really it is a 'Punky's Whips'-style oratorio for Steve Vai, including a hallucinogenic section ('with a hairbrush') that corresponds to a similar moment in 'Punky's Whips' ('you're an Angel!'). Like songs from *Thing-Fish*, 'Outside Now' proves exceptionally resonant away from its narrative context, as Ike Willis dreams of 'outside now' and Zappa's guitar takes off into some highly extrapolated rhythmic liberties. The sound here, engineered by Mark Pinske on the twenty-four-track digital, is quite spectacularly clear and ringing.

'Disco Boy' and 'Teen-age Wind', perfect summations of circular, self-defeating social attitudes, are played with blustering proficiency by the 1982 band; 'Truck Driver Divorce' has some viciously satirical meltdown before it cuts into a guitar solo that is the very opposite of the explosive xenochrony of *Them Or Us*,

---

[23]Frank Zappa, 'Titties & Beer', *Baby Snakes*, 1982.

a tight workout against the nimble bounce of the 1984 band. The entire 'Florentine Pogen' is attributed to 1979, when the opening is definitely the Roxy band with Napoleon Murphy Brock; only half-way through do we hear the unmistakable sounds of Ike Willis. Vinnie Colaiuta sounds exceptionally fervent on this Hammersmith cut. At the end we hear the famous synthesizer 'squirt' noise that so delighted the touring band in 1979 and was used extensively on 'A Little Green Rosetta'.[24] Its degradingly visceral noise introduces 'Tiny Sick Tears' from 1969. This is the same routine that Zappa performed at his orchestral concert at UCLA's Pauley Pavilion on 15 May 1970. It rubbishes Jim Morrison's mythic expansion of Oedipal themes in 'The End': when the protagonist declares 'father I want to kill you!' his father is 'beating his meat to a copy of *Playboy*' and says 'not now, son, not now'. Its delight in domestic banality connects to 'The Dangerous Kitchen'.[25]

'Smell My Beard' and 'The Booger Man' are fine examples of George Duke at play; 'Carolina Hard-Core Ecstasy' showcases a great Zappa guitar solo from 1984, exfoliating his spindly shapes over Scott Thunes's descending bass motif; eighty-nine seconds from the Mothers in 1969 has Zappa dealing with hecklers. Disc two closes with six songs from the 50s sung by the 1984 and 1982 bands. Zappa's instruction during 'The Closer You Are' ('we'll do it straight') shows how alien the emotional core of this music was to both bands. Bobby Martin's falsetto is terrific, though.

STAGE FIVE

Stage Vol. 5 has one disc devoted to the Mothers between 1965 and 1969 and another to performances by the 1982 band. Disc one opens with a 1965 tirade against police harassment of freaks, paying particular attention to the use of tape-recorders and cameras. This is the same strange period of acid and CIA involvement that led to Philip K. Dick's gruesome retrospective *Through a Scanner Darkly.*

> They pay him off in acid
> 'Cos he's a downtown talent scout

---

[24]Frank Zappa, 'A Little Green Rosetta', *Joe's Garage Acts II & III*, 1979.
[25]Frank Zappa, 'The Dangerous Kitchen', *Man from Utopia*, 1983.

He's got your name, he's got your face
He's got your ex-old lady's place[26]

For years Zappa's contention that the CIA were testing acid on the population was dismissed as paranoid fantasy, but now even gurus of acid like Timothy Leary are admitting as much[27] – something which makes one wonder about Zappa's allegation of connections between US government biological warfare research and Aids.

'Charles Ives' is prime Mothers abstraction with beautiful trumpet from Buzz Gardner. The drum section was used as the backing for 'The Blimp' on *Trout Mask Replica* when Antennae Jimmy Semens phoned in a Beefheart poem to Zappa while he was mixing the track at Whitney Recorders (it also appears in the extended 'Didja Get Any Onya' on the CD release of *Weasels*). 'Here Lies Love' illustrates what a mighty straight-R&B band the Mothers were; wonderful wobbly West Coast blues singing from Lowell George. The horn section also has some of the polish of West Coast cool jazz as arranged by people like Marty Paich.

'Piano/Drum Duet' illustrates what great music the Mothers could come up with using limited means. Ian Underwood plays electric piano and Art Tripp plays drums, using tunes later recycled for *200 Motels* and 'Bogus Pomp'. 'Mozart Ballet' is Zappa's revenge on the classics, Ian Underwood's consummate rendition (he was actually a prize-winning interpreter of Mozart) overlaid with band tomfoolery (including a guest appearance by Noel Redding from the Jimi Hendrix Experience, audience laughter, chicken brutality and snorks). 'Chocolate Halvah' is what would now be called a post-colonial fourth-world pan-African collision of muezzin cries, water drum, Appalachian yodel and art performance (intimations of Can, PiL, McLaren, etc.), but at the time was considered to be the Mothers fooling about.

For some critics, for example David Ilic, 'JCB & Kansas on the Bus #1' is simply an unforgivable example of Zappa's self-indulgence – a bus recording of Black's grotesquely out-of-tune singing – but it is precisely Zappa's recognition of personal aura that makes his deployment of musicians special. 'Right There' uses a bed recording of Bunk Gardner's that sounds like the germ of the idea of 'The Torture Never Stops': the Mothers respond with

---

[26]'The Downtown Talent Scout', 1965, *You Can't Do That on State Anymore Vol. 5*, 1992.
[27]Timothy Leary, interviewed by Andrea Juno, *Re/Search, #11 Pranks!*, 1988, p. 79.

falsetto cries and musical improvisation. This free crossover between documentary, live and studio sound uses the ideas of John Cage in a manner that challenges notions of private and public. Stripped of his liberal anarcho-mysticism, Cage's techniques become stringent and subversive, situated at a queasy interface that questions the limits of decorum.

'Return of the Hunchback' shows how rooted is the much-despised Flo & Eddie 'Mud Shark' routine in musical compositions played by the original Mothers. Though Zappa claims that he has to apply words to his compositions in order to make them sell, what is more remarkable is the way that his words invariably cause critical respect to evaporate. People seem incapable of hearing through the lyrics to the musical events themselves (which may explain the more elevated status of Zappa the composer in countries where English is not the first language).

'Proto-minimalism', a retrospective title, mocks the currently fashionable mode of classical music, while 'My Head?' is a recording of the Mothers assuming the 'mutant cluster-fuck pose' favoured in publicity photographs at the time. 'Baked-Bean Boogie' lays down the guitar-drenched sound (Zappa on wah-wah) that made the Mothers *the* definition of heavy 60s rock. 'Where's Our Equipment?' from 1967 in Copenhagen is accompanied by another sad story of sickness and disaster of the kind Zappa seems especially fond of, but the music is exceptional: a kind of weighty free improvisation that has only been equalled by Last Exit.

The 'FZ/JCB Drum Duet' recorded by Richard Kunc on a two-track analogue tape-recorder sounds so good that it begs the question whether the 'great advances' in recorded sound over the last two and a half decades are really bringing instruments any closer to us, or simply aggrandizing producer control. Over Jimmy Carl Black's steady shuffle, Zappa and Art Tripp sound absolutely brilliant. The special relationship between Black's dogged steadiness and Zappa's wit was one key to the success of the Mothers' sound. 'No Waiting for the Peanuts to Dissolve', recorded at Thee Image in Florida, opens with a characteristically sinuous solo from Lowell George, followed by a bubbling wah-wah solo from Zappa. Classic Mothers instrumental music, it has the power and invention that neither progressive rock nor fusion jazz captured in the ensuing decade: as Zappa says, 'underground psychedelic acid-rock freak-out music' (but in quotes, like everything in

Zappa's œuvre). In the classical aspirations of English progressive rock and the commercial hopes of fusion you hear the sound of accommodation: the abiding quality of Zappa's music is its resistance to social norms.

'My Guitar Wants to Kill Your Mama' was recorded at A&R Studios in New York in 1969 and has been around in bootleg form since the mid-70s. Though its audio quality is flat in comparison to the *Weasels* version, and it lacks its extraordinary *musique concrète* mid-section, it has a clipped urgency that is quite magical.

Although disc two is devoted to the 1982 band it scores – as the *Stage Vol. 4* disc two did not – by unleashing the band on songs worthy of its instrumental prowess. Only someone timelocked in the 60s could actually claim that there is no advance from the crude vigour of the Mothers of Invention to this staggering opening up of musical parameters, especially those of rhythm. The disc kicks off with 'Easy Meat', essentially a monstrously wide-ranging Zappa guitar solo bookended by the charging theme. Zappa was firing on all cylinders as a guitarist and the band's ability to both support him and leave him space to move is exemplary. The band are particularly sensitive to dynamics, making the classical filigree appear dainty and incongruous.

'Dead Girls of London' from L. Shankar's album *Touch Me There* is given a thrash treatment until

> Boutique frame of mind
> *Gee, I like your pants!*[28]

which uses weird harmonies and abrupt rhythms. This goes into the hitherto unreleased song 'Shall We Take Ourselves Seriously?': an insinuating jazz melody scrolls by words that attack fear of peer pressure and its block on personal evolution.

> Shall we take ourselves seriously?
> Shall we talk about it all night long?
> Shall we think we are so evolved?
> Will we be depressed if we're wrong?
> Shall we take ourselves seriously?
> Shall we take ourselves elsewhere?
> Shall we drink while we squat there in the middle of this stupid song?
> Shall we never go out there?

---

[28]Frank Zappa, 'The Dead Girls of London', 1982, *You Can't Do That on Stage Anymore Vol. 5*, 1992.

Shall we take us where we don't belong
When we notice the *sparkle* is gone?[29]

After the words 'Shall we weep in the box-office door?' there is a ludicrous falsetto chorus that could come straight from a 60s Lou Christie blue-eyed-Motown record. The uncertainties of American adulthood undo the very song as it concludes:

Shall we think we are so mature?
Shall we be very wrong at the end of the song?[30]

'What's New in Baltimore' is one of Zappa's extravagantly arching themes, similar to 'City of Tiny Lites' or 'Why Does It Hurt When I Pee?' It first appeared in an instrumental version on *Meets the Mothers of Prevention*. Its simultaneously rising and descending motifs are intricately woven, packing in some of the illusionistic power of 'Drowning Witch'; the musical ideas hurl themselves into a tangle to emerge with the soaring theme and an expansive Zappa guitar solo.

The Man from Utopia's 'Möggio' rattles itself out like a kinky salamander, delighting in its perverse twists and spikes, two minutes of incredibly concentrated musical thought. 'Dancin' Fool' is taken at a pace that makes the 1979 versions sound slack. 'Rdunzl' sounds more like 'Möggio' than it does anything played by the Roxy band, George Duke's jazzy looseness ironed out into bright, hard *pointillisme*. The transition between Zappa's guitar solo and the spook-corkscrew arrangement that introduces Tommy Mars's mad-professor solo is so abrupt that it resembles a tape splice, but is no doubt an illustration of this band's super-precision.

Apart from some inspired keyboard contributions from Tommy Mars, the 1982 'Advance Romance' is pretty much identical to the 1984 version on *Stage Vol. 3*, one of the few inclusions in the *Stage* series that does not seem very necessary, unless it is to showcase how disciplined both bands were: there is only five seconds' difference in total timing, not bad on a seven-minute song with a guitar solo recorded two years apart. 'City of Tiny Lites' has lost its 1978 Adrian Belew-spiked extravagance and become a lilting reggae vehicle for a considered, linear Zappa guitar

---

[29]Frank Zappa, 'Shall We Take Ourselves Seriously?', 1982, *You Can't Do That on Stage Anymore Vol. 5*, 1992.
[30]Ibid.

solo. Ray White exhibits bravura breath control for his vocal lines on the out-chorus.

'Pound for a Brown' is performed at a thrilling whack, with Ed Mann's virtuosity beautifully highlighted. Ray White scats along with his guitar solo (a habit of Johnny 'Guitar' Watson's) and Scott Thunes rumbles up some of his greasiest licks. Over what sounds like a spontaneously conceived shuffle, Ed Mann sprinkles inspired xylophone while Tommy Mars lets forth with sirens and whistles from his synth. Zappa floats in with an insouciant cool reminiscent of Miles Davis in a funk context. He spreads out into fluttering distortion that accentuates the rocking rhythmic give and take that has become the point of the piece, a highly original piece of collective improvising.

'Doreen' from the previous year's *You Are What You Is* hardly flexes Ray White's tonsils before 'The Black Page #2' cuts in, a slow-paced ten-minute version which features yet another gargantuan Zappa guitar solo. The reason Zappa's guitar solos work is that he is prepared to go *on* where others might seek to resolve or climb down. You can almost hear the relief as Chad Wackerman caps Zappa's concluding phrase in a great cymbal smash (at 8. 58), proving that the band has followed his parenthetical rhythmic deviations correctly, and Zappa resorts to his looped samples. The concluding 'Geneva Farewell' ends on a sour note as the band leave the stage in protest at the objects being hurled at them, reminding the listener of the fact that all this music has been played on stage in front of heaving rock audiences.

STAGE SIX

The idea of disc one of *Stage Vol. 6* was to collect together songs about sex, producing the wilful combination of manic rock songs and squirm-in-the-seat onstage raps that characterize Zappa's contempt for rules of decorum. It begins with more rock hysteria, this time in Florida in 1970, as Zappa informs the audience of the conditions under which they have been allowed to perform (Jim Morrison's notorious self-revelations had caused a ripple of concern in conservative areas). Remarks about the state of Florida's 'imbecilic' laws and 'rednecks' draw forth tumultuous applause as Zappa has the band recite 'The MOI Anti-Smut

Loyalty Oath' in which they swear not to reveal themselves. Of course Zappa turns it into an excuse for more gratuitous obscenity as Flo & Eddie promise not to reveal 'tube', 'pud', 'dingus', 'weeny' and/or 'penis' and declare that this does not exclude 'private showings in the motel later'.

This segues into 'The Poodle Lecture' in front of an equally excited Halloween audience at New York's Palladium in 1977. It tells the story of the woman who sends the man out of the Garden of Eden in order to earn money so that she can buy scissors in order to clip the poodle and turn it into a suitable fuck.[31] As often on these excerpts from the Palladium Shows that wound up on the *Baby Snakes* video, Zappa is importuned for a kiss by someone in the audience. The Edenic female then sings 'Dirty Love' to the dog while squatting on his face. Zappa evidently preferred the riotous atmosphere in New York to the cool reception he received in England, and he refers to 'simulated merriment here in London' as people clap along and he sings 'two paws stickin' up': cheap thrills, sex, common-denominator pleasures.

'Magic Fingers' is performed in a fancy arrangement by the 1980 band, both Willis and White on vocals. Zappa ends the song entreating an audience member to let go of the panties she is handing him. The next track is 'The Madison Panty-Sniffing Festival', with Zappa collecting knickers to a background of sleazy Hammond organ and commenting on them expertly before handing them to the band for perusal.

'Father O'Blivion' is an early version of the song from *Apostrophe (')*, with Zappa reciting the words over a vamp. On *Apostrophe (')* it tends to shoot by: here its obscenity is more blatant. After this blasphemous suggestion that priests might be susceptible to sexual desire – and that this is a laughing matter rather than a terrible thing – 'Is That Guy Kidding Or What' vilifies the commercial exploitation of sex in rock music. Zappa notes that people have T-shirts that say 'disco sucks', but he is not prepared to allow that the state of white music is any healthier as he mocks Peter Frampton for his album *I'm in You*. 'I'm So Cute' combines both themes – fear of sin and the oppressive nature of conformist good looks. Bob Harris's 'boy soprano' explodes with an anguish which is frightening. Zappa's low humour betrays an acute understanding of the way fear of recognizing the actuality

---

[31]For a full discussion of the poodle lecture, see 'Poodles and philosophy', Chapter 5: Bizarre to DiscReet.

of the material body allows religion and commerce access to their victims.

'White Person' is vocal improvisation by the 1977 band (similar performances were used for pieces like 'Duck Duck Down' on *Läther*) and 'Lonely Person Devices' is the story of 'Ms Pinky', recorded in rough quality on a two-track analogue tape-recorder in Copenhagen. As this low-fi commentary segues into 'Ms Pinky', recorded on twenty-four-track, it reveals the true splendour of the Zappa band in full flight, as do Flo & Eddie's marvellous operatic vocals on 'Shove It Right In', a sequence from *200 Motels* whose beautiful tunes have remained unappreciated due to the usual explicit-lyric problem. Remixing their tracks for the *Stage* series must have reminded Zappa just how strong their singing is and perhaps prompted the release of *Playground Psychotics*.

'Wind up Workin' in a Gas Station' features the rare vocals of Bianca Odin. Her strong voice and swaggering attitude were perfect, but apparently she could not handle the 'get 'em off' choruses that greeted her appearances on stage: Zappa's base in rock, the music of American male adolescence, claiming another aesthetic casualty. The song is Zappa's justification for his interest in the zones of human behaviour good taste says no to, a necessary preparation for 'Make a Sex Noise', a blush-inducing sequence where Zappa invites four Irish girls up on stage to prove that Irish people are, contrary to myth, sexy – by screaming at the top of their lungs – and 'Tracy is a Snob' and 'Emperor of Ohio' which use a female orgasm track in the manner of Bunk Gardner's bed recordings.[32] These sounds reproduce both the arousal and guilty panic induced by visual pornography and immediately provoke frenzied improvisations from Zappa's musicians.

The conclusion of disc one has the 1984 band steam through songs familiar as an encore threesome in the late 70s: 'Dinah-Moe Humm', 'Camarillo Brillo' and 'Muffin Man', invigorated by the Thunes/Wackerman bounce and fresh arrangements. The interpolation of 'He's So Gay' acknowledges – however grudgingly – that Zappa's heterosexist point of view does not encapsulate the whole story. The changed ending to 'Muffin Man',

> No cries is heard in the night as a result of him
> Stuffin' it in
> He shoulda been stuffin' it in[33]

[32]Frank Zappa, 'Right There', 1969, *You Can't Do That on Stage Anymore Vol. 5*, 1992.
[33]Frank Zappa, 'Muffin Man', 1984, *You Can't Do That on Stage Anymore Vol. 5*, 1992.

asserts Zappa's Reichian belief in sexual activity as an antidote to the exploitations of religion, commerce and fascism. Undeniably crude and maybe indefensibly offensive, disc one of *Stage Vol. 6* is a perfect summary of Zappa's low-budget sexual politics.

Disc two begins with the Halloween audience and another kiss. Like everything they played, the 1984 band's 'The Illinois Enema Bandit' is upfront and chunky. In his guitar solo, Zappa's staccato outbursts break up the music's scatological innuendo into something abstract and jagged. The authority with which Scott Thunes brings back the ensemble is impressive and it is a relief to hear Ike Willis have the district attorney say, *'No Silver jokes!'* 'Did you cause this misery?' has disintegrated into 'Did you cause this broccoli?', joining the long list of vegetables in conceptual continuity.[34]

'Lobster Girl' has Patrick O'Hearn show what a creative bassist he was before he decided to adopt new-age synthesizers: his hillbilly bass solo is reminiscent of the figures Charlie Haden supplies for Ornette Coleman. 'Black Napkins' – an out-take from *Zappa in New York* – has an intriguing solo by Michael Brecker: given just the two chords of the song to deal with he has to really crank up his melodic imagination. He twirls up some impressive architecture only to be thoroughly stomped on by the magisterial sense of space in Zappa's succeeding solo. Though the version is not substantially different from *Meets the Mothers of Prevention*, 'Alien Orifice' always bears repeated listening. 'Catholic Girls' and 'Crew Slut' played by the 1988 band do not have the impact they did on *Joe's Garage*, which was bound up with the extreme separation of elements in the mix, the mocking way different musical excitements – falsetto vocals, groovy bass, twanging guitar – swooped in and out. 'Catholic Girls', though, benefits from Chad Wackerman's manic drumming and a frenetic, snorting tenor break by Albert Wing, and there is the interest of Zappa using his Central Scrutinizer plastic megaphone for the link to 'Crew Sluts'. The relish with which he explains that Mary is 'backstage at the Tower Theater sucking cock so she can get a ticket to meet Ike Willis for free' shows no tiring in blow-job continuity.

---

[34]The pumpkin of *Absolutely Free*, the carrots of *We're Only in It for the Money*, the peaches of *Hot Rats*, *Fillmore East June 1971* and *Tinsel Town Rebellion*, the beans and celery of *Uncle Meat*, the grapefruit of *Overnite Sensation*, the watermelon of *Joe's Garage*, the string beans of *Drowning Witch* and *Them Or Us*, the frightful salad of *The Man from Utopia*, the mashed potatoes of *Thing-Fish*, the ketchup of *Broadway The Hard Way* and Steve Vai's zucchini in *Stage Vol. 4*.

L. Shankar's contribution to 'Thirteen' (named for its time signature, though its appearance in the thirteenth hour of the *Stage* series is also appropriate) was overshadowed by Zappa's guitar, but he really comes into his own on 'Take Your Clothes Off When You Dance', the folk element in the tune and its heavy beat bringing forth some scalding fiddle. Ed Mann also contributes some delightful lounge vibes while Hammond samples increment jazzbo cheesiness. Lisa Popeil, who sang 'Teen-age Prostitute' on *Drowning Witch*, proves that she can improvise on 'Lisa's Life Story'. Trained by the eccentricities of Zappa's guitar-playing, the 1980 band follow her shrieks and vagaries with joyful bravado: the sheer invention of moments like this outdoes most avant-garde performance art. Popeil's interest in labour-saving devices and sex make her themes entirely Zappaesque: her voice is arrestingly clear and powerful.

'Lonesome Cowboy Nando' uses a digital editing device called Sonic Solutions to blend two renditions of 'Lonesome Cowboy Burt': Jimmy Carl Black in 1971 with Frank Zappa in 1988, a compressed example of the strobing between decades that has happened throughout the *Stage* series. Flo & Eddie give their final, closing benediction from *200 Motels* at UCLA's Pauley Pavilion, where they originally went backstage to ask Zappa if they could sing for him. The *Stage* series concludes with an instrumental version of 'Strictly Genteel', an intricate arrangement from 1981. As well as a great tune, it is a secular goodbye and blessing, as if the whole series has been a single marathon concert. At thirteen hours it is certainly the most ambitious undertaking to have graced the annals of rock.

Zappa's closing remark to his New York Palladium audience also serves as a caution to his critics. What upsets people about Zappa's songs is frequently the reminder that they are subject to impulses they would rather not recognize. Zappa asks them not to respond by hurling back their personal problems in his direction: 'don't throw stuff on the stage'. A reasonable request.

CHAPTER 13
WEBERN VS. TELEVANGELISM

THE 1988 TOUR

Having sung the praises of the Synclavier and declared no more use for musicians, 1987 saw Zappa organizing an eleven-piece band for a world tour. Essentially it was the same band he had used throughout the 80s (Bobby Martin on keyboards, Scott Thunes on bass, Chad Wackerman on drums, Ed Mann on percussion) supplemented by a five-man horn section and newcomer Mike Keneally on guitar and vocals. Ike Willis, now the most long-standing vocalist associated with Zappa, played rhythm guitar as well. They practised for four months, starting in November 1987, in Zappa's rehearsal facility Joe's Garage (its three differently sized rooms are named Acts I, II and III). Scott Thunes called the shots. Like many mature leaders, Zappa now liked to delegate the basic work and merely add finishing touches himself. Being the straw boss is a tricky task and Thunes fell out with the band in June 1988; the band demanded that he be fired and Zappa retaliated by cancelling the West Coast and Southern legs of the tour. This is why one release was called *The Best Band You Never Heard in Your Life*. Altogether Zappa issued three albums (five CDs-worth of material) from the tour.

THE BEST BAND YOU NEVER HEARD IN YOUR LIFE

The *Best Band* double collected together old songs and covers of famous rock tunes. The opening 'Heavy Duty Judy', an arrangement of a guitar solo from *Shut Up 'N Play Yer Guitar*, makes use of the extended horn section to create a juicy ebullience that

501

had not been heard since the use of the Brecker brothers at the New York Palladium Halloween concerts.[1] The 'secret word' theme is celebrated as Zappa reads out a banner asking 'What is the secret word for tonight?'; he announces it is 'Ring of Fire', a song Johnny Cash said he would sing on stage with the band. Since Cash did not turn up, Mike Keneally sings it, in a stupid quavery voice that cropped up for the rest of the selections from the Würzburg show: 'Cosmik Debris', and the hippie monologue from 'Who Needs the Peace Corps?'

'Zomby Woof' benefits from the horn section and 'Zoot Allures' – recorded in Brighton, England – has some great, curdling Zappa guitar, something the tune's flavoursome harmonies frequently foment. 'Bolero' is muscular and tightly organized, compressing Ravel's overlong piece into a glorious chunk of architectonic saxophone reggae. As so often, the music gradually emerges out of dodgy onstage 'humor': disc one concludes with 'Mr Green Genes' and a suite from *One Size Fits All*. Ike Willis copes well with the task of being George Duke, Napoleon Murphy Brock and Johnny 'Guitar' Watson combined. Though these versions lack the surprising textural contrasts of the studio original, live rendition gives them a special thrust. As usual 'Inca Roads' provokes a beautiful guitar solo from Zappa. Paul Carman replaces George Duke's keyboard solo with some wiggly alto sax out of John Coltrane's soprano bag.

Disc two begins with 'Purple Haze' in Devo style, one of the generic beats – ska, reggae, heavy metal, Weather Report – Zappa cues with hand signals. Devo had already pulled such a stunt by covering 'Are You Experienced?' in 1984.[2] Replacement of guitar power chords with horn charts, absurd sex-baby-noise samples, a machine beat and facetious vocalizing by Ike Willis drain Hendrix of all his freedom and power. Cream's 'Sunshine of Your Love' is given the same treatment with Mike Keneally's Johnny Cash voice. Virtuosity tends to mannerism. As these songs are emptied of their utopian meanings the band makes them an excuse for delightful abstractions.

'Let's Move to Cleveland' is similar to 'What's New in Baltimore', alternating intricate parodics with a section of soaring pomp. Whereas on *Does Humor Belong in Music?* it had a driven, rockist quality, here it takes its time, sumptuous and expansive.

---

[1]Frank Zappa, *Zappa in New York*, 1977.
[2]Devo, 'Are You Experienced?', *Shout*, 1984, Warner Brothers 925097.

Zappa's guitar solo gains in intimacy what it lacks in keyed-up momentum, the notes moving towards the lower register with the ineluctable logic of hands groping towards the nether regions during heavy petting.

'A Few Moments with Brother A. West' has the graphic designer for *The Real Frank Zappa Book* and *Broadway the Hard Way* make a satirical right-wing speech – he did it with such conviction that Zappa had to assure his audience that he was not for real in order to secure his safety after the show. The idea of the stage as an arena of violence – emphasized in the *Stage* series by accounts of the projectiles Zappa and his musicians suffered in Italy – is here given disturbingly immediate form. A. West's TV preacher exhortations are interrupted by belch samples[3] and other effects. In beginning with American foreign policy – it is people 'like Mr Zappa' who prevented congress voting aid to the Contras – A. West is somewhat in advance of Zappa's own views.[4]

Disc two ends in a series of versions altered to vilify TV evangelist Jimmy Swaggart, caught in a New Orleans hotel with a prostitute in February 1988. This kind of tomfoolery is typical of Zappa's instinct for the perverse: he spent four months rehearsing this band to play an extravagantly wide selection of his songs with unerring accuracy, and then releases takes which feature on-the-spot changes. 'The Eric Dolphy Memorial Barbecue' exploits the jazz-sleaze capacity of the horns: Walt Fowler is beautifully sleek and burnished while Paul Carman revives some of Eric Dolphy's alto licks. A squeaky clean bounce and facetiousness has replaced the sense of sonic sorcery with which the original was performed on *Weasels*. An appearance of 'The Blue Danube' was presumably a salute to Vienna, one of the sites for its recording.

'Stairway to Heaven' is an example of Zappa's artistry at long distance. The horn arrangement of Jimmy Page's guitar solo was by a band member who knew it by heart. Ike Willis takes the lyric fairly straight: in comparison to the treatment he gave 'Purple Haze', he is downright sincere. Live, it seemed like a desecration of Zappa's outsider stance to devote time to such a massively overrated piece of progressive-rock baloney. However, when it appeared as a CD single coupled with 'Bolero', it revealed a preposterous overweightness that was gratifyingly grotesque. The

---

[3]See 'Meets the Mothers of Prevention', Chapter 11: Synclavier and Total Control.
[4]See the discussion of 'Rhymin' Man' below in 'Broadway the Hard Way'.

1988 big band plays its soaring kitsch with a cool and control that unravels each meretricious sentimentality (it took the cover of 'Stairway to Heaven' by no less than Rolf Harris to outdo Zappa in pissing on the behemoth of rock). The cover of the CD single used a photograph taken from a *Life* magazine for 1966 which gave another wonderful twist: it showed disused firescapes against an evening sky, the rusting metal structures forming 'Z's for Zappa.[5] Stairways leading nowhere indeed. In Zappa, materialism strikes where you least expect it.

MAKE A JAZZ NOISE HERE

The *Make a Jazz Noise Here* double CD collected together the more far-fetched instrumentals from the 1988 tour. Although only three numbers were première recordings, plentiful solos and collective improvisation made this much more than a live album of cover versions. The title was explained by Zappa: 'You ever heard of Erroll Garner, jazz pianist, who mumbles along with what he plays? "Ayee! Ayee!" It's the whole concept of jazz musicians who make jazz noises while they perform.'[6]

'Stink-Foot' was a common opener on the tour: here (from Boston, 20 February 1988) Zappa tells the audience about the stalls for registering voters and gives the 'great news' – Jimmy Swaggart is under investigation – before launching into the song. Den Simms notes with puzzlement that at Boston Zappa complained after his guitar solo that it was not mixed high enough in the monitors, yet nevertheless chose that performance (out of twenty-two possibilities) for release.[7]

'When Yuppies Go to Hell' is a free-form collage of orchestral moments from the tour threaded together in the manner of the instrumental music on *Weasels*. Access to such machinery for sound production (state-of-the-art samplers, a mixing desk that can balance five separate horn lines with electric guitar, real-sounding

---

[5]Thanks to Jonathan Jones for this observation.

[6]Frank Zappa, quoted by Den Simms, 'The Obsessive Analyst', *Society Pages*, No. 7, 30 September 1991, p. 41. Evidently this obsessive analyst hadn't heard of the composer of 'Misty', because he spells him *Earl* Garner.

[7]Den Simms, 'The Obsessive Analyst', *Society Pages* No. 9, 25 May 1992, p. 42. Technical observations about PA, recording dates and splices are dependent here on Simms's exhaustive studies in *Society Pages*, Nos. 7 (*Broadway, Best Band*), 9 (*Jazz Noise*, Disc 1) and 10 (*Jazz Noise*, Disc 2) – a staggering display of meticulous Zappography.

orchestral percussion, sampled string sounds) is generally reserved for the narrow musical scope required for backing pop vocalists: to hear the musicians engage in improvised multi-part dialogues with all these riches is quite giddying. Sections run the gamut from nephew Jade's belch samples to Webern-like purity, staggered funk, Jew's harp and Hammond organ. Bobby Martin comes into his own as he picks up phrases like 'outrageous filth' from the senatorial samples. As Zappa sings 'fire and chains' at the end, the whole piece reverberates like true dada cabaret, the joy of moving sonic material about vast auditoria used as a critique of religious obfuscation and pop sentimentality. 'Fire and Chains' is a guitar solo, the sounds curiously panoramic compared to those on *Guitar*. Use of sampled guitar loops gives a much denser texture than one would expect from what is essentially a guitar/bass/drums trio.

After the free-form expansion of the opening numbers, the band gallop through some themes from *Money, Weasels* and *Lumpy Gravy*, showing how far from rock and how close to show-time razzamatazz were themes like 'Let's Make the Water Turn Black' and 'Oh No'. 'Harry You're a Beast' recalls its original obscenities by reference to its complex metres alone. The rendition of 'Theme from Lumpy Gravy' in Rotterdam (3 May 1988) is preceded by Zappa crying, 'May you never hear *vloerbedekking* again!'

This is an example of Zappa's fastidious memory for location. On 27 November 1971 in Rotterdam Flo & Eddie performed a specially tailored 'Divan' routine which has them sing God's song to the sofa in Dutch: 'Geef mij wat vloer bedekking onder deze vette zwevende sofa' (Give me some floor covering under this fat floating sofa).[8] The reference is in keeping with the whole valedictory nature of the 1988 tour and the entire *Stage* series. It precedes the surf tune from *Lumpy Gravy* and refers to Jimi Hendrix's famous aside, 'May you never hear surf music again'.[9] Played on brass instruments, the tune sounds less like surf than circus music. After this pounding exhilaration, Mike Keneally's[10] evocation of George Duke's definitively funky intro to 'Eat That Question'

---

[8] First available on the early 70s bootleg *Pootface Boogie*, this routine is now spread among legitimate products: 'Once Upon a Time', 1971, 'Sofa #1', 1971, *You Can't Do That on Stage Anymore Vol. 1*, 1989; *Swiss Cheese/Fire!*, 1971, *Beat the Boots #2*, 1992; 'Stick It Out', *Joe's Garage Acts II & III*, 1979. For details, see above 'Sofa', Chapter 5: From Bizarre to DiscReet.
[9] Jimi Hendrix, 'Third Stone from the Sun', *Are You Experienced*, 1967, Polydor 847234.
[10] I'd assumed it was Bobby Martin; Zappa corrected me himself.

sounds beautifully unpressured and soulful, though the tune itself is used merely to announce a lush, brass-rich 'Black Napkins'. Walt Fowler (trumpet) takes his time, providing a special gleaming lyricism that keeps grabbing one's attention on *Jazz Noise*. Kurt McGettrick's rhythm-baritone is peculiarly effective as his scraping low notes answer the falsetto vocal chorus. Whereas Mike Brecker evidently found the tune a challenge for its lack of harmonic pressure – alternation between two chords is a device used by soul and rock bands rather than jazz-players – tenorist Albert Wing is relaxed and plaintive. A burst of applause after Wing's solo indicates that some members of the audience were aware of what was going on.

In the 1988 arrangement, 'Big Swifty' combines the gorgeous big-band sound of the Wazoo band with the rock drive of the 80s; the solos quote from such classical pops as Bizet's *Carmen*, Wagner's *Lohengrin* and Tchaikovsky's *1812 Overture*,[11] while a fully arranged crowd-pleaser has the entire brass section play music from *Carmen*. It is during this that Zappa announces 'Make a jazz noise here!', and starts parodying Erroll Garner's 'ayee! ayee!' grunt. Scott Thunes shows a nimbleness on bass during Paul Carman's alto solo that is very appropriately jazzy. What is entertaining about this music is that it can plunder jazz for flexibility and response without adopting the jaded virtuosity of fusion; there are jazz runs and solos but samples and percussion and vocal exclamations erupt with a freedom that is closer to free improvisation (or what jazz was doing before the political and economic retrenchments of the 70s). Anyone offended by the levity of Zappa's remarks or the 'yeah man!' comments from the band would be ignoring the genuine musicianship on display: in terms of control of his instrument Bruce Fowler has as much respect for the tradition as Wynton Marsalis.

Bobby Martin's variations on the *Carmen* theme show a delicate awareness of space entirely lacking when goaded to bellow out 'Whipping Post' at ninety miles an hour: the gruelling repetitions of Zappa's music in the 80s, the joyless run-throughs of anti-rock and cul-de-sac pop, suddenly evaporate into music as creatively interactive as it is funny and unpretentious. 'Big Swifty' dissolves into effects and samples and vocals that are worthy of *Weasels*. Then the musicians return to the head.

---

[11]Credit for noticing these quotes must go to Den Simms, 'The Obsessive Analyst', *Society Pages*, No. 9, 25 May 1992, p. 46.

'King Kong' is done reggae, with a snorting baritone solo from Kurt McGettrick. In a spoken interlude Bruce Fowler has a chance to expose his interest in palaeontology,[12] which resembles the rap that Zappa used to deliver in the 60s about King Kong: he was doing all right in the jungle, then a bunch of Americans found him, brought him to the States to make some money and killed him. In Fowler's tale an Upper Devonian intellectual placoderm-type fish is persecuted by religious fanatic sharks. Zappa carried on this eco-theme with *Outrage at Valdez*. Disc one of *Make a Jazz Noise Here* ends with 'Star Wars Won't Work', essentially the coda to 'Stairway to Heaven' at Stuttgart (24 May). According to Den Simms,[13] this piece of anti-cold-war politics had been triggered by a phone call from a Soviet official that evening, requesting that Zappa play a concert to commemorate the imminent Reagan/Gorbachev summit. Reagan had actually gone on record saying that it would be great if someone in 'say, Moscow, decided to ring Liverpool, England, and organize a concert – or vice versa'.[14] Excitement at the changes in Russia was echoing round the world. As the fade occurs we can hear Zappa scat in meltdown.

> Star wars won't work
> The gas still gets through
> It can get right on you
> And what about those germs now?
> Star wars won't work
> It's a piece of shit
> Why are they even talking about it anymore?
> It's just an expensive bunch of nothing[15]

Talking during fades is a sure way to make words resonate; once again, Zappa's ambivalence to technology manifests itself, as if military obsolescence is infecting all the hardware at America's disposal, including that being used by the current listener. As with 'A Little Green Rosetta' – 'throw the record away'[16] – the technological critique escapes nobody.

Disc two of *Jazz Noise* begins with what is called a 'new age'

---

[12] Found elsewhere in the name of the Fowler Brothers' record company, Fossil, and the album title *Breakfast for Dinosaurs*.
[13] Dens Simms, 'The Obsessive Analyst', *Society Pages*, No. 9, 25 May 1992, p. 47.
[14] A tape-recording of this message was played at Liverpool City Hall during Sergei Kuriokhin's performance there (which had been organized just like that) on 30 January 1989.
[15] Frank Zappa, 'Star Wars Won't Work', *Make a Jazz Noise Here*, 1991.
[16] Frank Zappa, 'A Little Green Rosetta', *Joe's Garage Acts II & III*, 1979.

version of 'The Black Page'. Whereas it used to burst on audiences as an impossible soundtrack for 'dancer participation', or in the midst of provocative songs like 'Titties & Beer' or 'The Illinois Enema Bandit', here it is given a gentle, chiming intro. Originally written to exact creative hysteria from Terry Bozzio, in the hands of these musicians it becomes a slow, tender jazz tune. It picks up momentum, but lush horn charts keep it from becoming the metrical thornbush of *Zappa in New York*.

'Dupree's Paradise' could have been written for this horn-rich line-up and features a wonderful trumpet solo by Walt Fowler, in the curious lean-limbed style of electric jazz that Zappa specializes in (and no one else has managed to emulate). The trumpet solo is introduced and then underlain by a tricky bass figure that is redolent of the illusions of mid-80s tunes like 'Tink Walks Amok'.[17] During a free-form section in the middle, there is some explorative trombone from Bruce Fowler and querulous tenor from Albert Wing. Then (at 6.24) Zappa unleashes the same looped guitar sample he used in 'Star Wars Won't Work': his voodoo slur on Reagan's high-tech war project evoked by just a few notes.

'City of Tiny Lites' is given a crunching bass part by Kurt McGettrick's baritone. Against a steady *clavé* beat Zappa's guitar is peculiarly robust and rugged. On the tour, mixer Harry Andronis (who had seen Zappa on every tour since 1973 and always taken exception to what he considered excessive amounts of mixing-desk effects) kept the sound natural,[18] though this is more likely to affect acoustic private recordings than Zappa's releases, which are remixes of the PA tapes. Playing music from all eras in quick succession meant some timbral levelling was inevitable: 'Sinister Footwear 2nd mvt' from *Them Or Us*, like the *One Size Fits All* tunes on *Best Band*, has lost some of the textural poignancy of the original (not helped by the heavy beat used for the first measures). However, it gains from the wit of Bruce Fowler's trombone breaks and the personality of the horns. The sudden eruption of 'Stevie's Spanking' in all this complexity is a reminder that it is precisely incongruity that makes Zappa's music valuable. 'Alien Orifice' again benefits from the horn section, emphasizing the sleaze factor of its introductory figure; most unusual to hear such loud and undistorted bass move beneath a horn section, or a

---

[17]Frank Zappa, 'Tink Walks Amok', *The Man from Utopia*, 1983.
[18]See *Zappa!* (a supplement from the publishers of *Keyboard and Guitar Player*), ed. Don Menn, 1992, pp. 91–2.

breakout into feedback guitar such as happens here. Chad Wacker-man's drumming is particularly responsive on the solo, full of strange spaces and sudden cymbal enthusiasms.

'Cruisin' for Burgers' has Zappa unfurl one of his great pieces of claustrophobic lyricism, a solo that appears to consist of one long melody. The tension between waiting for his rhythmic devi-ations to resolve and enjoying the dogged lilt of the band create a kind of oscillation of attention: towards the end Wackerman works himself into a frenzy to bring Zappa back to earth. Although the band feels a mite too unwieldy for the loose blues of 'Advance Romance' – a song that really requires a few big personalities close-miked – 'Strictly Genteel' has never sounded more multitud-inous, its mock pomp both amusing and moving.

According to Gail Zappa, cover artists 'seem to appear from nowhere'.[19] The cover of *Jazz Noise* by Larry Grossman shows a night-club named Zappa's built over still-combusting industrial waste. A sign reads: 'Last chance for live music'. Though Zappa seems unaware of the efforts made by musicians round the world to keep improvisation happening – at New York's Knitting Fac-tory, at Derek Bailey's Company Weeks, at countless tiny pub and club venues – his rock perspective at least deprives him of the option of becoming inured to the ghetto. Although this commen-tary is designed to draw attention to specific felicities, the totality of *Jazz Noise* evades comprehension: there is simply *too much* music happening here – one's listening imagination is gratefully stunned. *Jazz Noise* is a great boast, but given the music it contains, a boast to be proud of.

BROADWAY THE HARD WAY

Broadway the Hard Way presented the new songs of the tour on a single album: the most concertedly political record Zappa had made since *We're Only in It for the Money*. The album gatefold showed Zappa in a pantomime scenario staged by A. West. With hair standing on end and wearing a bow-tie and gross check jacket, Zappa poses as president. He is reading the magazine for private mercenaries, *Soldier of Fortune*. Prominent on the presidential desk is a jar of Hellman's mayonnaise, no doubt to help presidential

[19]Gail Zappa, interview with the author, 27 October 1993.

policies 'go down easy'.[20], Honker Video's blinkers that promise to obliterate all offensive materials and a 'have a nice day!' sign with a Smiley button (a 70s motif the graphic novel *The Watchmen* resurrected – with a dash of blood – and which was taken up by the English acid-house movement in 1988's 'summer of love'). Just in front of the American flag in the corner there is a telescope aimed at Congress. A sign also warns that 'all persons entering holding area are subject to search'. Sprayed on the wall is a quote from Ronald Reagan: 'facts are stupid things'. By Zappa's left hand is a copy of *Racing Form* with the headline 'Sunset ends meeting at Hollywood', perhaps referring to the failure of the 1988 band to make the West Coast. The calendar on the wall shows, not today's date but the next meeting of the Chamber of Commerce – an indication of presidential priorities.

Musically, *Broadway the Hard Way* is a far cry from the rock assault of records like *Them Or Us* or *Does Humor Belong in Music?*, featuring instead a combination of electioneering brass-band razzamatazz, showbiz sentimentality and songs that parody traditional American hymns in the manner of 'Heavenly Bank Account'[21] – long melody lines sung in multi-voice parts. In the same way that *Money* taunted the listener who wanted heavy rock, so *Broadway the Hard Way* uses dead musical forms in order to focus attention on the words rather than a musical massage. In doing this, the melodies – 'Any Kind of Pain', 'When the Lie's So Big', 'Jezebel Boy' – have some of the cynical beauty of Kurt Weill, tarnished structures looming beneath the tinsel. This musical content is well indicated by the title and the opening words of the first song: 'Ladies and gentlemen, Elvis has just left the building.' Rock 'n' roll is simply no longer up to the comments Zappa wishes to make. This announcement used to be made at the end of Elvis's appearances in Vegas in order to prevent his dressing room being mobbed: *Broadway the Hard Way* starts just where tarnished showbiz finishes.

'Elvis Has Just Left the Building' is a country song and, like 'Truck Driver Divorce',[22] satirizes blue-collar fantasies.

> So take down the foil
> From his hotel retreat

---

[20]Frank Zappa, 'Keep It Greasey', *Joe's Garage Acts II & III*, 1979.
[21]Frank Zappa, 'Heavenly Bank Account', *You Are What You Is*, 1981.
[22]Frank Zappa, 'Truck Driver Divorce', *You Are What You Is*, 1981.

And bring back The King
For the man in the street.[23]

The details – Presley's nappies, the tin foil over the windows – indicate that Zappa had been reading Albert Grossman's iconoclastic biography. 'Cher'bim and ser'phim / Whizz over his head' relates to an explanation of flying saucers Zappa heard from a store-front preacher back in the 60s[24] and evokes the parodic sci-fi of 'Inca Roads', as does the title of 'Dickie's Such an Asshole (The San Clemente Magnetic Deviation)', which refers to speculation by the Roxy band that Nixon was responsible for distortions to the earth's magnetic field.

He's up there with Jesus, in a big purple chair[25]

Given the powerful connections between rock 'n' roll and religion in the American south (TV evangelist Jimmy Swaggart is Jerry Lee Lewis's cousin, for example) to rubbish the Elvis myth is akin to blasphemy. The words

Elvis has just left the building
To climb up that heavenly stair[26]

need to be heard in conjuction with the nowhere-leading staircases on the cover of the contemporaneous 'Stairway to Heaven' single.

According to Den Simms, conductor of frequent detailed inquisitions with the man himself, Zappa says 'Planet of the Baritone Women' is about *male* Wall Street traders,[27] though this hardly seems to tally with the words.

The men carry purses wherever they go
Junior executives all in a row
Watch the Baritone Women do the Baritone show . . .
They do choreography still more unique!
They leave their legs open whenever they speak!
They roll their eyes upward and over again
And slam their legs closed
When they sing about men![28]

It seems more likely this voices the same sexual satire as 'Bobby

[23]Frank Zappa, 'Elvis Has Just Left the Building', *Broadway the Hard Way*, 1989.
[24]Frank Zappa, with Peter Occhiogrosso, *The Real Frank Zappa Book*, 1989, pp. 61–3.
[25]Frank Zappa, 'Elvis Has Just Left the Building', *Broadway the Hard Way*, 1989.
[26]Ibid.
[27]*Society Pages*, No. 7, 30 September 1991, p. 36.
[28]Frank Zappa, 'The Planet of the Baritone Women', *Broadway the Hard Way*, 1989.

Brown'[29] and 'The Legend of the Illinois Enema Bandit':[30] under-class resentment at feminism as the ideology of the new middle class. Whether it is men who seem like women or women who seem like men is hardly relevant: indeed the confusion as to who the song is 'actually' about increases its unsettling power. The early 80s boom saw the expansion of opportunities for female professionals just as it drew millions of women into low-paid, non-unionized employment; the song is about the hypocrisy of yuppie feminists of both sexes who equate progress with their own exploitative careers.

> They sing about wheat
> They sing about corn[31]

as Reaganomics produces poverty on a massive scale.

'Any Kind of Pain' shows Zappa responding to accusations that his lyrics are sexist. He describes the glamorous air-head invented by PR firms for appearances on talk shows, and then concludes:

> Yes, she's every bit as lame as me,
> Let us remember
> She gets only half the blame
> Only half the blame
> Only half the blame
> Unless we *extend* her – [32]

The last line recalls Carolina Hardcore Ecstasy after she has been trampled on the tile floor of the bathroom:

> She couldn't talk because her mouth had been *extended*[33]

This sadistic extension involves the listener's libido in the object of attack, a device that recalls the torture machine of Kafka's penal colony.

'Dickie's Such an Asshole' revives an anti-Nixon blues played by the Mothers in 1973/4. Ike Willis's rap about involvement in Nicaragua and losing crucial tape-recordings shows how Nixon's invasions of privacy finally backfired. On 'When the Lie's So Big', Ike Willis sings 'the Republican trick' with a relish that shows a keen attention to politics. The desperation of the lines

---

[29]Frank Zappa, *Sheik Yerbouti*, 1979.
[30]Frank Zappa, *Zappa in New York*, 1977.
[31]Frank Zappa, 'The Planet of the Baritone Women', *Broadway the Hard Way*, 1989.
[32]Frank Zappa, 'Any Kind of Pain', *Broadway the Hard Way*, 1989.
[33]Ibid.

People, wake up
Figure it out
Religious fanatics
Around and about[34]

have some of the urgency of 'Mother People' on *Money*.
In his micro-analysis of *Broadway*, Den Simms found the
following interpolations in Zappa's attack on Jesse Jackson,
'Rhymin' Man'. The figures refer to timings available with the CD
format.

Song	Timing
Chopin's *Piano Sonata Opus* 35	0.38–0.40
'Theme from Mission Impossible'	0.43–0.45
'Theme from the Untouchables'	0.50–0.54
'Happy Days are Here Again'	1.44–1.46
	1.48–1.51
	2.45–2.47
	2.50–2.53
'Entry of the Gladiators'	1.54–1.56
'Hava Nagila'	1.59–2.02
	2.10–2.12
'Hail to the Chief'	2.04–2.07
'La Cucaracha'	2.15–2.17
'Frère Jacques'	2.55–2.58
	3.01–3.03
The Knack's 'My Sharona'	3.03–3.08
	3.12–3.14
'Hallelujah, I'm a Bum'	3.37–3.50[35]

Zappa's politics are not as punctilious as his musical quotes. He
repeats the racist slur about Jesse Jackson faking his proximity to
Martin Luther King at the latter's assassination and mocks his
foreign policy.

Said he was a diplomat
Hobbin' an-a-knobbin' with Arafat
Castro was *simpatico*,
But the US voters, they said 'No!'[36]

In the 1984 primaries, Jesse Jackson's stand on foreign policy was
one of the few really radical proposals in American electoral politics for decades.[37] Zappa inveighs against the illiberalism used to

[34]Frank Zappa, 'When the Lie's So Big', *Broadway the Hard Way*, 1989.
[35]Den Simms, 'The Obsessive Analyst', *Society Pages*, No. 7, 30 September 1991, p. 37.
[36]Frank Zappa, 'Rhymin' Man', *Broadway the Hard Way*, 1989.
[37]See Mike Davis, *Prisoners of the American Dream*, 1986, p. 275.

mobilize voters for the right, but has little idea of the economic realities of the capitalist crisis. Democratic talk of economic restructuring to help the deprived parts of the population – poor white, black and Hispanic – was fraudulent if it did not take a serious look at where such money should come from. In suggesting that America give up its imperialist role, and therefore save the massive amounts of money it spends on arms, Jackson was being practical. The fact that he lost showed more about the concerns of the electorate (increasingly white and better-off), who saw their economic self-interest as aligned with Reagan's military-expansionist boom, than it does about Jackson's duplicity. Focus on the Democratic Party meant that Jackson had to make compromises that in the end obscured his argument, but Zappa's objection to meeting Arafat (a symbolic declaration of wishing to end support for Israel, America's watchdog in the Middle East) undermines his anti-Reagan polemic.

When discussing proposed cuts for the National Endowment for the Arts in 1985, Zappa compared the cost of a single aeroplane tyre for the Gulf War with sponsoring an orchestra, terms familiar to anyone involved with left anti-war campaigns. However, in 'Rhymin' Man', his own collusion with Reagan's views flaw his case. In *The Real Frank Zappa Book* he begins his description of his political stand with the demand for 'less intrusive government and lower taxes',[38] which is precisely what Reagan promised in his electoral campaign. 'Lower taxation' is the classic method of mobilizing petit-bourgeois opinion against welfare concessions won by the working class. Typically, such rhetoric is not really about dismantling state power, so much as allowing the state to restructure the economy in the interests of big business.[39]

In 1968, with *We're Only in It for the Money*, the prospect of concentration camps for freaks explodes any ideological credibility for the state as a usable instrument. By the late 80s, the meeting with Vaclav Havel in Czechoslovakia and the talk of running for president show Zappa entertaining the ideas that the state could be run by enlightened philosopher kings (between 1970 and 1985 any political comments had been cryptic and playful). Although it is possible to argue that Zappa's success with his cottage-industry record label has produced a stridently petit-bourgeois politics to replace *Money*'s sympathy for the dispossessed, the two

[38]Frank Zappa, with Peter Occhiogrosso, *The Real Frank Zappa Book*, 1989, p. 315.
[39]See Mike Davis, *Prisoners of the American Dream*, 1986, p. 228.

elements have always been there. Even in 1969 he was talking of 'cutting your hair' and 'infiltration'. In 1988 he has not forgotten the sinister aspects of bourgeois control either: the multiple references to 'confinement loaf' connect to the penal paranoia of *Money*.

Broadway the Hard Way is sprinkled with political brickbats Zappa had collected during his 1985 campaign against the PMRC. Political chat-show nonentities have no idea of state treatment of the underclass.

> When she's in a bold mood,
> *'Confinement Loaf'* sounds good[40]

As Zappa's introduction to side two of *Broadway* (in the vinyl version) explains, 'confinement loaf' is the term used by prison authorities for a special bean bread that is meant to keep 'problem' inmates docile: 'My question is – how long before confinement loaf is introduced into US high schools?'[41]

Zappa makes confinement loaf as disturbing a symbol for life under capitalism as anything on *Money*. During 'When the Lie's So Big' Zappa interjects the words 'ketchup is a vegetable!'. This casts into a phrase from 'Call Any Vegetable'[42] the absurd insistence by a cost-cutting federal agency that ketchup constituted a 'vegetable' in meals for underprivileged students.[43] Confinement loaf and ketchup as a vegetable: the bread and wine of life in modern America.

'Promiscuous' airs Zappa's belief that Aids is the result of CIA meddling with biological warfare. It is performed to imitation hip-hop modelled on Public Enemy by Scott Thunes. 'The Untouchables', the theme from the early 60s gangster TV series, was 'arranged by Bruce Fowler from a cassette miraculously obtained by Laurel Fishman [of 'Stevie's Spanking' fame] after Frank remarked that it might be a cool tune to play'.[44] Zappa shuffles the decades in a manner that resembles William Burroughs and his fast cuts between Hollywood clichés. Ike Willis enumerates various Republican luminaries, declaring that they're 'history', just like the cheesy vamp he is performing over. He calls up Dano

[40]Frank Zappa, 'Any Kind of Pain', *Broadway the Hard Way*, 1989.
[41]Frank Zappa, Introduction to 'Dickie's Such an Asshole', *Broadway the Hard Way*, 1989 (vinyl version only).
[42]Frank Zappa, *Absolutely Free*, 1967.
[43]Den Simms, 'The Obsessive Analyst', *Society Pages*, No. 7, 30 September 1991, p. 37.
[44]Mike Keneally, quoted by Den Simms, 'The Obsessive Analyst', *Society Pages*, No. 7, 30 September 1991, p. 37.

from *Hawaii Five-0* – the horns play a quick snatch of Morton Stevens' theme for the TV series – only to chase him away again. This song constitutes a kind of voodoo as Zappa gives current politicians the aroma of fictitious TV criminals.

'Why Don't You Like Me?' is 'Tell Me You Love Me' from *Chunga's Revenge*, rewritten for Michael Jackson. His controversial transformation into a white person is satirized as hatred for his family.

> I hate my mother
> I hate my father
> I hate my sister
> And Jermaine is a negro!
> A NEGRO! A NEGRO!
> A NEGRO! A NEGRO![45]

On the 1988 tour Zappa performed various Beatles songs – 'I am the Walrus' (which Paul McCartney had said was too much a studio product for the Beatles to reproduce live), 'Lucy in the Sky with Diamonds' (renamed 'Louisiana Hooker with Herpes') and 'Strawberry Fields Forever' (a section of which appears in *Broadway* during 'What Kind of Girl?') – with words changed to celebrate the Jimmy Swaggart scandal. When asked if he was going to release these tunes Zappa replied that after his vilification of the copyright-holder of Northern songs – Jackson himself – he was unlikely to get permission. Jackson himself puts down his striking change in skin colour to a congenital defect and points out that half of Hollywood has resorted to plastic surgery. Some defend Jackson's current appearance as an example of utopian self-transformation, others see it as capitulation to Aryan ideas of beauty. It is not surprising that Zappa, who has always pursued reverse psychology in the domain of aesthetics, should be in the latter camp.

An appearance by Sting (CD-only), with 'Murder by Numbers', a Police song Jimmy Swaggart denounced on TV as the work of the Devil, is preceded by a cover of 'Stolen Moments' by Oliver Nelson,[46] brilliantly played by Walt Fowler. The choice is appropriate, given Sting's patronage of neo-conservative jazz-players who are fixated on the music of the pre-rock-'n'-roll 50s and 60s. The band have no trouble backing Sting as his tune is

[45]Frank Zappa, 'Why Don't You Like Me?', *Broadway the Hard Way*, 1989.
[46]'Stolen Moments' is from Oliver Nelson's masterpiece *Blues and the Abstract Truth*, 1961, MCA, which features Eric Dolphy.

essentially a blues. Zappa conducted improvisation from the band to accompany Sting's anti-Swaggart verbals and joins him on guitar. Zappa had a low opinion of his own solos on this tour and, though his playing lacks the pyrotechnics of 1984, its non-feed-back directness, a reflection of the non-rock nature of the arrangements, is appealing.

Broadway the Hard Way is a vision of America from all points of the compass. Having started in the South with Elvis, gone East to Wall Street with 'Baritone Women', Zappa moves West with 'Jezebel Boy', a Chandleresque vision of upper-class depravity and sexual exploitation that continues the story of 'The Idiot Bastard Son'[47] and 'Teen-age Prostitute'.[48] Zappa's playing on 'Outside Now', the guitar showcase from *Joe's Garage*, has an appropriately tenuous relationship to the pulse of the rhythm section: he cuts across the mantra-like chiming with feisty fireworks that sound as if his live playing is now a form of xenochrony. 'What Kind of Girl?' revives the *Fillmore East* routine in order to snigger at Swaggart's demise.

In 'Hot-Plate Heaven at the Green Hotel' the couplet

> Republicans is fine if you're a multi-millionaire
> Democrats is fair if all you own is what you wear[49]

is, like his views on Jesse Jackson and busing,[50] another example of Zappa's middle-class politics. The idea that the Democrats offer any hope for the dispossessed can be seen only as a complete fantasy, now more than ever. The 80s saw a growth in the gap between rich and poor, a luxurious standard of living for some and immiseration for the majority, as the Fordist idea of mass-consumption (a house and car for every worker) was abandoned for financial deals and luxury markets. The result of this has been the decline of middle-class liberalism into outright reaction. In a contradictory way, *Broadway the Hard Way* is an attempt to deal with the worst aspects of this reaction. Despite Zappa's contradictions, the politics of 'Jesus Thinks You're a Jerk', for example, are perceptive and spunky. Although support for Reagan actually came from a middle class whose economic position he fostered,

---

[47]Frank Zappa, *We're Only in It for the Money*, 1968.
[48]Frank Zappa, *Ship Arriving Too Late to Save a Drowning Witch*, 1982.
[49]Frank Zappa, 'Hot-Plate Heaven at the Green Hotel', *Broadway the Hard Way*, 1989.
[50]BUSSTOP in California was one of the 70s middle-class pressure groups that helped roll back gains made by the civil rights movement in the previous decade. See Mike Davis, *Prisoners of the American Dream*, 1986, p. 222.

there is no harm in pointing out the roots of new-right ideology in old Southern racism.

Broadway the Hard Way, both tour and album, did tackle head-on one of the developments that paved the way for the economic and political ascendancy of the middle class in the America of the 80s. The CD and side one of the LP conclude with Zappa asking his audience to register to vote – a theme since at least *Fillmore East June 1971*. This was implemented on the 1988 tour by a registration drive at the concerts themselves. The statistics for voter participation in families of different incomes make interesting reading. After twenty years of relative stability, voting underwent a sharp decline in the 70s – an astonishing *eighteen million people* joined the 'former voter' category, mainly from lower income groups. This is a process which the recession of the late 1980s has merely accelerated.

Reported Voter Participation by Family Income (1976)

Income	Voters	Former voters	Never	1,000s
–5000	46%	27%	27%	21,801
5–10,000	53%	21%	26%	30,096
10–15,000	60%	19%	21%	30,921
15–25,000	70%	15%	15%	31,748
+25,000	77%	12%	11%	14,153[51]

When asked, at a press conference for *The Yellow Shark* concerts, if 'Food Gathering in Post-Industrial America' was a satire on the sharp differentiation between the super-wealthy and the homeless in New York, Zappa got a laugh by saying that he doubted the music would be heard by either constituency.[52] In producing art at his economic level Zappa would be fooling himself to think that he can address the fundamental aspects of oppression in society: admission to his œuvre is dependent on a certain solvency that excludes (increasingly) part of the American population. Given those limits, though, opposition to voter apathy – in however small a way – does oppose political disenfranchisement of the poor. His campaign against the PMRC in 1985 also contributed to the backlash that has led the Republican Party to separate itself from the evangelical right in the early 90s. As the band slip into 'Louie Louie' (a common habit of the 1988 band – and indeed all Zappa's bands) for the concluding lines

[51]Mike Davis, *Prisoners of the American Dream*, 1986, p. 224.
[52]'The Press Conference: Hotel Frankfurter Hof, Frankfurt, Germany, 21 July 1992', *Society Pages*, No. 10, 24 August 1992, p. 36.

Jim and Tammy!
Oh, Baby!
You gotta go!
You really got to go![53]

Zappa's politics appear perfectly traced upon his musical aesthetic.

PLAYGROUND PSYCHOTICS

The retrospection involved in assembling the *You Can't Do That on Stage Anymore* series resulted in two further historical releases: *Playground Psychotics*, which documented the Flo & Eddie band both on- and offstage, and *Ahead of Their Time*, a Mothers of Invention concert from 1968. Cal Schenkel provided brilliant graphics, recycling old motifs in an appropriately self-conscious manner. For *Playground Psychotics* he reprised the careless scribbles of *Fillmore East June 1971*, but using motifs – cogwheels and printed circuits, busted dynamos and classical columns – which had appeared before in both collages and oil paintings. The cover is based on the poster Schenkel had drawn for Zappa's appearance at UCLA's Pauley Pavilion on 7 August 1971,[54] while yellow and pink crayon provided an extra to the pencil monochrome of the *Fillmore East* cover, a graphic equivalent to the extra timing and dynamic range Zappa could use in a double CD format.

Playground Psychotics showcases Zappa's ability to frame complex and thought-provoking structures out of unpromising materials. Disc one begins with a recording made of the group as they wait for their airplane to lift off. Aynsley Dunbar's accent sounded to these Californians 'like a Beatles cartoon'. The disc ends with a concert recorded at the Fillmore with John Lennon and Yoko Ono: Zappa's fascination with representation versus reality is signalled right at the start (actually, Aynsley Dunbar's plummy tones sound nothing like Lennon's Liverpudlian). The disc starts with banal everyday life and builds outwards to public spectacle: to play the Fillmore in 1971 with Lennon and Yoko must represent some kind of mass-cultural apogee. The plane is held up for some extra baggage – 'Ours?' someone asks. Like Zappa's closing remark on the *Stage* series – 'Don't throw stuff

---

[53]Frank Zappa, 'Jesus Thinks You're a Jerk', *Broadway the Hard Way*, 1989.
[54]Frank Zappa, booklet for *Beat the Boots #2*, 1992, p. 23.

on the stage'[55] – this asks questions about both authorship and moral responsibility. *Playground Psychotics* definitely consists of cultural 'baggage' extraneous to the delivery of music, but – like *200 Motels* – it also asks very acute questions about the dividing line between the two.

The Mothers are met at the airport by a Reprise promo man who wants them to pose around a garbage truck for a press photo shoot: 'I really think it's gonna be a great idea,' he says, nervousness in the face of Zappa's glowering suspicion causing both logic and syntax to seize up. Like the contrast between the cartoon Beatles and John Lennon onstage, this hesitancy reveals ambivalence about the division between concept and reality: if the band refuse to go along with it, his bright idea turns to nothing but garbage – a hesitancy that *Playground Psychotics* keeps returning to.

The garbage truck had – probably unknown to the promo man – been prefigured in 'Mr Green Genes'.

> Eat your greens
> Don't forget your beans & celery . . .
> You'll pump 'em right through
> Doo-wee-ooo
> Eat your shoes
> Don't forget the strings
> And sox
> Even eat the box
> You bought 'em in
> That brought 'em in
> Garbage truck
> MMMMMMMMMMMMMouldy
> Garbage truck
> Eat the truck & driver
> And his gloves
> NUTRITIOUSNESS
> DELICIOUSNESS
> WORTHLESSNESS[56]

Lowell George made his name with a romantic truck-driving song, 'Willin' '. When he played it to Zappa, he was told that he had better quit the Mothers and form his own group. On a famous Little Feat bootleg, George introduced the song with the truck-drivers' slogan, 'If you got it, a truck brought it.' 'Mr Green

[55]Frank Zappa, farewell message, 'Strictly Genteel', 1981, *You Can't Do That on Stage Anymore Vol. 6*, 1992.
[56]Frank Zappa, 'Mr Green Genes', *Uncle Meat*, 1969.

Genes' sees Zappa applying the same logic, but tracing the passage of material the other way, to the garbage truck that will remove the box it was packaged in. Beatles cartoons, extra baggage, garbage: *Playground Psychotics* informs the listener of its status straight away.

' "This is Neat" ' has Howard Kaylan enthusing about the hotel the band are staying in: the lounge, the bar, the juke-box full of hokey country songs. Combined with documentary of sound-checks ('A Typical Sound Check', ' "Don't Take Me Down" ', 'Zanti Serenade'), the 'roving ears' of the Uher 7 1/2 ips portable tape-recorder give us an idea of the musicians' all-day movements: instead of being the sole event, the encounter with the audience becomes only one aspect of the tour. Zappa's method of creating musical material – noting musicians' behaviour and orchestrating it on stage – becomes a Borges-like hall of mirrors. 'The London Cab Tape' has Zappa, Aynsley Dunbar and Mark Volman listen back to a tape Volman has made of other members of the group. They are talking about leaving the Mothers to form a more commercial band. ' "It's a Good Thing We Get Paid to Do This" ' has the band rehearse a scene from *200 Motels* which pastiches this dialogue, including the name of the band they might form: Howard Kaylan World. Their disbelieving laughter and asides become indistinguishable from the script: we experience a tremor of fear, a vision of reality as constructed according to a masterplan.

There is actually a great deal of magnificent music on *Playground Psychotics*, but it is likely that only people alerted to the reverberating subtleties of the intervening chatter will persevere long enough to hear it. 'Zanti Serenade', which 'purports to be some sort of avant-garde extravaganza', but was 'really just a soundcheck with the audience in attendance',[57] has some extraordinary playing by Don Preston, while 'Sleeping in a Jar' and 'Sharleena'[58] utterly transform the material: Aynsley Dunbar's fluency and Flo & Eddie's vocal onslaught make the original performances seem plodding.

The Flo & Eddie band play a music that was best summed up in Oz's one-line review of *Fillmore East June 1971*: 'It rips and it snorts. I like it lots.' 'Cruising for Burgers' from *Uncle Meat* becomes ecstatic pop. 'Diptheria Blues' is an acoustic at-the-hotel

---

[57]Sleeve note, Frank Zappa, 'Zanti Serenade', 1971, *Playground Psychotics*, 1992.
[58]*Chunga's Revenge*, 1970 (not *Uncle Meat*, as the sleeve note has it).

recording with Aynsley Dunbar playing 'a bottle of scotch whisky and a wooden table': the sheer lift of Flo & Eddie's vocals reveals the kind of hysterical round-the-clock adrenalin this band was running on. Dunbar's clicking rhythms – strangely reminiscent of Prince's percussion or the classic wine-glass tapping that powers Marvyn Gaye's 'Got to Give It Up'[59] – are completely characteristic of his drumming, despite the limited means.

The Fillmore East recording with John Lennon and Yoko Ono that concludes disc one has already appeared on *Some Time in New York City*, released on Apple in 1972.[60] Phil Spector, John and Yoko only managed a blurred sound: here bass and guitar move in separate registers. Zappa has removed his preamble to Walter Ward's oldie 'Well', the song Lennon used to sing at the Cavern, ('For those of you in the band who have no idea what's about to happen, this is in the key of A minor and it's not standard blues changes – but it's close'). It is instructive to compare the segue from 'Well' to the next song in the two versions. *Some Time*'s generous audience applause obliterates the Mothers' sharp transition, which in Zappa's release has the shock of an Edgard Varèse sound-block (*Some Time* also cuts the guitar climax of 'Well'). At *Some Time*'s release Zappa complained that John and Yoko had renamed his 'King Kong' 'scumbag' and taken the royalty credits for themselves, but here he omits the statement of the tune and credits the improvisations to 'Lennon/Ono/FZ'. Due to the clearer sound on *Playground Psychotics*, Yoko Ono's final comment on Zappa ('He's the greatest') comes over much more forcibly. Despite this tribute, her six-minute free-form warble with the band is named 'A Small Eternity with Yoko Ono' (though she did end up being thanked on *The Yellow Shark*).

Disc two begins with an argument between the musicians about the ethics of pouring beer on each other while on stage. This segues into a mid-'Call Any Vegetable' account of the menstrual-champagne event[61] and then back to more arguments about poured beer and an interview with the front office manager at the Edgewater Inn, Seattle, the venue for the notorious activities with the mudshark (as featured on *Fillmore East June 1971*). The desk clerk is surprisingly urbane and unfluffed, making Zappa sound crude

---

[59]Marvin Gaye, *Live at the London Palladium*, 1977, Motown TMSP6006.
[60]John and Yoko/Plastic Ono Band/Elephant's Memory, *Some Time in New York City*, 1972, Apple PCSP716.
[61]Frank Zappa, with Peter Occhiogrosso, *The Real Frank Zappa Book*, 1989, pp. 216–18.

and prurient. His comment that sexual activities with a mudshark would be 'a little uncomfortable as the skin is so sandy'[62] suggests the primal beach on which fish first flopped on their way up the evolutionary ladder. The band's childish rows about splashed beer and Zappa's fascination for sex with fish coalesce in speculation about the watery origins of *Homo sapiens*.

In 'You Got Your Armies', Jeff Simmons remarks to a Dutch journalist that if you try and cross an army with a rock band, 'this is what you get'. This is followed by 'Status Back Baby', in which Zappa – having introduced the song with the words 'of course we'll send a penguin through the flaming hoop ... of course we'll play "Concentration Moon" for ya' – suddenly announces 'of course we'll play "Petrushka"!' and plays Stravinsky's line on guitar over 'Status Back Baby'. Both statements emphasize *incongruity* as a structuring principle: 'This has to be the tape with *all* the right notes in it'[63] coupled with 'what the fuck'.[64] Onstage clowning ('the Sanzini Brothers') and rehearsal of scripts derived from illicit recording of band-member conversations (' "It's a Good Thing We Get Paid to Do This" ') are sandwiched in a two-part rendition of 'Concentration Moon' from *We're Only in It for the Money*, squeezing the seemingly limitless ricochet of artistic paradox between social limits.

The introduction to another version of 'Billy the Mountain' – the theme that opens 'Music for Low Budget Orchestra' on *Studio Tan* – comes across as hauntingly delicate in the midst of Flo & Eddie's riotous rendition of *Money* tunes. One of the most misunderstood of Zappa's creations, this rendition of 'Billy the Mountain' shows how scripted and disciplined the piece actually was.

The freely improvised section that occurs while waiting for Studebacher Hoch's phone to ring in his secret briefcase is performed by Zappa, reduced to 'February 1975 ... 1986 ... March 1914 ...',[65] again suggesting some monstrous recasting of twentieth-century history.

Disc two finishes with excerpts from *The True Story of 200 Motels* video, backstage interviews in which participants explain the odd situation of being asked to 'act' yourself. Their descriptions are predictable, consisting of the familiar litany of

---

[62]Frank Zappa, 'The Mudshark Interview', 1971, *Playground Psychotics*, 1993.
[63]Frank Zappa, preamble to 'Bebop Tango (of the Old Jazzmen's Church)', *Roxy & Elsewhere*, 1974.
[64]Frank Zappa, sleeve note to 'The Sheik Yerbouti Tango', *Sheik Yerbouti*, 1979.
[65]Frank Zappa, 'Billy the Mountain', 1971, *Playground Psychotics*, 1993.

'isn't it amazing?' clichés endemic to on-set interviews, but – because of what has gone before – the remarks about life imitating art do not evaporate. Jeff Simmons's departure is explained as anxiety at performing lines that are so close to what he would say in 'real life'. 'The Worst Reviews' explains that Zappa expects the critics to pan him, because 'nobody's ready for it' (a boast that explains the title of *Ahead of Their Time*). Howard Kaylan talks about the 'management/employee' relationship of Zappa with his musicians. The final track is from Martin Lickert, Ringo Starr's chauffeur, who was recruited to replace Jeff Simmons; his anti-Zappa speech from *200 Motels* concludes with the line, 'I could be a star now.' *Playground Psychotics* is based on reverberating paradox and this conclusion is entirely apt. In a sense Zappa has proved that the Mothers were nothing without him: apart from George Duke, who is only featured in some scurrilous dialogue about the differences between the jazz scene and the rock world (' "There's No Lust in Jazz" '), no one involved has a name to equal Zappa's; but all Zappa can do to prove this fact is to release material that features such supposedly fly-by-night talents. Everywhere you look, *Playground Psychotics* has paradox etched into it like some genetic blueprint – which is why, despite the quantity of 'non-musical' material, it does repay repeated listening.

AHEAD OF THEIR TIME

Ahead of Their Time is the complete recording of a concert delivered by the Mothers of Invention at the Royal Festival Hall in London on 28 October 1968.[66] The title seems designed to forestall the kind of comments that would greet the release of his next CD, *The Yellow Shark*, orchestral music recorded at concerts in Frankfurt, Berlin and Vienna in September 1992 by the Ensemble Modern: 'former rock 'n' roll wildman Frank Zappa has turned his skills to serious music'.[67] The opening of *Ahead of Their Time*, in which members of the BBC Symphony Orchestra play neo-classical abstractions of a theme that later appeared in 'This Town

---

[66] Parts of this concert had appeared previously: part of 'Prelude to the Afternoon of a Sexually Aroused Gas Mask' on *Weasels Ripped My Flesh*, 1969.
[67] *Kaleidoscope*, BBC Radio 4, 20 April 1993.

is a Sealed Tuna Sandwich'[68] and 'Bogus Pomp',[69] could easily be part of the *Yellow Shark* programme. In accordance with Zappa's concept of people playing themselves, 'Progress?' casts Don Preston as a musical futurist.[70] An angry Bunk Gardner replies, 'You can take your progress and stick it under a rock!' This is of course how Zappa frequently uses avant-garde music – submerging it in rock – but it also recalls the issue of timelessness,[71] the idea of the artwork duplicating the unconscious and its lack of a historical dimension. Paradoxically, it is Zappa's 'progressive' abstractions, like the music played by the BBC musicians, which dates least. Listened to in conjunction with the orchestral music of *The Yellow Shark*, Zappa's classical music from 1968 asks many questions about both progress and the social inertia that prevents it.

The politics of *Ahead of their Time* also predicts that of *The Yellow Shark*. In 1968 Roy Estrada dressed up as the Pope and distributed Smarties in mockery of papal decrees against the pill; in 1992 'Food Gathering in Post-Industrial America' contained lines about unwanted babies and anti-choice legislation that provoked a burst of applause. Where Zappa orchestrated the Mothers in a charade about music and performance – Motorhead wants to join the classical 'robots', Jimmy Carl Black goes into the audience to 'hustle some action' – Zappa had the ballet troupe Lalala Human Steps from Montreal. The Mothers performed 'Agency Man' about the CIA marketing a president; 'Welcome' mocked the American chauvinism and its paranoia about immigrants.

Zappa's last word in his extensive liner note is that the concert was 'a fair – not outstanding – 1968 MOI rock concert performance'. Certainly the blending of classical instruments with the group is inspired, as conduction of falsetto cries and ensemble shouts punctuates delicate clarinet and violin lines. 'King Kong' features the composed mid-section – called 'The Ark' – missing from *Uncle Meat*. The rest of the concert is a potent example of the heavy exoticism of the Mothers in full flight: 'Help, I'm a Rock' (the title is particularly interesting in a context where Don Preston has been told to stick his progress under a rock: 'progress?' Zappa asks just before the song starts) is revealed as the basis of

---

[68]Frank Zappa, *200 Motels*, 1971.
[69]Frank Zappa, *Orchestral Favorites*, 1979, *London Symphony Orchestra Vol. II*, 1987.
[70]See 'Don Preston', Chapter 1: Origins.
[71]See 'Timelessness', Preface.

'Transylvania Boogie', whose gypsy modes provide an opportunity for some steaming Zappa guitar.

Cal Schenkel's graphics are cleverly adapted to the CD format: when the CD insert is unfolded the cover is revealed as an easel painting of the Mothers – in medieval dress but equipped with Ruben & the Jets dog-snouts – at the back of a castle hall. Everything has suffered millennial regression, rather in the manner of Philip K. Dick's *Ubik*. The record-player is a primitive wind-up, recalling Zappa's jokes about third-world listening devices on *Joe's Garage*,[72] its horn evidently provided by Emperor Cletus ('mystery horn' is inscribed on it in mirror-writing). CDs and vinyl records lie scattered on the floor. The 'doll's foot as a young rifle' from *Uncle Meat* has reappeared as a flintlock musket. A skull marked with the date 1348 can be made out under a maroon sofa. Uncle Meat's 'Tour Guide of Delaware' appears as a vellum manuscript, the Leonardo-style sketching of *One Size Fits All* ('N.G. Don't Work' scrawled over a cube-shaped Saturn) appears in a design for a lute. An upended chrome dinette chair recalls 'Sofa', while pink jello on the table recalls the slime from the TV set. A horse's head in the tapestry on the back wall is saying 'quack' as in *The Grand Wazoo*; the city beyond the portcullis resembles Uncle Meat's apparition. A tap on the boiler at the back marked 'hot' recalls the cover of *Hot Rats: Waka/Jawaka*.

Behind the doll's-foot-as-musket there is a (barely legible) sketch of a nude woman, recalling the palimpsests of femininity that aerated the cover of *Burnt Weeny Sandwich* and the back of *Waka/Jawaka*. Ubiquitous clocks and an hour-glass reinforce the theme of time. In a reference to the ex-Mothers lawsuit over royalties, a saucy knave (surely Don Preston) is reading 'Ye Olde Royalties' and burning pages in a furnace (which, appropriately enough, burns inside a suit of armour labelled 'law suits'); the bass drum used in the montage of *We're Only in It for the Money* has been slashed open to reveal coins and banknotes. His list has three items: the first, 'Noses', is ticked off; the second is 'Money'; the third is indecipherable. This connects to the man with dog-ears saying 'curses!' as last names are omitted from the chorus listing for *Lumpy Gravy* – dog-snouts for rank careerism. When he reappeared on the cover of *Tinsel Town Rebellion* he was seated

---

[72]Frank Zappa, 'A Little Green Rosetta', *Joe's Garage Acts II & III*, 1979.

at a table on which a strange geometric spheroid glowed; this reappears on the banqueting table, an eerie, anachronistic touch that might figure radioactivity or time travel. The reverse of the CD insert is a medieval version of the scribbles of *Playground Psychotics* – a primitive cannon firing notes, cogwheels that become geometric decoration – though there is a fly that appears to have escaped from John Williams's collage for *Joe's Garage Acts II & III*, and also appeared on Schenkel's programme for the Zappa's Universe concerts.[73] The two-tone style of the latter (black and dayglo-orange) predicts *Playground Psychotics*, though Schenkel's patent motifs are collaged via computer graphics rather than scribbled. Like Zappa and his use of onstage disorder and anything-goes field recordings, Schenkel has the ability to make what looks at first like careless doodles and botched design expand into something fascinating and evocative. The lack of any demonstrative skill – the very opposite of the smooth surface of a David B. McMacken or a Roger Dean – is precisely the achievement.

THE YELLOW SHARK

The Yellow Shark derived its name from a mysterious object that turned up on Zappa's doorstep and found a place in his basement studio: a ten-foot plastic shark. It came to be the name for a series of concerts of Zappa's music given by the Ensemble Modern, a musicians' co-operative based in Frankfurt who select a different composer to work with every year. Missing from the CD was perhaps the most impressive piece, an extended mixture of electronics and real-time musicianship called 'Beat the Reaper'.[74] Zappa's wry view of his new respectability manifests itself in his

---

[73]This event – which Zappa was too ill to attend – occurred at the Ritz in New York on 7, 8, 9 and 10 November 1991, with a band consisting of Mike Keneally on guitar and Scott Thunes on bass (veterans of the 1988 tour), plus Mats Oberg and Marc Ziegenhagen on keyboards, Morgan Agren on drums and Jonathan Haas on percussion. The 'Orchestra of Our Time' played music arranged and conducted by Joel Thome. Special guests included the Persuasions, Rockapella, Dale Bozzio, Warren Cucurullo, Dweezil and Steve Vai on guitar, Moon and Diva on go-go dancing and Jade on burps. A vast swathe of Zappa's back catalogue was played, along with Erik Satie's *Socrate*. Set designs included mobiles by Alexander Calder and backdrops by Cal Schenkel. A full account by Den Simms can be found – along with a special Schenkel cover that matches the programme – in *Society Pages*, No. 8, 13 February 1992, pp. 16–43. The concerts were issued on CD as *Zappa's Universe*, 1993, Verve/Polygram 513 575.
[74]Broadcast on German radio, 22 September 1992, and scheduled for release – in a Synclavier version – as the climax to *Civilization Phaze III*.

emphasis on the word 'fine' in his introduction and by his aside – 'and if you feel like putting underpants on stage you can put them over there'. Rather like his explanation of the name 'Mothers' (motherfucker as a word for a top notch musician[75]), saying 'underpants' neatly removes the sexist offence (in a way that, say, 'panties' or 'knickers' would not, at least, in an English context[76]), making the statement merely bizarre. In terms of the 'don't throw stuff on the stage' remark that concludes the *Stage* series, though, it is as if he is inviting the projection of personal fantasy into the music that he was rejecting earlier.

'Dog Breath Variations' and 'Uncle Meat' sound brilliant in this orchestral version, utterly different from their rock incarnations, like circus music gone haywire. The Ensemble Modern have a great group feel and sympathy for the separate events in the music – a patch of tender strings is delivered with the correct sense of inexplicable poignancy. 'Outrage at Valdez' – written for a Jacques Cousteau documentary about an Alaskan oil-spill – is here in its final form (Zappa had to finish the soundtrack before flying to Czechoslovakia and declared himself unhappy with it). This version of American pastorale – compare Charles Ives and early John Cage – is frequently used for landscape shots in cowboy films: here, though, Zappa's keen attention to timbre adds a sensation of scientific experiment. The relative weights of the instrumental sounds are measured with the delicate logic of a mobile by Alexander Calder.

American-sounding, too, is 'Time's Beach III', a wind ensemble. It has some of Milton Babbitt's super-real clarity, but also something mocking in its sequences of fast notes. Zappa's interest in speech-based rhythms provides a visceral intensity in the midst of the high-minded abstractions. 'III Revised', a piece of Webern-like atonal strings, is segued directly into 'Girl in the Magnesium Dress', a Synclavier tune from *Jazz from Hell*, here played on percussion and piano and mandolin. The glittering fireworks it sends up are the results of tight mathematical construction, offset by a romantic, somewhat satirical floridity. Whereas the earlier tracks comprised compendia of gangster movie and Tom and Jerry clichés, this has some of the cutting-edge innovation of Conlon

---

[75]Frank Zappa, *The Late Show*, produced by Nigel Leigh, BBC2, 11 March 1993.
[76]Zappa does actually say 'underpants' on 'Panty Rap', *Tinsel Town Rebellion*, 1981, but quickly follows it up with 'brassières' and 'small articles of feminine underclothing'.

Nancarrow, as piano and mandolin appear to occupy different rhythmic time zones.

'Bebop Tango' is the tricky tune from *Roxy & Elsewhere*, adding in patches of orchestra chatter in order to evoke jazz-lounge tawdriness. The theme wraps itself up into impossible-sounding complexities, delivering some of the hallucinogenic spin of fractal designs that reproduce patterns at ever-receding micro-dimensional thresholds: ending in a tiny, compressed dot of rhythm that seems to contain a sonic universe. The trumpet playing is burnished and clear: in this deliberately slurred jazz context it has the incongruous purity of Marcus Stockhausen's improvisations.

'Ruth is Sleeping' and 'None of the Above' are calm and classical, the first a piano sonata and the second a string quartet originally premièred by Kronos. Zappa's distaste for micro-tones means that only a few glissandi touch on the world of extended string technique opened up by Giacinto Scelsi, Helmut Lachenmann and Klaus Huber. However, Zappa's imaginative idea of rhythm gives the parts a paradoxical combination of freedom and closure that is bravura. The title 'None of the Above' – the box ticked in questionnaires by people refusing to accept the categories on offer – is a typically inspiring expression of Zappa's revolt against both conceptual and legalistic bureaucracy (a theme further developed with 'Welcome').

'Pentagon Afternoon' crosses sirens with Second Viennese School modernism and concludes with what sounds like an array of toy ray-guns, an obvious pun to those who opposed Ronald Reagan's Strategic Defense Initiative (Ronnie Ray-gun's Star Wars).

'Food Gathering in Post-Industrial America' extends conceptual continuity with rats and poodles as well as making a pro-choice gesture. 'Welcome', with Herman Gretschmar, quotes 'Louie Louie', being a modernized version of Lowell George's customs-officer routine[77] – though there is a delightful symmetry in the way that, here, a German mocks American restrictions. The piece is simply a recital of the questions on the US visa form with sound-effects and replies from the orchestra. Someone answers 'say – yes or no' with 'yes or no', a parallel form of resistance to 'none of the above'. Both the replies 'sea' and 'genocide' are given a similarly evocative orchestral effect, asking disturbing questions

---

[77]'German Lunch', 1969, *You Can't Do That on Stage Anymore Vol. 5*, 1992.

about beauty and suffering in the manner of the song title 'The Ocean is the Ultimate Solution'.

'Pound for a Brown' proves its elasticity in this arrangement, as Zappa's answer to Duke Ellington's 'Caravan' drives a complex path between arranged detail and ostinato pulse. 'Exercise #4' revives the dada clockwork of Sun Ra and Moondog.[78] The guitar writing catches the poignant claustrophobia of Zappa's improvised solos, while that for the clarinets recalls Eric Dolphy.

'G-Spot Tornado', in this arrangement, turns the urgent Synclavier Nancarrowisms of *Jazz from Hell* into a bionic Irish jig, recalling Zappa's enthusiasm for the Chieftains.[79] The title, implying a whirl of excitement around a centre that actually does not exist (the G-spot being a figment of mid-80s sexology), repeats the Zen argument of 'Apostrophe'. Questions of mortality being pressing at the time – Zappa missed some of the concerts due to ill-health brought on by his prostate cancer – the tumultuous applause that follows this final number suggests that Zappa's music, in the form of scores playable by note-reading ensembles, will outlive his physical demise.

Webern vs. Televangelism

In a programme on Zappa on Radio 3, the BBC's classical music station, music critic Michael Oliver was quick to make claims for Zappa's exemplary refusal to distinguish between high and low art forms. He did, though, voice disappointment with the politics of *Broadway the Hard Way*, calling them 'back-to-Roosevelt'.[80] It is not so much the narrowness of Zappa's politics that is the problem, though, as the narrowness of Oliver's aesthetic. Oliver seems to look at the records in a frame and ignore the impact of Zappa as a media entity. As the preceding analysis hopefully made clear, the negative dialectics of poodle play is far from happy with the politics of *Broadway* either: the inspiring aspect of Zappa's politics is not his declared positions, but his role as a spanner in the works

---

[78]Zappa declared his allegiance to Moondog as early as the 1970s, long before his 'rediscovery' by the likes of Steve Reich in the 1990s.

[79]In February 1993 Zappa held a soirée that combined the musical talents of the Chieftains, Tuvan throat-singers from beyond the Arctic circle, violinist L. Shankar and Johnny 'Guitar' Watson: *The Late Show*, produced by Nigel Leigh, BBC2, 11 March 1993.

[80]Zappa's politics are wide-ranging and contradictory – his pronounced anti-statist streak would look strange in a back-to-Roosevelt New Dealer.

of the recording industry; indeed, as a spanner in the works of culture itself.

Interspersed with Michael Oliver's comments was a side-splitting interview as presenter Adam Philips – in best Radio 3 tones – tried to ask Zappa questions about his beliefs and practices. The chasm between Zappa's observations on the music business and Philips's liberal idea of the arts was so wide that you could only laugh. Radio 1, the BBC's pop station, fared no better. Asked for a favourite record to play, Zappa chose Anton Webern, and then caused Nicky Campbell to gasp as he talked about payola in American radio[81] and the fact that the American media had suppressed coverage of anti-war protests in the build up to the Gulf War.

> NC: We got the impression, here, watching the news and stuff, that there was a lot of popular support for the Gulf War in America.
> FZ: Well you would have the impression simply because the news was managed. There were many many anti-war demonstrations in the United States and there was a standing rule on network television that they were not to be covered
> NC: Seriously?
> FZ: Yes.
> NC: Who imposed that rule?
> FZ: Who do you think? Somebody from the White House. There was a governmental agency that was set up by Ronald Reagan called the Department of Domestic Diplomacy and the goal of this organization is to manage the news.
> NC: That's like George Orwell – that's *1984*! This is the greatest democracy in the world?
> FZ: Says who?
> NC: The land of the brave?
> FZ: The land of the people who need to feel good about themselves because they blew up a bunch of Iraquis. It's shameful.[82]

Zappa then went on to give an informed account of US support for Saddam Hussein prior to his seizure of Kuwait and the involvement of the Christian right and TV evangelists in fomenting anti-Muslim feeling.

Zappa is irrefutably one of our great twentieth-century composers, but this is not merely a matter of some neat recordings or cool compositions. The grand design has been his net effect on the media: finally it is his *incongruity* as a cultural figure that is his most inspirational facet. He fits arts radio no more than he

---

[81]And recommended the essential work by Fredric Dannen, *Hit Men*, 1990.
[82]BBC Radio 1, 27 August 1991.

531

gets along with obsequious top-40 jocks. This sabotage of institutionalized class divisions comes as necessary balm to a subjectivity bruised and battered by the separations of capitalist society. It unleashes a wild energy, painful and healing at once.

Matt Groening, the cartoonist who created *The Simpsons*, has always found Zappa an inspiration, going so far as to start collecting material for a book on him. He remarked how creative is Zappa's refusal of acknowledged social levels.

> One of the things that always impressed me about Zappa was that he didn't allow anything to be beyond him – high culture, low culture . . . Most people say, 'Oh that area of culture over there is too grubby for me,' or, 'That area of culture is for rich fops,' and I tried not to let that get in the way.[83]

In a strange way this resembles the promise of postmodernism. Frank Zappa's achievement is to show how laughably distant – how painfully distant – that ideal is from realization.

---

[83]Matt Groening, *Zappa!* (from the publishers of *Keyboard and Guitar Player*) ed. Don Menn, 1992, p. 26.

Epilogue: Going to Meet the Man

Copyrights and Paranoia

Playground Psychotics showed that Zappa's concern with the issues of copyright and authorship – where private property impinges on creativity – remained undiminished in the 90s. On the cover of *Ahead of Their Time*, a musician is portrayed burning royalty statements. On the inner sleeve of *Man from Utopia*, the lyrics – which included the freely improvised road story of 'The Jazz Discharge Party Hats' – appeared with a ferocious copyright declaration:

> All rights reserved, including publication of lyric extracts for reviewing purposes. No portion of the music or lyrics herein may be altered or subject to quotation in any medium whatsoever without written consent from the copyright owner. Failure to obtain such permission may result in legal action.[1]

The law to do with quoting other people's words is vague. In literary publications – where prestige and fame tend to precede unit-shifting – it is generally considered fair game to quote who and what you like. Poets and authors are only too glad to have anyone air their work. However, copyright is still an issue. Following a beyond-the-grave edict against biographers, lawyers employed by T.S. Eliot's estate managed to prevent one writer from quoting a single line of his poetry. Once texts are widely disseminated the law steps in to administer the parting of monies. When the first stirrings of poodle play were published in the early 80s – in *A Vision Very Like Reality*[2] and *Reality Studios*[3] – print

---

[1] Frank Zappa, sleevenote, *Man from Utopia*, 1983.
[2] Out to Lunch, 'Frank Zappa: The Negative Dialectics of Poodle Play Part One', *A Vision Very Like Reality*, ed. Peter Ackroyd, Ian Patterson, Nick Totton, December 1979.
[3] Out to Lunch, 'Frank Zappa: The Negative Dialectics of Poodle Play Part Two', *Reality Studios*, ed. Ken Edwards, Vol. 5. Nos. 1–4, 1983.

runs were in such low numbers that seeking permission seemed superfluous. The same attitude prevailed when preparing the current work, until the publishers declared that, given the extensive amount of Zappa's material in the book and the official nature of the imprint, I had to seek proper copyright permission.

Casual listeners to Zappa may not be aware of the global network of hardcore fans who swap live cassettes and related material, a 'mail art' community Gail Zappa terms 'The Loop'. Bootleggers dip into the pool of available material, press up albums and fleece naïve purchasers and Zappa 'completists' – but hardcore fans amass their collections via swapping tapes. No money passes hands. The fact that *Society Pages* (very much a mouthpiece for the Zappas) encourages tape-swapping[4] shows that Zappa himself does not see it as an incursion on his rights or income. However, the written word is another matter. In 1972 *International Times* reported that Zappa had attempted to ban David Walley's *No Commercial Potential* and refused permission to quote lyrics.[5] Zappa's hostility to journalists seemed to extend to anyone who attempted to interpret his work. The preface to *The Real Frank Zappa Book* referred disparagingly to books which 'purport' to be about him.

Copyrights aside, there was also the issue of whether interpretation was a realistic endeavour in the first place. In 1975 Jeremy Prynne told a shocked gathering of undergraduates that any literary critical 'analysis' of the lyrics of Captain Beefheart or Frank Zappa was a vain exercise (though whether this was to do with the blinkers of educational privilege or the minimal cultural value of the material was unclear). Zappa has himself told interviewers that his lyrics are so packed with arcana that he is the only individual capable of understanding what they mean. Den Simms, who edits *Society Pages*, enumerated the difficulties:

> I'd advise you that, given the complex and peculiar nature of Frank's lyrics, with their abundance of bizarre, obscure and arcane 'inside' references, any attempt at a 'literary analysis' is certainly going to be fraught with infinite peril. I think that this would doubly apply for anyone who hasn't been submerged in American culture for several generations ... I would never attempt to do a 'comprehensive' lyric

---

[4] The regular rubric on the 'Subscriberz Adz' page runs: 'SOCIETY PAGES will not print ads for the SALE of unauthorized recordings, or other "bootleg" merchandise. We encourage the FREE EXCHANGE of unauthorized recordings, etc'. *Society Pages* may be contacted at PO Box 395, Deer Park, NY 11729–0395, USA.

[5] *International Times*, No. 140, November 1972, p. 22.

study. The best that one could ever hope to do, without help from the mad professor himself, is to chip away at that formidable obstacle, even having the benefit of being subjected culturally to all (at least most) of the Americanisms. I've been obsessively studying the stuff for two decades, and there's NO WAY that I myself would attempt such a feat . . . misinterpreting obscure lyrics is certain to lead to a great deal of embarrassment.[6]

On the other hand, the explanations Zappa has faxed to Simon Prentis[7] – who has the arduous task of translating Zappa's lyrics into Japanese – indicate a playful, expansive attitude at odds with Den Simms's literalness. The very density of reference becomes an excuse for semantic proliferation: puns and misunderstandings are built into the method itself. Thus the continual transposition of lyrics in live performance and the exploded syntax of *Thing-Fish*. Prentis's 'it takes one to know one' was transformed by Zappa into the Zen-like 'it takes one to no one'.[8] Note Zappa on sausages: 'It's a bit like eating a sausage: you don't know what's in it, you probably shouldn't know what's in there; but if it tastes good, well there you go.'[9] Den Simms's detective work is valuable, but it seems dry and dreary to restrict all commentary to lists of primary ingredients. Alchemical mixtures may be fraudulent, but even a mess is something different from its parts.

Zappa's combination of copyright paranoia and semantic suggestiveness creates a legal minefield. Poodle play was developed independently of Zappa's control. Poststructuralist distaste for criticism that reduces artworks to emanations of some integral personality provided an ideal excuse to avoid direct contact; given the treatment Zappa dished out to the English rock press in the late 1970s (his you-only-do-it-for-the-money cynicism versus their punk idealism), confrontation with Zappa was something any writer of my generation could only dread. However, poodle play's appearance on the horizon of official publication meant that some kind of contact was legally incumbent.

---

[6]Letter to the author, 22 September 1992.

[7]See *Zappa!* (a supplement from the publishers of *Keyboard and Guitar Player*), ed. Don Menn, 1992, pp. 86–7.

[8]Simon Prentis talking to the author, 18 October 1993. Prentis is preparing a *Zappa Companion* that will collate such horse's mouth 'explanations'.

[9]'Way Down in New Zealand: FZ Talks to Gary Steel, 5 December 1990, Part 2, *T'Mershi Duween*, No. 21, September 1991, p. 16.

ZAPPA THE MAN

The first question people asked on hearing that I was writing a book on Zappa was nearly always, 'are you going to talk to him?'[10] This is probably because famous people are hard to get to see (a topic dramatized by documentation of the groupie syndrome throughout Zappa's œuvre). Unlike dancing on stage at the Hammersmith Odeon,[11] presenting *Breeding from Your Poodle*[12] or bringing a 'Dinah-Moe Humm' encore to a halt[13] – activities which impact live performances and hence automatically enter the output macrostructure – confronting Zappa as a person is in many ways poodle play's nemesis: it was always about fomenting the paranoid creativity of Zappa fandom rather than gaining access to the court circle.

On the other hand, as the last line of this letter shows, the chance to make contact – and thus scuttle poodle play's dearest pretensions – was too tempting to pass by.

> 4 August 1993
>
> Dear Gail Zappa
>
> I don't know if you've seen it, but I'm the guy who asked Liz Wells to fax you an illustration from the poodle book. I talked to Dweezil and Ahmet in London last November about the book and how we passed it up on stage (a conversation I wrote up in Dweezil's fanzine Nos. 72 to 75). Spencer of G&S Music suggested I write to you after speaking to you at the Marquee.
>
> I've written a book about Frank Zappa's records – *not* another rock 'biography' (see Michael Gray's recent effort, which I thought was impertinent and stupid). It describes Frank as a radical artist in the tradition of the Marquis de Sade, William Blake and Conlon Nancarrow. I'm aware of Frank's annoyance with books about him that just rip him off. I don't want him to think I'm doing that – I've been a hardcore fan for eighteen years, I even danced on stage at the Hammersmith Odeon to 'The Black Page' (I had 'Out to Lunch' written on my raincoat).
>
> In order to do textual analysis you need to quote lyrics – so I'm writing to ask permission to do that. Out of a total of 196,412 words

---

[10]Don Preston registered weariness with such quizzing by writing a song which anticipates the inevitable: 'What was Zappa really like? Did he fly into a rage? Bet he got high all the time – and did he really shit on the stage?', 'The Eternal Question', 1981, *Vile Foamy Ectoplasm*, 1993, Muffin CDMR003.

[11]'Black Page #2', London, 26 January 1978: See 'We've Got to Get into Something Real', Chapter 7: Läther.

[12]'Pound for a Brown', London, 17 February 1979. See 'Shut Up 'N Play Yer Guitar', Chapter 9: More Guitars.

[13]'Dinah-Moe Humm', Newcastle, 13 February 1979. See 'John Ruskin and Dinah-the-dog', Chapter 5: Bizarre to DiscReet.

in the book, 9,279 are Frank's song lyrics (4.7%), often just a couple of lines or so from a total of 138 different songs. So would you accept 4.7% of my royalties as payment?

Would it be possible to fax me through a quick reply? It'd be a shame if Quartet gave up on the book because I couldn't clear copyright – especially when Barry Miles and Michael Gray get away with publishing such mediocre stuff. The way Frank manages to touch on some of the heaviest art themes of the millennium (there's a chapter on *Apostrophe (')* and *King Lear*) without anyone noticing is simply extraordinary.

My interest in Frank's music got started when I was studying English literature at Cambridge University. Imagine my surprise when I read these lines in William Blake about masturbation and religious hypocrisy [here I quoted Blake[14]]. I instantly thought of 'Evelyn, A Modified Dog'! You must be aware of these kind of strange coincidences around Frank's lyrics. Then there's the resemblance of 'Cheepnis' to Samuel Taylor Coleridge's *Kubla Khan*, and the way 'Stink-Foot' relates to Plato's dialogues about mortality in *The Phaedo* (Fido!). I'm not accusing Frank of plagiarism – it's more that I'm fascinated by how he independently discovers icons of cultural behaviour that have deep historical weight – I've traced poodle continuity back to the seventeenth century!

Rather like Frank's music, responses to it have been 'can you really be serious?' – but I think preposterousness is an underrated quality anyway. I'm not looking for 'endorsement' – there will obviously be things you won't agree with. I'm quite interested by the absurd, paranoid fantasies that so many Zappa fans come up with in interpreting conceptual obscurities.

I'm ready to fly over to LA with the manuscript if you'd like me on hand to answer any questions.

The package included the section '*Apostrophe (')* and *King Lear* from Chapter 5. Gail Zappa's faxed reply, 'We have called you Ben but apparently you're out doing something that is acceptable in public with your poodle(s). Please advise',[15] looked promising. After the traditional Barking Pumpkin delay, Gail telephoned. She told me that she and Frank had found the comparison of *Apostrophe (')* to *King Lear* hilarious – they both laughed and laughed – 'how much of this stuff is there?' she asked. 'How long have you been doing this? Where has it been in print? Why has it taken so long for you to get in touch?' She was so charming – relaxed and amused – I asked if I could bring over the manuscript in person, and the reply was yes.

[14]*Visions of the Daughters of Albion*, 1793, lines 178–86, *The Poetical Works of William Blake*, ed. John Sampson, 1928, p. 91. See 'The cosmic and the banal', Chapter 5: Bizarre to DiscReet.
[15]Gail Zappa, fax to the author, 18 August 1993.

THE FRIDAY NIGHT SOIRÉE

Even in October,[16] California is warm, and driving up the twists and turns of Laurel Canyon Boulevard is like driving in Greece – the road is in a similar state of disrepair, and there's only the polluted air and heavy traffic to inform you that you are not in the Mediterranean. After gazing into the eye of the security camera, I rang the bell. I was let into the house by Mark Holdom, who takes care of Barking Pumpkin business. The music of Edgard Varèse – in a stunning version I was to learn was Frank conducting the Ensemble Modern – was playing from six wall-mounted speakers, sounding deliriously beautiful. Framed on the back wall I spotted the famous letter from the old composer to Frank aged fifteen. Mark introduced me to Gail, who smiled and led me up to the kitchen/living room, where Frank was sitting. He had stopped shaving, his famous moustache lost in a pepper-and-salt beard that makes him look like an Old Testament prophet. He has a soft handshake. In a hoarse and frail voice he told me that he and Gail had so enjoyed my writing, 'because I can't stand the bard . . .', to which Gail made a noise of disagreement (I was to learn that they thrive on divergent views on practically everything). I was introduced to Faithe Raphael from Rhino Records and Spence Chrislu, Zappa's recording engineer. Frank said he would like to make the book a spoken-word project and had Spence time me reading out the first three pages, which clocked in at six minutes – at this rate we were talking about a sixteen-hour release! 'In your ten-day schedule that's not inconceivable,' said Frank, with the kind of deadpan confidence with which he must have presented countless projects to startled record company executives throughout his career. I had noticed him smile at the section heading 'Why Marx, why Freud'. Now his eyes twinkled as he offered to purchase my socialist soul – 'You see, I believe in marketing . . .' He said the spoken-word release should tie in with a college lecture tour.

He was keen that we see Dweezil's new video, hear disc one of *Civilization Phaze III* and check out the 'Al Malkin tapes' – which meant a trip down to the 'listening room'. Dweezil's video was 'Mommy', a heavy-metal-meets-slasher-movie rock promo, with a fast-cut sequence for a dazzling solo in which Frank's

---

[16]My first meeting with Frank took place on Friday, 22 October 1993. Early drafts of this chapter appeared in *The Wire*, February 1994; *Mojo*, March 1994.

portrait from *Sheik Yerbouti* appeared on Dweezil's guitar. *Phaze III* is a gigantic work for Synclavier that uses just about every sound Zappa has ever employed in a dense-packed continuum. Interspersed between dialogue that extends the speculation of *Lumpy Gravy* (ambiently edited using Sonic Solutions software), the music is unrelentingly abstract – on this listening the most ambitious he has undertaken so far. Spence Chrislu's first job for Frank was to provide a 'bible' for the Al Malkin tapes (a catalogue of digital transcriptions of twenty-five cassettes recorded by a school-friend of Warren Cucurullo's during the *Joe's Garage* era). Listening to Malkin's sexual braggadocio was too much for Faithe, who drifted back upstairs saying she thought she preferred Wild Man Fischer. Spence himself treated the material like a technician examining a disgusting centipede at the end of sterilized tweezers. Poodle play has always been fascinated by Zappa's emphasis on social behaviour without redeeming features. Al Malkin's exploits – the desperate attempts of someone 'with a recording contract from Frank Zappa' to get laid – are alternately hilarious and upsetting. I appreciated Faithe's disinterest, but found myself laughing despite my qualms. When a law student on the streets of New York critiques the legal disclaimer that Malkin wants her to sign so her voice can appear on the record, all the issues of copy-right and privacy and decorum – bad games with tape-recorders, playground psychotics – sparkle like a zircon. Malkin's joyful discovery of pus on Cucurullo's penis is so hysterically delivered it is practically music: the dishevelled moment that Zappa loves to dwell on.

It seemed like Frank was not only demonstrating the heights and depths of his art: he was also creating a bizarre social situation. What would Faithe think of me sitting still for such stuff? Does the Zappologist put up with anything? Worse, what kind of status did this give my book? Was I simply another Al Malkin? Back upstairs, we discussed what my book was trying to do. 'It's all entertainment,' said Frank. I tell Frank that despite the astonishing variety of what precedes it on *Civilization Phaze III*, the start of 'N-Lite' describes a new shape in sound, it packs a shock; 'But did you like it?' he asks, unaware that from a writer for *The Wire* there can be no greater praise.

On Friday nights everyone in the house – employees and family – collects together and drinks frozen margheritas (a drink which is like a snowball with a shot of tequila), a tradition started by Dave Dondorf after a particularly crisis-ridden day in the studio. Frank's friends started appearing: Matt Groening and Bobby Plotnik, an old friend of Frank who runs record shops in LA and New York. I was asked to read from the book, and delivered the section on the cover of *Uncle Meat*.[17] When I finished my dissertation on reification, Nazism and teeth Frank simply reached over and shook me by the hand.

Frank and Gail wanted me to read the *Apostrophe (')/King Lear* section,[18] which I did. Matt Groening called it 'demented scholarship'. I followed it with the conflation of Plato's *Phaedo* and Fido the poodle dog.[19] While Frank's feet were being rubbed with tiger balm to alleviate the pain caused by his prostate cancer, I discoursed about the last days of Socrates and the mortality of the soul (when Socrates drank the hemlock as ordered by the court, he first felt his feet go cold, then the coldness rose to his heart). Bobby was visibly moved and told about wanting to cut his hair after splitting up with his wife. Frank smiled as I quoted *Money* in reply: 'hair ain't where it's at'.[20] Bobby went to the record-player and put on some doowop records, including 'Can I Come Over Tonight' by the Velours. The quintuplets of the bass singer allow the falsetto to turn high weaslings into virtuosic curlicues. Ears full of the abstractions of 'N-Lite' had no problem at all in hearing Edgard Varèse in this R&B: the kind of insights you would expect sitting in Frank Zappa's kitchen.

The conversation moved on to the fact that Frank did not read philosophy, and therefore could not have consciously parodied *The Phaedo*. Frank remained enigmatically silent. I countered that artists deal intuitively with words and concepts, do not consciously plot every resonance of the symbols and themes they play with. Frank nodded. Certainly the Fido/*Phaedo* pun – hinted at eight years later (but never actually made) by Jacques Derrida[21] – is a stunning example of what Gail calls Frank's 'prescience'.

> There are many many many examples of things that Frank has said that have happened. Some of them really very inside, just silly references. A perfect example of that is just the title *Chunga's Revenge* – if you look in the artwork, there's the vacuum cleaner dancing around in the studio, a gypsy dancer ... and we didn't know this, but in Spain there's a very

---

[17] See '*Uncle Meat*', Chapter 2: Freakdom and the Hippies.
[18] See '*Apostrophe (')* and *King Lear*', Chapter 5: Bizarre to DiscReet.
[19] See 'Poodles and philosophy', Chapter 5: Bizarre to DiscReet.
[20] See 'Hair', Chapter 5: Bizarre to DiscReet.
[21] Jacques Derrida, *The Post Card from Socrates to Freud and Beyond*, 1980, trs. Alan Bass, 1987.

very famous dancer called La Chunga who does the flamenco dances with the castanets and everything. That's a bizarre example, not of prescience perhaps, but certainly of being in tune with something on a cosmic level – more of that cosmic debris.[22]

Gail's reference to 'Cosmik Debris' serves to remind us of Frank's hostility towards mystical 'explanations'. The materialist explanation, the one put forward by the surrealists and utilized by poodle play, is that form is sedimented content:[23] meditation on the concept of *faith* (central term for Christianity) via the material form of the Latin for 'I believe' – *fido* – pans out to consideration of the domestication of our animal nature (Fido, Faithe Raphael) and to the repression inherent in seeking pie in the sky (*Phaedo*). Plato's philosophy is packed into the very name of the dog.

SATURDAY

The next meeting[24] took place in the living room that adjoins the kitchen. One wall is decorated with a huge mural of fire-breathing dragons. Frank wants me to hear the second disc of *Civilization Phaze III* and we sit together listening for an hour. It goes even further than disc one. 'Beat the Reaper' (a sardonic reference to 'Perrier-breath yuppies who play tennis and think they'll live for ever', rather than Zappa's own personal defiance of mortality) is the climax,[25] truly the dog's bollocks (he laughed at the Anglicism): a little bit of everything and more, Webern tendrils aching out of sideshow sniggers and carnival firecrackers. Throughout the piece, there is a persistent noise like rain guttering down a roof. When it stops, it is as if the shelter we have been in has vanished, and the music has become thunder booming in the skies – truly a surrealist coup. Zappa tells me that the sounds come from a field-recording he made in San Fernando Valley at New Year 1987, 'assholes firing off automatic weapons' (this is Hollywood, where trespassers are met by signs reading 'armed response'). Random gunfire sounding like avant-garde percussion: suddenly the traditional American artistic meditation about the relationship of real

---

[22]Gail Zappa, talking to the author, 27 October 1993.
[23]'The campaign against formalism overlooks the fact that form ... is itself a sedimentation of content', Theodor Adorno, *Aesthetic Theory*, 1970, trs, C. Lenhardt, 1984, p. 209.
[24]Saturday, 23 October 1993.
[25]Although it was performed at the Yellow Shark concert on 22 September 1992, it was missed out from *The Yellow Shark* album – here it is realized on Synclavier.

life to art (something John Cage made his speciality) is coloured by pressing urban issues: private property, violence, politics. Like figuring the tensions of New York in recording circuitry on the cover of *Zappa in New York*, the sinister idea that art and reality have mysteriously exchanged places once again blooms. Is this experience life or art? You decide.

He asks for more of the book, and I read to him about *Zoot Allures*.[26] If he falls asleep while I read I'm not to be offended; the painkillers make him sleepy. I quote him Johnny 'Guitar' Watson on 'stressify' ('Ha. "Stressify" – and that's what I like about our native language.' Well in Johnny's case he uses the low E to make the talking guitar effects – you know, famous for making the guitar say 'you son-of-a-bitch!'). Zappa asks me if I play guitar; I tell him no.

> As you're not a musician, you won't realize this, but for guitarists, and electric guitarists especially, *tone* is so important. If you can get the right tone, you know your solo is going to go great whatever the notes. It's something spiritual, to do with the way the fingers respond to what the ear is hearing, a continual refinement and adjustment.[27]

He is describing the germ idea of 'Friendly Little Finger'. Earlier, he told a nephew he'd given a drum to, 'Don't hit the drum dead-centre – worry about *tone*, speed will come later.'

The humility of the man is hard to credit. Someone capable of such monstrous creativity is surely entitled to a modicum of arrogance: 'Ben,' he says, 'I'm so flattered that you would spend all this time to write a book on me . . .' When I take him up on this the next day, and say that it is logical for a critic to spend time writing about the greatest artist of the late twentieth century, he distances himself from such plaudits: 'That's *your* perception!'

We discuss Stravinsky and Webern. The box set of the complete Stravinsky had been sitting on the kitchen table when I first visited, and now it is in the living room. Gail pointed at it as she said:

> When I first met Frank we used to listen to records all the time, classical records, and now here we are again, listening to classical records all the time – we haven't done that for twenty-five years in between, it's very interesting.[28]

Frank talks about how few people can stand to listen to modern

---

[26]See 'Lyres, mortality, repression of the body' and 'Ulysses, twangs, death', Chapter 6: Guitars.
[27]Frank Zappa, talking to the author, 23 October 1993.
[28]Gail Zappa, talking to the author, 27 October 1993.

music. I tell him that I find fellow enthusiasts – people who mind about music outside commercial limits – in the field of free improvisation. I play him the latest Incus release, which features Derek Bailey on guitar and John Stevens on drums.[29] He asks me to take it off after two minutes: 'Not because I don't like it. It sounds to me like the music I wrote for *Lumpy Gravy* . . . improvised by me with a guitar in one hand and playing drums with the other.'[30]

As expected, he does not warm to an exposition of Bailey's anti-composer ideology. To him, musicians do not know what to play unless directed by a composer. I explain that in Europe, without the strong traditions of jazz and blues, free improvisers are fighting a whole system that denigrates improvisation as opposed to composition, active musicianship as opposed to conceptual thought. He immediately sees the connection to money: 'But that's about funding – why should *they* get this money and I don't – and it's so reactionary, just reacting against the situation and taking the opposite point of view.'[31]

Zappa and Bailey represent two sharply opposed poles: what is important is that all the significant movers in modern music pursue a dialectic best illuminated by such extremes.

> Extremism in art is a corollary of artistic technology; hence it is more than an expression of a rebellious attitude.[32]

> Objectively, art is intolerant not only of middling kinds of works, but also of a socially accepted pluralist norm where, to the delight of idealogues, different artistic spheres seem to coexist peacefully.[33]

Each time musicians consider the relative merits of recording and performance, composition and improvisation, they make social choices. The value of Zappa and Bailey (like Stravinsky and Schoenberg as theorized by Adorno[34]), is that the uncompromising pursuit of a particular method (one aiming at composerly realization, the other at improvising spontaneity) provides, for those who see the merits of both, a guide to the social significance of

---

[29]Derek Bailey/John Stevens, 1993, Incus CD14. Incus recordings are available from 14 Downs Road, London E5 8DS, England.
[30]Frank Zappa, talking to the author, 23 October 1993.
[31]Ibid.
[32]Theodor Adorno, *Aesthetic Theory*, 1968, trs. C. Lenhardt, 1984, p. 51.
[33]Ibid., p. 432.
[34]Theodor Adorno, *The Philosophy of Modern Music*, 1948, trs. Anne Mitchell and Wesley Blomster, 1973.

adopting such practices. All modern music worth its salt can be caught between these two arc-lights.

TUESDAY

On Tuesday, I tell Frank he is so good at answering nerdy journalist's questions that I have prepared twenty I would like him to answer. He tells me to get the tape-recorder running and fire away.

OTL: This relates to a point you were making about your musicians. It's rare that any musicians who've worked with you do any better when they're out on their own. If your musicians solo they do so at the peak of their intensity – how do you stop them coasting? Is it a matter of giving them instructions, or just the challenge of the musical environment they're given?

FZ: I don't understand the question.

OTL: It's because I'm reading it out without communicating it to you. Sorry. Your musicians always play – it seems to me – at the peak of what they're capable of doing. One of the things I really like about your records is that if there's a solo people don't noodle, they don't coast – they really play hard.

FZ: Yeah.

OTL: Is that because of what you tell them before they play? Or is it simply the challenge of the music?

FZ: The reason is that I tell them before they play and because all the live stuff is edited, so I look for the best work that each musician can do. It's not just a matter of kloodging something together, I try and make the performance of each tune exemplary in some way. So I'm not just optimizing what I write, I'm optimizing what they improvise.

OTL: I was thinking about seeing you at Hammersmith and watching Eddie Jobson play violin.

FZ: Yah.

OTL: He's free to play what he likes when he goes off on his solo.

FZ: Yeah, well, that's the way it is with all the guys. They know what key they're supposed to be in – they know what *kind* of a solo it's supposed to be and they know roughly how long it is they're supposed to play. So after that it's them, not me.

OTL: I've seen you many times, but your musicians never play that kind of up and down the fretboard fusion thing, that boring thing fusion players so often do.

FZ: You mean in my playing?

OTL: Not just yours – anybody in your band.

FZ: Well, they know the other guys are listening. It's a strong incentive to do a good job – it's a pretty critical audience up there on the bandstand, let alone who's out there in the seats. If you're playing shit, the other guys on the stage are certainly going to let you know about it.

OTL: People find the mixture of signals in your music – cerebral abstractions one minute, shocking moments of human dishevelment the next – people find this very confusing . . .

FZ: Why?

OTL: . . . Do you have any advice?

FZ: Well, that's the universe – it's the way the universe is.

OTL: How do you place the score in your work? Is it just a means to an end? In other words, is the art in the score or is it in the mastertape?

FZ: Well, there wouldn't even be a score if what was being requested of the musicians wasn't too complicated for me to hum it to 'em. In the most instances, for the rock 'n' roll stuff I find I get the best results if they're playing this stuff they've memorized rather than stuff they're reading. The point where the piece goes into muscle memory, you can then conduct it, do things with it that are impossible when they're reading [*Lights Marlboro*]. So – the final artistic result is the mastertape.

OTL: You've made me think harder about the relationship of art to life than any other artist. Do you have a formula to guide you?

FZ: Relationship of art to life? Well, I told you before, what I'm doing is entertainment. Choose between an entertaining life or the other kind – or the 'art' life. The answer becomes obvious.

OTL: Even though the music industry has done the most it can to suppress you, are you aware that it needs contrary figures in order to keep people interested in the product?

FZ: They don't care, they don't care.

OTL: It's as simple as that?

FZ: Yah.

OTL: Why have you chosen to talk to *Rolling Stone*?

FZ: Because after all these years, they have gotten so desperate about having me be interviewed, because I've complained so many times about what piece of shit kind of publication it is and I've got a new distribution deal and a new album coming out – I thought that it would probably be as good a time as any to do it if I'm ever gonna do it.

OTL: Why is James Joyce on the list of names on *Freak Out!*?

FZ: Well, I can't say that I've ever read anything by Joyce all the way through, but the few pages I looked at, I saw it and said, Now there's a real guy. It doesn't take much to have an influence on me.

OTL: There are signs that literary and academic people are at last coming round to appreciate the monstrous creativity of your œuvre. I think I can see signs of a Zappa industry in academia that one day might rival the Joyce industry.

FZ: [*Laughs*]

OTL: Do you have a message for such people?

FZ: Get a real estate licence.

OTL: Why did Spence Chrislu spend weeks editing the Al Malkin tapes?

FZ: He didn't edit them.

OTL: Catalogue them, sorry.

FZ: What he did was transfer them from normal cassette to digital cassette, he equalized them and catalogued them – so at a later date I can make a 'thing' out of it, and it's easier to 'make the thing' if it's a piece of tape with code on it ... That way you can find the line you're looking for.

OTL: I don't know if you want this known or talked about, but there was a letter from Terry Gilliam being passed around on Friday night – I was wondering if you'd like to say anything ...

FZ: Talk about being flattered!

OTL: Did you ever watch *Monty Python* or see *Brazil*?

FZ: Yes – *Brazil*'s my favourite movie.

OTL: It's one of mine, definitely. I always liked his things in *Monty Python* more than the sketches – his graphics.

FZ: Yah. He's so funny it's hard to imagine he's an American.

OTL: What kind of project is it?

FZ: Well I wrote a screenplay and I was looking for someone to direct it. I've been working on it for years.

OTL: This is a question from a friend of mine, Johnny Black, who's just written a long article about the Fugs and he wanted to know, Did they come and see you at the Garrick Theater?

FZ: I think we knew them from when they were playing in San Francisco. I don't know whether they came to the Garrick – we were both working there at the same time. They were working every night and we were working every night, so ...

OTL: What did you think of them?

FZ: Well, I thought it was a proper piece of entertainment for the time.

OTL: When I interviewed Dweezil and Ahmet they did a big routine about Lou Reed, attacking him. It was really funny. I sensed the rivalry going way back to the time of Tom Wilson and Verve and all the rest of it.

FZ: There wasn't any rivalry. I only met him once or twice back then.

OTL: When I talk to Velvet Underground fans I play them 'Venus in Furs' by Lou Reed followed by 'Penguin in Bondage' and I say, 'Venus in Furs' is just a list of sadomasochistic clichés everyone knows, while 'Penguin in Bondage' is something strange.

FZ: Huh-ha-ha. Yes, it is.

OTL: I find it pungent and practically hallucinogenic.

FZ: Huh-ha.

OTL: Is the point that you've experienced more than other people, or just that you care to write about experiences that a lot of people might have but not think to write songs about?

FZ: I don't know what the statistics are on the number of people who have experienced anything resembling 'Penguin in Bondage', but I just happen to choose song topics previously uncovered by other journalists, y'know – dental floss, stuff like that.

OTL: Do you think the way that women are attracted to famous musicians gives those musicians a special attitude? Isn't it strange that so much information given to young people about sex comes from men in a very favoured position?

FZ: I think so, I think that's true. There's always been a tradition of didactic blues artists – there's plenty of advice on how to treat your woman, what to do if she treats you bad, how to get one – these are common blues lyric topics.

OTL: Hmm. That assumes that the audience is male.

FZ: I think for most blues it's true. There's not too many female blues fans.

OTL: Does everyone have interesting dreams?

FZ: I don't know. I suppose to themselves they do. If you've ever had somebody tell you one of their dreams, it's usually presented in a way that now you're being given the opportunity to hear the most spectacular far-out fucking thing that anybody ever dreamed up – they're all very proud of their dreams even if what you're hearing is miserable.

OTL: Did you ever hear the expression '*Jeder Mann sein eigener Fussball*'?

FZ: No, never heard it.

OTL: It means, Everyone their own football.

FZ: [*Laughs*]

OTL: It was the name of a dada magazine that became a universal catch-phrase during the working-class revolts in Berlin at the end of the First World War.

FZ: You know, that was what was great about the 1920s, the way you could combine the concept of working class with dada. God, they don't know what they missed in those days.

OTL: The dadaists went on an anti-militarist procession through the working-class districts and got applauded by everyone. It was considered wild.

FZ: I've always appreciated dada and I keep trying to get Ahmet to read about it, because that's him in the flesh, he's a genetic carrier of that particular gene that has been pretty much bred out of the species. It's like Stravinsky says, It's not enough to want, you have to be. There are people that wish they were dada but they'll never make it. He doesn't even know what it means, but he exudes it.

OTL: What's your favourite colour?

FZ: It used to be Naples yellow, but I think purple.

OTL: I think a lot of people will be really surprised by purple ... Hendrix, Prince ... for what it means.

FZ: Well, it's a combination of red and blue, isn't it.

OTL: What would you do with radio?

FZ: Hmm. Bring back live dramas. There's no live drama on the radio in the US – I know there's still bits and pieces in Europe, maybe in the Far East, but it's a type of theatre that I really used to enjoy when I was a kid because it frees your imagination, and if there's one thing the US needs, it's a little bit of freedom.

OTL: The next question will need a bit of explanation. I don't know if you heard, but the British National Party – the Nazis – won an election in the Isle of Dogs recently. It is a very poor district of London which is near the Canary Wharf development. You've got this massive, prestigious office development, and then next to it these terrible slums and the BNP went round and said, Get the Bengalis out and improve your housing. It was like a protest vote. A lot of people have – since finding out who they were voting for – said they regret it, but they just managed to elect a councillor, which is the first time a fascist has been elected in Britain since the 70s. I was part of a big demonstration last Saturday calling for their headquarters to be closed down, which was hair-raising because it was attacked by the police. It wasn't the fascists we were frightened of – it was like science fiction, police with masks and shields and batons. There were about 60,000 of us, it was a good turn out for the anti-fascists and the anti-racists. The question was simply, Would you join the Anti-Nazi League?

FZ: No. I won't join anything. It's not that I like Nazis – I really hate them. I don't join shit.

OTL: It's just that in England, with the position in Europe – Le Pen in France and so on – the Nazis have grown very big. The idea is that everyone who hates the Nazis joins together and says, Not in England. That's why I'm a member of it.

FZ: Yeah. Well, I'd probably have to think twice about that if I thought that me joining would have any impact at all, but I'm pretty sure that it wouldn't, because you have to remember why those guys are in there in the first place – first of all it's a protest vote, and secondly no one knows who or what they're voting for. So, it could happen anytime anyplace.

OTL: I noticed certain 'new age' sounds in the music that preceded 'Beat the Reaper' on disc two of *Civilization Phaze III* – surely you're joking?

FZ: What's a 'new age' sound?

OTL: Sounds I associate with new-age music – shakuhachi or some kind of flute . . .

FZ: Mmm. [*Affirmative grunt*]

OTL: . . . and the throat-singing – quite atmospheric sounds. I was quite surprised to hear you use them. Normally . . .

FZ: Normally in new-age material there is no hint of dissonance, so no matter what you're orchestrating it with, the fact that you're not dealing with lush triads would set it apart anyway. The only thing it has in common with new age music is that the chords are held a very long time, but you couldn't go out and get a new age record contract with that tune, because there's too much going on in it.

OTL: Yeah – here's a . . . yes, I'll dare ask it: Was it necessary to be quite so cruel to Jumbo?

FZ: Why?

OTL: It's the only song of yours that really upsets me – because you talk about hitting her.

FZ: Well I'm not the one who's gonna hit her. That's a true story.

OTL: That's the reply I use for a lot of your songs to my friends. I say, This is documentary of people's behaviour.

FZ: Guy's name is Denny Walley, it happened.

OTL: Now, you can ... you will correct me if this is wrong ... but I sense a kind of underclass anger in your whole philosophy and music, a hatred of privilege, all the way from *Freak Out!* to *Thing-Fish*. What are the time-bombs you've concealed in *The Yellow Shark* ...

FZ: Ha.

OTL ... because *The Yellow Shark* looks like a very respectable thing.

FZ: Have you heard it?

OTL: Yes.

FZ: Well, 'Food Gathering in Post-Industrial America' ... 'Welcome to the United States' ...

OTL: It was funny for me when I came to read the immigration form on the airplane because I only knew it from *The Yellow Shark* – all I could hear was your music as I was looking at this piece of bureaucracy ...

FZ: It's bizarre. Here you have all these Middle Eastern terrorists just flying in and blowing up the World Trade Center, and you have all that bureaucracy dealing with that form to find out if you're a Nazi. It's like, if you fill it out properly, what happens – you get a job in the cabinet?

OTL: You always say you hate the rock press, but you're always such good copy. You won't collude with the basis of a question, you always say something that blows up the area from where the question's coming from.

FZ: The problem with doing a rock interview in the first place is that the person coming to talk to you (a) doesn't know anything about what you do, (b) doesn't know about music in general and (c) has already made up his mind in advance before he comes to you what the answer ought to be to his precious little question. There's no reason to collude. I'm not there to make his life miserable, but you know, by the same token, if you want facts I'll give them to you – you want something else, go someplace else. I still think it's one of the smartest things I ever said: 'Rock journalism is people who can't write interviewing people who can't talk in order to provide articles for people who can't read'.

OTL: I've always loved that one ... I also love another one, I think you said it round the same time: 'Some rock musicians make a bunch of money and stick it up their noses – I stick mine in my ear.'[35]

FZ: Yes, millions of dollars worth.

'Interview' over, Zappa returned with barely a pause to the matter in hand.

[35]Quoted by Hugh Fielder, 'Zappa', *Sounds*, 9 September 1978, p. 28.

FZ: Wanna read to me?

OTL: Sure. [*Fetches MS.*] I'm still waiting for the bit where you find the unacceptable thing that makes you want to stop the whole project...

FZ: You think there's something in there like that?

OTL: You never know. It's vaguely chronological, so if there's a record you'd be interested in I could dive in there...

FZ: [*Without hesitation*] Thing-Fish.

OTL: Right. [*Flips through MS.*]

FZ: I think that's a major work.

OTL: So do I... though it took me some time to come round to that opinion.

FZ: Well, you know it's like Tolkien.

OTL: [*Horrified*] Like Tolkien?

FZ: Yeah, to invent a whole language – Thing-Fish's dialogue doesn't grow on trees. Nobody of any species really talks that way.

OTL: Yeah. Yeah.

FZ: It's not as good as Tolkien, but...

OTL: Ah, come on – it's much better than Tolkien! Maybe I'm a bit too close to Tolkien, that literary tradition, it doesn't excite me.

FZ: He suffered a lot – who's that bastard who used to attack him all the time? He went to that private club and there used to be this one guy who'd be drunk all the time and lay on the couch, just ridicule and shit?

OTL: I don't know. I was helped a lot with *Thing-Fish* by this article which appeared in this Canadian magazine. [*Shows FZ Rampike*[36]] It's this weird shape. He reproduces the very type of every bit that he quotes – it's only a few pages – but...

FZ: Uh-huh.

OTL: ... it's like a collage and it's written by a guy called jwcurry, he runs a poetry bookshop in Toronto and he's interested in concrete poetry so he's always interested in the actual font used...

FZ: Yah.

OTL: ... the heaviness of the paper. It was the way he looked at *Thing-Fish* that really helped me see things about it, because he took it very literally.

[*OTL starts reading about* Thing-Fish[37] '... pricking an extremely unpleasant boil – which Broadway does indeed represent...' gets an appreciative 'ha-hmm'. Then, responding to the idea that the story of the moral corruption of a young couple came from the Rocky Horror Show:*]

FZ: You know I've never seen, heard or read *Rocky Horror*.

[*Then, responding to the comparison between Rhonda's use of her fountain pen and* The Sound of Music:*]

FZ: I've never seen *The Sound of Music* either.

---

[36]jwcurry, 'Grammatical Sabotage: Conversing with Frank Zappa's *THING-FISH*', *Rampike*, Vol. 7, No. 2, 1992, pp. 72–7.

[37]See '*Thing-Fish*', Chapter 10: Orchestras and Broadway.

OTL: It's this extraordinary way you pick on powerful things that reflect elsewhere.

[*After hearing Zappa quote from jwcurry's article, the section where he speaks live on stage about* 'cruel disregard':[38]]

FZ: Well, that's brilliant – I don't even remember saying that.

OTL: It's on a bootleg called *Show & Tell*, I don't have any date or anything for it.

[*After hearing the quote from Matt Groening* – 'not to suffer, but to offer *your scorn and ridicule'* – FZ *does an appreciative* 'ha-hmm'. OTL *reads the analysis of* 'Clowns on Velvet', *but breaks off on* '... gives a bell-boy an enema'.]

OTL: If I do a college lecture tour, it's going to be so absurd with me getting up and talking about this kind of stuff.

FZ: Well, since most people won't know what you're talking about, yes. But it sounds so grand with the English accent and all . . .

POODLE PLAY AND MISTER FRANK ZAPPA

I was secretly relieved when Zappa told me he could not bear to hear any more and that he would like me to spend the rest of my time in LA recording with Spence Chrislu (because of their more practical length, we decided to use the original poodle-play essays). Reading out the book had been taxing on us both. Frank pointed out that whenever I quoted Theodor Adorno he lost the thread. I replied that that was inevitable, since he did not come from a Hegelian-Marxist philosophical tradition: 'I've never read any philosophy at all,' he commented. When I compared my work to 'translation' – translating Zappa's art into a theoretical language – he agreed, and said the process was 'valid' (perhaps his experiences with Simon Prentis and his questions about precise meaning for producing Japanese lyric-sheets had mollified his hostility towards interpreters).

Some of Zappa's turns – the short hair of the 80s as he disputed with the PMRC on television chat shows, the suit-and-tie image for *Jazz from Hell* and *The Real Frank Zappa Book*, the 'respectability' of the involvement with the Ensemble Modern – have alienated fans, and there have been hints from some quarters that his welcoming attitude towards poodle play betrayed a similarly 'upwardly-mobile' attitude. However, someone keen to gain establishment approval does not direct his passport to respectability to hear material like the Al Malkin tapes (evincing precisely the

---

[38]Ibid.

'crass taste for smut' denounced by Michael Gray in the *Daily Telegraph*[39]). In fact, I would argue that it was Zappa's delight in *incongruity* and *preposterousness* that provided the bridge across to poodle play – across generations, educational backgrounds and politics. Later on, Gail came over with a message from Frank: he was tired and ill, listening was a strain – but he had not developed an aversion to my writing and he did not want me to draw that conclusion.

It is the dream of the critic to be approved of by the artist. Despite the warm reception – Frank actually called me a 'genius or something' at the Friday soirée – I had to recognize that we talk different languages, operate on different lines. A telling moment came when I defended Ice T from accusations of 'negative attitude' (though Frank conceded that Ice T was, contrary to received opinion, articulate and intelligent). How much in common can an SWP member have with a millionaire rock star in Laurel Canyon? How much in common can any pop-music consumer have with their idol? To the Big Note, poodle play is probably just another Al Malkin tape, 'stimulating digital audio entertainment for those of you who have outgrown *the ordinary*'.[40] Looking around at the cultural functionaries who assure us of their moral worth and ethical valour – whilst serving themselves liberally from the national economic stewpot – I am not sure that 'entertainment' status is really so reprehensible.

DEATH AND OBITUARY

Frank Zappa succumbed to cancer on Saturday, 4 December, and was buried at a private family funeral the next day. His death was announced to the press on Monday, causing a gratifying amount of obituary space in the dailies as various columnists sought to claim him for their own. Writing in the *Guardian*, Adam Sweeting declared that in his lifetime Zappa 'railed against America's corporate complacency and political lurch to the right and deplored racism and homophobia',[41] while *The Times* claimed that the songs 'He's So Gay' and 'Jewish Princess' 'had their respective pressure

---

[39] Michael Gray, 'The Double Life of Frank Zappa', *Daily Telegraph*, 18 September 1992, p. 16.
[40] From the Warning/Guarantee sticker on the cover of Frank Zappa, *Meets the Mothers of Prevention*, 1985.
[41] Adam Sweeting, 'Rock Irony from a Master Prankster', *Guardian*, 7 December 1993.

groups apoplectic with rage'.[42] Some mentioned his run-ins with the evangelical right and the fundamentalists over censorship, while *The Times* applauded his hatred for the 'half-baked and second-rate' culture of rock and his belief in private enterprise.[43]

However, simply to concentrate on his explicit political pronouncements (a failing of too much politically concerned 'analysis' of pop music) ignores the formal achievement of his music. He showed that 'resistant' or 'critical' culture is not the preserve of highbrow forms like theatre and novels; for him, blatant commercialism and vulgarity could become critiques of privilege. As demonstrated by the saga of Wilhelm Reich, radical ideas can go seriously awry in the reactionary climate of the States. Zappa's commitment to capitalism sat oddly with the rest of his surrealist principles (rabid opposition to mysticism, the church and the military). On the other hand, if Zappa hadn't built a cottage industry around his music, it's unlikely that he could have produced his monstrous, fifty-seven-album discography.[44] As with Duke Ellington, a certain business-mindedness is a requirement for producing a substantial body of music under a capitalist system.

In working with stadium-scale rock, Zappa managed to make enough money to finance abstract music which most avant-garde composers – either hopelessly underfunded, or constrained by the artistic expectations of respectable funding bodies – can only dream of. At a time when 'postmodernism' provides an ideology for compositional timidity, reinforcing the idea of classical music as a holiday from the challenge of modern life, he pioneered new rhythms and an utterly distinctive attitude towards harmony. Rooted in West Coast R&B, he showed that a defiant subcultural attitude could take on all the heroes of highbrow classical music and win. The release of *Civilization Phaze III* will force the classical world to admit, that, actually, someone in rock did it better. Not just a consistent irritant to moralists in any guise, Frank Zappa is a hero for anyone who thinks that the class system, along with its high/low cultural divide, is something that needs dismantling.

---

[42]Anonymous, 'Frank Zappa', *The Times*, 7 December 1993.
[43]Ibid.
[44]Though it looks as if Eugene Chadbourne, fusing Baileyite principles of spontaneity with the singing-hobo socialism of Woody Guthrie, might be pursuing an alternative path to discographical monumentality. Catalogue from 707 Longview Drive, Greensboro, NC 27403–2018, USA.

APPENDIX: A DISCOGRAPHY FOR NON-FETISHISTS

ALBUM	RELEASE DATE
FREAK OUT! (2)	Jul–66
ABSOLUTELY FREE	Apr–67
LUMPY GRAVY	Dec–67
WE'RE ONLY IN IT FOR THE MONEY	Sep–68
CRUISING WITH RUBEN & THE JETS	Nov–68
UNCLE MEAT (2)	Mar–69
MOTHERMANIA (BEST OF)	Apr–69
HOT RATS	15–Oct–69
BURNT WEENY SANDWICH	9–Feb–70
WEASELS RIPPED MY FLESH	Aug–70
CHUNGA'S REVENGE	23–Oct–70
FILLMORE EAST JUNE 1971	Aug–71
200 MOTELS (2)	Oct–71
JUST ANOTHER BAND FROM LA	Mar–72
HOT RATS: WAKA/JAWAKA	May–72
THE GRAND WAZOO	Nov–72
OVER-NITE SENSATION	7–Sep–73
APOSTROPHE (')	22–Mar–74
ROXY & ELSEWHERE (2)	10–Sep–74
ONE SIZE FITS ALL	25–Jun–75
BONGO FURY	2–Oct–75
ZOOT ALLURES	29–Oct–76
ZAPPA IN NEW YORK (2)	13–Mar–78
STUDIO TAN	15–Sep–78
SLEEP DIRT	12–Jan–79
SHEIK YERBOUTI (2)	3–Mar–79
ORCHESTRAL FAVORITES	4–May–79

JOE'S GARAGE ACT I 17–Sep–79
JOE'S GARAGE ACTS II & III (2) 19–Nov–79
TINSEL TOWN REBELLION (2) 11–May–81
SHUT UP 'N PLAY YER GUITAR (3) 11–May–81
YOU ARE WHAT YOU IS (2) Sep–81
SHIP ARRIVING TOO LATE TO SAVE A
 DROWNING WITCH May–82
THE MAN FROM UTOPIA Mar–83
BABY SNAKES Mar–83
LONDON SYMPHONY ORCHESTRA
 VOL.I 9–Jun–83
THE PERFECT STRANGER 23–Aug–84
THEM OR US (2) 18–Oct–84
THING-FISH (3) 21–Nov–84
FRANCESCO ZAPPA 21–Nov–84
THE OLD MASTERS BOX ONE (7) 19–Apr–85
MEETS THE MOTHERS OF PREVENTION 21–Nov–85
DOES HUMOR BELONG IN MUSIC? 27–Jan–86
THE OLD MASTERS BOX TWO (9) 25–Nov–86
JAZZ FROM HELL 15–Nov–86
LONDON SYMPHONY ORCHESTRA
 VOL.II 17–Sep–87
THE OLD MASTERS BOX THREE (9) 30–Dec–87
GUITAR (2) Apr–88
YOU CAN'T DO THAT ON STAGE
 ANYMORE VOL.1 (2) Apr–88
YOU CAN'T DO THAT ON STAGE
 ANYMORE VOL.2 (2) Sep–88
BROADWAY THE HARD WAY Nov–88
YOU CAN'T DO THAT ON STAGE
 ANYMORE VOL.3 (2) Oct–89
THE BEST BAND YOU NEVER HEARD IN
 YOUR LIFE (2) Apr–91
YOU CAN'T DO THAT ON STAGE
 ANYMORE VOL.4 (2) Jun–91
MAKE A JAZZ NOISE HERE (2) Jun–91
BEAT THE BOOTS (10) Jul–91
 AS AN AM ZAPPA 31–Oct–81
 THE ARK:MOTHERSOFINVENTION Jul–68
 FREAKS & MOTHERFU*%!!@# 5–Nov–70
 UNMITIGATED AUDACITY 12–May–74

555

Note: From 1988 onwards, numbers in brackets refer to multi-disc CDs rather than multi-disc vinyl albums. *Beat the Boots* dates refer to concert dates, not date of release. Those having difficulty obtaining material should contact: Zappa Records, Box 5265, North Hollywood, CA 91616, United States or G&S Music, 7 Ullswater Road, Leverstock Green, Hemel Hempstead, Herts HP3 8RD, England.

INDEX

NB: Figures in bold indicate the main entry for any topic.

bouzouki, 169, 359, 414
Bow Wow Wow, 50, 179, 231
Bowie, David, 278, 352, 454, 479
Bozzio, Dale, 67, 364, 366, 369, 527n
Bozzio, Terry, **286**, 288, 293, 294, 300, 309, 317, 320, 329, 339, 340, 341, 346, 347, 356, 358, 364, 408, 414, 476, 479, 508; adolescent uncertainty and 'Punky's Whips', 336–337; male bonding and 'Hands with a Hammer', 486; music-student hysteria and 'The Black Page', 334; diabolical pickles and 'Titties & Beer', 339–341; punk and 'I'm So Cute', 357
Bragg, Billy, xxix
Brainiac, The, 287
Braund, Simon, 288n
Braxton, Anthony, 66n, 304, 328, 329, 368, 427
Brazil, 546
Brecht, Bertolt, 57, 84, 130, 187, 355
Brecker, Michael, 337, 489, 499, 502, 506
Brecker, Randy, 337, 489, 502
Breeding from Your Poodle, **409–410**, 536
Brenna, Michael, 205n, 309n, 390n
Breton, André, xv
Breuker, Willem, 69, 427
Brevitz, Marshall, 196
Brewer, Don, 328, 346
Brian Lord & the Midnighters, 20
Bridge, Vanessa, ix
'Briefcase Boogie', 446
'Bringing in the Sheaves', 304
Brittini, 219
Broadside, the, 31
Broadway the Hard Way, 117, 503, **509–519**, 530, 555; cover, 509–510
broccoli, 499
Brock, Napoleon Murphy, 149, 176, **242**, 260, 264, 288, 294, 433, 447n, 451, 476, 481, 482, 485, 486, 491, 502
'Broken Hearts are for Assholes', 313, 315, 321, 354, 356
'Brown Moses', 446, 447n, 488

'Brown Shoes Don't Make It', 81, 82, **84**, 131, 194, 229–230, 380, 388
Brown, Arthur, 104, 191
Brown, Charles, 42
Brown, Clarence 'Gatemouth', 10
Brown, James, xxv, 7, 27, 482
Brown, Norman O., 73, 255
Brown, Paul, ix, xin
Browning, Tod, 13
Bruce, Jack, 149, 253
Bruce, Lenny, 35–6, **152–153**, 305, 487
Bruister, La Marr, 149
Bruitism, 6
Brylcream, xxiii
Brzeska, Gaudier, 261
BTO's, the, 151
Buckley, Lord (Richard), **69–70**, 102, 153
Buckley, Tim, 156
Buff, Paul, 18, 22, 25
'Bug, The', 13
'Building a Girl', 482
Burgen, Kenny, 16
Burnett, Chester – see Howlin' Wolf
Burnt Weeny Sandwich, 9, 97, 130, **168–170**, 371, 372, 526; cover, 168–9, 200
Burrage, Ronnie, 309
Burroughs, William, 23, 46, 72, 115, 127, 205, 317, 326, 366, 515
BUSSTOP, 517n
Butcher, Pauline, 121
Buttgereit, Jorg, 57
Buxton, Eric, 254
'Bwana Dik', 96, **189**
Byers, Bill, 200, 202
BYG label, 489
Byrds, the, 112, 178
Byrne, David, xxx

Cabbala, the, 95, 270
Cadillac Distribution, 42n
Cadillac Extravaganza, 453
Cage, John, xix, xvii, 47, 493, 304, 314, 456, 528, 542, 366
Calder, Alexander, 174, 527n, 528
Califia, Pat, 234, 282, 382

'Call Any Vegetable', 51, **82**, 180, 193, 236, 281, 522
Callinicos, Alex, xiiin
Calvi, Roberto, 137n
'Calvin' – see 'For Calvin (and his Next Two Hitch-hikers)'
'Camarillo Brillo', **220–222**, 223, 235, 260, 266, 286, 373, 498
Cambridge Rapist, 321
Campbell, Beatrix, 52
Campbell, Nicky, 531
Camper Van Beethoven, 305n
Can, 492
'Can I Come Over Tonight', 123, 540
'Canard du Jour', 414–415
'Canarsie', 376, **413–414**, 478
Canary Wharf, 548
Canterbury Rock, 210, 215n
Cantor's delicatessen, 34
Capital, 81, 222
Capitol label, 19, 20, 95
Caprimulgus, 331
Captain Beefheart – see Beefheart, Captain
Captain Beefheart vs. the Grunt People, 28, 437
Captain Glasspack and the Magic Mufflers, 31
Caraeff, Ed, 156
'Caravan', 530
Cardew, Cornelius, 104n, 334
Caretto, Jorge, ix
Carey, Timothy, 17
Carisi, John, 162, 432
Carman, Paul, 502, 506
Carmen, 51, 182, 388, 506
Carmina Burana, 465
'Carol, You Fool', 485
'Carolina Hardcore Ecstasy', **288–289**, 293, 491, 512
Carr, Wynona, 318
Carrie, 71
Carter, Elliott, 314, 317, 427
Carter, John, 77
Case, Brian, 360
Cash, Johnny, 148, 260, 502
Casswell, Rex, 480n

castration, 251–252, 260–261, 357, 409, 454
Castro, Fidel, xxii
'Catholic Girls', 365, 360, 499
Caygill, Matthew, ix, xivn, 382n
CBS label, 351, 410
censorship, 115–116, 467, 496–497
Central Scrutinizer, the, 116, 187, 291, 366, 373, 499
Ceraeff, Al, 22
Cerveris, Don, 15
Chadbourne, Eugene, 77, 305n, 553n
Chaffee Junior College, 15, 16
'Chalk Pie', 419–420
Chambers, Dennis, 294
Chambers, Joe, 59, 60
Chambers, Paul, 126
Chambers, Steve, 60n
'Chana in De Bushwop', 485
Chandler, Raymond, 259, 517
Chandrasekhar, Vinksu, ix
Channels, the, 448
Chantays, the, 339n
Chapman, Tracy, 52
Charing Cross, 266
'Charles Ives', 155, 172, 492
'Charlie's Enormous Mouth', **391**, 486n
'Charva', 12
'Chatanooga Choo Choo, The', 479
Cheech and Chong, 78
'Cheepnis', xi, 182, 259, **262–4**, 384, 481, 483, 537
Cheka, Mark, 36
Cher, xxxiii, 158
Cherry, Don, 296
'Cheryl's Canon', 26
Chess label, 42
Chester Music, 457n
Chevalier, Dominique, 17, 127n, 183n, 336n, 474
Chieftains, the, 316, 530
Childs, Andy, 21n, 63n, 136n, 169n
'China Girl', 454
Chinmoy, Guru Sri, 242, 364
'Chocolate Halvah', 492
Chopin, Frédéric François, 513
Chrislu, Spence, 538, 551, 545–546

577

200, 202, 202–203, 205, 207, 348, 483

'Marriage of Faustus and Helen, The', xin

Mars, Tommy, ix, 265, **352**, 379, 383, 391, 400, 419, 461, 463, 480, 487, 489, 495, 496, 409, 428, 447n; construction of 'Yo' Mama', 362–363; on recording sessions for 'Brown Moses', 447n; on Zappa's use of rhythm, 417–418; reads from *Breeding from your Poodle*, 409

Marsalis, Wynton, xxvii, 506

Marshal, Bob, xxxiin, 271n

Martian Time-Slip, 275

Martin, Bobby, 456, 461, 480, 487, 501, 505, 506

Martin, David Stone, 9

Martine, Bob, 252

Marx, Karl, xix, xxix, 6, 47, 48, 51, 52, 81, 217, 222, 228; thin crust of society rent by revolutions, 281; turning the royal sun into a bourgeois astral lamp, 272; why Marx, **xi–xiv**

'Mary Lou', 403

Mascara Snake, the – see Boston, Mark

Masmanian, John, 193, 267

Masoch, Sacher, 239

masochism, 231–4

'Masques' 432

'Massaggio Galore', 471–472

'Massive Improve' lence, The', 290, 446

Massumi, Brian, xixn, 96n

Masters and Johnson, 50

masturbation, 239, 256, **273**, 369, 488, 537

materialism, xxv, 109,111, 265, 282, 323; and the soul, 250–251; as guide to transcending limitations of genre, 7; as opposed to repressive purism, 425; as progressive, 326, 442; form as sedimented content, xxvii, 541; insistence on what *is* as reactionary, 277–278; Pierre Boulez and, 429; refusal of innerness, 279–280 – see also Lewis, Percy Wyndham;

sexual, 179–180; the Siren song as the voice of material truth, 308; versus stairways to heaven, 504; Zappa's compared to Hobbes, 275–6

Mattelson, Marvin, 200

Matthews, Dr Susan, xxvn, 50

Maxayn, 294

May 1968, xxi, xxiii, 209

Mayall, Jason, 386n

Mayall, John, 62, 106, 159, 163

Mayer, Louis B., 16

Mayfair Studios, 88

Mayonnaise, Hellman's – see Hellman's Mayonnaise

McAlmon, Robert, 259

McCambridge, Mercedes, 21

McCarthy, Senator, 36

McCartney, Paul, 42, 516

McClary, Susan, xxin, xxvi, 4, 53, 56, **48–57**, 129, 253n, 339, 383, 399

McColl, Ewan, 315

McElwaine, Bernard, 105n

McFarland, Gary, 235

McGettrick, Kurt, 506, 507, 508

McGhee, Brownie, 36

McGriff, Jimmy, 159

McKillop, Keith, 2

McLaren, Malcolm, xxi, 36, 179, 216, 231, 321, 405, 458, 492, 432

McLaughlin, John, 164, 197, 364

McLean, Ramsey & the Survivors, 68n

McMacken, David, B., 160, 219, 527

McMillan, Dr John, ix

McNeely, Big Jay, 4

McQueenie, John, 410

Meadows, Punky, 300, 336, 340, 345

Meatloaf, xix, 339

Medley, Bill, 157

'Meek Shall Inherit Nothing, The', 203, 203n, **393–394**, 443, 446

Meets the Mothers of Prevention, 460, **461–468**, 495, 499, 552n, 555

Mehta, Zubin, 117

Mekons, the, 66n

Melcher, Terry, 148

Mellers, Wilfrid, 129

romanticism, xv, 94, 201, 258, 309, 329, 403, 423, 424, 432, 463, 479; in 'Punky's Whips', 336–337; poodles and, 235; negative capability, 292–292; sofas and, 272; *Uncle Meat's* attack on, 140

Romero, George, 139

Romney, Jonathan, 382n

Romper Stomper, 325

Ronstadt, Linda, 199

'Room Service', 481

Rooney, Michael, ix

Roosevelt, Franklin, 530

Rorschach, Poison Ivy, 17

Rosen, Steve, 2n, 293, 301n, 410n, 419n

Ross, Michael, 149n

Rost, Doug, 16

Rosza, Miklos, 201

Rotations, the, 112

Rotella, Johnny, 63

Rotring pen, 211

Rotten, Johnny – see Lydon, John

Roxy & Elsewhere, xiin, xivn, 13, 97, 111, 127, 149, 176, 182, **260–265**, 478n, 480, 481, 523n, 529

Roxy Music, 346

Royal Albert Hall, 188

Royal Northern College of Music – see RNCM

Royal Philharmonic Orchestra, 183–184, 188

'Rubber Shirt', 303n, **358–359**, 361

Rubberneck, xxvi

rubbish epic, 94, 103

rubbish, **184**, 185, 187, 201, 253, 268, 280, 288, 377, 378, 399, 407, **431–432**, 520, 535n

Ruben & the Jets – see *Cruising with Ruben & the Jets*

Ruben & the Jets – *For Real*, 192n

Rude Boy, 405

'Rudolf the Red-Nosed Reindeer', 111

'Rudy Wants to Buy Yez a Drink', **182**, 346, 406

Ruhlman, William, 112n, 125n

Run Home Slow, 15, 21, 81

Rundell, Clark, xi, 426

Rundgren, Todd, 387

Rural Still Life, 160

Rush label, 158

Rushton, James, 457n

Ruskin, John, 231–234, 474n

Russell, Mark, ix

Russell, Mr, 15

Russell, Ross, 60n, 305n

Russolo, Luigi, 6

Rustic Protrusion, 171n

'Ruth is Sleeping', 529

'Ruthie-Ruthie', 476, 477n

Rybek, Christine, ix

Saatchis, the, 53

Saccharine Trust, 386

Sachs, Harvey, 57n, 139n

'Sad Jane', x, **423**, 425

sadomasochism, 282, 288, 316, 356, 393, 444; and Japan, 302; as a replacement for gendered polarities, 399–400; in Shakespeare, 244; on planet Gor, 381; sadism and desire for knowledge, 300

Safe As Milk, 154, 156, 287n

sailors, **314–316**, 318

Saint-Pont, Valentine de, 140

Salazar brothers, 13

Salewicz, Chris, 39n, 351n

Salomé, 275, 394

Sam the Sham, 31, 476

'Sam with the Showing Scalp Flat Top', 288–289

Sampson, John, 537n

Samuels, David, 347

San Andreas fault, 193, 263, 280

'San Ber'dino', 30, 124, 290, 437

San Francisco scene, 109

Sandall, Robert, 480n

Sanders, Ed, 72

Sanders, Pharoah, 173

Sandra, Miss, 151

Santana, Carlos, 302, 413

'Sanzini Brothers, The', 523

Sartre, Jean-Paul, xxii

Satie, Erik, 69, 249, 527n

satire-collage, 91

'Satisfaction, (I Can't Get No)', 41

595